A History of Housing in New York City

The Columbia History of Urban Life Series

D0840204

A History of Housing in New York City

DWELLING TYPE AND SOCIAL CHANGE IN THE AMERICAN METROPOLIS

Richard Plunz

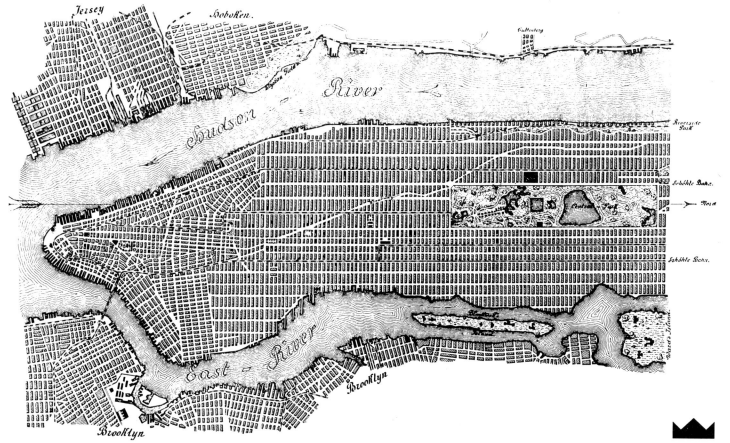

Columbia University Press
New York

COLUMBIA UNIVERSITY PRESS
New York   Oxford
Copyright © 1990 Columbia University Press
All rights reserved

Library of Congress Cataloging-in-Publication Data

Plunz, Richard.
  A history of housing in New York City: dwelling type
and social change in the American metropolis / by Richard Plunz.
    p. cm. — (The Columbia history of urban life series)
    Bibliography: p.
    Includes index.
    ISBN 0-231-06296-6
    1. Housing—New York (N.Y.)—History.
    2. Dwellings—New York (N.Y.)—History.
    I. Title. II. Series.
HD7304.N5P54 1989
363.5′09747′1—dc19
                                                                88-38831
                                                                CIP

*Casebound editions of Columbia University Press books are Smyth-sewn
and printed on permanent and durable acid-free paper*

Printed in the United States of America

For JAZ:

. . . She it was put me straight
about the city when I said, It

makes me ill to see them run up
a new bridge like that in a few months

and I can't find time even to get
a book written. They have the power,

that's all, she replied. That's what you all
want. If you can't get it, acknowledge

at least what it is. And they're not
going to give it to you. Quite Right.

William Carlos Williams
The Flower

Contents

Illustrations   ix

Preface   xxix

Acknowledgments   xxxvii

1 Early Precedents   1

2 Legislating the Tenement   21

3 Rich and Poor   50

4 Beyond the Tenement   88

5 The Garden Apartment   122

6 Aesthetics and Realities   164

7 Government Intervention   207

8 Pathology of Public Housing   247

9 New Directions   280

10 Epilogue   313

Notes   341

Bibliography   375

Illustration Credits   399

Index   407

FRONTISPIECE. Old houses on the corner of Broad and Garden streets, Manhattan, published in the *New York Mirror* in 1834. These houses were said to be among the last dwellings in New York City dating from the seventeenth-century Dutch Colonial period.

Illustrations

Frontispiece: Old houses on the corner of Broad and Garden streets, Manhattan, published in the *New York Mirror* in 1834. viii

1.1. Scene from the Great Fire of 1835. 3

1.2. Gotham Court, a notorious example of substandard new housing for the poor, completed by Silas Wood in 1850. 6

1.3. Section through Gotham Court from 1879. 7

1.4. John W. Ritch. The Workingmen's Home, built in 1855 to house working-class blacks. 8

1.5. Andrew Jackson Davis. Llewellyn Park at Orange, New Jersey, as developed by 1890. 9

1.6. Richard M. Hunt. Tenth Street Studio completed in 1857. 10

1.7. The southern half of Manhattan, showing the commissioner's gridiron of 1811 and Central Park, which was set aside in 1853. 12

1.8. System of subdivision of New York City gridiron blocks using 25-by-100-foot lots. 12

1.9. Evolution of New York City housing prior to the tenement house legislation of 1879. 13

1.10. Windowless interior room of a railroad flat, photographed by Jesse Tarbox Beals in 1910. 14

1.11. A notorious tenement on Mott Street known as the Rookery. 15

1.12. A Lower East Side tenement block with an unusual pattern of back building. 16

1.13. Typical back tenement on East 28th Street recorded in 1865 16

1.14. Two "improved" tenements from 1865. 17

1.15. Early "improved" tenement on Leonard Street. 17

1.16.   Edward T. Potter. An analysis published in 1879, showing two alternatives for the reorganization of the New York City gridiron.   18

1.17.   Edward T. Potter. Proposal made in 1878 for gridiron reorganization.   19

1.18.   Edward T. Potter. Proposal made in 1879 for a new house type based on the introduction of east-west mews streets within existing gridiron blocks.   19

1.19.   George Post. A proposal made in 1879 with George Dresser for the reorganization of the New York City gridiron.   20

2.1.   James E. Ware. The winning entry to the tenement house competition of 1878 sponsored by *Plumber and Sanitary Engineer*.   25

2.2.   Robert G. Kennedy, James E. Ware, George DaCunha. Placing entries in the tenement house competition of 1878.   26

2.3.   "Dumbell" tenement plan devised by James E. Ware and enforced under the provision of the Tenement House Act of 1879.   27

2.4.   Alfred J. Bloor. Proposal for a tenement made in 1880, using a single 25-by-100-foot lot with mediocre results.   28

2.5.   Nelson Derby. Proposal for a tenement made in 1877, using four 25-by-100-foot lots to produce an innovative organization around an internal courtyard.   28

2.6.   Edward T. Potter. Proposal for a tenement made in 1888, using a 37.5-by-100-foot lot.   29

2.7.   Edward T. Potter. Model of a proposed tenement expressing a "functionalist" approach.   30

2.8.   Edward T. Potter. Diagram from a study of building setbacks to provide increased light and air in housing, published in 1887.   31

2.9.   Tenement house plans published in 1887 as representative of those which could meet the approval of the Board of Health.   32

2.10.   Photo by Jacob Riis of an air shaft in an Old Law tenement.   35

2.11.   Photo of the air space between a tenement and its back building, on the Lower East Side block bounded by Canal, Forsyth, Bayard, and Chrystie streets. Circa 1895.   38

2.12.   Francois Rolland. Apartment house on the rue de la Chaussée d'Antin, Paris, published in 1859.   41

2.13.   Ernest Flagg. Tenement prototypes first published in 1894, using Parisian-influenced central courtyards and *port cochères* on multiple lots, compared with a typical dumbell tenement.   42

2.14.   Ernest Flagg. First Place entry to the tenement house competition of 1896.   42

2.15. James E. Ware. Second Place entry to the tenement house competition of 1896.   43

2.16. Henry Atterbury Smith. Third-place entry in the tenement house competition of 1900 sponsored by the Charity Organization Society.   43

2.17. R. Thomas Short. First Place entry in the tenement house competition of 1900.   44

2.18. Percy Griffin. Variations on the third-place entry in the tenement house competition of 1896 sponsored by the improved Housing Council.   44

2.19. I. N. Phelps Stokes. Entry in the tenement house competition of 1896.   45

2.20. Model of a typical Lower East Side tenement block, built for the Tenement House Exhibition of 1900.   46

2.21. Model of a typical dumbell tenement block, built for the Tenement House Exhibition of 1900, showing the definite increase in density over the "prelaw" tenement housing.   46

2.22. Ernest Flagg. Tenement plan submitted to the New York State Tenement House Commission of 1900, showing a refinement of his original plan types.   47

2.23. I. N. Phelps Stokes. Tenement plan submitted to the Tenement House Commission of 1900, using an organization quite close to the pragmatic possibilities of speculative development.   47

2.24. Typical tenement configurations permitted under the Tenement House Act of 1901 or New Law.   48

2.25. Typical speculative development of an Upper East Side gridiron block under the provision of the New Law.   48

2.26. Typical speculative New Law plan using a 50-by-100-foot lot.   49

2.27. Evolution of the New York City tenement from railroad flat, to the dumbell, to a New Law plan.   49

3.1.   Two plans illustrating typical uses for the cellar.   51

3.2.   Mulberry Bend, said to have been the most notorious slum in New York City throughout most of the nineteenth century.   52

3.3.   Photo taken by Jacob Riis of Bottle Alley.   53

3.4.   Depictions of squatters living in Central Park in 1857.   54

3.5.   Egbert Viele. The first plan for Central Park proposed in 1856.   55

3.6.   View looking east on West 86th Street in 1880.   56

3.7.   Views looking east along West 70th Street in 1885 and 1895 within the squatter community known as Dutchtown, showing the rapid transformation from shacks to upper-middle-class houses and apartments.   57

3.8.   John Kellum. Alexander T. Stewart mansion on Fifth Avenue completed in 1869, contrasted with the Five Points.   58

3.9.   Typical row house of the early 1830s, built on Washington Square.   59

3.10.   Upper-class house of the 1830s contrasted with a house of the 1880s.   60

3.11.   Bruce Price. Proposal for an upper-class brownstone row house made in 1879 for a 25-by-100-foot lot.   61

3.12.   A typical 1830s row house block contrasted with a typical 1880s brownstone block.   61

3.13.   Richard Morris Hunt. The Stuyvesant, also called the French Flats; credited in common history as the first apartment building for affluent tenants in New York City.   63

3.14.   Clavert Vaux. The Parisian Buildings, proposed in 1857 as an apartment building for affluent tenants.   64

3.15.   Bruce Price. Apartment house on East 21st Street built in 1878 using a 25-by-100-foot lot and six stories.   65

3.16.   Typical apartment house of the 1880s for tenants of modest means, using a single 25-by-100-foot lot, with three apartments on each floor.   66

3.17.   Apartment house of the 1870s for tenants of modest means, combining two altered single-family houses.   66

3.18.   West 133rd Street about 1877, showing the typical small-scale increment of development for housing of the period.   67

3.19.   Richard M. Hunt. Stevens House, completed in 1871 at Broadway and 26th Street.   68

3.20.   Arthur Gilman. High-rise apartment building proposed in 1874.   70

3.21.   Henry Hardenburg. The Vancorlear, completed in 1880.   71

3.22.   Hubert, Pirsson, and Company. The Chelsea, completed in 1883; probably the first high-rise apartment building in New York City.   71

3.23.   Henry Hardenburg. The Dakota, completed on the Upper West Side in 1884, at the center of the squatter community of Dutchtown.   72

3.24.   The Dakota plan, showing the internal courtyard with elevator lobbies at the four corners.   73

3.25.   James E. Ware. The Osborn, completed in 1885 and typical of the first generation of high-rise apartment buildings for the affluent in Manhattan.   74

3.26.   Hubert, Pirsson, and Company. Early photo of the Central Park Apartments, completed in 1883.   75

3.27.   Hubert, Pirsson, and Company. Block plan of the Central
        Park Apartments.   76

3.28.   Philip Hubert. View of the internal courtyards of the Central
        Park Apartments.   77

3.29.   Graves and Duboy. The Ansonia, completed in 1902 as one of
        the most innovative of the second generation of high-rise
        apartment buildings.   79

3.30.   Clinton and Russell. The Apthorp, completed in 1908, exceeding
        the Ansonia in size and luxury.   80

3.31.   Hiss and Weeks. The Belnord, completed in 1910, exceeding even
        the Apthorp in size.   81

3.32.   Graves and Duboy. Photo of the Ansonia in 1903; construction of
        New York City's first subway is being completed
        under Broadway.   82

3.33.   Hiss and Weeks. View of the Belnord, showing the
        Italianate facades.   83

3.34.   Warren and Wetmore. 270 Park Avenue, the last and largest of
        the luxury high-rise apartment buildings, completed in 1918. 83

3.35.   Charles W. Buckham. Proposal for a twenty-story apartment
        building made in 1911.   85

3.36.   Louis Korn and George Pelham. New Law tenement plans
        designed to middle-class standards.   86

3.37.   George Pelham. Middle-class apartment building designed
        in 1908.   87

3.38.   Plan showing new construction on upper Broadway, circa 1908,
        indicating the proliferation of new middle-class
        apartment buildings.   87

4.1.   Henry Roberts. Model working-class housing erected in the
        Great Exhibition of 1851 in London.   88

4.2.   Dwellings erected by Sir Sydney Waterlow's Improved Dwellings
        Company in London in 1863.   89

4.3.   Louis E. Dunkel. A philanthropic tenement built by the
        architect around 1865.   89

4.4.   William Field and Son. The Home Buildings, completed for
        philanthropist Alfred Treadway White in 1877 in Brooklyn.   90

4.5.   William Field and Son. The entire estate of philanthropic
        housing built for Alfred Treadway White in Brooklyn in 1879. 90

4.6.   William Field and Son. A portion of the Tower Buildings.   91

4.7.   William Field and Son. Warren Place Mews, completed in 1878. 91

4.8.   George da Cunha. Proposal for philanthropic tenements made for
        the Improved Dwellings Association in 1880.   94

4.9.   Vaux and Radford. Final plan adopted for the philanthropic tenements of the Improved Dwellings Association.   95

4.10.   Vaux and Radford. View of the philanthropic tenements for the Improved Dwellings Association, completed in 1881.   96

4.11.   William Field and Son. The Monroe philanthropic tenement, completed in 1879 for the Chichester Estate.   97

4.12.   William Schickel and Company. Philanthropic tenement for the Tenement House Building Company completed in 1886.   97

4.13.   Lamb and Rich. Astral Apartments, philanthropic tenement completed in 1887 for oil magnate Charles Pratt.   98

4.14.   Ernest Flagg. The Clark Buildings, the first philanthropic project to be built by the City and Suburban Homes Company, and the first realization of the Flagg-type plan, completed in 1898.   99

4.15.   James Ware. Proposal for the initial stage of the First Avenue Estate, the second philanthropic project to be built by the City and Suburban Homes Company.   100

4.16.   Harde and Short. Initial stage of the York Avenue Estate, the third philanthropic project to be built by the City and Suburban Homes Company.   100

4.17.   Sass and Smallheiser. Tenements at Broome and Mulberry streets completed in 1902.   102

4.18.   Plans used by the City and Suburban Homes Company to extend the York Avenue Estate.   102

4.19.   Henry Atterbury Smith. The East River Homes philanthropic project completed in 1912.   103

4.20.   Henry Atterbury Smith. Photo of East River Homes at the time of completion.   104

4.21.   Henry Atterbury Smith. The East River Homes stair and roof details.   105

4.22.   Henry Atterbury Smith. Study of the evolution of open stair planning under the regulation of the Tenement House Department.   106

4.23.   Grosvenor Atterbury. Roger's Model Dwellings, a philanthropic tenement built for Catherine Cossitt Rogers in 1915.   107

4.24.   Henry Atterbury Smith. Philanthropic tenement on West 146th and 147th streets completed in 1917 for the Open Dwellings Company.   107

4.25.   William Field and Son. The Riverside Buildings, a philanthropic project for Alfred Treadway White in Brooklyn, completed in 1890 as the largest and most refined perimeter block project in New York City.   108

4.26. William Field and Son. Photo by Jacob Riis of the internal garden of the Riverside Buildings, taken in the 1890s. 109

4.27. Hubert, Pirsson, and Company. Proposal for a perimeter block developed around 1890. 110

4.28. Julius F. Herder. Proposal for reorganization of the New York City gridiron made in 1898. 111

4.29. I. N. Phelps Stokes. Proposal for perimeter block made in 1900, with a provision for the internal park to be bought and maintained by the City of New York. 112

4.30. Workingmen's Model Home exhibited in 1893 by New York State at the World's Columbian Exposition in Chicago. 112

4.31. John Kellum. Garden City, Long Island, begun by Alexander T. Stewart in 1869 as a new town for the working class. 113

4.32. Plan of the village of Steinway in Queens, built by the Steinway and Sons Piano Manufacturing Company in order to relocate their workers from Manhattan. 115

4.33. Percy Griffin. Working-class cottages designed in 1898 for the Homewood Project in Brooklyn. 117

4.34. Frederick Law Olmsted, Jr., and Grosvenor Atterbury. Forest Hills Gardens, begun in 1908 in Queens by the Russell Sage Foundation, originally planned for deserving families of modest means. 118

4.35. Frederick Law Olmsted, Jr., and Grosvenor Atterbury. Forest Hills Gardens street layout compared with the New York City gridiron as initially planned for the area. 119

4.36. Frederick Law Olmsted, Jr. Two design alternatives for a typical block at Forest Hills Gardens. 119

4.37. Advertisement published in 1922 for building lots at Forest Hills West, where a commuter station just built by the newly electrified Long Island City Railroad contributed to the rapid development of the area surrounding Forest Hills Gardens. 120

4.38. Advertisement published in 1920 for building lots at Hempstead, Long Island. 121

5.1. Representative diagrams from the Building Zone Plan of 1916. 123

5.2. Delano and Aldrich. Proposed housing development for the United States Housing Corporation at Mariner's Harbor, Staten Island; made in 1918 but never built. 125

5.3. Sibley and Fetherston. First Place entry to the tenement rehabilitation competition of 1919. The existing Lower East Side block consisted of Old Law and pre-Law tenements. The proposal shows large light-courts carved out from the building interiors. 128

5.4. Clarence Stein. Proposal for a perimeter block project composed of three interlocking building types; made for the New York State Reconstruction Commission in 1919.   129

5.5. Map indicating the shape of influence of the New York City Subway System on population configuration in general and housing form in particular.   129

5.6. Advertisement published in 1917 for the newly completed Corona Line of the New York City Subway.   130

5.7. Emery Roth. Goldhill Court Apartments, the Bronx, completed in 1909.   133

5.8. Andrew Thomas. Proposal made in 1917 for a privately developed apartment building, planned for a 70-by-100-foot lot using higher standards than for tenements.   134

5.9. Charles Kreymbourg, William E. Erb, and Paul R. Henkel. Melrose Courts, the Bronx, completed in 1920.   134

5.10. Andrew Thomas. Entry to the tenement house competition of 1921. Sibley and Fetherston. First Place entry to the tenement house competition of 1921.   136

5.11. Comparative drawing of three entries to 1921 tenement house competition.   136

5.12. Andrew Thomas. Proposal for a perimeter block project composed of U buildings, made for the New York State Reconstruction Commission in 1919.   137

5.13. Paul Mebes. Charlottenburg II Project, built by the Berlin Civil Servants Dwelling Association between 1907 and 1909.   138

5.14 Queensboro Corporation formula for perimeter-type block organization applied to early projects.   139

5.15. George H. Wells. Front and rear views of the Greystone, built for the Queensboro Corporation at Jackson Heights, Queens.   140

5.16. Photo of the communal gardens behind the Greystone.   140

5.17. Andrew Thomas. Linden Court, completed in 1920 for the Queensboro Corporation in Jackson Heights.   141

5.18. Andrew Thomas. Linden Court site plan showing the integration of the internal garden with automobile access.   142

5.19. Andrew Thomas. The Château and the Towers building plans.   142

5.20. Andrew Thomas. The Château site plan, which attempted to increase the possibility for use of the internal garden over earlier Queensboro Corporation projects.   143

5.21. Andrew Thomas. Hayes Avenue Apartments, completed around 1922 in Jackson Heights.   144

5.22. Andrew Thomas. Proposal for a privately developed perimeter block project at Astoria, Queens, made in 1918.   144

5.23.   Frank Chouteau Brown. Plate from an analysis comparing U
         and "continuous" forms for perimeter block planning, published
         in 1922.   145

5.24.   George H. Wells. Operation No. 10, apartment cluster plan
         proposed to the Queensboro Corporation for Jackson Heights
         in 1920.   145

5.25.   George H. Wells. Cambridge Court apartment cluster plan.   146

5.26.   George H. Wells. Cambridge Court perimeter block project
         completed for the Queensboro Corporation around 1924.   146

5.27.   Horace Ginsbern. Noonan Plaza, completed in 1931 with one of
         the most elaborately appointed gardens of the era in the Bronx. 147

5.28.   Farrar and Watmaugh. London Terrace, a privately financed
         "slum clearance" project in Chelsea.   148

5.29.   King and Campbell. Pomander Walk, completed in 1921 between
         West 94th and 95th streets in Manhattan.   149

5.30.   Andrew Thomas. Addition to the Homewood Development of the
         City and Suburban Homes Company in Brooklyn in 1920.   150

5.31.   Andrew Thomas. Perspective view of typical block for the
         Metropolitan Life Insurance Company Project in Long
         Island City.   151

5.32.   Herman J. Jessor. Workers Cooperative Colony, second stage
         completed in 1927 on Bronx Park East.   152

5.33.   Springsteen and Goldhammer. First building in the cooperative
         apartment complex, developed by the Amalgamated Clothing
         Workers Union in the Bronx.   153

5.34.   Springsteen and Goldhammer. Photo of the internal courtyard of
         the first building built by the Amalgamated Clothing Workers
         Union in the Bronx, showing the elaborate development of
         the garden.   154

5.35.   Springsteen and Goldhammer. Grand Street building for the
         Amalgamated Clothing Workers Union, completed on the Lower
         East Side in 1930.   155

5.36.   Andrew Thomas. Thomas Garden Apartments, built by John D.
         Rockefeller, Jr., in 1928 along the Grand Concourse in the
         Bronx for middle-income white occupancy.   155

5.37.   Andrew Thomas. Photo of the internal courtyard of the Thomas
         Garden Apartments, showing the "Japanese garden."   156

5.38.   Shalom Aleichem Houses announcement of a celebration of the
         poet and playwright H. Leivick, held on Saturday night,
         January 30, 1930, with literary critic Shmuel Niger and actors
         Joseph Buloff, his wife Liuva Kadison, and Lazar Freed.   158

5.39.   Somerfeld and Saas. Lavanburg Homes, built as a philanthropic project in 1927 on the Lower East Side.   159

5.40.   Springsteen and Goldhammer. Project for the Academy Housing Corporation.   159

5.41.   Andrew Thomas. Paul Lawrence Dunbar Apartments, built in Harlem as a cooperative for blacks by John D. Rockefeller, Jr., in 1928.   160

5.42.   Clarence Stein. Phipps Garden Apartments, completed at Sunnyside Gardens in 1929.   161

6.1.   Springsteen and Goldhammer. Photo of the Grand Street building for the Amalgamated Clothing Workers Union.   166

6.2.   Andrew Thomas. Typical block plan for the Metropolitan Life Insurance Company Project in Long Island City.   167

6.3.   Andrew Thomas. Typical building plan for the Metropolitan Life Insurance Company Project in Long Island City, with eight apartments per floor, and very low rentals.   167

6.4.   Andrew Thomas. Typical apartment interior of the Metropolitan Life Insurance Company Project in Long Island City.   168

6.5.   Andrew Thomas. Photo of the Metropolitan Life Insurance Company Project in Long Island City shortly after completion in 1924.   169

6.6.   Clarence Stein, Henry Wright, and Frederick Ackerman. Sunnyside Gardens Development, begun in 1924 as a cooperative for the limited-profit City Housing Corporation.   170

6.7.   Clarence Stein, Henry Wright, and Frederick Ackerman. Sunnyside Gardens site plan showing the higher-density Phipps Garden Apartments, which was designed by Clarence Stein and completed in 1929.   170

6.8.   Photo of typical developer housing in Queens in the 1920s.   171

6.9.   Clarence Stein and Henry Wright. Analysis comparing Sunnyside Gardens with other projects.   172

6.10.   Clarence Stein and Henry Wright. Typical building plan for Sunnyside Gardens, showing the extreme simplification of the housing to a purely linear configuration.   172

6.11.   Henry Wright. Analytic sketches of possible techniques for joining apartment clusters, published in 1929.   174

6.12.   Henry Wright. Analysis of Sunnyside Gardens and Paul Lawrence Dunbar Apartments published in 1929.   174

6.13.   Henry Atterbury Smith. Analysis published in 1917 using a "sawtooth" geometry for the perimeter block form.   175

6.14.   Henry Atterbury Smith. Analysis published in 1917 applying the sawtooth geometry to a hypothetical suburban workingclass development with a large internal park and the exclusion of automobiles to garages at the periphery. 176

6.15. Henry Atterbury Smith. Cathedral Ayrcourt Apartments, a philanthropic project, competed in 1921 for the Open Stair Dwellings Company. 176

6.16. Frederick F. French Company. Apartment house at Forest Hills Gardens; completed in 1917, said to be the first residential elevator building in Queens. 177

6.17. Henry Atterbury Smith. The Mesa Verde site plan. Completed as a philanthropic project in 1926 by the Open Stair Dwellings Company in Jackson Heights. 177

6.18. Henry Atterbury Smith. The Mesa Verde, perspective and plan study for the perimeter block. 177

6.19. Henry Atterbury Smith. The Mesa Verde single-building plan. 178

6.20. Henry Atterbury Smith. Photo of Mesa Verde, contrasted with the surrounding developer, taken shortly after completion of the project. 179

6.21. Henry Atterbury Smith. Photo of the internal courtyard of Mesa Verde, with the "hurricane bridge" connecting two buildings. 179

6.22. Otto Haesler. Rothenberg Housing Project at Kassel, Germany. 181

6.23. Auguste Perret. Image of a city of *maisons-tours* drawn by Jacques Lambert from the sketches of Perret; published in 1922. 185

6.24. Le Corbusier. Proposal for the "city in a park." or *villes-tours*. 186

6.25. Le Corbusier. Typical image of the "city in the park," showing the continuous green space unaffected by buildings which are raised above the ground on *pilotis*. 186

6.26. Marcel Breuer. Proposal for "low-cost housing" using the slab block form. 187

6.27. Walter Gropius. Perspective of a slab block proposal using *Zielenbau* site organization with "intermediate green strips"; made in 1931. 188

6.28. Walter Gropius. Diagram from studies made in 1931 relating building heights to increased sunlight and higher density. 189

6.29. Walter Gropius. Typical slab block floor plan used in a project proposed for the Wannsee suburb of Berlin in 1931. 189

6.30. Howe and Lescase. Chrystie-Forsyth Street housing typical block, the first major "slab block" project for New York City. Maurice Deutsch and Gustave W. Iser. Chrystie-Forsyth housing proposal made in 1933 using a perimeter block configuration with interior gardens. 190

6.31. Howe and Lescaze. Chrystie-Forsyth housing proposal; perspective at ground level showing a transformation of the Corbusian image to the conditions of the Lower East Side. 191

6.32. Clauss and Daub. Site studies made for a housing proposal in Long Island City, showing an adaptation of the Gropius density studies to the context of the New York City gridiron. 192

6.33. Frank Lloyd Wright. Proposal for tower apartments on St. Marks Place made in 1930. 193

6.34. Representative diagram from the Multiple Dwellings Law of 1929, showing the dual-tower massing which was permitted for the highest of the high-rise apartment buildings. 195

6.35. Emery Roth. The Beresford, completed by 1930 on Central Park West, under the massing constraints of the Building Zone Plan of 1916. 197

6.36. Jacques Delamarre for the Chanin Construction Company. The Century, completed in 1931 on Central Park West; one of the first high-rise luxury apartment buildings characterized by reduced spatial standards and a modernist aesthetic. 198

6.37. Jacques Delamarre for the Chanin Construction Company. Typical six-room apartment plan for the Century. 199

6.38. Frederick Ackerman. Apartments on East 83d Street, completed in 1938 and the first centrally air-conditioned apartment building in New York. 199

6.39. Emery Roth. Proposal for an apartment building for the "average wage earner." 200

6.40. Robert Tappan and Rogers and Hanneman. Two-family "English garden homes" built in 1926 for the Queensboro Corporation at Jackson Heights. 201

6.41. Charles Schafer, Jr. Row houses completed on Hamden Place, the Bronx, in 1919, with integrated street-front garages. 202

6.42. Joseph Klein. Row houses on Holland Avenue, the Bronx, completed in 1940. 203

6.43. Arthur I. Allen. Row houses on 70th Street, Jackson Heights, built in 1927 with garages integrated at the rear, and street landscaping which becomes the equivalent of an elaborate public garden court. 204

6.44. Robert Tappan. Forest Close, completed at Forest Hills in 1927, with row houses along a garden mews and a garage court at one end. 205

6.45. Clarence Stein and Henry Wright. Radburn, New Jersey, site plan, begun by the City Housing Corporation in 1927 as a development for single-family houses planned with maximum recognition of the automobile.   206

7.1.   New York City Housing Authority Technical Staff under Frederick Ackerman. First Houses, the wholly government-built housing project in New York City, completed in 1936 with municipal funds through the NYCHA.   209

7.2.   John S. Van Wart and Frederick Ackerman with the Fred F. French Company. Knickerbocker Village, completed on the Lower East Side in 1933.   211

7.3.   John S. Van Wart and Frederick Ackerman with the Fred F. French Company. Knickerbocker Village Apartment cluster, designed with the reduced standards of the Multiple Dwellings Law in 1929.   211

7.4.   Richard Hutaff and Severin Stockmar. Winning entry in the Phelps Stokes Fund Housing Competition of 1933.   212

7.5.   Clarence Stein, Hillside Homes, completed in 1935 in the Bronx with a loan from the Public Works Administration.   212

7.6.   Clarence Stein. Hillside Homes, preliminary research into site-planning alternatives, using variations of the apartment cluster forms.   213

7.7.   Clarence Stein. Hillside Homes final site plan, comprising 1,416 apartments with a coverage of 39 percent.   213

7.8.   Ernest Flagg. Flagg Court, begun as a personal investment by the architect in 1933 in Brooklyn; it represented the fullest possible development of the garden apartment type.   214

7.9.   Charles F. Fuller, Horace Ginsbern, Frank J. Forster, Will R. Amon, Richard W. Buckley, John L. Wilson under Archibald Manning Brown. Harlem River Houses, completed in Harlem in 1937 by the Public Works Administration, closely following the design tradition of the 1920s New York City garden apartment.   215

7.10.   Photo from a promotional brochure for Harlem River Houses.   215

7.11.   James F. Bly, Matthew Del Gaudio, Arthur Holden, William Lescaze, Samuel Gardstein, Paul Trapani, G. Harmon Gurney, Harry Walker, John W. Ingle, Jr., under Richmond H. Shreve. Williamsburg Houses, completed in Brooklyn in 1938 by the Public Works Administration.   217

7.12.   James F. Bly, Matthew Del Gaudio, Arthur Holden, William Lescaze, Samuel Gardstein, Paul Trapani, G. Harmon Gurney, Harry Walker, John W. Ingle, Jr., under Richmond H. Shreve. Photo of Williamsburg Houses showing the abrupt schism between the geometry of the project and the surrounding area.   218

7.13. New York City Housing Authority technical staff under Frederick Ackerman. Plate from a 1934 analysis by the newly organized Housing Authority of twenty-three variations on the garden form. 220

7.14. New York City Housing Authority technical staff under Frederick Ackerman. Proposed PWA project for East Harlem, developed in 1935 using a perimeter block organization. 220

7.15. Horace Finsbern and John W. Ingle. Entries in the New York City Housing Authority Competition of 1934 using requirements similar to the actual site and program for Williamsburg Houses. 221

7.16. Brounn and Muschenheim. Proposal for an immense slum clearance project on the East Side made in 1935. 222

7.17. Frederick Ackerman and William Ballard. Plates from the study published as *A Note on Site and Unit Planning,* which demonstrated that higher long-term costs were associated with *Zielenbau*-type planning. 223

7.18. John Taylor Boyd, Jr. Rutgers Town housing proposal made in 1934 for the Lower East Side, covering approximately fifty gridiron blocks with twelve-story towers. 225

7.19. Public Works Administration Housing Division. Illustration from guidelines for design of low-rental housing published in 1935. 226

7.20. Henry Wright. Diagram published in 1935, which was a literal translation of the Gropius studies made several years earlier. 227

7.21. Aerial view of New York City looking west from Long Island, showing the network of new highways planned by the Department of Parks under Robert Moses and published in 1937. 228

7.22. Bullard and Wendehack. "America's Little House," a model suburban cottage constructed on Park Avenue near Grand Central Station in 1934 to promote private ownership of single-family houses. 229

7.23. Irwin S. Chanin. Green Acres, near Valley Stream, Long Island; 1,800 privately developed single-family houses organized on Radburn principles and sold beginning in 1936. 231

7.24. Richard Neutra. Second Place entry in the House for Modern Living competition sponsored by the General Electric Company in 1935 for a single-family suburban house on a 75-by-150-foot lot. 232

7.25. Charles C. Porter. Entry in the House for Modern Living competition; kitchen design with list of thirty-six General Electric appliances. 232

7.26. United States Housing Authority. Diagram of ideal site alternatives based on minimum dimensions between buildings for maximum light and air. 235

7.27. Federal Housing Administration, Rental Housing Division. Diagram of alternative apartment clusters to be considered for housing requiring FHA approvals for mortgage guarantees. 236

7.28. Federal Housing Administration, Rental Housing Division. Alternative "good" and "poor" apartment plans evaluated in relation to FHA mortgage guarantees. 236

7.29. New York City Housing Authority technical staff under Frederick Ackerman. Preliminary design proposal for Red Hook Houses in Brooklyn made in 1935. 237

7.30. William F. Dominick, W. T. McCarthy, William I. Hohauser, Electus D. Litchfield, Jacob Moscowitz, and Edwin J. Robin, under Alfred E. Poor. Red Hook Houses final site design. 238

7.31. William F. Dominick, W. T. McCarthy, William I. Hohauser, Electus D. Litchfield, Jacob Moscowitz, and Edwin J. Robin, under Alfred E. Poor. Red Hook Houses preliminary and final apartment plans. 238

7.32. New York City Housing Authority technical staff under Frederick Ackerman. Preliminary design proposal for Queensbridge Houses in Queens made in 1936. 239

7.33. William F. Ballard, Henry S. Churchill, Frederick G. Frost, and Barnett C. Turner. Final site design for Queensbridge Houses. 240

7.34. William F. Ballard, Henry S. Churchill, Frederick G. Frost, and Barnett C. Turner. Queensbridge Houses photo showing the abrupt schism between the site geometry of the project and the surrounding area. 241

7.35. William F. R. Ballard and Sylvan Bien under Richmond H. Shreve. Vladeck and Valdeck City Houses completed in 1940 on the Lower East side at Corlears Hook, using an offset variation on *Zielenbau* planning. 242

7.36. York and Sawyer, Aymar Embury II, and Burton and Bohm. Clason Point Gardens site plan, completed in 1941, using only two stories and quasi-*Zielenbau* site planning. 242

7.37. Le Corbusier. Proposal for reorganizing the Manhattan gridiron into megablocks using the "city in the park" image. 243

7.38. A cartoon published in *The New Republic* in 1938 criticizing the lack of technological progress in low-rental housing, in comparison with the concrete achievements of the military. 243

7.39. Voorhees, Walker, Foley, and Smith; Alfred Easton Poor; and C. W. Schlusing, under Perry Coke Smith. East River Houses preliminary and final site plans. 244

7.40. Voorhees, Walker, Foley, and Smity; Alfred Easton Poor; and C. W. Schlusing; under Perry Coke Smith. East River Houses aerial photo. 245

7.41.   Map of East Harlem prepared in 1950, showing Public Housing projects which had been planned up to that time.   246

8.1.   Philip Johnson. Proposal for a suburban "dream house," made in 1945 for the *Ladies Home Journal*.   252

8.2.   Gilmore D. Clarke, Irwin Clavin, Robert W. Dowling, Andrew J. Eken, George Gore, and Henry C. Meyer, Jr., under Richmond H. Shreve. Parkchester, a "city in the park" development for 12,273 families built by the Metropolitan Life Insurance Company in the outer Bronx.   254

8.3.   Gilmore D. Clarke, Irwin Clavin, Robert W. Dowling, Andrew J. Eken, George Gore, and Henry C. Meyer, Jr., under Richmond H. Shreve. Parkchester tower plan, showing the standardization of "unit" clusters.   255

8.4.   Irwin Clavin, H. R. Richardson, George Gore, and Andrew J. Eken, under Gilmore D. Clark. Stuyvesant Town, a "city in the park" development for 8.755 families built by the Metropolitan Life Insurance Company on the Lower East Side.   255

8.5.   Comparison of typical apartment plans for Stuyvesant Town and East River Houses.   256

8.6.   Riverton site plan, begun by the Metropolitan Life Insurance Company in Harlem in 1944, with residency intended only for blacks.   257

8.7.   Simon Breines. Analysis of Stuyvesant Town prepared for the Citizen's Housing Council in 1943, identifying some of the "dubious features" of the design.   258

8.8.   Serge Chermayeff. "Park-Type Apartments" study, published in 1943.   259

8.9.   Marcel Breuer. Alternative site plan for Stuyvesant Town, published in the interest of "comparative study" in 1944.   260

8.10.   Archibald Manning Brown and William Lescaze. Elliott Houses site plan in Manhattan, the first public housing project to be completed after World War II.   262

8.11.   Frederick G. Frost. Brownsville Houses site plan in Brooklyn, completed in 1948.   263

8.12.   Fellheimer, Wagner, and Vollmer. Albany Houses building plan in Brooklyn, completed in 1950 using fourteen-story "asterisk"-type towers.   263

8.13.   Four post-World War II public housing tower plans compared in a 1950 article in *Architectural Forum*.   264

8.14.   Skidmore, Owings, and Merrill. North Harlem public housing project proposed in 1951.   265

8.15.   Skidmore, Owings, and Merrill. Public housing slab block prototype floor plan as proposed to the Mayor's Committee on Slum Clearance for widespread use in public housing in New York City. 266

8.16. Skidmore, Owings, and Merrill. Sedgwick Houses public housing site plan, completed in 1951. 266

8.17. Le Corbusier. First study for the Unite d'Habitation at Marseilles. 267

8.18. Fellheimer, Wagner, and Vollmer. Farragut Houses public housing site plan, completed in Brooklyn in 1952. 269

8.19. Fellheimer, Wagner, and Vollmer. Farragut Houses construction photo. 269

8.20. Emery Roth and Sons. Baruch Houses public housing site plan, completed in 1959 on the Lower East Side. 270

8.21. Emery Roth and Sons. Baruch Houses site photo shortly after construction. 271

8.22. Baruch Houses and surrounding area of the Lower East Side. 271

8.23. Isadore and Zachary Rosenfield. Van Dyck Houses public housing project, completed in Brooklyn in 1955 using fourteen-story slab block towers. 272

8.24. Photo of Brownsville Houses public housing project in Brooklyn, with Van Dyck Houses behind. 273

8.25. Levitt and Sons. Plan of Levittown, begun at Hempstead, Long Island, in 1947 for mass-produced, inexpensive single-family houses. 275

8.26. Levitt and Sons. Model house built in 1949 for Levittown on Long Island. 276

8.27. Diagram from the *Bulletin of the Atomic Scientists* published in 1951. 277

8.28. Cover from a Federal Civil Defense Administration report from 1953, describing one of the atom bomb testing programs. 278

8.29. Illustration from an article, "Hiroshima, U.S.A.," published in *Collier's Magazine* in 1950, which described in detail the nuclear destruction of New York City. 279

9.1. Skidmore, Owings, and Merrill. Manhattantown (West Park Village) preliminary site plan and final built version. 283

9.2. Voorhees, Walker, Foley, and Smith. Fresh Meadows in Queens, the first of a series of postwar outer borough moderate income superprojects. 283

9.3. Leonard Schultz and Associates. Fordham Hill Apartments completed in 1949 in the Bronx using the "tower in the park" in its most reductive form. 284

9.4. Jack Brown. Lefrack City, Queens, completed 1962–67 and the largest privately financed housing project in New York. 285

9.5. Herman J. Jessor. Co-op city in the Bronx, completed in 1967–70 as the largest single housing development in New York. 286

9.6. Skidmore, Owings, and Merrill. Manhattan House, a luxury version of the slab block type, completed in 1950 on an entire Upper East Side block. 287

9.7. I. M. Pei and Partners. Kips Bay Plaza, completed 1960–65 with two pristine luxury slab blocks facing a private park. 288

9.8. Edvin Stromsten, Ricardo Scofidio, and Felix Martorano. Second Place entry to the East Harlem housing competition sponsored by the Ruberoid Corporation in 1963. 291

9.9. Lawrence Halpern. Proposal made in 1968 for reconstruction of the Penn Station South project. 293

9.10. Davis, Brody, and Associates. Riverbend, completed in East Harlem in 1976 and a significant departure from the orthodox slab block. 295

9.11. Riverbend typical duplex apartment section along a gallery "street," indicating the raised "yard" at the entry. 295

9.12. Richard Meier and Associates. Twin Parks Northeast in the Bronx, completed in 1973 and seen at the time as a breakthrough in high-rise massing. 296

9.13. Prentice, Chan, and Olhausen. Twin Parks Northwest, completed in the Bronx in 1973; a partial perimeter block integrated with the sloping terrain. 297

9.14. Giovanni Pasanella Twin Parks West duplex apartment sections, reminiscent of the Le Corbusier Unité organization. 298

9.15. Giovanni Pasanella. Twin Parks East; "pylon" and "gate" buildings opposite the Bronx Zoological Garden. 298

9.16. Philip Johnson and John Burgee. Roosevelt Island master plan designed for UDC in 1971, attempting to create a high-rise picturesque with a winding "Main Street" to reduce the scale of the project. 299

9.17. Sert, Jackson, and Associates. Eaaastwood on Roosevelt Island, completed in 1976, with open perimeters terracing toward the water. 300

9.18. David Todd and Associates. Manhattan Plaza on West 42nd Street, completed in 1977 as the archetype of the large raised plaza with parking and commercial space underneath. 300

9.19. Davis Brody and Associates. East Midtown Plaza, completed in 1974 with a large plaza spanning two blocks to unify the complex configuration of existing and new buildings. 301

9.20.   Hodne/Stageburg Partnership. 1199 Plaza, a union cooperative completed in 1974 along the East River in Harlem.   302

9.21.   Robert A. M. Stern and John S. Hagmann. Placing entry to the Roosevelt Island housing competition sponsored by the New York State Urban Development Corporation in 1975.   303

9.22.   O. M. Ungers. Entry to the Roosevelt Island housing competition using a miniature "Central Park" a community focus.   303

9.23.   Richard Kaplan. Crown Gardens in Brooklyn completed in 1971 as an informal perimeter block.   304

9.24.   Davis, Brody, and Associates. Lambert Houses in the Bronx, a philanthropic project of Phipps House completed in 1973.   305

9.25.   Ciardullo-Ehrmann. Plaza Boriquen at Mott Haven in the south Bronx.   305

9.26.   Urban Development Corporation and the Institute for Architecture and Urban Studies, with David Todd and Associates. Marcus Garvey Park Village in Brownsville, Brooklyn, completed in 1975 with walk-up apartments along mews cut across the mid-blocks.   306

9.27.   Roger A. Cumming with Waltraude Schleicher-Woods. Unbuilt 1973 proposal for Cooper Square on the Lower East Side.   307

9.28.   Perkins and Will. West Village Houses, the first and most controversial of the low-rise, walk-up projects, proposed in 1961 and not completed until fourteen years later.   308

10.1.   Richard Meier and Associates. Westbeth Artists Colony in renovated industrial building in the West Village.   316

10.2.   Jon Michael Schwarting. Loft on Broome Street in SoHo, one of the first architect's loft renovations to receive coverage in a major professional journal.   317

10.3.   The Gruzen Partnership. The Montana, completed on upper Broadway in 1984.   318

10.4.   Lichtenstein, Schuman, Claman, and Efron. The Saratoga apartment plan with one bedroom. Cesar Pelli and Associates Museum Tower apartment plan with one bedroom. Swanke, Hayden, and Connell, with Der Scutt. Trump Tower apartment plan with one bedroom.   319

10.5.   Johnson Burgee Architects. Trump Castle, proposed in 1984 for Madison Avenue at 59th Street.   319

10.6.   Alexander Cooper and Associates. Battery Park City master plan, completed in 1979.   321

10.7.   The New York "ring" of devastation that surrounds Manhattan.   324

10.8.   Permissible massing configurations for comparable conditions in an R-7 zone.   326

10.9.	Levenson-Thaler Associates. Rehabilitated tenements in Manhattan Valley.	327
10.10.	Prelaw tenement on East 6th Street, converted to an artist's loft.	328
10.11.	Rosenblum-Harb, Architects. Manhattan Valley townhouses completed on the Upper West Side in 1987.	328
10.12.	Beyer, Blinder, Belle. Crotona-Mapes Renewal Project in the shadow of Twin Parks Northeast in the Bronx.	329
10.13.	Ira D. Robbins with James D. Robinson. Nehiamiah Houses in Brooklyn, showing new row houses constructed as of 1986.	331
10.14.	Ira D. Robbins with James D. Robinson. Nehiamiah Houses typical block and unit plans.	332
10.15.	Ira D. Robbins with James D. Robinson. Nehiamiah Houses, typical street front yard with driveway.	333
10.16.	South Bronx Development Corporation. Charlotte Gardens Housing; typical single-family house with burned-out apartment building behind.	335
10.17.	Charlotte Gardens site plan, compared with the original neighborhood fabric, circa 1965.	336
10.18.	Scully, Thoresen, and Linard. Coney Island Townhouses completed in 1985.	338
10.19.	New York City Department of Housing Preservation and Development. Decal program for abandoned housing, 1980–83.	339

Preface

EXCEPT for a brief introductory background, this study begins at mid-nineteenth century when New York was quickly becoming the American Metropolis. At that moment the city moved out of the shadows of its colonial origin into the light of a new era characterized by changes in both physical form and culture. The fabric of the city's housing reflected these changes. By the 1830s the characteristic Dutch houses in lower Manhattan had already disappeared. By the 1850's a city composed almost exclusively of rowhouses was being transformed into a myriad of new housing types. By 1880, after only three decades, the cityscape was already changed to a degree unimagined at the beginning of the century. The new urban order and the speed with which it developed led to self-consciousness and self-doubt as to what the city would become: a collective crisis of identity. It is interesting to examine which changes people anticipated and which they did not. Many issues were raised that the twentieth century has hardly resolved and perhaps has only intensified.

To develop an understanding of the nature of housing design, which is fundamentally populist in nature, it is useful to study the cultural commentary of the popular press. Housing was a major concern of the press in the second half of the nineteenth century. In November and December of 1871 a telling series of exchanges appeared in the pages of two of New York's most prominent journals: *The World* and *Appleton's Journal*. Although most of the city as we now know it remained rural, dotted with hamlets, farms, and large estates, for the editors of the *Journal* planning for the growth of New York City loomed as a critical issue. The density of Manhattan was increasing, and the proliferation of railroad connections and elevated rapid transit lines created the potential for lateral expansion. The catalyst for this particular critical exchange, however, was the Great Fire of Chicago in early October of that same year, a disaster which destroyed much of that city. The fire led to discussion of the rebuilding of Chicago, and of the unique opportunity to implement a prototype city plan of a scale and conception unprecedented in American urban history; one that could affirm a great urban vision beyond the chaotic and haphazard growth that the unregulated marketplace had produced. In the exchange between the *World* and *Appleton's Journal* can be sensed the enormity of the debate that would preoccupy urban development in the United States for the next century. The debate helps to illuminate how unique the urban development of New York City and much of its housing stock was within mainstream American life.

For the *World*, if the calamity of Chicago could fortuitously stimulate reconstruction of an ideal city form, it would be one that would use the new technology of mass transportation toward the creation of a dispersed city. The business center would be placed in a setting of wide spaces, with housing spread over vast distances and taking the form of individual dwellings and yards. This "city of the future" was said to replace the obsolete city of proximity:

> Proper means of travel enable us to go ten or twenty miles as easily as our forefathers got over the few furlongs that separated their places of work from their places of rest. There is no reason why a man should not spend his days in the din and turmoil of the wharves and exchanges and walk in the cool of the evening amid the trees and vines of a rural home. Cities should be built so as to use to the utmost extent the great advantage of the age, and not as if we still dwelt in the barbarism of the middle ages . . . residences should be spread over a broad area beyond the limits of the tumultuous marts, where every house could have a goodly expanse of ground about it, filled with trees and shrubbery fanned by the pure breezes of heaven, and fully lighted by the health-giving sun. Noisome dens and crowded tenements for human beings ought to be numbered with the barbarisms of the past. When cities are laid out it ought to be a part of the plan that ample means should be provided for carrying the people from the centres of active work ten, twenty, or thirty miles in every direction through the wide and verdant suburbs where their homes should be.[1]

Appleton's Journal rebutted with another model, in strong opposition to the *World's*. This proposal was based on the idea that the emerging technology of the tall building could produce a vertical city of unprecedented density and civility:

> If the sole purpose of erecting cities were to afford the opportunity of exchanging commodities, an ideal city like that described in *The World* would be eminently practicable; but we apprehend that a city of splendid rural distances would scarcely answer to the needs or expectations of civilized communities. It is not sufficient for men having social and intellectual wants, that they are provided with rapid transit between their warehouses and their dormitories; nor in any just sense could that be considered a metropolis that simply multiplied the space and conditions of a village. A rich, specific, and munificent life arises from the compactness of settlement in cities, which diffusion and distribution would more or less impair. The opera and the theatre, the club, the reading room, the library, the art-gallery, the concert, the ball, the brilliancy and animation of the promenade, the inspiring contact of crowds, the magnetism of intercourse—all of these things largely depend upon neighborhood. No means of transit could bring people together from wide parts for social purpose that would be likely to meet the needs

of a scattered community, and hence the "ideal city" would be prone to divide the interest, weaken the intercourse, and abridge the pleasures of people. Men and women, moreover, often like the stir and bustle of cities; we all know the fondness of Dr. Johnson for the London streets, and this passion is by no means peculiar. And this model city, moreover, increases rather than ameliorates some of the greatest ills of modern life. . . . There are persons, of course, who would prefer suburban residences, and for these there will never be wanting means for the gratification of their tastes; but the ideal city, we imagine, must attempt to scientifically provide for the compact neighborhood of conditions that make up cities. Some months ago we argued, in these pages, for the utilization of air-spaces in great cities; we showed that buildings might be erected that would give, in immediate proximity to all the activities of the town, pure air, complete seclusion, and the maximum of household conveniences. We have just completed in New York two or three large and really splendid buildings for occupancy on the French-flat system . . . houses may now be constructed of fireproof material, and steam elevators enable occupants to reach the eighth story of a building easier than the second story of an ordinary structure; these two facts indicate the possibility of obtaining good air, seclusion, the charm of flowers and green vines [on the roof], in the heart of town, and within reach of all those things that give to great cities their social advantages.[2]

In retrospect we can observe that New York City housing possesses both of the extremes discussed in the pages of the *World* and *Appleton's Journal*. But it is precisely its density which makes metropolitan New York unique among American cities. By the 1880s high-rise living had already become associated with affluent Manhattanites. The optimism seemingly associated with technological innovation entered a realm of fantasy in which the present and future possibilities became blurred in the popular mind. At one point in its ongoing discourse, *Appleton's Journal* cited the recently completed Stevens House by Richard Morris Hunt (see Figure 3.19) as "The City of the Future," and indeed, it was so astounding in its innovations that the future seemed to appear before its time.[3] But the new urbanity was not limited to the vertical density of Manhattan. For example, there was the intense horizontal continuity of much of the Bronx, tempered by a large-scale conception of urban space and urban nature, in support of a culture which sociologist Louis Wirth characterized as "urbanism as a way of life."

Commonplace perceptions from our own century have read mainstream American culture as the by-product of an agrarian existence. In fact, the history of nineteenth century American culture is in large part a history of cities, and it was the city rather than the country which was the magnet for U.S. business and intellectal life.[4] In New York State, with New York port as anchor, a chain of cities grew westward along the path of the Erie Canal and the railroads, all remarkable for the urbanity of their form and life, superimposed on an equally remarkable agrarian landscape. It was the twentieth century that witnessed the dismantling of American urban centers, through a recent but dogged belief in the virtues of a decentralized city that dilutes both urban and rural values. To some degree the development of New York City has followed this pattern of reverse centralization. Its development is fraught with compromises and contradictions between lateral versus vertical growth, but the overwhelming density of its core remains unique in relation to the modern dispersed city.

New York grew to the metropolis stage quickly, outdistancing by far the great expectations of the New York State Commissioners' plan of 1811. In the unregulated marketplace that helped produce this agglomeration, little was understood of the consequence of rapid, uncontrolled growth, and in some instances, the desire to understand was even less. Just how little was understood is well-illustrated by the subject of health. The spread of epidemic disease as a by-product of poor housing conditions was widely suspected by the mid-nineteenth century when statistics began to indicate a correlation between the lack of light and air, and spread of disease. But the situation was hindered by misunderstanding of the mechanisms of disease. In the 1870s the medical profession was still debating germ theory. In the 1880s epidemics were still considered grave threats to the city;[5] Political interests prevailed and the New York State Supreme Court used the excuse that tenement house conditions had no relation to public health, effectively blocking government intervention and stymieing the tenement reform movement for over a decade.[6] By 1910 germ theory had gained popular acceptance; with it came naive gestures such as those incorporated in the East River Homes built for tubercular families (see Figures 4.19–4.21); for example, corners rounded so that the germs could be easily swept away like dust or dirt.

If modern technical understanding of disease was slow to develop, the psychological impact of disease was immediate and enduring. Cholera was the least understood and the most frightening of all:

> The first and in many ways the most significant of the altered disease relationships created by industrialization was the global peregrination of cholera. . . . It was caused by a bacillus that could live as an independent organism in water for lengthy periods of time. Once swallowed, if the cholera bacillus survives the stomach juices, it is capable of swift multiplication in the human alimentary tract, and produces violent and dramatic symptoms—diarrhea, vomiting, fever, and death, often within a few hours of the first signs of illness. The speed with which cholera killed was profoundly alarming, since perfectly healthy people could never feel safe from sudden death when the infection was anywhere near. In addition, the symptoms were peculiarly horrible: radical dehydration meant that the victim shrank into a wizened cariacature of his former self within a few hours, while ruptured capillaries discolored the skin, turning it black and blue. The effect was to make mortality uniquely visible: patterns of bodily decay were exacerbated and accelerated, as in a time-lapse motion picture, to remind all who saw it of death's ugly horror and utter inevitability.[7]

One source calculated that one out of every forty-six New Yorkers died annually in 1810, while one out of twenty-seven died annually by 1859, a reflection of the city's changing status.[8] In the following decades the death rate declined again, through sanitary reform and medical breakthroughs. In addition to cholera the common urban killers included smallpox, typhoid fever, malaria, yellow fever, and tuberculosis. Cholera, typhoid and diptheria vaccines were developed in the 1890s, and smallpox, malaria, and yellow fever had already declined as urban dangers. But they had all contributed to increased fears of urbanity which lingered long after the diseases themselves had been brought under control. So graphic was death by cholera that it was still frequently cited by the modern urbanists even though its impact had peaked before the beginning of this century. Such is the curious way that modern medicine and modern urbanism have coincided. For example, the discovery of penicillin in 1929 was contemporary with the first elucidations of the "tower in the park" urbanism that appears to have had as its most concrete motivation the question of hygiene: the introduction of "sun, space, and green" could foil the incubation of germs—moral as well as physiological. Like penicillin, the new urbanism was also a technical breakthrough: the product of the revolution in the technology of constructing tall buildings. Yet ironically it was the application of penicillin that made this radical new vision of urbanity obsolete, at least from the viewpoint of hygiene. By 1950, just as pencillin had conquered tuberculosis as the last of the traditional urban scourges, the "tower in the park" was being implemented in its most deterministic phase.

Mid-nineteenth century brought the first large-scale immigration through New York port, and with it came a profound change in the social outlook of the city. As one New York observer, E. Idell Zeisloft, would comment in *The New Metropolis:* "The German influx which began in 1845 made New York a dancing city, and the barricades with which Dutch dignity and New England Puritanism had encircled society were broken through."[9] New housing possibilities were correlated with a new class structure, which for the purposes of this study will remain the familiar triad of "Upper," "Middle," and "Lower." More accurate if not more complicated, however, was Zeisloft's depiction of these distinctions: "On the island of Manhattan, the people may be divided into seven classes: the very rich, the prosperous, the well-to-do comfortable, the well-to-do uncomfortable, the comfortable or contented poor, and the submerged or uncomfortable poor."[10] Housing evolved along class lines in part according to dwelling type. Like other aspects of social control, the relationship between housing and social class quickly became "institutionalized," with exaggerated differences between the upper and lower ends of the social spectrum. For these reasons, this study concentrates on the typology of building to help clarify distinctions between the architectural and social dimension of the history of housing.

Some aspects of the evolution of housing form in New York City were conscious and planned. Others were unplanned and unconscious. For architects the institutionalization of housing form was reinforced through a series of design standards and conventions; formal and informal controls imposed by business, governmental, and professional interests. They are most obvious in the evolution of housing for the poor, but they have affected housing for all levels of society. With the social housing programs of the 1950s the use of housing as a source of social control had probably reached its most deterministic phase. There is a parallel development with the institutionalization of the profession of architecture in the United States. For this reason, the outlook of the "culture" of architecture is of particular interest to this study, especially the dichotomy between the professional mainstream and the architects who were normally associated with housing concerns. The process of professional institutionalization began around mid-nineteenth century, most strongly manifested in the founding of the American Institute of Architects (AIA) in 1857 in New York City. The AIA was a professional lobby with national ambitions. Until this date only local professional organizations existed, although an earlier national effort was attempted and failed in 1837.[11]

The successful establishment of the AIA marked the transformation in meaning of the term "architect" from "master–builder" generalist to "design specialist" with a professional lobby. This change represented a different attitude toward the social role of built form than before, when "architecture" and "building" were less distinguishable. Of course "architects" existed, including Thomas Jefferson, who in 1781 envisioned a "reformation" in United States building to an "elegant and useful art."[12] But the primary architectural concerns were, of necessity, with the utilitarian problem of providing a young nation with shelter. Establishment of an architectural profession and proclamation of professional rights to building expertise required justification that was hard fought. Until a little over a century ago, the architectural profession as a legal entity was really only an adjunct of civil engineering. The technical expertise required of the civil engineer had created a *de facto* "profession" before architecture, and for some years distinctions between the two were informal. The two first academic programs in architecture were within the civil engineering curricula of West Point (1817) and Rensselaer Polytechnic Institute (1825). The American Society of Civil Engineers and Architects remained a professional lobby for architects as well as engineers from its founding in 1852 until 1969, when presumably the competition from the AIA caused its architectural membership to dwindle.[13] It was not until that year, when "Architects" was dropped from the society's title, that the split was formalized.[14]

In 1881 the founding of the Architectural League of New York gave this split further credence. The League sought to unite architects with sculptors, painters, and artisans, rather than with structural and mechanical engineers or technicians.[12] It was a private organization with a membership that combined the new commercial elite of the architectural profession such as Charles Follen McKim, with artist counterparts such as the academic sculptor Augustus St. Gardens. By 1893 the "turning point" of the World's Columbian Exposition in Chicago hung over the East Coast artistic establishment, further promoting the integration of architecture and art. The Fine Arts Society was established in its new building on West 57th Street (now entirely devoted to the Art Students' League), briefly uniting the Architectural League, the Art Students' League, and the Society of American Artists.[13] At the same time, the Municipal Art Society was founded to promote "civic art." Its membership was well-represented by architects, its first president, Richard Morris Hunt, among them. Hunt was also the first American to attend the Ecole des Beaux Arts in Paris.

Unfortunately, architecture and civil engineering became polarized through the respective guises of "aesthetics" and "utility." In relation to the unique complexities of housing, as both professions developed this polarization did not enhance the perspective of either side. Housing remains a unique challenge for its blend of both concerns. The profession of architecture, which quite logically assumed jurisdiction over housing design, has at the same time remained ambivalent toward it. The design sensibility needed to explore the problems of mass housing did not readily fit the conventional ideologies of design creativity which have dominated the culture of architecture to this day. Within the profession in general, there has never been a consistent pattern of innovation, evaluation, and learning applied to the design of housing. Still, the design of housing is probably closer than most other architectural activity to a long tradition in the United States of the social derivation of architectural form, with what has variously been called "social functionalism" of the sort to which the pioneering research of Lewis Mumford has attested.[14] This relationship has always caused problems for those who sought to promote stylistic concerns over social concerns; and housing as a valid subject for "high-style" architectural practice has always had its prominent detractors.

Although out of the mainstream of high-style practice, there has been a long historical involvement by some architects in the United States with housing. Among others, this study focuses on that particular lineage of architects who devoted much of their lives to it, in both practice and theoretical research. They have remained out of mainstream architectural history, and some are entirely unknown. A particularly remarkable group emerged in New York in the period after 1850 in the personages of such architects as Edward T. Potter, Ernest Flagg, Isaac Newton Phelps Stokes, Grosvenor Atterbury, Henry Atterbury Smith, Andrew Thomas, James Ford, Clarence Stein, Henry Wright, and Frederick Ackerman. In addition, given the restrictive nature of the avenues open to architectural practice, a kind of estranged body of housing work evolved parallel to the legitimate professional activity. It focused on the social aspects of domestic design that established architects tended to overlook entirely, beginning with diverse figures such as Catherine Beecher or Olivia Dow toward the mid-nineteenth century, proliferating into a unique legacy in its own right.[15]

The history of housing in New York City in some ways summarizes in microcosm the evolution of urban housing in the United States. Since the mid-nineteenth century, as the national Metropolis, New York has had the most severe housing problems. It has also led the nation in innovation and reform. While other cities have had their interludes in housing design, in New York can be found something of all of them. The horrors of the tenement were perfected in New York, and most reform legislation originated here as did most housing philanthropy. Wealthy New Yorkers embraced the technical innovations of the highrise as no other Americans did—or have done since. Public housing for the poor originated in New York, as did government subsidies for middle-class housing much later. The scale of New York City and the diversity of its geography—from Midtown Manhattan or the heart of the Lower East Side to the far reaches of the Bronx or Queens, or the wilds of Hempstead on Long Island—create a typology of housing combinations and permutations that is extraordinary for its range and completeness. For the researcher, the difficulties of scale are offset by several fortunate circumstances. The particular mode of development of the city left an impeccable record of detail for anyone willing to search for it. The great instruments of land development and speculation—the gridiron with its millions of lots, with the transactions of each carefully recorded—provide as complete and accessible a record of physical and economic development as could be desired. And as a Metropolis that achieved its world stature only after 1850, in a period of less than 100 years, New York gives an extraordinary record of the political and cultural milieu of modern American urbanism.

Acknowledgments

THIS study originated in 1976 with research made for an experimental interdisciplinary course on public housing in the United States which I organized, and which was supported by a Rockefeller Foundation grant through the Columbia University Committee on General Education. I am indebted to Professors Robert Belknap and Richard Kuhns of Columbia who encouraged that effort, and to Carl Burton who provided invaluable administrative support. A shorter version of this work was completed in 1980 and published in French by Pierre Mardaga Éditeur. I am very grateful to Professor Marcel Smets of the Katholieke Universiteit Leuven for his assistance, and especially to Professor Geert Bekaert of the Technische Hogeschool Eindhoven for encouragement and considerable editorial involvement. After several years of informal use by students and others in the Avery Architectural and Fine Arts Library, this earlier version was substantially revised and expanded for this edition. I wish to thank to Professor Kenneth Jackson of Columbia for his support of this recent effort. Over the years the Avery Architectural and Fine Arts Library has been a constant and invaluable resource. I am indebted to its staff, and especially to Avery Librarian Adolf Placzek for his encouragement early on in this study. Many Columbia students have contributed to this work directly with research assistance and indirectly by their enthusiasm and discussion. Especially important has been student feedback from the course "Historical Evolution of Housing in New York City" which I taught at Columbia several times since 1979. For valuable advice and extensive research I would like to acknowledge the help of Cynthia Jara, Thaleia Christidis, Laurie Lieberman, Margaret Bemiss, Marta Gutman, Wiebke Theodore, Stephen Day, and Nancy Josephson. Important contributions were also made by James Braddock, Christine Hunter, Ann Kaufman, David Smiley, Ludmilla Pavlova, Nancy Gorman, Tracy Dillon, Kate Owen, Debin Schliesman, Toby Chaum, Kevin Wolfe, Rachael Hoffman and José Alfano. At the Columbia University Press, Kate Wittenberg patiently guided this book to completion, with Joan McQuary, Susan Pensak, and Jennifer Dossin. Finally, throughout its entire evolution, Jerilea Zempel has lent a vigilant critical eye.

A History of Housing in New York City

1
Early Precedents

THE first government intervention in New York City housing design occurred within a year of the arrival of the first colonists in 1624. The Dutch West India Company devised a set of detailed rules regarding the types and location of houses that could be built in their new colony.[1] The rules proved impractical, however, and had to be abandoned. But as the city grew, laws were passed almost on a yearly basis, mandating one or another aspect of building and sanitation standards. Major advances were made less frequently, many times only after some major disaster.[2] The government was involved with housing first at the municipal and provincial levels, and only later at the state level. During the first two centuries of New York City's history, building law was concerned primarily with the prevention of fire and disease.

The first comprehensive construction law for fire prevention was enacted in 1648. This law forced the removal of wooden and plaster chimneys to eliminate fire hazards.[3] The city's fire laws were strengthened in 1683 when "viewers and searchers of chimneys and fire hearths" were appointed to report violations.[4] In 1775 drastic measures were approved which marked the beginning of the modern period in legislation against fire. The new law provided both for the prevention of fires and for controlling them once they started. Its provisions dealt with both new construction and the improvement of buildings already built.[5] The legislation was passed only a year before approximately one-quarter of the city was destroyed by fire and had to be rebuilt.[6] The use of fire walls was made mandatory by the New York state legislature in 1791. All adjoining buildings of three or more stories were required to be constructed of masonry party walls, with parapets at the roofs to prevent fire from jumping to adjacent buildings.[7]

The earliest comprehensive law covering hygiene was passed by the Council of New Netherland in 1657 prohibiting the disposal of rubbish and filth into the canals.[8] Until the turn of the nineteenth century, sanitary legislation remained concerned primarily with sewage and trash disposal. Some limited attention was also given to separating incompatible land uses and controlling the grazing of cattle, horses, and hogs. In 1695 the Provincial Legislature authorized the Common Council to appoint five "Overseers of the Poor and Public Works and Buildings" with the authority to impose a tax for relief to the poor and for public sanitation services.[9]

The eighteenth century began with a smallpox epidemic in 1702 that killed five hundred persons. Throughout the century, epidemics became more and more commonplace. By the end of the century, the New York City water supply was quite polluted. The yellow fever epidemics in the 1790s led to the first detailed and relatively objective reports on the sanitary conditions of the city.[10] In 1797 the New York state legislature appointed three commissioners of health for New York City who were given the power to make and enforce regulations regarding sanitation.[11] They constituted the first Board of Health. Also around this time, the city began to build sewers, and small sections of the city were supplied with running water. The first gaslight company was incorporated in 1823, offering an alternative to the hazards of the oil lamp and coal fire.[12] In 1835 the construction of an aqueduct from the Croton River forty miles north of the city was approved by public vote. By 1842 the cold and pure waters of the Croton Aqueduct were flowing to the city, providing the basis for a much-needed modern water distribution system.[13] Even as late as 1827, one of the major public sources of potable water had been the ancient "tea water pump" on Park Row.[14] Simultaneous with these technological improvements, however was the critical worsening of fire and hygienic conditions.

Between 1800 and 1810 the population of the city jumped from 60,515 to 96,373,[15] accompanied by great epidemics and social turbulence. The yellow fever epidemic of 1805 alone was estimated to have caused the death or illness of at least 645 persons.[16] During this decade the Board of Health was forced to define in greater and greater detail hygienic standards for the public. The laws began to reflect a naive understanding that the problems of health required measures that went beyond simple cleanliness. For example, hygienic concerns were related to population density in a law regulating lodging houses passed by the Common Council in 1804.[17] It was the first legislation to specify maximum densities for housing.

The first mandate for "professional" intervention in housing design came in 1806, when a Board of Health report suggested the hiring of a "scientific and skillful engineer" to assist builders.[18] A consciousness of the need for slum removal became more intense during this period, although there were many historical precedents for such activity. As early as 1676 the Common Council approved the right of the city to take control of abandoned and decayed houses, and to turn them over to new owners who were willing to fix them up or rebuild.[19] In 1800 the New York state legislature granted power to the city to purchase property within designated areas that violated building regulations. These parcels could then be disposed of in a manner as "will best conduce to the health and welfare of the said city."[20] Within the next several decades, the law was applied in various situations, usually to abandoned buildings. There were some important exceptions, however. In 1829 the law was used to raze four houses occupied by black families;[21] in 1835 condemned buildings at Christopher and Grove streets were replaced by a public park.[22]

Figure 1.1. Scene from the Great Fire of 1835, the largest in the history of New York City, and an important influence on building legislation in the following decades.

Major fires occurred in 1811, 1828, 1835, and 1845. Major epidemics of yellow fever and cholera occurred in 1819, 1822, 1823, 1832, 1834, and 1849. Minor crises arose almost every year. Reports and proposals proliferated, and they became the theoretical basis for preventive action. In a report on the cholera epidemic of 1819 written by Dr. Richard Pennell in 1820, the link between housing form and health was definitively established. Pennell compared the number of stricken residents who lived in cellars with the number who lived above cellars. In one comparison, he found that "out of 48 blacks, living in ten cellars, 33 were sick, of whom 14 died; while out of 120 whites living immediately over their heads in the apartments of the same house, not one even had the fever."[23]

Comprehensive legislation related to health was extremely slow to develop, partially because of moral and ethical issues. The worst cholera epidemics were in 1832, 1849, and 1866. The Metropolitan Board of Health was legislated in 1866, and thereafter, health measures had reached a degree of preventative measure such that no further massive outbreaks occurred.[24] The problem of fire was easier to legislate, although here, also, response was remarkably slow. The great fire of 1835, the worst in the history of the city, destroyed almost every building south of Wall Street and east of Broad Street—a total of 674 buildings valued at $26 million (figure 1.1).[25] Ten years later a last great fire occurred that was almost as destructive. But it was not until even later, in 1849, that the Common Council upgraded the fireproofing laws of the city to reasonable standards.[26]

Between 1820 and 1860 the population of the city grew from 123,706 to 813,699 persons, with another 266,661 persons living in Brooklyn.[27] The introduction of steam navigation on the Atlantic caused large increases in immigration toward the end of this period. Between 1820 and 1860 4 million immigrants reached the United States, most through New York City. By 1860 383,717 immigrants had settled in the city.[28] By mid-century New York had achieved its position as the North American metropolis.[29] During this time the dominant characteristics of the city's present-day culture of housing began to emerge; New York became a city not of "houses," but of "housing." A growing proportion of its inhabitants lived in collective accommodation that was unique in the nation. This condition crossed class lines from the tenements of the poor to the increasingly dense row housing of the upper middle class. Most fundamentally, the increased physical congestion was substantially altering both the house form and the culture of the colonial city. In 1847 a famous observer of the New York scene, Philip Hone, remarked that New York was appropriating certain characteristics of metropolitan Europe in the complexity of its outlook: "Our good city of New York has already arrived at the state of society found in the large cities of Europe; overburdened with population, and where the two extremes of costly luxury in living . . . are presented in daily and hourly contrast with squalid misery and destitution."[30]

Until the mid-nineteenth century, those aspects of fire and sanitation legislation that affected the poor were perhaps not intended as much to improve the condition of the poor as to protect the rich from the scourages of poverty. Laws were passed to control fire and disease because these were not easily contained within the area of origin, and on the occasion of calamity both rich and poor suffered. Improvement of the living conditions of the poor was in the immediate self-interest of the rich. But as the city grew and ghettos developed, the rich could put more distance between themselves and the poor. Legislation began to reflect more abstract ideas of social control.

By 1850 some new notions of the possible relationship between housing and social control had developed around the concept of private "philanthrophy." The extensive writings of Dr. John H. Griscom, who served as city inspector in 1842 and became one of New York City's first crusaders for housing reform, represent the first comprehensive treatment of the subject.[31] He appears to have been greatly influenced by the work in England of Sir Edwin Chadwick.[32] Writing in 1842 about the difficulties of enforcing housing standards for the poor, Griscom identified the landlords as having the resources and responsibility to improve housing conditions. Because he could find no sound economic reasons within the capitalist system for landlords to pursue such improvements beyond the minimums set by law, he was forced to call on their goodwill. His arguments implied that for all concerned, good intentions would be more profitable than exploitation. The landlords would be duly compensated with "the increased happiness, health, morals and comfort of the inmates, and good order of society, which cannot be estimated in money."[33]

Griscom believed that improved housing could best function as an instrument for societal betterment by incorporating some of the characteristics of educational institutions. He explained the mechanism for inducing betterment, using an argument that has been used in support of housing programs ever since. "A system of tenantage might be established, at so moderate a rent, as would form an inducement for the poor to live in it, even with such restrictions and supervisions as might be deemed necessary to maintain uniform cleanliness and good order."[34]

Griscom placed his faith in the capacity of the private landlord to improve housing conditions, yet he expressed outrage at the large-scale enterprise which was endemic to his proposal. Instead of owning single buildings and living alongside their tenants, landlords were investing in scores of buildings, and were increasingly removed from their tenantry. The new scale of housing enterprises was creating a system of absentee landlordism, rather than large-scale philanthropy:

> The *system of tenantage* to which large numbers of the poor are subject, I think, must be regarded as one of the principal causes, of the helpless and noisome manner in which they live. The basis of these evils is the subjection of the tenantry, to the merciless inflictions and extortions of the *sub-landlord*. . . . The *owner* is thus relieved of the great trouble incident to the changes of tenants, and the collection of rents. His income is from one individual, and obtained without annoyance or oppression on his part.[35]

In relation to the design of new housing, Griscom argued that the architectural plans should be subject to the same intensive review as the structural system or the materials:

> If there is any propriety in the law regulating the construction of buildings in reference to fire, equally proper would be one respecting the protection of the inmates from the pernicious influence of badly arranged houses and apartments. The power given to a magistrate to pull down a building, whose risk of falling endangers the lives of the inmates or passers-by, may with equal reason be extended to the correction of the interior conditions of tenements, when dangerous to health and life. The latter should be regarded by the legislator and executive, with as much solicitude as the property of citizens.[36]

Griscom identified the most crucial design issues as the provision of adequate light and ventilation. In 1850 the use of cellar apartments was widespread in the city; however, long after cellar apartments were outlawed, provisions of light and ventilation continued to dominate housing design well into the twentieth century. For many other matters as well, Griscom's prodigious output anticipated the housing issues of the next century in New York City.

Throughout the first half of the nineteenth century the predominant forms of housing for the poor in New York were either reconstructed space which had previously served other uses, or self-built squatter shacks. Former single-family row houses were frequently divided into substandard cubicles for poor families — by landlords "who only contrive in what manner they can stow the greatest number of human beings in the smallest space."[37] New housing was only for the af-

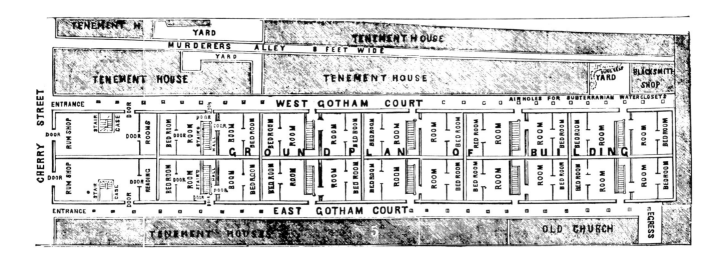

Figure 1.2. Gotham Court, a notorious early example of substandard new housing built for the poor, completed as an investment by Silas Wood in 1850.

fluent, and it consisted almost entirely of single-family houses. James Allaire has been credited with investing in the first substandard new housing for poor families. Located on Water Street, and built by Thompson Price, it was a "four story house designed for many tenants." Other sources cite a tenement on Cherry Street built in 1838, and there is some evidence of an earlier example, dating from the 1820s—a seven-story tenement at 65 Mott Street.[38] The earliest fully documented new project for the poor was Gotham Court, built in 1850 by Silas Wood on Cherry Street.[39]

Gotham Court consisted of two rows of six tenements back-to-back and six stories in height, organized along two narrow alleys intersecting Cherry Street (figure 1.2). Each tenement contained two dwellings measuring ten feet by fourteen feet, and were subdivided into two rooms, both without cross ventilation. A continuous cellar under each alley contained a long line of water closets and sinks. Small ceiling grates provided ventilation to the cellars. The building facing the alleys of Gotham Court blocked light to the extent that on cloudy days lamps had to be used continuously (figure 1.3).[40] Gotham Court was a lucrative investment. It was designed for 140 families, but by 1879 it was alleged to contain 240 families.[41] Overcrowding, filth, crime, and disease made it a notorious slum in New York for decades. It became a favorite target of reformers, including Jacob Riis, who succeeded in securing its demolition in 1895, under new provisions added to the Tenement House Law in that year.[42]

The first truly "philanthropic" housing in New York was the Workingmen's Home built in 1855 by the New York Association for Improving the Condition of the Poor. The AICP, founded in 1845, was a private organization which for over a century advocated for the poor in various ways, including sponsoring social welfare programs and several housing projects.[43] The AICP promoted private philanthropy in housing. In 1847 plans of a model block of buildings were drawn up and circulated to builders, hoping to attract interest. There was no interest, but

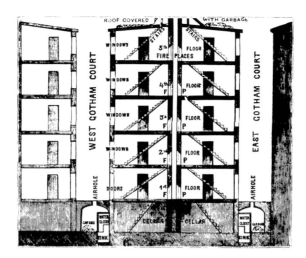

the plans were an important early attempt to deal with problems of light and air. The proposal was:

> to purchase, in some eligible part of the city, a plot of ground 200 feet square; to erect upon this a block of buildings four stories high, divided in one direction into two parts by a passage twenty feet wide, and in the other direction into four parts, by three passages, twenty, ten and twenty feet wide respectively;—each of the eight buildings thus made, consists of three houses;—each house having a single entrance, with a hall, piazza in the rear for each story, and upon each floor two rooms 15 feet by 11; each room (in turn) having two bedrooms 7 feet by 12 1/2, with sink, water closet, etc.—Thus there would be, in the four stories of each house 24 rooms for as many families;—and the block would accommodate as many families.[44]

The Workingmen's Home was more massive with higher ground coverage. It was designed by the prominent architect John W. Ritch for a narrow parcel was located between Mott and Elizabeth streets, north of Canal Street (figure 1.4).[45] Like Gotham Court, its plan was organized along an alley, which in this case connected the two streets. Exterior galleries provided access to the upper stories. The galleries were constructed of iron beams with brick arches spanning between, a fireproof construction technique that had only recently been developed for industrial buildings; probably this was the first residential application. The project is alleged to be the first tenement which provided each tenant with water and a water closet.[46] Gas lamps lighted the galleries. Standards for natural light and ventilation were slightly better than at Gotham Court, although interior bedrooms received no light.

In exchange for these superior amenities, the tenants had to abide by a strict moral and hygienic code that was enforced by the superintendent in charge. Tenantry was limited to blacks. Two large rooms on the top floor were used for con-

Figure 1.4. John W. Ritch. The Workingmen's Home, the first philanthropic housing in New York City, built in 1855 to house working-class blacks.

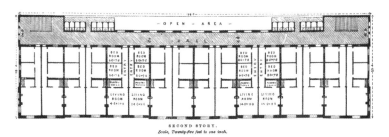

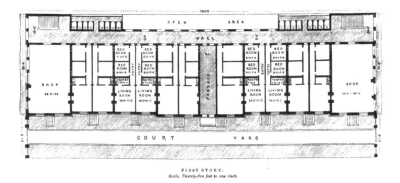

certs, moral indoctrination, and religious services. Apparently, the philanthropic goals of the establishment were successful for a time. In 1858 the annual report of the AICP noted that "at the opening of the 'Home,' and for some time afterwards, there was much disorder, disquiet, and even great indecencies of conduct; but all these evils gradually disappeared under the genial influences of their improved physical condition; and now a more orderly, cleanly, well behaved community of tenants in humble life, can nowhere be found."[47]

After twelve years the Workingmen's Home was sold to a private investor, and it became known as the Big Flat. The code of behavior was not strictly enforced, and the building became as degenerate, if not as notorious, as Gotham Court. The decline was apparently advanced by the impossibility of finding white tenants from the surrounding Irish neighborhood to rent dwellings formerly occupied by blacks.[48] By 1879 it was said to be occupied primarily by Polish Jews.[49]

In 1853, at this moment of housing innovation for the poor, an important precedent for the affluent was also established. Llewellyn Haskell, with the architect Andrew Jackson Davis, planned a 400-acre suburban community called Llewellyn Park, twelve miles from Manhattan in the Orange Mountains of New Jersey.[50] Development was limited to large houses built on five-to-ten-acre lots. The curvilinear system of roads and the landscaping of parkland were carefully studied to maintain a naturalistic setting (figure 1.5). Haskell was said to have been motivated in part by a desire to surround himself with like-thinking friends who philosophized in the popular traditions of nineteenth-century transcendentalism. The relationship of Llewellyn Park to New York City was very different from the rejectionist attitude of Brook Farm, where a decade earlier Elizabeth Peabody had asked, "What absurdity can be imagined greater than the institution of cities?"[51] Instead, Llewellyn Park was an urban extension for those who could afford it. The residents drew their economic livelihoods from the city, but could also turn their backs on it. The commute from lower Manhattan via private ferryboat and railroad coach took one hour, the same time required to reach the luxury houses near Central Park by trolley.

In 1850 commuting was not a new phenomenon in New York City. As early as 1819, Brooklyn Heights was offered as the first commuting community outside of Manhattan, and by mid-century similar expansion of the city's boundaries had occurred elsewhere.[52] The romantic preoccupation with the suburban ideal was

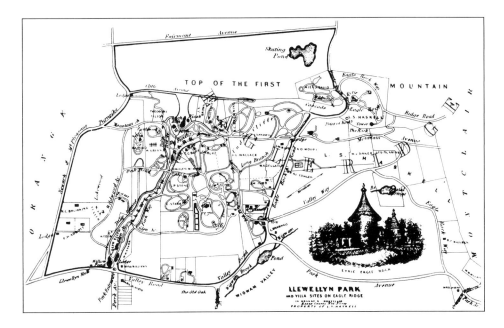

Figure 1.5. Andrew Jackson Davis. Llewellyn Park at Orange, New Jersey, as developed by 1890; begun by Llewellyn Haskell in 1853 as the first model suburban housing estate in New York City.

not new either, considering its fifty-year history in England, but Llewellyn Park was unprecedented in its extremism. The rustic guardhouse symbolized a degree of escape from urban intrusion that was unobtainable elsewhere. Similar communities for the affluent followed, such as Irving Park at Tarrytown in 1859, and Tuxedo Park in 1885.[53] By the second half of the nineteenth century, the same suburban ideals pervaded even model working-class housing. It was not until the mid-twentieth century, however, with the advent of federal highway building and FHA mortgage guarantee, that the fantasy of an escape to the suburbs could be realized by large numbers who would become a powerful new middle class.

By 1850 New York was assuming a definitive cultural dimension as the American metropolis; the New York art market had already begun to dominate other cities.[54] This factor helped formulate a unique sensibility toward housing, especially for the upper middle class. In general, the New York art scene influenced the cultural outlook of affluent New Yorkers who in turn dominated national taste at many levels. The tastes of its bohemia became a barometer of the preferences of the upper middle class, with each subsequent generation searching for new representation of its increasing wealth.[55] Housing form was an important ingredient in this equation. In this regard, an important mid-century precedent was the Tenth Street Studio, completed as artists' housing in 1857 by Richard Morris Hunt.[56] It was the first collective housing in New York designed specifically for artists, and the first of a long series of precedents that interconnected the mythic life-style of the artist with larger cultural ideals in relation to housing. The Tenth Street Studio was built by James Boorman Johnson, a leading art

Figure 1.6. Richard M. Hunt. Tenth Street Studio completed in 1857; public reception in 1868 in the studio of painter James M. Hart.

patron, who used the quasi-philanthropic project to help nourish the art scene. The building housed many of New York's most notable artists throughout the second half of the nineteenth century, and was a principal focus of artistic activity. Hunt also maintained his office in the building for many years. His background as the first American to attend the Ecole des Beaux-Arts in Paris was consistent with this cultural initiative.

The Tenth Street Studio provided both artists' studios and gallery exhibition space. The latter was a high courtyard at the center of the building, covered by a skylight. Twenty-five double-height studios surrounded the gallery, half with bedrooms attached, making the building one of the earliest apartment houses in New York City (figure 1.6). In some ways, its massing and sectional organization was a precursor, however unconscious, to the palazzo-type apartment house massing that appeared later toward the turn of the century (see figures 3.30 and 3.31). More obvious was its relationship to the duplex "artist studio" apartment that had also evolved by the early twentieth century. By then, this double-height space within a duplex apartment section had become a popular apartment type which few artists used or could even afford.

By 1865 a total of 15,309 tenements existed in New York City,[57] and the city's population was approaching 1,000,000. The new development at tenement densities was beginning to expose some generic problems with the Manhattan gridiron. The gridiron was established much earlier, when the city had a population of under 100,000, clustered at the lower end of the island. In 1807 the Common Council, recognizing that the inevitable growth of the city would require an impartial plan, requested that the New York state legislature appoint a commission to make recommendations.[58] The New York State Commissioner's Plan, which was adopted in 1811, became the sole basis for the phenomenal development of Manhattan in the nineteenth century (figure 1.7). The Commissioner's Plan organized all of Manhattan real estate above 14th Street in two thousand blocks of 200 feet by approximately 800 feet. These in turn were subdivided into 25-by-100-foot lots (figure 1.8). The long dimension of each block faced north-south, causing the majority of streets to run east-west between the Hudson and East rivers; 12 100-foot-wide north-south avenues and 155 60-foot-wide east-west cross streets were the result.

Even in 1811, the gridiron did not work well. For the small single-family row house which predominated at that time, the solar orientation of the gridiron was reversed from the ideal. Had the long dimension of each block faced east-west, both front and rear facades of each house would have received sunlight each day; however, with the north-south orientation, the south facades received all of the sun, and the north facades received none. In addition, no service alleys were provided through the centers of the blocks, although this was the usual practice in gridiron planning. The commissioner's rationalized that provision for commercial traffic along east-west streets and the maximization of negotiable land through the exclusion of service alleys were more important than adherence to the proven principles of gridiron planning. As a result, the Manhattan grid was substandard. Yet it remained inviolate for more than a century, except for Central Park, which

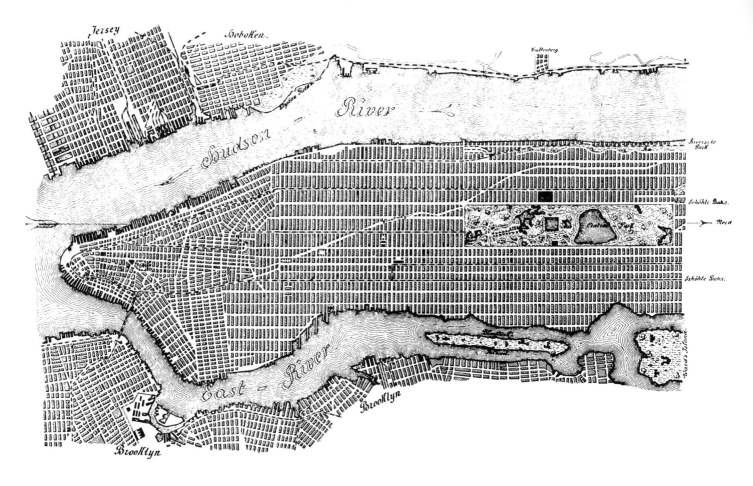

Figure 1.7. The southern half of Manhattan,
showing the commissioner's gridiron of 1811
and Central Park, which was set aside in 1853.

Figure 1.8. System of subdivision of New York
City gridiron blocks using 25-by-100-foot lots,
showing pattern of row house development
which was prevalent throughout the first half of
the nineteenth century.

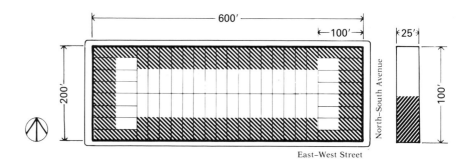

was set aside in 1853. Unfortunately, these flaws were repeated as Brooklyn, Queens, and the Bronx were developed. For housing design, it was not until well into the twentieth century that the gridiron was tampered with—in the large government-subsidized projects of the New Deal.

By 1865 the word "tenement" was a well-established term in the technical vocabulary of housing for the urban poor. As a housing type, the tenement was generated by the necessity to maximize densities within the constraint of the 25-by-100-foot building lot system. The 25-foot width of the tenement was dictated by practical structural constraints such as the maximum spans of wooden floor joists, and by the prevalent practice of building only in single-lot increments. The length of the tenement was often more than 90 percent of the 100-foot lot dimension. The height was five or six stories. The long tenements were commonly called "railroad flats" because the rooms were organized like cars on a train. Frequently older structures were converted to tenements by adding floors vertically, and by "back building" or filling in rear-yard areas with additional housing. By 1865 hundreds of Manhattan blocks had been overbuilt as tenement housing, with no standards for minimum space, light, or ventilation.

Figure 1.9 shows six steps in the evolution of the New York City tenements, from an original single-family row house to a typical railroad flat that covers 90 percent of a 25-by-100-foot lot. In many railroad flats, the rear yard was elimi-

Figure 1.9. The evolution of New York City housing prior to the tenement house legislation of 1879, from the single-family row house to the railroad flat.

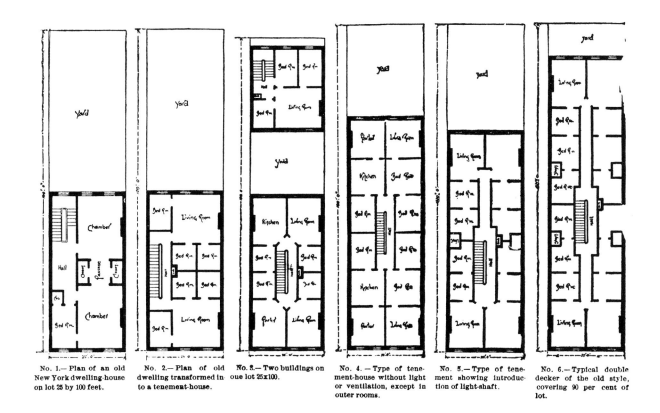

No. 1.— Plan of an old New York dwelling-house on lot 25 by 100 feet.

No. 2.— Plan of old dwelling transformed into a tenement-house.

No. 3.— Two buildings on one lot 25x100.

No. 4.— Type of tenement-house without light or ventilation, except in outer rooms.

No. 5.— Type of tenement showing introduction of light-shaft.

No. 6.— Typical double decker of the old style, covering 90 per cent of lot.

Figure 1.10. Windowless interior room of a
railroad flat, photographed by Jesse Tarbox
Beals in 1910.

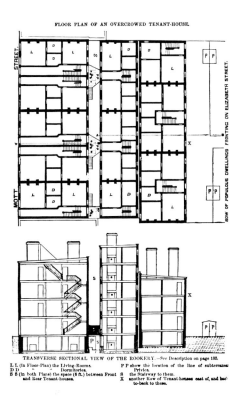

FLOOR PLAN OF AN OVERCROWED TENANT-HOUSE.

TRANSVERSE SECTIONAL VIEW OF THE ROOKERY.—See Description on page 185.

L L (In Floor-Plan) the Living-Rooms.   P P show the location of the line of subterranean
D D   "   Dormitories.   Privies.
S S (In both Plans) the space (6 ft.) between Front   S   the Stairway to them.
   and Rear Tenant-houses.   X   another Row of Tenant-houses east of, and back-
                                                     to-back to these.

Figure 1.11. A notorious tenement on Mott Street known as the Rookery, showing severe conditions of "back building," with windows entirely obstructed by the adjacent building.

nated entirely or might consist of only a few inches.[59] In these tenements, only the rooms on the street received light. A tenement floor often contained eighteen rooms, only two of which received direct sunlight—if the facade faced south. The interior rooms did not have any ventilation, unless air shafts were provided (figure 1.10). The practice of back building could lead to absurd results, such as the notorious Rookery on Mott Street between Bleecker and East Houston streets (figure 1.11).[60] Three parallel rows of housing were built on five small lots, with total street frontage of 90 feet. The inner and middle rows had only a foot of air space between them. The windows of one faced the brick wall of the other. The space between the outer and middle rows of housing was 6 feet wide, and filled with privies. In 1865 the Rookery housed 352 persons, at an extremely high density of 23 square feet per person.

Back building was common in every area of Manhattan where high densities prevailed. In 1882 the *New York Daily Tribune* placed rear tenements in "a class by themselves" for insalubrity in New York housing: "situated in dark courts and approached by narrow, foul smelling alleys . . . their position renders them not only dangerous from a sanitary point of view, but doubly perilous in case of fire."[61] Some interesting formal variations could be found, such as on East 11th Street between First and Second avenues, where the lot lines legislated by the gridiron had become confused with the earlier diagonal system of Stuyvesant Street (fig-

Figure 1.12. A Lower East Side tenement block with an unusual pattern of back building caused by the superimposition of a gridiron on an earlier street pattern.

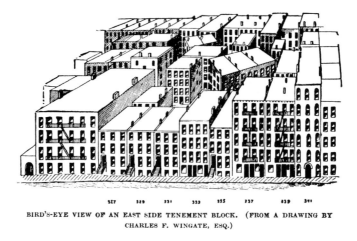

BIRD'S-EYE VIEW OF AN EAST SIDE TENEMENT BLOCK. (FROM A DRAWING BY CHARLES F. WINGATE, ESQ.)

Figure 1.13. Typical back tenement on East 28th Street recorded in 1865, showing privies and shacks in the leftover "yard" area.

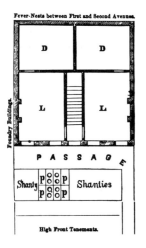

ure 1.12). An unusual juxtaposition between the orthogonal and diagonal buildings resulted. In the small areas of open space left over, the communal water taps and water closets were placed to be shared by families in one or more of the surrounding buildings (figure 1.13). The water closets were either privies or larger "school sinks," depending on whether the excrement was removed by hand or drained from the vault into the street sewer. Typically, hand removal was infrequent, or the sewer would be clogged up. School sinks were especially infamous sources of filth and disease.[62]

As late as 1865, the incorporation of small air shafts in tenement housing was still considered to be an improvement over standard practice. For tenements built to high densities on individual lots, there were no radical options for design innovation. The "improvements" of the period were limited to rather minuscule innovation in relation to standard building practice. A "diamond"-shaped air shaft might lend an aesthetic touch to an otherwise minimal improvement (figure 1.14). The principle of air shafts shared between adjoining lots was sometimes used to increase minimal ventilation.[63] Figure 1.15 shows an early version of the shared air shaft for an "improved" tenement located on Leonard Street. Its generous yard contains a luxurious number of school sinks.

The emerging profession of architecture generally did not involve itself with the problems of tenement design. The economic constraints which firmly controlled the form of tenements put their planning totally within the province of the builders. Moreover, there was little about the evolution of the profession which might encourage a concern for the housing problems of the poor. The architectural profession pursued the monumental and the unique, rather than the ordinary and repetitive. Already there appeared to have been some public recognition among officials interested in housing reform of the potential dangers of the professional limitations which were developing. The city inspector, George W. Morton, in his report of 1857, called for the establishment of a college of architecture with social purpose, including the

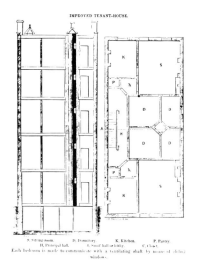

IMPROVED TENANT-HOUSE.

IMPROVED TENANT-HOUSE.

S S Sitting-Rooms.
K K Kitchens.
D D Dormitories.

S. Sitting-room.   D. Dormitory.   K. Kitchen.   P. Pantry.
H, Principal hall.   A, Small hall or lobby.   C, Closet.
Each bedroom is made to communicate with a ventilating shaft by means of sliding windows.

Figure 1.14. Two "improved" tenements from 1865; so-called because of the provision for rather minuscule airshafts.

diffusion of information as to the principles of hygiene, among the great mass of the population . . . for securing the united cooperation of architecture and agriculture, with the views of the medical profession, and for promoting, from time to time, all those specific improvements which their resources, assisted by the chemistry and the engineering of modern times may render it desirable to introduce.

In no place can a college of architecture be founded with such advantage, as in a large city such as New York, where so much building is in progress, and from which improvements will naturally extend to the whole American continent.[64]

Of course, no such college of architecture developed in New York City or anywhere else, at that time or since. The precedent set by Richard Morris Hunt in 1846, as the first American to enroll in the Ecole des Beaux-Arts in Paris, became the goal of every aspiring American architectural student. For the developing profession of architecture, it was the theory of the Beaux-Arts, rather than the reality of the tenements, which would become a preoccupation. By 1879 forty-six Americans had enrolled in the Beaux-Arts, including Hunt, Henry Hobson Richardson, Charles Follen McKim, Louis Sullivan, and John Carrère. They formed an elite group that quickly proliferated and dominated professional training for decades to come. The first "professional" school of architecture was established at the Massachusetts Institute of Technology in 1868, with a Beaux-Arts orientation. Its director, William Robert Ware, was a Beaux-Arts alumnus, as were several other faculty.[65] The pioneering MIT program bore little relation to the college of architecture advocated by the city inspector in 1857.

By the 1870s a consensus among architects had developed that the Manhattan gridiron was a deterrent to the city's architectural advancement. Objections were aesthetic, as well as functional. They believed the possibilities for a great architecture in New York City were hampered by the gridiron. The landscape architect Frederick Law Olmsted wrote in 1876 that

Figure 1.15. Early "improved" tenement on Leonard Street, with a luxurious number of privies in the rear yard area.

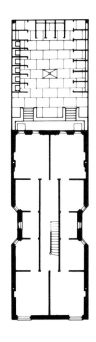

EARLY PRECEDENTS   17

Figure 1.16. Edward T. Potter. An analysis published in 1878, showing two alternatives for the reorganization of the New York City gridiron to permit greater possibilities for improved tenement design.

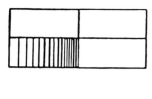

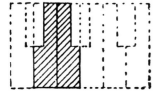

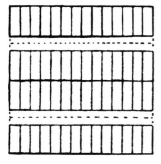

New York, when the [gridiron] system was adopted, though vaguely anticipating something of the greatness that has since been thrust upon her, viewed all questions of her own civic equipment, very nearly from the position which a small, poor, remote provincial village would not be expected to take.

There are numerous structures, both public and private, in London and Paris, and most other large towns of Europe, which could not be built in New York, for want of a site of suitable extent and proportions. The trustees of Columbia College sought for years to obtain the privilege of consolidating two of the uniform blocks of the system, into which their own property had been divided, in order to erect sufficient buildings for their purposes, in one unbroken group, but it was denied them.[66]

Olmsted also noted that the lack of service alleys hindered building at higher densities by eliminating the possibility of developing legitimate streets at the interior of the blocks whenever necessary. He argued that without alleys, only 100-ft lots were possible, when shorter ones could be more useful for certain applications:

In New York, lots of 100 feet in depth cannot be afforded for small, cheap houses. The ground-rent would be in too large proportion to the rent of the betterments. In no prosperous old city are families of moderate means found living, except temporarily in the outskirts, in separate houses on undivided blocks measuring 200 feet from thoroughfare to thoroughfare. It is hardly to be hoped that they ever will be in New York under the plan of 1807.[67]

By the 1870s, such ideas were in the air. In 1875, Dr. Stephen Smith, the well-known reformer in the health field, advocated reallocation of the New York lot system to blocks reduced to 50-ft-widths rather than 200 feet.[68] Architects began to explore similar ways to adjust the gridiron at the scale of individual blocks, in order to overcome its limitations. In 1878 Edward T. Potter, who was to become one of the most interesting nineteenth-century theorists for housing,[69] began publishing his research on modification of the gridiron to improve light and ventilation in tenement housing. The analysis indicated that by building on multiple lots, rather than single lots, the restrictions of the twenty-five-foot module could be overcome to increase manyfold the design possibilities for tenement plans.[70] For example, a series of double lots would allow a system of back-to-back air slots. Light and ventilation would be vastly improved over the railroad flat (figure 1.16). The principle proved to be an important one for future tenement house legislation.

Potter's study contrasted light and ventilation conditions for typical row house development within the Manhattan gridiron with those for a modified block in which small north-south streets were introduced to permit houses to have east-west solar orientation (figures 1.17 and 1.18). It showed that light could be improved, while retaining a land coverage comparable to tenement back building. An embryonic version of the small connector or "mews" street had been used previously in both Gotham Court and the Workingmen's Home. It was developed further in a number of model housing proposals made during the 1870s. In 1879

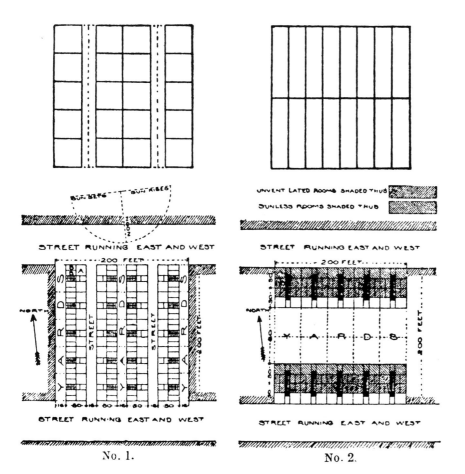

Figure 1.17. Edward T. Potter. Proposal made in 1878 for gridiron reorganization achieved by introducing new east-west "mews" street within existing gridiron blocks (No. 1), compared with the traditional New York City row house pattern (No. 2).

No. 1.

No. 2.

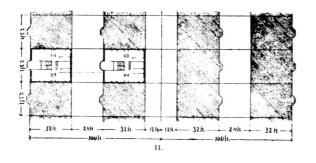 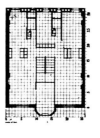

Figure 1.18. Edward T. Potter. Proposal made in 1879 for a new house type based on the introduction of east-west mews streets within existing gridiron blocks.

Figure 1.19. George Post. A proposal made in 1879 with George Dresser, an engineer, for the reorganization of the New York City gridiron through the introduction of east-west mews streets.

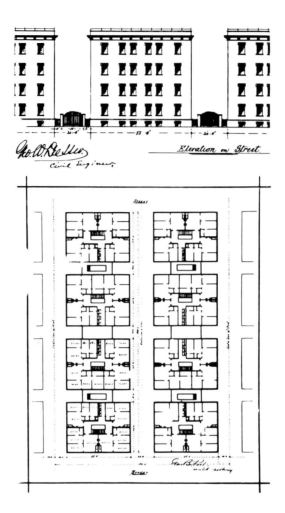

the well-known architect George Post, with George Dresser, an engineer, published a housing design using a mews reorganization of the Manhattan gridiron (figure 1.19).[71] In addition to Potter and Post, other architects, including Nelson Derby, published similar proposals.[72]

The logic behind the east-west reorganization schemes was sound. Had the principle been widely applied, light and ventilation in New York City tenements could have been vastly improved without sacrificing density. The mechanics of Manhattan land speculation however, did not permit removal of potentially salable land from each block for the connector streets. Even if the city had doubly reimbursed owners, permanent removal of the land from the market would have reduced potential profits for an infinite future. The original gridiron was designed to maximize profits. Land speculation was big business. The rights of its practitioners were not easily infringed upon.

2

Legislating the Tenement

B Y the 1850s, political pressure was building for legal intervention in the tenement house problem in New York City. The condition of the poor was steadily worsening, aggravated by disaster. For example, the great cholera epidemic of 1849 took approximately 5,000 lives. Yet another cholera epidemic in 1854 caused 2,509 deaths.[1] The national economic difficulties of 1857 were so severe that the Common Council was forced to provide jobs for the unemployed and distribute food to the poor. In 1858 there were 25,000 unemployed, who with their families represented approximately 100,000 in dire need.[2] The annual reports of the Association for Improving the Condition of the Poor in those years depicted suffering unprecedented in the history of the city. The New York state legislature had to take action. In 1856 the first legislative commission was set up to study the housing problem. Its work, which was continued in 1857, described in detail the conditions of the tenements, but no legislation was advanced.[3]

Conditions in the city were beginning to take their toll in terms of the general social order. Major riots in 1849 and 1857 pointed toward the increasingly pathological state of the tenement population. The most traumatic civil disturbance, however, was the "draft riots" in July 1863.[4] On the surface they were a reaction to newly imposed involuntary conscription for military service in the Civil War. But the violence was also a product of the intolerable condition of the city's poor. The wretched and diseased population of the tenements, and especially of the Sixth Ward, poured out into the city streets. They demonstrated beyond question the connection between the housing problem and the threat of civil disturbance. Immediately following the draft riots, a group of influential private citizens formed the Citizens' Association of New York to advocate improvement in the sanitary conditions of the city.

The Citizens' Association appointed a subcommittee called the Council of Hygiene and Public Health to undertake a comprehensive survey of conditions. The monumental report, published in 1865, remains a unique document for its scope and thoroughness. Each of twenty-nine "Sanitary Inspection Districts" was analyzed in detail, and the report included a degree of architectural documentation unknown in previous surveys. The most sensational statistic cited in the report stated that of a population of more than 700,000 in New York City (not including Brooklyn), a total of 480,368 persons lived in 15,309 tenement houses with substandard conditions.[5] One year later a committee on tenement houses appointed by the New York state legislature published another report which supplemented the architectural documentation of the Council of Hygiene. This report provided physical and social analysis of a number of tenement case studies.[6]

In 1866 and 1867 the pressure for serious government legislation yielded the first initiatives toward change. In 1866 the state legislature approved a comprehensive law defining standards for building construction in New York City.[7] The following year the legislature passed its first comprehensive housing law, the Tenement House Act of 1867, which marked the beginning of its long involvement with raising the standards for low-cost housing design. The "tenement" was at last legally defined: "Any house, building, or portion thereof, which is rented, leased, let or hired out to be occupied or is occupied, as the home or residence of more than three families living independently of one another and doing their own cooking upon the premises, or by more than two families upon a floor, so living and cooking and having a common right in the halls, stairways, yards, water-closets, or privies, or some of them."[8]

The purpose of the Tenement House Act was to supplement the new building construction regulations in relation to the special problems of tenements. Both documents required additional construction as an increased precaution against fire, including mandatory provisions of fire escapes for nonfireproof buildings. In relation to hygiene, the Tenement House Act specified that there had to be at least one water closet for every twenty tenants. Tenement house spatial standards were only slightly improved, with minor attention paid to distances between buildings. The cellar dwelling was prohibited, unless the ceiling was one foot above the street level.

The 1860s also saw major advances in the enforcement of building standards, as the first moves were made toward the development of a modern building bureaucracy for New York City. Between 1813 and 1849 building laws had been enforced by city-appointed surveyors; between 1849 and 1860, by fire wardens within the Fire Department. In 1860 the state legislature created the office of superintendent of buildings within the Fire Department, with a staff of inspectors to enforce structural safety laws. In 1862 this office was made independent of the Fire Department and renamed the Department of Survey and Inspection of Buildings. All architect's plans were subject to its review, and appeals went directly to the supreme court of the City of New York. The legislature created the Metropolitan Board of Health in 1866 to replace the old Board of Health which dated from 1801. In 1867 the Metropolitan Board of Health became the body responsible for enforcing the new Tenement House Act. Yet in the same year, the powers granted to the Department of Survey and Inspection of Buildings over tenement houses were also strengthened.[9] This dichotomy between the authority of the "health bureaucracy" and the "design bureaucracy" remained problematic until the turn of the century. The enforcement of tenement legislation was most affected by this structure. For tenements more than any other building type, "health" and "design" were inextricably intertwined.

With the growth of enforcement, the review of architectural plans for compliance with building regulations was made mandatory. The 1862 law placed this responsibility within the Department for Survey and Inspection of Buildings. But in 1874 appeals were relegated to a Board of Examiners instead of the supreme court. Under the corrupt conditions of the Tweed years, the relationship formed between architects and the city building bureaucracy was apparently troublesome. As a result, appeals were set up entirely outside of the judicial system.[10] With enforcement of review procedures, the growing architectural profession found a new way to justify its existence: technicians were needed to translate building practice into the terms of accountability required by the city. Nevertheless, the symbiotic relationship between architects and the city building bureaucracy did not always work to strengthen the profession. The relationship was clouded by the lack of an independent mechanism for judging the professional competence of architects.

For large and aesthetically pretentious building, the position of the architect was becoming well established. Generous budgets simplified meeting minimum building standards. But for low-budget and aesthetically simple building, the architect's claim to expertise was not as strong. By the close of the 1870s, there was considerable agitation within the profession to fix qualification standards for the practice of architecture. The arguments cited the need to strengthen the profession by "forbidding non-architects to do architects' work," and to protect the public interest by "requiring that architects do their work well."[11] Strangely enough, in New York State, the location of the largest city in the nation, an independent professional examination for architects was not established until 1915, after eight other states had already approved similar systems.[12] The licensing of plumbers, however, was made mandatory in 1881.[13]

The mere existence of a building bureaucracy did not guarantee enforcement of the law. One of the most blatant failures involved the provision of fire escapes as mandated by the Tenement House Act of 1867. By 1900, out of a sample of 2,877 tenements, 98 had no fire escapes at all, and 653 had only rear fire escapes.[14] In their special report to the New York State Tenement House Commission of 1900, housing reformers Lawrence Veiller and Hugh Bonner placed the blame on architectural vanity:

> There is no reason why fire escapes should be omitted on the front of such buildings except the pride of the architect and the owner, who dislike seeing cheap iron balconies upon the front of their buildings. If these balconies offend their artistic sensibilities, they have two remedies: one to make balconies artistic; the other to build their buildings fireproof. We believe that the protection of human life is of much greater importance than anything else.[15]

The fire escape clause of the Tenement House Act of 1867 legislated a major impact on the aesthetic character of New York streets, yet the reaction of architects and owners to the challenges of this problem was limited. Frequently, fire escapes were haphazardly attached to the most elaborately designed facades, with no consideration given to the relationship between the two. The facade was within the realm of architecture, and the fire escape in the realm of the law.

Architects were involved with housing for the poor typically as liberal supporters of housing reform movements, rather than as professionals actively engaged in the elaboration of knowledge concerning design innovation. Architectural innovation came indirectly through legislation which, in a sense, acted as a buffer between professional ideals and the problems of producing low-cost housing in a capitalist society. But the circumstances surrounding the Tenement House Act of 1879 show that even this level of involvement had its difficulties. The act of 1879 revised only Sections 13 and 14 of the Tenement House Act of 1867, but the revisions were substantial.[16] The most radical provision was that no new tenement house could occupy more than 65 percent of a 25-by-100-foot lot. Another important provision prohibited the practice of tenement back building unless adequate light and ventilation were maintained. More water closets were required than in 1867. Unfortunately, the Board of Health's power to enforce the specific provisions was discretionary. The board yielded to real estate interests, and the new provisions were, in effect, nullified. The famous "dumbell" tenement, also commonly called "Old Law Tenement," was enforced as a kind of compromise. Its coverage was usually at least 80 percent of a 25-by-100-foot lot.

This design interpretation of Sections 13 and 14 of the Tenement House Act of 1879 by the Board of Health bore a curious relationship to a tenement house design competition for architects, sponsored in the previous year by an influential new magazine called *Plumber and Sanitary Engineer*. The program called for a tenement plan that could be repeated on 25-by-100-foot gridiron lots. There was to be particular emphasis on improving the typical railroad flat in terms of light, ventilation, sanitation, and fireproofing.[17] In addition, the schemes had to be economically real, accommodating enough families to pay as an investment. Of the 209 schemes submitted to the competition, the prizewinning schemes were undoubtedly the most conservative, with only minimal modification of prevailing practice in the building of railroad flats.[18] First prize was given to James Ware, a New York architect, who was to become a major figure in tenement design. His design was a variant of the dumbell-type plan, which covered approximately 90 percent of the lot (figure 2.1). Four dwellings on each floor surrounded a central core that contained a water closet and stairway. Light shafts on both sides of the core could be combined with those of adjacent tenements, to increase their effectiveness.

Of the twelve placing entries, most were as conservative as the Ware scheme. Several used innovative approaches, however, going beyond simple rationalization of the status quo (figure 2.2). The scheme by George Da Cunha of New York placed open-air galleries at the center of the plan, to help expand the dimensions of the interior courtyard. A second scheme submitted by James Ware, which placed ninth, used another variation of the internal gallery, achieving considerable open space at the center of the plan. The scheme of Philadelphia architect Robert G. Kennedy was designed to leave a five-foot-wide slot along the entire length of

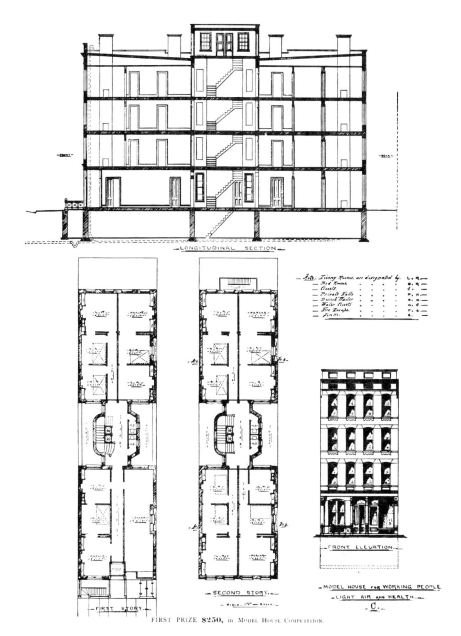

Figure 2.1. James E. Ware. The winning entry to the tenement house competition of 1878 sponsored by *Plumber and Sanitary Engineer*.

the lot. Presumably this space could adjoint an adjacent slot, creating ten feet between buildings. In order to maintain a high coverage, Kennedy built along the entire hundred-foot dimension of the lot. The open wall was crenellated to maximize light and air.

LEGISLATING THE TENEMENT   **25**

Figure 2.2. Robert G. Kennedy, James E. Ware, George DaCunha (*top* to *bottom*). Placing entries in the tenement house competition of 1878; all three maintained higher design standards than the winning entry.

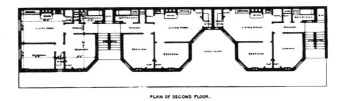

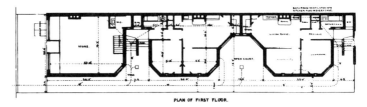

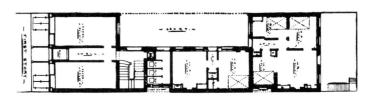

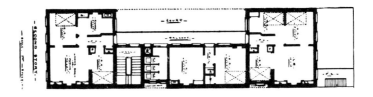

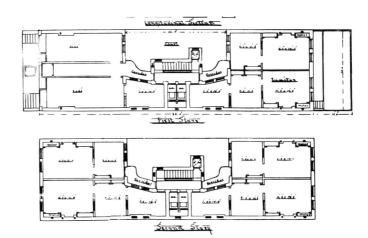

When the winning entries were announced, an article in the *New York Times* expressed what came to be widespread popular criticism of the dumbells:

If the prize plans are the best offered, which we can hardly believe, they simply demonstrate the problem is insoluble. The three which have received the highest prizes offer a very slightly better arrangement than hundreds of tenements now do. They are simply "double houses" front and rear, with the space between occupied by halls and water closets. They have all of the disadvantages of "double houses" which have so often called forth sanitary censure and even adverse legislation. The only access to air, apart from the front, is through the courts in the small spaces between the houses; for the rear, if these plans were generally adopted, would also be closed up by the rear wall of the house in the next street. To add to their ill effects, each suite on the second storey has apparently that old nuisance, a dark bedroom which under the present arrangement, is such a prolific source of fevers and disease. In some of the plans, this room ventilates through other rooms, and in others by a small well. The only advantages offered, apparently, over the old system, are in fireproof stairways, more privacy of halls, and the ventilation of the water closets.[19]

The *Plumber and Sanitary Engineer* competition was crucial to the passage of the Tenement House Act of 1879. Several of the competition's organizers founded the New York Sanitary Reform Society, which in turn drafted the legislation and lobbied for its enactment by the New York state legislature during the winter of 1879.[20] After enactment by the legislature, the Board of Health was only willing to enforce the standards represented by the winning dumbell scheme of the competition, in spite of the severe criticism directed against such schemes (figure 2.3). Charles F. Chandler, the respected president of the Board of Health, could not enforce the law because, as the *New York Times* expressed it, he "no doubt feared the political influence which the landlords could bring to bear on the Legislature."[21] Real estate interests were undoubtedly satisfied. No one could argue that the dumbell was not an improvement over the railroad tenement; yet coverage remained very high, insuring continued maximum profitability. The housing bureaucracy was also satisfied. Ostensibly, they could still maintain control over tenement building. Unfortunately, the young architectural profession was forced to lend its credibility to the compromise through the use of the "open" competition. There appears to have been a kind of gentlemen's agreement between the profession and the city building bureaucracy, if not explicitly arranged, at least implicitly encouraged by professional reticence.

The uncomfortable position forced upon architects in relation to the enforcement of the Tenement House Act of 1879 was typified in the stance taken by Alfred J. Bloor, secretary of the New York chapter of the American Institute of Architects. In a long paper read to the Fourteenth National Convention in November 1880, Bloor condemned the tenement house competition and the resultant dumbell enforced by the Board of Health: "The recent tenement house competition, so much exploited in the current newspapers, resulted in the prizes being awarded for designs each of which included the dark middle room, which is the horror of physicians and visitors among the poor, which has been so strenuously

Figure 2.3. "Dumbell" tenement plan devised by James E. Ware and enforced under the provision of the Tenement House Act of 1879. Also known as the Old Law tenement, it used a coverage of approximately 80 percent.

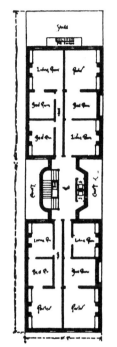
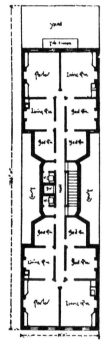

No. 10.—First prize plan -- model house competition of March, 1879, awarded to James E. Ware, architect.

No. 11.— Mr. Ware's modification of his prize plan.

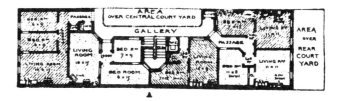

Figure 2.4. Alfred J. Bloor. Proposal for a tenement made in 1880, using a single 25-by-100-foot lot with mediocre results.

inveighed against by the Board of Health, and which, in practice, would have necessarily involved the official condemnation of the plans by the Building Department."[22] Bloor argued that the 25-by-100-foot lot could not produce satisfactory results anyway: yet he could not resist producing his own "solution" for the 25-by-200-foot lot (figure 2.4). Beyond this contribution, he could only express the vague hope that new improvements in rapid transit might eventually provide "independent homes for many of the better sort who now live in tenement houses, which . . . might well be in the shape of disconnected cottages."[23] This latter vision was to become the dominant national design ideology for housing the working class in the next half century.

In spite of the reluctance of the mainstream architectural profession to address such issues, by the decade of the 1880s there was a growing body of housing research which presented design alternatives to the railroad flat. Many of these unbuilt schemes prefigured the innovations which eventually would be mandated by law, though in some cases, not until well into the twentieth century. As early as 1877, the architect Nelson Derby published a tenement proposal for a 100-by-100-foot lot which bore many similarities to plans produced by the tenement legislation of 1901 (figure 2.5).[24] His use of four 25-foot lots permitted an arrangement of four buildings around an internal courtyard. The three stairs were open and roofed over in glass. The sensibility of Derby's proposal was also echoed in

Figure 2.5. Nelson Derby. Proposal for a tenement made in 1877, using four 25-by-100-foot lots to produce an innovative organization around an internal courtyard.

Richard Morris Hunt's advocacy of central courtyard planning for tenements, whereby the air shafts of several single-lot tenements would be combined within a larger building.[25]

Among the most important of the early housing researchers was Edward T. Potter, who continued investigations into tenement design throughout his long career. His model tenement proposal published in 1888 was probably the best known (figure 2.6).[26] Potter enlarged the gridiron lot to 37.5 feet, thereby achieving greater possibilities for a good dwelling arrangement using the principle shown in figure 1.14. Large "light slots" penetrated into the building mass from the street, reversing the normal prototype which placed the slots facing rear yards. The stairwells were entered through the slots from the street. Potter's proposal was completely outside the realm of any established stylistic precedent—having been generated by a purely functional analysis of the problems at hand (figure 2.7). A series of undulations in the side walls of the buildings were carefully calculated to secure an oblique view to the street for each dwelling. All dwellings had cross ventilation, and the solar orientations were adjusted so that every one would receive sea breezes on hot summer evenings, and at least one hour of direct sunlight daily. Steel, masonry, and glass were used exclusively. All stairs were roofed in glass, and the building entrances were enclosed with stained glass. Some windows were covered with vertical translucent louvres to insure privacy; others incorporated solar shading devices. The roofs were abundantly planted with vegetation.

Edward T. Potter traveled to the International Congress on Low Cost Housing held at Brussels in 1897 to present his housing designs, including the large maquette of his model tenement. He emphasized the need to put to good use the developing building technology, such as new materials and techniques, electricity or hydraulics, for solving the problems of tenements as well as other building types.[27] His ideas were apparently well received. Potter was the first of several relatively unknown but important New York architects who took up the architectural side of housing reform. They tended to work in a vein of functionalism which remained outside of mainstream architectural aesthetics until the 1930s. For example, Potter's high-rise building proposals published in 1887 postulated a radically new vision for the form of tall buildings in New York City, based on extensive research into the problems of providing sufficient light and air for this emerging building type (figure 2.8).[28] The principles behind his setback diagrams did not appear in New York City building legislation until 1916; they appeared more fully in 1929. Alfred J. Bloor, writing at the time of Potter's death in 1905, described an architect who had

> devoted most of his adult years not to securing commissions giving him opportunities to gratify his taste and talent for the production of fine architecture, ecclesiastical, domestic or (and best paying) the financial sky-scraping variety, but for the solution of the momentous problem of how to render fasible the providing of proper homes for the vast majority of all communities, those not rich, the poor, the very poor—homes, whether urban, suburban or rural, by which everything possible, under the unavoidable restrictions of expenditure, local or-

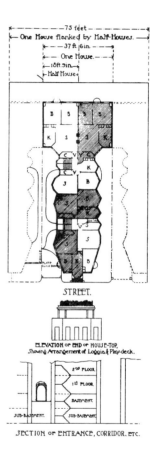

Figure 2.6. Edward T. Potter. Proposal for a tenement made in 1888, using a 37.5-by-100-foot lot, with a multitude of detailed functional criteria for the organization of the plan.

Figure 2.7. Edward T. Potter. Model of proposed tenement expressing a "functionalist" approach in its radically innovative appearance.

MODEL
Of An Improved
TENEMENT HOUSE

dinance, site, environment, etc., for the supply of sunlight, thorough draught, heating, cooling and ventilating of quarters, with the privacy and convenience of their occupants, has been thoroughly thought out and planned.[29]

By 1900 more than 80,000 tenements were built in greater New York City. These buildings housed a population of 2.3 million, out of a total city population of 3,369,898. Approximately 60,000 of the tenements had been built after 1880,[30] all of them Old Law. Most were designed to the dumbell standards which con-

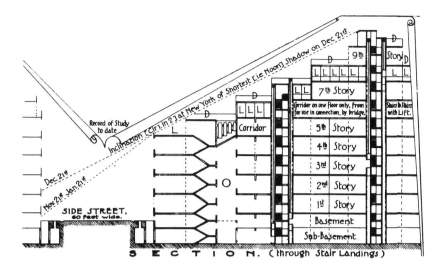

tinued to meet the approval of the city building bureaucracy until 1901 (figure 2.9). No significant advances in tenement standards were made during this critical twenty-year period, when the population of the metropolitan area increased from 1,844,785 to 3,369,898.[31] There was only minor legislative reform, much of it unenforceable. The building bureaucracy went through a series of reorganizations, starting in 1880 when the Department of Buildings was placed within the Fire Department as a result of economic cutbacks. In 1892 it was made independent again, and its jurisdiction was extended to the light, ventilation, plumbing, and drainage of buildings — powers formerly exercised by the Board of Health. The department retained these powers after the enactment of the Greater New York Charter of 1897, which placed Manhattan, Brooklyn, the Bronx, Queens, and Richmond under the central control of the Department of Buildings.[32]

The first effort to unify New York City building legislation came with the Consolidation Act of 1882. This law was an attempt to remove inconsistencies between jurisdictions by creating a single document governing building construction laws. The building laws for tenements and for general building were integrated for the first time, yet retained separate enforcement bureaucracies in the Department of Buildings and the Tenement House Department.[33] The "health" side of legislation remained with the tenement house laws, although by the turn of the century, bureaucratic transformations had gradually weakened the old dichotomy between design and health for enforcement. The familiar problem of the examination of the architect's plans became more acute. The situation was clearly exposed at the hearings of the New York State Assembly Special Committee of 1899, which investigated the offices and departments of New York City government. The architect Ernest Flagg testified that:

All those [architects] that I have talked to seem to think that the present arrangement, or the present board, is very bad . . . because it is responsible to no one, and the people who compose it have not received the training that people

Figure 2.9. Tenement house plans published in 1887 as representative of those which could meet the approval of the Board of Health.

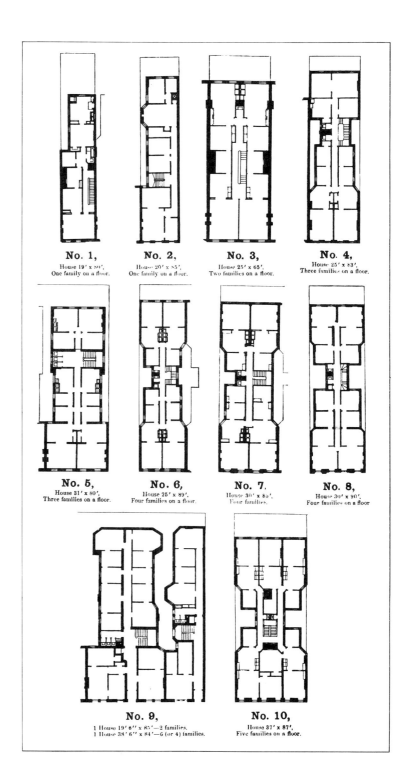

No. 1,
House 19' x 80',
One family on a floor.

No. 2,
House 20' x 85',
One family on a floor.

No. 3,
House 25' x 65',
Two families on a floor.

No. 4,
House 25' x 83',
Three families on a floor.

No. 5,
House 31' x 80',
Three families on a floor.

No. 6,
House 25' x 89',
Four families on a floor.

No. 7,
House 30' x 85',
Four families.

No. 8,
House 30' x 90',
Four families on a floor

No. 9,
1 House 19' 6'' x 85'—2 families.
1 House 38' 6'' x 84'—6 (or 4) families.

No. 10,
House 37' x 87',
Five families on a floor.

holding that position should have. I understand that it is a matter of general knowledge in the profession that these men have been closely associated together in business enterprises. . . . It is my opinion that there is favoritism, if not worse, in the conduct of the Board of Examiners. It is an opinion that has been shared in by others. The builders and architects are under great difficulty in coming out publicly against this system. We can be annoyed beyond endurance, and I expect to be annoyed for this testimony that I give now.[34]

The New York state legislature appointed a second Tenement House committee in 1884, after considerable agitation led by the activist founder of the Society for Ethical Culture, Felix Adler. This committee reported that the requirements of the Tenement House Act of 1867 of one water closet for every twenty persons had been largely ignored. They found, in fact, that only 30.1 percent of the tenements examined had any water closets at all, and almost none had running water above the first floor.[35] The committee recognized that in order to legislate the form of the tenement, a definition of scientific criteria for sanitary standards was necessary. The report hinted that the development of "preventive" measures required legislation of substantial architectural design controls:

The chief practical difficulty in dealing with sanitary problems is to establish a sufficiently clear and satisfactory statement of what constitutes unwholesome conditions. At present the law defines an unsanitary building as one which actually contains infection by which sickness may be conveyed to other inmates in the building. In the present state of knowledge, however, this definition should be extended so as to include conditions which general experience has shown favor the spread of infection and not wait until infection actually appears. . . . Hitherto, the sole standard which has been applied by the health authorities to test the wholesomeness of the building has been the amount of air space allotted to each individual, but it is now desirable to apply other standards which would cover the necessities of ventilation, dryness of site, and sunlight.[36]

The design recommendations of the Tenement House Committee of 1884 were extensive. They included the enforcement of the 65 percent coverage specified in the Act of 1879; the elimination of all privies; the provision of water supply on each floor of tenements; direct light through external windows for all inner hallways and rooms; and the provision of electric street lighting in tenement districts. The tenement house laws were not amended until 1887, three years after the committee made its report. At that time, several enforcement provisions were added, but no additional design controls were imposed.[37] The committee report had little impact on the legislation.

The lack of substantial new legislation and the recalcitrant atmosphere for enforcement was partially caused by the threat of legal recourse on the part of anti-reform interests. These fears were given ample credence by a New York State Court of Appeals decision in 1885. The Court struck down an amendment to the Tenement House Law passed in the previous year which had broadened the base for reform by imposing controls on non-residential uses permitted in tenements.

Specifically, the bill had been sponsored by the Cigar-Maker's Union to prohibit manufacturing tobacco products in homes, forcing the manufacturers to assume more responsibility for conditions in the workplace.[38] Also addressed was overcrowding, later described in graphic terms by Theodore Roosevelt, a New York State Assemblyman who was a member of the legislative committee that visited tenements while preparing the bill:

> In the overwhelming majority of cases. . . . there were one, two, or three room apartments, and the work of manufacturing the tobacco went on day and night in the eating, living, and sleeping rooms — sometimes in one room. I have always remembered one room in which two families were living. On my inquiry as to who the third adult male was I was told that he was a boarder with one of the families. There were several children, three men, and two women in this room. The tobacco was stowed about everywhere, alongside the foul bedding, and in a corner where there were scraps of food. The men, women, and children in this room worked by day and far into the evening, and they slept and ate there. They were Bohemians, unable to speak English, except that one of the children knew enough to act as interpreter.[39]

Using the most emphatic language possible, the court found the bill to be a threat to "personal liberty and private property," presumably that of the cigar company proprietors:

> Such legislation may invade one class of rights today and another tomorrow, and if it can be sanctioned under the Constitution, while far removed in time we will not be far away in practical statesmanship from those ages when governmental prefects supervised the building of houses, the rearing of cattle, the sowing of seed and the reaping of grain, and governmental ordinances regulated the movements and labor of artisans, the rate of wages, the price of food, the diet and clothing of the people, and a large range of other affairs long since in all civilized lands regarded as outside of governmental functions. Such governmental interferences disturb the normal adjustments of the social fabric, and usually derange the delicate and complicated machinery of industry and cause a score of evils while attempting the removal of one.[40]

The court decision was a conservative reaction to the previous housing and health reforms, and a definitive victory for real estate and manufacturing interests. It cast a pall over the entire reform movement. Public officials had to enforce existing legislation conservatively for fear of inducing further damaging litigation, and the introduction of substantial new bills in the New York state legislature could only be considered as an uncertain exercise. Roosevelt later described the severity of the impact: "This decision completely blocked tenement-house reform legislation in New York for a score of years, and hampers it to this day [1914]. It was one of the most serious setbacks which the cause of industrial and social progress and reform ever received."[41]

On the positive side, however, the impasse appears to have simply intensified the determination of the reform movement. During the decades of the 1880s and 1890s populist reformers became a driving force that focused national attention

Figure 2.10. Photo by Jacob Riis of an air shaft in an Old Law tenement.

on the tenements. This movement fully exploited new possibilities relating to the expansion of a mass national media. New tools, such as a photojournalism, added an element of realism to the documentation of tenement house conditions (figure 2.10). Jacob Riis was the giant among the reformers, almost turning tenement reform into a political crusade. Riis, an immigrant who worked as a newspaper reporter, published his first crusading article, "How the Other Half Lives," in *Scribner's* magazine in 1889, followed by his first book of the same title in 1890.[42]

Throughout the next decade he published a series of popular books and campaigned widely for reform, appealing to the moral sensibilities of the "first half." Dr. Stephen Smith, who had been largely responsible for the creation of the Metropolitan Board of Health in 1866 and served as commissioner of health between 1868 and 1875, launched a campaign for a National Board of Health. This bill was passed by the U.S. Congress in 1879. Like Riis, Smith's activities helped focus national attention on conditions in New York City. And like his predecessor, Dr. John Griscom, Smith helped build a scientific basis for health and housing legislation.[43] In another vein, with the founding of the Charity Organization Society in 1882 the activities of charitable organizations in the city were centrally coordinated. In general, the COS enlarged the concerns of the Association for Improving the Condition of the Poor.[44]

The Tenement House Committee of 1884 had expressed some frustration at finding an adequate "scientific" basis for tenement legislation. But these disappointments were soon placated by a "moralist" outcry which grew with the populist reform movement. Charles F. Wingate, who had been a member of the committee, used incredibly unscientific arguments in 1885 when he wrote on the "moral side of the tenement house problem":

> Probably seventy-five percent of the maladies in the cities, which often pass over into the better quarters, arise from the tenement houses. Ninety percent of the children born in these dens die before reaching youth. The amount of sickness is proportioned to the death rate. There is a gradual physical degeneracy. Wasting diseases prevail. Infantile life is nipped in the bud; youth is deformed and loathsome; decrepitude comes at thirty.

Wingate went on to describe the remedy:

> What New York wants is a revival of civic pride in her citizens to stimulate them to give their time and thought as well as their money to public duties. Our people are too absorbed in their private affairs and content to delegate responsibilities to ill-paid and harassed officials. Self-interest should teach them, if necessity does not, that a different course of action is imperative. But above all the clergy and all who feel the urgent necessity of mastering and reaching a practical solution of this vast problem.[45]

One aspect of the populist movement was its reaction against the social disruption caused by the massive presence of immigrants. By 1890, immigrants made up 42 percent of the city's population, and occupied almost all of the tenements.[46] Wingate did not hesitate to judge some of them as "ignorant, filthy, and more or less debased, especially the Italians, Poles, Russians and the Bohemians."[47] Such "moral" issues aside, the political containment of the immigrant population did pose practical problems. Already nearly half the total population of the city, immigrants held political views which were regarded as dangerous by some critics. Allen Forman wrote in *American* magazine in 1888: "The Poles, Russians and lowest class of Germans come to us imbued with Anarchistic notions—notions which are fed by the misery and disappointment of their life in this country where they had looked for affluence without work, and fostered by the freedom of speech which is permitted by laws which were framed to govern a people of entirely different character to those who have been pouring in upon us from the slums of Europe."[48]

Two major studies relating to tenements emerged by the mid-1890s, and both remain documents of major importance. The first was the report of the Tenement House Committee, established by the New York state legislature in 1894. The report traced in detail the evolution of tenement house reform, and produced unprecedented documentation of conditions based on a survey of 8,441 houses occupied by 255,033 persons. While New York ranked sixth among world cities in population, it was found to rank first in density, at an average of 143.2 persons per acre. Paris was a distant second, with 125.2 persons per acre. A portion of the Lower East Side was found to have reached a density of 800.47, which surpassed the highest known foreign agglomeration—a section of Bombay with 759.66 persons per acre.[49] The prolific use of such statistical analysis within the report served to push the "scientification" of the tenement problem to new levels.

The committee's report indicated that over one-half of the New York population lived in tenements, and it devoted considerable attention to an analysis of their design evolution, and to a discussion of improved tenement plans. It was the first official document to use photography to supplement a written description of tenement conditions (figure 2.11). The report was also innovative for the extensive comparative charts and mapping of citywide conditions—a precedent which contributed to the genesis of the discipline of city planning. The recommendations included increasing the 65 percent coverage of the 1879 Tenement House Law to a more enforceable 70 percent, with the elimination of the discretionary power the Board of Health had used to circumvent enforcement. Another interesting recommendation was to develop rapid transit as quickly as possible to alleviate overcrowding in tenement districts. As in the case of its predecessor nine years earlier, the recommendations made in the report of the committee of 1894 had little effect on the Tenement House Act which was passed in the following year,[50] especially in relation to standards for design.

In 1895 the federal government tackled the housing problem for the first time and produced the second major tenement study of the decade. The large special report of the Department of Labor, called *The Housing of the Working People*,[51] used material which had been amassed by Elgin R. L. Gould, an economist and housing reformer who held a post within the department. It was the first extensive survey of private and public initiatives for housing reform, documenting events not only in the United States, but also in England, France, Belgium, Germany, Austria, the Netherlands, Sweden, and Denmark. Previously, the only foreign design initiatives to have been published in the United States were the philanthropic housing projects built in England, dating from mid-century. The Department of Labor report presented critical new information about European developments, including considerable architectural documentation.

By 1895 numerous European municipalities had resorted to direct government home building for the poor, and the report of the Department of Labor documented examples at Huddersfield and Liverpool in England, at Glasgow in Scotland, and at Duisberg in Germany. These precedents in no way biased the

Figure 2.11. Photo of the air space between a tenement and its back building, on the Lower East Side block bounded by Canal, Forsyth, Bayard, and Chrystie streets. Circa 1895.

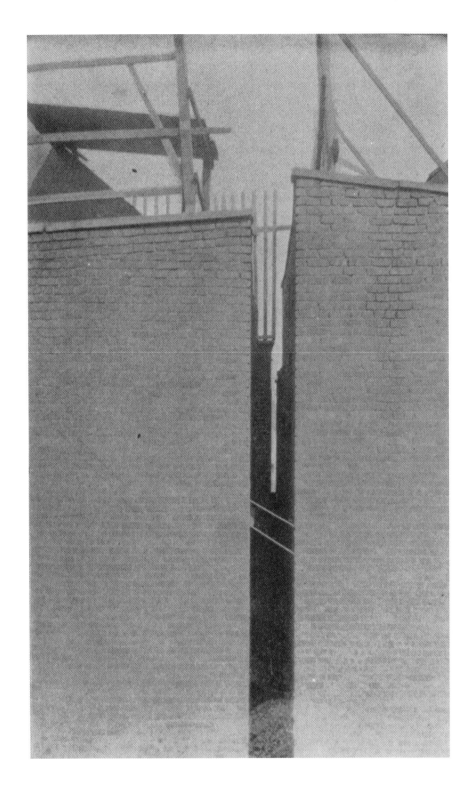

conclusion of the report, which clearly expressed its faith in the private sector to house the poor, within the constraints of government standards. Government abstinence from homebuilding was not due to a lack of lobbying to the contrary. From the 1880s onward pressure increased from the most progressive sector of the housing reform movement, led by Felix Adler and the Society for Ethical Culture. A lecture in Chickering Hall on March 9, 1884, on "The Helping Hand of Government," typified Adler's arguments:

> The evils of the tenement house section of this city are due to the estates which neglect the comfort of their tenants, and to the landlords who demand exorbitant rents. The laboring classes are unable to build homes for themselves, and the law of morality and common decency binds the Government to see to it that these houses shall not prove fatal to the lives and morality of the inmates. If the houses are overcrowded the government must interfere. It must compel a reduction of the number of inmates, enforce renovation at the expense of the landlord, and where that is no longer possible, must dismantle the houses and remove them from existence.[52]

Such pleas were to no avail, however. For example, it was not until the crisis of production in World War I that the first government-initiated home-building program was attempted—not for the poor, but for wartime factory workers. The government did not take initiatives toward the poor until the Great Depression of the 1930s, long after the governments of Europe had begun to do so.

The two decades between 1880 and 1900 were critical ones for the final formation of a professional identity for architecture. With the completion of the Columbian Exposition in 1893 in Chicago, architecture laid claim to a separate but equal role with engineering in the realization of building. The exposition was an engineering masterpiece, fully exploiting new technological breakthroughs—from electrical to mechanical to structural. But the engineering marvels were painstakingly clothed in the architecture, at all scales, from the electric light fixtures to the system of canals. Charles Emery, the famed engineer, described this extremist duality:

> The ghostly skeletons of great buildings arose, designed to imitate in architectural treatment those built in early historical times in enduring stone by millions of slave laborers during long years of toil. To attempt the real was prohibited by time and the enormous expense, notwithstanding the advances of modern improvements. The sham realistic was made possible by the knowledge of the engineer as to the strength of all parts of the flimsy frames, which carried the so-called "staff" or clothing of the walls, and the architectural features of the buildings.[53]

In the famous debate which preceded the exposition, the style chosen for the architectural clothes was that of ancient Rome. This was carefully translated through the Ecole des Beaux-Arts in Paris to the New York architectural establishment, to the Midwest, where the Exposition was skillfully orchestrated by Daniel Burnham. The style had the enthusiastic backing of big business. Business interests were aware of the usefulness of the symbolism of Rome and its importance for nurturing their own imperial ambitions for the United States for centuries to come.[54] For the discourse on urbanism and housing, this development emphasized the monumental concerns of the "City Beautiful" rather than the details of daily life. While the City Beautiful movement was important in counterbalancing the growing anti-urban sentiment of the day, its concerns left little recourse for the largest urban constituency, the poor tenement dwellers. Charles Mulford Robinson, the most prominent proponent of the City Beautiful, left no doubt as to the limits of its domain:

> We have first to remind ourselves, then, that our own subject is not sociology but civic art. The themes merge again and again—a fact that is the chief glory of the modern conception of civic aesthetics—so that the distinctions have sometimes to be purely arbitrary. We may reasonably assert, however, that civic art need concern itself only with the outward aspect of the houses, and therefore that for such details—sociologically pressing though they are—as sunless bedrooms, dark halls and stairs, foul cellars, dangerous employments, and an absence of bathrooms, civic art has no responsibility, however earnestly it deplores them.[55]

Louis Sullivan, who was working within a tradition of functionalism based on a more socialistic conception of architecture, was on the losing side of the discourse. He saw Burnham as the new breed of architect, who would "corner" the market on "style" in much the same way as the barons of commerce could form a monopoly: "During this period, there was well under way the formation of mergers, combinations, and trusts in the industrial world. The only architect in Chicago to catch the significance of this movement was Daniel Burnham, for in its tendency toward bigness, organization, delegation, and intense commercialism, he sensed the reciprocal workings of his own mind."[56]

Monopolies on style have come and gone since, but none was more monolithic than that of the Beaux-Arts. Its protagonists proclaimed a complete triumph in 1898 with the results of the Antwerp Competition, for the new campus of the University of California at Berkeley, to be financed predominantly by the Hearst family.[57] One hundred and eight entries were submitted in an international competition. Of the eleven placing designs, six were from the United States, and the majority of these were by architects trained at the Beaux-Arts. As one United States columnist related: "It was a question of America against the world—and America carries off the palm. But another phase of the question interests observers of things artistic—the question of the Beaux-Arts training against the rest of the world. And the Beaux-Arts wins."[58]

So the Beaux-Arts became the vehicle for raising the hope of an American imperialism for culture, as well as for commerce. The "English System" was said to have been "defeated," as evidenced by the lack of winning English entries; a state of affairs which even the English juror Richard Norman Shaw admitted was regrettable, but deserved.[59] The English System, as the term was used, appears to have been a branch of the same functionalism and social architecture that interested Sullivan. In spite of the "triumph" of the Beaux-Arts, that tradition

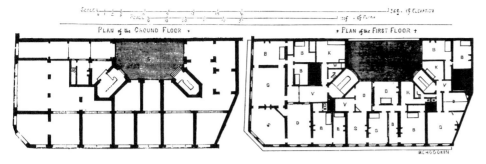

PARIS ARCHITECTURE: HOUSE IN RUE DE LA CHAUSSÉE D'ANTIN.——M. ROLLAND, ARCHITECT.

Figure 2.12. Francois Rolland. Apartment house on the rue de la Chaussée d'Antin, Paris, published in 1859, and typical of Parisian upper-middle-class housing of the Second Empire.

continued to evolve in the Midwest and West Coast regions of the United States, forming a continuity which continues to the present day.

On the East Coast, the Beaux-Arts dominated the profession, and New York City was its epicenter. It was also the center of big business. The scale of Burnham's architectural activities, which was so unique in Chicago, was the order of the day in New York. So were his business tactics. Yet, within the New York profession, at least three names stand above the normal practice of the day: Grosvenor Atterbury, Ernest Flagg, and Isaac Newton Phelps Stokes. All were graduates of the Beaux-Arts, but they never joined the ranks of the sycophants. All had an intense interest in issues related to the production of housing, and each made invaluable contributions. Ernest Flagg's were earliest, and perhaps the most influential. In 1894, as a recent graduate of the Beaux-Arts, he published his first studies for tenement housing. Flagg, like Phelps Stokes, had studied New York tenement problems at the Beaux-Arts. His prototypes were a clever translation of the courtyard apartment house, so prolific in Paris and elsewhere on the Continent, into terms which responded to the New York tenement dilemma (figure 2.12).

The Flagg prototypes made ingenious use of the Parisian *porte cochère* and internal courtyard (figure 2.13). Four 25-by-100-foot lots were combined into a single building incorporating an internal central courtyard entered directly through an opening from the street. The building itself was entered from the courtyard, usually by stairs located at each of the four corners; 18-foot-wide light slots opened to the rear, between each 100-foot module. Other plans showed how the model could be modified for 75-foot and 50-foot buildings. The 100-foot version was preferred, however, as it redistributed the identical amount of square footage typically contained in four dumbell tenements, but with vastly superior light and ventilation for each apartment.

The influence of Flagg's studies was immediate and widespread. The reasoning articulated by his prototypes was obvious and realistic in response to both the gridiron impasse and the economics of private speculative development. In 1896 he submitted a variation on his studies to the tenement house design competition sponsored by the Improved Housing Council of the Association for Improving the Condition of the Poor.[61] It won first place (figure 2.14). James Ware,

Figure 2.13. Ernest Flagg. Tenement prototypes first published in 1894, using Parisian-influenced central courtyards and *port cochères* on multiple lots, compared with a typical dumbell tenement (plan D).

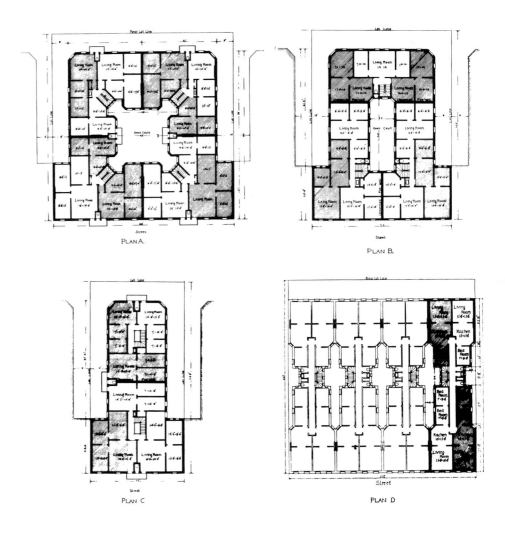

Figure 2.14. Ernest Flagg. First Place entry to the tenement house competition of 1896, sponsored by the Improved Housing Council of the Association for Improving the Condition of the Poor. The plan was a variation on the most generous version of his earlier prototypes.

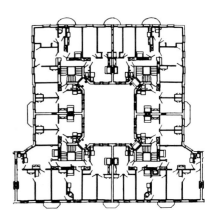

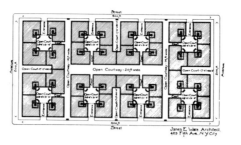

Figure 2.15. James E. Ware. Second Place entry to the tenement house competition of 1896; ideal block configuration using a plan similar to the Flagg submission.

of dumbell fame, also submitted a variation on the Flagg plan. He placed second (figure 2.15). The same Flagg-type plan dominated a second tenement house competition in 1900, which was sponsored by the Charity Organization Society.[62] Innovative variations were developed, such as the third-place submission designed by Henry Atterbury Smith, which adapted the Flagg-type plan for use with open stairs and toilets vented onto them (figure 2.16). The first-prize submission, designed by R. Thomas Short, skillfully manipulated the interior massing to further increase the penetration of light over the original Flagg prototypes (figure 2.17).

The 1896 competition sponsored by the Improved Housing Council required the design of six-story housing covering not more than 70 percent of a 200-by-400-foot piece of the New York gridiron. The Charity Organization Society competition in 1900 required the same coverage and height requirements, but with a tighter focus on categories of 25-, 50-, 70-, and 100-foot-wide lots.[63] The combined competitions produced a wide range of possible tenement configurations. Both competitions served to develop the architectural vocabulary which was needed to translate the tenement studies of the past two decades into a clear, legislatable new form, more satisfactory than the dumbell. Many entries experimented with configurations which were less complex than the Flagg-type plans. A common approach simply enlarged the dumbell air shaft, opening it toward front or rear

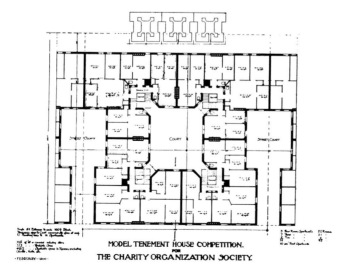

Figure 2.16. Henry Atterbury Smith. Third-place entry in the tenement house competition of 1900 sponsored by the Charity Organization Society, combining the Flagg-type plan with use of open stairs.

LEGISLATING THE TENEMENT   43

Figure 2.17. R. Thomas Short. First Place entry in the tenement house competition of 1900, using a variation on the Flagg-type plan with reduced massing at the interior courtyard.

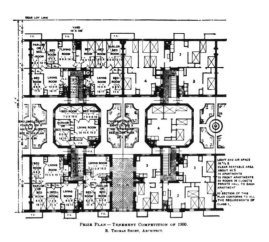

to create a light "slot" instead of a light "well." Percy Griffin placed third in the competition of 1896, using this approach, and he continued to develop it in the following years (figure 2.18). A more studied variant on the same strategy was submitted by I. N. Phelps Stokes. Its origins date from Stokes' studies at the Ecole des Beaux-Arts in Paris (figure 2.19).[64]

In February of 1900 the discourse on the ideal architectural form for the legislated tenement was further developed in an exhibition on tenements sponsored by the Charity Organization Society, and organized by reformer Lawrence Veiller.[65] Many of the recent design proposals were shown publicly. The exhibition included architectural models, more than a thousand photographs and a hundred maps, and many charts and diagrams. A series of conferences were held to discuss different aspects of the tenement house problem. There was also considerable documentation of model dwellings built in Europe. A housing exhibition of such size and scope has not been seen since in New York City.

Figure 2.18. Percy Griffin. Variations on the third-place entry in the tenement house competition of 1896 sponsored by the improved Housing Council; an attempt to enlarge the courtyard of the Flagg-type plan to form an open light "slot" and to simplify stair configurations.

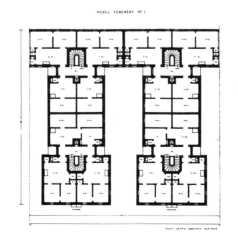
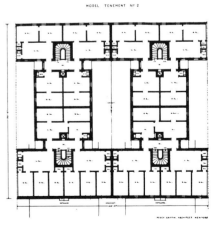

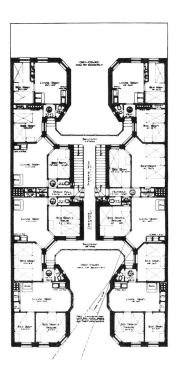

Figure 2.19. I. N. Phelps Stokes. Entry in the tenement house competition of 1896, based on previous studies made while a student at the Ecole des Beaux-Arts in Paris, using a clear alternative to the Flagg plan, incorporating light slots and open-air galleries, carefully calculated for maximum light and air.

One of the exhibition's architectural models depicted a Lower East Side tenement block, bounded by Chrystie, Forsyth, Canal, and Bayard streets (figure 2.20). The 200-by-400-foot block housed 2,781 persons at an astounding density of 1,515 persons per acre, far above the figures revealed by the Tenement House Commission of 1894. For 605 dwellings, there were only 264 water closets. Only 40 were supplied with hot water. Of 1,588 rooms, 441 rooms received no light or ventilation, and another 635 rooms faced air shafts.[66] By comparison, a model of a typical dumbell tenement block was also exhibited, furnishing proof that the 1879 legislation had only succeeded in further aggravating the conditions (figure 2.21). This block, also 200 feet by 400 feet, was said to house over 4,000 persons at a density of over 2,000 persons per acre.

In 1900, under pressure from the Charity Organization Society, the New York state legislature appointed its fourth Tenement House Commission. Robert DeForest served as chairman, and Lawrence Veiller as secretary. The two-volume study *The Tenement House Problem* was the end product. It provided the most complete survey to that date of the evolution of tenement house legislation and reform, in New York and in other American and European cities as well. Apart from the report, there were other interesting aspects of the commission's work. For the first time, studies by architects on the design ramifications of alternative tenement controls were seriously considered. Various architects were invited to prepare plans to test the provisions of proposed legislation.[67] The tenement plan submitted by

Figure 2.20. Model of a typical Lower East Side tenement block, built for the Tenement House Exhibition of 1900, sponsored by the Charity Organization Society.

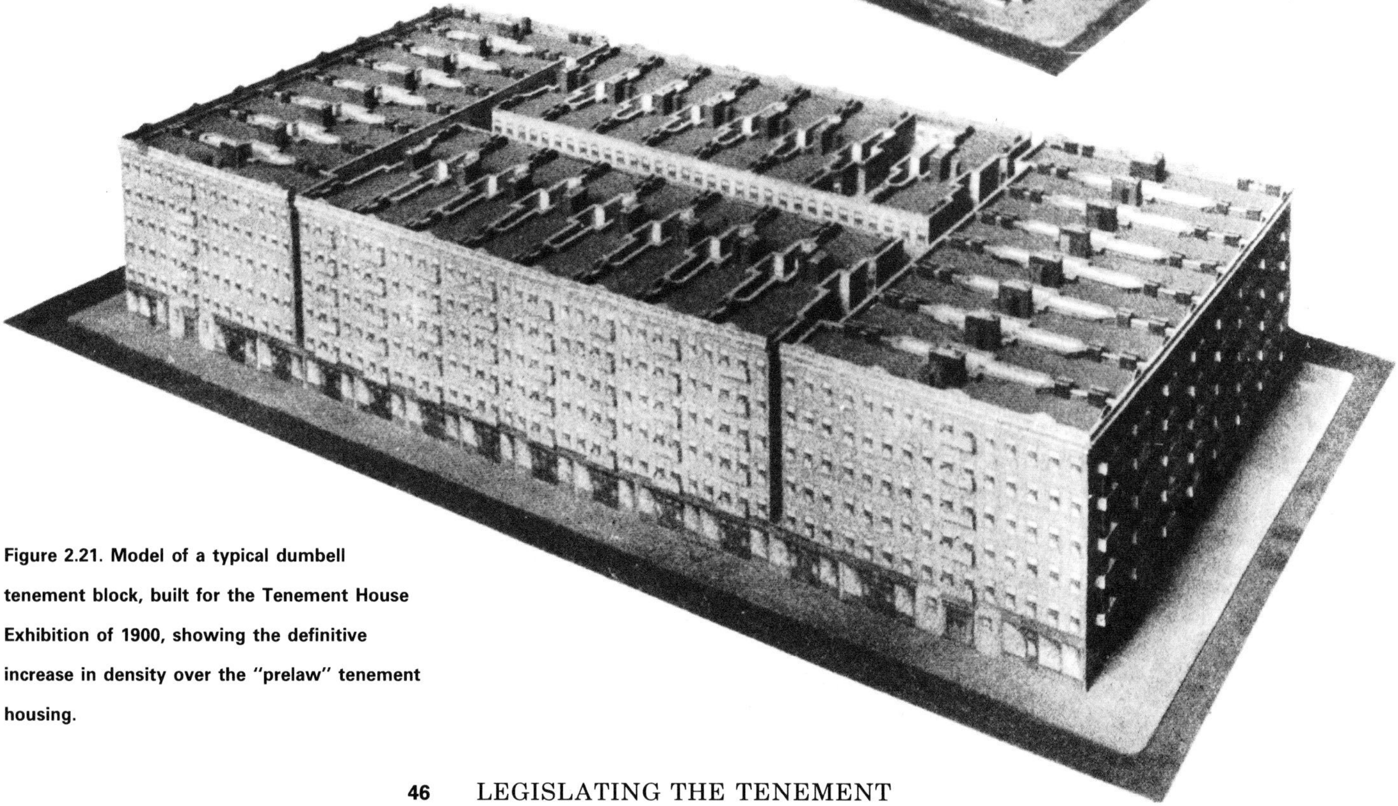

Figure 2.21. Model of a typical dumbell tenement block, built for the Tenement House Exhibition of 1900, showing the definitive increase in density over the ''prelaw'' tenement housing.

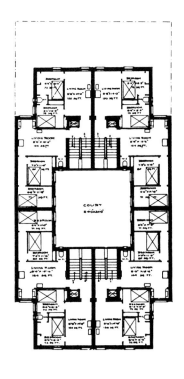

Figure 2.22. Ernest Flagg. Tenement plan submitted to the New York State Tenement House Commission of 1900 (left), showing a refinement of his original plan types, but with some of the same inefficiencies related to stairs and circulation.

Figure 2.23. I. N. Phelps Stokes. Tenement plan submitted to the Tenement House Commission of 1900 (right), using an organization quite close to the pragmatic possibilities of speculative development.

Ernest Flagg (figure 2.22) was an interesting hybrid based on his earlier proto-types, combining internal courtyards with moderately crenellated walls on both exterior sides. Another study, submitted by I. N. Phelps Stokes, came closer to a usable prototype for the speculative builder (figure 2.23).

In 1901 the state legislature finally made a definitive legislative response to the agitation of the previous decades. The Tenement House Act of 1901, commonly called the "New Law," set the national standard for tenement legislation.[68] Although it has since been modified extensively, its provisions are still the basis for the regulation of low-rise housing design in New York City. Its most important provision revised the Old Law coverage requirements which had been established in 1879. The unenforceable 65 percent coverage was increased to 70 percent in the New Law, with a mandate for strict enforcement. The dimensions for the dumbell air shaft were increased to courtyard proportions, which in effect eliminated the enclosed air shaft. The minimum dimensions for interior enclosed courtyards were 12 feet by 24 feet on the lot line, and 24 feet by 24 feet at the building center, to be increased for buildings over 60 feet high. Minimum dimensions for courtyards opening to the outside had to be 6 feet wide at the lot line and 12 feet wide at the building center, with increases for buildings over 60 feet high. The rear yard had to be at least 12 feet wide, again with increases for buildings over 60 feet high. No building could be higher than one and one-third of the width of the street it faced. Every apartment had to have running water and a water closet. Every room had to have an exterior window of specified minimum

Figure 2.24. Typical tenement configurations permitted under the Tenement House Act of 1901 or New Law, which enlarged the dumbell air shafts and enforced a maximum coverage of 70 percent; only plans using multiple lots could produce efficient organizations.

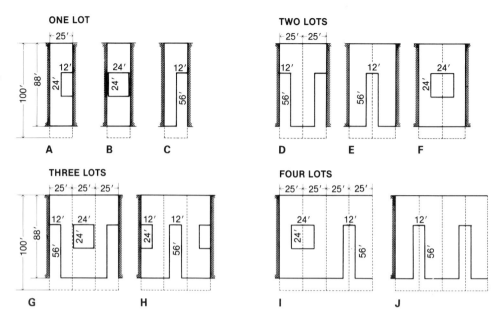

dimensions, and a series of construction and egress requirements to limit the likelihood of death from fire.

The minimum dimensions established by the New Law could produce only a few efficient floor plans. Figure 2.24 shows the possibilities allowed for one, two, and three 25-by-100-foot lot increments, all using the 70 percent maximum coverage which was permitted. Of the single-lot possibilities, only B works at all, and then with a very inefficient plan. Among the double-lot possibilities, E and F work, but are also highly inefficient. B, E, and F work better when coverages are reduced to below 60 percent. Only on triple lots can efficient plans be obtained while maintaining the full 70 percent coverage. G shows the great affinity of the New Law dimensions for Flagg-type plans. In general, the New Law prevented efficient development from occurring on lots of less than 40-by-100-foot dimensions.

Figure 2.25 shows a typical New York block, using 40-foot lots, as the majority of speculative developers interpreted the 1901 legislation. The New Law

Figure 2.25. Typical speculative development of an Upper East Side gridiron block under the provision of the New Law, using 40-by-100-foot lots.

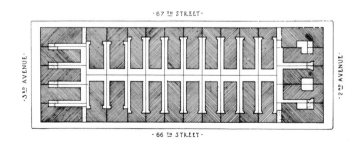

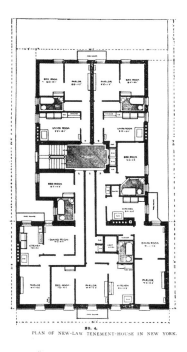

NO. 4.
PLAN OF NEW-LAW TENEMENT-HOUSE IN NEW YORK.

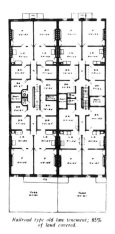

Railroad type old law tenement; 85% of land covered.

Dumb-bell type of old law tenement; 82% of land covered.

New law tenements; 70% of land covered. Erected by a limited dividend company.

was enforced through a new Tenement House Department comprising a Bureau of Records, a new Buildings Bureau, and a Bureau of Inspection. With the 1901 legislation, in combination with the political consolidation of the Greater New York Charter of 1897, it was no longer possible to build a blatantly substandard new dwelling in New York City. This increased control, combined with the constriction of possible plan types, meant that standards which had originated with the impasse of the high-density areas of Manhattan tended to unduly influence the form of housing throughout the outer boroughs as well, just as the earlier precedent of the commissioners' gridiron for Manhattan tended to be reproduced elsewhere in rote fashion.

The dimensional constraints of the New Law in effect eliminated single 25-foot lot development from the mass market. For higher density tenements, the small developer who built on a lot-by-lot basis could no longer control housing production (figure 2.26). Large capital began to monopolize the tenement market. The spatial complexities of the New Law, together with its mandate for larger-scale projects, assured architects a share of this market. Their position had not been so secure under the Old Law, whose requirements could be translated by any builder. For the housing bureaucracy, the New Law firmly established housing design control both on paper and in practice. For the general public, it radically improved the quality of tenement housing. In comparison with the Old Law, the New Law managed to achieve a successful balance between real estate interests, the architectural profession, and the building buraucracy. Ultimately, it was this balance which made the law enforceable (figure 2.27).

Figure 2.26. Typical speculative New Law plan using a 50-by-100-foot lot (left).

Figure 2.27. Evolution of the New York City tenement from railroad flat to the dumbell, to a New Law plan (right).

LEGISLATING THE TENEMENT   **49**

3

Rich and Poor

THE second half of the nineteenth century in New York City saw technological innovation in the form and production of housing which was unique in world history. By 1885 new building technology had brought changes in the form of housing which had been unimagined only two decades earlier. The steel skeleton frame, the elevator, electricity, and modern sanitation had created the high-rise New York apartment house. With this momentous development came a period of the greatest inequity between the housing of the rich and the poor that New York City has known. The upper class immediately embraced the new technology and its offspring; the lower class could not afford it, and continued to live in their cellars, rookeries, and squatter shacks, sometimes in the shadow of the high-rise palaces.

Of the possible housing options for the poor, the cellar dwelling was the most ubiquitous and the most hazardous (figure 3.1). The cellar was inevitably the nexus between the poor and disease. Overcrowded, filthy, airless, wet, dark, and frequently filled with gases from primitive sewers or with effluent from the school sinks, cellars were the breeding ground for cholera, malaria, and tuberculosis. The great cholera epidemic of 1849 originated in a cellar on Baxter Street near Five Points. It was described by the visiting physician William P. Buell: "At my first visit, on the 16th of May, five human beings, one man and four women, lay upon the floor in different stages of cholera. There was nothing under them but mud and filth, and nothing over them but a few mats of the filthiest description. Civilization and a great city could scarcely afford a parallel to the scene."[1]

Municipal advancements in sanitation sometimes worked to the disadvantage of the poor. The Croton Aqueduct for example, brought pure water into upper-class homes, heralding vast sanitation improvements at that level. Yet conditions worsened in the cellar dwellings. As individual wells were replaced by the Croton, water tables in the city rose, flooding the cellars.[2] The cellars represented the worst housing conditions in the city, and became a favorite target of early reformers. The number of cellar dwellings began to decline as early as 1859, when only 20,000 cellar dwellings were reported, 9,000 less than in 1850.[3] Gradually

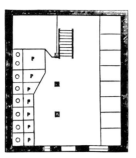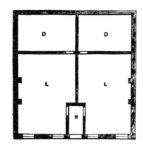

Figure 3.1. Two plans illustrating typical uses for the cellar; one was the privy (left), the other was the dwelling for the poor.

the cellar was replaced by the tenement, which at least eliminated the most subterranean aspect of housing affliction for the poor.

The "rookery," a term which also predated "tenement" and held different meaning, was as notorious as the cellar. Rookeries were not "designed" to be tenements. They usually were discarded buildings haphazardly reinhabited at tenement densities. Many were formerly single-family houses built of wood frame construction in the days before inexpensive brick. Like the cellars, rookeries began to disappear after mid-century. They were also popular objects of reform. They tended to burn or fall down easily. The most notorious rookeries in the city were located in the vicinity of Mulberry Bend and the adjacent Five Points, where Worth, Park, and Baxter streets intersected (figure 3.2).[4] The Five Points consisted of a cluster of wooden buildings. Mulberry Bend, one of the city's worst slums, contained both wood and brick structures, with extensive back building. Slum clearance proposals for the area dated from 1829, when the Common Council contemplated ridding the city of that "place of great disorder and crime."[5] Yet it took the city sixty-seven years to realize that mandate. The descriptions of its horrors are remarkably consistent over that long period.

In 1842 Charles Dickens, visiting the Five Points, wrote about it in his *American Notes:*

> What place is this, to which the squalid street conducts us? A kind of square of leprous houses, some of which are attainable only by crazy wooden stairs without. What lies beyond this tottering flight of steps, that creak beneath our tread! A miserable room, lighted by one dim candle, and destitute of all comfort, save that which may be hidden in a wretched bed. Beside it, sits a man: his elbows on his knees: his forehead hidden in his hands. "What ails that man?" asks the foremost officer. "Fever," he sullenly replies, without looking up. Conceive the fancies of a fevered brain, in such a place as this![6]

The Tenement House Committee of 1884 devoted special consideration to Mulberry Bend and the Five Points, finally recommending that it be razed. The committee revealed that of the 659 deaths recorded for Mulberry Bend in the previous three years, 65 percent were children under five years of age.[7] Such official statistics were amplified by the housing reformers. Jacob Riis devoted an entire chapter of *How the Other Half Lives* to Mulberry Bend, and it was due in

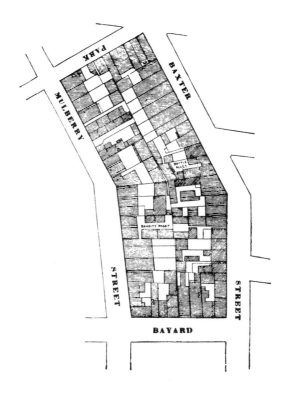

Figure 3.2. Mulberry Bend, said to have been the most notorious slum in New York City throughout most of the nineteenth century.

large part to his efforts that the slum was finally razed. By the time of Riis, Mulberry Bend had passed from the Irish to the Italians, who made some surface changes: it became "more like some town in Southern Italy than a Street in New York—all but the houses; they are still the same old tenements of the unromantic type."[8] Riis described "Bottle Alley"(figure 3.3), within the interior maze of the bend, as "a fair specimen of its kind . . . look at any of these houses, everywhere the same piles of rags, of malodorous bones and musty paper, all of which sanitary police flatter themselves they have banished to the dumps and the warehouses."[9] Another reformer, Allen Forman, expresses the more conservative side of public opinion which clearly placed the blame on the victims: "By all odds the most vicious, ignorant and degraded of all immigrants who come to our shores are the Italian inhabitants of Mulberry Bend and the surrounding tenements . . . an eddy in the life of the city where the scum collects, where the very offscouring of all humanity seem to find a lodgment."[10] After innumerable delays, the city finally acquired possession of Mulberry Bend and began demolition in 1894. By 1896 Columbus Park covered the site. It was one of the first slum clearance projects on a modern scale in New York City.[11]

As a type, the squatter's shack appears to have been less perilous to its inhabitants than the cellar or the rookery. New York City had large squatter settlements, a condition typical of large urban areas in developing countries. In New York squatter housing was considered illegitimate and temporary, rarely coming under the same legislative scrutiny as cellars and rookeries. Therefore, the squat-

Figure 3.3. Photo taken by Jacob Riis of Bottle
Alley, one of the interior courtyards of Mulberry
Bend which was inhabited by rag-and-bone
pickers, the poorest of the poor; published in
1890 in *How the Other Half Lives*.

ter settlements were not well documented. It is possible to establish, however,
that throughout much of the second half of the nineteenth century, large areas
of Manhattan above 57th Street were covered with "shantytowns." In 1864 the
New York Times estimated that "there is a population of 20,000 on this island
that pay neither rent for the dwellings they occupy, nor municipal taxes as hold-
ers of real estate. They comprise that portion of the population know as squat-

Figure 3.4. Depictions of squatters living in Central Park in 1857 who were removed in the same year as the landscaping of the park was begun.

FASHIONABLE RESIDENTS OF THE PARK.

ters."[12] The *Times* deplored the "hundreds, or . . . thousands [of squatters] who have grown rich on the exempt system."[13] Their figure of twenty-thousand was undoubtedly conservative, especially with the extended definition of squatting, to include the widespread practice of land speculators who charged "rent" to "squatters" while they held their land for the inevitable boom.[14] This "rent" covered the original cost of the land and yearly taxes, assuring clear profit for the speculator. The family who "leased" the land and built their shack on it had no rights whatsoever when the time came for the landowner to build.

The report published by the Council of Hygiene in 1865 gives some information about the extent of squatting on the Upper East and West Sides by that date. The Upper East Side had yielded to permanent urbanization sooner than the West Side, and attracted a more affluent population. By 1867 the East Side of Manhattan north of 40th Street contained 3,286 one- or two-family houses, 1,061 tenements, and 1,016 squatter shacks. Most of the squatters were concentrated to the east of Central Park. On the West Side, above 50th Street, there were only 516 one- and two-family houses, 1,760 tenements, and 865 squatter shacks.[15] Over the next two decades this pattern shifted, with squatting confined to the area west of Central Park, where land speculators held out the longest.

Prior to 1857 squatting proliferated within Central Park (figure 3.4).[16] The practice was probably most widespread after the city began acquisition of the parkland in 1853. In 1856 the city produced its first proposal for the park, designed by Egbert Viele (figure 3.5).[17] Fifth Avenue adjoining the park already was viewed by some as New York's next and most luxurious neighborhood, with the wealth moving ever northward from downtown.[18] As a first step, Frederick Law Olmsted, appointed commissioner of Central Park in 1857, dutifully removed the three-hundred squatter shacks in the park.[19] The creation of Central Park, like that of the Croton Aqueduct, had differing effects on rich and poor; it must have been with some sense of irony that the Common Council temporarily hired the squatters to help grade the new park.[20] For a period the squatters clung to the park edges. In 1864 the New York Times complained bitterly that shacks could still be found in the middle of Fifth Avenue adjacent to the park, "on that high ground which promises to be in a few years the most magnificent terrace on the continent."[21] These soon made way, however, for the mansion building.

The 1865 report by the Council of Hygiene provides an invaluable description of the squatter's shack, or shanty:

The shanty is the cheapest and simplest domicile constructed in civilized communities. The typical shanty is built of rough boards, which form the floor, the sides, and the roof. It is built either on the ground, or but little raised above it. It is from six to ten feet high, and its ground area varies much in different cases; but it is always of moderate extent. It contains no fireplace or chimney, but a stovepipe, the pipe from which passes through a hole in the roof. It has from one to three or four windows, with single sash, each containing from four to six panes of small size. Some shanties have but one room; others an additional small apartment, used as a bedroom. The better shanties are lathed and plastered. It is evident that, to the occupants of the shanty, domiciliary and personal cleanliness

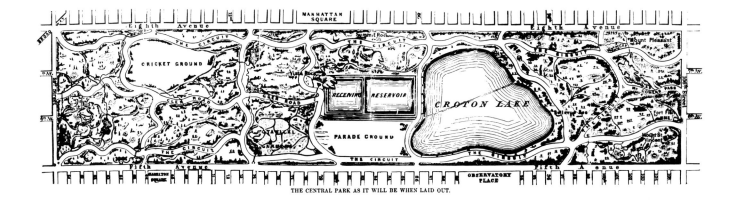

THE CENTRAL PARK AS IT WILL BE WHEN LAID OUT.

is almost impossible. In one small room are found the family, chairs, usually dirty and broken, cooking utensils, stove, often a bed, a dog or cat, and sometimes more or less poultry. On the outside, by the door, in many cases are pigs and goats, and additional poultry. There is no sink or drainage, and the slops are thrown upon the ground. The water used is sometimes Croton, which is brought to the shanties in pails, usually from one of the avenues. In other places, where the Croton hydrants are too far away, and the ground is marshy, the water is obtained from holes dug a little below the surface. This water often has a roiled appearance, and unpleasant flavor. Shanties are usually built promiscuously over the ground, without the least regard to order.[22]

Obviously, health hazards existed, especially given the swampy ground where shacks were frequently built. When squatter settlements grew up, such problems were worsened by the higher densities. But on the other hand, compared with the conditions at Mulberry Bend, squatter living could also appear to be idyllic. In 1880 *American Architect and Building News* described one of the "worst" remaining Upper East Side squatter settlements, located in the area around East 67th and 68th streets, indicating the coexistence of both squalor and charm:

The condition of the district is extremely bad, the ground soaked with filth, and the huts unusually crowded and close. It appears that the effluvium which hangs about the place is so offensive that the officers of the neighboring foundling asylum are obliged to keep their windows closed on that side, and several of the rooms are considered uninhabitable. The Mount Sinai Hospital, also, which is situated on high ground nearby, is so invaded by the pestilential atmosphere that erysipelas, dysentery, and diptheritic troubles are constantly prevalent in the wards nearest the foul village. Under these circumstances the Board [of Health] ordered the removal of the shanties as a public nuisance. It may seem hardly becoming a journal which upholds a high sanitary ideal to regret the disappearance of these filthy dens, but we confess that we never pass a village of them without being irresistibly attracted by their extreme picturesqueness. Less gloomy and vicious-

Figure 3.5. Egbert Viele. The first plan for Central Park proposed in 1856, but replaced by the plan of Olmsted and Vaux in the following year. It launched the prospect of a redevelopment of upper Manhattan for the affluent.

looking than city rookeries, the habitations of the squatters, with their white-washed walls of rough boards leaning in all directions, their roofs of rusty tin, torn in a crumpled sheet from some demolished warehouse, their dilapidated stovepipes projecting unexpectedly through roof or walls, and their groups of goats and children climbing about in the sunshine through the circuitous paths among the rocks, have a naive charm peculiar to themselves.[23]

Throughout the 1870s most of the Upper Side between Central Park and the Hudson River was undeveloped. Many streets were still not opened, and most others were only dirt tracks.[24] Two large squatter settlements existed: one called Dutchtown, bounded by West 65th Street, West 85th Street, Ninth Avenue, and Central Park,[25] and another bounded by West 58th Street, West 68th Street, Tenth Avenue, and the Hudson River. The latter was said to be as dense as any neighborhood of the city.[26] Much of the remaining land was covered by shacks, surrounded by small gardens interspersed with little villages such as Shantyhill at West 79th Street, and Wallhigh to the southeast of it.[27] As permanent urbanization began, the shacks and new row houses stood side by side, causing a striking but temporary building contrast (Figure 3.6).[28]

The livelihoods and living conditions of the squatters varied widely. Some shacks were squalid; others were neat and comfortable. A large proportion of the Upper West Side squatter population maintained small gardens, and it was said that they produced "a large proportion of all the green stuff consumed in the city . . . the lettuce, the parsley, the celery, the cabbages, and the potatoes."[29] Raising hogs was also commonplace. Other squatters were scavengers, the most lowly being the rag and bone pickers and the cinder gatherers. The squatters could be seen daily before dawn beginning their long trek southward to the Washington Market

Figure 3.6. View looking east on West 86th Street in 1880 showing the elevated railroad on Columbus Avenue, a new row house, and a cluster of squatters' shacks.

SEVENTIETH STREET BETWEEN CENTRAL PARK WEST AND COLUMBUS AVENUE
IN 1882, THEN KNOWN AS EIGHTH AND NINTH AVENUES.

SEVENTIETH STREET TO-DAY, BETWEEN CENTRAL PARK
WEST AND COLUMBUS AVENUE.

to sell their produce. As the city inspector complained in 1856, their presence permeated the entire city;

> The class of persons coming under this definition are mainly residents of the up-town wards, but the nature of their daily avocations, subjects every quarter of the city to their presence, and the effluvia of their filthy gatherings. The neighborhood of the shanties where they dwell, is a perfect hotbed of foul vapor, and no language could adequately describe the stench arising from a close inspection of the cauldrons containing bones, putrid meat and rancid fat, which they boil for various purposes of traffic; nor is this all, rags, possibly containing the virus of disease, examined, re-examined, washed and exposed to dry, within and around their dwellings, contribute their quota to a nuisance which should be rooted from our midst without delay.[30]

Official action was unnecessary, however, given the force of developmental change. In a massive and rapid transformation, the entire Upper West Side yielded to permanent urbanization within the ten years between 1885 and 1895 (figure 3.7). Even large settlements such as Dutchtown were decimated, quickly replaced by tenements as well as upper-class houses. Throughout the city, the indigenous shacks and rookeries were being eclipsed by the dumbell tenement. The tenement had far greater potential for economic exploitation of the tenants: its production was not only lucrative, but mandated by law. The marketplace conquered all, and land speculation paid off handsomely at every turn. By one account, a tenant living at the northwest corner of West 84th Street and Eighth Avenue was offered $900 in 1865 for thirty-nine lots, including his own. He refused. In 1895 his lot alone was worth $35,000[31] Even technology came to the aid of the market. By the 1880s, with the perfection of the pneumatic rock drill, Manhattan's troublesome rock was quickly excavated. Building lots could be literally carved out of stone, cheaply and with ease, using machinery unknown only a decade earlier.[32]

Figure 3.7. Views looking east along West 70th Street in 1885 and 1895 within the squatter community known as Dutchtown, showing the rapid transformation from shacks to upper-middle-class houses and apartments.

Figure 3.8. John Kellum. Alexander T. Stewart mansion on Fifth Avenue completed in 1869 (*above*), contrasted with the Five Points (*below*); from the frontispiece of a popular book on New York City life by Matthew Hale Smith published in 1869.

While the poorest housing comprised cellars, rookeries, and squatter shacks, until 1880 the predominant dwelling type for the affluent was the row house. Only the less affluent middle class lived in multiple dwellings. The upper middle class and upper class clung tenaciously to the ideal of the individual house on a lot. By 1880 however, that ideal was undermined by economic and physical constraints. Only the mansions of the most wealthy were unaffected, growing larger and larger as the successes of the city's business establishment proliferated. A precedent was set by the Alexander T. Stewart House, the earliest of a series of elephantine mansions constructed on Fifth Avenue.[33] Designed by John Kellum and completed in 1869 for the millionaire merchant, it provided the city with a sharp new contrast to the Five Points (figure 3.8). It was massive and freestanding. Built of marble in the "Second Empire style," it occupied six lots at West 34th Street.

The Stewart mansion was widely noted as evidence of the new wealth of the growing metropolis. Also noted was the parvenu nature of this wealth. Anthony Trollope, visiting New York in 1861, commented on the "aristocracy of Fifth Avenue":

> I own that I have enjoyed the vista as I have walked up and down Fifth Avenue, and have felt that the city had a right to be proud of its wealth. But the greatness and beauty and glory of wealth have on such occasions been all in all with me. I know no great man, no celebrated statesman, no philanthropist of peculiar note who has lived in Fifth Avenue. That gentleman on the right made a million of dollars by inventing a shirt collar; this one on the left electrified the world by a lotion; as to the gentleman at the corner there,—there are rumours about him and the Cuban slave trade; but my informant by no means knows that they are true. Such are the aristocracy of Fifth Avenue. I can only say that if I could make a million dollars by a lotion, I should certainly be right to live in such a house as one of those.[34]

It was only in the 1840s that the term "millionaire" was invented, with only a handful of New Yorkers possessing wealth of that magnitude. By 1870 there were calculated to be 115 millionaires in the city.[35] But more significantly, the Civil War had created fortunes large and small, which increased the housing expectations of all affluent New Yorkers, shaded, perhaps, by a certain penchant for overstatement of their newfound status.

For the merely affluent, the single-family "brownstone" had to suffice. It was a large row house, with a front facade normally faced in the plentiful local stone which gave the type its name. It was normally built on a single 25-by-100 foot gridiron lot. The cost of land in built-up parts of Manhattan prohibited the use of multiple lots for any but the most exclusive mansions. The brownstone type was the logical culmination of the evolution of the row house in Manhattan.[36] Around 1800 the relatively modest Federal-style town house, typically three or four stories with six or eight rooms, covered no more than one-half of a lot (figure 3.9). The evolution which followed puts in evidence the growth in the wealth of the city, and especially of its mercantile class. For example, by 1830 the growing affluence was expressed in the increased height of the Greek revival row houses which outscaled their lower Federal neighbors. But by 1850 the ever-increasing size was beginning to produce an impasse. Charles Astor Bristed, a prominent observer of the social scene; described such a dilemma:

> It has been hinted more than once that land in fashionable localities is expensive, and the Gothamites, when they build, are consequently economical of ground. A "lot" of the ordinary size is twenty-five feet front by a hundred deep. The desire to make one's house a *little* superior to the ordinary standard has caused many of the lots . . . to be arranged . . . with fronts of twenty-six or twenty-seven feet. It will be evident that such a width allows only one front room alongside of the not very wide hall; the house can only be extended perpendicularly and longitudinally. Thus Mr. Vanderlyn's twenty-six feet are carried up into four pretty stories, and back over nearly seventy feet of the hundred which the lot contains, leaving the smallest possible quantity of yard, but allowing three rooms en suite

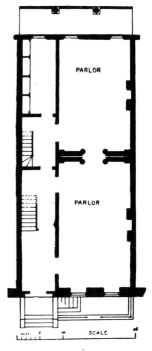

Figure 3.9. Typical row house of the early 1830s, built on Washington Square in the period when it was becoming an upper-class neighborhood.

Plan 1.—A Washington Square House, New York, about 1830.

THE FIRST HOUSE LIGHTED WITH GAS,

No. 7 Cherry Street, residence of Samuel Leggett, First
President of the New York Gas Company.

HOUSE IN FIFTY-SIXTH STREET.
BRUCE PRICE, ARCHITECT.

on each floor. One inconvenience of this arrangement is, that either your hall shrinks into very small dimensions . . . or you must dispense with a private staircase altogether. Mr. Vanderlyn has chosen the latter alternative.[37]

By 1880 the evolution was complete. An ostentatious brownstone, typically four or five stories high, with sixteen or twenty rooms, might cover over 90 percent of a lot. Behind the brownstone facade the houses got bigger and bigger, pushing up to five stories and out into the rear yards. At the same time, real estate prices were likely to make the lots narrower, rather than wider (figure 3.10). Even the architect-designed brownstone could not escape the typological problems of dimension. For example, a house designed in 1879 by Bruce Price covered 90 percent of the lot (figure 3.11).[38] It contained internal spaces which would receive no more light or ventilation than might be found in a dumbell tenement.

The inadequacies of the Manhattan gridiron, so obvious a detriment to the evolution of tenement standards, also affected the design of single-family houses for the affluent. Overbuilding on the 25-by-100-foot lot meant poor light and ven-

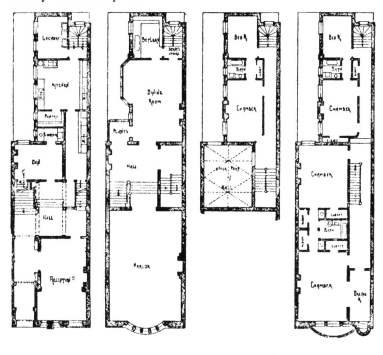

ALTERNATIVE DESIGNS FOR A CITY HOUSE, NEW YORK, N. Y.
MR. BRUCE PRICE, ARCHITECT, NEW YORK.

As shown by the appended plans the house is to cover an ordinary twenty-five foot city lot.

Figure 3.11. Bruce Price. Proposal for an upper-class brownstone row house made in 1879 for a 25-by-100-foot lot.

tilation, whether for a single family or for many (figure 3.12).[39] As the row house grew to fill the lot, the outer rooms remained sunlit, but the mid-sections grew larger and darker. At the center of the brownstone was the most up-to-date plumbing, but these marvels, fed by the water of the Croton Aqueduct, were placed in cryptlike spaces, usually without light or adequate ventilation.

There were other disadvantages associated with the scale and form of the brownstone. At least four servants were required to maintain one house. The servants, in turn, required supervision by the family, as well as considerable expen-

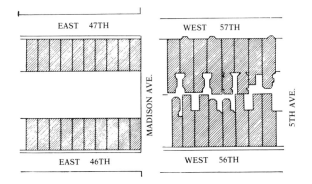

Figure 3.12. A typical 1830s row house block (*left*), contrasted with a typical 1880s brownstone block (*right*), showing the overbuilding which was occurring in upper-class single-family housing by that time.

diture. In addition, brownstone living was rather public. In the 1870s and 1880s, which have been called the most violent decades in United States domestic history,[40] the brownstone provided only a window between the parlor and the street, or a skylight between the roof and the stair hall. For the affluent New York businessman, an inevitable target of street crime, subject to the hounding of his malcontents, and terrorized by threat of anarchism, his home was not entirely his "castle."

Until the 1880s, in spite of the disadvantages of the brownstone, New Yorkers of means steadfastly refused to live in apartments, or French flats, as they were called. The term "French flat" generally referred to multiple dwellings for the middle class: large apartments as opposed to small tenements.[41] The Parisian apartment house was considered to have set the standard of perfection for the type. What Haussman had done for the bourgeoisie of Paris was the considerable envy of the New Yorker.[42] Yet in spite of the growing predilection for all things French, the French flat was not popular among those who could afford a brownstone. This was a result at least in part of the peculiar strength of an Anglo-Saxon bias toward "house" and ownership. This predilection had become even more of a fixation in United States middle-class culture than in the England of its origins. Fears associated with the French flat involved extremes, including adultery and the destruction of family life.[43] There was also the issue of the home as a particular expression of social class in the United States. In 1880 Sarah Gilman Young explained:

> There are no objections to apartment houses in American cities, except prejudice, and this is stronger in the United States than elsewhere. To Americans it is a question of rank. Anything that resembles what we term a tenement house is tabooed. There being no fixed caste in America, as in foreign states, we have established a certain style of living and expenditure, as a distinctive mark of social position. . . . Especially do we seek an exterior of respectability and wealth in our homes. The desire to live in a fine house is particularly American. Europeans of distinction, of all countries, think much less of the exterior of their residencies.[44]

Young partially blamed the quality and management of American apartment houses: "There is no doubt that apartment houses would gain rapidly in favor in America, if properly constructed and rightly managed. They should at first be designed by architects who have completed their studies in Europe, especially in France, where this system has reached its greatest perfection."[45]

Actually, Richard Morris Hunt, the first graduate of the Ecole des Beaux-Arts from the United States, is credited with designing the first apartment buildings in New York for affluent tenants. Around 1855 he is said to have designed an apartment house on Wooster Street.[46] His best-known early building, however, was the Stuyvesant, also known as the French Flats, which was located on East 18th Street, and completed in 1869 (figure 3.13).[47] The Stuyvesant consisted of two identical five-story walk-up buildings, each occupying two 25-by-100-foot gridiron lots (not unlike the configuration explored in figure 1.16. Each building provided a public stair and a service stair shared by both sides. This arrangement

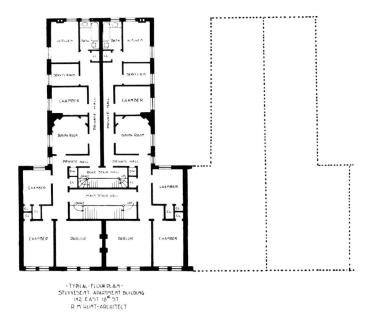

- TYPICAL · FLOOR PLAN -
STUYVESANT APARTMENT BUILDING
142 EAST 18ᵗʰ ST
R M HUNT · ARCHITECT

Figure 3.13. Richard Morris Hunt. The Stuyvesant, also called the French Flats, completed in 1869 using four 25-by-100-foot lots with five stories; always credited in common history as the first apartment building for affluent tenants in New York City.

allowed more spatial flexibility than was possible with two isolated stairs, and it introduced the concept of a private service stair segregated from the public area. Each floor was no larger than a typical brownstone floor, but the stair arrangement permitted a far more efficient organization of space than in a brownstone. Still, with between six and ten rooms, the apartments were of modest size when compared with a brownstone.

Hunt's Stuyvesant plan was relatively successful, especially in comparison with apartment designs by his contemporaries. The key was his use of multiple lots. By contrast, in 1857 Calvert Vaux presented a paper to the American Institute of Architects, which described his "Parisian buildings," a proposal for upper-class apartments on a single lot. Vaux argued that the subject "ought, doubtless, to be responded to by professional architects, as far as possible, inasmuch as it is the duty of science and art to popularize as well as to discover, and to assist in developing, in an economical form, all those refinements of convenience that education teaches us are healthful and agreeable."[48] Unfortunately, his design succeeded only in showing the impossibility of achieving reasonable standards for a large building on a single lot, even if architect designed (figure 3.14). Vaux proposed one apartment on each floor, but added a change of level between living and sleeping areas, to better approximate the spatial dimension of a single-family house. A public stair was shared with the adjacent building of the same plan. In order to obtain sufficient space on each floor for the modest three-bedroom apartments, each lot had to be entirely covered, with three air shafts for the provision of ventilation. Another approach (figure 3.15), was designed by Bruce Price in 1878 for a single lot on East 21st Street.[49] The massing, which is similar to one eventually mandated by the New Law, forced the apart-

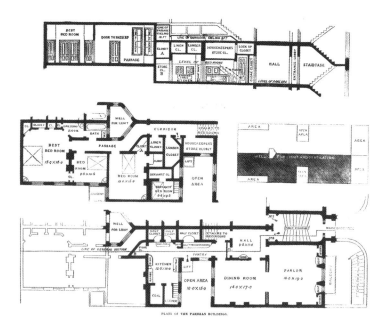

Figure 3.14. Calvert Vaux. The Parisian Buildings, proposed in 1857 as an apartment building for affluent tenants, using a single 25-by-100-foot lot, and a name which clearly identified the source of its pretension.

ment into an awkward linear configuration. It had better light than Vaux's design, however. In spite of its impressive facade, it still could not equal the social emblem of the single-family brownstone, which it attempted to emulate.

By 1880 buildings similar to the proposal of Bruce Price were adopted primarily for the burgeoning middle class. This portion of the city's population wished to remain within densely populated neighborhoods, but could not afford single-family housing.[50] One such plan by a developer shows an identical massing to the Price proposal, but with three apartments per floor (figure 3.16). Another common type of housing for the middle class was converted row houses, broken into small apartments. Floors of adjacent row houses could be combined by breaking through the party walls and reorganizing stairs (figure 3.17). The majority of these renovations were not to middle-class standards, but the same could be said for new construction. In 1879 *Appleton's Dictionary* recorded that there were "several hundreds of these buildings . . . now distributed over the city, and others constantly being erected."[51] According to their list, less than fifty were considered expensive. Many of the rest were hardly adequate even for the middle class.

Appleton's Dictionary made a careful distinction between "tenements" and "apartments," citing not only the higher rents and services of the latter, but also their more elaborate physical organization, including dual stairs for segregation of services. For much of this new high-density housing, however, the line between apartment and tenement was a fine one, especially for modest income. And by this time the middle class was being forced out of the highest-density areas of Manhattan because of a lack of adequate moderate-cost housing, a condition which has since proved to be chronic for the city. As one observer wrote in 1885: "New York is distinctly a city without homes. Two-thirds of its population live in ten-

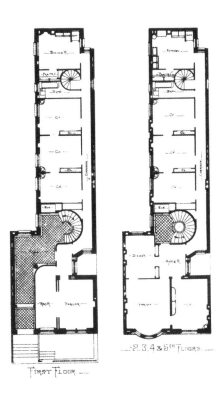

ements, and the remainder either occupy palatial but cheerless brownstone fronts on Murray Hill and its vicinity, or board. The rich and poor are increasing, while the great middle class of thrifty and intelligent people are being crowded into the suburbs."[52]

Improvements in mass transportation encouraged the middle class to move to the periphery, in Harlem or Brooklyn, where single-family ownership of a modest row house was still possible (figure 3.18). As for the center, in 1874 *Scribner's* magazine reported that

> there are . . . ten times as many houses three, four, and five stories high planned . . . for the accommodation of one family each, as there are families large enough to support them. On the other hand, not one tenth of the families who live, or would live in the City, can find shelter for the maintenance of homes; that is, apartments containing the required number of rooms and no more, grouped for easy and economical housekeeping and shielded from undue publicity. . . . From time to time . . . French Flats were erected on the avenues, especially on the West Side, but without meriting much success. Sham elegance and general inconvenience were their most prominent characeristics; marble mantels and much paint vainly striving to atone for the abundant presence of dark rooms, narrow passages, and back-breaking stairs.[53]

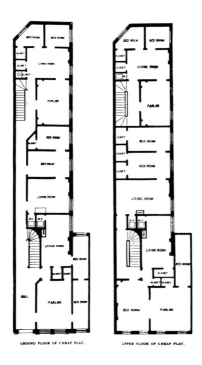

Figure 3.16. Typical apartment house of the 1880s for tenants of modest means, using a single 25-by-100-foot lot, with three apartments on each floor.

GROUND FLOOR OF CHEAP FLAT.   UPPER FLOOR OF CHEAP FLAT.

Figure 3.17. Apartment house of the 1870s for tenants of modest means, combining two altered single-family houses in a single new structure.

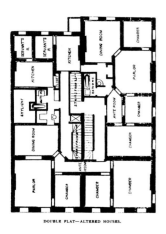

DOUBLE FLAT—ALTERED HOUSES.

For the upper class, the break in the housing impasse came in the 1880s, with the perfection of the passenger elevator for residential use. A barrier to living in the French flat had always been the necessity of climbing the public star—up to four stories—which was considered to be unacceptable for all but tenement dwellers. The elevator replaced the drudgery of the stair with a futuristic symbol of status. The fireproof, independent structural frame already used for commercial buildings, when combined with the passenger elevator, obviated height limitations for residential buildings. The high-rise revolution in housing came swiftly. It was only in 1858 that the first mechanically powered residential elevator in New York City was installed in the five-story Astor House, a prominent hotel on Broadway between Barclay and Vesey streets.[54] It was powered by primitive steam machinery. In 1859 a primitive "screw-type" elevator was in use in the six-story Fifth Avenue Hotel, between West 22nd and 23rd streets.[55] Throughout the 1870s experimentation with elevators increased, together with the increasing heights of the buildings. In 1870 the five-story Haight House was completed on Fifth Avenue and West 15th Street, incorporating a steam elevator. It was converted from existing buildings while retaining a patina of domesticity such that "nobody in passing along Fifth Avenue or Fifteenth Street would imagine that it was anything else than the private residence of some private individual."[56] Twenty family apartments and fifteen bachelor apartments were served by hotel facilities. Tenants were given the possibility of taking their meals communally and receiving domestic services. This option became popular among the early developers, pro-

Figure 3.18. West 133rd Street about 1877, partially built up with single-family row houses for middle-income families, showing the typical small-scale increment of development for housing of the period.

THE "STEVENS HOUSE," CORNER OF TWENTY-SEVENTH STREET AND BROADWAY.

viding a competitive edge over the brownstones, which required costly private domestic staffing.

A key precedent in the evolution of the high rise was Stevens House, designed by Richard Morris Hunt and completed in 1872 on Broadway between West 26th and 27th streets.[57] With eight stories and only eighteen apartments. Stevens House considerably advanced the state of the art for both height and apartment size over previous projects (figure 3.19). Unlike the Stuyvesant, it was organized around a single internal courtyard, prefiguring the configuration of those luxury projects of the next three decades which rejected the air-shaft plan types. Hunt's involvement with the project helped insure its acceptability to upper-income tastes. The project was less than successful economically however, and after only several years it was remodeled into a hotel. Its extravagance proved unprofitable. Perhaps Stevens House was slightly ahead of its time, and perhaps, as well, it was a victim of the financial volatility of the period. But more than any other apartment building of the 1870s, it was seen as heralding a new age in New York City. In the popular mind Stevens House represented the "city of the future," miraculously arrived before its time. The extraordinary height, steam heating, steam elevator, forced mechanical ventilation, gas ranges, and various other modern contrivances of daily life, made Stevens House a technological landmark.

Stevens House also was seen as a cultural landmark. More than the other apartment buildings before it, Stevens House embodied the potential for launching a new kind of urban civility. With its overscaled mansard and other detailing, its archetype was Parisian. Stevens House was an exaggerated version of much of the housing built in Second Empire Paris. But *Appleton's Journal* saw it as much more than that. Stevens House represented a move from Parisian antecedents toward a fundamentally new urbanity, fueled by U.S. technology:

> We all know something, and have heard much of the European method of living in flats. Handsome buildings have been erected in this city for the purpose of naturalizing the Parisian plan of living. . . . But it is possible for us to improve greatly on the European method, which was in use before steam began to be applied to domestic purposes. By simply establishing steam communications between each floor and the street, we may carry our buildings as high as we please, and render the topmost floor the choicest suite of them all.[58]

With this new era of "sky homes" and "huge compact structures with their hives of families" would evolve a new form of urban intercourse created by unprecedented density organized according to a "method of scientific compactness." In the "pure empyrean above" would be roof gardens which would contrast some of the "best features of suburban life" with the metropolis below, creating a particular admixture of built form and nature unknown in previous epochs.

The "method of scientific compactness" foreseen by *Appleton's Journal* was slow to evolve. The new luxury high-rise construction was not exempt from many of the same issues of light and air which plagued the brownstone or tenement, especially as the buildings began to cluster. The absence of design precedents for high-rise housing also meant that the new and complex functional problems of the large high-rise residential building were frequently handled naively by their designers. An early plan proposed by Arthur Gilman in 1874 was typically problematic (figure 3.20).[59] The proposal incorporated all of the design contrivances of the high rise, but still retained the mentality of tenements rather than housing of the future. The massing resembled a tenement plan simply enlarged. Many of the rooms faced light wells, although these were much larger than those in tenements. The inadequacies of Gilman's design are only underscored by his long experience with apartment house design. Gilman was involved with the design of what was possibly the first apartment hotel in the United States, the Hotel Pelham in Boston, completed in 1857.[60] The appearances of the luxury apartment building were strictly upper class from the start, but it would be another decade before the planning standards matched the social standards of the tenantry. Gilman

Figure 3.20. Arthur Gilman. High-rise apartment building proposed in 1874, with seven stories, elevators, a monumental Second Empire facade, and planning standards which were vaguely reminiscent of tenements, with oversized air shafts and no views for many rooms.

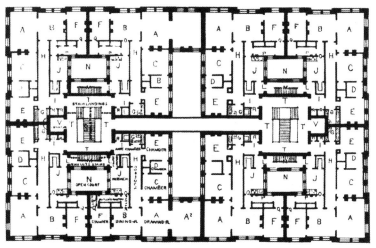

GILMAN'S PLAN OF APARTMENT HOUSE.

placed his building behind an imposing Second Empire facade, so grandiose that in Paris it would have been considered appropriate only for an important public building.

The Vancorlear, designed by Henry Hardenbergh and completed by 1880, was an important step in the evolution of high-rise planning.[61] While it was only six stories, the building plan incorporated two water hydraulic elevators, which were more advanced than steam. The developer, Edwin Severin Clark, incorporated other technological advances which would soon appear in higher buildings. Most important however, was the plan organization. Located at the end of a block facing Seventh Avenue between West 55th and 56th streets, the building enclosed a large central courtyard with sufficient dimension in relation to the height to provide adequate light. This organization prefigured the palazzo plan type, which became one of the important approaches to apartment house massing in New York (figure 3.21). Hardenbergh used the same approach at the Dakota several years later, for the same developer.

A different approach was embodied by the Chelsea, completed in 1883. In contrast to the Vancorlear, the Chelsea was a monolithic slab, relying entirely on the exterior facades for light. Located on West 23rd Street, it was designed by Philip Hubert for Hubert, Pirsson, and Company. Philip Hubert was the initiator of several luxury high-rise projects through Hubert, Pirsson, most of them co-operatives known as Hubert Home Clubs.[62] Cooperative "home ownership," like hotel services, was pioneered by Hubert, Pirsson to entice tenants away from the brownstone.[63] The Chelsea was one of the city's first cooperatives. This eleven-story structure contained ninety apartments from three to nine rooms with accompanying hotel facilities. Each floor had a central vertical core consisting of two elevators and a stair. A double-loaded corridor ran the length of the building (figure 3.22). Its organization was strikingly similar to the genre of high-rise slab blocks commonly built after World War II; however, these latter schemes did not solve the problem of cross ventilation as well. Hubert lined the corridor with large ventilation shafts, which extended to the roof, providing each apartment with a large interior flue for movement of air. Like all of the earliest apartment buildings, an independent skeleton frame was not used. Instead, massive masonry-bearing walls were spaced at twenty-two-foot intervals, acting like huge eleven-story party walls reminiscent of the typical tenement house structural organization, but much higher.

The Dakota, which opened in 1884, overshadowed the other luxury high-rise projects in extravagance and opulence, a status highlighted by the irony of its location at West 72nd Street and Central Park, in the center of the large squatter community of Dutchtown. The shanties and their population soon disappeared in the face of new development (figure 3.23). The roughly square mass of the Dakota rose ten stories around a central courtyard, as in the Vancorlear (figure 3.24). Its sixty-five apartments varied in size from four to twenty rooms; some parlors were immense, measuring twenty feet by forty feet.[64] Four passenger and four freight elevators were powered by water hydraulic machinery. Like Stevens House and the Vancorlear, the Dakota seized all of the latest technology, using every advance the burgeoning fields of mechanical and electrical engineering could offer.

Figure 3.21. Henry Hardenburg. The Vancorlear, completed in 1880 with six stories and elevators; a precursor to the high-rise perimeter plan type.

Figure 3.22. Hubert, Pirsson, and Company. The Chelsea, completed in 1883; probably the earliest truly high-rise apartment building in New York City, with eleven stories and elevators. The structural system was primitive, however, with enormous parallel bearing walls, reminiscent of the row house party wall.

Figure 3.23. Henry Hardenburg, The Dakota, completed on the Upper West Side in 1884, at the center of the squatter community of Dutchtown; shown in a view published in 1889.

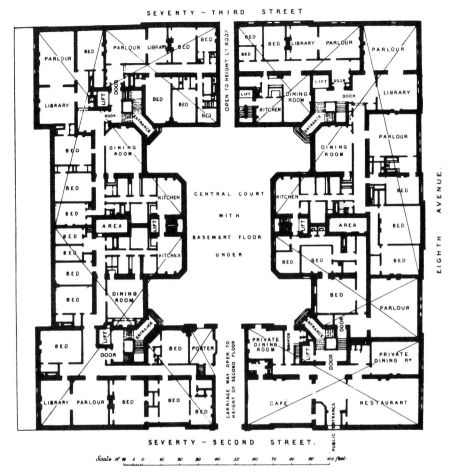

SEVENTY - THIRD STREET

EIGHTH AVENUE

SEVENTY - SECOND STREET.

Scale of 10 5 0 10 20 30 40 50 60 70 80 90 100 feet

THE DAKOTA APARTMENT-HOUSE, NEW YORK.

GROUND FLOOR PLAN

Figure 3.24. Henry Hardenburg. The Dakota plan, showing the internal courtyard with elevator lobbies at the four corners; notice the increase in scale from the Vancorlear and Chelsea to the Dakota.

A large vault under the great lawn contained steam boilers and engines to power the pumps and dynamos. The building was electrified. On the roof, six tanks supplied two million gallons of water per day, through two-hundred miles of piping. Structurally, the independent frame was not yet used. Masonry-bearing walls supported floors spanned with rolled steel beams three to four feet apart with arched masonry infill. All partitions were fireproof brick. The spread of fire was close to impossible either horizontally or vertically.

By the early 1880s numerous plans were being filed with the Bureau of Buildings for high-rise luxury apartment structures in Manhattan using elevators. One report states that between July 11, 1881, and March 15, 1883, permits were granted for the erection of forty-two buildings exceeding one-hundred feet in height, of which the majority were for housing.[65] A number of the new apart-

ment buildings were located near the south side of Central Park. Each year set some new precedent for either height or amenity. For example, the nine-story Dalhousie on Central Park South, completed in 1884, boasted duplex apartments, refrigerators, and steam heat.[66] In the following year it was eclipsed by the lavishly appointed Osborn, a 10 story apartment building designed by James Ware, on West 57th Street at Seventh Avenue (figure 3.25).[67] Nearby was the Wyoming, and several cooperatives designed by Philip Hubert.[68]

The technological feat of high-rise building received immediate notice among architects, especially in Europe. In 1883 *The Builder* in London announced the planning of the Osborn, reassuring its readers with a quote from an American source that "high quarters will surely come into great demand for offices or homes."[69] The English architect John Gale wrote at great length about the emerging New York City high rise after his visit of 1882.[70] His infatuation was more with the technology alone, rather than with the aesthetic changes it might bring. American architectural style was considered at best derivative, or as a critic writing in *The Builder* in 1883 pointed out, it was becoming "Europeanized." But the critic admitted that American building technology was unique: "In regard to some more practical matters connected with building, however, there is more difference

Figure 3.26. Hubert, Pirsson, and Company. Early photo of the Central Park Apartments, completed in 1883, showing the enormous massing of the ten-story structure, which remained the largest apartment building in New York for the next two decades.

Figure 3.27. Hubert, Pirsson, and Company. Block plan of the Central Park Apartments, with the eight interconnected buildings and internal courtyards.

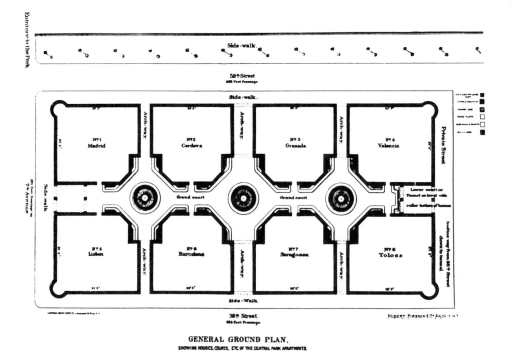

GENERAL GROUND PLAN,
SHOWING HOUSES, COURTS, ETC OF THE CENTRAL PARK APARTMENTS.

between England and America than in matters of purely architectural taste, and we may have more to learn from our Transatlantic cousins on these subjects than on architecture as an art."[71]

The most expansive of the first generation of high-rise apartment buildings was the Central Park Apartments, or Spanish Flats, on Central Park South, a cooperative completed in 1883 by Hubert, Pirsson, and Company (figure 3.26). The eight ten-story buildings occupied over half a block between Sixth and Seventh avenues (figure 3.27). Some apartments occupied entire floors (7,800 square feet); others, half floors on two levels.[72] The effect was as close as possible to having a brownstone "in the air." A private courtyard ran the length of the block, large enough to accommodate some landscaping, with limited light and ventilation. It provided no view, however, for the rooms facing into it, and its scale was considerably diminished by the massive ten-story walls (figure 3.28). Still, its standards for light and air were relatively decent in comparison with other examples; both the Dalhousie and the Osborn used air wells which were far smaller than those of the Central Park Apartments. Frequently light and view were less than ideal, even in outside-facing rooms, as the new high buildings began to impinge on each other.

High-rise living had other problems as well. Many were simply endemic to the type and not easily corrected. Privacy, both acoustic and visual, probably ranked among the most troublesome, especially given the bias of Anglo-Saxon culture toward the individual. Whatever disadvantages high-rise living may have had however, they were outweighed for affluent New Yorkers by its positive characteristics.[73] In 1882 an article in *Harper's New Monthly* magazine related:

Although flats have proved a partial failure in solving the [housing] problem for the mass of Americans, they have been warmly welcomed by people of liberal incomes. They have become a fashion, and in a certain way are very convenient. Some of those that are very elegant bring from $2,500 to $4,000, and are readily taken. One might not believe that an apartment could be leased at such a price, when whole houses, and handsome ones, may be had at those figures. But it should be remembered that very expensive apartments are saving, in that they require less furniture and fewer servants, a smaller outlay of every kind than an entire house, and at the same time enable their tenants to present an equally fair appearance in the eyes of the world. This last point is one of grave consequence for New Yorkers, who will, as a rule, keep up appearances at almost any sacrifice. They save too, by the new method of living, much trouble, much friction. A flat simplifies housekeeping greatly, and they feel that they can safely leave it, and go to the country, or abroad, for an indefinite period. If they had a house, they would continually be afraid, and with reason, of its being entered by burglars; and to people who travel so frequently as New Yorkers do, freedom from such fear is not to be disesteemed. Thus, socially and practically, there are arguments in favor of flats, and arguments of weight.[74]

The high-rise luxury apartments had much to offer in terms of social appearances which the single-family brownstone could not have, particularly immense scale and extravagant details and materials. There was a certain status associated with being above the dirt and noise of the city, with views unseen previously. For the first time in New York City, apartments on upper floors commanded higher rents than those near the ground, a reversal of normal convention in buildings where tenants had to climb stairs. The lofty heights were celebrated with an entourage of elegant and efficient door, hall, and elevator men, who screened visitors, operated the elevators, and provided tenants with essential services while reinforcing the expression of opulence. Some of the technical innovations within the new apartment buildings were not yet available for single-family dwellings, or even for the millionaires' mansions. For example, before the institution of municipal service, electricity could be installed only in the large new buildings with private dynamos, like the Dakota. It was prohibitively complicated and expensive for single houses. Finally, as an article in 1893 *Cosmopolitan* pointed out, for the efficiency of its layout, the apartment far surpassed the brownstone:

There is more available floor-space in an ordinary apartment, containing from seven to ten rooms, all one level, than in a four storey house with a frontage of thirty feet, in which the space is taken up by storage and the attic room and stairways is wasted.

. . . [The wife] is a queen, as truly as Victoria in Windsor Castle, with this improvement over isolated housekeeping, that all the responsibility for protection, heating, lighting, and attendance is assumed by the general management. Only the lighter duties of personal service need be performed by her maids. The elevator conductors are always on watch at the entrance to her home. She has her own kitchen, reception room and private hall. Her house is absolutely safe from

Figure 3.28. Philip Hubert. View of the internal courtyards of the Central Park Apartments, showing the ten-story walls and limited view.

THE COURT OF THE "SPANISH" FLATS.

fire and robbery. During the summer, she locks up her apartments and leaves them undisturbed until she returns in the fall, knowing that there are no rear windows unguarded, no skylight to admit burglars, through the roof, and no necessity for the employment of special watchmen. This perfect security from unwelcome intrusion is a peculiarity of the apartment-house, that has recently acquired increased value in the estimation of men who, on account of their financial or political influence, are being constantly sought after. The narrow escape of Mr. Russell Sage from death at the hands of a bomb-thrower has had the immediate and universal effect of increasing the natural shyness of rich men. Mr. Gould, the Vanderbilt and the Rockefeller brothers, and other millionaires, employ special policemen in front of their residences, while Mr. Henry Villard, John W. Mackay, Jr., and other cliff-dwellers, live at an elevation as safe from invasion as the eyrie of the American eagle.[75]

Thus, among other things the high rise was a welcome fortress during a period characterized by the greatest economic instability and civic insurrection in United States history, first in the 1870s and then in the 1890s. The threat of violence did not discourage some from building ostentatious mansions along upper Fifth Avenue. By 1881 the Stewart mansion was already outclassed by the William K. Vanderbilt mansion on several lots at 52d Street and Fifth Avenue.[76] Designed as a François I château by Richard Morris Hunt, it set the precedent for a progression of mansions which marched up Fifth Avenue, culminating in the Frick, built in 1914.

During the decades between 1890 and 1910, the form of high-rise luxury housing evolved steadily from the pioneering efforts of Stevens House, the Chelsea, the Dakota, and the Central Park Apartments. The technological advances came quickly. Steam and water hydraulic elevators were soon replaced by oil hydraulic and electric traction machinery. Electric elevators were more versatile, and could even be used during construction, speeding up the building process.[77] The cumbersome combination of masonry-bearing walls and iron beams, infilled with vaulted brick, was replaced by the independent steel skeleton with concrete fireproofing. On the facades, ornate cast terra-cotta began to replace the heavier and more expensive worked stone. Steam heat, electricity, and central refrigeration systems were commonplace. In Manhattan, high-rise luxury housing pushed its way northward past 57th Street, up Broadway, West End Avenue, Riverside Drive, and Park Avenue. The completion of the Interborough Rapid Transit subway on upper Broadway in 1904 encouraged the building of many new luxury projects on the Upper West Side.[78]

In the design of early high-rise apartment buildings, two different approaches to the problems of massing and light seemed to emerge. An "extroverted" approach tended to cut into the building mass from the outside, creating large air slots which penetrated toward the center. The Ansonia at West 72d Street and Broadway, designed by Graves and Duboy and completed in 1902, was a good example of this approach (figure 3.29).[79] By contrast, Graham Court, completed by Clinton and Russell in 1901 on Adam Clayton Powell Jr. Boulevard between West 116th and 117th streets,[80] used an "introverted" approach. Here, the center

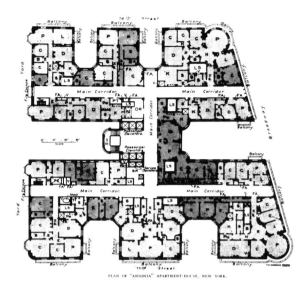

Figure 3.29. Graves and Duboy. The Ansonia, completed in 1902 as one of the most innovative of the second generation of high-rise apartment buildings. It used an "extroverted" approach to plan organization, with an unprecedented height of seventeen stories.

PLAN OF "ANSONIA" APARTMENT-HOUSE, NEW YORK.

of the building was hollowed out, creating a large internal courtyard surrounded by perimeter walls of housing. In 1908 the same architects completed the Apthorp a similar but larger version at West 79th Street and Broadway (figure 3.30).[81] This introverted or palazzo type was expensive. Relatively few such projects were built; one of the largest was the Belnord at West 86th Street and Broadway, designed by Hiss and Weeks and completed in 1910 (figure 3.31).[82] The massing characteristics of the palazzo type presented difficulties for the design of efficient corners, and this type tended to work best at less site coverage than other types of massing—the Belnord used only 67 percent coverage, in comparison with 86 percent for the Apthorp. In return, however, the palazzo courtyards frequently solved light problems better than the light slots of the extroverted types. Ernest Flagg attacked the design of the Ansonia fiercely, criticizing the lack of light in the apartments. He was probably equally incensed by the fact that the huge project was not architect designed, having been planned principally by its builder, William E. D. Stokes, in collaboration with the architect Paul Duboy.[83]

In 1903, when the seventeen-story Ansonia was completed, it was the largest apartment house in New York City and, by consequence, in the world. Ironically, in spite of its historicist facade, it was also the most technically advanced apartment house in the world (figure 3.32). Flagg's criticism of the Ansonia's lack of light may have been well taken, but its tenants were undoubtedly more interested in the incredible dimension of its technical servitude. The 340 apartments received lengths of service conduit which was measured in miles: 44.01 miles of water pipe, 18.56 miles of steam pipe, 37.30 miles of gas pipe, 15.81 miles of sanitary waste line, 39.28 miles of electric conduit. There were 2,440 sanitary fixtures, 2,100 gas outlets, 2,071 steam radiators, and 7,849 electric outlets fed by a network of 83 miles of copper wire. Power was supplied by four steam boilers and five electric dynamos. There were seventeen elevators, piped ice water at 147

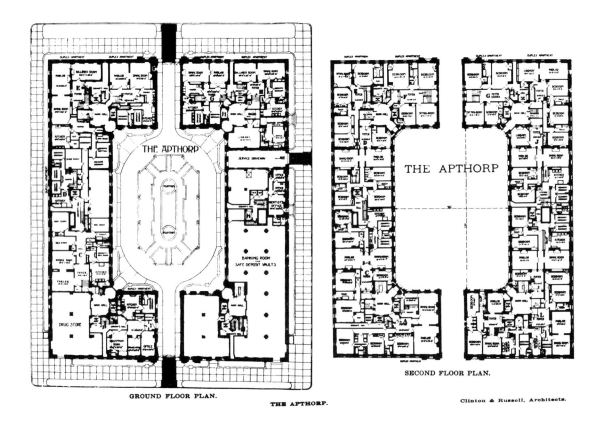

GROUND FLOOR PLAN.

THE APTHORP.

SECOND FLOOR PLAN.

Clinton & Russell, Architects.

Figure 3.30. Clinton and Russell. The Apthorp, completed in 1908, exceeding the Ansonia in size and luxury and using an "introverted" perimeter plan, around a large internal courtyard.

outlets, and 365 telephone outlets. Pneumatic tubes transported messages and packages to all floors. In anticipation of the perfection of a centralized vacuum cleaning system, the necessary tubing was installed. Two hundred forty employees were required to run the building. A laundry service had a capacity of 25,000 pieces per day. Other amenities included a private dairy, barber shop, swimming pool, and baths. The anticipation of technology not yet materialized extended to the automobile. A basement garage housed twenty-four automobiles, complete with repair shop, scarcely after the automobile had begun to make its way up and down Broadway.[84]

The Ansonia was soon exceeded in size by the Apthorp, which in turn was immediately exceeded by the Belnord (figure 3.33). Both were designed in the style of the Italian Renaissance, but completely dwarfed the Florentine palazzi that inspired them, just as the Ansonia increased to absurdity the scale of the Hausmann street which inspired its image. In 1918 270 Park Avenue, one of the last and largest of the palazzo apartment buildings, was completed between Park and Madison avenues and East 47th and 48th streets (figure 3.34). Designed by Warren and Wetmore to exceed in size and cost "anything ever attempted of its kind,"[85] the building massing was actually a broken perimeter, forming two U-shaped sections. Otherwise, it followed closely the tradition of the Apthorp and

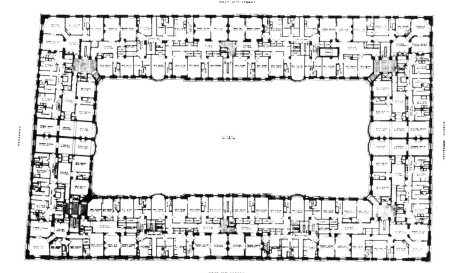

THE "BELNORD"—TYPICAL FLOOR PLAN.

Figure 3.31. Hiss and Weeks. The Belnord, completed in 1910, exceeding even the Apthorp in size, with the same plan organization.

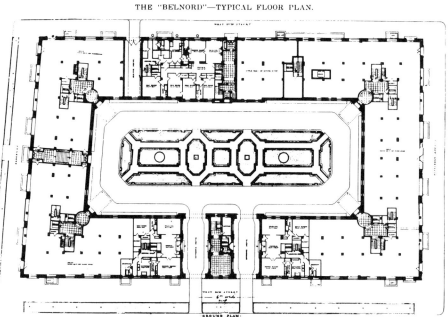

THE "BELNORD"—GROUND FLOOR, SHOWING THE COURT.

Hiss & Weekes, Architects.

Figure 3.32. Graves and Duboy. Photo of the Ansonia in 1903, showing the monumentalized Second Empire facade; construction of New York City's first subway is being completed under Broadway.

Figure 3.33. Hiss and Weeks. View of the
Belnord, showing the Italianate facades,
intended to be reminiscent Renaissance palazzi.

Belnord, including the Italianate facades and garden. From this point on, little
new ground was broken for the luxury palazzo building. Noteworthy, however,
were two other Park Avenue perimeters: 277 Park Avenue was completed by
McKim, Mead, and White in 1925,[86] and 1185 Park Avenue was completed by
Schwartz and Gross in 1928.[87]

Just as sophistication in overall apartment-building massing and organization grew toward the turn of the century, so did the planning of individual apartments. From the earliest days of the tall apartment house, experimentation with
units attempted to replicate the spatial amenity of the brownstone, which logically led to duplex units organized around private internal staircases.[88] By 1884
duplex sections were employed at both the Central Park Apartments and the
Dalhousie. The use of two levels helped to resolve the problems of social propriety
involving privacy for the bedroom areas. As time went on, the spatial potential
of the duplex was more fully developed as a unique apartment type called the
"studio," with a double-height living or studio area. This organization developed
from the idea of the artists' studios, with a high room and large expanses of north-
facing fenestration. It served as work space and informal exhibition area, with
the private areas attached. The origins of the type date from 1857, with Hunt's
Studio Building (see figure 1.6). For a period, the studio remained the province
of artists, with several cooperatively owned studio buildings completed by artists'
initiative. By the early twentieth century, however, it was adopted for luxury
housing, with an interesting array of such buildings completed in Manhattan.[89]
It was these prototypes which pioneered the revolutionary spatial potential of the
independent structural frame. Because no bearing walls were needed, the spatial

Figure 3.34. Warren and Wetmore. 270 Park
Avenue, the last and largest of the perimeter-
type, luxury high-rise apartment buildings,
completed in 1918.

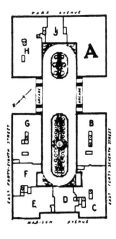

volume of the apartments was free to move vertically. Later on, with the development of modernist spatial conceptions, this freedom was exploited even further. This new spatial order appealed to the affluent, along with the connection to bohemianism. According to one observer in 1920:

> If space in this type of [studio] building were in demand only by artists . . . fewer buildings would supply the demand. But many other people have come to appreciate the possibilities of a studio from a decorative standpoint and many prefer a comfortable, informal big studio room to the usual apartment living room. Whatever the reasons may be, so many other people have taken studio apartments that, it is safe to say, the artists are in the minority in some buildings at least. Probably in the last analysis the motive is in most cases the same that has brought the big living room into favor in moderate-size houses—a desire for simplicity and breadth, for at least one room big enough so that one does not feel restricted.[90]

For many decades in New York City, high-rise luxury housing was not given the same legal scrutiny as tenements, especially in relation to building height restrictions. The legal definitions of "tenement" used after passage of the Tenement House Act of 1867 could be construed to include high-rise apartments—that is, any building with three or more rental dwellings, with independent living and cooking, and more than two per floor.[91] The building height restrictions imposed by the tenement house laws, however, were completely ignored by developers of high-rise housing. This practice caused an outcry each time a building of unprecedented new heights appeared. The developers of high-rise apartments tired to avoid the jurisdiction of the laws by calling their buildings "apartment-hotels," as hotels were clearly outside of tenement legislation. Cooperative apartments, as privately owned rather than rental dwellings, also were exempt.[92] Thus a great portion of developer motives in marketing "home ownership" and hotel amenities within apartment buildings had to do with attempting to escape the scrutiny of housing legislation. This practice led to a new category of housing enterprise commonly known as the "bootleg hotel."[93]

In 1900 Edward T. Potter complained bitterly to the Tenement House Commission of the New York state legislature about inequities between housing legislation for the poor and for the rich, arguing that the same set of laws should be applied to everyone:

> I would like the sting to be taken out of the word "tenement" wherever it is applied; and, as to law, what is bad in itself is bad wherever it is to be found. I do not like having one law for Peter and another for Paul, nor exempting noblemen from prosecution for debt, nor approve of any form of creating privileged classes. Apart from other more excellent reasons, it is contrary to the trend of civilization, the spirit of the age, as well as the development and ennobling of humanity. The well-meant law hampering land-division led to the evils this commission are benevolently wishing to lessen; the well-meant law forbidding rear tenements led to intensifying those evils; and now, to introduce laws, or mitigations of law, founded

A PROPOSED TWENTY-STORY APARTMENT HOUSE
ON UPPER FIFTH AVENUE

PLAN A. TYPICAL FLOOR PLAN OF LARGE APARTMENTS

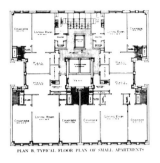

PLAN B. TYPICAL FLOOR PLAN OF SMALL APARTMENTS

Figure 3.35. Charles W. Buckham. Proposal for a twenty-story apartment building made in 1911, intended to be the highest in New York City, but using a plan derived from the Tenement House Laws.

on, and tending to intensify class distinctions, would be another mistake, and a very sad and far-reaching one.[94]

It was not until 1916 with the introduction of the height and setback laws for all types of building in New York City that the form of high-rise luxury housing came under any form of strict control. The definitive legislation, however, did not come until 1929, with passage of the Multiple Dwellings Law, which uniformly controlled all types of housing. With passage of the New Law in 1901, however, tenement house legislation did have some effect on the emerging category of middle-income apartment buildings. Frequently variants of New Law plans were arbitrarily projected vertically. A 1911 proposal by Charles W. Buckham for the first twenty story apartment building in New York City used a Flagg-derived plan, with an elevator and stair core filling what would normally be a light slot (figure 3.35).[95] Coverage was obviously greater than permitted by the New Law, however.

New Law plans also were often adapted for use with primitive self-service elevators in buildings which followed the New Law height restriction of no more than one and one-third of the street width. These were usually five-to-seven story buildings for middle-income occupancy. At this time, New York City building regulation restricted self-service elevators to low buildings, where walking up stairs was also practical.[96] Figure 3.36 shows two typical New Law plans designed by Louis Korn and George Pelham, with small elevators inserted.[97] Figure 3.37 is a

Figure 3.36. Louis Korn and George Pelham. New Law tenement plans designed to middle-class standards, with six stories and small elevators inserted, circa 1903.

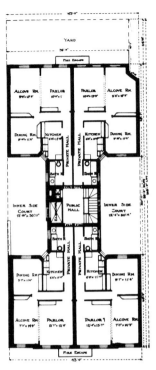

FOUR-FAMILY-ON-A-FLOOR "ELEVATOR APARTMENT HOUSE."

Nos. 82 and 84 West 12th Street.   Louis Korn, Architect,
                                          No. 31 West 33d Street.
Lot 43 feet wide by 103 feet 3 inches deep: 4 four-room apartments; 16 rooms and 4 baths on each floor.

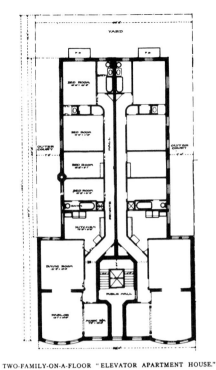

TWO-FAMILY-ON-A-FLOOR "ELEVATOR APARTMENT HOUSE."

North side 113th Street,   Geo. Fred. Pelham, Architect,
325 feet west of 7th Avenue.   No. 503 Fifth Avenue.
Lot 50 feet wide by 100 feet 11 inches deep: 2 apartments of
8 rooms and 2 baths each.

more elaborate plan by George Pelham for Rafford Hall, a six-story building on upper Broadway.[98] It is a derivation of the Flagg-type plan, adapted to a central stair and elevator. It was a plan type which was widely used in the expanding middle-class periphery of the city. For example, on upper Broadway and Riverside Drive between West 135th and 165th streets, construction of no fewer than sixty-three such apartment houses was begun between 1905 and 1908 (figure 3.38).[99] Most were six stories, with New Law plans and frequently with elevators, typical of hundreds of buildings under construction in upper Manhattan and the Bronx by the early part of the twentieth century.

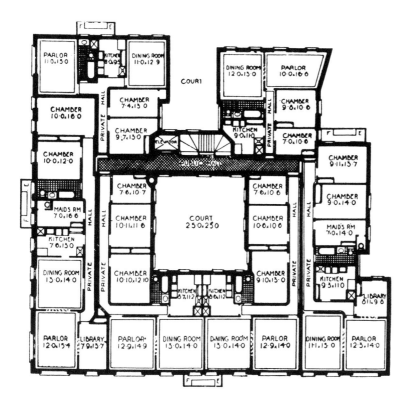

Figure 3.37. George Pelham. Middle-class apartment building designed in 1908, with six stories and a small elevator incorporated into a derivative of the Flagg-type plan.

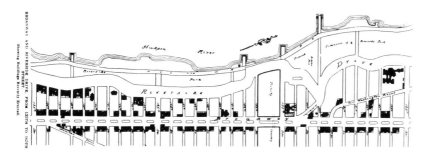

Figure 3.38. Plan showing new construction on upper Broadway, circa 1908, indicating the proliferation of new middle-class apartment buildings.

4

Beyond the Tenement

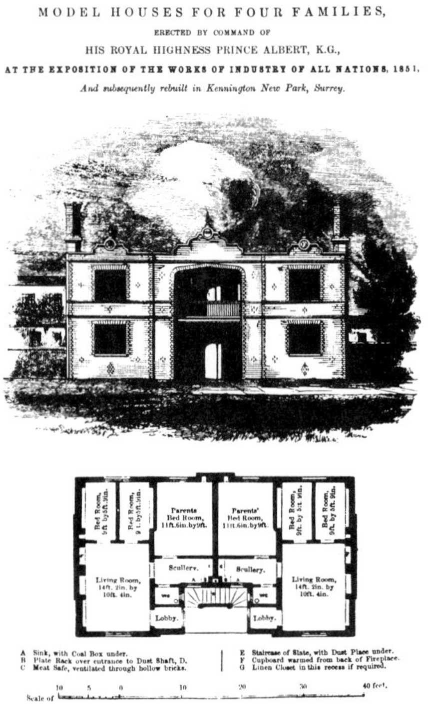

MODEL HOUSES FOR FOUR FAMILIES,
ERECTED BY COMMAND OF
HIS ROYAL HIGHNESS PRINCE ALBERT, K.G.,
AT THE EXPOSITION OF THE WORKS OF INDUSTRY OF ALL NATIONS, 1851.
And subsequently rebuilt in Kennington New Park, Surrey.

Figure 4.1 Henry Roberts. Model working-class housing erected at the Great Exhibition of 1851 in London; the system of open stair and gallery access eventually found its way to philanthropic projects in New York City.

PHILANTHROPIC tenements built in New York City between 1880 and 1920 were minuscule in number, compared with the overall tenement construction: however, they received considerable notice among reformers and architects. Usually their design was carefully and scientifically studied, and correlated very carefully with social programs for their tenants. For these projects, the exploration of a conscious "social architecture" could be dealt with more concretely than for most other buildings.

Much of the earliest design investigation for philanthropic tenements looked to precedents in England, especially in London, by organizations such as the Improved Dwellings Company, the Peabody Trust, and the Metropolitan Association.[1] The rationalized form for the improved English tenement included several unusual practices. Public stairs tended to be open to the exterior, frequently with "gallery access" to each dwelling, eliminating the dark, unventilated internal stair found in most row housing. The open stair and gallery on the front facade of the building did not hinder the penetration of light and air to the rooms behind it. This device dated from the model dwellings designed by Henry Roberts and built at the Great Exhibition of 1851 in London by Prince Albert, at the instigation of the Society for Improving the Condition of the Laboring Classes (figure 4.1).[2] Within each dwelling, the area containing the water supply or water closet was usually placed against the rear facade, with a window for ventilation. Frequently, this area actually protruded from the facade, in order to further improve light and ventilation. The first such English plan published in New York appears to have been in the *Report of the Council of Hygiene* in 1865.[3] The plan was for the first building by the Improved Dwellings Company, organized by Sir Sydney Waterlow (figure 4.2). Erected in 1863 in London, the building incorporated both gallery access and protruding "wash house" areas from the rear.

The reasoning behind the Waterlow plan type also was applied to improved tenement design in New York. A very early example ingeniously attempted to combine both stair and water closets in an extension to the rear of a single 25-foot-wide tenement (figure 4.3). The alteration was made in an existing tenement

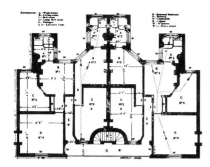

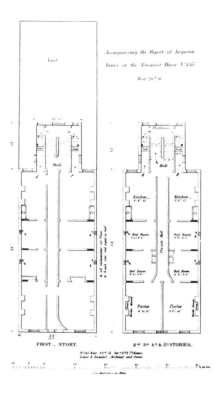

Figure 4.2. Dwellings erected by Sir Sydney
Waterlow's Improved Dwellings Company in
London in 1863 (left), using open stairs and
galleries and protruding wet areas; the plan
was later applied to philanthropic housing in
New York City.

Figure 4.3. Louis E. Dunkel. A philanthropic
tenement built by the architect around 1865
(right), using some characteristics of the
Waterlow-type plan.

around 1865 on West 26th Street by the architect, Louis E. Duenkel, who also
owned, managed, and lived in the building.[4] The first literal translation of the
Waterlow type was a philanthropic project of Alfred Treadway White in Brooklyn—
the Home Buildings designed by William Field and Son and completed in 1877
(figure 4.4).[5] Located on the corner of Hicks and Baltic streets, the Home Buildings became part of a larger concentration of White's projects, completed during
the following two years. The two Home Buildings, both six stories in height, housed
forty families each. The building facing Baltic Street used open stairs, but without
gallery access, and with only partially protruding wet areas. Each stair served a
25-foot module on either side. A variation in dwelling sizes from two to four rooms
was accomplished through a system of laterally "borrowed" spaces between mod-
ules. The plan of the other Home Building facing Hicks Street was much closer
to the Waterlow version, although unfortunately it included an interior room which
received no direct light or ventilation. Both plans were luxurious by tenement
standards, with living rooms, one or two bedrooms, and the separate wet areas
which included sink, washtub, and water closet—the prefiguration of the modern
kitchen and bath.

By 1879 William Field and Son had completed several other projects for White,
all adjacent to the Home Buildings (figure 4.5). The Tower Buildings, with 146
dwellings, were built on three sides of the block between Baltic and Warren streets.
Another Waterlow-type plan was used which eliminated the problematic interior
room (figure 4.6). In the same year, with the completion of the Warren Place

Figure 4.4. William Field and Son. The Home
Buildings, completed for philanthropist Alfred
Treadway White in 1877 in Brooklyn, using an
adaptation of the Waterlow-type plan to the
New York City gridiron.

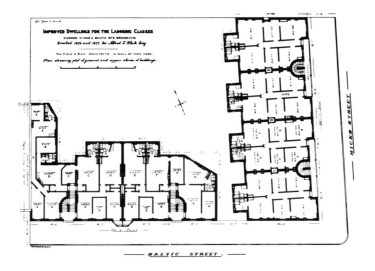

project to the rear of the Tower Buildings, an internal courtyard was formed, and
it was devoted to a lawn, drying racks, a central gazebo, and an encircling promenade. The Tower Buildings covered only 52 percent of the land, in contrast to
the 80 percent coverage of the Old Law tenements. The Warren Place project
organized 34 houses along an east-west mews between Baltic and Warren streets,
using the same principle as shown in figure 1.14. The two rows of single-family
houses faced a 24-foot-wide "parkway," with service alleys behind (figure 4.7).
Eight larger houses at the ends of the mews contained nine rooms each, while
the smaller houses on Warren Place contained only six rooms. In its critique of
the results of the 1879 tenement house competition, the *New York Times* singled

Figure 4.5. William Field and Son. The entire
estate of philanthropic housing built for Alfred
Treadway White in Brooklyn in 1879, consisting
of the Home Buildings (1 and 2); the Tower
Buildings (3, 4, and 5); and Warren Place (6).

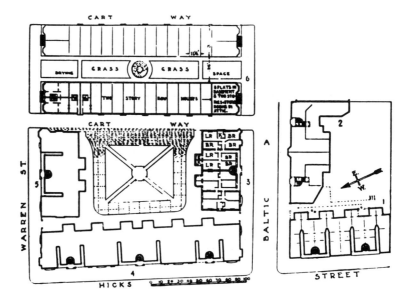

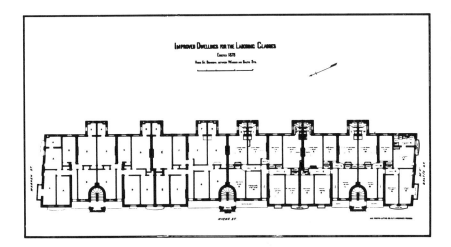

Figure 4.6. William Field and Son. A portion of the Tower Buildings, showing improvements in the plan organization over the Home Buildings.

out White's Warren Place project as one potential "solution of this vexed question of tenement houses." The newspaper advocated building villages of such mews "cottage houses" for workingmen, to be financed by building associations, in locations where low land costs and reasonable transit connections would make them economically feasible.[6] In spite of such interest, almost no other mews cottage

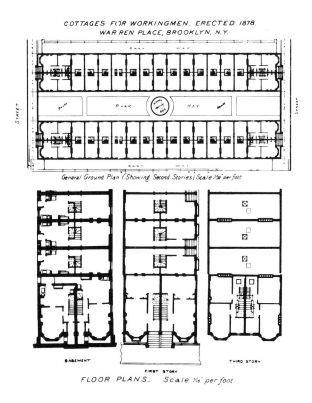

Figure 4.7. William Field and Son. Warren Place Mews, consisting of modest single-family row houses along a private "parkway," completed in 1878.

projects were realized in New York City, and none of them for working-class housing. And as for all of White's projects, the intention was clearly for rental to families of more than subsistence means.

For the first time in New York City, with the initiative of White, communal outdoor space of substantial magnitude was included within housing for families of modest income. In general, the 218 dwellings of the Home and Tower buildings and the Warren Place project together represented the first major philanthropic investment in housing by private capital in the United States.[7] Through the realization of these projects, and through his writing and other activities, Alfred Treadway White had an extraordinary impact on tenement reform in the United States. White graduated in civil engineering from Rensselaer Polytechnic Institute in 1865. Shortly afterward he became interested in divesting family wealth from a mercantile fur business into limited profit housing for the "working class." He went to England in 1872, where he became especially interested in the theories of Sir Sidney Waterlow.[8] Undoubtedly he found them compatible with the prospects for a private housing philanthropy in the United States. White's arguments came to reflect attitudes in United States housing philanthropy which have prevailed to present day: he advocated strong legislative measures against substandard housing, while his real hope was that the housing impasse could be solved within the private sector of the economy. In his first tract, published in 1877, the recurrent theme appeared:

> Legislation is not the only thing needed; *private endeavor* must show the possibility of improving existing dwellings, or erecting improved dwellings which shall yield a *fair return on the capital invested*. It is not worth while to consider the Old World experiments in providing homes for the poor furnished in whole or in part *as a charity,* for this is neither necessary nor to be commended. The laboring classes now pay rents in New York which would yield a large interest on the cost of well-constructed and well-aired houses; but beyond this, the reception of a home as a species of charity is quite as harmful to the poor, quite as discouraging to the industrious, as the direct receiving of alms without adequate return in labor.[9]

White develops his arguments further, however, to the conclusion that "the ideal city is, of course, one in which every family should own and occupy a separate house."[10] He continued: "It is a fact that the poor are too poor and the rich are too rich to care whether City Government is well and economically administered or not. The presence of the middle classes in their own houses is essential to the lasting prosperity of the metropolis."[11] The housing problem became a moral issue, and even in the theories of its chief protagonist, philanthropy was limited to providing transitory housing for the future middle class, and to strengthening the private sector of the economy. What was totally lacking was a cohesive strategy for transforming the half of the city's population which was considered poor into the ideal middle class.

White correctly identified excessive land costs inflated by the private sector as the primary barrier to achieving his goals of improved housing and increased private ownership. He hoped that improved transportation technology could offer a way out of this deadlock, reasoning that until "far better methods of transit exist than any now promised, New York and, to some extent, Brooklyn, will depend upon tenement houses or 'flats' to house a large part of its population."[12] This latter observation was in fact prophetic. With each extension of the transportation network over the next eighty years, another group entered the middle class, and each new influx came closer to achieving the ideal of the single-family suburban house. White himself was forced to locate his projects in Brooklyn to save on land costs.

As White also noted, the high cost of land in New York prevented effective use of cooperative savings and loan associations for private home building. These organizations, which could have given small wage earners the opportunity to invest their money and enjoy lending privileges, were generally unavailable in New York City. In Philadelphia by the 1880s they had provided the mortgages which created a city of predominantly private single-family houses.[13] In New York State, a law passed in 1851 permitted the organization of savings and loan associations. By 1888 there were approximately 275 associations in the state, but only 48 were in New York City and Brooklyn. In Philadelphia by 1888 there were 450.[14] By 1900, the domestic fabric of the two cities could not have been more different. In Philadelphia, 84.6 percent of the population lived in single-family houses, while only 1.1 percent lived in buildings with six or more families. In New York, 50.3 percent lived in buildings containing six or more families, while 17.5 percent lived in single-family houses.[15]

By 1900, for all classes of housing, domesticity in New York had achieved an affinity for density which was unique among U.S. cities. Yet for philanthropic housing, doubts persisted as to the ideal housing type. Ideological and economic constraints caused dual foci to develop, alternating between city and suburb. In his Home and Tower buildings, White proposed the philanthropic tenement as an interim step in advancing the poor into the middle class and, ultimately, into the suburban single-family house. The architectural plans, codes of conduct, and managerial policies he followed were carefully designed to promote this purpose. As in all subsequent philanthropic projects, White's tenants were upwardly mobile and well-screened, despite his insistence that "of all of the families . . . only one was known to either owner or agent in advance of their application for rooms, and it would have been easy to secure many in better circumstances than those accepted as tenants."[16] The income requirements alone would have eliminated families in dire need. The aura was more of a finishing school than of reform school.

Another approach to housing philanthropy in the city were the "reeducation" schemes patterned after the work of Octavia Hill in London.[17] These pragmatic efforts focused on improving conditions in existing tenements through educational programs for tenants and physical rehabilitation of the building—usually the small-scale initiatives of private individuals. In New York, projects by people such as Olivia Dow or Ellen Collins received some notoriety. Dow's work at Gotham Court in 1881 had a positive, if brief, effect on that infamous slum.[18] Collins bought a building on Water Street in 1890, which she proceeded to rehabilitate, along with its tenants.[19] Suburban philanthropic projects also were planned. The confusion between urban and suburban strategies is clearly reflected in the wide range of

Figure 4.8. George Da Cunha. Proposal for philanthropic tenements made for the Improved Dwellings Association in 1880, improving dumbell design standards and including a large courtyard at the interior of the block.

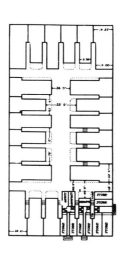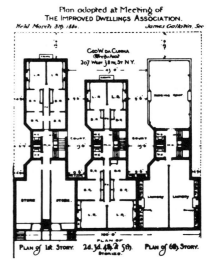

architectural proposals which had evolved by the turn of the century—from generous cottages to tenements with only minuscule improvements by comparison.

To a large extent, the architecture of philanthropy in urban housing became equated with reductions in coverage, and with vague communal uses planned for the leftover space. Open spaces were intended ostensibly to permit a greater penetration of light into the dwellings, but they also took on a larger significance of almost mystical dimensions. The provision of open space for the use of residents was always equated with "good," even if in reality it was only left over. Frequently the "courtyard" was just an oversized air shaft with concrete pavement. Toward the turn of the century, however, the amount of leftover space in some proposals increased sharply, rivaling the important precedent set by White's complex in Brooklyn.

The most common method of reducing ground coverage was to open air shafts onto the rear yards. This strategy was used in 1880 by the architect George Da Cunha in a proposal to the newly formed Improved Dwellings Association for several lots between First and Second Avenues, at East 71st and 72nd streets (figure 4.8).[20] He widened the standard dumbell air shaft to more than nine feet, and opened it toward the interior of the block to obtain better light and ventilation. The block plans used a coverage of only 67 percent. As in the complex built by Alfred Treadway White, a perimeter of housing surrounded a communal space for the use of adjacent residents. The "perimeter block" approach was destined to create as much interest for its application to reduced-coverage philanthropic schemes as it did for luxury buildings (such as the Apthorp or Belnord, figures 3.16 and 3.17). Da Cunha discarded the 25-foot lot as the design module, using thirty-three and a half feet instead to improve the efficiency of the plans.

The Improved Dwellings Association was formed in 1880 on the recommendation of a committee appointed by Mayor Edward Cooper to devise means of

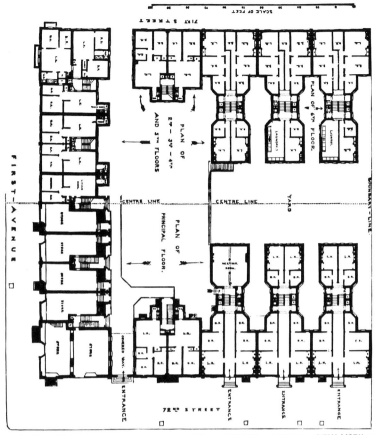

Figure 4.9. Vaux and Radford. Final plan adopted for the philanthropic tenements of the Improved Dwellings Association; further development of the previous Da Cunha proposal used both Waterlow-type plans and a "fishtail" variant on the dumbell tenement.

implementing tenement house reform.[21] The association dividends were to be limited to 5 percent. An initial capital of $300,000 was raised by several men of wealth and power, including Cornelius Vanderbilt, who had in the same year completed his own residence on Fifth Avenue at a cost of $750,000.[22] George Da Cunha was replaced as project architect by Vaux and Radford, who completed a final design using only one-half of the original site. They retained the interior of the block as a courtyard which served "the purposes of a place for recreation, and entrance to the dwellings, and an open space which will supply an abundance of light and air" (figure 4.9).[23]

Da Cunha's dwelling plans, as modified by Vaux and Radford, were used for some of the houses facing East 71st and 72nd streets. The remaining dwellings used a variant on the Waterlow plan type: they had protruding wet areas, but the stairs were enclosed, without galleries. The buildings achieved a sophistication of architectural detail which made their presence far more commanding than the normal middle-class flat of the same period in New York (figure 4.10). They were

BEYOND THE TENEMENT   95

GENERAL VIEW OF BUILDINGS being erected on 71st and 72d Streets and 1st Ave. New-York, for THE IMPROVED DWELLINGS ASSOCIATION—Vaux & Radford, Arch'ts.

the only project built by the Improved Dwellings Association. In 1879 a Waterlow plan type was also applied to the Monroe, a philanthropic project designed by William Field and Son and built on Monroe Street on the Lower East Side (figure 4.11). The architects used the plan of White's Tower Buildings. The project was built as a limited profit investment by the estate of Abner Chichester.[24] A single six-story building contained twenty-five two-room apartments and fifteen three-room apartments. The construction was entirely fireproof, except for minor partitions within each dwelling. In 1886, on the Lower East Side, another philanthropic project was built on Cherry Street, fashioned after the familiar "light slot" New York tenement plan (figure 4.12). The project was designed by William Schickel and Company, and built by the Tenement House Building Company.[25] The Tenement House Building Company was formed in 1885 with more than $150,000 in capital raised by its directors, due in large part to the efforts of Felix Adler. Dividends were limited to 4 percent. The Cherry Street plan used forty-two-foot-wide frontage modules, which could be halved to twenty-one feet. Rooms were single or double loaded, in an organization similar to a railroad flat (see figure 1.8). But these dwellings were better lit than the railroad flat. The excessive forty-two-foot width of the lots permitted use of the light slots. The slots became inordinately long, approaching fifty-feet in order to allow outside windows in each room, and were given irregular forms to improve window placement and view in some rooms. The scheme was subsequently published as a recommended plan to conform with the standards of the Board of Health (see figure 2.8).

The Monroe Model Tenement.

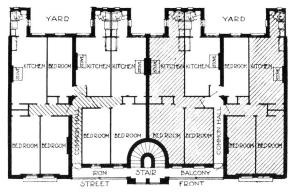

Figure 4.11. William Field and Son. The Monroe philanthropic tenement, completed in 1879 for the Chichester Estate, using their variant on the Waterlow-type plan.

PLAN OF 1878—THE MONROE

The Cherry Street building covered 70 percent of the site, with the light slots creating long and narrow exterior open spaces. These spaces were paved, and available for tenant use—primarily as play areas. The entire roof was developed for tenant use, presumably because the ground area was severely limited. The roofs were paved in brick, and enclosed by an iron fence, making an excellent open-air playground. From the laundry room in the basement, clothes could be sent by dumb waiter to the roof for drying. On hot summer nights many of the

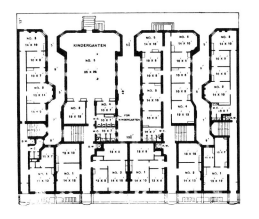

Figure 4.12. William Schickel and Company. Philanthropic tenement for the Tenement House Building Company completed in 1886, using highly refined version of a speculative tenement plan.

BEYOND THE TENEMENT   97

Figure 4.13. Lamb and Rich. Astral Apartments, philanthropic tenement completed in 1887 for oil magnate Charles Pratt, following a design approach which was similar to projects built by the Peabody Trust in London.

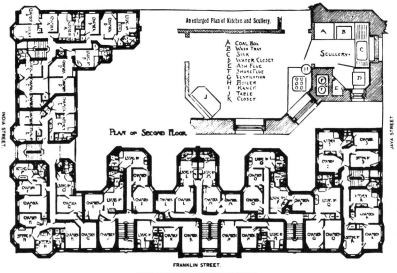

108 tenants used the roof for sleeping. A kindergarten on the ground floor accommodated about 50 children, primarily from within the building. The kindergarten also was used for other community-related activities, such as sewing classes and boys' club meetings.[26] The Cherry Street building was the only project built by the Tenement House Building Company.

In 1887, with the opening of Astral Apartments in Brooklyn, a new plan type appeared in New York philanthropic housing. The project was built on Franklin Street by the oil magnate Charles Pratt, near his refinery for the manufacture of Astral Oil in the Greenpoint area of Brooklyn. The architects Lamb and Rich had apparently studied in some detail the new philanthropic housing in London, especially the buildings recently erected by the Peabody Trust.[27] The Peabody Trust was one of the most successful of the London housing companies and was funded by the American philanthropist George Peabody. The eighteen Peabody projects built by this time tended to follow a somewhat different design approach from that of Sir Sydney Waterlow's Improved Dwellings Company. They were characterized by more internal circulation and wet areas. This approach combined with the constraints of the New York City gridiron to produce an interesting prototype in the Astral Apartments (figure 4.13). Stairs and corridors were internal and enclosed, and wet areas were incorporated into much larger protrusions than in the Waterlow type. The light slots were wider and shallower than in the normal improved New York City tenement. The development of the facades was influenced by the Peabody Trust buildings; they had a rather heavy and institutional appearance which many prospective tenants apparently disliked. The six-story structure housed ninety-five families, with a building coverage of 62 percent. A free library and kindergarten were provided for tenants. The cooperative stores on the ground floor were to apply a portion of their profits to a reduction in the price of rents.[28]

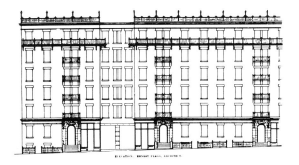

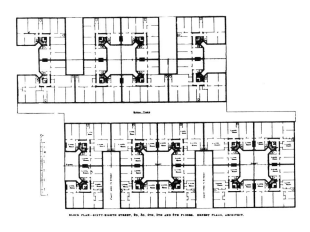

BLOCK PLAN—SIXTY-EIGHTH STREET, 2D, 3D, 4TH, 5TH AND 6TH FLOORS. ERNEST FLAGG, ARCHITECT.

Figure 4.14. Ernest Flagg. The Clark Buildings, the first philanthropic project to be built by the City and Suburban Homes Company, and the first realization of the Flagg-type plan; completed in 1898.

After the introduction of Ernest Flagg's prototypes in 1894 (see figure 2.12), the theoretical basis for architectural experimentation with philanthropic projects shifted to his ideas. The first Flagg-type plans to be built in New York City were for the Clark Buildings, designed by Flagg for the City and Suburban Homes Company and completed in 1898 (figure 4.14).[29] These plans were only slightly modified from Flagg's winning entry to the competition held by the Improved Housing Council in 1896. (See Figure 2.14). Located on West 68th and 69th streets, between West End and Amsterdam avenues, the six-story buildings housed 373 families. In 1900 the City and Suburban Homes Company built a modified version by James E. Ware of his second place entry to the same 1896 Competition (see figure 2.15). These buildings, located on First Avenue between East 64th and 65th streets and became the initial segment of the First Avenue Estate. Ware used Flagg-type plans with slight improvements over the Clark Buildings (figure 4.15).[30] The dwellings were designed to middle-class apartment standards, with an entrance hall, modern bathrooms, central hot water and steam heat, gas fixtures and ranges, and built-in closets. Eventually City and Suburban developed the entire block between First and York avenues. Ware completed three more segments, each using a Flagg-type plan. Philip Ohm completed the final segment in 1915.

Another large City and Suburban Homes Company block was built on the Upper East Side during the same period. Called the York Avenue Estate, it was

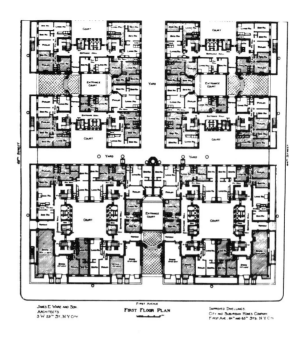

Figure 4.15. James Ware. Proposal for the initial stage of the First Avenue Estate, the second philanthropic project to be built by the City and Suburban Homes Company. The bottom portion was completed in 1900. Subsequent stages continued to explore Flagg-type plans.

bounded by York Avenue, East 78th and 79th streets, and the East River. The first segment, facing York Avenue was completed by Harde and Short in 1901 (figure 4.16).[31] Percy Griffin completed another segment in 1904. The remainder of the block was completed by Philip Ohm in seven segments between 1907 and 1914. Each of the succession of extensions of both estates attempted to further perfect what had come before, within the constraint of the Flagg-type plan. A careful study of the plan differences reveals the subtlety and intensity of this search. The City and Suburban estates were important design laboratories, upholding a commitment and high purpose in advancing the state of the art of tenement design.

The City and Suburban Homes Company was formed as a consequence of the deliberations of the Improved Housing Council, organized in 1896 by the Asso-

Figure 4.16. Harde and Short. Initial stage of the York Avenue Estate, the third philanthropic project to be built by the City and Suburban Homes Company. Completed in 1902 it was followed by several other variants on the Flagg-type plan.

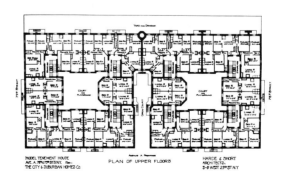

ciation for Improving the Condition of the Poor. In March 1896, the Council sponsored an "Improved Housing Conference" in which disillusionment was prevalent. Private philanthropy had proven to be ineffectual given the magnitude of the tenement house problem causing participants to argue for a major new initiative. Felix Adler posed the question in the strongest possible terms:

> Philanthropy! Bah! I am ashamed of the word. Thirty years ago we were tinkering away at this question. New York was then startled out of its stupor by the fear of cholera. Then, and not until it was frightened for its own safety, did it begin to look around. To what extent have we improved the life of the working classes who live in the tenements? Certain things have been accomplished, it is true. Better houses are going up, but more than half are still houses built before 1879. I do not understand why the city of New York is not afire, why it is not aflame over this matter.[32]

A hidden agenda for renewed efforts was undoubtedly the economic instability and civic insurrection of the decade. The immediacy of concerns of the conference led to the 1896 Tenement House Competition held by the Improved Housing Council in May (see figures 2.14 and 2.15). The Council's determination to build the two winning entries of Flagg and Ware fueled the formation of the City and Suburban Homes Company by the Council membership, including Felix Adler, and Elgin R. L. Gould who served as company president until 1915. This latest attempt at philanthropy was far more determined than its predecessors, and the City and Suburban Homes Company was destined to become the largest builder of model tenements in the country.[33] Both Adler and Gould advocated the familiar elixir of suburban workingclass development, including provision of mass transit.[34] The company's name reflected the familiar dichotomy between city and suburb, the foci for its philanthropic concerns. It built single-family houses in the suburbs as well as tenements in Manhattan. By 1938, after forty years of operation, the company had paid stockholders an average dividend of 4.2 percent, increased its capital stock from $489,300 to $4,255,690, and initiated fifteen projects related to low-rent housing.[35]

Until the 1920s, Flagg-type plans proliferated in privately developed middle-income housing, usually supplemented with amenities such as elevators, which were not used in philanthropic projects (see figures 3.36 and 3.37). For privately developed low-income housing, the ordinary New Law plan with light slots opening to rear yards was probably more common than the more complicated Flagg-type interior courtyard plans (see figure 2.25). A plan designed in 1902 for the corner of Broome and Mulberry streets by Sass and Smallheiser is typical of this approach (figure 4.17).[36] The small group of architects who experimented with philanthropic companies using Flagg-type plans inevitably attempted to improve on one another's accomplishments. Ernest Flagg himself designed several additional projects after his Clark Buildings, using variants on the same plan. In 1899 he completed the New York Fireproof Tenement Association buildings on Tenth Avenue between West 41st and 42nd streets;[37] in 1911 he completed another building of similar plan on West 47th Street for the same company.[38] Much of the experimentation with Flagg-type plans appears to have tried to create more ef-

Figure 4.17. Sass and Smallheiser. Tenements at Broome and Mulberry streets completed in 1902, showing the influence of the tenement house legislation of 1901.

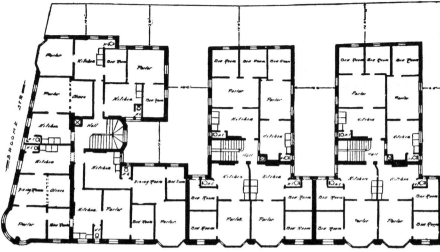

PLAN OF TENEMENTS ON BROOME STREET, NEW YORK. MESSRS. SASS & SMALLHEISER, ARCHITECTS.

Figure 4.18. Plans used by the City and Suburban Homes Company to extend the York Avenue Estate, Harde and Short, 1901 (*above left*), and Philip Ohm, 1906 (*above* right); and the First Avenue Estate, James E. Ware, 1900 (*below left*), and James E. Ware, 1905 (*below right*). Each explored ways to further perfect the Flagg-type plan.

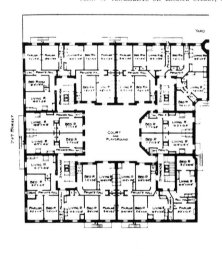

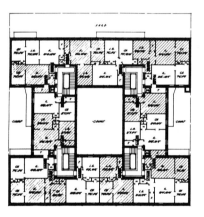

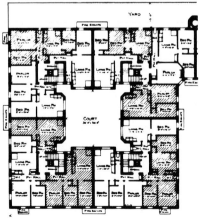

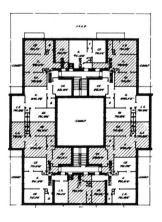

ficient circulation through shifting positions of the stairs, sometimes reducing their numbers or removing them entirely from the courtyards. An interesting example was the variation used by Grosvenor Atterbury in 1906 for the first housing in New York City to be built by the philanthropist-industrialist Henry Phipps.[39] In this project, located on East 31st Street, the stairs were removed completely from the internal courtyards, and reduced in number to two for each building. Also of particular interest was the evolution of plans used for the City and Suburban Homes Company's First Avenue and York Avenue Estates (figure 4.18). The series explored variations within a complex horizontal and vertical matrix of service and circulation cores, correlated with requirements for light and ventilation within the generic Flagg-type massing configuration.

The most remarkable Flagg-type philanthropic tenement to be built in New York City was the East River Homes, designed by Henry Atterbury Smith and completed in 1912.[40] Located between East 78th and 79th streets, adjoining John Jay Park, the four six-story buildings housed 383 families (figure 4.19). The project was amply funded by Ann Harriman Vanderbilt as an experiment in the physical rehabilitation of poor families with tubercular infections. The strategy, modeled after an earlier experiment in Sweden, involved the preventative removal of families from the environments which were the cause of their sickness, rather than simple application of curative measures in a sanatorium. Infected families were to remain intact in the city, leading quasi-normal lives throughout the long period of rehabilitation and even afterward, in order to prevent the relapse which would inevitably occur if they returned to their former dwellings. The unique functional requirements for the housing permitted Smith to exaggerate further the familiar preoccupation with light and air of the housing movement. He used an open stair plan, similar to the one he pioneered in the Charity Organization

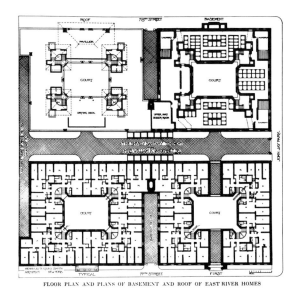

FLOOR PLAN AND PLANS OF BASEMENT AND ROOF OF EAST RIVER HOMES

Figure 4.19. Henry Atterbury Smith. The East River Homes philanthropic project completed in 1912 using a Flagg-type plan with open stairs; funded by Ann Harriman Vanderbilt as an experiment in rehousing tubercular families.

Figure 4.20. Henry Atterbury Smith. Photo of East River Homes at the time of completion, showing the extensive use of iron, glass, balconies, and roof areas.

Society Competition of 1900 (see figure 2.16). Four corner stairs opened on each courtyard. Every dwelling had a balcony, and the roof area was extensively developed to further promote fresh-air activity (figure 4.20).

The combination of unusual functional requirements and ample subsidy permitted Smith to achieve a level of innovation in the architectural design and detailing of the East River Homes that was unprecedented in philanthropic housing. He paid great attention to the sixteen open stairs, with their iron and glass awnings and roof structures (figure 4.21). The stairs, which opened onto the internal courtyards, became the symbol of innovation, celebrated openly and effectively, without resorting to the traditional architectural rhetoric used for the exterior facades of the building. Even a small "window seat" was integrated into the ironwork of each stair landing, presumably to encourage the taking of health-giving air. Apartment interiors showed the same innovative attention to detail. The bathrooms were designed as much as possible with continous surfaces and used moulded tile intersections and built-in bathtubs for sanitary as well as aesthetic purposes. The buildings were completely electrified so that the negative effects of gaslight on air quality could be avoided. Hoods over gas ranges in the

Figure 4.21. Henry Atterbury Smith. The East River Homes stair and roof details.

kitchens were even equipped with electric fans to remove impure cooking fumes. East River Homes was by any standard the most advanced model tenement to be built in New York City up to 1912, and quite possibly since. It represented an apex in technical innovation, and launched a new functionalist tradition in housing design, free of the excessive economic constraints of private capital, and free of the excessive historicism which controlled the mainstream of architectural expression at that moment. In many ways, Smith's concerns paralleled those of Edward T. Potter before him.

Henry Atterbury Smith remained a key figure in the evolution of New York City housing design throughout his career, until the close of the 1920s. Much of his earliest effort in housing was devoted to promoting the open stair. It became a kind of cause among some reformers. In 1891 a lobby called the Tenement Economies Society was organized by Charles Chandler and others to secure an amendment to the Tenement House Law which would permit open stairs to be substituted for air shafts in meeting minimum square foot requirements.[41] Some critics, including Lawrence Veiller, opposed open stairs. Gradually, through political intrigue, the Tenement House Department was forced to severely limit open stair possibilities (figure 4.22). Smith remained at the center of the controversy for five years, between 1912 and 1917.[42] In 1910 the Open Stair Tenement Company (later the Open Stair Dwellings Company) was formed under the leadership of Champlain L. Riley.[43] It was a limited dividend company devoted to building philanthropic open stair housing. Smith built several company projects, including the John Jay Dwellings, completed in 1913, in collaboration with William P. Miller, across from the East River Homes on East 77th Street; and the Open Stair Dwell-

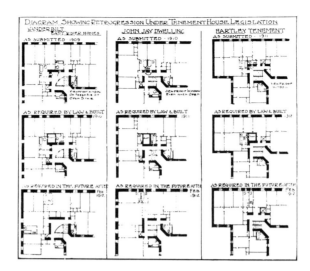

ings on West 147th and 148th streets, completed in 1917.[44] In 1913 he also completed the Hartley Dwellings, a philanthropic project, for Helen Hartley Jenkins, on West 47th Street.[45]

In 1916 the *Report* of the Tenement House Department listed eighteen "model tenements" in Manhattan, providing 5,249 apartments for approximately 18,000 tenants.[46] There were additional projects as well; all were variants of Flagg-type plans and all were philanthropic. Even for philanthropy the cost of Manhattan real estate prevented more radical approaches to tenement massing, using greater reductions in coverage. In spite of the architectural restrictions, many of these projects were programmatically innovative, from the Tuskeegee in 1901 to the Emerson in 1915. The Tuskeegee on West 62nd Street, designed by Howells and Stokes for the Phelps Stokes Fund, was the first philanthropic project for black tenants since the Workingman's Home in 1855 (see figure 1.4).[47] It was later acquired by the City and Suburban Homes Company. The Emerson, designed and built by the architect William Emerson, devoted the entire ground floor to communal amenities, including a cooperative store, day nursery, community baths, and a kitchen for teaching homemaking.[48]

Grosvenor Atterbury took unprecedented liberties with the Flagg-type plan in the Rogers Model Dwellings on West 44th Street, a philanthropic project built in 1915 for Catherine Cossitt Rogers (figure 4.23).[49] The entire middle courtyard zone of the plan was only two stories high, and devoted to communal amenities. The plan was an adaptation of the winning entry to the Charity Organization Society competition of 1900 (see figure 2.14). This reduction in building mass improved considerably the penetration of natural light to many rooms. In spite of such drastic alteration, the Flagg plan began to outlive its usefulness; one of the last such philanthropic plans was Smith's design for the Open Stair Dwellings Company project on West 146th and 147th streets (figure 4.24).[50] The generous open space running through the block used with enclosed building courtyards pro-

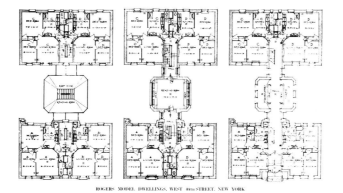

ROGERS MODEL DWELLINGS, WEST 44th STREET, NEW YORK
MR. GROSVENOR ATTERBURY, ARCHITECT

Figure 4.23. Grosvenor Atterbury. Roger's Model Dwellings, a philanthropic tenement built for Catherine Cossitt Rogers in 1915, with the massing at the interior reduced to a two-story building which served as a library.

PERSPECTIVE OF OPEN-STAIR APARTMENTS ON WEST 146th AND 147th STREETS,
NEW YORK CITY.

Figure 4.24. Henry Atterbury Smith. Philanthropic tenement on West 146th and 147th streets completed in 1917 for the Open Stair Dwellings Company; site coverage was only 52 percent, making strict adherence to the Flagg-type plan unnecessary.

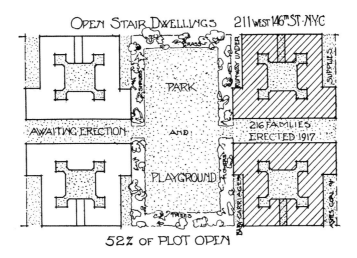

Figure 4.25. William Field and Son. The
Riverside Buildings, a philanthropic project for
Alfred Treadway White in Brooklyn, completed
in 1890 as the largest and most refined
perimeter block project in New York City.

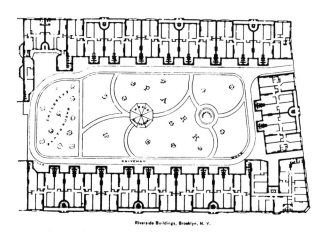

Riverside Buildings, Brooklyn, N. Y.

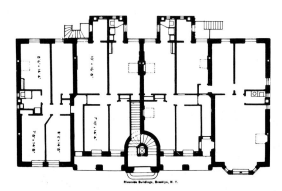

Riverside Buildings, Brooklyn, N. Y.

duced a questionable plan. The building mass could have responded more to the open space, perhaps by opening courtyards into it. With a coverage of only 52 percent, other site configurations would have been more desirable. The perimeter block was one such option. By the turn of the century, the perimeter block had been applied to philanthropic housing as well as to high-rise luxury housing like the Apthorp and Belnord (see figures 3.30 and 3.31). For privately developed housing, the low coverage of the perimeter approach had been limited to high-rise applications in order to maintain the high densities dictated by economics. But for low-rise philanthropic housing, as the reduction in coverage began to approach 50 percent, the perimeter form could be given serious consideration as well.

Alfred Treadway White's last philanthropic project, the Riverside Buildings, was a six-story perimeter block completed in 1890.[51] It covered most of a Brooklyn block bounded by Joralemon and Furman streets and Columbia Place. Designed by William Field and Son, Riverside Buildings used the same Waterlow plan type as in the earlier Tower Buildings (figure 4.25). According to White, the plans were not modified because "twelve years experience with the earlier constructions failed to develop any important suggestions for improvement."[52] The six-story

Figure 4.26. William Field and Son. Photo by Jacob Riis of the internal garden of the Riverside Buildings, taken in the 1890s.

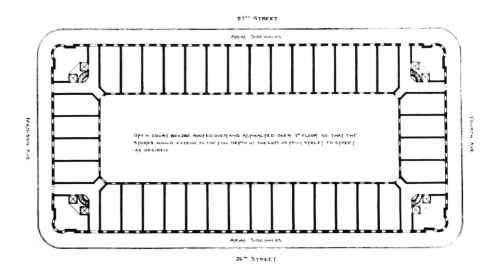

buildings housed 280 apartments and nineteen stores. The project faithfully produced a dividend of about 5 percent for many years.[53] The Riverside Buildings covered only 49 percent of the land—an equivalent of twelve gridiron lots were devoted to the internal park for the use of the tenants (figure 4.26). A White brochure described the character of this semipublic space as "laid out with grass, trees, fountain, and walks. . . . At the South end space of 50 by 80 feet is provided with swings, sand heaps, etc. In the center of the park is a large shelter and music pavillion, where every Sunday from May to November, from 4 to 6 p.m., a band furnishes music at the expense of the company."[54]

Semipublic space on the scale of the Riverside buildings was unprecedented for all types of housing in New York City in 1890—even for upper income projects. Only the few private squares, such as Gramercy Park, built a half century earlier, were comparable. For high-rise housing built with private capital, the size of perimeter block courtyards was restricted by economic constraints, rarely permitting lower coverages than the 67 percent used at the Belnord. Around 1890 a perimeter block proposal developed by Hubert, Pirsson, and Company attempted to circumvent the coverage constraint by covering the entire ground level of the block with a one-story commercial space (figure 4.27).[55] Its roof became the open space for the twelve-story housing above, with a coverage of 65 percent. Presumably the large rental income generated by the excessive building height and large commercial area would pay the cost of the generous roof area. The scheme was planned for an entire block between Madison and Park avenues and East 26th and 27th streets. It was never built. The architects attributed the difficulties to the ambiguities of the Tenement House Law, which sometimes hampered the construction of high apartment buildings.

Perimeter schemes used unusually small blocks, less than 400 feet in length. For normal 600- or 800-foot gridiron blocks, the form tended to be unwieldy, especially the long and narrow internal courtyard. By the turn of the century, as

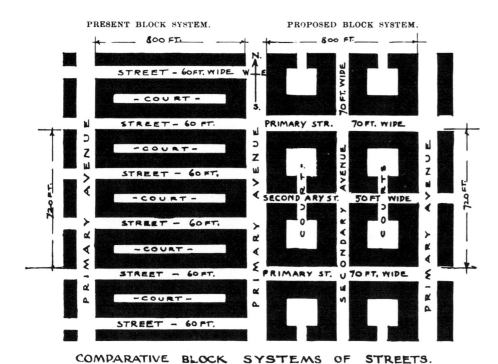

Figure 4.28. Julius F. Herder. Proposal for reorganization of the New York City gridiron made in 1898, with the introduction of "secondary avenues" and a perimeter block housing configuration.

interest in the high-rise perimeter increased, proposals for reorganization of the gridiron using perimeter forms appeared. These were descendants of earlier reorganization proposals which advocated the introduction of new north-south streets for improving the pattern of housing in relation to light and air (see figures 1.14 and 1.17). For example, in 1898 the architect Julius F. Harder published a perimeter proposal which introduced "secondary avenues" through the middle of blocks, and reduced the number of east-west streets by one-third (figure 4.28).[56] He argued that this new organization would introduce a hierarchy of principal and service avenues, as well as preferable solar orientation for buildings, with "cooler houses in summer and warmer in winter," and "50 percent more light and 33 1/3 percent less shadow in the streets."

White's projects were the only pre–World War I philanthropic housing where semipublic space covered almost 50 percent of the site. Even private philanthropy could not provide such amenities. When private initiatives could go no further, public discussion began to focus on government provision of semipublic space in housing. In 1901, as part of the report of the Tenement House Commission, I. N. Phelps Stokes described his plan for a perimeter block development in which the forty-foot-wide perimeter was to be developed as six-story housing, with the internal courtyard retained by the city as a park.[57] Housing coverage was only 33 percent (figure 4.29). The project was proposed as a slum clearance strategy, which would serve to renew housing, as well as provide parkland. Phelps Stokes estimated that approximately two-thirds of a 200-by-400-foot tenement block could

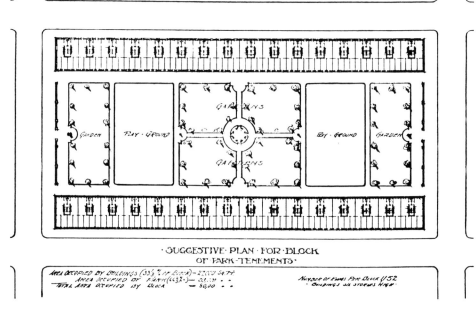

Figure 4.29. I. N. Phelps Stokes. Proposal for perimeter block made in 1900, with a provision for the internal park to be bought and maintained by the City of New York; the first argument for government participation related to housing philanthropy.

Figure 4.30. Workingmen's Model Home exhibited in 1893 by New York State at the World's Columbian Exposition in Chicago; a harbinger of government sensibility in relation to the question of working-class housing.

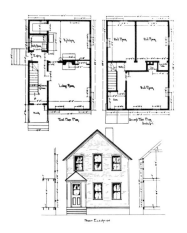

be rehoused with no increase in the cost per room, if the city bought the internal land. This was the first detailed economic argument for direct government intervention in housing production in New York City—an intention which would not be realized until the federal initiatives of the 1930s. The Phelps Stokes argument was prophetic in linking open space with economic arguments for public intervention.

In general, government interest in working-class housing before 1930 focused more on suburbia than on cities. The State of New York set an important precedent when it addressed the issue of housing production in 1893, with its exhibition of a model suburban working-class cottage at the Columbian Exposition in Chicago (figure 4.30).[58] New York excluded any representation of high density housing even though it was the most populous state in the Union and the home of the North American metropolis. Throughout the nineteenth century the suburban working-class cottage was built as a routine matter by industry. As urban boundaries were extended, factories moved with them, seeking more and cheaper land. In rural areas the mill town, with its factory housing and stores, was a staple of working-class existence.[59] In New York City, the working-class commuting suburb, however, did not appear until well into the second half of the century, around the same time that the sequels to Llewellyn Park, such as Tuxedo Park north of New York City and Short Hills in New Jersey, were being planned.[60]

In New York City, the suburban worker cottage was a difficult model to realize because of the necessity for inexpensive rapid transit. Workers had to be moved to and from the workplace, which was frequently far removed from under-developed suburban land. It would be prohibitively expensive, for example, for workers to commute from outlying areas in the Bronx or Queens into the manufacturing core in lower Manhattan. Nonetheless, schemes proliferated, although few were realized. Perhaps typical was the early project for cooperative housing initiated by the German Cabinetmakers Association of New York. In 1869 the organization bought ninety-one acres of land in Astoria in Queens, and in the following year, organized a railroad to connect their development with Hunters Point and the East River ferry.[61] Another proposal for Astoria was advanced in 1880 by the Clerks' and Mechanics' House Company Limited, which planned to build row houses for only $1,000 each.[62] And in 1891 an investment syndicate proposed to build one hundred wood frame cottages for workers in the Bronx.[63]

In 1869 the most ambitious scheme for a suburban working-class housing estate was commenced by Alexander T. Stewart, the New York department store magnate. Stewart already was well known for his initiatives to improve working conditions for his employees. He purchased a large tract of land near Hempstead on Long Island and publicized his intention to build a new town for the working population of Brooklyn and Manhattan, including his own employees. Stewart chose the name Garden City (figure 4.31).[64] With his architect, John Kellum, he began to plan the town which according to one contemporary description was "so gigantic that it throws into the shade every attempt of the kind hitherto made."[65] In 1873 he completed the necessary railroad connection from the center of Garden City to Flushing. In addition to a railroad station, Stewart built a hotel, a water supply, streets, a park with a lake, stables, commercial structures, and a number of large houses, which could hardly be described as "working class."

The design of the town plan itself represented no particular breakthrough. The initiative was entirely a private investment; at the outset only rental housing was offered. Stewart's detractors charged that he was simply setting up a captive community to maximize the return on his investment. After Stewart's death in 1876, the town remained the property of his estate until 1893, when the Garden

Figure 4.31. John Kellum. Garden City, Long Island, begun by Alexander T. Stewart in 1869 as a new town for the working class. Located at Hempstead on Long Island, it required building a special railroad connection to Manhattan.

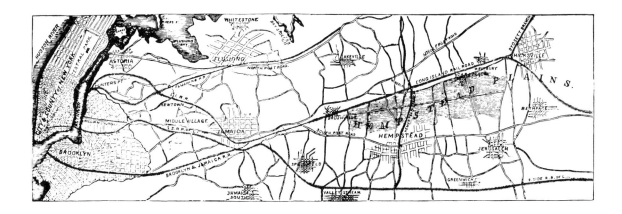

City Company was formed as a private corporation. After a period of economic difficulty, it evolved into a typical Long Island suburb. Garden City was never realized, or even planned as a cohesive conceptual undertaking, from the aspect of its relationship to the metropolis. But it was an important precedent which prefigured many similar and important initiatives in the United States and Europe in the following decades.

Stewart's vision was the most radical of its kind, given Garden City's great distance from Manhattan and the scale of transportation infrastructure it required. Far more realistic were the numerous post–Civil War housing and community proposals which were limited to a few miles from Manhattan. Long Island City in Queens became an important focus for such activity. After 1871 William Steinway, of the famous piano manufacturing firm, began a large-scale model town at Astoria, then a completely undeveloped area. It was an attempt to move the company's factories from their location on East 52nd and 53rd streets in Manhattan.[66] Like Stewart's Garden City, Steinway was partially the conseqence of its founder's effort to profit from real estate investment. The value of his company's holdings in Queens was promoted at every opportunity. Unlike Garden City, Steinway was clearly a company town, built with some expression of concern about the condition of the working class. In the violent decade of the 1870s this concern inevitably assumed a political dimension. As William Steinway wrote many years later: "We wished to escape the machinations of the anarchists and socialists, who even at that time—25 years ago were continually breeding discontent among our workmen and inciting them to strikes. They seemed to make us a target for their attacks, and we felt that if we could withdraw our workmen from contact with these people and other temptations of city life in tenement districts, they would be more content and their lot would be happier."[67]

Like that of Garden City, the physical plan of Steinway represented no particular design innovation (figure 4.32). The speculative gridiron configuration of local streets was retained, presumably to maintain the option of normal sales of building lots for the areas unaffected by the factories and housing. An existing mansion built for Benjamin Pike, Jr., in 1865 was occupied by the Steinway family as its summer home, and served as an informal focus of the town, which covered the surrounding area of approximately four hundred acres. In 1871 a lumber mill and foundry were established with a small port on Long Island Sound for delivery of lumber, foundry sand, and pig iron. In the same year, sewer and water lines were laid out following a typical New York gridiron pattern. In 1873 the first worker housing was completed, using three types: four-bedroom single cottages, three-bedroom double cottages, and three-bedroom row houses. Class distinctions were reinforced, with the most substantial houses placed in the eastern area on the highest ground. Steinway sold the houses to his workers, which he recognized would help contribute to community stability as well as provide immediate financial gain. He further enhanced his profits and strengthened his investment by selling building lots to unaffiliated outsiders.

In general, through skillful manipulation of the community and the Long Island City municipality, Steinway was able to provide community amenities at minimal cost to himself while enhancing the value of his investment. Over two

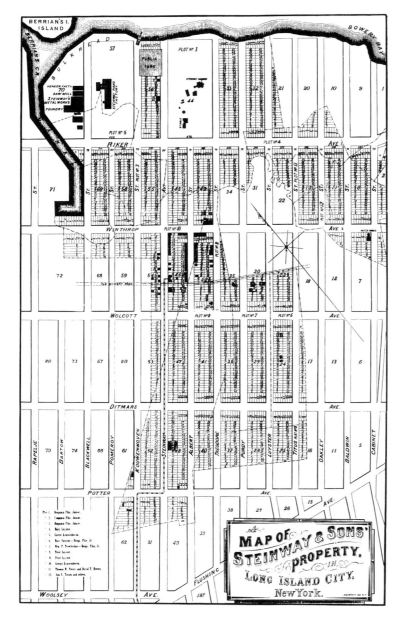

Figure 4.32. Plan of the village of Steinway in Queens, built by the Steinway and Sons Piano Manufacturing Company in order to relocate their workers from Manhattan. Development is shown to about 1880; included was a factory, housing, school, and other civic amenities, and a transportation link with Manhattan.

decades, a Protestant church, park, library, kindergarten, public bath, fire house, post office, were all built on land given by Steinway, while construction used public funds. He recognized the importance of good transit connections, both to shuttle workers back and forth to Manhattan and to increase the value of his real estate. He promoted sales to "well to do and refined people," presumably not necessarily his workers. Initially he used the Astoria Ferry and an extension of the Long Island Shore Railroad. Electric trolley service was instituted in the early

1890s. He also was involved in an unsuccessful venture to construct a bridge across the East River at East 77th Street. It was not until 1909, with the completion of the Queensboro Bridge, that Queens was finally connected to Manhattan by roadway. Steinway also unsuccessfully lobbied for the first mass transit tunnel to Queens. Like the bridge, this was eventually realized, but in its own time.

In 1881 Steinway had 130 houses with more than 1,200 occupants. By the 1890s it had a population of more than 7,000. The area had become a relatively self-contained community and remained somewhat isolated for many years, partly owing to the efforts of Steinway. To retain an inward focus for the community life, the company subsidized the teaching of music and German in the public school, and German remained the everyday language of the factory for years. In spite of such attempts at paternalism, the freedoms enjoyed by workers were considerable. Unlike George Pullman's similar experiment in Chicago, Steinway workers could own houses and enjoyed some of the same financial rewards of building in the community as the company. But the attempt to retain isolation was unenforceable. Much of the Steinway production remained in Manhattan. There the factory became the nexus of the famous piano strikes between 1878 and 1880, which were among the most important nineteenth-century labor struggles in New York City. All of Steinway's worker initiatives, which had been triggered by the disputes of the early 1870s, seemed to come to naught. A long series of wage disagreements between workers and piano manufacturers climaxed in February 1880, when Steinway varnishers struck, and the company threatened to close out all workers rather than increase wages. Piano workers for other companies took action. At Steinway there was a full strike for five weeks, before the company finally acquiesced to the rights of labor in negotiating wages.[68]

In 1898 the suburban working-class cottage became the object of housing philanthropy for the first time. The City and Suburban Homes Company planned a parcel of approximately 530 city lots between 16th and 18th avenues and 67th and 74th streets at Homewood in Brooklyn.[69] The company developed the entire project, including grading, macadam streets, curbs, sidewalks, sewers, gas, water, and landscaping. The modest brick and wood frame single-family houses designed by Percy Griffin each occupied a 30-by-100 foot lot (figure 4.33). The company provided twenty-year mortgages, with only a 10 percent down payment and 5 percent rate of interest. Each owner held title immediately, but was required to subscribe to a life insurance policy for at least two-thirds of the amount owed for the house. The policy was underwritten by the City and Suburban Homes Company, and proved to be a considerable factor in the success of the project. In 1898 66 detached houses were built, and by 1909 a total of 112 detached and 136 single-family row houses were constructed.[70] The financial arrangements, which permitted working-class home ownership through life insurance and the mortgage guarantee, became widespread within the next several decades. Eventually they were taken over by the government initiatives of the New Deal and after. As cheap transit connections were built in the first decades of the twentieth century, permitting working people of modest means to commute to Manhattan, the numbers of such single-family suburban developments increased. Homewood was only fifty-five minutes from City Hall in Manhattan, for only a five-cent fare.

HOMEWOOD COTTAGES.

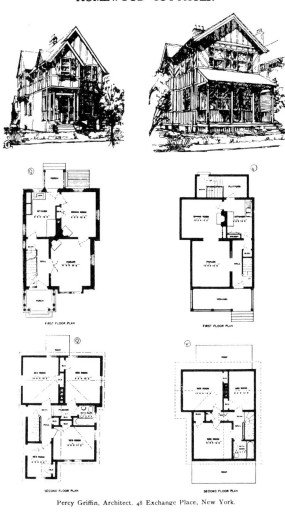

Figure 4.33. Percy Griffin. Working-class cottages designed in 1898 for the Homewood Project in Brooklyn; developed by the City and Suburban Homes Company, it was the first philanthropic project in New York City to provide suburban cottages.

Percy Griffin, Architect. 48 Exchange Place, New York.

In 1908 the Russell Sage Foundation invested in an experiment similar to Homewood. Forest Hills Gardens in Queens was to be a limited profit investment, clearly distinguishable from standard private suburban cottage development.[71] The initial foundation brochure related that

Mrs. Russell Sage, and those whom she has associated with in the Foundation, have been profoundly impressed with the need of better and more attractive housing facilities in the suburbs for persons of modest means, who could pay from twenty-five dollars a month upward in the purchase of a home. They have thought that homes could be supplied like those in the garden cities of England, with some greenery and flowers around them, with accessible playgrounds and recreation facilities, and at no appreciably greater cost than is now paid for the same roof

Figure 4.34. Frederick Law Olmsted, Jr., and Grosvenor Atterbury. Forest Hills Gardens, begun in 1908 in Queens by the Russell Sage Foundation as a quasi-philanthropic suburban estate, originally planned for deserving families of modest means.

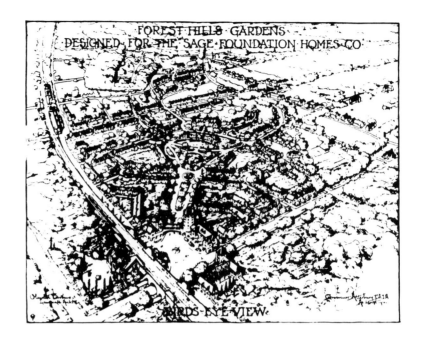

room in bare streets without any such adjacency. They have abhorred the constant repetition of the rectangular block in suburban localities where land contours invite other street lines. . . . They have hoped that people of moderate income and good taste, who appreciate sympathetic surroundings, but are tied close to the city by the nature of their occupation, might find some country air and country life, within striking distance of the active centers of New York.[72]

The plan of Forest Hills Gardens was by Frederick Law Olmsted, Jr., with Grosvenor Atterbury as the architect of most of the initial buildings (figure 4.34). A location was chosen along the main line of the Long Island Railroad, at the area adjacent to Forest Park, at that time the largest public park in Queens. The new Pennsylvania Station in Manhattan was approximately fifteen minutes away by rail via the East River tunnel. The street layout distorted considerably the city's plan for the area, using a curvilinear, irregular, and picturesque gridiron (figure 4.35). Atterbury designed a rail station and public square with a high-rise hotel as a focus for the community. Two curvilinear avenues radiated from the square, connecting the entrance to Forest Park. Several local streets followed the city's gridiron, but according to Olmsted, most attempted to respond to topography, while evoking a "cozy, domestic character . . . where the monotony of endless, straight, windswept thoroughfares which represent the New York conception of streets will give place to short, quiet, self-contained and garden-like neighborhoods, each having its own distinctive character" (figure 4.36).[73] Forest Hills Gardens appears to have been the first major violation of the gridiron within the boundaries of the city.

Olmsted and Atterbury provided considerable residential variety within the

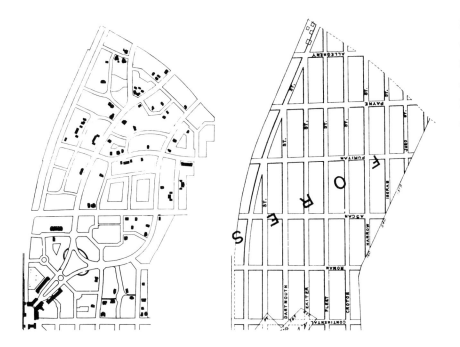

Figure 4.35. Frederick Law Olmsted, Jr., and Grosvenor Atterbury. Forest Hills Gardens street layout (*left*) compared with the New York City gridiron as initially planned for the area (*right*); Forest Hills was the first large-scale residential distortion of the gridiron within the city.

Figure 4.36. Frederick Law Olmsted, Jr. Two design alternatives for a typical block at Forest Hills Gardens.

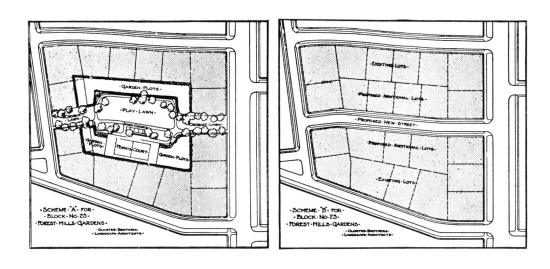

planning, from a "village green," defined by continuous row houses, to isolated single- and double-family houses on individual lots. Many of these initial houses were built using sophisticated prefabrication techniques, based on the research of Grosvenor Atterbury. A series of seven demonstration projects were completed by 1920, using totally panelized construction of precast concrete.[74] Atterbury's methods undoubtedly represented the most sophisticated thinking of the day. In spite of such innovation, however, by the end of the decade, construction at Forest Hills Gardens appears to have begun to decline to the level of standard developer practice—perhaps owing to the sale of undeveloped lots to individual owners. And if throughout its initial years Forest Hills Gardens had acquired a patina of philanthropy, the Russell Sage Foundation Homes Company advertising of 1920 made it clear that such impressions were mistaken:

> Lest confusion and an indefinite impression exist as to just what Forest Hills Gardens is and represents, and in order to confute any opinion that it has been developed and undertaken with certain charitable or philanthropic objects in view, it is well to state that this is not the aim. Forest Hills Gardens is a high-class suburban residential community conducted upon strictly business principles. It is a new type of high-class home community not to be confused with the usual ephemeral development filled with absurd fancies and individual idiosyncrasies. It is a successful project along garden city or model town planning lines and contains the basis of a liberal education in this work.[75]

New York City's early working-class experiments in the suburbs had some superficial similarities to developing English new town theory. Stewart's Garden City predated Ebenezer Howard's proposal of the same name, and was organized using several of the same assumptions, including its rail link to the metropolis and its expansive natural setting.[76] The design of Forest Hills Gardens, consciously followed the precedent set at Letchworth. In general, the reasoning behind Garden City, Steinway, or Forest Hills Gardens responded to the same goals as Howard's: improved housing at lower cost through the availability of inexpensive land, and increased productivity and happiness of the residents through isolation from the evils of urban environments. The differences were economic. All three were far more dependent on the parent metropolis than Howard envisioned, and

Figure 4.37. Advertisement published in 1922 for building lots at Forest Hills West, where a commuter station just built by the newly electrified Long Island Railroad contributed to the rapid development of the area surrounding Forest Hills Gardens.

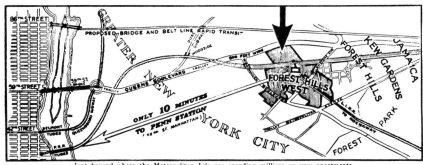

Just beyond where the Metropolitan Life are spending millions on new apartments.

they were developed through private investment, rather than cooperative ownership. Forest Hills Gardens was slowly absorbed by the repetitive gridirons of the surrounding privately developed housing, especially with the development of Forest Hills West after 1922, where the Long Island Railroad opened a new station and 1,500 lots were auctioned (figure 4.37).

Forest Hill Gardens spawned a number of imitations along the Long Island Railroad and Queens Boulevard. None matched the conception of the original, but developments like Kew Gardens or Rego Park still represented a significant alternative to the anonymous suburban tracts. Among these developments, the organization of Rego Park was most distinctive, with radial and circumferential roads forming a cresent facing the rail station. Built between 1924 and 1929, Rego Park was far more populist than its philanthropic predecessor. It was developed by the Rego Construction Company, founded by two German immigrants who promoted its "real good" housing.[77]

In Queens, the potential for residential development grew with the advances in transportation: the completion of the Queensboro Bridge in 1909, the East River tunnel and the electric rail service on the Long Island Railroad in 1910, the Queensboro subway in 1915; the subway across the Queensboro Bridge in 1917; and the Brooklyn Rapid Transit tunnel under the East River at 60th Street, with connections to Astoria and Corona, in 1920.[78] The situation in other boroughs of New York City was similar. Alfred Treadway White's hypothesis that a transportation infrastructure was essential to mass improvement of working-class housing was accurate. Even as far away as Hempstead on Long Island, in the vicinity of Stewart's Garden City of fifty years earlier, cheap lots were advertised as the answer to the "housing problem," only forty-two minutes from Pennsylvania Station by the newly electrified Long Island Railroad (figure 4.38). And the suburbs were gradually moving closer to the great mass of moderate-income households in New York City.

Figure 4.38. Advertisement published in 1920 for building lots at Hempstead, Long Island; within easy commuting distance from Manhattan via the Long Island Railroad.

5

The Garden Apartment

THE decade of the 1920s produced an advance in housing form and production of a significance to middle-class New Yorkers equal to the upper-class apartment revolution in the 1880s. A confluence of economic, technological, and sociological phenomena created new housing types, which in their various forms came under the loose rubric of the "garden apartment." It was an advance which focused on the developing outer boroughs rather than in Manhattan, where stagnation of residential development was already in evidence. While the term "garden apartment" comprised many possible approaches and contexts, all involved the fundamental premise of building coverage reduced to the point of opening up a possibility of integrating "garden" courtyards within the mass of the housing, so that the design conventions associated with the tenement air shaft were altered beyond recognition. For New York, the closest similar approach historically was the palazzo type, although it had evolved to a much higher and tighter form, and upheld strictly upper-class standards. The specifics of the garden apartment varied widely depending on geography, social strata, and ethnicity; but the key ingredient in this innovation was the open land of the outer boroughs, inexpensive in comparison with Manhattan, and made newly accessible to the middle class by the completion of the New York City subway system.[1] This fertile new ground for design innovation was unparalleled before or since, reinforced by the general prosperity of the 1920s once recovery from the wartime economy had begun.

The 1920s produced a volume of new housing which has never again been equaled, quantitatively or qualitatively. Between 1921 and 1929 420,734 new apartments, 106,384 one-family houses, and 111,662 two-family houses were constructed. The total of 658,780 new dwellings averaged 73,198 units per year, a figure unmatched even in the 1960s, also a period of substantial growth. In the most prolific year, 1927, 94,367 dwellings were built, compared with 60,031 in 1963, the peak year since. The quantitative aspect of this growth involved increased dwelling space standards for the new construction, combined with the first substantial reduction in the number of older substandard tenements. Between 1920 and 1929 43,200 Old Law tenements were removed from the New York City housing stock.[2] The economic and technical groundwork for the 1920s development was laid well before; the boom in housing construction was reinforced by a new constituency created by the massive immigration of the prewar years. In 1905, 1906, 1907, 1910, 1913, and 1914 more than 1,000,000 immigrants entered the United States; most came through New York City, and many stayed.[3] Between 1900 and 1920 the city's population increased from 3,437,202 to 5,620,048. By 1920 2,028,160 New Yorkers were first-generation immigrants. The upward mobility of these immigrants led to a large demand for apartments designed to middle-class standards, rather than tenements.[4]

The shift in expectations in relation to design standards was reflected in the changing definition of the word "apartment." Since 1880, the term "apartment" suggested large and luxurious dwellings, usually in high-rise elevator buildings. "Tenement" referred to smaller dwellings of minimal standards within walk-up buildings. As the twentieth century progressed, however, the term "tenement" was abandoned and "apartment" was used to describe any dwelling other than houses. Lawrence Veiller's study *A Model Housing Law*, published in 1914, dropped the word "tenement" completely, and used instead "private dwelling," "two-family dwelling," and "multiple dwelling."[5] According to one source, between 1914 and 1920 only 5,134 "tenements" were built in New York City, in contrast to 89,356 "apartments."[6] By 1920 the middle-class expectations created a category between "apartment" and "tenement," of moderate size, with modern baths and kitchens, and with better light and ventilation than the minimum established by the New Law. In response to the widespread demand for higher standards, developers could build in the outlying areas of Brooklyn, the Bronx, and Queens, where land values were relatively low. Laws were passed to protect this new housing production. The *Building Zone Plan* was of great importance, shielding growing middle-class housing areas in the outer boroughs from adjacent uses that were considered undesirable. Of course, this legislation is better known for establishing high-rise building height restrictions based on street width (figure 5.1).[7] It was under these provisions that the great Manhattan residential canyons along West End Avenue and Park Avenue were completed in the 1920s. In another important reflection of the new middle class, the Tenement House Act was revised in 1919 to permit conversion of large single-family houses such as brownstones into apartments for less affluent occupants.[8]

The form and intensity of the outer borough development was defined by certain advances in building technology, most principally centered on the elevator. From the inception of the residential elevator in the 1870s, elevator apartment buildings were limited to the realm of tall structures and upper incomes, because of the excessive costs of machinery and elevator operators. Both were required by law. By 1920 both of these constraints had changed. Cheaper alternating-current machinery came into use,[9] and, more important, the New York City Building Code was revised to permit the use of automatic self-service elevators in large apartment buildings.[10] The legalization of self-service meant that the long-term cost of elevators could be drastically reduced because operators were no longer required. A whole class of tenants who had formerly been relegated to walk-up

Figure 5.1. Representative diagrams from the Building Zone Plan of 1916, which regulated the massing of all building types including housing.

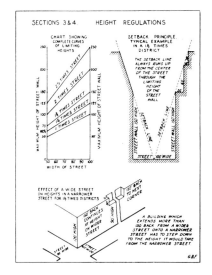

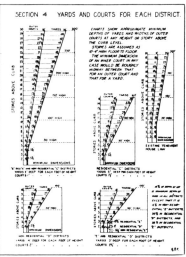

buildings could enjoy the convenience of the elevator. Even class distinctions within buildings changed. Suddenly the upper floors were more desirable than lower floors, with superior light, air, views, and without the need to climb stairs. In Manhattan this development stimulated construction of tall buildings with small apartments for middle-income tenants. In the outer boroughs it stimulated an evolution of new housing types, the most important being the garden apartment.

Outer borough high-density development remained primarily four to six stories in spite of the introduction of the elevators. This seeming contradiction was the result of an intricate balance between building law, construction costs, and land economics. For buildings of five stories or less, nonfireproof construction was permitted throughout except for the ground floor. Compared with any other possible housing configuration in New York City, the construction cost of a five-story building was cheapest. For six-story buildings, the first two floors were required to be fireproof, raising the costs only slightly. For buildings of seven or more stories, however, fireproof construction was required throughout, increasing costs substantially. The cost of an elevator, therefore, could be offset by the cheaper construction in buildings under seven stories. Given the low cost of outer borough land, more return could be realized on four-to-six story elevator buildings than on higher ones. As a result, large areas of the outer boroughs witnessed a surge in middle-income elevator building construction in the 1920s with virtually no increase in building height over tenements.[11]

Of considerable importance to the evolution of the new housing was a new generation of architects who were assimilated into the profession in the 1920s. They were different from the stereotypical gentlemen who dominated the formative years of the profession in the second half of the nineteenth century. This earlier generation was largely upper middle class. They could afford the requisite Beaux-Arts education, and they were tied to the WASP establishment, which was a critical source of patronage. With few exceptions, they expropriated design ideology which was almost anathema for housing, except in relation to the upper class. In the 1920s, for the first time, a generation of "housing architects" emerged, finally fulfilling in a limited way the call of earlier thinkers like Edward T. Potter. The sheer volume of 1920s housing production allowed the new generation to show its face. A few of these architects became well known, but most practiced silently in their respective boroughs where they lived and where the bulk of the new housing work was. Many were from ethnic backgrounds, which reinforced their secondary status. Many were first- or second-generation immigrants, and many had received no formal university training. If they attended a formal program, it was at the nonelite local schools like Cooper Union, Pratt, or New York University, perhaps Columbia, but never Harvard, Yale, or Princeton. Among the better known was Emery Roth, who entered the United States from Czechoslovakia at age thirteen as an orphan, apprenticing to an architect in the following year. Andrew Thomas was born on lower Broadway and by age thirteen was also orphaned. He never formally studied architecture. George Springsteen, born in Brooklyn, attended night classes at Cooper Union and Pratt Institute. Horace Ginsbern graduated from Columbia.[12]

A development of considerable importance to the new generation was the U.S.

government war housing programs initiated in 1917, which were the first direct federal involvement in large-scale housing production.[13] These programs helped pave the way for the larger initiatives of the New Deal in the 1930s, and helped introduce the architectural profession to the potential for government intervention in housing. Many young architects spent their war years working for these agencies, where they gained invaluable experience. Although the federal programs emphasized one- and two-family houses, they provided important training in the large-scale organization of housing production, which served the architects well in the 1920s when the scale of private production increased enormously. Among them, were Frederick Ackerman, Clarence Stein, Andrew Thomas, and Henry Wright, all key housing architects in the 1920s and 1930s.

Prior to 1917 the government built homes only for government workers. During the war, with the pressure to provide housing for the private work force near the hastily constructed wartime factories, the U.S. government was forced to begin building homes for civilians. In 1917 the Emergency Fleet Corporation within the U.S. Shipping Board began construction of housing related to naval installations. In 1918 the United States Housing Corporation within the U.S. Department of Labor began another housing program for all industries connected with defense. The federal government could use these organizations either to loan money for housing construction to limited dividend corporations, or to construct housing itself. By 1919, for example, the United States Housing Corporation already had plans for housing 21,983 families.[14]

The only federal wartime project proposed for New York City was made by the USHC for Mariner's Harbor, Staten Island, designed by Delano and Aldrich. A thirty-six unit apartment building was combined with seventy-eight two-family houses.[15] It was apparently the only project nationwide that included an apartment building, further evidence of the government bias toward the worker cottage (figure 5.2). The project was not built, and in general, nationwide, the number of projects completed fell far short of the proposals. By fall 1919 the USHC had provided housing for 5,998 families and 7,181 individuals, at a cost of $52 million. After the conclusion of World War I, in July 1919, Congress directed that these projects be sold at a loss of $32.5 million. Similarly, the Emergency Fleet Corporation, which had built housing for 9,185 families and 7,564 individuals at a cost of $67.5 million, was forced to sell the buildings after 1920 at a loss of $42

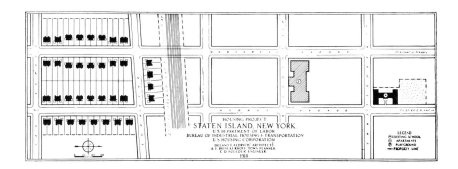

Figure 5.2. Delano and Aldrich. Proposed housing development for the United States Housing Corporation at Mariner's Harbor, Staten Island; made in 1918 but never built.

million.[16] The hasty termination of these programs by Congress reflected an agenda to return the nation to free enterprise housing production, yet the war had precipitated a housing crisis of unprecedented dimensions.[17] This state of affairs provoked a radical protest by architects that has not had an equivalent since, and reflected the new order which had arrived within the profession.

The campaign for government production of housing was largely the result of the economic chaos caused by the war. By 1919 new housing production in New York City had decreased from a prewar high of 54,884 dwellings in 1906, to only 1,624.[18] In New York City the vacancy rate fell from 5.6 percent in 1916 to only .15 percent by 1921, the lowest ever.[19] This condition reversed many of the housing advances of the prewar years. For example, 38,251 Old Law tenements which were vacant in 1916 were back in use by 1921.[20] The overcrowding caused by the shortage was exacerbated by more endemic conditions such as the lack of adequate enforcement of the Tenement House Law. Between 1910 and 1921 the number of employees of the Tenement House Department had been cut by 361 persons or 45 percent. And while the total city budget had doubled in the same period, the Department budget decreased slightly.[21]

The housing shortage led to opportunism among real estate interests. For example, landlords had managed to secure a new law which granted them the right to remove tenants and increase rents at will only thirty day after signing a lease.[22] A cartel among building materials suppliers was designed to create an artifical shortage in order to raise prices. Banks found investment in high-profit speculative securities more interesting than housing; whatever mortgage money was available was tinged with an aura of favoritism and corruption.[23]

Tenant resistance to the massive evictions led to the formation of the Greater New York Tenants League. A series of rent strikes were intertwined with the forces of socialist politics, which reached its zenith at that time. The tenants movement endured the Red Scare, which was fanned by paranoia about events in Russia as well as political activism at home. Red-baiting and nativism emerged not only from the landlords, but from the politicians and courts. By state law passed in 1919, Red flags could not be waved from striking buildings;[24] by local ordinance passed in October 1919, foreign languages could not be used in street meetings.[25] The Greater New York Tenants League was denounced as "Bolshevist" by the Office of the District Attorney.[26]

It was within this political milieu that a progressive voice within the profession emerged. By 1920 it had achieved a new level of maturity and power. Architects had finally won legal legitimacy. In 1915, thirty-four years after the legal requirement for registration of plumbers, the New York state legislature passed registration laws authorizing the Board of Regents to license architects who proved their competency through examination.[27] At the conclusion of World War I, the American Institute of Architects took an active role in the effort to force Congress to continue government housing programs into peacetime. The New York chapter was especially active. Its membership witnessed firsthand the unfolding of the tenants' extraordinary struggle. The *Journal of the American Institute of Architects* was filled with advocacy of government programs. In 1920 an article even endorsed the New York Labor party housing platform, which appeared to call for a complete government takeover of housing production.[28] Since that time, no professional group of architects has fought with such vehemence for government production of housing. With the prosperity of the 1920s waiting just around the corner to silence the dissenters, Congress remained unmoved. Bills were introduced in the state legislature to authorize the cities within the state to acquire land and build housing for rental at cost. They were never passed and were widely denounced as "socialistic" by business interests, predictably including the Real Estate Board of New York.[29]

From the point of view of design, the force of political events led to a moment of innovative thinking at the beginning of the decade which was important to the housing of the 1920s. At one end of the spectrum, the chairman of the Board of Standards and Appeals even suggested that the crisis could be solved by adding an extra story to existing tenements, making seven-story walk-ups, with enabling amendments to the Tenement House Laws.[30] In general, the strategy of systematic rehabilitation of the nineteenth century tenement housing stock was raised as a possible way out of the housing impasse. After Governor Alfred E. Smith appointed the Reconstruction Commission in the New York state legislature in 1919, one of the first efforts of its Housing Committee was to organize an architectural competition for the rehabilitation of a tenement block on the Lower East Side.[31] The competition was the first in New York City to be sponsored by a governmental body, underlining the aura of crisis of the period. The winning scheme by Sibley and Fetherston cut a series of eight courtyards in the pre-Law and Old Law buildings in order to gain light and air (figure 5.3). But rehabilitation was controversial; many opposed the principle of trying to create decent housing from substandard buildings.

Thus began the debate on rehabilitation which remains unresolved to this day. The older tenement portion of the New York housing stock was relegated to the lowest level of the underclass who remained below the reach of reform efforts. It seemed logical, therefore, to attempt to tie rehabilitation to housing reform. New construction was moving toward standards affordable only to a generation of upwardly mobile moderate income families. Yet there was also the hope that new construction could phase the older tenements out of existence through filtering. Within this context, Andrew Thomas, who served on the competition jury, argued that not only were the standards for rehabilitation lower than for new construction, but the process was more costly. On the other side, those who supported rehabilitation argued that there was no choice in the matter; 50,000 remaining Old Law tenements were not going to disappear, and should therefore be improved by whatever means available. In time, the prosperity of the 1920s did produce an extraordinary amount of new moderate income housing. And the following five decades have produced little rehabilitation of the quality which the 1919 competition envisioned.

Apart from the rehabilitation study, the Housing Committee of the Reconstruction Commission produced an important body of other work, informed by the young architects in its membership like Frederick Ackerman, Andrew Thomas, and Clarence Stein who had recently gained housing experience in the government war housing effort. Both Thomas and Stein produced hypothetical studies

Figure 5.3. Sibley and Fetherston. First Place entry to the tenement rehabilitation competition of 1919, sponsored by the Joint Legislative Committee on Housing and the Reconstruction Commission of the New York State Legislature. The existing Lower East Side block (*above*) consisted of Old Law and pre-Law tenements. The proposal (*below*) shows large light-courts carved out from the building interiors.

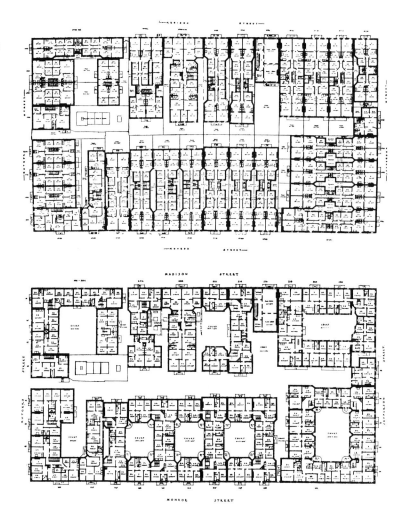

of ideal new housing configurations for urban blocks. Stein, for example, developed an ingenious prototype which interlocked two-family houses with higher-density apartments, in an effort to support diversity of scale and building types (figure 5.4). At the center of the block were communal gardens and playgrounds. Stein built a single version of the two-family prototype in 1920 on West 239th Street in the Bronx.[32] As a result of this research, the committee concluded that the housing shortage in New York City could be addressed only through large-scale building operations on the periphery of the city where land was inexpensive.[33] There was already ample evidence to support this view, especially in the Bronx, where enormous growth had already occurred since the turn of the century. Clarence Stein's proposal typified the concerns of the committee in its development of innovative new "suburban" apartment configurations.

The Bronx was the first of the outer boroughs to experience accelerated development as a portion of the consolidated urban entity of Greater New York City

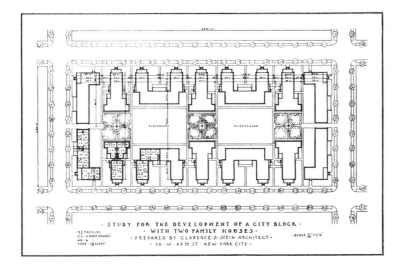

enacted by charter in 1897. The political unification of Manhattan with the outer boroughs crystallized a physical symbiosis which had been present in New York development since the mid-nineteenth century. Even Brooklyn, an independent political entity and already the fourth largest city in the United States by 1855, could still be seen in certain ways as subservient to Manhattan.[34] After 1897 the symbiosis was clinched, not so much by political unification as by the physical infrastructure the new political order permitted, principally through construction of the subway system. In the Bronx, for example, before subway development, some village development had occurred, mainly along rail lines. But the first wave came only after 1886, with completion of the Third Avenue Bronx extension of the Manhattan Second Avenue elevated line up through the central Bronx. This brought Manhattan densities to the Bronx for the first time. Waves of dense development followed.[35] In 1904 the Westchester Avenue elevated line was opened, and connected to the Lenox Avenue subway in 1906. In 1908 the Broadway Interborough Rapid Transit (IRT) line to Van Cortlandt Park was completed. Several major lines opened between 1917 and 1920, expanding the possibilities for the 1920s wave of development. In 1917 the White Plains line extended the Westchester Avenue elevated to the northernmost edge of the borough; in 1917–18 the Jerome Avenue IRT lines opened to Van Cordlandt Park; and in 1920 the Lexington Avenue IRT was extended to Pelham Bay Park. Finally, in 1933 the IND line along the Grand Concourse was completed (figure 5.5).[36]

For the Bronx, alignment along the north-south axis of Manhattan was a fortunate circumstance in terms of transit connections. Brooklyn's geography was not quite so opportune, and Queens was even more isolated. Brooklyn's original connection to Manhattan was by the hundreds of ferries which plied the East River. But in Brooklyn, the river became an obstacle to the development of the early mass transit connections the Bronx enjoyed. The heroic Brooklyn Bridge, completed in 1883, was testament to this crucial problem. Brooklyn subway de-

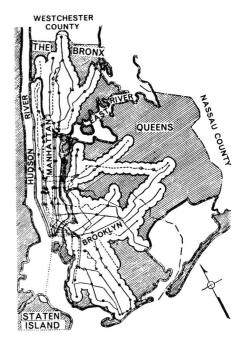

velopment lagged slightly behind that of the Bronx. The IRT was first, completed along Eastern Parkway in 1908. No additional line was in place for another decade, when a number of BMT lines were completed. The far-reaching IND lines were not completed until the 1930s and 1950s. Brooklyn urbanization was, therefore, stretched over a long period, beginning well over a half century before the Bronx and ending after Bronx urbanization had peaked. Major urbanization in Queens began last. In 1920 its 115 square miles still awaited development: 78 were productive farms, and 54 were within a 10-mile radius of Grand Central Station.[37] But this changed as well, with rapid transit and the 1920s boom. The first segment of the Queensboro IRT subway was completed as far as Jackson Heights in 1917; it was extended to Flushing in 1928. The BMT line through the new East 60th Street tunnel was completed to Astoria in 1917 and to Queensboro Plaza in 1920. Midtown Manhattan was only fifteen minutes from open farmland (figure 5.6).[38] The other major Queens lines were completed in the 1930s and 1950s.

The garden apartment was not just the product of the new access to cheap outer borough land. It also reflected the reorganization of capital for the production of middle-income housing to match the scale of the large outer borough parcels. After the turn of the century, the private production of housing shifted to larger and larger scales. The small-scale lot-by-lot development of the nineteenth century lapsed as the economic milieu changed. The modern development corporation emerged, involving large private investment. These corporations managed all of the activity related to the production of a new generation of middle-class housing, from real estate acquisition to design and construction, to rental and maintenance. An important example was the Queensboro Corporation, one of the earliest, largest, and most innovative. Queensboro was formed by Edward A. MacDougal in 1909, just as the completion of the Queensboro Bridge opened up a vast new land area in Queens. At Jackson Heights MacDougal acquired six adjoining farms of 325 acres total area—the equivalent of three thousand building lots, located at the highest elevation in Queens.[39] The site was along Jackson Avenue, which connected directly to the Queensboro Bridge. With intense pressure from the Queensboro Corporation, the IRT and BMT transit lines were subsequently built adjacent to Jackson Heights, increasing the accessibility of the land to midtown Manhattan, and in effect subsidizing the development of a residential area. This use of public transit to subsidize private development typified the mass transit undertaking in New York City, from the earliest period.[40]

Jackson Heights was for many years the largest development in Queens, but by 1920 the Queensboro Corporation had begun similar projects at Corona and Douglaston in Queens.[41] Its large scale spawned a number of innovations in the mass marketing of housing. The Queensboro Corporation pioneered mass media advertising, including radio commercials, and it emphasized cooperative apartment ownership for moderate incomes, instead of luxury housing as in the past. Most importantly, the scale of production could be used to promote an idealized community plan. In 1925 promotional literature for Jackson Heights boasted that the scale of development was the largest community of cooperatively owned garden apartment homes under single management in the world. If this garden section of New York City were superimposed on Manhattan, it would extend from 34th to 57th Streets, Third to Seventh Avenues. The garden apartments already erected at Jackson Heights, if constructed on Fifth Avenue would extend from 42nd Street on both sides of Fifth Avenue to 62nd Street and represent an investment of approximately $20,000,000. With such a large area under one management, it was possible to carefully lay out the entire property on a comprehensive plan, and by careful selection of co-operative owners to encourage to the fullest extent the community life which is enjoyed by residents of this section.[42]

The Queensboro Corporation projects were marketed to the middle class of the city, which could afford the move from Manhattan; and they reinforced the continuing geographical stratification of the city's population based on ethnic and economic characteristics. As one Jackson Heights resident reminisced in 1975, there were "no Catholics, Jews, or dogs in those days."[43]

In relation to the evolution of housing types, each of the boroughs colored the developments of the 1920s in its own way. Brooklyn, with its long history, remained most diverse. The Bronx and Queens present sharp contrasts. By the end of the 1920s, the Bronx was the borough of apartments. Only 18.5 percent of the 198,151 dwellings constructed in the Bronx between 1920 and 1930 were one- or two-family houses. This was the lowest proportion of any of the outer boroughs. Brooklyn followed with 40 percent, and Queens had the highest total, outside of Staten Island, with 70 percent one- and two-family houses.[44] The low density of most Queens development in comparison with the Bronx was in some ways a straightforward expression of its vast size. With 117 square miles, it is over one-third of the total area of New York City, in contrast to the 43 square miles of the Bronx. But the contrast was also a consequence of timing.

Bronx development, which was earlier than Queens', did not lose the strand of continuity with what had come before in Manhattan. Built as it was on the eve of a new age, it adopted a modern infrastructure of mass transit, parkways, and parks within a nineteenth-century outlook in the best sense. The "core" of the Bronx development, which extends from Harlem up its central axis, is characterized above all else by urban density, tempered by a large-scale conception of urban space and urban nature. It is not the vertical density of Manhattan, but tight and intense horizontal continuity. There is a dialogue between urban and rural in the evolution of housing types found in the Bronx which has contributed to the unique quality of its urbanism. By 1914 an extraordinary 17 percent of the total area of the Bronx had been devoted to public parkland, in contrast to 11 percent for Manhattan, 2 percent for Brooklyn, and 1.5 percent for Queens.[45] Queens was considered the "Garden Borough," but its nature was more privatized, in the form of low-density housing with yards rather than public parks. In the Bronx a much firmer line was drawn between housing and nature, with great urban walls facing equally impressive parks. It was these boundaries that were most highly prized for housing, resulting in high densities and an innovative formal tension between city and country.

There is also a side to the differing sensibilities of Bronx and Queens urbanism which is related to the ethnicity and social mobility within New York in the early twentieth century, principally focused on Jewish resettlement. By 1930 the Bronx had the highest concentration of Jewish population in the city (and, by extension, in the United States). While Brooklyn led in absolute numbers with 851,000, the Bronx population of 585,000 Jews out of a total population of 1,300,000 was by far the highest proportion at 46.2 percent, followed by 33 percent in Brooklyn and 16 percent in Manhattan. In Queens the 88,000 Jewish population out of 1,100,000 reflected its differing path of development.[46] Of course, the most concentrated areas in the Bronx and elsewhere had higher densities than the averages show. This condition of density became a kind of celebration of proximity which the sociologist Louis Wirth came to call "urbanism as a way of life."[47] The melding of high-density development with Jewish culture in twentieth-century New York has been the source of considerable commentary. This phenomenon resolutely countered the growing anti-urban ideals of mainstream middle-class culture.[48] These characteristics of dense urbanism accompanied the various Jewish extensions into the outer boroughs in places like the Eastern Parkway and Ocean Parkway areas of Brooklyn, or Queens Boulevard in Queens. But it was in the Bronx where the ideals were most comprehensively realized. Perhaps it was the "explosiveness" of the various Bronx "booms" which facilitated the Jewish presence by opening it to investment, unlike the slower and more controllable Queens growth.[49] The scale of the Jewish exodus from Manhattan to the Bronx peaked in the 1920s, reflected in the reduction of the Jewish population on the Lower East Side from 706,000 in 1923 to 297,000 in 1930. Two-thirds of this number went to the Bronx, where the Jewish population climbed from 382,000 to 585,000 during the same seven years.[50]

Bronx development could be considered suburban development. But for the first Jewish generation in the Bronx, the public emblems associated with their new status were not private cottages surrounded by lawns. The ideal was closer to a people's palazzo, involving a monumentality not possible through individualism. The cottage yard with grass and flowers became a courtyard instead, elaborately landscaped and collectively maintained for the common good. The minimum dimensions of the New Law light court were rejected in favor of an internal garden. The suburban Bronx harbored a Lower East Side population released from what had been described in 1894 as the most concentrated urban agglomeration in the world.[51] For this group, the trip to the single-family cottage involved more than one generation. The urbanistic legacy of the Lower East Side could not be easily eradicated. Material comforts were increased in the Bronx, while the remarkably strong sense of "metropolis" was retained and in fact celebrated as nowhere else in New York. The Grand Concourse and Pelham Parkway became the twentieth-century equivalents of Chrystie and Forsyth streets; Third Avenue and East Tremont were the equivalents of Orchard Street. The private marketplace built almost all of the 1920s housing in New York, but circumstances accrued to produce more than a formula product for profit taking. Within the predictable economic constraints, experimentation prevailed, and was even keenly pursued.

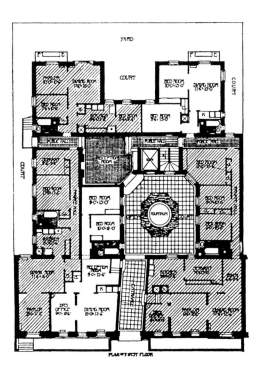

Figure 5.7. Emery Roth. Goldhill Court
Apartments, the Bronx, completed in 1909 with
a New Law light court made pretentious
through the inclusion of garden elements and a
fountain.

For moderate-cost private market housing, the impetus for reduced coverage had already appeared in an embryonic stage in the adjustments developers were making in the New Law tenement by 1920. Frequently, the minuscule internal courts of the Flagg plan type euphemistically became "gardens," as at Goldhill Court, completed in 1909 on Union Avenue in the Bronx.[52] It was one of Emery Roth's earliest apartment buildings (figure 5.7). A large fountain filled a small New Law light court, disguising its utilitarian origins. Its middle-income pretentions were reinforced by an elevator and an elaborate polychromatic facade. Another common approach took greater liberties with New Law massing by cutting light slots from both the street and rear sides. An interesting illustration was a proposal by Andrew Thomas for East 45th Street near Queens Boulevard. Here, light and ventilation were superior to the Flagg-type plan, with only slightly less site coverage for a 70-by-100-foot lot (figure 5.8).[53] The need for fire escapes was eliminated by a dual stair system, and Flagg's interior courtyard was replaced by two exterior courtyards. The front courtyard was envisioned as a slightly raised and lightly planted entry for the building. Subsequently, this idea became a widely used prototype for builders.

Beyond this small-scale innovation in unit planning, design experimentation entered the realm of the perimeter block. An important example in the Bronx was Melrose Courts, completed in 1920 on an entire block bounded by East 163rd and 164th streets and Park and Teller avenues. The original architect was Charles Kreymbourg, with completion of the project by William E. Erb and Paul R. Henkel.[54]

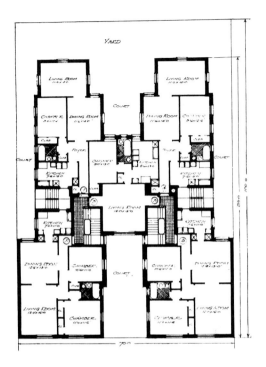

Figure 5.8. Andrew Thomas. Proposal made in 1917 for a privately developed apartment building, planned for a 70-by-100-foot lot using higher standards than for tenements.

A large interior court, 100 by 200 feet, was developed as a garden with fountains (figure 5.9). The traditional street relationship was reversed so that automobiles could cross the block through the garden. This reversal caused the function of the New Law light slots to change from unused rear "yards" to outdoor entry foyers

Figure 5.9. Charles Kreymbourg, William E. Erb, and Paul R. Henkel. Melrose Courts, the Bronx, completed in 1920 adapting New Law plans for the perimeter of a large interior court.

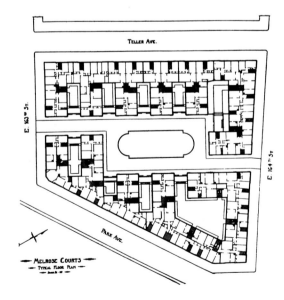

for the lobby of each building. At 65 percent, the building coverage was relatively high, yet the interior garden court appeared spacious, as a result of the ingenious incorporation of the light slots.

The garden apartment would not have emerged unless it was profitable. In this aspect the garden apartment represented a major change in developers' perceptions of profitability in relation to the issue of coverage for moderate-income housing. Prior to the 1920s, it was always assumed that of reduction of coverage would increase costs and reduce profits. The arguments for reduced coverage remained exclusively within the realm of social good, or of marketing, in the belief that apartments associated with better conditions for light and air could be expected to demand higher rents. This common wisdom changed, especially with the new accessiblity to cheap outer borough land. It became apparent that reduced coverage on low-cost land might reduce costs enough to increase profits, in spite of the lower number of apartments. Thus, the financial imperative in New York City for moderate-income housing evolved from the 25-by-100-foot lot mandated by the Tenement House Act of 1879 to the 100-by-100-foot lot of the Tenement House Act of 1901, to the perimeter block of the 1920s. A key to these larger-scale developments was the use of a unified open space, which simplified construction detailing and reduced investment costs per room while raising rental rates. Higher tenement densities with less open space were less desirable because they required more complex and expensive spatial organization in order to provide adequate light and ventilation. The new economic formulas applied especially to housing for the arriving middle class, whose space standards were far less stringent than for tenement design. In the developing outer urban areas, open land and reduced values permitted reduced site coverages.

A definitive step in the consolidation of the new economic theory came from the debate which surrounded the tenement house competition sponsored by the Phelps Stokes Fund in 1921[55] The program required a proposal for twenty-four rental rooms on a 50-by-100-foot lot, or forty-eight rental rooms on a 100-by-100-foot lot, with not less than 56 percent of the lot for living space on any floor. These restrictions produced coverages of 70 percent with the inclusion of circulation and other service space. Andrew Thomas submitted a scheme which did not meet these requirements, using only 60 percent coverage. He argued that not only had he increased design standards by providing better light and air, but that the plan would be more profitable because of its lower coverage (figure 5.10). The winning entry submitted by Sibley and Fetherston, used a more conventional New Law plan type with 68 percent coverage. A placing scheme by Raymond Hood used only 64 percent coverage.

The Thomas scheme could not qualify, but his arguments received considerable credence through a subsequent study of the three schemes by Frederick Ackerman (figure 5.11). Ackerman concluded that the Thomas scheme would be 10 percent cheaper to build because of its reduced cubic footage.[56] Although the Thomas scheme contained four fewer rooms, reducing its gross income per year, it would still produce .2 percent more profit than the winning entry. As Ackerman pointed out, the difference in construction cost was actually much greater than 10 percent, a figure based only on the reduced cubic footage. Because of the re-

Figure 5.10. Andrew Thomas (*left*). Entry to the tenement house competition of 1921, sponsored by the Phelps Stokes Fund; disqualified due to its low coverage of 60 percent. Sibley and Fetherston (*right*). First Place entry to the tenement house competition of 1921, using used 68 percent coverage.

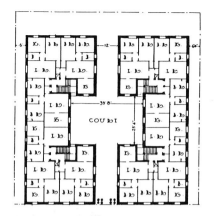
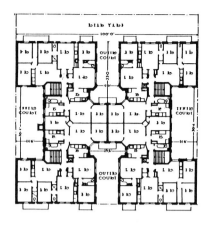

Figure 5.11. Comparative drawing of three entries to 1921 tenement house competition: Sibley and Fetherston (*1*); Raymond Hood (*2*); Andrew Thomas (*3*).

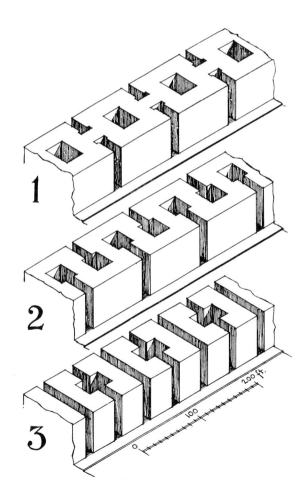

duced site coverage, the architect could vastly simplify construction through a simpler configuration of exterior walls and less complicated interior partitioning. The Thomas scheme produced a better balance between rental income and form, as represented by its rental income per room and construction cost per cubic foot. The plan also provided superior light and ventilation, because of reduced site coverage. Ackerman's study was seminal. For the first time, reduced coverage was seen not simply as a moral imperative, but as an economic advantage. Still, at the conclusion of his analysis. Ackerman could not resist a wry commentary about all of the schemes: "After many thousand years of progress man has gained such mastery over the material world that a large percentage of one-half the population may choose circumstances permitting between these several types as his place of abode."

By 1922 Thomas had publicized numerous proposals incorporating his ideas about reduced coverage. In 1919 he submitted a proposal to the Housing Committee of the New York State Reconstruction Commission for fourteen U-shaped buildings placed around the perimeter of a 200-by-650-foot block with a large interior garden (figure 5.12).[57] The U form was derived from a careful analysis of the ideal relationship between building mass and constructional configuration in order to minimize cost while maximizing light and air. In his report, Thomas argued that this configuration, with a coverage of only 67.7 percent, could provide a 7.5 percent return, while the normal 70 percent coverage schemes would return only 6.9 percent. Thomas' economic arguments represented a turning point in housing design in New York City. Not only was proof given that reduced building coverage schemes had an economic imperative, but the argument could be extended to monolithic planning for entire blocks. Larger-scale developments could permit efficiencies in design and insure even greater construction savings. With this type of block configuration, the upper-class palazzo of the late nineteenth

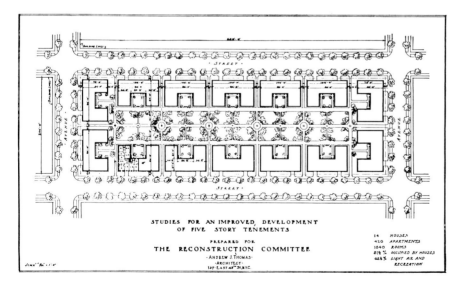

Figure 5.12. Andrew Thomas. Proposal for a perimeter block project composed of U buildings, made for the New York State Reconstruction Commission in 1919; with this scheme Thomas began to develop his arguments in favor of reduced coverage, based on increased profitability.

THE GARDEN APARTMENT   137

century was evolving toward a more loosely assembled "perimeter" massing, with lower height and coverage, and lower-income tenantry.

In Europe by the turn of the century, the development of new prototypes for reduced coverage had reached a level of sophistication unknown in New York until the 1920s. Similarities existed between the two situations, including the annexing of large new land parcels through the development of rapid transit. The earlier European innovation was fueled by working-class social housing programs involving various forms of public and private philanthropy which could support large-scale experimentation. In London the London County Council had completed an impressive array of reduced-coverage projects by the beginning of World War I.[58] In Paris building societies for low-cost housing (HBM) had realized a number of remarkable new projects toward the periphery, where the obsolete walls were being removed.[59] Other cities had achieved similar results; in Berlin, for example, the royal holdings at Charlottenburg had been developed to include a large assemblage of good worker housing realized by philanthropic building societies.[60] In both England and Belgium, the first industrialized nations, the working-class "garden suburb" in its various forms had become a well-established tradition.[61]

In all cases, the European efforts far surpassed the scale and quality of anything that could be found in New York. Given the intensity of international exchange which surrounded housing and planning activity around the turn of the century, it was inevitable that these projects would influence New Yorkers. These influences were widespread, reaching directly to the new housing entrepreneurs. The directors of the Queensboro Corporation visited Europe in 1914, where they saw new housing in several cities. They claimed to have been impressed by the new housing at Charlottenburg.[62] It is likely that they visited the extraordinary Charlottenburg I and II projects, designed by Erich Kohn and Paul Mebes for the Berlin Civil Servants Dwellings Association, completed between 1904 and 1909 (figure 5.13).[63] These developments could be considered garden apartments—five- or six-story buildings whose perimeter massing incorporated ample recreation or other shared communal space. They bear striking similarity to much of the housing at Jackson Heights. Charlottenburg, which had developed at the turn of the century after the introduction of mass transit, no doubt presented the directors of the Queensboro Corporation with a reassuring argument that a similar potential existed in Queens for both housing design innovation and profits. By around 1910 the new housing at Charlottenburg had begun to receive considerable notice

Figure 5.13. Paul Mebes. Charlottenburg II Project, built by the Berlin Civil Servants Dwelling Association between 1907 and 1909, visited by the directors of the Queensboro Corporation in 1914.

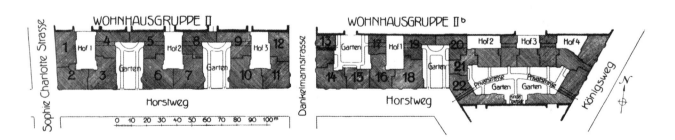

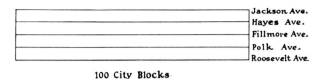

100 City Blocks

Figure 5.14. Queensboro Corporation formula for perimeter-type block organization applied to early projects; later construction increased the coverage well above 40 percent.

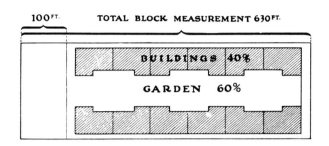

in the United States architectural press, furthering the legitimacy of the new type.[64]

The first housing built by the Queensboro Corporation at Jackson Heights was the Laurel, completed in 1914 on 82nd Street at Northern Boulevard. It was a single apartment house, incorporating a small courtyard.[65] At Jackson Heights, for a brief period of time, a combination of land economics and the new transportation produced conditions more favorable to innovation for the new garden housing type than in any other area of the city. Its legacy is unique for the variety of massing approaches which were employed. Compared with the Bronx, the Jackson Heights perimeters tended to be lower density and less continuous, with a stronger presence of the garden. In the initial stage of development, coverage was only 40 percent, although this increased subsequently when the blocks were fully built up (figure 5.14).

The Queensboro Corporation claimed to be the first to use the term "garden apartment" for its project called the Greystone, which was designed by George H. Wells and completed in 1918 on 79th Street, between 34th Avenue and Northern Boulevard (figure 5.15).[66] As a garden apartment, it was quite primitive, enclosing the street rather than the block interior, with most rooms oriented toward the street and minimal development of any rear "garden" space. It was not until subsequent projects that the potential of a garden began to evolve. The corporation marketed as fully as possible the ideal of apartment living in a rural setting. Every piece of unbuilt land was temporarily devoted to gardens, parks, and outdoor recreation. For example, the block ends, which were initially left open, were used for formal gardens, tennis courts, and a skating rink, as a marketing strategy to attract the initial tenants. There was even a golf course. At the beginning of the Jackson Heights development, land was so plentiful that the corporation was able to provide individual gardens for tenants who desired them. This tradition dated from the Victory Gardens of World War I, and continued

THE GARDEN APARTMENT   139

Figure 5.15. George H. Wells. Front and rear views of the Greystone, built for the Queensboro Corporation at Jackson Heights, Queens, completed in 1917 and 1918; said by the corporation to be the first garden apartments in New York City.

Figure 5.16. Photo of the communal gardens behind the Greystone, built on undeveloped land owned by the Queensboro Corporation, circa 1918.

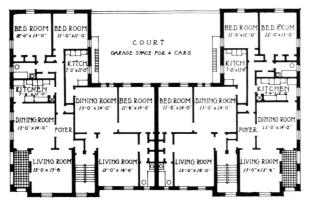

Figure 5.17. Andrew Thomas. Linden Court, completed in 1920 for the Queensboro Corporation in Jackson Heights. It used a variation of the U prototype which incorporated garages for automobiles.

Typical Floor Plan of 107 Foot Unit
8-5 Room and 8-4 Room Apartments, Area 4190 Square Feet

through the 1920s until the open land had become entirely built up (figure 5.16). This marketing strategy left the block ends free allowing a characteristic perimeter configuration consisting of a unified middle section and separate ends. The garden provided the cohesion for the block as a whole.

Given the interests and prominence of Andrew Thomas, it was inevitable that he would become involved with the Queensboro Corporation. He realized several of his most important projects at Jackson Heights. All were variations on U-shaped buildings, organized into perimeter configurations, which further explored his study for the New York State Reconstruction Commission (see figure 5.12). The earliest was Linden Court, completed in 1920 at Jackson Heights (figure 5.17).[67] Five buildings, each four stories in height, lined each side of a gridiron block bounded by 84th and 85th streets between 37th and Roosevelt avenues. Limited garage space was incorporated at the rear of each building. The presence of the automobiles was tempered by a raised garden level, which was more decorative than functional; access from the apartments was rather indirect (figure 5.18). The entire project housed 144 families. The other Thomas perimeter blocks which incorporated variations on U buildings included the Château and the Towers projects. Both modified considerably the U organization to incorporate self-service elevators (figure 5.19). Both were built as upper-middle income cooperatives, which is reflected in their generous standards for space and light.

The Château was completed first, on a block bounded by 80th and 81st streets and 34th and 35th avenues.[68] The site plan was Thomas' typical perimeter block arrangement with twelve U buildings around an interior open space (figure 5.20). The Towers, built on the adjacent block between 34th Avenue and Northern Boulevard, used a similar approach, but with larger apartments and a more elaborate furnishing of the courtyard.[69] The courtyard of the Château, however, with its raised landscaping running down the middle (like Linden Court), seems much more effective as a green oasis. Both projects were designed for the most elite of the Queensboro Corporation tenants and were sold as cooperatives. Both projects

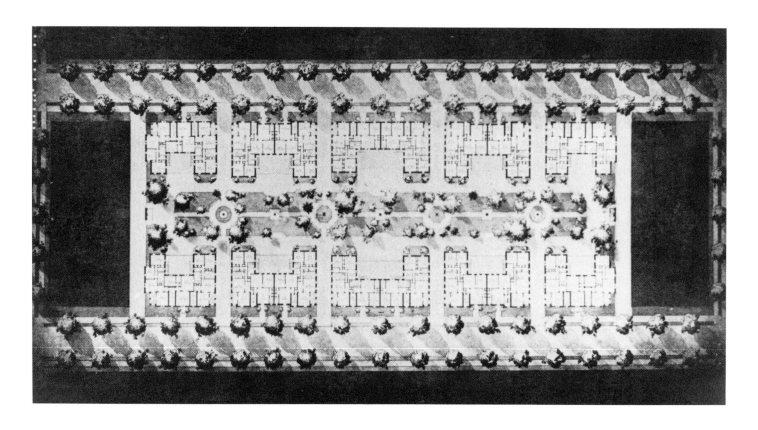

Figure 5.18. Andrew Thomas. Linden Court site plan showing the integration of the internal garden with automobile access.

Figure 5.19. Andrew Thomas. The Château (*left*) and the Towers (*right*) building plans, completed for the Queensboro Corporation in 1922 and 1923, respectively, as upper-middle-income cooperative projects, incorporating automatic push-button elevators.

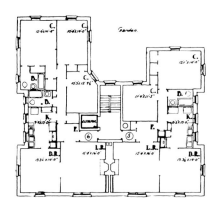 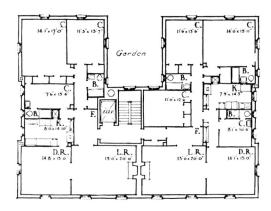

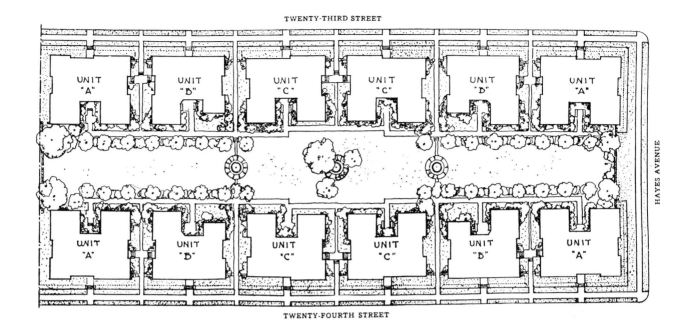

TWENTY-THIRD STREET

UNIT "A" UNIT "B" UNIT "C" UNIT "C" UNIT "D" UNIT "A"

HAYES AVENUE

UNIT "A" UNIT "B" UNIT "C" UNIT "C" UNIT "B" UNIT "A"

TWENTY-FOURTH STREET

were extremely well conceived and executed with the careful attention to detail which was Thomas' mastery. Stylistically, the use of the château and villa motifs reinforced each project's claim to social status. They also represented a shift in the conception of "perimeter," from urban palazzo to suburban villa. They were looser configurations of free-standing buildings, which in their architectural expression sought to adopt the images historically associated with free-standing buildings in the countryside.

Thomas' other project at Jackson Heights was the Hayes Avenue Apartments, which applied his U prototype in another way, to solve the generic problem of the block end inherent to the Jackson Heights plan (figure 5.21).[69] Built in 1923 on 34th Avenue between 82nd and 83rd streets, two U buildings completed a small courtyard with a passage between the street and a loggia along the garden side. The interior elevations were carefully developed to heighten the presence of the garden. Elsewhere, Thomas had been experimenting with similar massing in a variety of contexts, such as his interesting 1918 proposal for a four-story perimeter block development for lower-middle-income families on Ditmars Avenue at Hallett Street in Astoria, Queens (figure 5.22).[71] The same form was applied to another project at 190th Street and Morris Avenue in the Bronx.[72] Other architects questioned the economy of the U form. One analysis calculated that by interconnecting the isolated buildings, an additional apartment per floor could be provided at no extra cost (figure 5.23).[73] This impetus for efficiency and economy would, for a period, lead to continuous and highly crenellated perimeter walls, or "double perimeter" massing, which by the end of the 1920s became commonplace

Figure 5.20. Andrew Thomas. The Château site plan, which attempted to increase the possibility for use of the internal garden over earlier Queensboro Corporation projects.

Figure 5.21. Andrew Thomas. Hayes Avenue
Apartments, completed around 1922 in Jackson
Heights, using only two U builings to create an
extremely well-scaled courtyard.

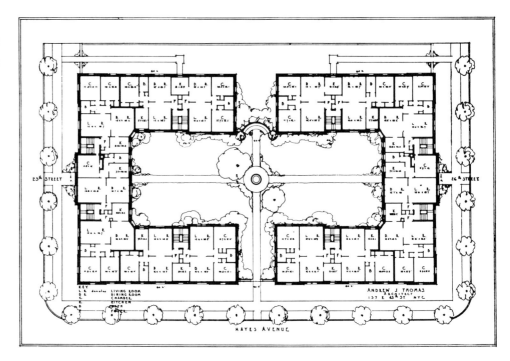

for the garden apartment type. Such ideas were closer to the direction taken by
George H. Wells. He developed several early continuous perimeter proposals for
the Queensboro Corporation, including Operation No. 10 in 1920 which was never
built (figure 5.24).[74] These early schemes typically did not resolve the conflict
within apartment plans between the street and garden sides. Later, at Cambridge

Figure 5.22. Andrew Thomas. Proposal for a
privately developed perimeter block project at
Astoria, Queens, made in 1918.

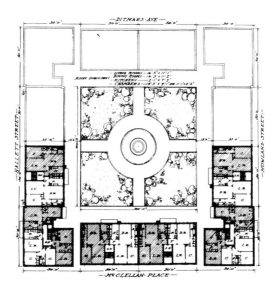

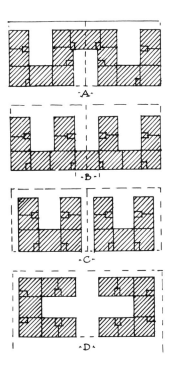

Figure 5.23. Frank Chouteau Brown. Plate from an analysis comparing U and "continuous" forms for perimenter block planning, published in 1922.

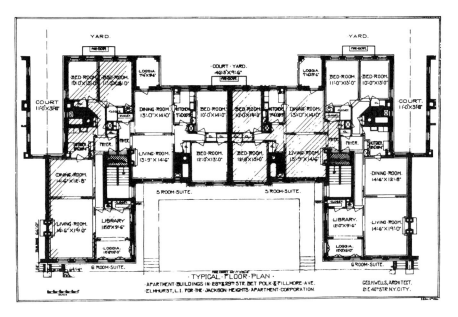

Figure 5.24. George H. Wells. Operation No. 10, apartment cluster plan proposed to the Queensboro Corporation for Jackson Heights in 1920, showing early experimentation with a continuous "double" perimeter form.

THE GARDEN APARTMENT 145

Figure 5.25. George H. Wells. Cambridge Court apartment cluster plan, which attempted to increase contact between the internal living space and both street and garden; a different approach from earlier Queensboro Corporation projects.

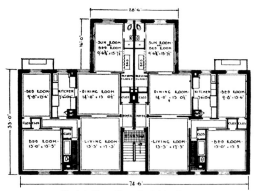

Typical Floor Plan—Cambridge Court.

Court, Wells used simple through-units, permitting all apartments to face both street and garden (figure 5.25).

Throughout the 1920s the function of the garden within the garden apartment became more and more an issue, especially as building coverage for middle-class garden apartments continued to decrease. By 1924 the Queensboro Corporation constructed Cambridge Court at Jackson Heights, with a coverage of only 35 percent (figure 5.26).[75] The four-story perimeter block project was located on 70th and 80th streets, between 34th and 35th avenues. The architect, George Wells, included gardens at the street front and in the interior of the block. At Jackson Heights the uses planned for such garden-type open space were reconsidered after several projects had been built and occupied. For example, at Linden Court, completed in 1920 (see figure 5.18), the garden was designed only to be looked at. For the Château, completed by Thomas two years later (see figure 5.20), the design approach was changed:

> As the earlier garden was an experiment, it was not thought desirable to encourage people to gather in it. Experience had induced the Queensboro Corporation to go further, and this later garden is definitely a social place, where the people of the apartments are invited to come. This object is contained in the design by means of a complete system of circulation and by the use of little paved spaces or terraces, where people may sit outdoors.[76]

Figure 5.26. George H. Wells. Cambridge Court perimeter block project completed for the Queensboro Corporation around 1924, using only 35 percent coverage and a highly developed internal garden.

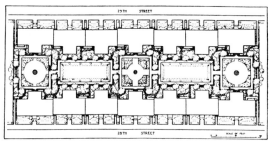

Block Plan of Cambridge Court.

As the identity of the Jackson Heights development materialized, the scope of the enterprise and the design conventions of its garden apartment perimeters attracted visitors from abroad, just as the directors of the Queensboro Corporation had earlier visited innovative European housing. As early as 1922, British housing officials were shown the first buildings,[77] and in 1925, the delegates to the International Regional Planning Conference surveyed the further progress.[78] Included were Ebenezer Howard and Raymond Unwin of England, Joseph Stubben of Germany, and Eliel Saarinen of Finland.

Jackson Heights is unusual for the notable concentration of a wide range of garden apartment types, but similar building was prominent throughout the entire city for moderate-income private housing development until the end of the 1930s. The "garden" spaces tended to become more elaborate as time went on. The Queens, Bronx, and Manhattan versions varied, however, with coverages reflecting their differing conditions of density. One well-known urban example was Noonan Plaza, located on West 168th Street at Nelson Avenue in the Bronx, designed by Horace Ginsbern and completed in 1931.[79] An eight-story perimeter structure, it was designed with a Mayan Deco motif and a garden courtyard which boasted a waterfall and ponds stocked with goldfish and swans (figure 5.27). What the garden lacked in size was compensated in its embellishments.

Elsewhere in the Bronx are found numerous excellent examples of the U type. The Greystone, completed in 1929 by Charles Kreymbourg on Greystone Avenue at West 238th Street, is one of the most elegant. The irregular building, formed by the angle of the street and enclosing a lawn and gardens, is raised from side-

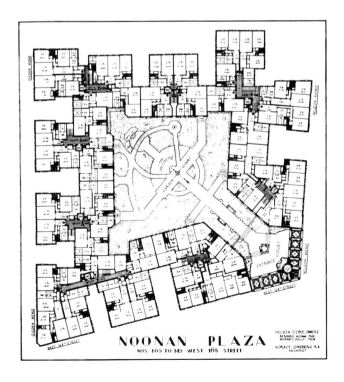

Figure 5.27. Horace Ginsbern. Noonan Plaza, completed in 1931 with one of the most elaborately appointed gardens of the era in the Bronx, including ponds with goldfish and swans, and a waterfall.

THE GARDEN APARTMENT   147

walk level to give partial seclusion. The enclosure is generous enough to accommodate several large pine trees, flower beds, and walkways, with an entrance framed by a covered gate and guardhouse. The Pelham Parkway area contains a number of excellent examples: prominent among them is the Alhambra, completed in 1927 on Pelham Parkway between Holland and Wallace Avenues by Springsteen and Goldhammer.[80] This deep U at the block end is highly reminiscent of turn-of-the-century Berlin examples. Other similar buildings line Holland, Wallace, and Muliner avenues; in some cases, U buildings face each other, capturing the street space between. On Brady Avenue, between Holland and Wallace avenues and Antin Place, a garden mews completed by Robert E. Golden around the same time, represents one of the finest examples of the type in New York. Six shallow U buildings line a terraced garden passage which cascades downward from Brady Avenue to Antin Place.

In Manhattan, garden apartment examples were scarce because of high land costs, with consequent overbuilding. In the 1920s undeveloped land still existed at Washington Heights on the northern tip, however, where several important garden projects were realized. The best known was Hudson View Gardens, completed in 1924 by George Fred Pelham on Northern and Pinehurst avenues at 182nd Street.[81] For most of southern Manhattan, however, the large parcels needed for garden apartment projects required the redevelopment of existing blocks. By this time, "slum clearance" had become a practical reality. It had been practiced in a number of locations throughout the city; the most notable private project was the immense Tudor City, developed by the Fred F. French Company on approximately three square blocks east of Grand Central Station between First and Second avenues. The land had been bought in 1919 for a record $7.5 million. A series of tall "apartment hotels" lined Prospect Place, a garden mews which connected East 40th and 43rd streets.[82] London Terrace, another notable private slum clearance project, was completed in 1930 on a block between West 23rd and 24th streets and Ninth and Tenth avenues in Manhattan (figure 5.28).[83] Unfortunately, the "slum" which was destroyed was an important nineteenth-century terrace row of the same name along West 23rd Street, completed by Andrew Jackson Davis in 1846.[84] Farrar and Watmaugh, the architects of the new London Terrace, followed a variation on perimeter planning, with an internal garden formed by the massive sixteen-story buildings. The "gardens" of both projects were overwhelmed by the building heights, which presumably were a product of Manhattan real property values. But they still represented the highest standards possible in the Manhattan

Figure 5.28. Farrar and Watmaugh. London Terrace, a privately financed "slum clearance" project in Chelsea, using a sixteen-story perimeter block.

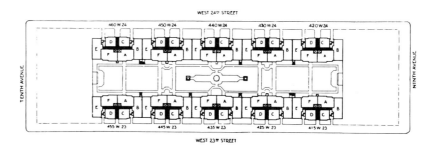

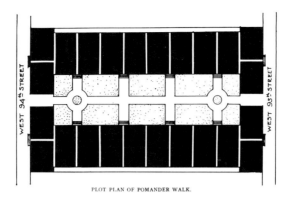

PLOT PLAN OF POMANDER WALK.

Figure 5.29. King and Campbell. Pomander Walk, completed in 1921 between West 94th and 95th streets in Manhattan; one of the few mews projects ever built in New York.

of the 1920s. Their patrimony was limited to the few palazzi of the turn of the century (see figures 3.30, 3.31).

In the 1920s in comparison with the outer boroughs, there was little radical housing innovation in Manhattan, with only an occasional project of more than routine interest. One important exception was Pomander Walk, completed by King and Campbell in 1921 (figure 5.29).[85] Organized as a "mews" linking West 94th and 95th streets, between Broadway and West End Avenue, it is one of the few built examples which address gridiron reorganization along the lines proposed by Edward T. Potter in the nineteenth century (see figures 1.17, 1.18, 4.5). The origins of Pomander Walk, however, did not lie in rationalist planning, and the twenty-four small "Queen Anne" row houses were an anachronism in the Manhattan development of that era, standing in surreal contrast to the adjacent wall of apartment buildings on West End Avenue. They were the eccentric vision of the developer, Thomas Healey, based on the stage set for a Broadway production of Louis N. Parker's play "Pomander Walk" several years earlier. Nevertheless, it was a poignant commentary on the phenomenon of overbuilding, which had reached serious proportions in much of Manhattan by this time.

The garden apartment development was as important for philanthropy as for the private marketplace. In fact, it was innovation in social welfare, in combination with the garden apartment form, which provided the most powerful exemplars of the type. The notion of medium-density living, tempered by a garden, fit well into the well-established reform ideology which saw the reduction of building coverage as an inevitable consequence of innovation. With the completion of the subway, the older philanthropic companies looked to the advantages of the outer boroughs, just as did the private developers. And they looked to higher-density housing, rather than the worker cottage which had been the somewhat elusive focus of their suburban activity in the previous decades. For example, the City and Suburban Homes Company, which had constructed almost 250 single-family homes for their Homewood project by 1900 (see figure 4.33), shifted to the garden apartment type in 1920, with an extension to Homewood designed by Andrew Thomas (figure 5.30).[86] Located on 17th Avenue between 73rd and 74th streets, one hundred families were housed in four buildings which elaborated further on

THE GARDEN APARTMENT   149

Figure 5.30. Andrew Thomas. Addition to the Homewood Development of the City and Suburban Homes Company in Brooklyn in 1920; the U buildings were organized around an internal garden designed after Tuscan motifs.

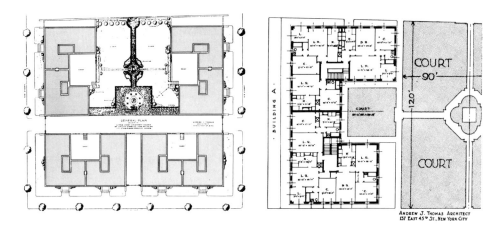

the U configuration, with only 52 percent coverage, a central garden, and facades that evoked "Tuscan" scenography.

In many ways, Thomas' Homewood project represented a new level of quality for philanthropic housing, especially in comparison with the impasse which permeated the last of the Flagg-plan-type projects in Manhattan (see figure 4.24). Philanthropic standards were finally merging with middle-class expectations, such that the philanthropic garden apartment became the standard for the type, rather than a second-class version. Partially this change was related to the new land economics. The City and Suburban Homes Company concluded in its *Annual Report* of 1917 that because of the vastly increased availability of cheap land, building quality rather than land value would become the prime source of real estate income in the future.[87] This judgment reversed an assumption that had always been the basis for building housing in New York. Allan Robinson, the company president, reasoned that, in the face of peaking land values, building value would assume more importance. Thus free market speculation would encourage higher design quality. To some extent, the prosperity of the 1920s proved his theory correct.

New forms of "philanthropy" began to appear in the early 1920s, which expanded the realm of traditional private activity. These involved government interventions, which attempted to respond to the housing crisis by stimulating the private marketplace in various ways.[88] The garden apartment was a dominant ideal model. Thus, simultaneous with the highly visible public opposition to direct government intervention in housing was a private offensive in support of a lucrative indirect subsidy to private production. In 1920 the New York state legislature approved a bill which permitted ten-year real estate tax exemptions for construction of buildings completed between April 1920 and April 1924, but begun before April 1922. This law contributed to the housing boom under way by 1922.[89]

In 1922 the legislature passed an amendment to the New York State Insurance Code granting life insurance companies temporary permission to invest in housing projects.[90] Insurance company investments were highly regulated, and the rapid growth of the insurance industry created a lack of adequate investment opportunities. After passage of the amendment, insurance companies could invest their burgeoning earnings in housing with the stipulation that rent not exceed a very modest nine dollars per room per month. The amendment was intended to stimulate postwar housing starts and to prove the capability of big business to contribute to the public good while making a profit at the same time. The Metropolitan Life Insurance Company, which had lobbied extensively for the right to invest in housing, began construction almost immediately.[91] By 1924 the company had constructed the largest single housing project in New York City to date, designed by Andrew Thomas in Long Island City in Queens. His U prototype was adapted to reflect the severe economies required to meet the low rentals required by the law. Fifty-four such buildings housed 2,215 families in three locations near the Bliss Street, Woodside, and Ditmars Avenue stations of the Queensboro subway (figure 5.31).[92]

In 1923 economic inducement for reduction of coverage was renewed by the state legislature, which extended permission for real estate tax exemptions to new housing completed between 1920 and 1926, but begun before April 1924.[93] The Limited Dividend Housing Companies Law passed by the legislature in 1926 further enhanced the generally favorable economic climate for reduced coverage.[94] This latter legislation granted condemnation rights and local tax abatements to housing companies which limited their dividends to 6 percent, restricted their rent schedules, and selected tenants with low incomes. The awarding of condemnation rights reflected the increasing scarcity and cost of undeveloped land on the city's fringes, as well as a recognition of the need for large-scale slum clearance. The State Housing Board was set up to supervise the law. The first projects built under its jurisdiction were completed toward the end of the decade.

The political climate of the 1920s encouraged a number of interesting experiments with cooperative workers' housing built by labor and other organizations. Some used the benefits of the 1926 Limited Dividend Law—like the Amalgamated Housing Corporation, organized in 1927 by the Amalgamated Clothing Workers Union, and the Farband Housing Corporation, sponsored by the Jewish National Workers Alliance of America in 1928. Other collectives were developed independent of government subsidy—for example, the Workers Cooperative Colony and the Yiddish Cooperative Heimgesellschaft (Shalom Aleichem Cooperative). Both date from 1926. All of these organizations built cooperative worker housing projects which served as important catalysts within larger socialist political move-

Figure 5.31. Andrew Thomas. Perspective view of typical block for the Metropolitan Life Insurance Company Project in Long Island City.

Figure 5.32. Herman J. Jessor. Workers
Cooperative Colony, second stage completed in
1927 on Bronx Park East, making the
development the largest of the labor
cooperatives for a number of years.

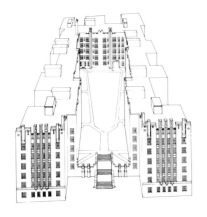

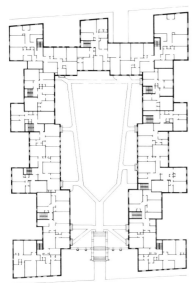

ments. Most were located in the Bronx. Each cooperative had a well-defined ideology, related to the diverse currents in leftist Jewish politics.[95]

The first and largest of the cooperatives was the United Workers Cooperative, which completed its first building, the Coops, in 1927, designed by Springsteen and Goldhammer. Located in the Bronx, the six-story garden apartment covered a block bounded by Britten and Allerton streets, facing the Bronx Park.[96] A deeply crenellated "double perimeter" enclosed the garden, which was traversed by an axial connection with the park. In the following year, an adjacent second project was completed, designed by Herman Jessor (figure 5.32). In this latter project, the approach to the massing was changed to two elongated U buildings which opened directly on the park. The coverage was reduced from 56 percent to 46 percent, to make more garden area. Both projects developed elaborate garden landscapes, with fountains and planting, and both used to some advantage the existing changes in grade, raising garden levels above the street.

The United Workers was founded in 1913, when a group of Jewish workers leased a small tenement on East 13th Street and initiated a housing cooperative, which included a cooperative kitchen and a cultural program with readings, discussions, and invited lecturers and entertainers. The political stance of the leadership appears at that time to have been Zionist and territorialist in relation to the Jewish homeland issue. Over the next years, the group grew larger and leaned politically toward communism, especially after the Russian Revolution. After some years, they rented a larger apartment building in Harlem. A cooperative cafeteria was opened on Second Avenue, which included a library, and publication of a magazine was initiated. In 1924 a summer retreat, Camp Nigedaiget ("No Worries") was founded at Beacon, New York, on a large tract of land bordering the Hudson River. Finally, in 1925, plans were begun for the new Bronx housing complex, which was completed over the next several years with a total of 697 apartments. The project included cooperative stores, a restaurant, a day-care center, and a library of books on political thought in English, Yiddish, and Russian.[97]

The Workers Cooperative Colony was the first large-scale socialist housing project. Next came the Shalom Aleichem Houses (Yiddish Cooperative Heimgesellschaft), completed in 1927 by Springsteen and Goldhammer for 229 families on a site overlooking the Jerome Park Reservoir at Giles Place, West 238th Street, and Cannon Place.[98] The irregularly shaped perimeter enclosed a hilltop site, with a central garden and large fountain overlooking the west Bronx. The relatively high coverage of 55 percent was reconciled by the hilltop view. The contrast with the normal gridiron figuration was striking, evoking the character of a lofty urban oasis. The origins of Shalom Aleichem membership focused on the Workmen's Circle, where a year or so before a small group had formed to make a cooperative, based on shared ideals related to the perservation of secular Yiddish culture. They took the name of the famous Yiddish writer as a symbolic reference to that concern.[99] Compared with the United Workers, the organization was much less avowedly political in the normal sense of the word. Its genesis arose from issues associated with the condition of second-generation immigrant culture and with assimilation. Around the same time, the Jewish National Workers Alliance (Natsionaler Yidisher Arbeter Farband) began planning Farband Houses, a coopera-

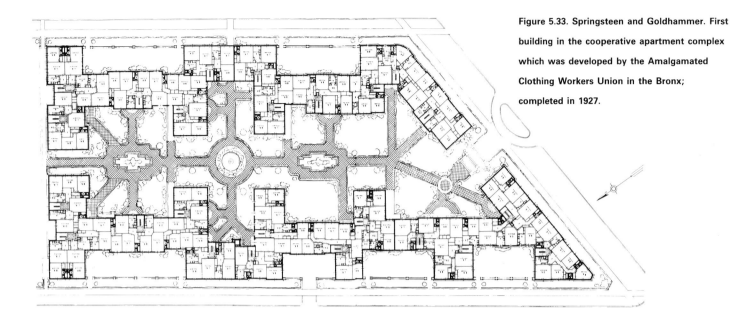

tive consisting of two buildings for 127 families on Williamsbridge Road between Barnes and Matthews avenues, completed in 1928 by Meisner and Uffner.[100] The Jewish National Workers Alliance was founded in 1912 as a fraternal association not unlike the Workmen's Circle, but it was Zionist in orientation and became the bulwark of Labor Zionism in the United States.[101] Slightly later, the Typographical Union, another Jewish organization, constructed two apartment houses for 60 families at Daly Avenue and East 180th Street.[102]

The largest of the labor housing initiatives was begun by the Amalgamated Clothing Workers of America in the Bronx in 1927, with completion of its first garden apartment at the edge of Van Cortlandt Park between Saxon and Dickinson avenues (figure 5.33). It was designed by Springsteen and Goldhammer for 308 families. The six-story walk-up was a highly indented double perimeter, with a coverage of 51 percent and an elaborate formal garden (figure 5.34). Subsequent additions by the same architects were made in 1928, 1929, and 1931, all similar in character to the first, but all incorporating elevators.[103] The Amalgamated also constructed another project on the Lower East Side of Manhattan during the same period. By 1931, with 700 families in the Bronx, the Amalgamated rivaled the scale of the Workers Cooperative Colony. Like the latter, the Amalgamated provided a cooperative store, cultural facilities, and extensive social services. In the period after the war, the Amalgamated estate expanded considerably through the addition of several high-rise buildings.

The Amalgamated Clothing Workers of America was the most powerful union in the garment industry, with a membership of 175,000 by the early 1920s. Its membership included a broad spectrum of persons involved in the garment industry, and its politics were moderately socialist, having resisted communist in-

THE GARDEN APARTMENT   153

Figure 5.34. Springsteen and Goldhammer.
Photo of the internal courtyard of the first
building built by the Amalgamated Clothing
Workers Union in the Bronx, showing the
elaborate development of the garden.

cursions of the early 1920s.[104] This moderation was said to have been reflected in the majority outlook of the Amalgamated tenants, in comparison with the more radical aura associated with the Workers Cooperative Colony.[105] And unlike several of the other projects, the Amalgamated housing included non-Jewish tenants, although in a minority.

The Amalgamated's Lower East Side project was the first large urban renewal development to come under the terms of the 1926 Limited Dividend Law. Completed in 1930 on an entire block bounded by Grand, Columbia, Sheriff, and Broome streets, it was a cooperative housing 233 families.[106] Springsteen and Goldhammer designed the six-story elevator complex. Coverage was only 60 percent (figure 5.35). The garden, with its large pool and fountain, remains today one of the most extraordinary housing courtyards in Manhattan. Like the Bronx projects, considerable space was devoted to an auditorium, meeting rooms, and day care. Amalgamated took advantage of the demolition provisions of the new law and cleared the site of a former factory. Only nine months lapsed between demolition and the occupation of the new housing by tenants, providing a successful early experiment with accelerated construction techniques.

Another important labor initiative was the Thomas Garden Apartments in the Bronx, originally developed by the Labor Homes Building Corporation, an amalgam of four unions, which included the International Ladies Garment Workers Union.[107] The 170-apartment project experienced financial difficulties and was purchased by John D. Rockefeller, Jr., before its completion. The five-story walkup building was located along the Grand Concourse in the Bronx, between East 158th and 159th streets (figure 5.36).[108] Individual apartments were reached through a carefully planned garden sequence, cascading down the sloping site from the

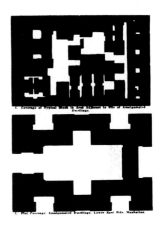

Figure 5.35. Springsteen and Goldhammer. Grand Street building for the Amalgamated Clothing Workers Union, completed on the Lower East Side in 1930. It was a seven-story perimeter block with elevators and was developed as a slum clearance project.

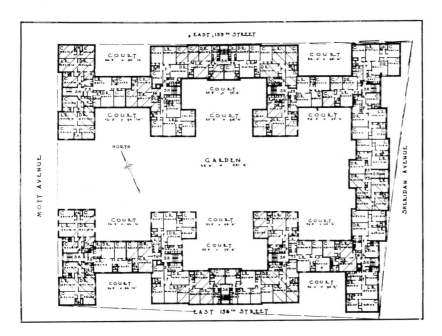

Figure 5.36. Andrew Thomas. Thomas Garden Apartments, built by John D. Rockefeller, Jr., in 1928 along the Grand Concourse in the Bronx for middle-income white occupancy.

Figure 5.37. Andrew Thomas. Photo of the internal courtyard of the Thomas Garden Apartments, showing the "Japanese garden" which contained an artificial water course and bridges; the garden aspect of the garden apartment type was developed to its fullest potential.

Concourse. The design was influenced by Japanese gardens, with concrete lanterns, bridges, and a course of running water. It is one of the landmarks in the garden architecture of that era in New York housing (figure 5.37).

For the earliest of the labor cooperatives, financing came directly from the sponsor organizations, or from sympathizers, who usually shared the same political views. The Workers Cooperative Colony was financed with a bond issue, which was subscribed through a campaign launched by the *Morgen Freiheit,* a Yiddish-language daily newspaper aligned politically with the United Workers Cooperative Association. Individual tenants were required to pay $375 per room to purchase their stock, and rent was $12 per room per month. Potential tenants were recruited using any means, from word of mouth, to tables set up on street corners.[109] For the Shalom Aleichem Houses, financing followed a similar course, including the formation of *mikelets,* or small investment banks, within the membership to raise funds.[110]

But by the time of the Farband Houses, and the Amalgamated project, the assistance provided by the Limited Dividend Housing Companies Law of 1926 could also be applied. Tenants' purchase costs appear to have been reduced. The first building at Farband Houses, which did not receive tax exemption, required only $200 per room, rather than $375 for the Workers Cooperative Colony. The

$16 rent per room was higher, however. The second building at Farband received exemptions, which reduced the monthly cost to $11 per room, in accordance with the law. The purchase price was higher, at $400 per room.[111] The Amalgamated also received a tax exemption and required a tenant investment of $500 per room, with the mandatory $11 per room monthly cost.[112] The Amalgamated enjoyed more secure financing, given the scale and power of the union, which backed a large mortgage from the Metropolitan Life Insurance Company. Mortgages also came from the *Jewish Daily Forward* and the Amalgamated Bank, which belonged to the union.[113] As with the *Morgen Freiheit* for the Coops, the *Jewish Daily Forward* shared political ideology and connections with the Amalgamated.

In general, the monthly cost in the cooperatives was said to represent a savings of 25 percent over the private market.[114] Additional savings were accrued through other cooperative enterprises. For example, the Coops, the Shalom Aleichem Houses, and the Amalgamated all had cooperative stores which offered groceries and filled other daily needs at reduced cost. In the case of the Coops and the Amalgamated, these were large enterprises, with extensive separate buildings.[115] All of the projects provided day care and education programs for young children, giving an economic advantage to parents, who could each work. Beginning in 1929, the Amalgamated as well as the Workers Cooperative Colony developed a summer camp for children. The summer camps included adults and provided families with the possibility of a holiday which might normally have been out of the question for their economic strata.[116] Over the years, the Amalgamated developed extensive consumer services, including self-generated electricity which was sold to families at a cost below Consolidated Edison. They also initiated their own bus service, which, among other uses, carried people to and from the subway. Milk and ice were distributed at cost, and laundry service was provided.[117]

The character and scale of the cooperative services varied from project to project, but all were dedicated to ideals of communal life which went far beyond simple economic advantage. A prerequisite for all of the projects was the library, which was a source for the political and cultural literature essential to the ideological development of each community. There were countless clubs for men, women, and children devoted to personal development and focused on art, music, and crafts. There were workshops, and at the Shalom Aleichem Houses, several artists' studios were incorporated into the design, in order to encourage working artists to join the cooperative. The sculptor Aaron Goodelman and the painter Abraham Maniewich lived there for years. At the Shalom Aleichem Houses and later on at the Amalgamated, there was an auditorium for lectures, concerts, and dramatic productions. All three had cooperative "cafeterias," which served various functions, from banquets to teas. All of the cooperatives had their own newspapers and journals. At the Coops there was a Russian dance group and the J. B. S. Haldane Scientific Society, named after the famous British biologist and leftist activist. The Amalgamated had a garden club, with garden plots and a "Grange." At Farband there was a gymnasium, a chorus, a drama club, and a child study group.

Perhaps at the Shalom Aleichem Houses the cultural activities were most

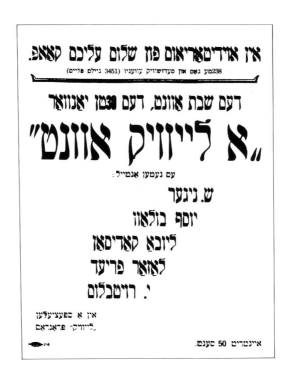

extensive, in keeping with the strength of that particular mandate within the organization. There exists a vast legacy of programs and events amassed over the years. For example, on Saturday night, January 30, 1930 there was a typical program in which the work of H. Leivick, Yiddish poet and playwright, was celebrated with Shmuel Niger, literary critic, Joseph Buloff and his wife Liuva Kadison, actors, Lazar Freed, another actor, and others (figure 5.38). This activity spanned four decades, into the 1960s.[118] Indeed, with the labor cooperatives the working class in New York City had achieved a vision of incredible dimensions. They were outposts in the labor movement, which was already showing signs of political co-option and outposts in the whole of American life as well, which was already showing signs of a tendency toward the homogenization of mass culture.

In the beginning, the Bronx cooperatives were also physical outposts. The massive buildings were placed on the urban periphery, among open fields and private single-family cottages. The urbanity of the Lower East Side or of Hunts Point was transformed, but never discarded. From the point of view of the co-operators, it was simply improved upon. The Shalom Aleichem Houses, for example, was a great castlelike building perched on a hill, in sharp contrast to its surroundings. Possibly the site could equally well have been developed by the cooperative with radically different housing; for example, suburban worker cottages like those around it. But a fundamental part of the cooperative's philosophy had to do with proximity and therefore lent itself to high-density living. The symbolism of the massive structure was not lost on its non-Jewish and less urbane

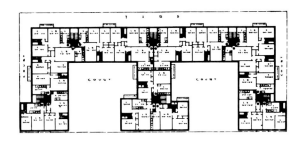

Figure 5.39. Somerfeld and Sass. Lavanburg Homes, built as a philanthropic project in 1927 on the Lower East Side, incorporating an extraordinary number of social services.

neighbors, apparently leading to conflicts in the early years.[119] The cooperatives were in a sense also a microcosm of the whole of the Jewish Bronx. The life within the elite private buildings of the Grand Concourse was less intense and less directed, of course, but all the same, these buildings shared a common "culture of housing" which imbued similar urbanistic ideals and cultural heritage, regardless of specific differences of social class or politics.

By the late 1920s several other innovative projects had been completed with more conventional "philanthropic" financing. In 1927 the Lavanburg Foundation built the Lavanburg Homes project on the Lower East Side on Goerck Street, between East Houston and Stanton streets (figurer 5.39).[120] This project was entirely nonprofit, and experimented with the provision of social services, including a tenants' council and extensive adult education courses. During the depression, its rents were scaled to match family incomes. The architects, Sommerfeld and Sass, with Clarence Stein as consultant, managed to place 113 apartments in a six-story walk-up structure that covered one-quarter of a gridiron block and provided two large courtyards. In 1931 Springsteen and Goldhammer completed a limited dividend project for the Academy Housing Corporation, located at Rosedale, Lacombe, Commonwealth and Randall Avenues in the Bronx (figure 5.40).[121] It was the largest single project built during this period under the 1926 Limited Dividend Law. Eight six-story elevator buildings bordered the sides of a gridiron block, using 44 percent coverage, with a pedestrian mall running down the middle.

Andrew Thomas completed the Paul Lawrence Dunbar Apartments in Harlem in 1928. Located between West 149th and 150th streets and Seventh and

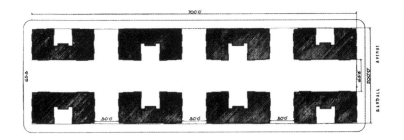

PLOT PLAN

Figure 5.40. Springsteen and Goldhammer. Project for the Academy Housing Corporation. Completed in 1930 in the Bronx, it was the largest limited dividend project at the time.

THE GARDEN APARTMENT   159

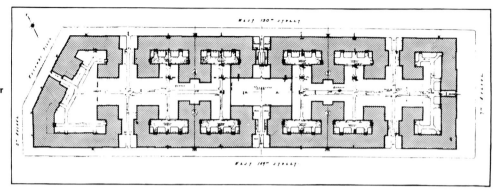

Eighth avenues, they were built by John D. Rockefeller, Jr., as a cooperative ownership project limited to black occupancy. It was considered a companion project to Thomas Gardens, which was restricted to whites. It was one of the few black ownership projects to be built in New York City, and won an award from the New York AIA in 1928 (figure 5.41).[122] Six-story walk-up buildings containing 511 apartments were placed around the perimeter of the slightly irregular block and created a large internal common space. The double perimeter was more articulated on the interior side than the simple U forms used by Thomas at his earlier Metropolitan Homes in Queens. The massing protrusions permitted many double exposure apartments and corner rooms, so that all apartments were well lit and ventilated.

In the context of Harlem, the introverted characteristics of the perimeter form could be seen as a buffer to the deterioration of the surrounding neighborhood, and provided an architectural device for protecting Rockefeller's investment. Rockefeller protected his investment in other ways. He held all preferred stock in the corporation, carefully selected the building's middle-class tenants, and encouraged tenants to place their savings in the Dunbar National Bank, created specially for them. In spite of such precautions, Dunbar's tenants could not survive the depression. Rockefeller foreclosed on their individual mortgages in 1936 and sold the project in the following year.[123]

The extreme articulation of the internal facades at Dunbar became commonplace in many innovative perimeter block projects toward the end of the decade. The approach was used at Thomas' Fourth Avenue project, completed for Brooklyn Garden Apartments, Inc., a limited dividend company, in 1929,[124] and the Phipps Garden Apartments at Sunnyside Gardens in 1928. Designed by Clarence Stein and sponsored by the Phipps Fund, the Phipps Garden Apartments project was a large complex with a mix of four- to six-story walk-up and elevator buildings. A perimeter block configuration with 43 percent coverage was used to accommodate 344 lower-middle-income families (figure 5.42)[125] The organization of the Phipps perimeter was generated by a comparative study of interlocking "cluster" segments, each reflecting differing formal and programmatic characteristics. This research led to the development of a crucial T cluster, which incorporated the elevators and was knit into the continuous perimeter mass with more neutral I and L walk-up segments. The result was a highly varied wall, with all pieces working efficiently within their specific locations. Applied in this manner, the approach produced an advance in the organization of the double perimeter type. As research, the strategy of decomposition, however, was also a premonition of what was to come in housing, which would produce far more mixed results.

All cooperatives were placed in serious economic jeopardy during the Great Depression, but the labor cooperatives suffered interminably, given the denial of their ideals which the crisis soon brought. Unfortunately, it struck before they had achieved economic maturity, making its effects doubly difficult. Even the Amalgamated, which had the strongest financial outlook, had difficulty:

> The first five years were spent in constructing and developing the organization . . . During the greater part of these five years, plans were being formulated on how to round out and strengthen the development. Few of the members gave due consideration to the financial setup of the organization. The low-rental and other privileges that they enjoyed were taken for granted. No protective measures were introduced because, at that time, the demand of applicants to join the enterprise was fairly strong—the outgo comparatively light. The economic storm in its full fury began to be felt in 1932. Large numbers of cooperators found themselves totally unemployed. A good many could not maintain their apartments. Some, in fact, not only did not pay the fixed monthly rental, but had to be helped by extending them credit in the service departments of the organization. Ugly rumors were being circulated that the development would not survive the storm. The income of the corporation dropped to about 60% of its former receipts. Measures to remedy the difficult situation were introduced. Operating expenses that could be deferred were eliminated. Changes calculated to reduce the cost of operations were affected and a method of repurchasing the equity held by the outgoing members on an installment basis were put into effect. By way of illustrating the gravity of the situation, suffice it to say, that at the end of this period more than 1/3 of the total stock equity of the housing corporation was offered to the A. H. Consumers Society for re-purchase.[126]

Although the cooperatives' political stance placed them in opposition to the capitalist system which was in demise, they were still victims of that system like everyone else. They had nowhere else to turn. In addition, the rather utopian and otherworldly nature of the cooperatives left them particularly vulnerable to the economic crisis. There were stopgap measures, like the Rent Relief Fund at Farband, which provided interest-free loans for several months to tenants who were unable to pay their monthly charges.[127] At the Coops, the fate of those unable to pay became divisive, reflecting the lack of realism about the nature of the situation:

> They were reluctant, for instance, to evict workers who could not pay their rent; in fact, they led anti-eviction campaigns and took in people who had been evicted from other buildings. According to an early resident of the Coops, one woman

Figure 5.42. Clarence Stein. Phipps Garden Apartments, completed at Sunnyside Gardens in 1929. An evaluation of perimeter configuration possibilities was used to arrive at the final site plan. The analysis was typical of the increasingly self-conscious and non-historicist design methods which developed in the 1920s, especially in relation to housing.

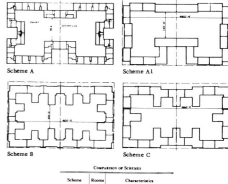

Scheme A   Scheme A1

Scheme B   Scheme C

Scheme	Rooms	Characteristics
Scheme A	214	1 exterior court — good interior court
Scheme A1	244	4 exterior courts — fair interior court
Scheme B	256	12 elevator "T" units — crowded interior courts
Scheme F	256	10 elevator "T" units — crowded interior courts
Scheme C	246	8 elevator "T" units — crowded interior courts
Scheme S	228	6 elevator "T" units — good interior courts
Final	236	6 elevator "T" units — good interior courts

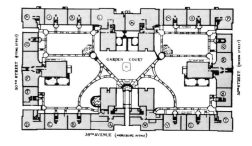

simply refused to pay her rent on the theory that she "couldn't be evicted—it would cause too much of a scandal if the *Daily Forward* found out." By the early thirties, the board of directors maintained control of the buildings only by working out a moratorium on amortization payments with the mortgage holder. In the early forties, when another plan to keep control in the board's hands would have required raising rents one dollar a room, the cooperators voted against the raise, partly on political grounds. By 1945, the Workers Cooperative Colony was officially out of business—its members merely tenants of two privately owned buildings on Bronx Park East.[128]

The Shalom Aleichem Houses experienced economic failure first, having passed into receivership of the bank in 1929. By 1931 it had been sold to a private landlord. During this transition, the cooperative continued to function, oblivious to the impending new financial order. Around June 1932 it set up a rent relief fund, and worked out a verbal agreement with the landlord to pay half of unemployed tenants' rents, with the remainder to be delinquent until each had found a job. In August, however, the landlord began evicting forty tenants anyway, and one of New York City's most publicized rent strikes ensued. Within a week, forty of the tenants who refused to pay rent out of sympathy were also given eviction notices, and four tenants had already been removed from their apartments. The tenants claimed gross injustice, citing the cooperative character of the buildings. They argued that unlike other buildings emptied by the Depression, theirs remained occupied. They advertised for another building, threatening to move en masse. They picketed constantly while unsuccessfully taking their case to what they termed a "capitalistic" municipal court. They fought the possibility of punitive loss of welfare assistance from the Emergency Home Relief Bureau because of their activities. The tenants were also addressed by Norman Thomas, Socialist candidate for President, who helped fight a "blacklisting" of the strikers which was threatened to be circulated by the Bronx Landlord's Protective Association. Following a number of eviction orders, an agreement was finally reached directly with the landlord, who reduced rents by 5 percent, and placed 2 1/2 percent of rent totals in a fund for unemployed tenant arrears, with abandonment of all eviction proceedings.[129] With this agreement, a truce was begun which lasted, with frequent difficulties, until 1949, when the building changed hands.

Like all of the cooperatives, the original communal ideals at Shalom Aleichem lasted through the differing economic circumstances until the founding generation began to fade. Over the years there were many crises, most prominently and inevitably ideological, between the socialist and communist factions. But the real political death knell came at the beginning of the 1950s, with the McCarthy-era political repression, when the elders of the cooperatives were old. Commitments of the second generation were tempered by the promise of the 1950s prosperity, and by mainstream American values which by then had moved far from the urbane socialist vision in the Bronx. Calvin Trillin wrote of the Co-ops that "simply having the address 2700 Bronx Park East was thought to be enough to put people in jeopardy. Some people chose to move away for the same reason that they had chosen to move in twenty-five years before—living in the Coops could be considered part of their political identity."[130] Presumably, like thousands of others, many moved to the new suburbs, which fit so well into this massive transformation of American culture. By the time of the third generation, there could be no question. By 1967 the *New York Post* had made it official. Those who could not make it to Westchester could leave for Co-op City,[131] for an urbanism of very different ideological significance, and for a cooperative lacking ideology. At the Amalgamated, the economic advantages of cooperative life have survived, but the ideology has waned. All else of the other cooperatives has disappeared, except the buildings. At the Shalom Aleichem Houses, the Woman's Club was the last to go, having passed from the scene in 1979.[132]

6

Aesthetics and Realities

HE garden apartment was a short-lived phenomenon in New York City development, reaching its apogee in the 1920s. It was (and still is) among the most livable housing in New York. It set a standard for urban housing that has remained unmatched since. Fundamental to the success of the garden apartment was the balance between building mass and open space so that a level of proximity was maintained which involved a strict definition of the public realm to be shared by neighbors. Important to this neighboring was a sense of theater, which required use of architectural language bordering on the scenographic. The language of the "garden" of the garden apartment, together with its enclosing facades, was critical to the transformation of housing from a consequence of economic formulas to a unique environment. This entered a realm of fantasy, providing every building with an identity that called forth particular places or tenants. The garden was a critical symbol of arrival for the new middle class, while also facilitating the making of a kind of public theater in which the most joyous myths of urban existence could be acted out.

The scenographic devices tended to reflect rather eclectic sources which relied primarily on the realm of the architect's invention. Andrew Thomas was one of the most inventive. From his earliest projects, Thomas carried his garden apartment experimentation through to stylistic explorations of considerable latitude. One of these, built in 1917 at Kew Gardens, Queens, on Metropolitan Avenue near Lefferts Avenue, was typical. It was described as "an adaptation of the Indian style with open courts, characteristic roof lines of belvederes, and spacious garden effect." Even the light gray and green color scheme was carefully calculated to be in "harmony with the rural surroundings of the building."[1] At Homewood, the reference was Tuscan; at the Château, French Renaissance, and at the Towers, Moorish; at Thomas Garden Apartments, it was Japanese. Thomas' sensibility was not unique. Ginsbern's courtyard entry at Noonan Plaza, with its pond and stream, bridge, goldfish, and swans, surrounded by Mayan Deco facades, was one of the best-known examples of the genre (see figures 5.30, 5.20, 5.36, 5.27). While this kind of architectural scenography proliferated in the 1920s, it was nevertheless a fragile sensibility, not functional in the strictest sense of economy, and subject to competition from many of the other stylistic currents then emerging.

Several of the stylistic currents of the 1920s involved a relationship to European developments of the same period. These were promulgated primarily on an informal basis. Some of the most important connections were made by the European architects who worked in New York offices, attracted by the jobs the 1920s boom provided. This situation led to the transliteration of certain contemporary strains in European architectural language to a very different New York context. An interesting example was the contrast between the two buildings designed for the Workers Cooperative Colony in the Bronx (see figure 5.32). There were variations in the plan organization of both projects, but the most notable differences were evident in the facades. The first project, designed by Springsteen and Goldhammer, was clothed in the conservative English Tudor which was a staple of New York's middle-class housing, not exactly a proclamation of the progressive ideals of the colony. The second project, designed by Herman Jessor, was highly influenced by the Teutonic expressionism prevalent in Germany and Austria, incorporating decorative brick and stucco patterns integrated with highly abstract and decorative massing. This latter departure was said to have been the work of Stefan S. Sajo, a young Hungarian architect employed by Jessor, who undoubtedly brought expressionist influences with him from Europe.[2]

Like the second building of the Workers Cooperative Colony, the Amalgamated project on the Lower East Side was significant for its stylistic initiatives—again coming from Germany and Austria. The large arched entries to the internal courtyard bore a strong resemblance to the Karl Marx Hof in Vienna, one of a number of municipal projects completed in Vienna in the 1920s.[3] For modest housing, the decoration was rich. It included abstract geometrical articulation at the building entrances and textured brickwork on the building facades (figure 6.1). The architect who designed the project was Roland Wank, another young Hungarian working in the office of Springsteen and Goldhammer.[4] Wank went on to become the chief architect of the Tennessee Valley Authority, where he brought a modernist influence to bear on an extraordinary range of work. When the Lower East Side project received an award in 1930 from the New York chapter of the American Institute of Architects, the press noted that it had been judged in direct competition with some of the most prestigious and expensive housing in Manhattan. The AIA especially commended the "complete elimination of meaningless ornament and the sincerity with which they used the essential elements of the design to achieve aesthetic results."[5] Thus the new aesthetic approach, arriving via Hamburg or Vienna, was admired above all for its economy of means, in preference to the more ostentatious Beaux-Arts idiom.

The roles of both Sajo and Wank in bringing European modernist vocabulary to the United States were undoubtedly typical of countless other situations in American architectural offices as the influence of the Beaux-Arts began to wane. These accounts typify how new developments in Europe tended to be transformed in the United States, where the marketplace cleansed European stylistic conventions of their political impurities, and where the conscious use of architectural language as a means of political expression was quite uncommon. Perhaps typi-

Figure 6.1. Springsteen and Goldhammer. Photo of the Grand Street building for the Amalgamated Clothing Workers Union, showing the strong visual similarity to the Germanic Expressionist work in Europe in general and to the Karl Marx Hof in Vienna in particular.

cally American was the fact that the Amalgamated Clothing Workers or the Workers Cooperative Colony saw little connection between their extensive political agendas and their new buildings. Styles passed freely from one purpose to another in a most eclectic fashion, as witnessed by the diversity of language. This eclecticism was fed by the enormous prosperity of the decade, with its exuberance and experimentation. But the contribution of transient foreign labor in architectural offices cannot be discounted as an important factor contributing to this diversity. Attracted by the lucrative New York market, this work force came and went. Given the nature of American design practice, these architects were frequently assigned significant design responsibility within architectural offices.

The same period also witnessed stylistic changes which were far more indigenous to New York and to the specific political economy of the moment. These changes shared characteristics with European developments, but tended to be isolated in their origins. A new American functionalism was developing around the issue of housing. As in Europe, this had to do at least in part with the growth of the middle class, and the resultant increase in new housing production for a significant proportion of the population. The expansion of outlook brought into view the real issues of cost and efficiency. At the same time, the ideal of reduced coverage was lurking behind much of the new compositional experimentation which emerged. Andrew Thomas always managed to combine both concerns in his eclecticism. At his Metropolitan Life housing, which was generated by the most stringent economies because of the rent restrictions imposed by law, the new social functionalism was prefigured (figures 6.2 and 6.3). Thomas attempted to meet economic constraints through a rational and exhaustive analysis of the balance between site coverage and construction efficiency (figure 6.3). The site plan was somewhat better than earlier ones, especially in relation to construction simplicity. The apartments were tight, with nothing wasted. Using new techniques from the social sciences, Thomas had organized public meetings with a representative tenant sample to help formulate the unit designs. Innovations included the "Pullman" or "breakfast nook," a small built-in eating space which was rented only

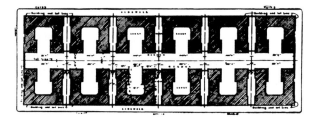

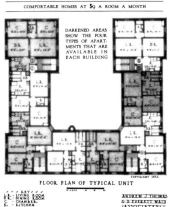

Figure 6.2. Andrew Thomas. Typical block plan for the Metropolitan Life Insurance Company Project in Long Island City (left). Completed in 1924, it used a highly efficient version of the U prototype, with a coverage of 53 percent.

Figure 6.3. Andrew Thomas. Typical building plan for the Metropolitan Life Insurance Company Project in Long Island City (right), with eight apartments per floor, and a very low rentals.

AESTHETICS AND REALITIES   167

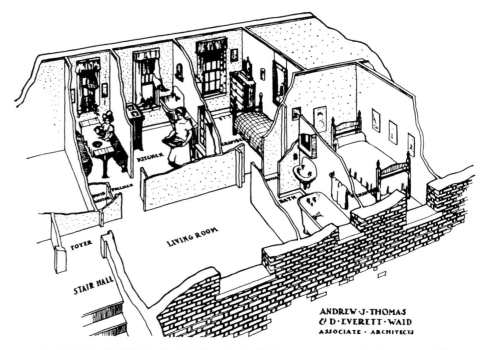

SECTION OF INTERIOR OF TYPICAL APARTMENT—APARTMENT HOUSES FOR THE
METROPOLITAN LIFE INSURANCE COMPANY, NEW YORK CITY.

as a half room.[6] Compared with tenements, the Metropolitan units achieved a
degree of spatial amenity that definitively placed them in the category of "apartment," for approximately the same rent (figure 6.4). The functionalism of the
planning is apparent in the appearance of the project (figure 6.5). No decoration
was applied to the facades. Instead, visual interest was created by the scale of
the massive brick volumes and a repetitive pattern of different openings. The
buildings were a severe composition of solid and void, reflecting the function of
the spaces behind. At the roof, the traditional cornice was replaced by a simple
horizontal band and a parapet that stepped up at the stairs to represent that
change in function. This approach constrasted sharply with the elaborate Beaux-
Arts facades of West End Avenue, or even with Thomas' own eclecticism in other
projects.

Thomas' functional arguments balanced the limits of plan efficiency with a
coverage of 52 percent. But soon thereafter, projects began to further reduce coverage, paving the way for a new urbanism in which nature, rather than building,
became the dominant presence. A key precedent in this transition was Sunnyside
Gardens, developed by the City Housing Corporation in 1924. The City Housing
Corporation was a limited dividend company that extended the philanthropic legacy of the City and Suburban Homes Company as "socialized business at six percent." It was formed to "improve living conditions, reduce rents, and influence
the future of cities."[7] Sunnyside became the first important public platform for

Figure 6.5. Andrew Thomas. Photo of the
Metropolitan Life Insurance Company Project in
Long Island City shortly after completion in
1924.

Figure 6.6. Clarence Stein, Henry Wright, and Frederick Ackerman. Sunnyside Gardens Development, begun in 1924 as a cooperative for the limited-profit City Housing Corporation; located along the Queensboro Subway in Long Island City.

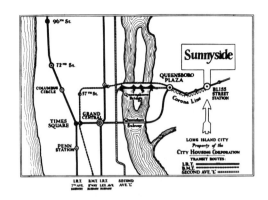

Figure 6.7. Clarence Stein, Henry Wright, and Frederick Ackerman. Sunnyside Gardens site plan showing the higher-density Phipps Garden Apartments, which was designed by Clarence Stein and completed in 1929.

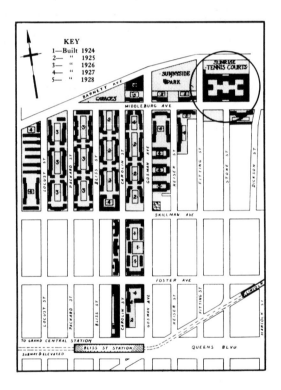

A plan of the Sunnyside development on Long Island, showing the location of the Phipps Garden Apartments

the ideas of the corporation's architects, Clarence Stein, Henry Wright, and Frederick Ackerman. It was developed on 1,100 building lots in Long Island City, near the Bliss Street station of the Queensboro subway (figures 6.6 and 6.7). Sunnyside was admittedly biased toward middle incomes, and competed directly with the private single- and two-family tract houses that comprised much of the housing

stock in Queens in the 1920s (figure 6.8). The density at Sunnyside was almost five times less than that of Metropolitan Homes. This was reflected in the site development costs per family, which were approximately four times greater than those for Metropolitan Homes. Metropolitan's 58 percent coverage was reduced to 28 percent (figure 6.9).[8]

Sunnyside's coverage remained the lowest of any garden apartment development completed in the 1920s. The impact of the increased site cost was partially offset by the extreme simplification of the building forms. These were reduced to linear rows in order to minimize construction costs (figure 6.10). The extremely low coverage at Sunnyside was incorporated into the same 200-by-800-foot gridiron as the surrounding developer housing. Instead of private yards, continuous landscaping completely surrounded the rows of two- and four-story houses and apartments, even on the street sides. Subsequent additions to Sunnyside between 1924 and 1928 gradually increased densities and coverage. When completed in 1928, Sunnyside housed 1,231 families,[9] totaling slightly over 1 family per lot of the original 1,100 building lots within the site. The Sunnyside block plans were extremely simple in comparison with the mainstream 1920s garden apartment. The traditional perimeter block form was compromised by the use of row housing, which did not have the same capacity to turn the corners of the block, resulting in discontinuous walls. Crenellation of the facades was reduced to several mini-

Figure 6.8. Photo of typical developer housing in Queens in the 1920s, which was an object of reform as represented by Sunnyside.

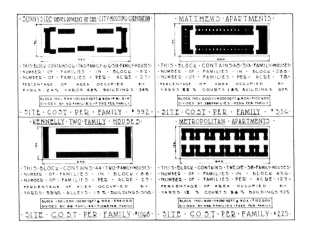

mal offsets. In general, the level of spatial enclosure and functional articulation of the public area was minimal, justified only through vaguely defined social activities, supported by a quasi-socialistic conception of community life. The eclectic scenography of the garden apartment was replaced by a less refined naturalism, which in its time was no less powerful a source of community cohesion, especially in the political ideals it embodied.

Lewis Mumford, a longtime Sunnyside resident, argued that its new architectural order was more politically powerful than the old, presumably because Sunnyside embodied political ideals at all. The labor cooperatives, for example, which built in an eclectic expanse of styles, seemed oblivious to the potential for

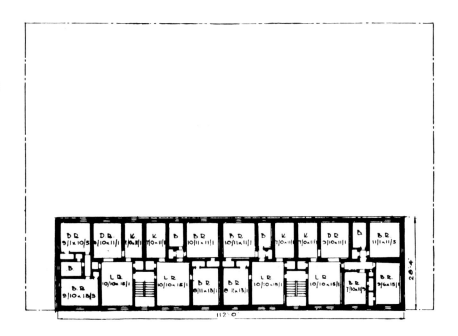

an architecture that directly expressed their political ideals. According to Mumford, it was Sunnyside's "visible coherence in the architecture with a sufficient number of local meeting rooms for group activities" that provided a catalyst whereby "a robust political life with effective collective action and a sense of renewed public responsibility has swiftly grown up." Mumford argued against the scenographic, advancing what became a principal argument for the new architecture:

> It is on the purely instrumental physical services that we must practice the most stringent economy, even parsimony; it is on the political and educational services that we must spend with a lavish hand. This means a new order of design and a different type of designer: It means that emphasis will shift progressively from the stage-set to the drama, and that the handling of the social activities and realtionships will engage the fuller attention of the planner.[10]

In spite of Mumford's arguments, the Sunnyside community did not possess the same degree of political coherence as the Workers Cooperative Colony or Shalom Aleichem Houses, but then, it lacked an equivalent religious and cultural adhesive. Sunnyside had to politicize the uninitiated, which it did accomplish with good results, to the extent that the community has retained a strong identity to this day. Like the labor cooperatives, it had to survive the famous rent strikes of 1933. During the strike residents withheld mortgage payments when the Depression forced the City Housing Corporation to sell to an insurance company. The insurance company began evicting residents who could not keep up their payments. Almost 60 percent lost their homes.[11]

Toward the end of the 1920s, the large number of housing projects built using reduced coverage had become the object of considerable study, providing the genesis for modern "housing research."[12] Such study led to improved techniques, not only for the design of the projects, but for their analysis as well. The "design" and "analysis" began to be seen as an interrelated process. Project plans were dissected into fragments, analyzed, and then recombined in various ways, creating detailed structuralist studies that usually led to comparisons of social and monetary costs for a series of alternative physical schemes or parts of schemes. Such studies could also work in reverse. Hypothetical schemes, assembled from various combinations of design fragments, were analyzed in order to choose the most workable solution. Thus an aesthetic of assemblage began to evolve, and reinforced the socioeconomic impetus for fragmentation. While similar methods had always been used in the design of buildings, the process was becoming increasingly systematic and self-conscious. More than Sunnyside, for example, the design of the adjacent Phipps Garden Apartments by Clarence Stein in 1929 (see figure 5.42) evolved from a systematic evaluation of a number of hypothetical schemes which combined fragmentary cluster units in various configurations.[13] Henry Wright was perhaps the most prominent advocate of the new design research. He recognized that certain properties of housing form could be categorized into types and used for analytic description and study. Typical of his approach was an analysis, published in 1929,[14] which explored the properties of fragments commonly used by designers in the assemblage of housing (figure 6.11).

Wright also engaged the issue of reduced coverage. In 1929 he expanded

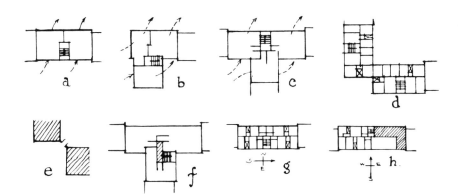

Figure 6.11. Henry Wright. Analytic sketches of possible techniques for joining apartment clusters, published in 1929.

Figure 6.12. Henry Wright. Analysis of Sunnyside Gardens and Paul Lawrence Dunbar Apartments published in 1929, attempting to show the greater internal spatial efficiency of the Sunnyside buildings, owing to their simpler configuration permitted by the lower densities.

FIRST·FLOOR·PLAN
"A"—SIMPLE PERIMETER, SUNNYSIDE PLAN.

PLAN OF 2ⁿᵈ 3ᵈ 4ᵗᴴ & 5ᵗᴴ FLOORS
"B"—DOUBLE PERIMETER. DUNBAR PLAN.

PLAN OF FIRST FLOOR
"C"—DOUBLE PERIMETER, DUNBAR PLAN.

Thomas' earlier reduced coverage argument based on building shape to include the effects of site composition on construction efficiency, comparing the early Sunnyside plans with a portion of the Dunbar plan.[15] Sunnyside, because of its simple linear configuration and lower site coverage, was shown to contain 1.6 percent more usable square footage overall than Dunbar (figure 6.12). According to Wright, a key factor in the reduced efficiency of Dunbar was its higher coverage, which necessitated a tight perimeter development, with valuable ground floor space removed by the passageways linking internal courtyards to the street. The amount of such "pass through" space is shown in the shaded portions of plan C. By comparison, Sunnyside, with its extremely low coverage and isolated buildings, required practically no internal circulation space, since circulation could occur around the buildings rather than through them. Wright was careful to point out, however, that in terms of "social" cost, the analysis was not as definitive. Dunbar appeared to have certain advantages over Sunnyside, including more rooms of ideal shape (approximating a square), and more rooms with double exposure. For recreation, Wright favored the large, concentrated open space of Sunnyside, in comparison with the smaller, fragmented spaces at Dunbar. This was an expedient judgment, however, since Sunnyside was cheaper to build. In any event, the use of concentrated open space soon became a hallmark of the new site planning.

In the 1920s the work of Henry Atterbury Smith, who had pioneered an earlier generation of philanthropic housing including the open stair tenement (see figure 4.22), paralleled Thomas' and Wright's housing research. His work was far more exploratory, however. In 1917 Smith set a precedent with the first theoretical work proposing that building geometry could deviate from the geometry of the New York gridiron. He suggested that buildings did not have to be oriented along lot lines and argued that other geometries, based on purely functional considerations such as light and view, might be superimposed on the gridiron. Smith published a series of diagrams illustrating an open stair building in the form of an L, arranged at forty-five degrees to a gridiron street, to maximize light, ventilation, and view (figure 6.13).[16] This "sawtooth" plan produced a number of identical entry spaces adjacent to the street, and the scale of the large interior garden became somewhat reduced by the pattern.

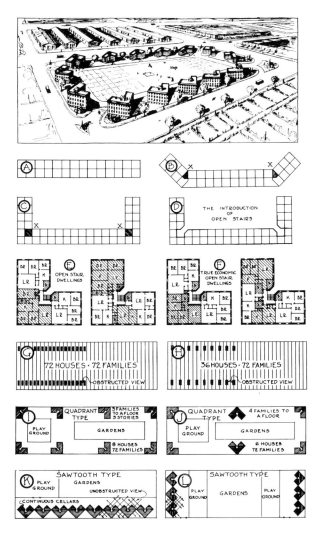

Figure 6.13. Henry Atterbury Smith. Analysis published in 1917 using a "sawtooth" geometry for the perimeter block form; the first housing proposal in New York City to advocate breaking the rectilinear geometry of the gridiron.

This series of diagrams represented a methodological precedent consistent with the attitude found in Smith's earlier work. The design solution was a direct outgrowth of the method, which used a composite of functional rules to eliminate formal possibilities. The almost total lack of historicist influence was notable: the sawtooth forms were even more purist than the stairs of the Vanderbilt East River Homes project (see figures 4.19, 4.20, 4.21). Smith also applied his analysis to a hypothetical project for suburban worker housing (figure 6.14).[17] A plot of land 100 acres square was organized along a service road which circled a private "park." The sawtooth housing was placed around the inner edge of the service road and created a circular enclosure of 1,500 feet in diameter. Automobiles were parked in garages at the entries to the site to enforce an entirely pedestrian environment.

By the early 1920s Henry Atterbury Smith was experimenting with further

AESTHETICS AND REALITIES   175

 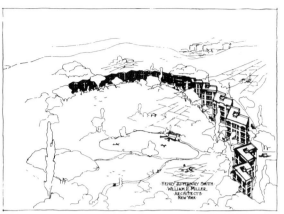

Figure 6.14. Henry Atterbury Smith. Analysis published in 1917 applying the sawtooth geometry to a hypothetical suburban working-class development with a large internal park and the exclusion of automobiles to garages at the periphery.

economies involving adaptation of low-rise housing form to the elevator. In 1921 he designed the Cathedral Ayrocourt Apartments in Manhattan between West 122nd and 123rd streets on Amsterdam Avenue and Broadway, which was typical of his approach (figure 6.15).[18] A single elevator in each of two six-story buildings (only one is shown) carried tenants on the upper floors to the roof, from which they could walk down to their apartments. Tenants close to the ground walked up in the usual way. The roof was landscaped as an amenity for all the tenants. This scheme succeeded in reducing both the number of elevators and the cost of each elevator by eliminating stops. The 1919 law permitting automatic elevators was a source of design innovation for Thomas as well as Smith. Both were interested in the moderate-cost application of elevator technology to emerging middle-income housing, especially to the moderate-height garden apartment. When the low-cost self-service elevator first appeared, its potential to change housing form remained unexplored by most architects. For example, the first elevator garden apartment building in Queens was a six-story structure at Forest Hills Gardens, poorly organized along a double-loaded corridor (figure 6.16). It was designed and built by the Frederick F. French company in 1917.[19]

Smith's Mesa Verde housing was more radical. The project, which was com-

Figure 6.15. Henry Atterbury Smith. Cathedral Ayrcourt Apartments, a philanthropic project, completed in 1921 for the Open Stair Dwellings Company, and an important experiment with elevator economies; tenants on the upper floors went directly to the roof, from which they walked down to their apartments.

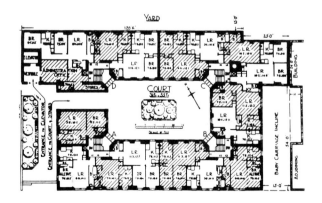

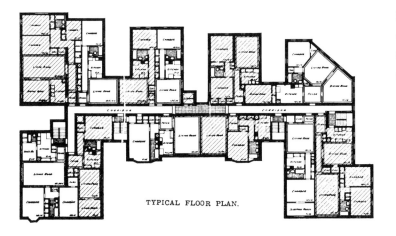

TYPICAL FLOOR PLAN.

Figure 6.16. Frederick F. French Company. Apartment house at Forest Hills Gardens; completed in 1917, said to be the first residential elevator building in Queens.

pleted in 1926, assimilated many of his ideas of the previous decade. The Mesa Verde was constructed by the Open Stair Dwellings Company in Jackson Heights, on an entire block between 90th and 91st streets and 35th and 36th avenues. It was the only built example of Smith's 1917 block analysis. Six closed L buildings lining both sides of a block were organized at forty-five degrees to the gridiron (figures 6.17 and 6.18).[20] The ends of the block provided recreation space with the possibility of later substituting four more buildings. Each building was six

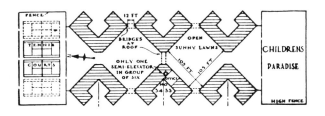

Figure 6.17. Henry Atterbury Smith. The Mesa Verde site plan. Completed as a philanthropic project in 1926 by the Open Stair Dwellings Company in Jackson Heights, it uses the sawtooth principle as developed previously.

Figure 6.18. Henry Atterbury Smith. The Mesa Verde, perspective and plan study for the perimeter block.

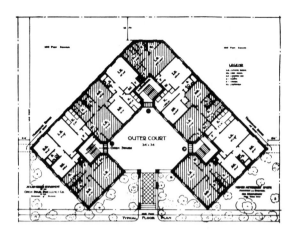

stories high, modeled on a Flagg-type plan with one corner removed. Together they contained 323 apartments (figure 6.19). In contrast to Thomas' Metropolitan Homes, this project incorporated an elevator. Smith applied his walk-down system, using only one central elevator to the roof. A series of "hurricane bridges" connected the elevator building to the roofs of the other buildings. Depending on the location of their apartments, tenants could either walk up from the ground level or walk down from the roof.

Like Metropolitan Homes, the Mesa Verde facades used little applied decoration except for simple horizontal bands to differentiate bottom, middle, and top. Visual interest came from the building massing (figures 6.20 and 6.21). The spactial composition was extraordinary, with the intersecting diagonals of the buildings connected by the bridges and walkways which helped frame the ground-level interior garden, and created a striking pattern against the sky. The project was significant from almost any point of view, even for its name. "Mesa Verde" was taken from the Southwest Native American cliff dwellings in Colorado, which Smith visited in 1925. Smith attempted to make the connection between the ancient dwellings, "four and five stories high, with open, ladder-like stairs and flat, useful roofs," and his own project, with "open stairs, roof gardens, bridges connecting the roofs."[21] The analogy was significant for its conscious use of historical precedent outside of the influence of European culture.

The rigorous emphasis on "functionality" in numerous projects and proposals by the mid-1920s, including both Metropolitan Homes and the Mesa Verde, was largely a reaction to the economic constraints of housing philanthropy. In spite of the general level of economic prosperity, the budgets of architect-designed, moderate-cost housing and public works did not promulgate the same historicist eclecticism that was still the hallmark of most building. Through experimentation with new sources of visual organization, architectural sensibilities gradually changed. This process spread from housing and public works to other building by the 1930s. The new sensibilities emerged both in housing, with the work of architects like Edward T. Potter and Henry Atterbury Smith, and in public works, where engineering considerations took precedence over historicism. By the early

Figure 6.20. Henry Atterbury Smith. Photo of Mesa Verde, contrasted with the surrounding developer housing, taken shortly after completion of the project.

Figure 6.21. Henry Atterbury Smith. Photo of the internal courtyard of Mesa Verde, with the ''hurricane bridge'' connecting two buildings.

AESTHETICS AND REALITIES   179

1920s the great national public works projects like the hydroelectric developments on the Tennessee River at Mussel Shoals began to substitute social-functionalist vocabulary for historicism. In both housing and public works a functionalist approach connoted progressive political and economic views. But unlike the new work in Europe, the architectural expression was at best guarded. The Mesa Verde remained about as radical a conception as can be found in New York. Even Roland Wank, who contributed heavily to the early years of modernism in the United States, could not reconcile the inertia of building tradition with a new social vision: "We cannot make revolutionary improvements any more than we can pull rabbits out of a hat. Until mass production puts materials of the twentieth century—steel, concrete, aluminum, glass, cork, rubber, resin compositions, etc.— closer within our reach, we are confined to much the same materials as our forefathers used, and they have already made a pretty thorough job of exploring all the possibilities of lumber, brick, stone and mortar."[22]

By 1926 the Mesa Verde was as radical an alternative to traditional housing as anything realized in the Netherlands or Germany. But in the United States it had little company. In Europe a prodigious amount of new work and thinking had developed in the postwar years, much of it far more challenging to the inertia of building tradition. All of it was far more directly tied to the expression of the progressive politics of the era.[23] The large new suburban garden apartment projects, such as the German *Seidlungen,* were built with direct government subsidy, while in New York City private housing development was widespread until the depression. The scale of design for the European work was vast in comparison with that of New York City. Frequently the *Seidlungen* were designed totally according to one architect's conception, while in New York City design was done on a block-by-block basis, even for large-scale developments like Jackson Heights. The limitations of the New York gridiron block tended to create isolated housing clusters with strong perimeters and clearly defined spaces. In the new European work, the lack of formal site constaints produced larger and less defined public spaces.

While the 1920s suburban extensions within New York City were derivative of an earlier generation of European perimeter housing like Charlottenburg (see figure 5.13), the avant-garde European work had moved to functional concerns having to do more exclusively with open space and idealized exposure to the sun. And in comparison with the eclectic functionalism of the Mesa Verde, they appeared to be rather academic and reductive in their outlook. Called *Zielenbau* by the Germans, the new planning consisted of parallel rows open at the ends, and usually organized in single directions to obtain ideal east-west orientation. In Europe the nexus of this tendency was the Congrès International d'Architecture Moderne (CIAM), founded in 1928 to promulgate the new modernist ideals. In 1930, the third CIAM meeting in Brussels was dedicated to "Rational Lot Division," and provided an extensive documentation of the new *zielenbau* projects.[24] The widely publicized Rothenberg Housing Project at Kassel, Germany, designed by Otto Haesler in 1930, was typical of the approach (figure 6.22). The project was introduced to United States architects in the housing section of the Inter-

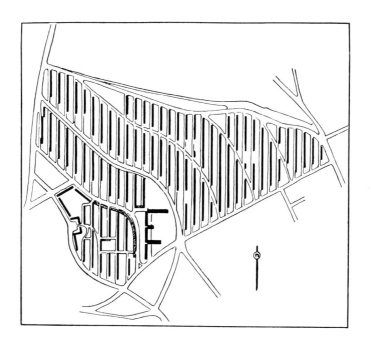

Figure 6.22. Otto Haesler. Rothenberg Housing Project at Kassel, Germany. Completed around 1930, it used the *Zielenbau* configuration of parallel rows which had developed in Europe; exhibited and acclaimed at the International Exhibition of Modern Architecture at the Museum of Modern Art in 1932.

national Exhibition of Modern Architecture at the Museum of Modern Art in New York in 1932.[25] By then the stage was set in the United States for the new European academic functionalism, loosely defined as the "International Style." In the evolution of urban housing in the United States, the introduction of the international style in 1932 represented a watershed for the dominant ideology of the next half century.

In many ways the period of the early 1930s proved to be reminiscent of Chicago in 1893, strengthening a developing United States tradition of open competition in the stylistic marketplace. But the critical difference in 1932 was the Great Depression. At no previous point in United States history was the priority for a new architectural expression so transparent; in the depths of capitalism's greatest crisis, a "revolutionary" declaration of its renewal was an imperative. For architectural patronage, the international style addressed this need. Philip Johnson and Henry Russell Hitchcock, Jr., conceived this breakthrough after returning from their European tour of 1931, with the complicity of the forces behind the Museum of Modern Art, newly opened in 1929. In the face of crisis, the attempt to redefine "architecture" was a desperate one. The new currents in European modernism were considered superior to the approach of "American functionalists," who were accused of "claiming to be builders first" and "surely seldom architects in the fullest sense of the word."[26] Within this framework, the tradition of United States social functionalism was set aside, replaced by a more intellectualized functional style with European origins. It coincided with the establishment in 1932 of a Department of Architecture within the museum, under the directorship of Philip Johnson. In the same year as the exhibition, Johnson and

Hitchcock published *The International Style,* a pattern book for the new tendency, which included an aesthetic criticism of seventy-five selected architectural projects and a revisionist history of the previous half century of architectural development.

The 1920s produced a great stylistic confluence in the United States that ranged from Beaux-Arts historicism to the lineage of Sullivan and Wright, from the new social-functionalism of housing and public works, to the reconstituted decoration of Deco-Moderne. In New York City, however, most monumental building was obliged to continue Beaux-Arts historicism until new economic and cultural realities could be absorbed in another aesthetic of equal cultural status. It was the new European academic functionalism which provided a way out of the dilemma.

The new European work was said to be "functionalist," but its superiority was linked to the new academicism. Philip Johnson wrote that "the best work of the [European] functionalists is . . . distinguished more in theory than in practice from the work of those who accept the new aesthetic possibilities of the art of architecture."[27] Practitioners of Deco-Moderne were said by Hitchcock to have "borrowed the tricks of design and ornament of the Paris Exhibition of 1925 without any real conception of what modern architecture may be."[28] The Sullivan lineage was heralded, and Beaux-Arts historicism was denounced. Frank Lloyd Wright was designated as the most important American architect. His influence on pre–World War I Europeans was emphasized. Johnson argued that the new European work had healed the nineteenth-century schism between architecture and engineering, "based . . . on modern engineering and on modern provision for function."[29] His perception, however, seems to have been limited to architects' aesthetic interpretations of contemporary engineering accomplishments, rather than to an integration of the two disciplines which had long since gone their disparate ways.

While Hitchcock and Johnson took particular care to distinguish between "architecture" and "building,"[30] it was "housing" which appears to have been the most problematic category. "Housing" was segregated into a separate section of the exhibition, organized by Catherine Bauer, Clarence Stein, and Henry Wright, with a separate introduction within the exhibition catalogue by Lewis Mumford. This segregation was curious, especially in light of the new European work which tended to legitimize housing as an architectural problem. One could even argue that the whole conception of the new European architectural sensibilities revolved around housing—or at least around a definition of housing expanded to include the utilitarian uses of architecture for the enrichment of daily life.

In his introduction to the exhibition catalogue, Mumford argued that "the building of houses constitutes the major architectural work of any civilization," and that "the house cannot remain outside of the currents of modern civilization."[31] In *The International Style,* Hitchcock and Johnson disagreed with this position, arguing that only under certain circumstances could housing be considered worthy of the term "architecture." They noted that the European functionalists might avoid doing a single-family house because of its lack of progressive political significance. But Hitchcock and Johnson countered that individual minimum dwellings within housing projects were not architecture because they were "so simple and so little specialized that they are well within a realm of building." The large-scale project, however, was said to "offer so many opportunities for arbitrary choice that it may become architecture."[32] And in any event, for Hitchcock and Johnson the compositional principles of the new European *Seidlungen* pattern making represented the most likely way to elevate housing to a realm of architectural significance.

In the United States, by the 1930s, a strong national "movement" had evolved for housing problems and town planning, reaching beyond provincial tenement reform efforts in isolated cities. This development was said to have passed a critical threshold between 1910 and 1912 when the formation of the National Housing Association created the first organization to deal with housing issues on a national basis.[33] It also reflected a period of unprecedented international exchange within the emerging housing and planning disciplines, in which Americans had participated substantially. International activity ranged from the development of the garden cities movement to town planning, to housing reform. These were also related to the larger political movements of the day, including the pre–World War I peace movement. In the period between 1900 and 1913 alone, it is estimated that 2,271 international conferences on various subjects were held in Europe and North America.[34]

In the United States the new housing and city planning activity was partially a reaction against the "City Beautiful" movement of the previous two decades, which was more devoted to the architectural adornment of cities than to the architecture of daily life. It also reflected the emergence of new methods related to urban studies, especially in the social sciences, and the beginning development of the city planning profession.[35] Concerns for housing and town planning developed credibility. Among those architects with an interest in the social side of practice, the new activity was a refuge from the limitations of the Beaux-Arts. By the 1920s "housing" had become a strong component of architectural activity. By 1930 a new discipline had begun to emerge, as the work of figures such as Henry Wright and Carol Aronovici in New York demonstrated.

In spite of its appellation, the international style was a reaction against the previous era of internationalism, and sought to cleanse from architectural discourse most of the social agenda which had evolved to form the revolutionary body of new work in Europe. For the United States, the "American *Seidlungen*," presumably the 1920s garden apartments which had grown from these same concerns, were dismissed by Hitchcock and Johnson as "sometimes excellent illustrations of sociological theory, but . . . seldom examples of sound modern building and never works of architectural distinction."[36] In dismissing this work, and in an attempt to drive a wedge between "architecture" and "housing," Hitchcock and Johnson contributed to a trend which by the 1950s had destroyed the legitimacy of urban moderate-cost housing as a challenge worthy of the attention of the architectural profession. In general, the stance of Hitchcock and Johnson can be interpreted as unsympathetic to the broader housing movement in the United States and the implications for architectural values and practice it represented. With the Great Depression as a catalyst, the two men served to reinforce the "aesthetic" side of architectural practice in the face of economic crisis, providing an antidote to the growing political radicalism of a profession racked with unemployment and uncertainty. They promoted a moralism grounded in aesthetics rather than political action.

Throughout the 1920s, while most American experimentation in housing tended to be limited to the "apartment in a garden," the avant-garde in France and Germany was focused on a fundamentally new kind of urbanism. The infrastructure of the nineteenth-century city was replaced by vast parklike settings, with the traditional streets and building walls sublimated by nature. These ideas had begun to surface in their most archaic form after the turn of the century in France, most notably with the work of Tony Garnier and his "Industrial City."[37] In contrast to that of the United States, much of the European housing design and theory incorporated a consciously polemical approach. While Europe had many practical housing researchers, such as the German architect Alexander Klein, whose studies Henry Wright admired,[38] there was also a strong utopian movement. It had no equivalent in the United States. In the United States even the most radical innovations of the 1920s were part of a historical continuum extending from before the turn of the century, and were directly responsive to the practical realities of the economics of housing production. In New York City only the work of Henry Atterbury Smith came close to the sensibility of the European avant-garde.

In Europe the "city in the park" first surfaced in its most radical form with the theories of Auguste Perret, who envisioned an urbanism of high towers within a park (figure 6.23). In the early 1920s Perret's images were elaborated by his pupil Le Corbusier. While Perret was an architect and engineer best known for his pioneering work in reinforced concrete, his urban vision represented a precedent of far-reaching significance.[39] His thinking was substantially influenced by the first tall commercial buildings in Manhattan, such as the 55-story Woolworth Building designed by Cass Gilbert. At the time of its completion in 1913, the Woodworth Building was the tallest building in the world. Perret envisioned such structures adapted to a myriad of urban functions, including housing. He viewed his proposals as an answer to the question of housing production, with a massive application of the legacy of technological innovation that had produced the early high-rise apartment. Perret's fascination with architectural developments in the United States assumed a different dimension than that of other Europeans like Berlage, Oud, and Widjeveld, for example, who limited the scope of their interests to Richardson, Sullivan, and Wright.

Around 1922 Le Corbusier began to publish his tenets for the "tower in the park," based on the theories of Perret. In that year, *L'Esprit Noveau* published his "Villes-Tours," a "modernist" interpretation of Perret's proposals (figure 6.24). The "Ville Contemporaine" published in 1927 further elaborated his ideas.[40] Le Corbusier obliterated the traditional urban elements of street and building by increasing them to a scale which was comprehensible only in terms of the entire city. Skyscrapers of unprecedented height and breadth were placed at wide intervals in unbounded park space, threaded by continuous lower "redent"-type buildings. Le Corbusier's lyric and seductive drawings of this new urbanism often showed buildings raised on columns so as not to interrupt the continuous land-

L'AVENUE DES MAISONS-TOURS. — Un extraordinaire projet pour résoudre la question de l'habitation dans la région parisienne. Composition de JACQUES LAMBERT, d'après les maquettes de l'architecte AUGUSTE PERRET.

Figure 6.23. Auguste Perret. Image of a city of *maisons-tours* drawn by Jacques Lambert from the sketches of Perret; published in 1922.

AESTHETICS AND REALITIES   185

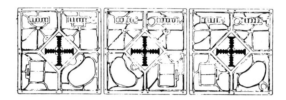

Figure 6.24. Le Corbusier. Proposal for the "city in a park" or *villes-tours*, which began to be publicized around 1922, based on Perret's earlier ideas.

scape (figure 6.25). All of this was supposed to fulfill the socialistic goal of giving every inhabitant equal access to the precious amenities of "sun, space, and green." In the 1920s Le Corbusier's proposals, like those of Perret, remained entirely within the realm of utopian visions. During the same period, the "city in a park" was translated into buildable form by the German architects Marcel Breuer, Walter Gropius, and Ludwig Hilbersheimer. Their proposals for "slab blocks" were literal towers in parks: high-rise elevator buildings, simple rectangles in form, dispersed in a green setting. Breuer first developed the slab block as a form for low-cost housing around 1924 (figure 6.26).[41]

Figure 6.25. Le Corbusier. Typical image of the "city in the park," showing the continuous green space unaffected by buildings which are raised above the ground on *pilotis*.

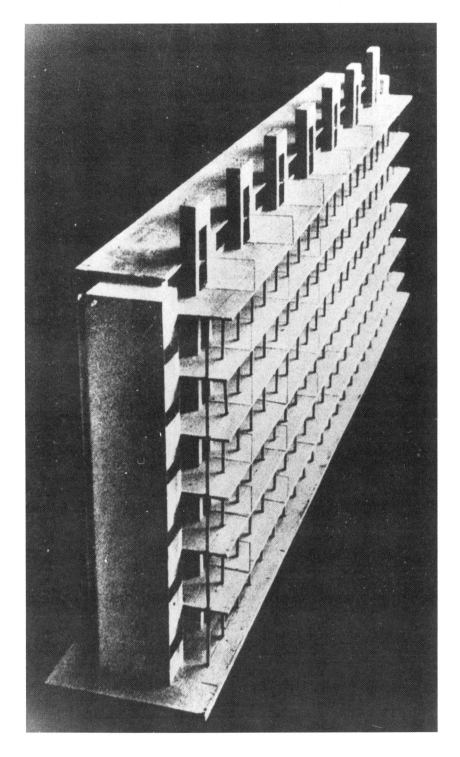

Figure 6.26. Marcel Breuer. Proposal for "low-cost housing" using the slab block form. Made around 1924, it was among the earliest practical proposals to use the slab block in its pure form.

Figure 6.27. Walter Gropius. Perspective of a
slab block proposal using *Zielenbau* site
organization with "intermediate green strips";
made in 1931.

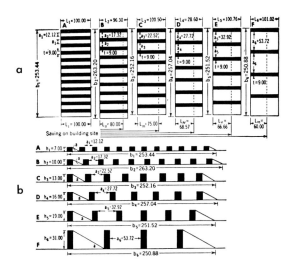

Figure 6.28. Walter Gropius. Diagram from studies made in 1931 relating building heights to increased sunlight and higher density. It made a widely influential argument for the "city in the park," using a *Zielenbau* organization.

By 1930 Gropius had considerably expanded Breuer's work (figure 6.27).[42] Typically in his research, Gropius would advocate a coverage of approximately 15 percent combined with a requirement of north-south orientation so that no building should place another in shadow. In his widely published studies, Gropius documented the efficiencies of the isolated high-rise block over other housing forms. A series of site plans from a study made in 1931 demonstrated that by combining increased height, density, and space between buildings, more sunlight could be obtained,[43] in contrast to traditional low-rise housing, where increased densities always meant less sunlight (figure 6.28). The efficiency, in terms of density, of each site plan was represented by the additional length of building permitted for increased height, beyond the minimum set by a scheme two stories in height (scheme A). A series of site sections showed how increased length permitted the increase of open space, if the density of the two-story scheme was maintained. Both diagrams supported Gropius' fundamental argument that high-rise slab-block planning would simultaneously increase density, reduce coverage, and improve light and ventilation. Gropius' slab-block configurations typically used a simple linear shape,[44] which was efficient and cheaper to build than the more complex perimeter garden apartment (figure 6.29).

The combined sentiments of Gropius and Le Corbusier produced a formidable

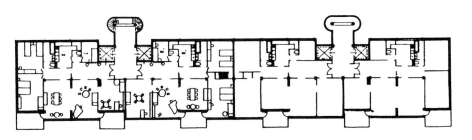

Figure 6.29. Walter Gropius. Typical slab block floor plan used in a project proposed for the Wannsee suburb of Berlin in 1931.

polemic, both social and aesthetic, visual and verbal, which conformed perfectly to the economic realities confronting housing design in Europe and America. Through the confluence of a number of critical factors, the slab block in a park was destined to become a hallmark of twentieth-century urbanism. In the twilight of the prepenicillin age, the ideal hygienic city had at last emerged, with the old urbanism of insalubrity replaced by a perfect elixir for urban ills, real and imagined. In the utopian mind, the "new" building technology made it possible. That the technology had already existed for almost a half century in New York was of no consequence in the argument; the interpretation of the technology was radically new. In New York this attitude meshed very well with the emerging preoccupations of the International Style. Perhaps the most seductive aspect of the new urbanism was its economy. For the first time, social housing was definitively linked to low cost of construction. Previously, the issue of cost had been limited to providing affordable housing through philanthropy, rather than economy. Beginning with Breuer's initial proposals, the slab block was consistently conceived as a breakthrough in the realm of cost. Nothing could be cheaper, and therefore more housing could be built with limited resources. It was an elusive dream, inextricably tied to the emerging morality of the modern welfare state.

The "tower in the park" was quickly incorporated into the New York context. In 1931 the firm of Howe and Lescaze designed the first housing project for New York which was clearly derivative of the new European slab-block. George Howe was an established Beaux Arts practitioner who took a young Swiss architect, William Lescaze, as his partner in 1929 in an effort to change his style to the "modernist" idiom. Their proposal was for a narrow strip of land running between

Figure 6.30. Howe and Lescaze (*above*). Chrystie-Forsyth Street housing typical block; proposed for the Lower East Side in 1931 as the first major "slab block" project for New York City. Maurice Deutsch and Gustave W. Iser (*below*). Chrystie-Forsyth housing proposal made in 1933 using a perimeter block configuration with interior gardens.

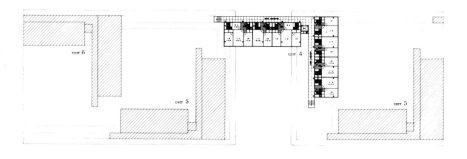

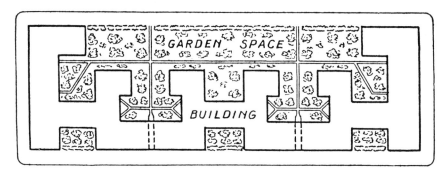

Chrystie and Forsyth streets from East Houston to Canal Street on the Lower East Side.[45] In the following years the site became the object of many proposals, all in the tradition of the garden apartment perimeter (figure 6.30). The Howe and Lescaze proposal differed radically from the traditional approach, using L-shaped slab-blocks raised on *pilotis,* faithful to the Corbusian ideal (see figure 6.25). They even produced a romantic view of the project from under the slab, through the forest of columns in the manner of Le Corbusier (figure 6.31). The wall of tenements which paralleled the site were appropriately neutralized in the rendering in an effort to present a context closer to the European ideal than the Lower East Side. But the context succeeded in directing the scheme, and the L-shaped slabs, presumably necessitated by the constraint of site dimensions, were quite foreign to the reductive simplicity of the Breuer and Gropius visions. The Chrystie-Forsyth proposal was one of the few United States housing designs represented in the International Exhibition at the Museum of Modern Art in 1932. Subsequently, schemes in the new style proliferated. Another of the earliest was proposed by the young "modernist" New York firm of Clauss and Daub for a block in Long Island City (figure 6.32).[46] Like many others to follow, they used the

Figure 6.31. Howe and Lescaze. Chrystie-Forsyth housing proposal; perspective at ground level showing a transformation of the Corbusian image of continuous green space and *pilotis* to the conditions of the Lower East Side.

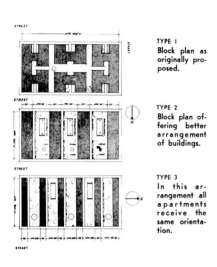

TYPE I
Block plan as originally proposed.

TYPE 2
Block plan offering better arrangement of buildings.

TYPE 3
In this arrangement all apartments receive the same orientation.

Gropius site analysis, which would prove to be a very seductive convention for the new site planning. It was, in fact, destined to become perhaps the single most important housing diagram of the coming decades.

In 1930 *Architectural Record* published a scheme by Frank Lloyd Wright for tower apartments on St. Mark's Place in New York City (figure 6.33).[47] Wright proposed to raze the nineteenth-century buildings which surrounded St. Mark's-in-the-Bowery Church. They were replaced by four Usonian towers which were versions of those he later used in his Broadacre proposals.[48] He attempted "towers in the park," although the "park" was compromised by the surrounding tenements. The project was said to realize "some of the most advanced aims professed by the European architects, without attendant anomalies." Thus a circle was completed, as the old master and rebel who had influenced an earlier generation of Europeans looked, probably with uncertainty, at the new polemic, and at a strange city, both of which he later professed to dislike. His towers were a radical departure from the low-rise terrace housing projects he had proposed for Chicago many years earlier.[49]

In general, the "utopianism," which was indigenous to the culture of architecture in New York, shared little with either the Howe and Lescaze slab-blocks or Wright's Usonian towers. Visions of the "city of the future" which emanated from New York tended to dramatize the unique existing urbanism which had evolved from the nineteenth century. At the end of the 1920s, a number of New York architects produced ideal urban visions, at least partially as rejoinder to the new European work. The proposals of Arthur J. Frappier, Raymond Hood, Harvey Wiley Corbett, and Hugh Ferriss, all heightened the physical and technological dimension of the city, using Beaux Arts planning principles as a paradigm.[50] They employed gigantuan buildings of unprecedented dimension and proximity, integrated with the new movement technology and building systems at hand. Hugh Ferriss' study, *The Metropolis of Tomorrow,* published in 1929, gives the most coherent view of this genre.[51] Ironically it was a utopianism realized in its own time, at least in fragments like Rockefeller Center.

By the end of the 1920s the actual state of the high-rise type in New York reflected a far different outlook from that of "tower in the park" envisioned by the utopians. Parts of Manhattan, especially the West Side, had become overbuilt with high-rental tower apartment buildings.[52] The type had begun to suffer from weakening demand, a condition which could be corroborated with unconsidered repetition and poor design standards. Because the high-rise buildings were luxury housing built for profit, there was an imperative for innovation. Following the demands of the open marketplace, the upper income hold on the high-rise form had eroded. New buildings whose exteriors suggested rambling twelve- or fifteen-room apartments might actually contain one- and two-bedroom apartments.[53] The elaborate Beaux Arts facade was retained as a symbol of affluence, in much the same manner that in an earlier epoch the brownstone facade frequently masked the presence of middle-class flats. But even the Beaux Arts facade had begun to be cheapened, with much of the expensive cut limestone replaced by terra-cotta reproductions. Usually only the facades facing the street were decorated. Concern

Figure 6.33. Frank Lloyd Wright. Proposal for tower apartments on St. Marks Place made in 1930. Wright claimed its superiority over the new European urbanism.

AESTHETICS AND REALITIES   **193**

over the increased use of terra-cotta was such that in 1920 Mayor John F. Hylan attempted to restrict its use for public building in the city, judging it to be aesthetically and structurally inferior to stone.[54] But such measures were futile given the cheapness of terra-cotta, especially as the last generation of stonecutters began to disappear.

The plans of the high-rise, luxury buildings on Park Avenue, Fifth Avenue, Riverside Drive, Central Park West, and West End Avenue in many cases were based on the conventions of the Tenement House Act of 1901. Typically, some variant on the 100-by-100-foot New Law plans would be projected vertically to the twelve-to-fifteen-story maximum permitted by the height restrictions of 1916. In some cases, heights were increased beyond the maximum permitted by law. A second generation of high-rise towers had developed by 1929. The newer towers, like many of the earlier high-rise projects, were frequently classified as "apartment hotels," partly to avoid the restrictions of the Tenement House Law. In 1927 this practice was challenged in court by the Tenement House Department, which first lost the suit but then won a reversal.[55] In 1924 height restrictions imposed on Fifth Avenue since 1921 were removed by a court decision opening up its development.[56] In 1926 the first luxury high rise appeared in Brooklyn adjoining Prospect Park.[57] While the highest housing towers proposed in Manhattan in 1924 had been twenty-eight stories,[58] by 1928 fifty-eight-story towers were being proposed.[59] In 1925, with the completion of the forty-one-story Ritz Tower at Park Avenue and 57th Street, designed by Emery Roth and Carrere and Hastings,[60] a definitive precedent was realized for the height of apartment buildings. Although it was classified as an apartment hotel, some suites were inordinately large, with up to eighteen rooms.

The widening discrepancies between New York City building law and common practice for high-rise residential building were the most important reason behind the appointment of a Tenement House Commission within the New York state legislature in May 1927. In its report, published in January 1928, the commission advocated comprehensive legislation governing all "dwellings" in the city, from tenements to luxury high-rise apartments.[61] The report, like Lawrence Veiller's prophetic *Model Housing Law* of 1914, did not use the word "tenement" at all. This mirrored the market situation at the time, when a steadily decreasing proportion of new housing was being built to tenement standards. By the end of the 1920s housing boom, Old Law vacancies were high.[62] Real estate interests also were becoming more and more flagrant in their use of the "bootleg hotel" in order to construct high-rise apartments outside of the Tenement House Department controls, a source of continuing litigation with the city. Clearly, comprehensive new housing legislation was needed.[63]

The Tenement House Commission's most innovative proposal involved a new approach to the structure of the housing law, based on density as reflected in land value assessments. One set of design standards was to be applied to lots assessed less than $2 per square foot, another for lots more than $4 per square foot. This system was proposed to prevent standards which applied to lots assessed at more than $2 per square foot, amounting to less than 7 percent of the area of the city, from governing the remaining 93 percent. The device sought to discourage massive high-rise housing where alternatives existed. This and other controversial recommendations prevented the bill from passing in the legislature during the 1928 session. The committee was reconvened. New and more conservative recommendations were passed in the 1929 session as the Multiple Dwellings Law.[64] The legal differentiation of design standards based on lot valuation was dropped, but the principle of singular legal jurisdiction over all housing types remained.

The Multiple Dwellings Law only minimally affected existing tenement design standards, although it reduced the practicality of 50-by-100-foot lots through some increase in minimum courtyard sizes. The law most drastically affected the form of the high-rise apartment tower, and placed all high-rise housing firmly under its control. The "bootleg hotel," which for years had remained exempt from tenement house legislation, was now definitively placed under legal jurisdiction.[65] The law mandated bulk and height restrictions for high-rise housing which covered a range of possibilities going far beyond the setbacks of the 1916 Building Zone Plan. Many more massing options were available, and high buildings were fully considered.

For the largest new apartment buildings, on building lots of 30,000 square feet or more, housing "towers" were allowed to rise three times the street width, providing they did not exceed one-fifth of the area of the lot. The lower bulk of such buildings was limited by the same regulations as buildings on smaller lots — approximately one- and three-quarters times the street width. For very large lots, two towers were permitted (figure 6.34). The new law led to a brief proliferation of luxury dual-tower high-rise buildings along Central Park West, consisting of towers and a base. First was the San Remo at West 74th Street, designed by Emery Roth,[66] followed by the Eldorado at West 90th Street, designed by Margon and Holder with Emery Roth;[67] the Majestic at West 71st Street, designed by

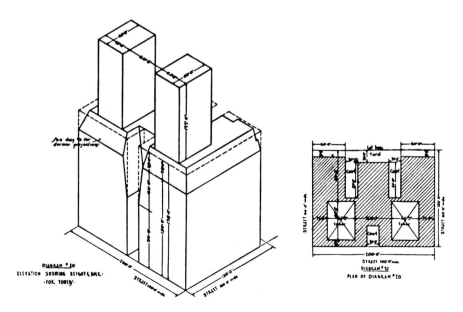

Figure 6.34. Representative diagram from the Multiple Dwellings Law of 1929, showing the dual-tower massing which was permitted for the highest of the high-rise apartment buildings.

Jacques Delamarre with the builder Irwin S. Chanin;[68] the Century at West 62d Street, also designed by Jacques Delamarre with Chanin.[69] The identical massing of each of these projects was wrapped in radically differing architectural clothes, consistant with the pluralism of the times: from the Italian Renaissance of the San Remo to the Mayan Deco of the Eldorado.

Ironically, the Multiple Dwellings Law, the first legislation to deal comprehensively with high-rise design standards, was partially responsible for the decline of the high-rise form as luxury housing. The Multiple Dwellings Law sanctioned inferior design standards, which had not even been permitted under the Tenement House Act. Most notable were those concerning exernal light and ventilation. For the first time since 1901, interior public corridors or stairs were not required to have openings to the exterior, even to air shafts or courtyards. "Mechanical ventilation" was considered sufficient. In effect, the new law legalized the double-loaded interior corridor. This provision facilitated efficient spatial organization for minimum high-rise apartments, but cross ventilation within apartments was frequently eliminated. Fortunately for the affluent, the technological advance of air-conditioning was just around the corner.[70]

The contrast between the Beresford and the nearby Eldorado, Majestic, and Century on Central Park West indicates the extent of the design transformation which occurred in high-rise housing at the close of the 1920s. Designed by Emery Roth, the Beresford was probably the last of the long succession of grand and luxurious New York high-rise apartment houses that had begun with the Dakota and Central Park Apartments in the early 1880s and ended with the market crash of 1929.[71] The Beresford occupied the entire end of a block between West 81st and 82d streets. Its setbacks, which were governed by the 1916 law, were elaborately wrought with Italian Renaissance decorative motifs (figure 6.35). The Eldorado, Majestic, and Century also occupied block ends, but their massing reflected the new requirements of the Multiple Dwellings Law. All had far smaller apartments. The Majestic was caught in mid-construction by the stock market crash, so that the developer was forced to drastically reduce the apartment sizes.[72] The Eldorado followed, incorporating less luxurious apartments for a less affluent clientele.[73] But it was the Century which most drastically cut apartment sizes, while still attempting to maintain an aura of absolute luxury.

The Century was completed last, in 1931. Its massing consisted of two 14-story towers on a 19-story base (figure 6.36). Stylistically, the Century most emphatically expressed the new age, departing most radically from the Italianate Beresford. Its simple, abstract geometrical patterns were partially derived from an attempt to dramatize the massing of the building. Broad bands and massing of materials were substituted for the Beresford's elaborately carved cornices and railing. The Century's facade, like those designed earlier by Thomas and Smith for their quasi-philanthropic projects, recognized economic imperatives. Yet the decoration of the Century was not comparable to that of Smith's Mesa Verde (see figures 6.20 and 6.21). The Century was a chic answer to the new economic realities, the Italianate high style of the Beresford transformed to the high style of Deco-Moderne, transposed from Paris to the New York context through American eyes by Jacques Delamarre.[74] The Mesa Verde had none of these pretensions. Its

Figure 6.35. Emery Roth. The Beresford, completed by 1930 on Central Park West, under the massing constraints of the Building Zone Plan of 1916; one of the last of the succession of grand and luxurious high-rise apartment buildings dating from the 1880s.

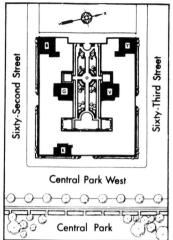

functionally and aesthetically innovative design was a more direct response to both economic necessity and social issues.

The Century's developer and tenants were undoubtedly less interested in its new imagery than its drastic reduction of apartment sizes. Significantly, no proportionate reduction in rents accompanied the reduction of space standards. The rents were equivalent to those in older, larger luxury apartments. Irwin Chanin, the developer, argued in an article in the *Real Estate Record and Guide* that one of the Century's six-room apartments was worth the rental normally charged for a seven-room apartment because of its spatial efficiency and the addition of time-saving conveniences and appliances (figure 6.37).[75] The argument that functional utility could compensate for reduced apartment size accompanied the rapid decline of housing quality for the affluent in New York City. A proliferation of household appliances cushioned the fall. In 1925, at the Eighteenth Annual Electric and Industrial Exposition held in New York, great advances were recorded toward the perfection of radios, vacuum cleaners, irons, washers, mixers, etc. The low-cost electric refrigerator appeared. Manufacturers claimed that the cost for current was less per month than the cost of ice.[76] The old and formerly uncompromised amenity of space, whether in the single-family brownstone or rambling high-rise apartment, gradually gave way to modest apartment sizes, and immodest amounts of consumer gadgetry.

In 1938 the long-awaited precedent of the first centrally air-conditioned apartment house in New York City was realized.[77] Designed by Frederick Ackerman at Madison Avenue and East 83d Street, the well-organized plans reflected the small apartment standards for luxury housing, with only one- and two-bedroom units. But the appearance of the twelve-story structure was revolutionary, with a large proportion of glass block which had the advantage of providing abundant light while obtaining sufficient insulation to reduce the heat gain (figure 6.38). The somewhat brutal grid of glass block, operable steel sash, and varied brick coursing introduced to luxury housing a modernism based on strict functional and

ROOM COUNT AS STANDARD FOR APARTMENT
RENTALS OBSOLETE, CHANIN DECLARES

Figure 6.37. Jacques Delamarre for the Chanin Construction Company. Typical six-room apartment plan for the Century, which was claimed by the developer to be the functional equivalent of larger and older apartments because of its increased organizational efficiency.

Figure 6.38. Frederick Ackerman. Apartments on East 83d Street, completed in 1938 and the first centrally air-conditioned apartment building in New York; the technological impact of this breakthrough is reflected in the facade expression.

AESTHETICS AND REALITIES   199

technological criteria, in a spirit which was closer to the spirit of the Mesa Verde than that of the Deco-Moderne of the Century.

By the end of the 1920s, severe limits had evolved on the range of new housing types available for moderate-income families in Manhattan. A combination of real estate costs and limitations on availability of land permitted few alternatives to a small apartment in an elevator building. In 1929 one study indicated that since 1918, the average number of rooms per apartment had declined from 4.19 to 3.37 in 1928, and in the same period, the proportion of newly constructed housing with apartments of four or more rooms fell from 66.8 percent to 32.7 percent.[78] In Manhattan the situation was far worse. For families with children, the temptation to join the exodus to the outer boroughs was reinforced by this prospect. Architects could produce no viable alternatives. In 1930 borough president Julius Miller commissioned a number of architects to produce housing studies for the "average wage earners," who were leaving Manhattan en masse for the less expensive housing of the outer boroughs.[79] Two solutions were accepted as having the greatest potential; one was designed by Charles Lengh, the other by Emery Roth. Each used a 100-by-100-foot lot (figure 6.39). Both reflected the new standards of the Multiple Dwellings Law, including double-loaded corridors without windows. The 12-story towers contained only small apartments of one, two, or three rooms. All were inferior in terms of spatial amenities to the developers' frame houses on the outskirts of Queens, lacking adequate bedrooms, yards, or accommodation for the most momentous consumer product of all, which was the automobile. Economics or aesthetics aside, it was the automobile which provided the single most revolutionary force in the urbanism of housing in this century.

Already by the decade of the 1920s, the automobile was beginning to substantially affect United States culture. Clarence Stein, who became one of the

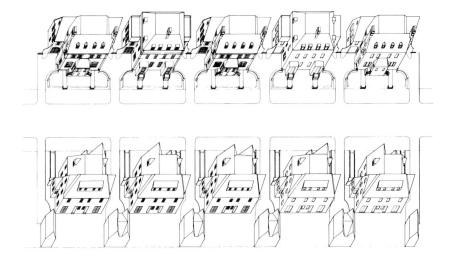

Figure 6.40. Robert Tappan and Rogers and Hanneman. Two-family "English garden homes" built in 1926 for the Queensboro Corporation at Jackson Heights; each of the two prototypes differs in approach to integrating garages for automobiles.

chief protagonists of "housing for the motor age," pointed out that in 1910 there were only 458,000 automobiles in the United States. By 1928 that number had multiplied by almost fifty times to 21,300,000.[80] The influence of the automobile penetrated to all aspects of daily life, including housing. Most principally affected were lower-density house types, which tended to function well with the integration of the automobile. By the end of World War I, for example, the number of building permit applications for the addition of garages to existing one- and two-family houses had increased noticeably in the outer boroughs. And the house form itself began to adapt with the inclusion of garages attached in various ways to the new houses.[81] Of particular interest for this approach were the two-family "English garden homes" built by the Queensboro Corporation in 1926 on 86th Street between 34th and 35th avenues in Jackson Heights (figure 6.40).[82] The houses on the west side of the street were designed by Rogers and Hanneman following the more common convention of providing detached rear garages with a shared driveway between each of the houses. More interesting from an organizational point of view was the east side of the street, designed by Robert Tappan. The garages were integrated at the side of each house, one-half level below the front entrances, to form a shared paved auto court between the houses. Both prototypes were well studied, such that the integration of the automobile did not compromise use of the private yard, while the landscape development at the street gave the impression of a spatious public amenity.

The most radical architectural response to the automobile was its integration into the house proper, with access provided directly from the street. The row house was modified for this approach. Frequently the drive ramped down slightly from sidewalk level, with the major living space on the second floor, reached by steps and outdoor porch. With elimination of a passage to a rear garage, a continuous street wall could be employed, permitting development at higher densities. The automobile could be prominently displayed, with the garage as the most dominant element within the composition of the facade. Some of the earliest examples were

Figure 6.41. Charles Schafer, Jr. Row houses
completed on Hamden Place, the Bronx, in 1919,
with integrated street-front garages; an early
example of the domestication of the
automobile.

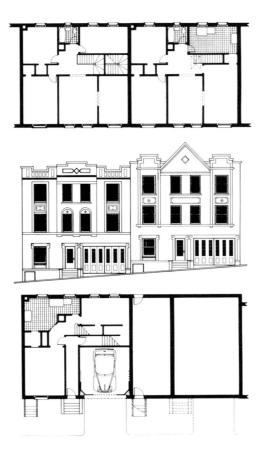

row houses with garages inserted on the ground floor, as are found on Hampden Place in the Bronx, completed by Charles Schafer, Jr., in 1919 (figure 6.41).[83] These three-story, single-family houses devoted most of the ground level to the automobile, at some sacrifice to the organization of the living space. They were relatively primitive, but as the type evolved, the place of the automobile became more domesticated, while the identity of each row house became more pronounced, with devices such as gable roofs and bay windows creating more individualistic expression. Frequently the garage was placed below grade, so that the living space above could be closer to the ground. An excellent example is the row of houses on Holland Avenue in the Bronx completed by Joseph Klein in 1940 (figure 6.42).[84] The Tudor gables and facade details, as well as the chimneys, terraces, and stoops, help to establish an individual identity for each house, with the automobile tucked beneath the terraces. This particular type can be found in many locations in the pre-1940 outer boroughs, but it has continued to be built until the present day.

In general, the juxtaposition of the row house with the exigencies of the automobile age became the catalyst for countless modifications of the basic type. A primitive approach presented a unified block row at the street edge, with a de-

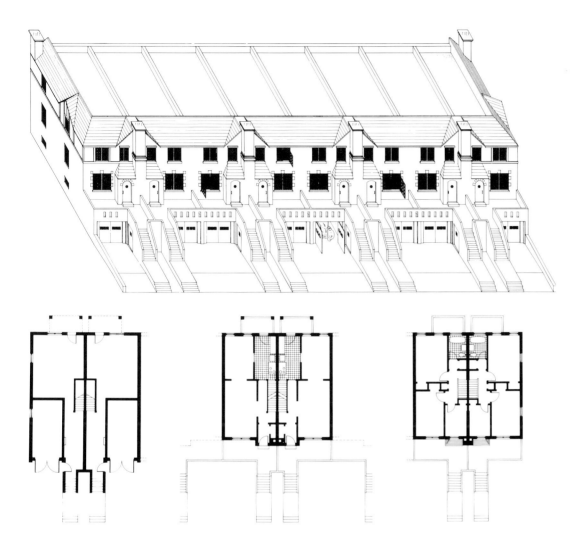

tached row of garages behind like those built in Jackson Heights on 73rd Street between 34th Avenue and Northern Boulevard by Benjamin Dressler, Jr., in 1929.[85] In such cases the garage access completely destroyed the potential for development of rear yard areas. A slightly simpler approach to this problem placed the garage within the houses at the rear; found, for example, in Jackson Heights on 70th Street between 34th Avenue and Northern Boulevard (figure 6.43).[86] It was designed by Arthur I. Allen and built in 1927. Nineteen houses line both sides of the street and are arranged in a unified group, with the central and end houses emphasized to reinforce the cohesion of the entire cluster. Access ramps to the garages are at the ends. Unfortunately the garages cut off the possibility of integration of the rear yards with the houses. At the street side, however, elaborate landscaping is integrated with each house, transforming the street into lush linear park.

Figure 6.42. Joseph Klein. Row houses on Holland Avenue, the Bronx, completed in 1940; by this date the automobile was skillfully integrated beneath street-front terraces with a minimum disruption of living space.

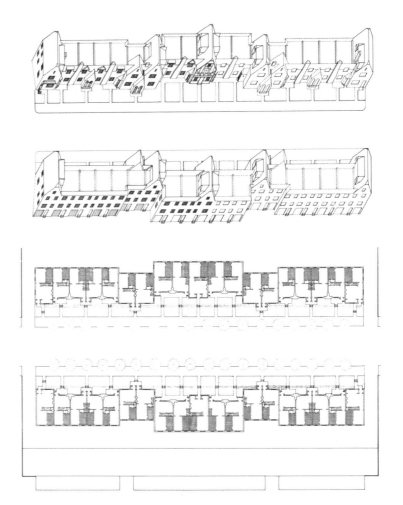

Figure 6.43. Arthur I. Allen. Row houses on 70th Street, Jackson Heights, built in 1927 with garages integrated at the rear, and street landscaping which becomes the equivalent of an elaborate public garden court.

Other interesting responses to the automobile were closer to the garden apartment in the genesis of their site organization. At the highest density, there was the precedent of Linden Court (see figure 5.18), with its garages integrated into the internal garden space. But at lower densities, row houses were also reconfigured to accommodate the automobile while enclosing central gardens. For example, at Forest Close in Forest Hills, Queens, completed by Robert Tappan in 1927, thirty-eight row houses share a common green mews which connects to a garage court at one end (figure 6.44).[87] Located on Austin Street between 75th Road and 76th Avenue, the domain of the automobile garages adjoins a commercial strip development along Queens Boulevard. An adjacent twin development, Arbor Close, was completed in the previous year.

In addition to house form, the automobile began to alter the traditional neighborhood fabric. The commercial development along the major traffic arteries of the outer boroughs, Queens Boulevard or Northern Boulevard in Queens, for example, or Fordham Road in the Bronx, began to exhibit the characteristics of

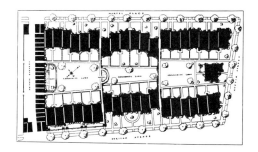

Figure 6.44. Robert Tappan. Forest Close, completed at Forest Hills in 1927, with row houses along a garden mews and a garage court at one end.

automobile-oriented strip development, with the requisite change in spatial structure and use. By the 1920s Fordham Road was called the "Forty-second Street of the Bronx."[88] But it possessed striking differences from its older namesake. It was as much automobile oriented as transit oriented, with its excellent connections to the parkways, including the new Bronx River Parkway completed in 1923. Apart from the new movie palaces, it was the home of burgeoning automobile dealerships and of chain stores, the "strip" in its infancy. The suburban extension of New York City which would come three decades later was prefigured here.

For Joseph P. Day, the real estate entrepreneur whose earlier fortunes had depended heavily on New York City's transit extensions, and whose success depended in large part on his ability to anticipate new patterns of development, the omens were clear by 1925. Conventional urban modes of transportation, and therefore retail marketing, were in transition. Day pinpointed a major symptom: "The chain store has become an important factor in the development of the business centres of the Bronx, for with the increase in local population these foresighted organizations saw their opportunity and grasped it. . . . As the population of the Bronx has grown greater year by year, the smaller shopkeeper of the past has developed into the representative merchant of today."[89] The symptoms of a mass culture, whether automobile, chain store, or movie palace, were well in evidence. Day went on to generalize: "The automobile has been, perhaps, the foremost factor in the development of large areas located at a distance from the subways, elevated and trolley lines. It is no longer a question of living directly along the route of a transit line and homeseekers generally have come to realize that some of the most desirable home-building sites in the Bronx are those that are located some distance from the transit lines, but which, nevertheless, are easily accessible by automobile."

Perhaps the ultimate harbinger of things to come was Radburn, begun in 1927 in Fairlawn, New Jersey. It was a community planned by Clarence Stein and Henry Wright for primarily single-family houses, the first planned suburb for the "motor age" (figure 6.45).[90] It was the second philanthropic project developed for middle-income families by the City Housing Corporation, which had begun Sunnyside in 1924 (see figure 5.39). Radburn was the first suburban development of this kind by a limited dividend company. Fairlawn, about 13 miles from New York City, was physically isolated from the metropolis by the Hudson River and poor transit connections. With the opening of the Holland Tunnel in

Figure 6.45. Clarence Stein and Henry Wright. Radburn, New Jersey, site plan, begun by the City Housing Corporation in 1927 as a development for single-family houses planned with maximum recognition of the automobile.

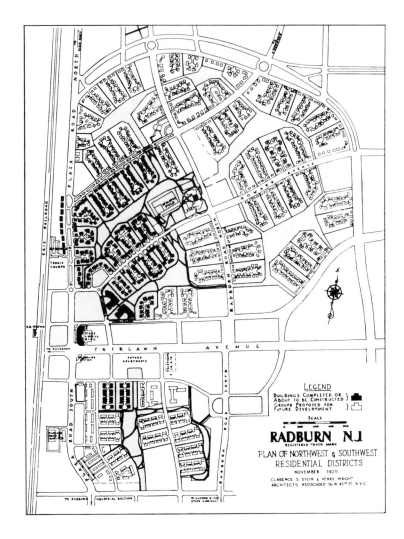

1927 however, it was possible to commute quickly by private automobile without the inconvenience of ferries. The well-known Radburn planning principles separated vehicular and pedestrian realms, with extensive provision of parks and greenways. Radburn represented a turning point. The development signaled the formative influence which the automobile would take in the coming generation of urban extension. It achieved a degree of sophistication in subdivision planning which was much discussed, but unfortunately seldom emulated in the following decades. By this time, the private automobile had taken a formative role in planning and architectural theory and practice. As early as 1923, Robert Moses had been planning the parkway system of Long Island through his Long Island State Park Commission; in 1927 the George Washington Bridge to New Jersey was begun. With the publication of the New York Regional Plan in 1929, the scenario was established.[91] Only New Deal money was needed to realize it.

C ONGRESS disassembled the United States Housing Corporation and the Emergency Fleet Corporation in 1920. Not until
the Great Depression did the federal government again intervene directly in housing production. Between 1932 and 1938 the
government tried several approaches to stimulate housing production before the methods and ideology that dominated the following decades began to take shape. The first consensus for federal intervention
came out of the President's Conference on Home Building and Home Ownership,
held in Washington in December of 1931. Although privately organized, the conference was under the aegis of the Hoover administration.[1] Participants num-
bered three thousand. Their generally conservative recommendations proved influential. Direct government competition with private enterprise was to be
minimized; provision of fiscal incentives to private developers and home owners
was recommended to stimulate home building.

One such stimulant was the Federal Home Loan Bank Board, established in
1932 to provide reserve credit for home financing institutions.[2] Another was the
Reconstruction Finance Corporation (RFC), established in the same year to advance low-interest loans to limited-dividend housing corporations through state
or municipal agencies. Both programs were intended primarily for middle-income
families, as was most subsequent government intervention. The Federal Home
Loan Bank Board was an impetus for suburban home building. This trend was
reinforced by other devices such as the Federal Housing Administration Loan
Guaranty Programs begun in 1934. In contrast, the Reconstruction Finance Corporation was short-lived; it made only two loans. One of these loans, $8 million
went to New York City for the construction of Knickerbocker Village on the Lower
East Side. The funds were channeled through the New York State Board of Housing, which had been established in 1926.

In 1933 the National Industrial Recovery Act, a part of Roosevelt's New Deal,
created the Public Works Administration (PWA). The Housing Division of the
PWA took over the loan program of the Reconstruction Finance Corporation.
Knickerbocker Village was completed as a PWA loan project. Other PWA loan

projects that originated with the RFC included Hillside Homes, built in 1933 in the Bronx, Boulevard Gardens in suburban Woodside, Long Island, and the Spence Housing Estate in the Bronx, which was never built.[3] The PWA could award grants through state or municipal agencies for up to 30 percent of a project's cost, or it could act directly as the project developer. The PWA became the first federally owned "philanthropic" organization for building housing. In 1935 Williamsburg Houses in Brooklyn received approval as the first PWA direct intervention project, closely followed in 1935 by Harlem River Houses. The PWA loan program was abandoned in 1934, and policy shifted to project development through direct intervention. Within three and a half years, fifty-one projects in thirty-six cities were completed under the PWA Housing Division.[4]

In 1934 the New York state legislature passed the Municipal Housing Authority Act. This act amended the 1926 State Housing Law, permitting municipalities to form local authorities to develop housing projects which would be financed by the sale of municipal bonds or by federal funds.[5] The New York City Housing Authority (NYCHA) was founded immediately after passage of the Municipal Housing Authority Act. Later on, state programs were instituted to augment local resources.[6] In his book *Slums and Housing,* James Ford pointed out a very critical difference between the State Housing Law of 1926 and its amendment by the Municipal Housing Authorities Law of 1934.[7] Both laws were intended to promote production of housing for low-income families, but their definition of this type of housing differed significantly. The 1926 law defined low-income housing by placing upper limits on the average monthly rentals per room: $12.50 in Manhattan and $11.00 elsewhere within the city. The 1934 law placed no limitation on rent, but instead emphasized "low cost," implying that reduction in construction costs would be passed along to tenants in terms of reduced rents—a strategy which has produced questionable results.

Although the 1934 law equated government-subsidized housing for low-income families with low-cost housing, for several years it had no effect because of the availability of generous federal monies under the New Deal. The earliest government-subsidized housing projects were considered experimental, and low cost was never given priority over livability. As a result, the New Deal projects remain among the best-designed government housing in New York City. But as government housing programs became less experimental and more institutionalized, a conflict between high project costs and low rentals developed. Obviously, limitations on rents had to be enforced in order to fulfill the goals of the programs. At the same time, in order to fulfill the national political ideology of "free enterprise," superior housing could not be provided at below-market rents. Reductions had to be made in housing construction costs, and project livability had to be compromised.

Costs, however, entered the housing question in more insidious ways than simple construction economics, or even ideology. For example, cost could be used as a foil in resolving political complexities involving site selection.[8] Controversy over the redevelopment of the Chrystie-Forsyth corridor provided ample evidence of this nuance. The city had acquired the land in 1929, and by 1931 had proceeded to raze the tenements with the hope of constructing a major early precedent for public housing. By 1933, an interesting range of proposals had surfaced including those of Andrew Thomas, John J. Klaber, Howe and Lescaze, Sloan and Robertson, Holden, McLaughlen, and Associates, Jardine, Murdock, and Wright and Maurice Deutsch and Gustav W. Iser (see figure 6.30).[9] Yet the project became engulfed in a political morass, earning the distinction of being the first casualty of the public housing era. At least partially to blame was the political patronage which had so inflated the initial clearance costs that further investment in rebuilding was thrown into question.[10] The Chrystie-Forsyth site became a park instead. In 1934, his first year as Commissioner of Parks, Robert Moses seized this opportunity created by indecision over the site, making a coup of sorts which helped crystallize his power early on.[11] And within a few years, his ambitions were no longer limited to parks, but to housing as well.

The first wholly government-built housing project in New York City was an anachronism and atypical of what was to come in the following three decades of public housing. Called First Houses and completed by the New York City Housing Authority in 1936, it was a series of rehabilitated prelaw tenements covering a partial block at Avenue A and East 3rd Street on the Lower East Side.[12] Frederick Ackerman, Howard McFadden, and George Genug of the Technical Division of the Housing Authority designed the project. A group of twenty-four tenements were rebuilt with selective removal of buildings to provide adequate light and air. The 123 new apartments shared a highly developed recreation space created by combining yards (figure 7.1).

The choice of rehabilitation over new construction was dictated by the project's complex status as the first public housing in New York City. Financing came

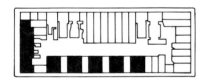

Figure 7.1. New York City Housing Authority Technical Staff under Frederick Ackerman. First Houses, the first wholly government-built housing project in New York City, completed in 1936 with municipal funds through the NYCHA; involved was the rehabilitation of an existing row of tenements (*above*), through the demolition of every third building and the extensive renovation of the others (*below*).

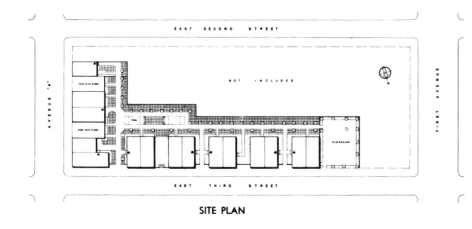

SITE PLAN

directly from the Federal Relief Administration and indirectly from a real estate arrangement with Vincent Astor, who owned most of the site. The development of the project was controversial, both for the financial gains alleged to have been accrued by Astor, and for the fact that the tenements were being rehabilitated rather than demolished. Rehabilitation was apparently seen as giving a public relations advantage for the Housing Authority.[13] First Houses was also seen by some as a definitive answer to the tenement rehabilitation question, and in fact, the quality of its architectural design has yet to be surpassed. The project was extremely expensive, however. It cost three times more than other pre–World War II government projects involving new construction in New York City.

The majority of the early federally supported projects in New York City followed the design traditions established by the innovations of the 1920s or earlier; for example, Boulevard Gardens, completed in 1935, was a limited-dividend PWA project designed by Theodore H. Englehardt in the tradition of Sunnyside. The suburban site at Thirty-First Avenue and Hobart Street in Woodside, Queens, permitted a large open lawn. Ten six-story buildings used only 22.4 percent coverage.[14] Another example was the RFC loan project, Knickerbocker Village, designed by John S. Van Wart of the Fred F. French Company with Frederick Ackerman as a limited-dividend project. Located on the Lower East Side between Cherry, Catherine, Monroe, and Market streets, the project consisted of two perimeter block buildings, projected to a height of twelve stories with 46 percent coverage (figure 7.2).[15] Completed in 1933, it was the first application in low-rental housing of the "introverted" courtyard form which had been used earlier for luxury projects such as the Apthorp or the Belnord. In contrast to its high-rental predecessors, Knickerbocker Village used automatic push-button elevators, instead of employing an elevator staff, and its 1,593 apartments were tiny (figure 7.3). The plan reflected the standards of the 1929 Multiple Dwellings Law with a narrow, double-loaded, and windowless corridor. In order to address the lack of through ventilation, the exterior walls were "crenellated" to admit additional light and to provide better circulation of air.

The interior courtyards of Knickerbocker Village were small relative to the surrounding twelve-story walls, a consequence of trying to obtain maximum density and coverage within the constraints of the perimeter type. It was a dilemma well known to tenants of the luxury palazzi at the turn of the century (see figures 3.30 and 3.31). But especially for social housing, with its emphasis on light and air and on economy of means, the perimeter with its difficult corners presented an enigma. Still, for a brief period the perimeter remained the focus of architects' thinking for high densities at moderate heights. The housing competition that was sponsored by the Phelps-Stokes Fund in 1933 gives ample evidence of this preoccupation. The program called for a block of housing with a "small park" at the interior, leaving little option for other approaches. The winning entry was especially interesting in its attempt to address this problem (figure 7.4).[16] The designers, Richard Hutaff and Severin Stockmar, rejected the stock answer of reducing density and coverage in order to increase light and efficiency. Instead they increased density and coverage, in order to gain more apartments, while radically changing the traditional perimeter massing in order to solve light prob-

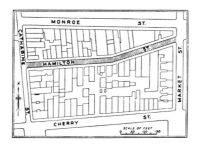

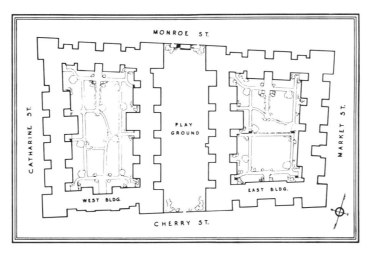

Figure 7.2. John S. Van Wart and Frederick Ackerman with the Fred F. French Company. Knickerbocker Village, completed on the Lower East Side in 1933 with a loan from the Reconstruction Finance Corporation, using the high-rise perimeter form previously associated with luxury housing.

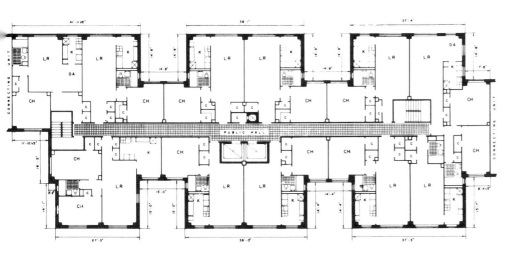

TYPICAL UNIT PLAN

Figure 7.3. John S. Van Wart and Frederick Ackerman with the Fred F. French Company. Knickerbocker Village Apartment cluster, designed with the reduced standards of the Multiple Dwellings Law of 1929, but with "crenellated" exterior walls for light and ventilation.

GOVERNMENT INTERVENTION   211

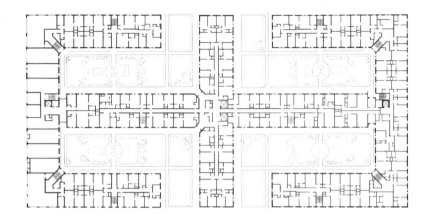

Figure 7.4. Richard Hutaff and Severin Stockmar. Winning entry in the Phelps Stokes Fund Housing Competition of 1933; the efficiency of the perimeter block was maximized by filling the center of the block with a tall cruciform building, surrounded by a lower perimeter.

Figure 7.5. Clarence Stein, Hillside Homes, completed in 1935 in the Bronx with a loan from the Public Works Administration; it used extensive preliminary research for the determination of apartment cluster forms.

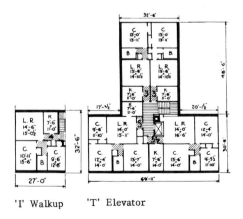

'I' Walkup   'T' Elevator

lems. This strategy was accomplished by filling the center of the block with a thirteen-story cruciform mass, surrounded by a lower perimeter at the exterior, producing four interior courtyards instead of one.

In the design of Hillside Homes, the first PWA loan project, Clarence Stein continued to develop the ideas pioneered earlier with Henry Wright at Phipps Garden Apartments. The large site occupied approximately five irregular blocks in the outer Bronx at the intersection of Eastchester and Boston roads.[17] The preliminary program for the housing was flexible. The objective of the design was to reduce rents to very moderate levels through an optimal balance of the number, configuration, size, and cost of building on the site. Stein used the Phipps configuration as a starting point (see figure 5.42), while hoping to reduce the Phipps rent of sixteen dollars per room per month to eleven dollars. Rather than beginning with large monolithic forms encompassing the entire site, Stein used smaller design components as analytic tools, combining them in various ways to produce alternative schemes. These smaller components were derived from the plan of the Phipps Garden Apartments. He used primarily walk-up, I-shaped pieces, walk-up, T-shaped pieces, and six-story elevator serviced, T-shaped pieces (figure 7.5). Eventually the walk-up T was eliminated because of its excessive cost in comparison with the I shape.

Two of the site alternatives studied used continuously joined pieces to define grassy courtyards on the scale of the Phipps project (figure 7.6). Scheme A was designed earlier, using both T and I walk-ups, and four T elevator pieces, shown shaded. In Scheme B, the T walk-ups were replaced by I pieces. The plan as built comprised 1,416 two-, three-, four-, and five-bedroom apartments with a 39 percent coverage, excluding streets (figure 7.7). The design method was an important innovation because the site plan configuration could change through the final stages of design. This method gave both architect and developer a new flexibility in design development which was especially useful in large-scale projects. It also allowed adjustment of the mixture of apartment sizes through the final stages of design. This mixture, and the planning of each apartment type, was influenced by

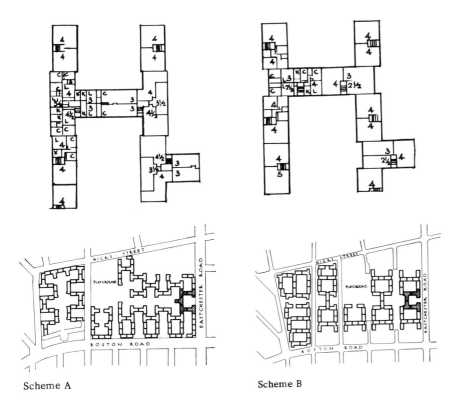

Figure 7.6. Clarence Stein. Hillside Homes, preliminary research into site-planning alternatives, using variations of the apartment cluster forms.

Scheme A   Scheme B

sociological studies of the types of families expected as tenants, followed a precedent set by Thomas for Metropolitan Homes.

Another significant 1930s project which continued the garden perimeter tradition was the Celtic Park Apartments, which was the last development of the City and Suburban Homes Company. It was designed by Ernest Flagg, who had

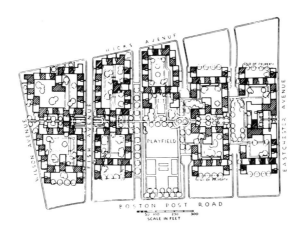

Figure 7.7. Clarence Stein. Hillside Homes final site plan, comprising 1,416 apartments with a coverage of 39 percent.

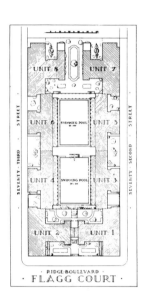

also designed their first project, the Clark Buildings, completed in 1898 (see figure 4.14). Flagg, now at the end of his important career in housing, completed a circle with this most significant of the private philanthropic companies in New York history.[18] Located in Long Island City on a block bounded by 48th and 50th avenues and 43rd and 44th streets, it was a large double perimeter, with an elaborately landscaped central garden axis.[19] Flagg constructed the block end buildings, while Springsteen and Goldhammer designed the sides. Together they formed a unified massing.

During the same period, Ernest Flagg also built another perimeter project: the most elaborate of the New York philanthropic blocks, called Flagg Court and completed between 1933 and 1936 on Bay Ridge Boulevard between 72nd and 73rd streets in Brooklyn. It was initiated by Flagg using capital from his Model Fireproof Tenement Company. The ten-story buildings incorporated a courtyard unequaled in its amenities, with two swimming pools, a tennis court, and an auditorium. Other social features of the project included recreation rooms, a bowling alley, and large roof playground (figure 7.8).[20] Most extraordinary was the manner in which these facilities were physically integrated into the courtyard to form a kind of public "agora," with colonnades along the sides bounding the swimming pools and gardens, lined by the indoor public rooms within the building. Flagg Court was as public and civil an expression of social housing as has been achieved in New York. There also was technological innovation, including the circular wall opening in each apartment containing an electric fan for mechanical ventilation; and exterior window shades for solar control. The complex was stylistically unified through the use of a Hindu motif in the garden and rooftop architecture and in some elevation detailing. Thus it continued the scenographic tradition in garden apartment architecture which had enjoyed such prominence a decade earlier. Change was in the air, however, and Flagg Court must have been seen by the new generation as an anachronism. It was built in the depths of the depression and at the height of excitement over a new social vision in architecture.

In no way was the new architectural vision better exposed than in the contrast between the two New Deal housing projects which had been completed by 1938 in New York City: the Harlem River Houses in Manhattan and the Williamsburg Houses in Brooklyn. Both were direct interventions by the PWA, and they differed radically in their design approaches. Harlem River Houses was designed by the PWA staff under Archibald Manning Brown. Horace Ginsbern was chief designer, with Charles F. Fuller and four associates. The design approach closely followed the New York City garden apartment tradition (figure 7.9).[21] The project, which was completed in 1937, contained 574 apartments on four irregular blocks in upper Manhattan between West 151st and 153rd streets and Macombs Place bordering the Harlem River. West 152nd Street was closed to traffic and incorporated into the landscaping. Coverage was 32 percent. Unlike Williamsburg Houses, the project was intended only for black occupancy (figure 7.10).

The apartments in Harlem River Houses varied in size from two to five rooms. Building massing assumed four- and five-story L-, T-, and Z-shaped sections, which were interlocked to fit the irregular blocks while producing a number of pleasant

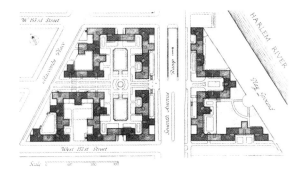

Figure 7.9. Charles F. Fuller, Horace Ginsbern, Frank J. Forster, Will R. Amon, Richard W. Buckley, John L. Wilson under Archibald Manning Brown. Harlem River Houses, completed in Harlem in 1937 by the Public Works Administration, closely following the design tradition of the 1920s New York City garden apartment.

Figure 7.10. Photo from a promotional brochure for Harlem River Houses showing the project as a continuation of the evolution from the Old Law tenement, the New Law tenement, and the Paul Lawrence Dunbar Apartments, all found in the adjacent blocks.

courtyards. The courtyards were well furnished, planted, and paved in brick. The massing of the project carefully responded to surrounding streets and buildings, as well as to changes in grade, which produced a variation in ground levels. The detailing of the buildings, while sometimes banal, was, at the same time, of the highest utility and permanence. Today the Harlem River Houses remains among the highest-quality public housing projects in New York City, and is one of the showpiece projects of the New York City Housing Authority. The architects incorporated all of the experience and learning of the previous decade. Nothing was left unconsidered. Murals and sculpture were included in the buildings and landscape design. A team of artists headed by Heinz Warnecke and including the famous black sculptor Richard Barthe was hired by the New Deal Treasury Art Projects Program to collaborate with the architects.[22]

Williamsburg Houses was designed by a PWA-commissioned team headed by Richmond H. Shreve, principal of Shreve, Lamb, and Harmon, architects of the Empire State Building. The chief designer was William Lescaze, with Matthew Del Gaudio, Arthur Holden, James F. Bly, and five associates. Williamsburg Houses was the first limited-income housing in New York City to depart radically from the spatial traditions of the garden apartment. The project, which was completed in 1938, covered ten standard blocks in Brooklyn, between Bushwick Avenue and Leonard, Maujer, and Scholes streets. Cross streets were closed to form three large "superblocks." Twenty articulated H- and T-shaped buildings housed 1,622 apartments with a coverage of 32.1 percent (figure 7.11).[23] The buildings could have been more continuous, but instead they tended to become isolated objects. The disparate effect was heightened by the placement of the buildings fifteen degrees out of alignment with the gridiron streets. The orientation was chosen primarily for aesthetic reasons, in contrast to the earlier proposals of Henry Atterbury Smith, which introduced a second geometry through careful analysis of functional criteria such as light and view (see figures 6.13 and 6.14). In Williamsburg Houses there was no economic justification for the isolated building approach. In fact, Williamsburg's construction cost was more per rental room than Harlem River Houses.[24]

The geometrical alignment of Williamsburg Houses produced an abrupt schism between the project and its surrounding environment (figure 7.12). The substitution of two-dimensional interest in the plan for three-dimensional spatial development related to site usage caused some basic functional problems. Solar orientation was not improved by the fifteen-degree angle, and the effects of the strong winter winds were definitely worsened in the courtyards. Talbot Hamlin wrote in 1938:

> Strangely enough, this [angle], so important in plan, in the actual group is not apparent except in a few places; so great is the number of buildings, and so large the area covered, that the impression . . . [is that] the *streets* were laid out crooked. . . . Certainly the unsymmetrical, sawtooth type of effect on the street fronts is neither inviting or informal; it has an aggressive formality of its own, a rhythm . . . that emphasizes rather than detracts from the institutional character of the whole group.[25]

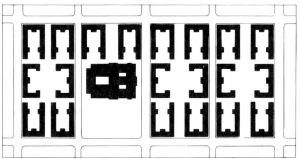

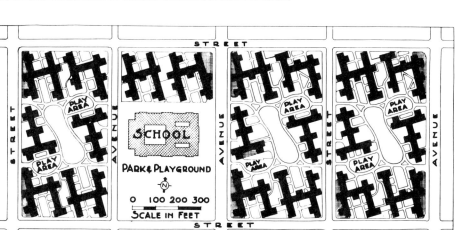

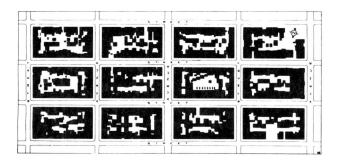

Figure 7.11. James F. Bly, Matthew Del Gaudio, Arthur Holden, William Lescaze, Samuel Gardstein, Paul Trapani, G. Harmon Gurney, Harry Walker, John W. Ingle, Jr., under Richmond H. Shreve. Williamsburg Houses, completed in Brooklyn in 1938 by the Public Works Administration. Original site before demolition (*below*); preliminary proposal by the NYCHA technical staff under Frederick Ackerman, which followed the New York City garden apartment tradition (*above*); final site plan, which represented a radical shift in design approach (*middle*).

Figure 7.12. James F. Bly, Matthew Del Gaudio, Arthur Holden, William Lescaze, Samuel Gardstein, Paul Trapani, G. Harmon Gurney, Harry Walker, John W. Ingle, Jr., under Richmond H. Shreve. Photo of Williamsburg Houses showing the abrupt schism between the geometry of the project and the surrounding area.

Beginning with the planning of Williamsburg Houses, a brief but intense struggle appears to have occurred in relation to the design sensibility of the new government housing projects. On one side was the technical staff of the New York City Housing Authority headed by Frederick Ackerman. He was a unique figure in American architecture. He pursued a lifetime interest in housing, and his work for the New York City Housing Authority included some of the most serious housing design research carried out in the United States. Lewis Mumford called him "perhaps with Grosvenor Atterbury and John Irwin Bright the first important architect, after Louis Sullivan, to be fully alive to the social responsibilities — and the economic conditioning—of architecture."[26] Early in his career, during World War I, Ackerman had a critical role in the development of government housing programs, especially through his study and application of British methods in housing.[27] In his later period with the Housing Authority, he upheld the design tradition of garden apartment perimeter planning, although he favored what he called a more "open-type" site plan. He opposed both "enclosed courts and long rows."[28] For most of the earliest NYCHA projects including Williamsburg, Queensbridge, and Red Hook Houses, the technical staff under Ackerman produced perimeter-type site plans in their preliminary proposals, which were changed in design development by the project architects, invariably to less defined configurations.

Ackerman's ideas were held in opposition to the generation of architects who were influenced by the new European modernism, which was also embraced within the highest circle of economic and political power. In the depths of the Great Depression this new architectural expression was seen as an affirmation of the potential for renewal of the capitalist system along liberal humanitarian lines, as put in abundant evidence by the architectural preferences and broader cultural advocacy of important forces like the Rockefeller family.[29] Ackerman, on the other hand, looked toward the rich heritage of the 1920s upon which to build the new social vision. One of the earliest research projects of the technical staff was a comparative study in 1934 of twenty-three low-rental housing projects in New York City. Most were 1920s garden apartments, and most could be considered starting points for the new government housing (figure 7.13).[30] Indicative of the approach favored by Ackerman was the 1935 technical staff proposal made for a third, unbuilt PWA project on an entire Manhattan block, between East 98th and 99th streets and First and Second avenues (figure 7.14).[31] Ackerman proposed a perimeter which opened at one end and at the middle. A similar prototype was repeated in his preliminary studies for the Williamsburg site.

For Williamsburg Houses, this approach was articulated by Ackerman early on. The Housing Authority technical staff had produced the early plan studies which retained the geometry of the gridiron through use of long U-shaped housing perimeters.[32] In addition, the Housing Authority had used Williamsburg as the basis for a competition to qualify architects for the new NYCHA housing work. This competition, carefully organized by Ackerman, produced 278 entries covering a broad range of design approaches. As a result, twenty-two architects were qualified. But none of these were named to design Williamsburg. Instead, the

Figure 7.13. New York City Housing Authority technical staff under Frederick Ackerman. Plate from a 1934 analysis by the newly organized Housing Authority of twenty-three variations on the garden apartment form. All were for moderate-income tenants and had been built by the end of the decade of the 1920s.

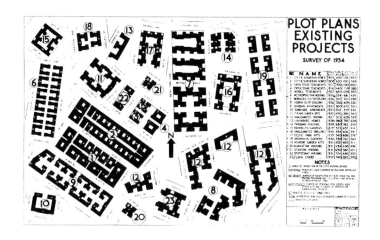

team chosen was the Housing Authority's Executive Board of Architects. This board had been named as advisers to the Housing Authority, and had not entered the competition, having judged it instead. The fact that the Lescaze team was chosen indicates that extraordinary influence was brought to bear. The stakes were high in the struggle for jobs and for design ideology alike. Protest was lodged from within the NYCHA technical staff, but to no avail.[33] Lescaze succeeded in employing the arbitrary geometrical alignment and the fragmented building forms which were closer to the *Zielenbau*-type organization of the much-admired *Seidlungen*.[34] His approach was rewarded as the only New York City housing included in the tenth anniversary exhibition at the Museum of Modern Art in 1939. The exhibition catalogue praised Williamsburg Houses as: "An oasis of open space and comfortable orderly buildings in the middle of a blighted slum area. Only 30 percent of the land is built on. The regular gridiron of the city street system has been modified to triple-size superblocks. . . . This reduces the dangerous through-streets and permits a more advantgeous arrangement of the buildings."[35]

At Williamsburg, the building elevations were equally important to the new architectural expression as plan and massing. They departed radically from the

Figure 7.14. New York City Housing Authority technical staff under Frederick Ackerman. Proposed PWA project for East Harlem, developed in 1935 using a perimeter block organization.

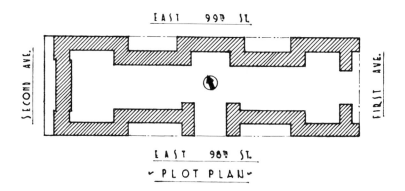

earlier projects of the 1920s. In place of the typical punched openings and eclectic detail, Williamsburg used the abstract geometry of horizontal bands and strip windows, arranged more according to interior function than for definition of hierarchies of public space. The reference was to precedents in industrial architecture rather than housing, which Ackerman faulted rather severely based on cultural criteria:

> I will admit that I cannot set up a very convincing argument why habitations in their effect or appearance should be differentiated from factories. It may be that we should not attempt to differentiate in the architectural expression of habitations, factories and schools. . . . However, we are living in a world where people have habits and points of view and judge structures under them. There is some ground for assuming that we should take all this into account.

Ackerman went on to question the validity of the functional criteria which had presumably been the basis for the aesthetic:

> Here is a case where fenestration is not ordered, nor is it random, nor is it wanton. It is simply a bunch of windows punched in a wall without the slightest "interest" in their arrangement. I am not objecting to the wide horizontal windows; those are certainly required in a plan in which a very large percentage of the windows in important rooms are located in positions where light values are minimum. It is the pattern of fenestration which results from such a condition that disturbs me. But given the site plan there is not much that one can do about that.[36]

The same simplistic and reductive tendency in site planning was evident in the entries to the New York City Housing Authority competition of 1934, with the influence of the *Zielenbau* plan appearing even in the entries of older, traditionalist architects such as John W. Ingle (figure 7.15).[37] By this time, the barracks "style" was spreading quickly to more and more questionable applications. In 1934 the architects Brounn and Muschenheim, in collaboration with the Tenement House Department, proposed an immense and very literal translation of *Zielenbau* principles for a section of the Upper East Side between East 60th and 70th streets, Second Avenue, and the East River (figure 7.16).[38] Muschenheim, who received his architectural training at the Academy of Fine Arts in Vienna, was one of the most literal early interpreters of European functionalism in New York. The project envisioned parallel rows of five- and twelve-story slabs, up to 720 feet long, the largest-scale *Zielenbau* plan to appear in New York City. The absurdity of the gigantism aside, this scheme typified the manner in which the new European work came to be misapplied in the United States. The *Zielenbau* form, which had evolved in Europe as a suburban housing type for relatively low densities (such as the Rothenberg Estate at Kassel; see figure 6.22), was applied to vastly different contexts in New York City. Even Catherine Bauer's important book, *Modern Housing,* published in 1934, exhibited much of the same ambivalence. While it indicated an unusually good understanding of the political origins of the new European housing, it suffered from the same lack of recognition of the fundamental difference in the physical-spatial dimension between the European and United States social housing applications. Descriptions of the European *seid-*

Figure 7.15. Horace Ginsbern (*above*) and John W. Ingle (*below*). Entries in the New York City Housing Authority Competition of 1934 using requirements similar to the actual site and program for Williamsburg Houses.

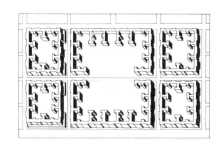

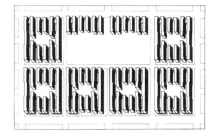

Figure 7.16. Brounn and Muschenheim. Proposal for an immense slum clearance project on the East Side made in 1935. It covered approximately fifty gridiron blocks and employed a very literal translation of European *Zielenbau* techniques.

SLUM CLEARANCE HOUSING PROPOSAL / DIST 5 / MANHATTAN

lungen and New York tenements were interspersed as if the two were interchangeable.[39]

Ackerman's most ambitious critique of the *Zielenbau* was published in *A Note on Site and Unit Planning,* co-authored with William Ballard.[40] It was an extensive economic analysis of a range of site configurations derived from the 1934 Housing Authority competition, and it provided definitive evidence that the long-term costs for *Zielenbau*-type plans were higher than for continuous perimeter massing. An important related project constructed massing models of fifty-eight existing housing projects with a spatial and demographic analysis of each.[41] These studies rank in importance with Ackerman's earlier analysis of the Phelps-Stokes Fund tenement competition of 1921 (see figures 5.10 and 5.11). Using data compiled through the Works Progress Administration, a carefully chosen series of forty-two site alternatives were evaluated for short- and long-term cost charac-

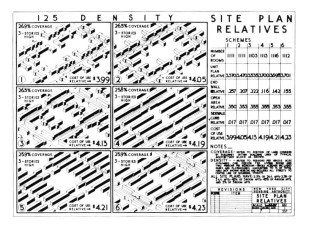
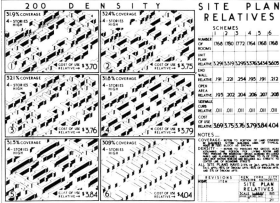

teristics. Continuing maintenance costs, an item rarely included in site design analyses, was a significant aspect of the study.

The site analysis used incremental densities of between 100 and 250 people per acre (ppa). Each density was assigned a series of alternative massing approaches ranging from simple "ribbons" to complex, articulate U forms, between three and six stories in height. Two important conclusions of the study were that lower coverage and simple ribbon forms did not necessarily guarantee lower costs, as shown by the 200 ppa alternatives (figure 7.17). This result questioned what was becoming low-rental design dogma: that for low-rise, low-rental housing, lower costs were synonymous with low coverages and simple forms. Ackerman suggested that one of the decisive factors related to lower costs was long-term maintenance or "cost of use." But the combination of aesthetic preferences and a concern only for reduction of initial costs caused Ackerman's arguments to be ignored.

In the end, however, Ackerman himself was ambivalent about how to address the cost issue without evoking the need for larger societal change. In his comparative study of twenty-three low-rental housing projects built in New York City (see figure 7.13), he expressed disappointment that not one of these philanthropic projects rented for less than eight dollars per room, which placed them above the reach of "the majority of families then occupying the decayed and obsolete structures of our slums." He added that "it is not surprising, therefore, that a somewhat skeptical attitude toward the 'better housing movement' has developed within the lower income groups."[42] At the same time, he was pessimistic about the possibility of combining excellent housing design with low costs. He saw the fundamental problem as helping families out of poverty, rather than providing cheap and substandard housing:

> The survey exposes the compromises made while groping for an answer to a problem which technique could not solve due to the incongruous relationship between the inevitable cost-of-use and the incomes of those for whom the projects were designed. This survey . . . makes one thing plain. Technique cannot solve the

Figure 7.17. Frederick Ackerman and William Ballard. Plates from the study published as *A Note on Site and Unit Planning,* which demonstrated that higher long-term costs were associated with *Zielenbau*-type planning.

problem as stated. It must first be stated in congruous terms: incomes of the lower income groups must be raised; cost-of-use must be cut down—one or both.[43]

His views were counter to the emerging ideology which held that modern building technique could solve the dilemma. Soon this elusive dream spread to the high-rise housing type.

As early as 1934, the newly formed Housing Study Guild, a private civic group, published a study which attempted to prove the economic advantage of the high-rise cross-plan tower over low-rise *Zielenbau* patterns. The analysis of the Housing Study Guild marked the beginning of the debate over high-rise versus low-rise buildings for lower-income families. It challenged prevailing "dogma . . . [that] the two-story flat was the cheapest form of housing."[44] However, the arguments for low-rise housing extended beyond issues of cost. For example, other objections to the high rise were sociocultural in their origins. Opponents argued that high-rise tower projects were incompatible with the way in which low-income families used neighborhoods. This position was taken by Clarence Stein in 1934 when he said that "elevator buildings are undesirable socially for families of limited means. The children should be near the ground where they can play freely."[45] And from elsewhere, the old bias remained that the poor should not be permitted the luxury of elevators.

The high-rise versus low-rise debate figured prominently in controversy over funding the proposed Corlears Hook renewal area on the Lower East Side, which comprised over fifty acres along the East River between the Manhattan and Williamsburg bridges. It was New York's first "superproject," and beginning around 1932 a number of development proposals had been reviewed by city and federal officials, including plans by the Housing Authority Technical Division, Andrew Thomas, Howe and Lescaze, Holden, McLaughlan and Associates, and John Taylor Boyd Jr. The schemes varied widely, between high- and low-rise; between garden perimeter and modernist configurations; and between private and public initiative.[46] Banking interests and private developers tended to argue, as Fred F. French did in 1934, that no large residential building under twelve stories should be built south of Fourteenth Street in order to meet the housing requirement of Lower Manhattan.[47] The Corlears Hook proposal by John Taylor Boyd Jr. followed that reasoning. Sponsored by the privately initiated Rutgers Town Corporation as a limited dividend project, it was the most developed proposal, evolving over several years. One hundred and one massive twelve-story towers were proposed, housing a total population of 30,000 persons[48] (figure 7.18). The Rutgers Town Corporation requested a $40 million loan from the PWA. The loan was turned down in May, 1934, ostensibly due to lack of funds.[49] Critics in the PWA, however, were also said to represent the other side of the high-rise debate, voicing the fear that the project would be likely to create "vertical sanitary slums."[50] By comparison, Queenstown, a companion project housing 37,000 persons in Queens, was proposed as resettlement housing for families displaced by Rutgers Town.[51] Designed by Voorhees, Gemlin, and Walker, it used two-story *Zielenbau* planning exclusively. The Rutgers Town Corporation managed to keep its scheme alive until 1939, when it finally abandoned its proposal, accusing Mayor LaGuardia of fa-

Figure 7.18. John Taylor Boyd, Jr. Rutgers Town housing proposal made in 1934 for the Lower East Side, covering approximately fifty gridiron blocks with twelve-story towers; criticized as likely to create "vertical sanitary slums."

voring public housing as a way of nurturing political patronage.[52] Eventually much of the site was covered with high-rise housing projects anyway. All were government housing. Beginning with the Vladeck Houses completed by the New York City Housing authority in 1941, the fate of the area was sealed for public housing rather than the white-collar housing envisioned by private interests.[53]

In spite of the relatively small size of the PWA program, it strongly influenced the development of housing design methods and ideology, and it laid the groundwork for the more extensive federal housing efforts which followed. An approach to control of its initiatives nationwide was established. It had to account for the widely varied local contexts of U.S. cities. The most obvious justification for government control over design decisions was simply that government money was used. Government design guidelines were needed to insure that quality was maintained. In the early days of the RFC and PWA, such guidelines were informal, largely working memos for the use of inside staff, not unlike the design guidelines of the earlier U.S. Housing Corporation and Emergency Fleet Corporation. But informal guidelines began to harden into specific design images by 1935, the year in which the PWA published its first comprehensive design document, called *Unit Plans*.[54] It was a catalogue of acceptable design possibilities for repetitive housing units, with some suggestions regarding site planning. The

March 1935 issue of the *Architectural Record* further elaborated PWA design expectations.[55]

The PWA's design guidelines were more specific in relation to apartment design than site planning. In general, apartment design standards were very high; room size, light, and ventilation were equal to the best of the 1920s garden apartments. *Unit Plans* systematically codified an array of interlocking apartment clusters that were named "T-units," "corner units," "ribbon units," and "cross plans." Altogether, fifty-four plans were presented and evaluated for a variety of criteria. Nine arbitrary site plans were discussed briefly. The *Architectural Record* article recommended that site planning be accomplished by arranging wooden blocks representing apartment clusters on a site model until a pattern evolved which recognized site characteristics and satisfied PWA critera (figure 7.19). To suggest much more would have been difficult without discussion of specific sites. Architects were cast in the role of children playing with blocks and a puzzle whose outcome was largely predetermined. The PWA simplified site issues by emphasizing certain trite criteria such as the removal of through traffic from project sites. Community participation was discouraged since the living habits of future residents were considered to have a negative influence on design; social workers would translate "usable information." While the recommendation of a 25 percent site coverage fulfilled the social reformers' goal of the "city in the park," it also meant also that almost any building geometry could work anywhere, and it facilitated the bureaucratic acquisition of design control.

Figure 7.19. Public Works Administration Housing Division. Illustration from guidelines for design of low-rental housing published in 1935. It advocated that design alternatives should be studied by arranging wooden blocks on a site model.

The PWA architect's fee structure encouraged massive repetition of PWA apartment clusters on open sites. According to an explanation published in the *Architectural Record,* "the fee for architectural service is in accordance with a definite schedule, and varies from 6 percent of construction amounting to $100,000 to 2 percent on $10,000,000. The fee is based on repetition of units with no unusual ground conditions."[56] This schedule obviously discouraged architects from breaking away from repetitive schemes for larger housing projects which were less well funded in relation to the volume and cost of construction. In addition, PWA suggestions for minimum unit standards also had a negative influence on housing quality, because "minimum standards" could easily be turned into "maximum standards," especially without a provision of incentives to produce better design. These "guidelines" quickly became frozen into laws written and unwritten, for bureaucratic design control.

The PWA guidelines did not appear until after the first New York City projects were already under construction. In comparison with the PWA projects already built in the city, the guidelines were strangely abstract and unreal. In the six years between the publication of Henry Wright's informal sketches of housing "joints" (see figure 6.11) and the PWA *Unit Plans,* analytic design tools had already degenerated into the simplistic legalities of guidelines. Surprisingly, Wright himself seemed to contribute to this simplification. The 1935 PWA issue of the *Architectural Record* included Wright's rendition of the Gropius Solar Study (see figure 6.28), a prime example of the rationalization of *Zielenbau*-type planning (figure 7.20). Nevertheless, Wright remained ambivalent toward, if not critical of, that approach. Only two years earlier he had written: "the more theoretic studies of the German architects, including those of the Bauhaus . . . seemingly result in a community organization even more rigid and monotonous than heretofore (and my own observation leads me to believe that this mania for universal exposure loses more in other living qualities than it gains in its one acknowledged aim)."[57]

In general, New Deal money built little social housing. Instead it nurtured the impending middle-class suburban housing boom by funding the construction of bridges and roads. In New York City this strange set of priorities was controlled by Robert Moses.[58] By the mid-1930s his plans for the city's new highway infrastructure were well on the way toward completion (figure 7.21). During the same period, both the government and private enterprise promoted extensively the small single-family suburban house as the American dream come true.[59] The dream was realized, of course, through the Federal Housing Administration (FHA) Loan Guaranty Programs, begun in 1934. The importance housing reformers and other progressives attached to the PWA involvement in New York City housing was hardly matched by financial expenditure. The direct grants to Harlem River Houses and Williamsburg Houses amounted to less than half of the $53 million that the PWA gave for the building of the Triborough Bridge alone, which opened in 1936. In 1937 the New York City Housing Authority freely admitted that Harlem River Houses and Williamsburg Houses "were undertaken primarily to create employment and stimulate the building industry rather than to wipe out the social evil of the slum."[60]

Figure 7.20. Henry Wright. Diagram published in 1935, which was a literal translation of the Gropius studies made several years earlier.

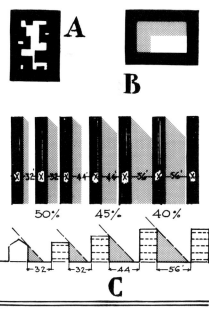

(A, B AND C) COMPARISON OF OLD AND NEW METHODS OF BLOCK DIVISION.

Figure 7.21. Aerial view of New York City looking west from Long Island, showing the network of new highways planned by the Department of Parks under Robert Moses and published in 1937.

New Deal economic policies saw the production of the single-family suburban house as a critical ingredient to the economic resurgence of the country. The strategy was not new; in the difficult economic period following World War I, the federal government had also sought to encourage private ownership of single-family houses.[61] For example, in 1919 the United States Department of Labor sponsored a national "Own Your Own Home Week," featuring a "home show" exhibition in New York City which was repeated for the next three years.[62] In the 1930s however, the technique became more sophisticated. By 1935 both government and private enterprise, frequently in collaboration, applied newly developed marketing techniques to economic recovery strategies. Their goal was to create a mass market for the single-family house simultaneously with the development of homeowner mortgage opportunities through the FHA.

The "model house" became a popular sales device. Every new suburban subdivision and every "home show" had its ideal home built to full scale. It became a repository for the latest technological advances in housing, almost all of which were related to appliances and equipment. Aggressive sales campaigns used the techniques of big business.[63] In 1937, with the unveiling of the *Ladies Home Journal* model house at the New York Home Show, this form of mass advertising became the province of the architectural profession as well as the automobile industry. The *Ladies Home Journal* replaced the traditional builder model cottage with a slick, modernistic "House of Tomorrow."[64] Designed by architects Wallace K. Harrison and J. Andre Fouiboux, it not only glamorized the normal array of consumer appliances, but also included architectural features such as a semicircular living room with huge motor-driven plate glass windows which disappeared into the floor in order to open the house to the outdoors. Record crowds visited the house.

One of the more bizarre model houses in New York City was built in 1934 on Park Avenue at East 39th Street on an abandoned construction site which had been planned for a gentlemens' club. Called "America's Little House," the small suburban cottage, complete with lawns and a picket fence, was designed by Bullard and Wendehack. It sat surreally among the tenements and high-rise office buildings within three blocks of Grand Central Station (figure 7.22).[65] The house was

Figure 7.22. Bullard and Wendehack. "America's Little House," a model suburban cottage constructed on Park Avenue near Grand Central Station in 1934 to promote private ownership of single-family houses.

built by the New York committee of an organization called National Better Homes in America, and the Columbia Broadcasting System maintained it. The National Better Homes in America was an amalgamation of local businesses and civic organizations which promoted private ownership of single-family houses. It had grown quickly in the 1920s, assisted by the United States Department of Commerce and Department of Agriculture. By 1930 its membership had grown to include 7,279 local committees.[66]

In 1936 the same Park Avenue location became the site of a far more interesting experiment. "America's Little House" was replaced by the "House of the Modern Age," a prefabricated design by William Van Alen for National Houses, Inc.[67] Using a steel panelized system, Van Alen worked at many levels to produce a number of innovative details, even including special exterior finishes developed with Du Pont engineers. The system was said to take many configurations, up to four stories in height; the cubistic forms contrasted with the "colonial" or other cottage styles used for most of the builder model houses. In these early years of the single-family house campaign, innovation in both design and construction was far more common than for the period of massive building later on, when design mediocrity was standard practice.

From the end of World War I, the architectural press reinforced the small house activities of government and business by attempting to make the small single-family cottage a legitimate concern of architects. In the mid-1930s this journalistic advocacy intensified. Every architects' and builders' magazine devoted issue after issue to the subject. The October 1935 small house issue of *Architectural Forum* was typical. It proclaimed "the profession's acceptance of the new approach to the small house" and devoted exhaustive coverage to "101 New Small Houses; All Within the Price Range for FHA Insured Mortgages." The 101 houses were supplemented with another 50 in 1936, and 50 more in 1937.[68] The architectural profession, plagued by unemployment, was ready to consider any design opportunity legitimate. In the face of larger and less comprehensive problems, the single-family suburban home became a preoccupation for architects and, perhaps, even a relief.

By 1936 Irwin S. Chanin, the builder of the Century and the Majestic on Central Park West (see figure 6.36), was completing the first houses in his suburban subdivision called Green Acres near Valley Stream, Long Island. It was built for upper-middle-class families, presumably those who could not cope with the expense and space limitations of Manhattan apartments like the Century. Chanin's planning borrowed heavily from Radburn, including the aphorism "A Community for the Motor Age." The 1,800 homes were convenient to a major highway which entered Manhattan at the Queensboro Bridge—only twenty-five minutes away. The "principle of traffic separation" combined with a "park system" and "playgrounds for children" were said to deliver the residents from the "menace of the automobile."[69] Most of the houses fronted on eighty-five private cul-de-sac streets with access to a park at the rear (figure 7.23). Each house contained between five and eight rooms, and included "garages, wood-burning fireplaces, complete insulation, oil burners, scientific kitchens, and landscaping." Green Acres was a harbinger of even greater things to come on Long Island.

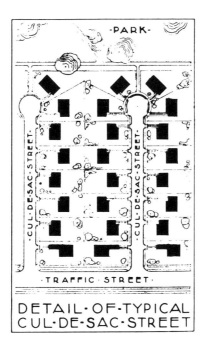

Figure 7.23. Irwin S. Chanin. Green Acres, near Valley Stream, Long Island; 1,800 privately developed single-family houses organized on Radburn principles and sold beginning in 1936.

The inherent inefficiencies of the single-family house made it more profitable than multiple-family housing. For example, a 200-apartment project in Manhattan might use only two oil-fired boilers, while a 200-house development on Long Island would require 200 oil burners, miles more wiring and piping, repetitive laundry equipment and utilities, and so on. General Electric, one of the most aggressive promoters of home ownership of the single-family house, collaborated frequently with government agencies. The company donated air time for the FHA's weekly radio broadcast entitled "What Home Means to Me."[70] On its own, General Electric launched massive advertising campaigns for appliances, using sales tactics which were often questionable.[71] During the 1920s and 1930s General Electric invaded the field of consumer goods, having concentrated previously on capital goods. The company became the largest manufacturer of household appliances. In 1941 appliance sales reached a high of $100 million.[72]

In 1935 General Electric sponsored an architectural competition whose subject was the single-family house.[73] The program called for a small- or medium-size house in a northern or southern climate to be sited on a 75-by-150-foot lot (figure 7.24). Entrants were required to incorporate a list of General Electric appliances in their designs (figure 7.25). One architect used seventy-six appliances. The $21,000 in prize money was the largest sum ever afforded for a housing competition, and the economic condition of the profession at that moment made it even more significant. The competition attracted 2,040 submissions, surely a record for any architectural competition in the United States. Entries were publicized in the media; an entire issue of *Architectural Forum* was devoted to the subject. During the following two years, the plans for 18 winning entries were

Figure 7.24. Richard Neutra. Second Place entry in the House for Modern Living competition sponsored by the General Electric Company in 1935 for a single-family suburban house on a 75-by-150-foot lot.

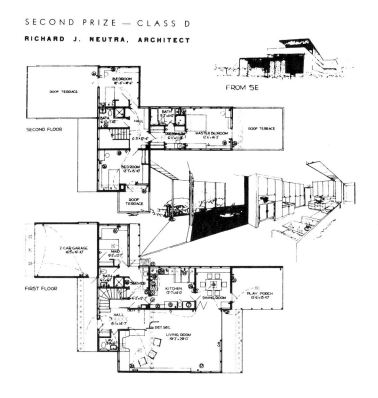

Figure 7.25. Charles C. Porter. Entry in the House for Modern Living competition; kitchen design with list of thirty-six General Electric appliances. The record number of appliances among the entries was seventy-five for a single house.

1	MODERN RADIO	ALARM-LITE CLOCK	19
2	REFRIGERATOR	HEATING PAD	20
3	WALL VENT FAN	SEWING MACHINE	21
4	MIXER	CEILING SUN LAMP	22
5	CHEF CLOCK	RADIANT HEATER	23
6	SINK & DISHWASHER	CURLING IRON	24
7	IMPERIAL RANGE	IMMERSION HEATER	25
8	COFFEE MAKER	RAZOR BLADE SHARP.	26
9	TOASTER	INFRA RED LAMP	27
10	STREAMLINE IRON	WATER HEATER	28
11	CLEANER	OIL FURNACE	29
12	NEO-CLASSIC RADIO	AIR CONDITIONER	30
13	PURITAN CLOCK	WORKSHOP	31
14	FLOOR SUN LAMP	SOLDERING KIT	32
15	URN SET	WASHING MACHINE	33
16	WAFFLE IRON	TWIN HOTPLATE	34
17	ILLUM. HOUSE NO.	FLATPLATE IRONER	35
18	MODERN SC RADIO	DRYER	36

made available to selected builders. As a result, some five hundred General Electric model houses were erected, with extraordinary publicity.[74]

Many other large corporations devised their own extensive advertising campaigns, including Johns-Manville, Kelvin, and Reynolds. Numerous other small house competitions followed, including those held by the *Ladies Home Journal* in 1938[75] and by the American Gas Association in 1938 and 1939.[76] The latter competition, like the General Electric competition, emphasized the maximum use of energy-consuming utilities and appliances. This attitude gained in acceptance, especially in the decades after World War II. Promotion of the new appliances penetrated even the domain of new public housing. Williamsburg Houses boasted all-electric kitchens, but the Housing Authority had to organize cooking classes for the housewives who had never used an electric stove.[77]

The response of government and big business to the economic crises of the 1930s molded the ideals of mainstream life and culture of the United States for the next forty years. They correctly understood that the building of the nation was essentially complete, and that the economy would have to shift from one of heavy production to a consumer orientation. The impacts on the culture of housing were profound, centered on the ownership of the suburban single-family house and maximum use of the automobile. During the New Deal era, the activities which reinforced these ideals impregnated every aspect of national life. Perhaps the most devastating activity to have recently come to light was the systematic destruction of the national light rail mass transit system. Beginning in 1932, General Motors started to purchase municipal electric railway systems and converted them to diesel buses.[78] Fifty-six cities were affected. In addition, General Motors sought to eliminate electric trains and replace them with diesel locomotives at the same time when every other technologically advanced nation was developing efficient electric railroads. Apart from selling diesel buses and locomotives, all of this was strengthened further by the New Deal highway programs. By gaining control of competing methods of transportation, General Motors was able to exert undue influence on a critical determinant of the way of life in the United States during the following decades.

In 1939 "The World of Tomorrow" as promoted by the New York World's Fair showed the holistic new vision in minute detail. A "Town of Tomorrow" had evolved into a well-defined physical entity including an exhibit of fifteen model houses sponsored by fifty-six building products manufacturers. The suburban revolution and its life-style were projected by Norman Bel Geddes for the General Motors "Futurama"; the "Perisphere" Theme Building posed "Democracity" by Henry Dreyfus, a vision which definitively pushed the urban dispersal ideology into the realm of the consumer age.[79]

Government philanthropy in housing became a permanent reality in 1937, when Congress passed the Wagner-Steagall Bill.[80] This legislation, known as the United States Housing Act, set up a permanent structure for federal low-rental housing, based on the PWA experience. In contrast to the PWA programs, this act did not authorize direct federal intervention at the local level. State and local authorities were empowered, as public corporations, to administer federal programs. The United States Housing Authority (USHA), also a public corporation, was formed to supervise these programs at the federal level. Local authorities entered into contracts with the USHA for project planning and construction. The 1937 act authorized the USHA to issue bonds and other obligations up to $500 million, an amount that varied in subsequent amendments. In just a year, funding was increased to $800 million. During the two decades between 1937 and 1957, the act was amended fourteen times. Jurisdiction over USHA shifted from the Department of the Interior in 1937 to the Federal Works Agency in 1939, to the National Housing Agency in 1942, to the Housing and Home Finance Agency in 1949. The label "public housing" came from the administrative organizations which handled the business of the USHA; first the Federal Public Housing Authority and then the Public Housing Administration. Between 1937 and 1957 545,594 low-rental apartments were built in the United States with USHA money.[81]

In 1938 the State of New York was permitted to begin building public housing through a public referendum which authorized a total expenditure of $300 million in funds for such purposes. In the following year a state public housing bureaucracy was formed through the creation of the Division of Housing, to replace the State Board of Housing, and the first $50 million in state bonds for public housing was authorized. In 1941 $25 million more was added.[82] These funds paved the way for a state housing program which, in general, replicated the philanthropic intentions and quality of design of the program of the USHA.

In effect, the USHA was more powerful than the earlier PWA. Although it required administration of its program through local agencies, the USHA retained the power to intervene in the formation and staffing of local authorities and to control both funding and design ideology.[83] In New York City, where the New York City Housing Authority had already been in existence for three years when the 1937 Housing Act was passed, such influence was undoubtedly minimal. The New York City Housing Authority became the local municipal corporation required by the new federal law. Between 1937 and 1957 the Housing Authority built 33,355 low-rental apartments under federal programs. An additional 29,601 low-rental apartments were built under state programs and 24,787 under city programs. As of 1975 a total of 165,892 apartments were being operated by the New York City Housing Authority.[84]

With the introduction of the large new federal and state housing funds totaling more than $1 billion, the domain of government housing production assumed greater local political significance than ever before—a condition which was underscored by Robert Moses' aborted attempt in 1938 to gain control of New York City's public housing programs. In his capacity as commissioner of parks, Moses prepared a brochure called *Housing and Recreation,*[85] outlining proposals for ten new public housing projects at a total cost of $245 million, completely ignoring the program of the New York City Housing Authority. Through a heavy media campaign and political lobbying, he hoped to be able to gain sufficient political support to control the Housing Authority. His attempt was foiled by Mayor LaGuardia, however, and he had to wait until 1948 to add public housing to his burgeoning sphere of influence.[86] His implied tactics alienated a broad spectrum of the architects who were then working on public housing. Objections were raised to the projected high cost of land, high densities, excessive slum clearance, and methods of raising revenues.[87] In general, however, Moses' brochure indicated a design approach which was sympathetic to the new modernist urbanism. It made perfect sense for the Commissioner of Parks to make his foray into housing via the "city in the park."

After the creation of USHA, federal design guidelines proliferated, becoming more stringent, more abstract, and more rigid in terms of aesthetic imagery. The USHA study *Planning the Site,* published in 1939, presented an extensive series of rather specific project images for idealized sites.[88] A revised and enlarged version, called *Public Housing Design,* dealt with site configurations identical to those of the 1939 study, with the addition of four more site alternatives.[89] One important design determinant was the USHA's specification of the minimum dimensions between buildings based on building heights. These this ranged from fifty feet for one-story buildings to 75 feet for six stories. Such rules did not lend themselves to easy graphic representation for complex building forms. They were usually represented by simple "ribbon" shapes, not unlike the guidelines published by Gropius ten years earlier (figure 7.26). Unfortunately, what was easy to represent was also easy to approve.

Among the other federal agencies besides the USHA which became involved with housing design controls, the most notable was the Federal Housing Administration. The FHA, with its vast program of mortgage guarantees, all involving design approvals, became the single most influential source of housing design standards in the United States. Virtually all privately financed housing was subject to its review through direct and indirect controls. *Architectural Planning and Procedure for Rental Housing,* published by the FHA in 1938, outlined design methods and solutions which would insure FHA approval of mortgage guarantees under the provisions of the 1937 Housing Act.[90] The preoccupation with categorizing types of units was presented in the accustomed bureaucratic manner (fig-

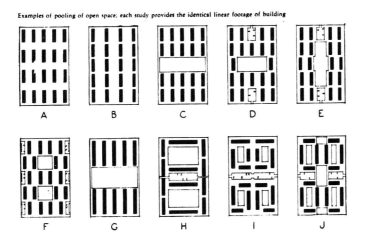

Examples of pooling of open space: each study provides the identical linear footage of building

A   B   C   D   E

F   G   H   I   J

Figure 7.26. United States Housing Authority. Diagram of ideal site alternatives based on minimum dimensions between buildings for maximum light and air; each provides an identical linear footage of housing. First published in 1939 and revised by the Federal Public Housing Authority in 1946.

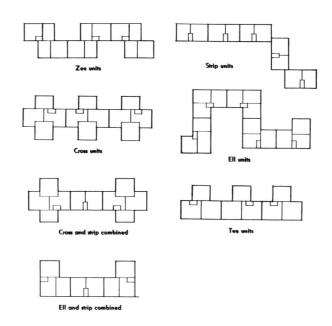

Figure 7.27. Federal Housing Administration, Rental Housing Division. Diagram of alternative apartment clusters to be considered for housing requiring FHA approvals for mortgage guarantees; published in 1938.

Zee units

Strip units

Cross units

Ell units

Cross and strip combined

Tee units

Ell and strip combined

Figure 7.28. Federal Housing Administration, Rental Housing Division. Alternative "good" and "poor" apartment plans evaluated in relation to FHA mortgage guarantees, showing a standard arrangement of New York City apartments as "poor and unsatisfactory."

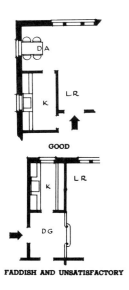

GOOD

FADDISH AND UNSATISFACTORY

ure 7.27). But in the same brochure, the FHA went beyond simple enumeration of standards to analyze "good" and "poor" plans. In one case, the "sunken" living room with "raised" kitchen and dining area, long a standard feature of New York middle-class apartments, was criticized as "faddish and unsatisfactory." A single-level alternative was suggested (figure 7.28).

The Housing Act of 1937 and its subsequent interpretations, mandated limitations in initial cost and building coverage. The total cost of housing projects for cities with a population of over 500,000 was limited to a maximum of $1,250 per room.[91] This figure represented a considerable reduction of PWA allowances, 40 percent less than Harlem River Houses, which was $2,103 per room.[92] Under the assumption that higher coverage would lead to higher costs while reducing open space amenities, the USHA refused to approve any project of more than 35 percent coverage.[93] Even 35 percent was considered high, and lower figures were generally obtained. Thus, government-assisted, low-rental housing became synonymous with low cost and, by extension, low coverage. The official argument for low-cost construction was that given a constant amount of money, many more people could obtain good housing if costs were kept down.

The first USHA-funded project in New York City was Red Hook Houses in Brooklyn, between Dewight, Clinton, Lorraine, and West 9th streets. Completed in 1939, it demonstrated what "low cost" meant in design terms. Alfred Easton Poor headed a design team of associated architects including William F. Dominick, W. T. McCarthy, William I. Hohauser, Electus D. Litchfield, Jacob Moscowitz, and Edwin J. Robin. As completed, it contained 2,545 apartments in twenty buildings, with a 22.5 percent coverage.[95] As at the Williamsburg Houses, the preliminary site design for Red Hood had been influenced by Frederick

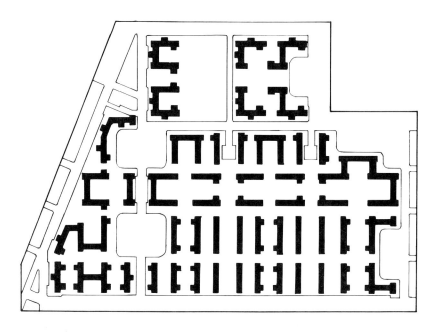

Ackerman and the technical staff of the Housing Authority.[96] Their proposal was limited to three- and four-story buildings, organized along a central axis fed by repetitive variations on the perimeter form (figure 7.29). The final scheme retained the central axis, but drastically weakened the hierarchy and structure of the public space through use of a rather literal interpretation of prevailing federal standards. Six-story, cross-shaped building "units" were joined together to form two articulated Z-shaped buildings for each block over a sixteen-block area (figure 7.30). The final design for the site had begun before the formation of the USHA with a $16 million allocation for construction. In keeping with the new USHA cost policy however, the project allocation was reduced to $12 million in 1938. Of course, cutting costs by one-quarter necessitated substantial changes in the original design.

Cost cutting meant that Red Hook's cross-shaped buildings underwent three stages of revision (figure 7.31). The result was a reduction of the gross floor area per room from 221 square feet to 172 square feet, justified as an elimination of "waste space." Each apartment was allotted one closet with a door; curtains were installed on the remaining closets. No interior doors were permitted to separate kitchens from living areas. Plaster lath and studs were used instead of masonry for many of the interior partitions. Although elevator service was considered necessary because of the six-story height of the buildings, stops on the second, fourth, and sixth floors were omitted. The buildings were not made higher, in spite of the elevators, because New York City building law required a second fire exit for seven or more stories. Lower building heights would have increased the coverage, thereby increasing the cost of expensive footings needed because of poor soil conditions on the site. They also would require additional roof, corridor, and base-

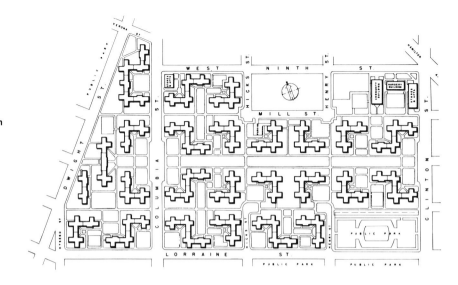

ment areas; six stories were considered the ideal height. Red Hook's only claim
to innovation was cost reduction. The final cost per room was only $1,137, con-
siderably less than the federal maximum. Previously, innovative philanthropic
projects had always aimed at improving housing standards. Red Hook reversed
this trend for the next two decades of housing philanthropy in New York City.

Red Hook Houses' immediate successor, Queensbridge Houses, was designed
by William F. Ballard, Henry S. Churchill, Frederick G. Frost, and Burnett C.
Turner. The project was located in Queens, between Vernon Boulevard, 21st Street,
40th Avenue, and 41st Road and completed in 1940. It contained 3,149 apartments
and was built at a cost per room of $1,044—8 percent lower than at Red Hook.[97]
Frederick Ackerman and the technical staff of the Housing Authority had influ-

Figure 7.31. William F. Dominick, W. T.
McCarthy, William I. Hohauser, Electus D.
Litchfield, Jacob Moscowitz, and Edwin J.
Robin, under Alfred E. Poor. Red Hook Houses
preliminary and final apartment plans, showing
changes made after the United States Housing
Authority cut the budget.

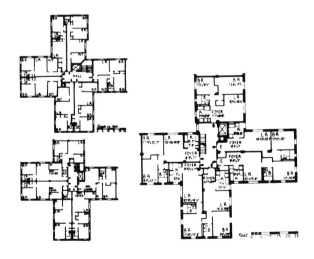

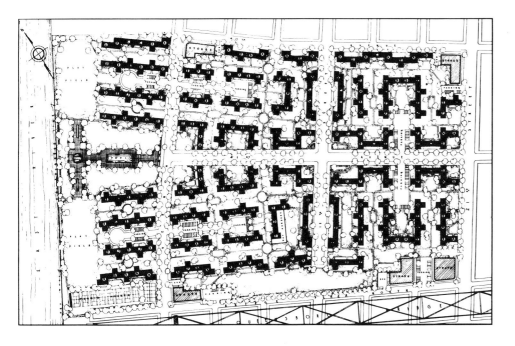

Figure 7.32. New York City Housing Authority technical staff under Frederick Ackerman. Preliminary design proposal for Queensbridge Houses in Queens made in 1936; using a central axis with variations on the garden apartment form, it was limited to three- or four-story buildings.

enced an earlier site plan,[98] as they had for Williamsburg and Red Hook (figure 7.32). Like the others, the earlier plan used three and four-story buildings. The approach to the public space was more structural and hierarchical, especially when compared with the final plan, which was generated principally by repetition of the Y-shaped units.

The Y was desirable because it contained more facade area than conventional T units, and therefore it allowed more rooms to cluster around a single elevator core and still receive adequate light (figure 7.33). Unfortunately, the Y units produced rather bewildering relationships between buildings on the site. With the Y system, any given street might be fronted with buildings oriented at up to six different angles. Aesthetically, in relation to the traditional tenement patterns, the Queensbridge Houses site plan offered a bold new image in terms of both decreased coverage and nonrectilinear geometry (figure 7.34). But in the end, this "revolutionary" geometry was no more convincing than at the earlier, more conservatively planned Williamsburg Houses. By 1940 the New York City Housing Authority had completed Vladeck City Houses, its first municipally-financed housing, comprising 240 apartments incorporated with Vladeck Houses, a much larger federal project.[99] Located between Henry, Water, Gouverneur, and Jackson Streets on a portion of the controversial Rutgers Town site, the Vladeck Houses was the first of the long succession of government projects which eradicated much of the old Lower East Side. The designers, headed by Richmond H. Shreve of Shreve, Lamb, and Harmon with William F. R. Balland and Sylvan Bien, organized the massing in *Zielenbau* fashion. The massing of the rows was somewhat ecclectic, however, with the barracks line broken by offset geometry (figure 7.35).

Figure 7.33. William F. Ballard, Henry S.
Churchill, Frederick G. Frost, and Barnett C.
Turner. Final site design for Queensbridge
Houses. Completed in 1940, it used a six-story
Y-shaped units which negated the possibility of
a strong spatial definition of either street or
garden.

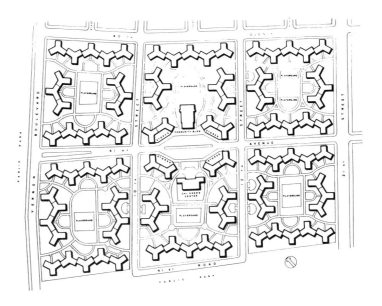

Still, given consideration of solar orientation, the planning made more functional sense than the site design of Williamsburg Houses that Shreve had also participated in. Williamsburg and Vladeck typified the two public housing site approaches which became standard for the era: the centroidal cluster and the linear barracks.

Prior to 1941 the New York City Housing Authority avoided building high-rise housing by seeking inexpensive sites which offset the higher costs of low-rise construction. This policy was in keeping with the provisions of the Housing Act of 1937, which prohibited the use of high rise except where low rise was impractical. The Red Hook land was cheap because of bad bearing conditions. At South Jamaica Houses and Clason Point Gardens, completed in 1940 and 1941, the land was cheap because it was located in the outer boroughs. The use of inexpensive, low-rise, quasi-*Zielenbau* site planning augmented this savings. The Clason Point project, designed by York and Sawyer, Aymar Embury II, and Burton and Bohm for a site on Metcalf, Noble, Story, and Seward avenues in the Bronx, was only two stories high with a coverage of 20.8 percent (figure 7.36). At the opening dedication, the USHA administrator, Nathan Straus, related: "I have always believed that men and women were not intended to live in tall, crowded buildings and that children can best enjoy a happy and healthy childhood if, instead of being crowded into even the best six, eight, and ten-story buildings, they are enabled to live amid the surroundings that you see as you look about you today."[100]

Despite the prevalence of these attitudes, aesthetic, social, and economic arguments were beginning to reinforce the idea of high-rise design. Le Corbusier had visited New York City in 1935 and, with a flourish of salient observations,

Figure 7.34. William F. Ballard, Henry S. Churchill, Frederick G. Frost, and Barnett C. Turner. Queensbridge Houses photo showing the abrupt schism between the site geometry of the project and the surrounding area.

Figure 7.35. William F. R. Ballard and Sylvan Bien under Richmond H. Shreve. Vladeck and Vladeck City Houses completed in 1940 on the Lower East side at Corlears Hook, using an offset variation on *Zielenbau* planning.

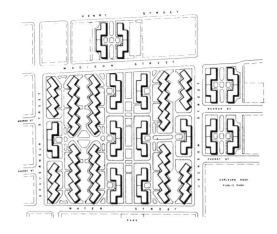

Figure 7.36. York and Sawyer, Aymar Embury II, and Burton and Bohm. Clason Point Gardens site plan, completed in 1941, as one of the few low-rise, low-density public housing projects built in New York City, using only two stories and quasi-*Zielenbau* site planning.

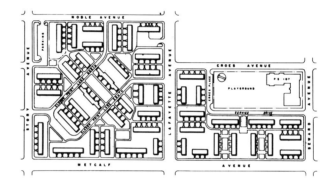

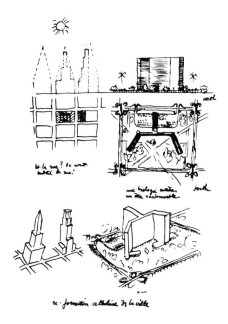

Figure 7.37. Le Corbusier. Proposal for reorganizing the Manhattan gridiron into megablocks using the "city in the park" image (left); sketched after his visit to New York City in 1935.

Figure 7.38. A cartoon published in *The New Republic* in 1938 criticizing the lack of technological progress in low-rental housing (right), in comparison with the concrete achievements of the military.

advocated transforming Manhattan to his "city in a park" image. He said that the "skyscrapers were to small" and sketched Manhattan blocks recombined into megablocks. Oversized and formally idealized skyscrapers were placed in the middle and surrounded by a continuous green park (figure 7.37). In 1937 Le Corbusier outlined his criticism and vision in *Quand les cathedrales etaient blanches.*[101] The book lent authority and respectability to various scaled-down versions of the "city in the park." A cartoon published by the *New Republic* in April 1938 expressed the dominant progressive view that the poor were entitled to as much technological advancement as the military, an ideal which the high-rise tower seemed to realize (figure 7.38).

The first high-rise tower project in the history of New York housing philanthropy was East River Houses, completed in 1941 as the city's fifth USHA-financed development. The site was a slum clearance area in East Harlem, bordered by East 102nd and 105th streets and the East River Drive.[102] The design team consisted of Voorhees, Walker, Foley and Smith, Alfred Easton Poor, and C. W.

Figure 7.39. Voorhees, Walker, Foley, and Smith;
Alfred Easton Poor; and C. W. Schlusing, under
Perry Coke Smith. East River Houses preliminary
and final site plans, showing the transformation
from a low-rise *Zielenbau* pattern to high-rise
towers combined with lower buildings.

Schlusing, with Perry Coke Smith as chief architect; all had previous experience in low-rental public housing. The site plan completely obliterated two streets and created one large superblock. The architects offered no functional explanation for the forty-five-degree orientation of the buildings in relation to the Manhattan gridiron, not even for solar orientation. The angle chosen was apparently an aesthetic decision, based on the shape planned for the adjacent city park, which Robert Moses made triangular to allow a longer side with a river view. (Eventually, a footbridge was built over the East River which connected the park to Wards Island.) Two alternatives were developed for the site: one used six-story elevator buildings; the other mixed six-, ten-, and eleven-story buildings (figure 7.39). The high-rise scheme was cheaper than the low-rise by a factor of 3 percent for almost the same number of apartments (1,170 as built). Only six of the twenty-eight buildings were high-rise, accounting for the relatively small difference in cost between the two schemes; had the entire project been high-rise, the difference would have increased immensely. With the completion of East River Houses, the decades-old prejudice that the poor should not live in towers was reversed by the realities of housing cost (figure 7.40).

The high-rise, government-subsidized precedent set by East River Houses remained the exclusive model for housing development in East Harlem. A report published in 1945 by the Manhattan Development Committee shows all of East Harlem redeveloped with high-rise towers in parklike settings (figure 7.41).[103] By 1950 a second high-rise project had already been completed, and Robert Moses' Mayor's Committee on Slum Clearance identified four more sites. He slated the remainder of the entire area for demolition.[104] Eventually thirteen additional sites were developed, four by the NYCHA and nine by other agencies. The result is that today approximately one-third of East Harlem is covered with postwar subsidized housing, almost all designed according to the "tower in the park" image. A similar scenario was developed on the Lower East Side, where by the close of the 1950s tenements had been replaced by massive concentrations of "tower in the park" projects.

Figure 7.40. Voorhees, Walker, Foley, and Smith; Alfred Easton Poor; and C. W. Schlusing; under Perry Coke Smith. East River Houses aerial photo; completed in 1941 as the first public housing in New York City to incorporate high-rise towers.

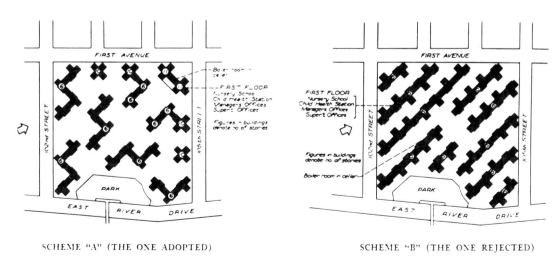

SCHEME "A" (THE ONE ADOPTED)

SCHEME "B" (THE ONE REJECTED)

Figure 7.41. Map of East Harlem prepared in 1950, showing Public Housing projects which had been planned up to that time.

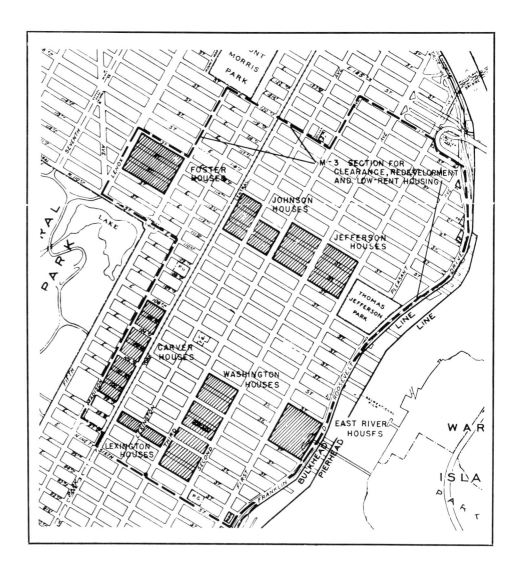

8

Pathology of Public Housing

L IKE World War I, World War II forced the United States government to take extraordinary action in relation to national housing production. Unlike the earlier precedent, however, the government interventions of World War II were facilitated by well-established social housing programs, from the mortgage guarantees of the Federal Housing Administration (FHA), to the comprehensive agenda of the United States Housing Authority (USHA). All existing government housing activities were diverted. In 1940, Congress authorized the USHA to channel its funds to housing projects for persons engaged in national defense activities. In 1941 Title VI was added to the National Housing Act, authorizing liberal mortgage insurance to builders who provided new homes in critical defense areas. This provision generated 962,000 new dwellings nationwide before it was discontinued in December 1947. In addition, the 1941 Lanham Act provided separate funds for construction of temporary and permanent housing for persons engaged in national defense work. By December 1947 this act had generated another 945,000 new dwellings. The Division of Defense Housing Coordination was established in 1941 to coordinate government defense housing activities. In 1942 an executive order from President Roosevelt consolidated the various government housing agencies into the National Housing Agency.[1]

Public housing for low-income families in New York City benefited little from World War II national defense activities in housing. Only three new projects were built under these programs, and all were occupied by families of middle-income defense workers. More than six hundred public housing apartments formerly occupied by low-income families were turned over to families of U.S. servicemen by November 1943. This new influx was accomplished by waiving the requirement that public housing applicants demonstrate need based on proof that they were living in substandard conditions.[2] It was only after the war that the projects were returned to poor families.

The first national defense housing project to be completed in New York City was Wallabout Houses in 1941. The project was built with USHA money, and was designed by William Y. Hohauser, Carl A. Vollmer, and Walter Wefferling. Two

13-story towers housed 207 families at 25 percent coverage. The project was located near the Brooklyn Navy Yard bordering the Brooklyn-Queens Expressway between North Elliott and North Portland avenues. Wallabout Houses was reserved for families of enlisted navy personnel, and room sizes were increased over previously built federally funded projects. At the opening dedication, the address of Rear-Admiral Adolphus Andrews captured the new spirit of purpose in public housing: "[This project] will mean that these sailor men of ours will serve our country with a better spirit, with greater confidence, with higher morale, if they know that their wives and children are safely located in a home like this, surrounded by their friends and healthy environment."[3]

The second federally funded national defense project, Edwin Markham Houses on Richmond Terrace on Staten Island, was completed in 1943. Designed by DeYoung and Moscowitz and Frederick Mathesius, it housed 360 workers' families from nearby shipyards and defense industries. Following the precedent of the earlier Clason Point Gardens, the project was only two stories high with 26 percent coverage (see figure 7.36). The first New York State public housing project, Fort Greene Houses (now called Whitman-Ingersoll), also was used as national defense housing. Designed by a consortium of nine firms and completed in 1944 on a site bordered by Prince, Carlton, Myrtle, and Park avenues in Brooklyn, Fort Greene Houses contained 3,501 apartments with 22 percent coverage. Room sizes were increased beyond USHA requirements. The buildings consisted of the ordinary T-, L-, and X-shaped units. Heights varied between six, eleven, and thirteen stories, following the precedent of East River Houses.

In the period between the Great Depression and the end of World War II, the outlook and interests of United States architects had changed considerably. The vast amount of building that resulted from the prosperity of the 1920s was abruptly extinguished by the market crash. During the next five years, architectural activity was almost nonexistent. This period of extreme hardship for architects led to professional social welfare activity on a scale unprecedented before or since. By 1931, the Architects' Emergency Employment Committee had been organized in New York to explore job opportunities outside of the devastated private offices. It remained active throughout the period of crisis.[4]

Similar organizations were begun in other cities including Philadelphia, Boston, and Cleveland. In the same year, the American Institute of Architects (AIA) annual convention authorized a lobby for federal employment of architects. The government responded,[5] with New Deal programs. Architects, especially the younger generation, had little choice but to join and espouse the New Deal's social rhetoric, designing according to its particular public works type of functionalism. Within the milieu of economic disaster, human suffering, and the uncertainties of European fascism, the profession was forced to develop a new social consciousness. As architects began to question existing professional institutions, "alternative" architectural organizations, publications, and schools began to appear.

The first alternative magazine was *Shelter*, which emerged in 1932 from a parochial publication of the T-Square Club in Philadelphia. Published until 1933, and again from 1938 to 1939, *Shelter* expressed concern for social issues in architecture and published some of the new modernist work that also had started to make its way into the established architectural media. The first professional alternative to the American Insitute of Architects was the Federation of Architects, Engineers, Chemists, and Technicians (FAECT), founded in 1933. Among other things, FAECT acted as a labor union for architects and draftsmen. FAECT's membership was the workforce, rather than the managers who continued to sustain the AIA. This period represented the first and only time that this particular constituency obtained a strong voice within the architectural establishment. FAECT was affiliated with the CIO and had a distinctive socialist bent. Between 1934 and 1938 the organization published a magazine, *Technical America*, which gave considerable coverage to architectural issues. The architectural workforce was not the only group to feel the winds of change, however. Architectural education also stirred. The first alternative architectural curriculum in the United States was initiated by Joseph Hudnut at Columbia University. The new curriculum was vastly different from its Beaux-Arts predecessor, and included significant programs in housing under the direction of Henry Wright and Carol Aronovici.[6]

The labor unions were frequently the source of the most interesting of the political activity that was interwoven throughout the culture of architecture in the 1930's. FAECT was the most powerful of these, dominating this brief but intense period of advocacy for the architectural workforce. The organization was founded at a mass meeting held in New York in 1933 in response to a "Code of Practice" that the American Institute of Architects had submitted to the federal government.[7] The code included wage guidelines proposed for use under the newly passed National Recovery Act. The guidelines scheduled architectural draftsmen with two or more years of experience to receive only fifty cents per hour. Enraged by the meager figure and the apparent lack of concern about the welfare of workers so directly related to the AIA membership, the 1933 mass meeting was organized to fight the code. As *Technical America* editorialized on the union's fourth anniversary: ". . . almost totally without economic organization, full of illusions as to their role in industry, with strong prejudices against unions or contact with the organized labor movement, architects and engineers suffered the worst kind of degradations and demoralization. Some dared to fight back."[8]

FAECT sponsored a number of job actions by architects through the end of the 1930s against both private and government practice. In June 1936 FAECT members organized what was probably the first "sit-down" strike by architects.[9] Employed by the New York City Department of Parks, the strikers barricaded themselves in their offices after being harassed by Robert Moses and his assistants, who opposed union-organizing activities. The Architectural Guild of America (AGA), was another prominent labor organization for architects and draftsmen, with an active chapter in New York. In September 1936, through the combined efforts of both FAECT and AGA, a major wage increase was secured for the seven thousand architects and engineers working for the WPA.[10]

The war tended to sublimate the architectural concerns of labor organizations. After the war the organizations remained silenced, undoubtedly because of the peculiar political economy of the architectural profession. However, many of the issues raised in the pages of *Technical America* remained with the profession: for example, questions of accessibility of the architectural profession to lower-income groups; increasingly rigid requirements for professional licensing; and the changing nature of academic architecture programs. Conditions in architectural offices were also criticized, particularly the obvious issues of economic exploitation of young architects. The dichotomy between the architect-businessman and the nameless design-draftsmen was a recurring theme. And the established architectural journals were viewed with some humor and anger. Many of these same themes were central to the concerns of the Designers of Shelter in America (DSA), another alternative professional organization founded in 1936 in New York. The DSA concerned itself with the welfare of the general population instead of the traditional clientele of wealthy individual patrons. The DSA stressed that issues of "style," whether modernist or otherwise, were secondary to issues of purpose and function.[11]

Toward the end of the 1930s the progressive thinking and activity of U.S. architects began to be augmented by immigrant Europeans who were escaping Fascism. Many of the most prominent were invited to take academic posts, where their influence was enormous. Radical new design programs were implemented by Laszlo Moholy-Nagy at the New Bauhaus in Chicago in 1937, Walter Gropius and Marcel Breuer at Harvard University in the same year, Ludwig Mies van der Rohe and Ludwig Hilbersheimer at the Armour Institute (which became the Illinois Institute of Technology) in Chicago in 1938, and Serge Chermayeff at Brooklyn College in 1942 (and later in 1947 at the New Bauhaus in Chicago).[12] Others, such as Jose Luis Sert at Yale, were influential visiting professors.

The European influx channeled American activism into directions that it might not have taken otherwise. Gropius, a figure crucial to the European architectural revolution 30 years earlier, had great influence on American architecture. His ideas were quickly embraced by United States progressives. For example, Joseph Hudnut, who left Columbia University for Harvard in 1935, found his ideas eclipsed by those of Gropius, whom he hired at Harvard in 1937. The program that Hudnut began at Columbia withered, an unfortunate development because the Columbia program had been different in its emphasis and was potentially as interesting as the program subsequently developed at Harvard. If, in retrospect, the results of European dominance are questionable, the union of the United States and European movements at the time produced boundless optimism about the changes which would occur in architecture in the United States. As if on cue, in 1938 the Bauhaus was given the official ritualistic blessing of a major retrospective at the Museum of Modern Art.[13]

The list of progressive activities in architecture continued to grow through the 1940s. In 1940 in San Francisco, a group called Telesis was formed to research and publicize issues concerning architecture's "relation to society."[14] In 1941 the magazine *Task* was founded at Harvard, taking up many of the concerns *Shelter* espoused. New organizations also appeared at this time in New York. Architects' committees were formed by the National Council of Soviet-American Friendship and the Committee of the Arts, Sciences, and Professions. Both organizations pursued a broad range of progressive political causes. The American sections of the Congrès Internationaux d'Architecture Moderne (CIAM) were established in New York and Boston.[15] Founded in 1928, CIAM had been one of the key organizations that contributed to the unification of a modernist polemic in Europe.[16] Even the New York chapter of the AIA, the Architectural League, and established professional media such as *Architectural Forum* assumed more progressive stances.

Perhaps the most prestigious alternative professional organization was the short-lived American Society of Planners and Architects (ASPA), founded in New York in 1944 with additional chapters established in Boston, Philadelphia, and Washington. Its select membership of architects and theorists included seventy persons who would shape the direction of United States architecture in the 1950s. During its four years of existence, the executive board included Serge Chermayeff, Walter Gropius, George Howe, Louis Kahn, Carl Koch, Jr., Oscar Stonorov, and Hugh Stubbins, Jr. Among its other members were Alfred H. Barr, Jr., Marcel Breuer, Gordon Bunshaft, Wallace K. Harrison, Henry Russell Hitchcock, John M. Johansen, Philip Johnson, Edgar Kaufman, Jr. Richard Neutra, I. M. Pei, Jose Luis Sert, Eero Saarinen, and Konrad Wachsmann. Its membership roster represented the next generation of architect-manager, rather than the office workforce of the earlier labor organizations. The literature of the ASPA expressed a commitment to urbanism and stressed the necessity for the integration of aesthetics, economics, technology, and sociology within architecture.[17]

Immediately after World War II, the architectural profession was swept by an overwhelming current of conservatism. By the end of the war, architects hardly resisted the long campaign by government and industry to make legitimate the transformation of United States urbanism, together with the concurrent architectural problem of the modest single-family house. Undoubtedly an invisible carrot over the heads of many architects was the certainty, after years of hardship, of a postwar economic boom. Even more important was the common knowledge that the boom would take place in the trouble-free wilds of suburbia rather than in the increasingly problematic center cities. The essential ingredient for suburbanization, the road infrastructure, had been provided by the public works programs of the New Deal, and the postwar priorities for industrial production had been fully formulated. A typical case was General Electric, the largest manufacturer of household appliances. As early as 1941 (before Pearl Harbor), GE began to plot its strategy for expansion of production after the conclusion of World War II, so that it could redeploy its increased war-time production capacity toward the needs of the new consumer culture.[18]

During the war, government and industry played up the suburban house to the families of absent servicemen. Between 1944 and 1946, some of the profession's most promising young architects published their "dream houses" in a series in the *Ladies Home Journal.*[19] A part of the same series was exhibited at the Museum of Modern Art in 1945 in a show called "Tomorrow's Small House." The exhibition predictably included Frank Lloyd Wright, who had long advocated the ideal of the single-family house in the pages of the *Ladies Home Journal.* Wright's "Broadacre City" ideal also paralleled precisely the new urban vision of the government and business planners.[20] Other names were less predictable. All of the houses were modest, perhaps best characterized by the phrase applied to Philip Johnson's entry, "Not a miniature mansion, but a concisely stated small house" (figure 8.1).[21] All emphasized the glass wall, the carport, and the design simplicity

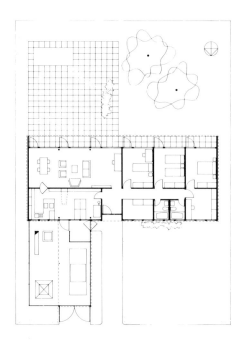

needed for FHA mortgage approvals. By 1949 the *Ladies Home Journal* was publishing built dream houses, as a sequel to their earlier series.[22] The architects represented included many of those who would dominate the profession in the 1950s. By the 1950s, the ASPA, along with most other progressive groups and activities, no longer existed. The surge of professional conservatism obviously affected architects' stances toward housing design and production. Provision of social housing, together with the general improvement of the urban condition had been at the core of all of the political agendas of the unions and the other new professional organizations. The former ASPA members either eased into influential commercial practice or assumed influential ideological and pedagogical positions: Breuer, Gropius, and Sert adapted the conventions of their practices in Europe to situations in the United States; Pei and Bunshaft mass-produced a respectable "international style"; Johnson, having long forgotten the international style, sailed in the breezes of eclecticism; Saarinen and Kahn developed their craft at a more personal level of expression. Only Chermayeff, who was a leading practitioner in England in the 1930s, resisted the United States marketplace. By 1954, he had resigned from the AIA and devoted his career to teaching and research. In 1963 he published *Community and Privacy,* which today remains the seminal architectural critique of the 1950s suburban house.[23]

Toward the close of the Depression, it was already obvious that the economics of housing production in New York City would prevent private enterprise from producing adequate urban middle-class housing, able to compete with what was available in the suburbs. In response, beginning in 1938 economic incentives were applied to urban middle-income housing, which gradually erased the distinction between low- and middle-income beneficiaries. The incentives became more and more broad, with more direct government involvement, and with increasingly complex adaptation of private enterprise. Like its equivalent for the poor, government philanthropy for the middle class was used to help shape attitudes toward the design of housing in the city of the 1950s. By 1950 the urban alternatives to suburbia for the middle class had been reformulated.

As a first step, in 1938 the New York State Insurance Code was temporarily amended by the state legislature to permit life insurance companies to make direct investments in moderate-rental housing projects. As in 1922, this legislation was passed following advance negotiations with the Metropolitan Life Insurance Company.[24] In contrast to the 1922 legislation, however, no maximum rents were specified—an advantage only slightly tempered by the lack of tax exemptions. The result of this legislation was that Metropolitan Life embarked on four projects in New York City, comprising almost 25,000 apartments. They were Parkchester, Stuyvesant Town, Peter Cooper Village, and Riverton.[25] Slightly later, Equitable Life and New York Life also began housing projects in New York City. The insurance company projects represented an important precedent for urban middle-income housing. Previously, innovative middle-income housing always differed physically from philanthropic low-income housing of the same period. But now the growing use of similar high-rise tower forms would change the direction of housing for both groups.

Parkchester was the first and largest insurance company project built in New York City at the time. Located at the junction of White Plains Road and East Tremont Avenue in the Bronx, it was designed by a team headed by Richmond H. Shreve, who was also head of the design team for Williamsburg Houses (see figures 7.11 and 7.12). Completed in 1940, its fifty-one high-rise buildings housed 42,000 persons in 12,273 apartments.[26] A comparison between the site plan of the built scheme and a plan showing the maximum development allowed by city zoning on the gridiron reveals that the project came as close to the "tower in a park" imagery as could be realized in New York City (figure 8.2). The built scheme reduced the density on the site to 320 ppa, which was one-half the allowable maximum. Coverage was 27.4 percent, with building heights between seven and thirteen stories. Each building was a composite of several core types (figure 8.3). Because the project was isolated from midtown by poor subway service, a special bus line provided commuter connections. With a population equivalent to that of most medium-sized cities and with its own shops and institutions, Parkchester was about as self-sufficient as possible. Culturally, as well as geographically, Parkchester was intended to be an independent city, a new middle-class enclave well removed from the uncertainties of old inner city neighborhoods many of its residents left. Parkchester was an omen of the mass isolation that would be heightened for all forms of middle-class housing after the war. The towers of Parkchester were prophetic of the tower in the park form of public housing that evolved after the war and came to be used exclusively. And the project became an important part of that evolution, every bit as much as Williamsburg Houses was.

Figure 8.2. Gilmore D. Clarke, Irwin Clavin, Robert W. Dowling, Andrew J. Eken, George Gore, and Henry C. Meyer, Jr., under Richmond H. Shreve. Parkchester, a "city in the park" development for 12,273 families built by the Metropolitan Life Insurance Company in the outer Bronx, completed by 1940; plan as constructed compared with a hypothetical plan developed to the highest density and coverage permitted at that time, for 24,800 families.

Stuyvesant town also was an omen, and an enclave, but an urban one located on the Lower East Side, between Avenue C, First Avenue, East 14th and East 20th streets. The clearance of the eighteen-block area was made with the considerable assistance and tutelage of Robert Moses, who demonstrated for the first time his capacity to implement what came to be called the "bulldozer approach" to urban renewal. Moses succeeded in clearing even more land for the adjacent Peter Cooper Village, completed by Metropolitan Life slightly later for a higher income tenancy.[27] Stuyvesant Town provided 8,755 apartments, housing 24,000 persons in thirty-five thirteen-story buildings with a coverage of 23 percent.[28] Like Parkchester, it was designed by a team, in this case headed by Gilmore D. Clark. The tower floor plans combined several core types into single large blocks, and the site was designed for maximum security against unwanted external intrusion (figure 8.4). A combination of brick walls and low commercial and parking structures surrounded the perimeter of the development; pedestrian and vehicular access was limited to eight entry points. The Manhattan gridiron was completely obliterated and the internal open spaces heavily landscaped. In the central lawn the roads formed the "Stuyvesant Oval," which framed a patrol booth for police at its center. This panoptic placement of the housing blocks allowed most of the ground area to be surveyed from a single point. The "tower in the park" was advantageous in terms of control, from the "inside out" as well as the "outside in."

Figure 8.3. Gilmore D. Clarke, Irwin Clavin, Robert W. Dowling, Andrew J. Eken, George Gore, and Henry C. Meyer, Jr., under Richmond H. Shreve. Parkchester tower plan, showing the standardization of "unit" clusters which could be recombined in various ways to achieve the site configuration.

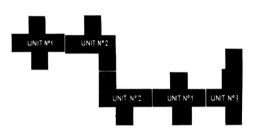

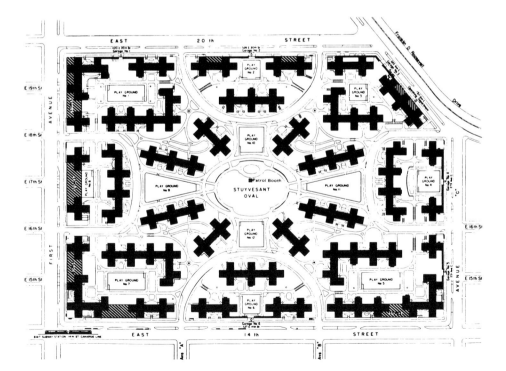

Figure 8.4. Irwin Clavin, H. F. Richardson, George Gore, and Andrew J. Eken, under Gilmore D. Clark. Stuyvesant Town, a "city in the park" development for 8,755 families built by the Metropolitan Life Insurance Company on the Lower East Side. Begun in 1943, but not completed until 1949, the panopticon-like site organization included a patrol booth for police at the center for the security of the residents; residency was intended only for whites.

Figure 8.5. Comparison of typical apartment plans for Stuyvesant Town (*left*) and East River Houses (*right*), showing the inferior plan for Stuyvesant Town, which cost double the rent of the public housing plan.

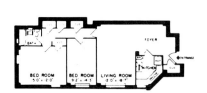

Although site acquisition for Stuyvesant Town began in the early 1940s, work on the project was interrupted by the war, and it was not completed until 1949. Much publicity was given to the 200,000 tenant applications which had been received by 1948. While the apartments were attractively priced for the middle-income Manhattan market, their design and space standards were no better, and perhaps even lower, than public housing apartments. The relationship is shown by a simple comparison of a two-bedroom apartment in East River Houses with a two-bedroom apartment in Stuyvesant Town (figure 8.5). The latter cost double the rent for a decidedly inferior apartment plan in terms of the delineation of the spaces. Another important contrast between Stuyvesant Town and public housing tower projects concerned the interpretation of the "park." In middle-class Stuyvesant Town, the park simply reinforced the role of the tower as a symbolic and secure residential fortress, in the tradition of fortress towers for New York's affluent since the 1880's. For public housing the park also reinforced the fortress aspect of the tower, but it came to symbolize the antithesis of security, which was the containment rather than the protection of the tenants. The "tower in the park" was emblematic of a new era of racial and economic disparity, isolating the differences rather than similarities in society.

The insurance company projects of the 1940s were clearly intended for white middle-income occupancy, and only Riverton in Harlem, admitted black tenants. Apparently, it was planned partially as a response to the accusations of racism which had surrounded Stuyvesant Town from its inception. Stuyvesant Town was approved in 1943 by the New York City Planning Commission and the Board of Estimate with no guarantee that tenants would be chosen without racial bias, even after a rather vocal public effort was made to have such a clause entered into the agreement.[29] Since Stuyvesant Town was intended to be a white, middle-class enclave, in 1944 Metropolitan Life was obliged to announce Riverton, its project for blacks. It placed six of the Stuyvesant Town towers in Harlem between East 135th and 138th streets and the Harlem River Drive (figure 8.6).[30] Its 1,200 families were to pay $12.50 per room per month for rent, rather than Stuyvesant Town's $14 per room. Riverton was a symptom of the new generation of racism endemic to the emerging postwar culture. James Baldwin described one side of the community reaction to the project:

> Harlem got its first private project, Riverton . . . because at that time Negroes were not allowed to live in Stuyvesant Town. Harlem watched Riverton go up, therefore, in the most violent bitterness of spirit, and hated it long before the

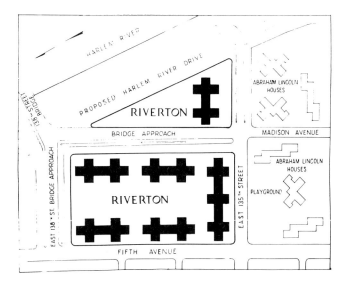

Figure 8.6. Riverton site plan, begun by the Metropolitan Life Insurance Company in Harlem in 1944, the year after Stuyvesant Town, using the same tower building forms; built for 1,200 families, with residency intended only for blacks.

builders arrived. They began hating it at about the time people began moving out of their condemned houses to make room for this additional proof of how thoroughly the white world despised them.[31]

In the 1940s much architectural criticism from progressives centered on the emerging United States application of the "tower in the park" ideology. Stuyvesant Town was a particularly vulnerable target not only because of its design but also due to the circumstances surrounding its development (figure 8.7).[32] The creation of the Stuyvesant Town site meant that Metropolitan life received without charge the 16.9 acres of land that previously had been publicly owned streets. Metropolitan also received tax waivers for twenty-five years. As critics pointed out, such public subsidies conflicted with Robert Moses' claim that the project was "private," a misrepresentation that even the *New York Times*, which supported Moses and Metropolitan Life, faithfully confirmed.[33] The company's openly racist tenant selection policy especially outraged critics in view of the large public subsidy that Metropolitan recieved,[34] and eventually it was challenged in court.

Critics of Stuyvesant Town also challenged the scale and monotony of the project and questioned whether it could provide a humane environment for families. In a heated exchange between Robert Moses and Lewis Mumford in *The New Yorker* in 1948, Mumford wrote: One must not be deceived by the fact that new developments like Stuyvesant Town and Jacob Riis Houses, nearby, have more open space than the old slums. What matters in their case is not merely the percentage of the land covered by the buildings, but the number of people crowded together in a given area. Like Le Corbusier, Moses confused visual open space with functional (habitable) open space.[35]

In spite of such criticism, the "tower in the park" prevailed as the most economical answer to mass housing production. Political circumstances dictated its continued use for public housing, but for a typical middle-income family,

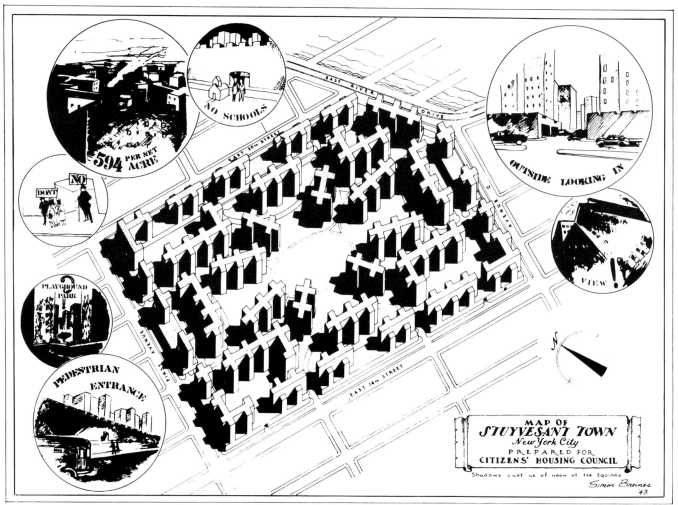

In this map Architect Breines has visualized Stuyvesant Town in its most favorable light—on the day and hour when shadows are shortest. The site plan on which the building elevations have been drawn is that proposed by the Metropolitan Life Insurance Company. The seven small cartoons, of course, do not pretend to be drawn to scale, but serve to dramatize dubious features of the Stuyvesant Town plan.

Figure 8.7. Simon Breines. Analysis of Stuyvesant Town prepared for the Citizen's Housing Council in 1943, identifying some of the "dubious features" of the design.

Parkchester or Stuyvesant Town could not compete with the single-family suburban house. Notably, no more middle-class Stuyvesant Towns were forthcoming in Manhattan after the suburban boom began. And Parkchester remained the largest development in the outer boroughs until the construction of Co-op City in 1972 (see figure 9.5). By then, the shifting economics of housing production had begun to halt the suburban dislocation.

Both Stuyvesant Town and Parkchester were glaringly deficient in family-size apartments. Out of 8,755 apartments at Stuyvesant Town, only 491 had more than two bedrooms; at Parkchester, only 562 out of 12,273.[36] Architecturally, there were no constraints except cost, which would have prohibited including large

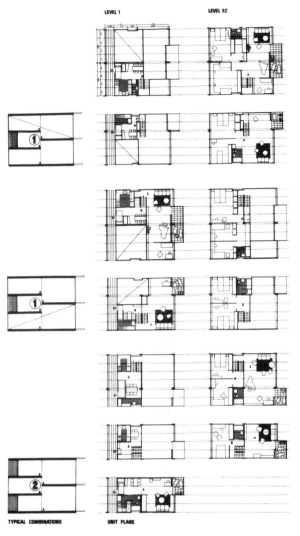

LEVEL 1   LEVEL ±2

①   ①   ②

TYPICAL COMBINATIONS   UNIT PLANS

Figure 8.8. Serge Chermayeff. "Park-Type Apartments" study, published in 1943 to demonstrate the possibilities for the efficient incorporation of a wide range of apartment sizes and types within conventional slab block massing, exhibited at the Architectural League coincidental with announcements of the design for Stuyvesant Town.

apartments in either project. A study published by Serge Chermayeff in 1943 demonstrated an extremely efficient system that enabled a variety of large, family-size, one- and two-level apartments to fit within a conventional high-rise, slab block structural grid, with gallery access (figure 8.8).[37] The study, called "Park-Type Apartments" and timed to coincide with announcements of the design for Stuyvesant Town, was sponsored by *Architectural Forum* and exhibited at the Architectural League. Other architects also challenged the Stuyvesant Town proposal. Marcel Breuer developed an alternative scheme for the Stuyvesant Town site[38] in the interest of "comparative study" (figure 8.9). His proposal replaced the concentric planning with an axial organization, while reducing the coverage

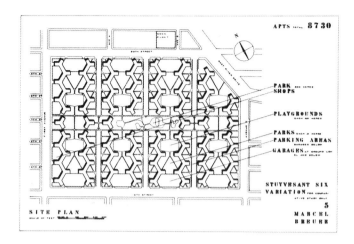

by 5 percent and the density by 20 percent. Yet in terms of scale, Breuer's scheme hardly seemed to address the issues raised by the original plan.

The low cost of the suburban single-family house was subsidized heavily by the federal government, indirectly through the building of the highway and service infrastructure, and directly through mortgage insurance and tax laws. In his study for the Brookings Institution, Henry Aaron documented the degree to which the single-family house was subsidized by government policy after World War II. By the end of the war, all of the enabling mechanisms for the mortgage guarantees had been long established. Most dated from the New Deal: the Federal Home Loan Bank system in 1932, the FHA loan guaranty programs in 1934, and the Veterans' Home Loan Guaranty Program in 1944. More important than the mortgage guarantees were the income tax laws, which even today continue to give substantial advantage to home owners. According to Aaron:

> If the homeowner were taxed like other investors, he would have to report as gross income the rent he could have obtained on his house. He would be allowed deductions for maintenance, depreciation, mortgage interest, and property taxes as expenses incurred in earning income. The difference, or net rent, would be his taxable income. In fact, rather than paying a tax on his imputed net rent, he is allowed to deduct mortgage interest and property taxes from his gross income.[39]

Aaron calculated that for a typical year (1966), the government subsidy provided to the poor by public housing programs was $500 million, while the subsidy provided primarily to middle-class home owners through the income tax law was almost $7 billion.[40] There were a myriad of other subsidies that supported the new lifestyle. Many were focused on the road and services infrastructure needed to sustain the massive infusion of private automobiles.[41]

At the close of World War II, optimism regarding the postwar boom together with priorities given to housing the returning veterans almost completely destroyed the established government housing programs for the poor. Legislative efforts to renew them, begun in 1944, were unsuccessful. In that year, the Senate created the Special Committee on Postwar Economic Planning and Policy, which drafted the Wagner-Ellender-Taft (WET) Bill. The bill called for the creation of a permanent National Housing Agency that would operate through the existing Federal Home Bank, Federal Housing, and Federal Public Housing administrations. According to the provisions of the bill, the Federal Home Bank and Federal Housing Administration would increase aid to private enterprise. The Federal Public Housing Administration would enlarge the public housing program by placing greater emphasis on local needs, especially through new programs for slum clearance, with increased government sponsorship of housing research. The WET Bill caused so much opposition when it was proposed to Congress in 1945 that it was not until four years later that a drastically modified version, which became the United States Housing Act of 1949, could finally be passed.[42]

Within the architectural profession, support of the WET Bill drew a firm line between conservatives and progressives. Conservatives saw no need to tamper with a free market economy in housing, given the certainty of the postwar boom. Progressives saw the postwar boom as an opportunity to expand much-needed programs. The American Society of Planners and Architects passed a resolution enthusiastically supporting the WET Bill in January 1946;[43] however, it was not until two years later that the AIA finally issued a mild and conditional statement of support by its Board of Directors.[44] In a scathing rebuke delivered at the annual AIA convention in April 1947, Carl Koch of the ASPA criticized the AIA's failure to support the WET Bill. Koch called attention to the contrast between the AIA's reticence following World War II and its earlier activism after World War I when it had organized an intense lobby for government housing programs.[45] But it seemed that this time the AIA's interest was elsewhere. It is important to note the historical change in prevalent AIA attitudes toward housing legislation at three critical times: the "gentlemen's agreement" over the dumbell tenement in 1879, dictated by the insecurity of a new profession; the aggressive support in 1919 of a young, secure, and activist profession; and the disinterest in 1946 of a conservative establishment.

By 1946 United States housing stock for both low- and middle-income families was showing the ill effects of economic depression and the war. With the return of servicemen from abroad, a severe housing shortage was inevitable. The federal government's response was limited to emergency measures for veterans and the liberalization of mortgage insurance programs, assistance which was beneficial only to the middle class. The most notable legislative action was the Veterans' Emergency Housing Act of 1946, which revised and extended FHA authority to insure mortgages, thus stimulating single-family house construction. Public housing received no such attention; state and local governments were left to their own devices. Nevertheless, between 1945 and 1950 nine state-financed and twelve city-financed public housing projects were completed in New York City, against considerable financial odds. Therefore, if before the war "low cost" had been the ideological preference, after the war it became an economic necessity. In fact, low cost was to have an incalculable effect on the large number of public housing projects planned for the future as well as those constructed contemporaneously.

The first public housing project completed in New York City after the war

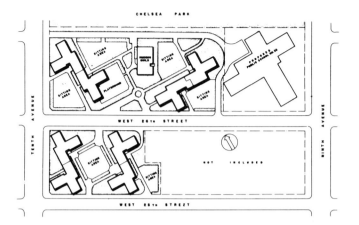

Figure 8.10. Archibald Manning Brown and William Lescaze. Elliott Houses site plan in Manhattan, the first public housing project to be completed after World War II; also the first public housing to consist entirely of high-rise towers (eleven and twelve stories); completed in 1947.

was Elliott Houses in Manhattan on West 25th Street between Ninth and Tenth avenues. The project was designed by Archibald Manning Brown and William Lescaze and completed in 1947. Significantly, Elliott Houses was the first public housing project (other than the Wallabout Houses national defense project) to consist entirely of high-rise towers (figure 8.10). The project's four eleven- and twelve-story towers occupied a two-block site with 22 percent coverage. Like many other early postwar projects, its planning sensibility dated from the prewar period; however, several of the new cost-saving techniques that dominated later NYCHA postwar construction were introduced. These included the use of a column and slab concrete structure with cavity wall construction.[46] The undersides of the monolithic floor slabs were left unfinished for the ceilings below. Brownsville Houses in Brooklyn, designed by Frederick G. Frost, was the second postwar project. Twenty-seven low-rise buildings with 338 apartments were distributed over eight blocks between Sutter, Dumont, Stone, and Rockway avenues. The coverage was 22.6 percent (figure 8.11). The project combined three-story walk-ups and six-story elevator buildings.

Like all of the twenty-one postwar city and state projects, both Elliott Houses and Brownsville Houses used variants of the "cross" plan. This approach consisted of building "wings" radiating from a central core of circulation, usually in L, T, or X configurations. The cross plan tended to consolidate circulation by cutting down on excess corridor area, and it provided a maximum amount of light and ventilation to apartments in the protruding wing forms. Albany Houses, on Park Place and Albany, Troy, and St. Mark's avenues, completed in Brooklyn in 1950 and designed by Fellheimer, Wagner, and Vollmer, took the cross concept to an extreme. It used a five-pronged asterisk form with a compact core consisting of two elevators and a scissor stair (figure 8.12). The disadvantage of the cross form was its relatively high cost owing to excessive exterior wall surface and the complexities of joining the wings at the core. The simple rectilinear slab was cheaper.

In an article published in *Architectural Forum* in 1949, the cross form was found to be obsolete when it was compared with a new "in-line" plan that was

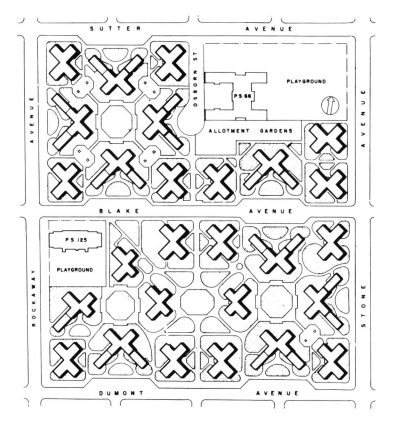

Figure 8.11. Frederick G. Frost. Brownsville Houses site plan in Brooklyn, completed in 1948, consisting of twenty-seven three-story walk-up and six-story elevator buildings organized at forty-five degrees to the existing gridiron.

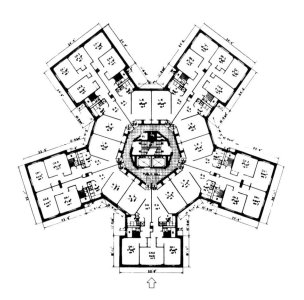

Figure 8.12. Fellheimer, Wagner, and Vollmer. Albany Houses building plan in Brooklyn, completed in 1950 using fourteen-story "asterisk"-type towers which attempted to improve on the efficiency of the "cross" type through maximizing the number of apartments served by the core.

PATHOLOGY OF PUBLIC HOUSING   263

Figure 8.13. Four post–World War II public housing tower plans compared in a 1950 article in *Architectural Forum,* in which the evolution from the articulated slab to the pure slab block is equated with positive design innovation.

PARKSIDE HOUSES
Architects: Walker & Poor
Number of buildings: 3 14-story, 9 7-story and 2 6-story units
Number of apartments 879
Site coverage 19.8%
Persons per acre 257.09
Gross area per room* ... 230.9 sq. ft.
Construction cost per room* $2,201

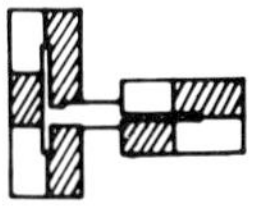

GUN HILL HOUSES
Architects: Alfred Hopkins & Associates
Number of buildings: 6 14-story units
Number of apartments . 733
Site coverage 13.9%
Persons per acre 322
Gross area per room* . 233.7 sq. ft.
Construction cost per room* $2,204

DYCKMAN HOUSES
Architect: William F. Ballard
Number of buildings: 7 14-story units
Number of apartments 1,167
Site coverage 13.1%
Persons per acre 290
Gross area per room* .. 230.8 sq. ft.
Construction cost per room* $2,166

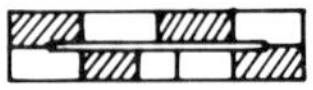

SEDGWICK HOUSES
Architects: Skidmore, Owings & Merrill
Gordon Bunshaft, Partner-in-charge
Number of buildings: 7 14-story units
Number of apartments . 786
Site coverage 18.7%
Persons per acre 346.9
Gross area per room* .. 235.8 sq. ft.
Construction cost per room* $2,181

* The word "room" refers to construction, not rental rooms. It includes laundry, storage space, etc.

based on the use of straight-line, double-loaded corridors. This development was billed as a "major revolution in the housing field," since the cross plan had "until the last few years . . . in all forms . . . represented the peak achievement of housing design."[47] The *Forum* article described four new public housing projects for New York City which were awaiting passage of the United States Housing Act. All had in-line plans. The projects were Gun Hill Houses in the Bronx, designed by Alfred Hopkins and Associates; Parkside Houses in the Bronx, designed by Walker and Poor; Dyckman Houses in upper Manhattan, designed by William F. Ballard; and Sedgwick Houses in the Bronx, designed by Gordon Bunshaft of Skidmore, Owings, and Merrill (figure 8.13).

Gun Hill Houses broke the in-line form into two pieces and formed a T. The others were simple slabs. Parkside and Dyckman had articulated facades to pro-

vide cross ventilation. The pure slab block, used by Bunshaft at Sedgwick Houses, pared high-rise costs to a minimum, but had disadvantages, such as excessive corridor areas. It lacked cross ventilation in all but end apartments. In addition to Sedgwick Houses, Bunshaft designed slab buildings for two other public housing sites in upper Manhattan and Brooklyn (figure 8.14). In the proposal reports,[48] prepared in 1950, different building heights were compared for a single slab plan (figure 8.15). According to the analysis, the total cost of two two-story towers would be no more than the total cost of three fourteen-story towers, except for the expense of larger and faster elevators required by the taller towers. But the reports echoed the earlier theme of Gropius that with higher towers there could be fewer buildings on the site and consequently more open space (see figure 6.28). Higher buildings cost no more per square foot while saving on site development.

Figure 8.14. Skidmore, Owings, and Merrill. North Harlem public housing project proposed in 1951; one of the eight almost identical applications of the SOM public housing slab block prototype, proposed in 1951 to the Mayor's Committee on Slum Clearance.

**Figure 8.15. Skidmore, Owings, and Merrill.
Public housing slab block prototype floor plan
as proposed to the Mayor's Committee on Slum
Clearance for widespread use in public housing
in New York City; included were economic
arguments for building to twenty stories rather
than the usual fourteen stories.**

TYPICAL FLOOR PLAN

**Figure 8.16. Skidmore, Owings, and Merrill.
Sedgwick Houses public housing site plan,
completed in 1951, as an application of the
SOM public housing slab block prototype, using
fourteen- and fifteen-story towers with a
coverage of 18.7 percent.**

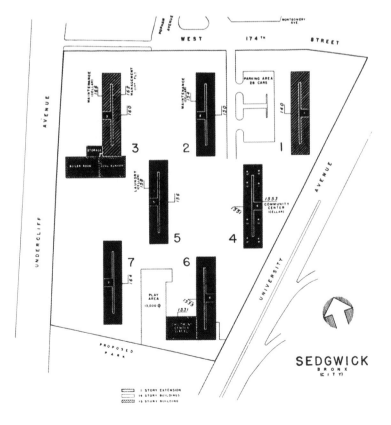

Figure 8.17. Le Corbusier. First study for the Unite d'Habitation at Marseilles. Begun in 1945, it received wide publicity in the United States.

Sedgwick Houses used only 18.7 percent coverage with a density of 300 ppa (figure 8.16).

The economic legitimacy of the slab block was by now unquestioned. The aesthetic and social legitimacy remained more problematic, although the slab block had the ideological blessing of the modern movement dating from the Breuer and Gropius proposals of twenty-five years earlier (see figures 2.26 to 6.29). A more recent influence was Le Corbusier's widely published proposals for his Unité d'Habitation, based on the same form (figure 8.17). Since 1946, the architectural press had been carefully following his first Unité proposals: a plan for the bombed-out city of St. Die and a single Unité which was completed at Marseilles by 1951.[49] The same silhouette of widely spaced rectangular slabs used by Le Corbusier at St. Die soon appeared in proposals for New York City. Another influence was the prolific literary output of the "tower in the park" proponents, many associated with CIAM activities, which by now had gained exposure in the United States. Much of it was a response to the massive urban rebuilding in Europe required after the destruction of World War II.

Jose Luis Sert became one of the most dedicated public proponents of CIAM thinking in the United States. His book *Can Our Cities Survive?*, a product of the CIAM 5 meeting in Paris in 1937, was published by Harvard in 1942.[50] It became an important ideological influence for the next two decades, summarizing all of the social and aesthetic arguments for the "tower in the park." *Can Our Cities Survive?* was followed by *The Heart of the City* in 1952.[51] Based on proceedings of the CIAM 8 meeting held in Hoddesdon, England, in 1951, it focused on design strategies for rebuilding urban centers. For U.S. cities, all that was needed was an equivalent to the wartime urban destruction in Europe. This equivalent materialized with the "slum clearance" and "urban renewal" programs of the 1950s. Ironically, the alteration of European ideals in the United States was filtered back to Europe in the period of postwar domination, most notably through the Marshall Plan, which was instrumental in rebuilding European cities.

In postwar New York development, an important confluence developed around the "tower in the park." From the point of view of members of the liberal establishment, like Nelson Rockefeller for example, the "tower in the park" made sense. The "tower in the park" conformed to the myths of the desirability of reducing costs and coverage in social housing. In theory, more housing could be built for the money, while also exorcising the nineteenth-century city of its tenements. From the point of view of the architects, theorist-practicioners such as Sert or corporate practicioners such as Gordon Bunshaft, the "tower in the park" was legitimized as a progressive vision by its association with European theory, especially with Le Corbusier, who was emerging as the most powerful single international architectural "hero" of the postwar period. From the point of view of Robert Moses, New York's most powerful bureaucrat, the "tower in the park" was ideal as a forceful emblem of reform, which could sustain universal application in a myriad of neighborhoods, and at a low cost that tended to maximize profits to the development community. In 1948, after trying for a decade, Robert Moses finally gained control of public housing in New York City through his appointment as chairman of the Mayor's Committee on Slum Clearance.[52] He in turn sought out the new modernist corporate practicioners, such as Gordon Bunshaft. For postwar public housing, Robert Moses was the catalyst and buffer between theory and practice. He gave the "tower in the park" final economic and political credibility, and also its incredible design mediocrity.

Almost without exception, public housing projects built in New York City in the 1950s were high-rise towers with coverages of under 20 percent. Many were under 15 percent. The geometrical organization of the sites tended to be quite arbitrary since low coverage removed the constraints of designing for buildings in close proximity. Often the towers were simply lined up, like the three offset rows of Sedgwick Houses; or they were placed on sites with no systematic rationale at all, like the asterisk-shaped towers of Farragut Houses, a companion project to Albany Houses (see figure 8.12), designed by the same architects, Fellheimer, Wagner, and Vollmer. Farragut was completed in Brooklyn in 1952 on a site between York, Nassau, Navy, and Bridge streets (figure 8.18). Floating randomly in a sea of green with 13.9 percent coverage, the towers lacked any connection to the surrounding environment (figure 8.19). Only the apartment plans appeared to have been seriously considered and were significant for their separation of through circulation from the living rooms. By this time, the isolation of public housing sites was functionally complete to the extent that even commercial space was eliminated from the projects. Stores had been built in all of the early projects: the First Houses, Williamsburg, Harlem River, Red Hook, Queensbridge, and Fort Green projects collectively contained over one hundred. In 1944, however, the Housing Authority decided to eliminate commercial space from all postwar projects, following the specious argument that it was only in the business of providing housing, and that it did not want to compete with private enterprise.[53]

The spatial pathology of public housing in New York City during the 1950s culminated in the Baruch Houses project, which was completed in 1959 on a site on the Lower East Side bordered by the East River, Columbia, Delancey and East Houston streets. The project, designed by Emery Roth and Sons,[54] consisted of seventeen towers scattered over fifteen Manhattan blocks with a coverage of 13.4 percent (figure 8.20). Because there were no discernible criteria for site organi-

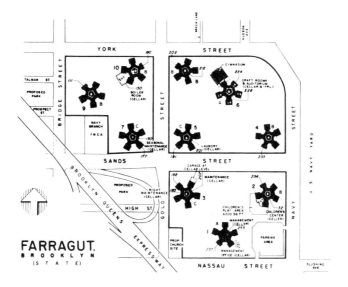

Figure 8.18. Fellheimer, Wagner, and Vollmer. Farragut Houses public housing site plan, completed in Brooklyn in 1952, the second and last public housing project in New York City to use asterisk-type towers, which floated randomly in a sea of green space.

Figure 8.19. Fellheimer, Wagner, and Vollmer. Farragut Houses construction photo, showing the ultimate spatial pathology between a public housing project and the surrounding context.

Figure 8.20. Emery Roth and Sons. Baruch

Houses public housing site plan, completed in

1959 on the Lower East Side, with crenellated

slab blocks, randomly distributed in the park.

zation, the orientation of the buildings was quite random. However, the individual buildings were an interesting hybrid form that combined the characteristics of the slab and the asterisk (figure 8.21). Along the East River, Baruch Houses adjoins many other philanthropic versions of the "tower in a park." As in East Harlem, these projects are concentrated to a degree unequaled elsewhere in New York City (figure 8.22). In *adhoc* fashion, the dream of Rutgers Town was realized (see figure 7.18).

The "tower in the park" provided a radically new kind of urbanism that represented the culmination of an evolutionary reduction of building coverage from the nineteenth century tenements with 90 percent coverage to only slightly more than 10 percent. But the open space was not accountable. There was no criteria for structure or use, beyond creation of the parklike settings. In public housing, especially, the social characteristics of the parks within the tower projects were far different from those of the tenement streets they replaced, and they contributed to a myriad of problems. This pathology of public housing design was not unique to New York City. The "tower in the park" had become a national standard for housing the urban poor. By the end of the decade, it was obvious that the "tower in the park" was problematic everywhere, as was the public housing ideology that produced it. Other United States cities experienced greater difficulty than New York. At least in New York, there was widespread experience with high-rise apartment living, in comparison with St. Louis for example, where such traditions did not exist. Also, to its credit, the New York City Housing Authority was well-managed in contrast to counterparts in many other cities.

Perhaps everywhere the most widespread problem attributed to the "tower in

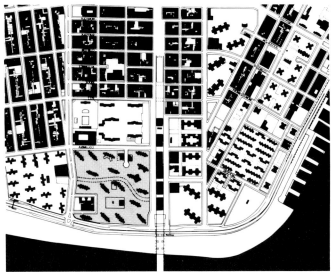

Figure 8.21. Emery Roth and Sons. Baruch Houses site photo shortly after construction (top), showing the crenellated towers and the development of the "park" area for automobile parking.

Figure 8.22. Baruch Houses and the surrounding area of the Lower East Side (left), showing the heavy concentration of public housing "city in the park" projects, similar to the transformation of East Harlem.

the park" was its tendency to increase crime, especially in neighborhoods that already had crime problems. In his important study, *Defensible Space,* Oscar Newman developed an interesting comparison between two adjoining projects in Brooklyn: low-rise Brownsville Houses built in 1948 (see figure 8.11) and the newer high-rise Van Dyck Houses completed in 1955.[55] Van Dyck Houses was designed by Isadore and Zachary Rosenfield, on a site west of Brownsville Houses, bounded by Sutter, Powell, Livonia, and Stone avenues (figure 8.23). Both projects were of similar size and tenant composition, but Brownsville had three-to-six-story buildings with a coverage of 23 percent, while Van Dyck used fourteen-story towers with 16.6 percent coverage. In a typical year (1969), Van Dyck Houses was found to have 50 percent more total crime incidents than Brownsville and required 39 percent more maintenance work, even though the two projects were adjacent to each other (figure 8.24). Newman argued that the difference in design approach accounted for much of the difference in statistics. For example, the scale of towers prevented normal exercise of family territoriality. The removal of large numbers of units from visual contact with open space prevented proper public surveillance.

The slum clearance provisions of the United States Housing Act, as it was finally passed in 1949, stipulated that public housing be built in the areas where slums were to be razed. It was forbidden explicitly to raze a slum in an urban center and rehouse the inhabitants in the suburbs; the slum had to be replaced by public housing near the same spot. Moreover, families left homeless by slum clearance were given priority for rehousing; thus, most ended up in public hous-

Figure 8.23. Isadore and Zachary Rosenfield. Van Dyck Houses public housing project, completed in Brooklyn in 1955 using fourteen-story slab block towers; adjacent to the earlier Brownsville Houses public housing project.

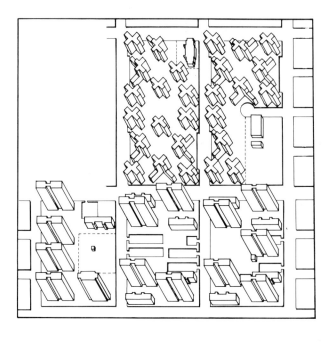

ing. The effect was a policy that ensured that one ghetto was replaced by another. In addition, the housing authorities lost their power to select tenants. In the 1930s the New York City Housing Authority could exercise the strictest criteria for tenant selection, "using the same credit reference schemes employed in high-class apartment houses, and adaptations of principles used in European low-rental government housing."[56] The homes of applicants were visited. An enormous amount of investigative activity was compiled into a point system similar to one developed for the municipal housing in Vienna. By 1950 the sole criterion might be that a family had been displaced by urban renewal. Management staffs were not prepared to deal with a mandatory influx of what previously might have been considered problem families. From the point of view of tenants' interests, a remarkable network of tenant unions had existed before the war. They were an invaluable vehicle through which tenants could combat the paternalism and institutionalization normally associated with housing philanthropy. But in the new era, as tenants became poorer and more estranged from the culture at large, this valuable resource lost its clout as well.[57]

Figure 8.24. Photo of Brownsville Houses public housing project in Brooklyn, with Van Dyck Houses behind; within two years of its completion, Van Dyck developed social problems which were more serious than anything experienced at Brownsville Houses, completed five years earlier.

PATHOLOGY OF PUBLIC HOUSING   273

In 1938 Catherine Bauer, then director of research and information for the United States Housing Authority, wrote: "Today there are no longer any doubts. The public housing program is here to stay, and it is on the way toward vast concrete achievements."[50] Twenty years later she was writing about the "dreary deadlock of public housing."[59] But if the old progressives were worried, the newly ensconced suburban middle class was not. The suburban house in Westchester was well removed from the problematic towers of East Harlem. All possibility of contact had been eliminated, except for the slight visual discomfort experienced from the windows of a commuter train passing along upper Park Avenue or an automobile passing along Harlem River Drive. And for the architect, the lucrative and busy practice of the 1950s did not permit much time for soul-searching. The impossible design standards and the undercurrent of corruption associated with social housing led most architects to shun such work.[60] Public housing became the "bread and butter" work for the "bread and butter" architectural firms. The "stars" of the profession had other interests. The prosperity of the 1950s had a far different effect on housing innovation than the prosperity of the 1920s. The city was no longer the backbone of the culture of housing. "Urbanism as a way of life" was eclipsed by the suburbs.

In March 1960 the Panuch Report commissioned by Mayor Wagner painted a rather grim picture of housing progress in New York City between 1950 and 1960. Slums were worse, and the housing shortage was still desperate. Citing the 1950 census, which showed a shortage of 430,000 units, the report argued that the same shortage still existed in 1960, and it emphasized the need to view housing issues holistically, for all income groups.[61] A rebuttal to the Panuch Report, published by the Housing and Redevelopment Board (HRB) in November 1961, indicated that the number of "substandard units" had decreased and "recalculated" the housing shortage. The number of substandard units was reduced to 356,000 units, based on a technical change in the definition of a "dwelling unit" in 1960.[62] This implied that the 1950s housing programs had succeeded in reducing the housing shortage, but noticeably lacking in the rebuttal was any reference to who lived where.

One census statistic was not cited by either report, although everyone knew it anyway. For the first time, during the 1950s, New York's suburban population exceeded its urban population. The suburban population had increased by 2,180,492, while the urban population decreased by 109,973.[63] If the housing programs had "worked," it was only because the city was being emptied of its middle class. In Suffolk County alone, the fastest-growing area, population had increased by 141.5 percent. Resettlement on such a massive scale was bound to produce optimistic figures on the city's housing needs. But what the city really received was nothing more than fewer people—a side effect of the displacement. The census figures for 1960 showed that 66 percent of all inhabitants of the New York metropolitan area, or 9,742,100 persons, changed homes in the 1950s.[64] The 75,403 public housing units built by the New York City Housing Authority during the same period seem negligible by comparison. The real government effort was in the suburbs, and entirely consistent with the previous twenty years of planning. Public housing design limitations were only a relatively minor symptom of a mentality that pervaded every aspect of United States culture. By the end of the 1950s, a newly constituted middle-class majority had written off the large cities and those citizens who were destined by choice or coercion to live in them.

The archetype for the 1950s suburban single-family house was built by Levitt and Sons at Levittown on Long Island between 1947 and 1950.[65] Just as the "tower in the park" can be seen as the culmination of the typological progression for high-rise housing in New York City, the Levitt house represents a comparable culmination for the garden apartment. It was built on 60-by-100-foot lots with 12 percent coverage for four and one-half rooms. The gridiron of streets was deliberately irregular, removing all visual resemblance to the gridirons of the city (figure 8.25). The incredibly low price of $7,990 permitted families only one gen-

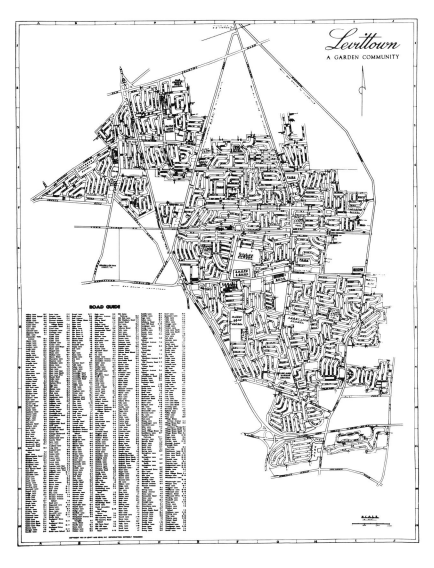

Figure 8.25. Levitt and Sons. Plan of Levittown, begun at Hempstead, Long Island, in 1947 for mass-produced, inexpensive single-family houses; located near Alexander Stewart's Garden City of 1869.

Figure 8.26. Levitt and Sons. Model house built in 1949 for Levittown on Long Island, shown on the standard 60-by-100-foot lot; 4,200 were produced in a single year.

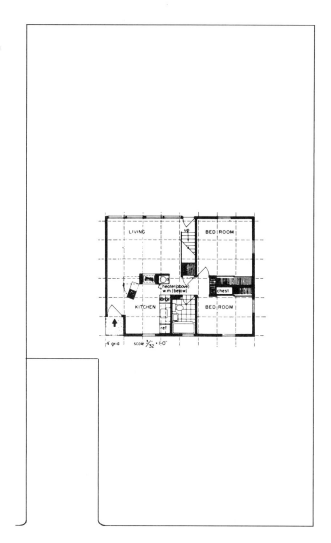

eration away from the 25-by-100-foot dumbell of the Lower East Side to escape the city entirely. By 1948 William Levitt began to construct the first six thousand houses on 1,400 acres, and he played the role of populist entrepreneur for the American "dream house." Although he lived in Manhattan, Levitt's political views found dangers in urban housing, even the garden apartment. He favored the suburban single-family house, arguing that "no man who owns his own house and lot can be a communist."[66]

The 1949 Levitt model, with 750 square feet gross, and an expansion attic, influenced housing production and form nationwide (figure 8.26). The plans were distributed nationally through department stores by *Better Homes and Gardens*. By 1951, Levitt had built 15,000 houses for 51,000 persons, making it the largest housing project in the New York region.[67] For financing, Levitt developed to a high art the use of public guarantees, dating from the 1934 Federal Housing Administration Loan Guaranty Programs. FHA mortgage guarantees made it possible for him to organize financing on a large scale, before selling a single house. Levitt was also an innovator in marketing for the housing field, applying some of the techniques developed previously by big business. He understood the principles of consumerism, and in this he had the ample advice of mentors like the General Electric Company and the Bendix Corporation. As he wrote for a General Electric advertisement, "A dream house is a house the buyer and his family will want to live in a long time . . . an electric kitchen-laundry is the one big item that gives the home-owner all the advantages and conveniences that make his home truly livable."[68]

Although skepticism about the virtues of urbanity had been present in all stages of United States cultural development, this time the symptoms were manifest in ways that had been unthinkable previously. Even the 1950's hysteria about civil defense, which led to programs ostensibly for the protection of city dwellers from the threat of nuclear attack, was futile and absurd. In 1951 the *Bulletin of the Atomic Scientists* devoted an entire issue to "Defense Through Decentralization."[69] It advocated dispersing existing large cities into smaller settlements to avoid concentrated targets for nuclear attack. The ideal model suggested was a drastically reduced city core surrounded by small satellite towns (figure 8.27). The proposals represented a suburban ethic dictated by national sentiment. And if the widely publicized nuclear tests were any indication, the suburbs were all that mattered anyway. Few of the tests simulated urban situations: suburban houses were blasted away, and automobiles in mock-up suburban parking lots were crumpled (figure 8.28).[70]

Many of the intellectual elite, especially those who represented the interest of the military or industry, quite frankly advocated obliteration of the city.[71] In 1950, when the U.S. Civil Defense Agency was beginning its vast public relations campaign concerning nuclear attack, *Collier's magazine* published an article by John Lear called "Hiroshima, U.S.A.," describing the nuclear destruction of New York City by Soviet Russia.[72] Full-color illustrations and a long narrative related the events in terrifying detail (figure 8.29). The article was part of a national

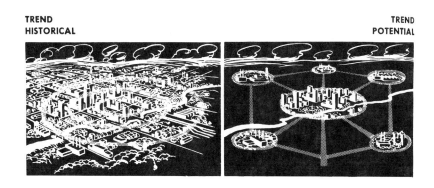

TREND
HISTORICAL

TREND
POTENTIAL

Figure 8.27. Diagram from the *Bulletin of the Atomic Scientists* published in 1951, arguing for defense against nuclear attack through the decentralization of United States cities.

Figure 8.28. Cover from a Federal Civil Defense Administration report from 1953, describing one of the atom bomb testing programs in which suburban houses and shopping center parking lots were subjected to atomic blasts, as the representative icons of mainstream United States culture.

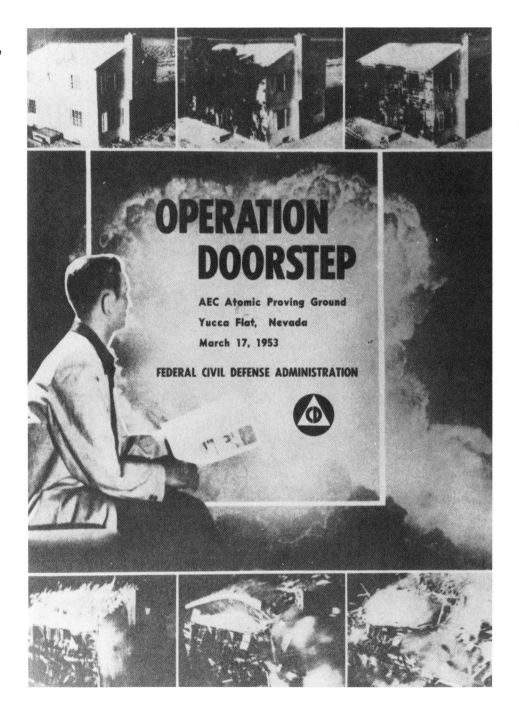

IMMEDIATE CONFIRMATION UNAVAILABLE. WIRE CONNECTIONS WITH MANHATTAN ARE DOWN.

Figure 8.29. Illustration from an article, "Hiroshima, U.S.A.," published by *Collier's Magazine* in 1950, which described in detail the nuclear destruction of New York City; with "ground zero" targeted for the Lower East Side, calculated by the U.S. Department of Defense to be the optimal position for leveling the city.

mass media campaign, made with the complicity of the federal government, which shamelessly contributed to the destruction of whatever remained of credible, urban middle-class life. John Lear exploded his bomb in the location the Defense Department had calculated as the optimal position for the destruction of the city. This was the heart of the Lower East Side, where, ironically, destruction was already under way, using the same sentiments, but with economic and political means.

9

New Directions

THE 1960s represented a watershed for the resistance to doctrinaire postwar urbanism in city and suburb alike. By then, the "tower in the park" had become the object of particularly fervent criticism. For social housing, a hybrid high-rise urbanism developed, sustained by the general prosperity which expanded the design concerns of programs for the increasing numbers of disenfranchised poor. In addition, efforts to preserve a middle class in New York City caused government philanthropy to move into the realm of middle-income housing through implementation of new public mechanisms for development. For domestic high-rise urbanism, the 1960s were arguably the most innovative period in New York City history, at least from the point of view of site planning for nonluxury development. The immense economic and cultural transformation represented by the suburb and its single-family house also began to show the first signs of blemish. This was most evident in the generation who had come of age in the early days of suburban underdevelopment, and whose "youth culture" was pointing them back toward the city by the end of the 1960s.

In spite of the tradition of high-rise living in New York City, orthodox "tower in the park" urbanism had been the object of controversy and resistance from the time of its inception. As early as 1924, Lewis Mumford objected to the "sanguine people . . . who fancy that it is possible to have residential buildings surrounded by open space and gardens; they even talk as if the problems of housing might be solved on a grand scale by erecting such buildings."[1] By 1947 Mumford was attacking Le Corbusier's "Marseilles Folley," including the various scaled-down versions that were being built in United States cities, especially for the urban poor.[2] But in spite of criticism, the "tower in the park" saw a universal proliferation after World War II. The mandate for this particular approach as a panacea for postwar social housing needs penetrated far deeper than the objections of critics could reach. It represented a confluence of forces with diverse prerequisites, including political containment, low construction cost, high development profits, and an architectural imagery identified with social reform. By the 1960s however, as philanthropy moved into the realm of the middle class, these priorities began to soften.

In New York City the single most important champion of the "tower in the park" was Robert Moses. As chairman of the Mayor's Committee on Slum Clearance during fourteen critical years in the postwar era, Moses was able to dominate design ideology for social housing. In 1956 for example, all of the seventeen projects proposed by Moses' committee used high-rise slab blocks placed in park-like settings.[3] Even in 1968, at the close of his long career, Moses still insisted that to "accommodate large numbers of people more comfortably, the answer is vertical construction on less land. Instead of building four or five stories, covering 80 or 85 percent of the land, you go up four or five times as high on 20 percent coverage. This will leave plenty of open space, playgrounds for the kids, and better views."[4] Moses was able to enforce his ideas through his control of the Title I money for slum clearance from the federal government. In this process, the city acquired slum property by condemnation and then resold it at a reduced price to private developers. The federal government paid two-thirds of the resale price difference.

With or without Moses and Title I, the fact that no low-rise alternatives to the "tower in the park" were developed throughout the 1950s was due in large part to the tremendous initial economy of the high-rise tower. No other high-density form could be simpler or more profitable to construct. Initial construction economies justified the high-rise tower, outweighing the longer-term costs, both economic and social. Before the decade of the 1960s, the typical reaction among architects to the problems of the high-rise tower was exemplified by the alternative solutions produced in response to the Stuyvesant Town controversy in 1943 (see figures 8.8 and 8.9). The alternatives made by Breuer, for example, did not question the high-rise tower form. Rather, he tried to perfect it. For the early moderns like Breuer and Gropius, the equation of social housing with low cost, and by consequence with the tower, held out the possibility of vastly increasing housing production. In the postwar period in the United States however, this equation at best simply amounted to an increase in profits to banking interests and developers.

The Limited Profit Housing Companies Law passed by the New York state legislature in 1955 also had a critical impact on the design and construction of government-subsidized housing in New York City, extending over the next two decades.[5] Popularly known as the Mitchell-Lama program after the originators of the legislation, it was the first program to openly provide government philanthropy for the middle class. It was designed to promote construction of urban middle-income housing, which neither the public housing program nor unsubsidized private developers were producing. Developers could receive mortgages from either New York State or New York City for 90 percent of project costs at lower interest rates than on the private market. They could also receive property tax exemptions. In return, limits were placed on profits. Design, construction, operating costs, and rents were also subject to public control—either by the state or by the city, depending on the source of financing. Frequently Mitchell-Lama projects were initiated in conjunction with the Title I slum clearance program, which provided the sites.

By its second decade, the Mitchell-Lama program had begun to influence "tower in the park" design orthodoxy, becoming oriented toward middle-income design standards and higher building budgets. With the loosening of the ideology of low-cost housing production, the severity of the 1950s high-rise tower could be reduced. This change provided an initial foothold for the erosion of the "tower in the park" urbanism by the mid-1960s. By 1969, more than 57,000 Mitchell-Lama apartments had been built in New York City; more than half were occupied by upper-middle-income tenants.[6] A similar federal program followed in the footsteps of Mitchell-Lama. Known as Section 221d3, it was written into the National Housing Act of 1961.[7] It was focused on somewhat lower income levels, however, and it did not permit quite the same level of amenities as were possible under Mitchell-Lama.[8]

In the formative years of the 1950s, Title I slum clearance projects cleared away poor and working poor areas, substituting lower-middle-to-middle-income developments. Brownstones and tenements were replaced with towers, obliterating the traditional streetscape. In Manhattan, West Park Village (formerly Manhattantown), designed by Skidmore, Owings and Merrill, and Penn Station South designed by Herman Jessor were typical of this genre. These projects carried on the tradition of the inner city enclave like Stuyvesant Town, although they were smaller and lacked some of its most deterministic features related to site planning and rental policies. In 1952, construction of the sixteen slab-blocks of West Park Village began on six blocks between Amsterdam Avenue, Central Park West, and West 97th and 100th streets (figure 9.1).[9] Similarly, in 1957 the six slab-blocks of Penn Station South replaced tenements on six blocks bounded by Eighth and Ninth avenues and West 23rd and 29th streets.[10] Both projects used Title I subsidies and bore the stamp of Robert Moses' Mayor's Committee on Slum Clearance. West Park Village became embroiled in scandals which considerably delayed its completion.[11]

The same design approach on a far larger scale was applied in the outer boroughs, where land values were much lower than in Manhattan, and where problems of slum clearance were far easier to deal with. These projects typically housed a large segment of the lower middle class that had not left for the suburbs. Parkchester in the Bronx, which was completed before the war, was the definitive prototype (see figure 8.3). It was followed by a succession of projects, each boasting more tenants and more amenities than the previous. Fresh Meadows was the earliest of these postwar projects, completed by the New York Life Insurance Company in Queens in 1949, along the Long Island Expressway between 186th and 197th streets.[12] It housed three thousand families and was designed by Voorhees, Walker, Foley, and Smith, using a mixture of high- and low-rise buildings in a "park." The housing was integrated with schools, shops, and other community amenities (figure 9.2). Beyond easy reach of the subway, Fresh Meadows was intended to be an independent community for a lower middle class estranged from the inner city urban condition. For Lewis Mumford, who had vociferously at-

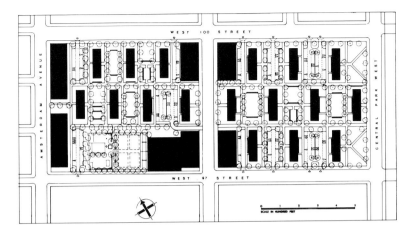

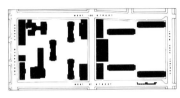

Figure 9.1. Skidmore, Owings, and Merrill.
Manhattantown (West Park Village) preliminary
site plan (above) and final built version (below);
completed toward the end of the 1950s, it
became the most prominent focus of criticism
of New York's slum clearance program.

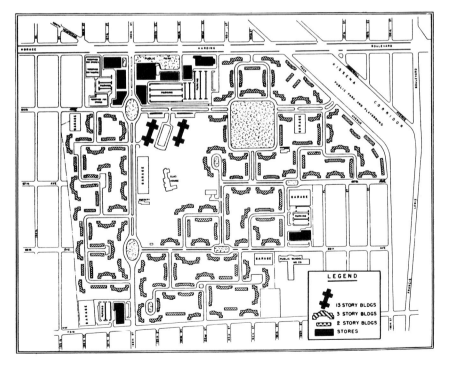

Figure 9.2. Voorhees, Walker, Foley and Smith.
Fresh Meadows in Queens, completed in 1949.
The first of a series of postwar outer borough
moderate income superprojects, it was the only
one which followed low rise, garden city
planning principles.

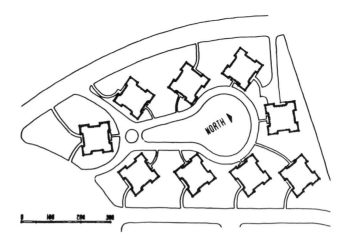

tacked the "tower in the park" in all its forms, Fresh Meadows was closest to his ideal of the horizontal garden city. He called it "perhaps the most positive and exhilarating example of large-scale community planning in this country," and he saw it as an "antidote" to the urban gigantism of Stuyvesant Town or the New York City Housing Authority projects, which he called "painful lessons in how not to rebuild New York." Fresh Meadows was "the City of Tomorrow—not the futuramic city of Hugh Ferriss' theatrical (and moonstruck) charcoal architectural sketches, but a place that will stand up under the closest critical inspection."[13]

High-rise gigantism persisted in spite of such criticism. For example, Fordham Hill Apartments, completed in 1949 in the Bronx by the Equitable Life Assurance Company shared many of the sociological goals of the Fresh Meadows project.[14] But it differed in that it pioneered the postwar version of high rise, high density towers for moderate income families. The 1,118 families were housed in nine 16-story towers in a park, designed by Leonard Schultze and Associates (figure 9.3). Located on high ground at Sedgewick and Webb Avenues, the towers enjoyed spectacular views across the northern tip of Manhattan, but their principal justification was said to be economic. The towers of Fordham Hill were said to represent a future which was mandated by a 25 percent savings in maintenance costs over a comparable low-rise development. Indeed, Fordham Hill was prophetic in many ways. By the 1960s, similar developments proliferated, encouraged by changing demographic and cultural characteristics of the city, including the dislocations and overcrowding caused by the inner city Title I projects.[15]

The "tower in the park" ideal was given final economic sanction in 1961 with passage of a new zoning resolution,[16] the first new approach since the original 1916 *Building Zone Plan* (see figure 5.1). The new plan encouraged use of towers and large open spaces. Areas which were the domain of continuous low-rise, high-density building, including large portions of the outer boroughs and north of 96th Street and the Lower East Side in Manhattan were most affected. Like earlier building controls, the new zoning was biased toward certain high-density Manhattan conditions and tended to "Manhattanize" other areas. For higher densities, the 1961 zoning resolution shifted control of building bulk and coverage from simple height and exposure restrictions. A more complex regulation of interrelated factors governed open space, ratio of rooms to lot area, floor area, and minimum lot size.[17] Central to this formulation was the Floor Area Ratio (FAR), which correlated the total square footage of the building with lot area. A bonus system encouraged the developer to increase the open space in exchange for taller and slimmer buildings. Ironically this change came at precisely the time when the housing tower was coming under increasingly critical scrutiny, reflecting the problematic lag between building practice and its institutionalization in legal terms. Unfortunately, the new zoning resolution not only helped tear apart the fabric of low-rise, high-density areas, but also contributed toward the stagnation of private housing production. Only large-scale interventions were encouraged, wiping out the more incremental small-scale private development of the past.

Early among the other outer borough superprojects was Lefrak City in Queens, completed between 1962 and 1967 along the Long Island Expressway between Junction Boulevard and 99th Street.[18] Designed by Jack Brown Lefrak City was built by Samuel J. Lefrak, who became the largest single private landlord in New York City. With 5,000 families, Lefrak City remains the largest single private development in New York City. In comparison with Fordham Hill, the site planning was even more reductive, consisting only of six enormous X-shaped towers with a haphazard inclusion of one-story shopping structures (figure 9.4). A dismal irony was the name given to each tower, which recalled a number of great world cities. The Lefrak City project was followed by others such as Trump Village,[19]

Figure 9.4. Jack Brown. Lefrack City, Queens, completed 1962–67 and the largest privately financed housing project in New York; its six cruciform towers, each with over eight hundred families, came as close as any other project to the scale of the Corbusian *villes-tours*.

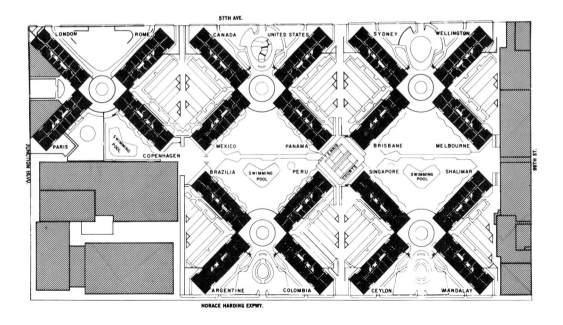

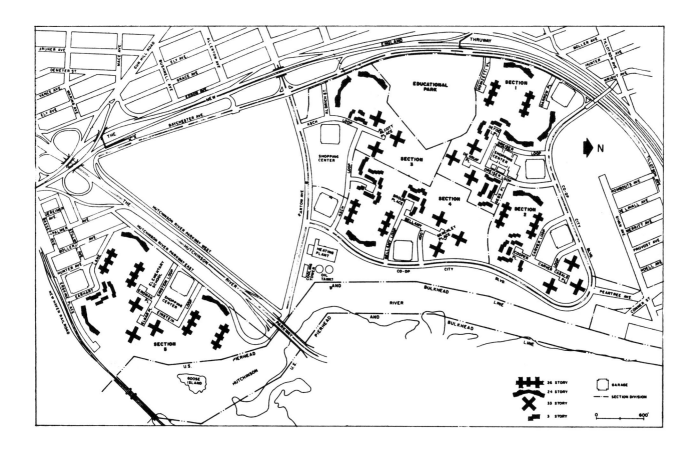

Figure 9.5. Herman J. Jessor. Co-op city in the Bronx, completed in 1968–70 as the largest single housing development in New York, with thirty-five towers set in a vast "park."

a Mitchell-Lama development on Coney Island built by Fred C. Trump for 3,800 families; and by Starrett City, another Mitchell-Lama development completed in 1976 in Brooklyn.[20] Designed by Herman J. Jessor, it housed 6,000 families.

All of the outer borough superprojects were overshadowed by Co-op City with 15,500 families, completed between 1968 and 1970 in the Bronx.[21] One of the final housing monuments to Robert Moses, Co-op City is the largest single housing development in New York City. It was designed by Herman J. Jessor, with thirty-five towers of thirty-five stories each set in a vast "park," with a sprinkling of two-family houses and commercial and community buildings (figure 9.5). Co-op City's site planning was readily distinguished from the previous superprojects only in terms of the megalomaniacal scale, part of a vast new Moses housing vision undauntedly forged even at the twilight of his power.[22] It was also consistent with the scale of Governor Nelson Rockefeller's particular social vision, and it marked the close of Herman J. Jessor's long career in housing. The design of Co-op City was a far cry from the sensibilities of Jessor's early projects, such as the Workers Cooperative Colony (see figure 5.32). This project is perhaps as clear an indication as anything else of the dilemmas facing those architects who chose to continue to work in the realm of social housing in the postwar era. Political progressivism had long since passed and social institutionalism had taken charge along with its requisite design conventions.

Building the superprojects helped to destabilize older middle-income neighborhoods of New York City, particularly those with developing economic and social problems like the Grand Concourse in the Bronx.[23] As the ethnic and class composition of the older neighborhoods began to change, the new outer borough superprojects provided an affordable escape for those who were left behind by suburbia. They were also a refuge from other displacements; for example, the Cross Bronx Expressway which created a swath of destruction across the South Bronx and contributed significantly to its rapid decline. The entire community of Crotona Park was wiped out in order that the suburbs might be better reached by automobile.[24] By the mid-1960's, a state of fear was exacerbated by popular coverage in the press. For example, in 1967 the *New York Post* announced the demise of the Grand Concourse, tracing many of the Co-op City applicants to the Concourse, where panic along race and class lines was quickly developing.[25] What was lost in this kind of exodus was tragic for all concerned, as witnessed by the decline of the concourse, and by the problematic mediocrity of the projects substituted in its place. Co-op City, with economic and construction problems coupled with design mediocrity and ghettolike isolation from the rest of the city, has not proven itself to be a desirable alternative to what the Grand Concourse could have become. Amid the outcry against Co-op City, Denise Scott Brown and Robert Venturi's "revisionist" argument that it was "almost alright" was too simplistic an interpretation of its problemmatic economic and cultural impact.[26] Continuing problems with the project in more recent years has only raised further questions.

The evolution of the high rise from "cross" plan to "slab-block" was not limited to application for social housing. The slab block enjoyed an extended period of acceptability in the realm of high style, even in Manhattan, where the economic constraints of land values tended to limit the requisite "park" setting. In 1950, with the completion of Manhattan House by Gordon Bunshaft of Skidmore, Owings, and Merrill, the slab-block entered the domain of the upper middle class.[27] Built by the New York Life Insurance Company to complement its lower-middle-income Fresh Meadows development, Manhattan House occupied an entire block between Second and Third avenues and East 65th and 66th streets (figure 9.6). The massive single crenellated slab of twenty-two stories was more than six hundred

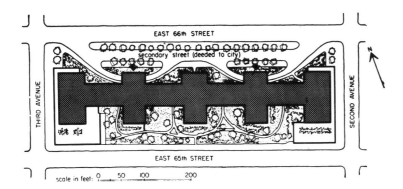

Figure 9.6. Skidmore, Owings, and Merrill. Manhattan House, a luxury version of the slab block type, completed in 1950 on an entire Upper East Side block.

Figure 9.7. I. M. Pei and Partners. Kips Bay Plaza, completed 1960–65 with two pristine luxury slab blocks facing a private park with parking and commercial buildings integrated at the edges.

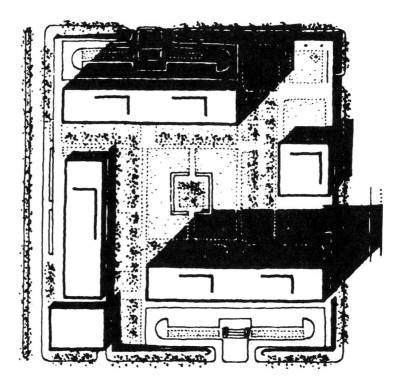

feet long—larger than Le Corbusier's Unité d'Habitation at Marseilles from which the form was derived. Low commercial structures at both ends of the block helped to integrate the project with the neighborhood, and the gardens contributed to the space of the street. Compared with Bunshaft's Sedgwick Houses public housing project of the same period (see figure 8.16), the extensive amenities of Manhattan House amply demonstrated the wide differential between the slab block as applied to social housing and luxury housing. More than three decades later, Manhattan House remains a fashionable New York address.

Between 1960 and 1965 I. M. Pei and Partners with S. J. Kessler completed the most pristine version of the Le Corbusier Unité in New York City at Kips Bay Plaza in Manhattan.[28] Two similar slab blocks faced a large plaza between First and Second avenues and East 30th and 33rd streets (figure 9.7). The facades were large undifferentiated grids of precast concrete and glass, derivative of the Unité and one of the more elegant of the many such likenesses which proliferated in New York in that era. The plaza was actually a planted garden over the parking garage, integrated with low commercial structures on the avenue ends. In this way the "park" was woven into the urban context. Yet from within, the planting gave the feeling of isolation and respite from the city. A similar but larger project was Washington Square Village which used two enormous slabs spanning three blocks between LaGuardia Place and Mercer Street bordering West 3rd and Bleeker streets. It was completed between 1958 and 1960 by S. J. Kessler and

Sons with Paul Lester Weiner.[29] Like Kips Bay, the slabs were separated by a garden with parking below. Innumerable upper-middle and upper-income slab block projects followed suit with varying degrees of innovative site planning, indicating that at least for some socioeconomic groups, the "tower in the park" could function well urbanistically, given sufficient attention to design detail. But these projects were relatively discreet urbane modifications of the slab block. They served primarily to pave the way for the more radical reconciliations with the high-rise that were beginning to emerge around the same time.

Washington Square Village originated with the notorious Washington Square South plan proposed in 1951 by the Mayor's Committee on Slum Clearance.[30] The scheme extended Fifth Avenue through Washington Square and razed most of the area between the Square and Spring Street. It become one of the important rallying points for opposition to Robert Moses and the "bulldozer approach." Apart from the desecration of Washington Square, protest focused on the massive displacement of local businesses and families, and the aura of corruption which surrounded the acquisition for Title I projects everywhere.[31] Eventually, only a fragmented version of the project was realized, without the Fifth Avenue extension. Included was University Plaza, "three towers in a park" completed by I. M. Pei and Partners in 1966.[32]

A powerful general critique of postwar urbanism had already coalesced by the end of 1950s in New York City, with roots touching both populist and theoretical concerns. For example, the Women's Club of New York made a detailed study of the relocation problems associated with the Title I slum clearance projects, specifically for Manhattantown (West Park Village). Completed in 1954, with a follow-up in 1956, it was a pioneering effort to understand the social disruption associated with large-scale urban redevelopment.[33] The extensive tenant interviews and locational analysis conclusively indicated that urban renewal in New York City was creating slums faster than it was removing them. In a different realm, Serge Chermayeff's pioneering housing studies at Harvard University beginning around 1954 proposed that high densities might be better achieved through low-rise housing types. This work made a broad impact with the publication of *Community and Privacy* in 1963.[34] Within the New York scene, however, no one was able to coalesce such diverse arguments better than Jane Jacobs, whose *The Death and Life of Great American Cities,* published in 1961, provided the first significant, broad basis for the growing attacks on urban renewal policies in New York City and throughout the United States.

Jane Jacobs argued for a return to all of the things orthodox modernist urbanism had removed from cities. In this sense her book was an antithesis to Jose Luis Sert's *Can Our Cities Survive?,* which had been published exactly two decades earlier. Jacobs attacked the simplistic and reductivist conceptions of the city inherent in such axioms as the separation of urban "functions" into habitation, work, and leisure. She urged a return to smaller-scale, diverse, and more incremental rebuilding rather than massive renewal. She argued that the high-rise tower had destroyed the residential patterns endemic to normal urban life, at a social cost far outweighing questionable short-term construction economies. Jacobs also questioned the totalitarian aesthetics of large-scale urban form-making proposals, from Burnham's "City Beautiful" to Le Corbusier's "Ville Radieuse." She wrote:

> To approach a city, or even a city neighborhood as if it were a larger architectural problem, capable of being given order by converting it into a disciplined work of art, is to make the mistake of attempting to substitute art for life.
>
> The results of such profound confusion between art and life are neither life nor art. They are taxidermy. In its place, taxidermy can be a useful and decent craft. However, it goes too far when the specimens put on display are exhibitions of dead, stuffed cities.[35]

The effect of Jacobs' ideas on housing design was immediate and forceful. For example, her influence was obvious on the competition for new housing in East Harlem sponsored by the Ruberoid Corporation in 1963.[36] The program, developed in coordination with the New York City Housing and Redevelopment Board (HRB), focused on a four-block renewal area between East 107th and East 111th streets and the FDR Drive. The 1,500 subsidized middle-income apartments were to be developed with particular attention paid to integration with the neighborhood. Within the zoning and building code restrictions, any combination of high- and low-rise massing was permitted, but the jury seemed particularly interested in low-rise possibilities. The winning scheme, by Hodne Associates, placed four towers within a small-scale gridiron of walkways and streets lined by lower buildings. A more radical approach placed second, designed by Edvin Stromsten, Ricardo Scofidio, and Felix Martorano. It proposed a fine-grain low-rise massing, with narrow walkways and automobile access limited to the periphery (figure 9.8). Both projects evoked a world far closer to nineteenth century Greenwich Village than to the "Ville Radieuse," as the traditional New York urban texture began to reassert itself in architects' thinking.

In 1968, the Brighton Beach Housing Competition presented another opportunity for the latter team to further explore the same low-rise issues.[37] Scofidio and Stromsten, joined by Berman, Roberts, placed second, with six buildings stepping down to the beach on an oceanfront site in Brooklyn. Their scheme contrasted with the winning entry by Wells-Koetter, which reflected the mainstream upscale social housing genre of the period: a twenty-five story tower with lower buildings surrounding a public plaza facing the water. Most public attention, however, was focused on the third place project submitted by Venturi and Rauch, an indication of the growing influence of Venturi's ideas, especially after publication of *Complexity and Contradiction in Architecture* two years earlier.[38] Two-story townhouses were interspersed among two large thirteen-story brick boxes which the designers argued were contextual in that they were evocative of the surrounding builder vernacular. This strategy was admired by some jury members as a sophisticated application of "existing possibilities." Others were critical, arguing "that the buildings look like the most ordinary apartment construction built all over Queens and Brooklyn since the Depression, that the placing of the blocks was ordinary and dull."[39] Whatever else, the discourse represented the first time in New York that "ugly and ordinary" were said to be virtues for social housing.

Figure 9.8. Edvin Stromsten, Ricardo Scofidio, and Felix Martorano. Second Place entry to the East Harlem housing competition sponsored by the Ruberoid Corporation in 1963. The fine-grain low-rise high density massing made a definitive break with the "tower in the park" approach.

It was a harbinger of a coming period when cultural nihilism could be considered germain to the issue of design quality in housing.

The first significant weakening of the New York City housing bureaucracy's support of the "tower in the park" came in 1960 with Robert Moses' resignation from the Mayor's Committee on Slum Clearance. Moses left under overwhelming criticism of the handling of Title I money allocated to New York City by the federal government. Accusations included corruption in the purchase of land for slum clearance and general use of political influence for private profit in expediting the Title I program.[40] There also was a growing public resistance to Moses' slum clearance tactics, involving massive evictions and relocations of the sort publicized at Manhattantown. Anticipating the demise of Moses, Mayor Robert Wagner appointed a management consultant, J. Anthony Panuch to study the reorganization of the city housing bureaucracy.[41] After Moses' resigned, Panuch's recommendations were followed. A Housing and Redevelopment Board was formed to coordinate the functions of several existing agencies, including the Committee on Slum Clearance. The public received assurances that the "bulldozer" approach to housing renewal was abandoned. For the first time in New York City, Title I money was to be used for rebuilding housing as well as for clearance.

After taking office in 1966, Mayor John Lindsay promoted a major reorganization of the New York City government, including the housing bureaucracy. He proposed a new "superagency" which would consolidate all of the existing housing agencies under a single administrator whose powers would substantially exceed those of the former chairman of the Housing and Redevelopment Board. In 1967 the new agency, named the Housing and Development Administration (HDA), was approved by the City Council.[42] Immediately it became the nexus of the new directions in housing design and urbanism which had been fomenting. The demise of the "tower in the park" became one important focus. The HDA, for example, quickly commissioned Lawrence Halpern to study the redevelopment of open space within tower housing projects in New York City in an attempt to correct some of the design problems of the previous generation of social housing. Halpern's report, published in 1968, included the first proposal for reconstruction of a "tower in the park" project, made for Penn Station South less than a decade after its completion.[43] The proposal suggested building new low, continuous structures in the "parkland" which would reestablish human-scale spaces and reintegrate the towers with the surrounding urban fabric (figure 9.9). Ideas involving the same sensibility as Halpern's were also proposed by other architects commissioned by the Housing and Development Administration, and by the staff of its Office of Planning, Design, and Research. Design proposals evolved toward a vision of the highrise tower as an eroded form which could be more readily integrated with lower building. The realization of some of these proposals helped establish a new generation of high-rise housing design, which was completed by the mid-1970s. The HDA also further explored Halpern's ideas about "tower in the park" redevelopment. Its proposal for Independence Houses in Brooklyn showed similar concerns.[44] Other important initiatives included the Brighton Beach Housing Competition.

The HDA was not the only source of new ideas. By 1969 the newly formed New York State Urban Development Corporation (UDC) started to promote many of the same design values as the HDA. Created by the New York state legislature in 1968,[45] the UDC was a public authority with vast powers which could be brought to bear on the issue of design quality. The UDC could override local zoning codes and government bodies to condemn land for site acquisition. Architects could be hired without following civil service codes, thus eliminating the mediocrity caused by a reliance on those whose qualifications were dominated by their local political connections. UDC also enjoyed a certain financial independence. The authority

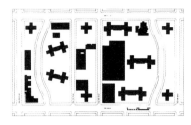

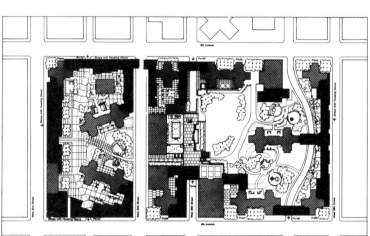

Figure 9.9. Lawrence Halpern. Proposal made in 1968 for reconstruction of the Penn Station South project; the existing "towers in a park" are reintegrated with the surrounding city through the introduction of new low, continuous buildings in the "parkland."

could issue its own bonds backed by a "moral obligation" from the State of New York to pay the debt service. The independence of the UDC led to the development of its own design standards, which were higher than the FHA's. In general, the UDC has left a unique legacy, not only of important built projects, but also of programming and research.[46]

Other new design thinking was generated by neighborhood planning and design organizations. These groups reached their maturity by the end of the 1960s, with political and monetary support provided by the Kennedy and Johnson era social programs. One of the more notorious "community-initiated" projects was a 1967 proposal for the redevelopment of Taft Houses in East Harlem, made by architects working through the United Residents of Milbank-Frawley Circle-East Harlem Association.[47] A high-rise public housing project completed only two years earlier, Taft Houses had been designated by the HDA as a site for new low-rise infill housing. The United Residents felt that the HDA proposal would only contribute to further neighborhood deterioration. They developed an alternative plan to include middle-income as well as low-income apartments. As families within the project became more affluent, they could move to better housing without leaving. Their architect, Roger Katan, proposed a system of horizontal "shelves" from three to eleven stories high, which would have covered the entire Taft Houses "parkland" and surrounding area, even using air rights over streets. The proposed structure was filled with prefabricated houses. Many community facilities were planned, such as health care centers, cooperative shops, and offices for public and private agencies, which were expected to contribute to the self-sufficiency of the neighborhood. The scale of the project proved unrealistic, and the false hopes it had raised in the community made it the target of criticism.

Around the same time, Oscar Newman undertook a research project at the Columbia University School of Architecture on security in urban residential environments, funded by the U.S. Department of Justice. Newman found a correlation between the design characteristics of the "tower in the park" and increased frequency of crime and vandalism. This study resulted in the publication of *Defensible Space,* a controversial book which had a wide impact.[48] For the first time, a well-documented argument was presented that placed an aspect of the blame for the social pathology of the high-rise public housing tower on its physical design. Included was the comparison between Brownsville and Van Dyck Houses in Brooklyn, which forcefully argued this point (see figure 8.23). Thus, it took more than three decades of New York City Housing Authority programs before the admonitions of its first architectural director, Frederick Ackerman, were given the empirical credence he lacked. But, indeed, his studies proved to be correct. It was confirmed that the long-term costs in housing were intricately tied to housing type, at least in relation to social class.

During the period between 1967 and 1976, the new government agencies produced a large amount of new subsidized housing in New York City, all influenced by changing architectural attitudes. An important new generation of architectural firms knowledgeable about housing came of age. Several significant concentrations of housing were completed, including large-scale projects in the Twin Parks area of the South Bronx, and at Coney Island. Even larger in scale were the "new towns" planned for Roosevelt Island and on the landfill extension of lower Manhattan at Battery Park City. The latter, begun in 1968, was the first of the extensive plans for redevelopment of the West Side of Manhattan. This included the planning for Westway, a waterfront project which envisioned rebuilding most of the western edge of Manhattan south of 42nd Street. The UDC alone had built thirty-two projects totaling 15,514 new units in New York City by 1977 when the program was terminated, less than a decade after its inception.[49] The Mitchell-Lama program produced even more housing, 33,718 units for the same period. These numbers did not match the peak figures of the mid-1960s, but the crucial difference was the relative increase in the quality of this later generation of social housing.

Of the many innovative projects completed during this period, several stand above the others for the significance of their influence. Although not always applauded in the long term, they were greeted with considerable initial interest and became prototypes for subsequent projects. The first and most influential was Riverbend Houses, a Mitchell-Lama project designed by Davis Brody and Associates and completed in 1967.[50] Located between East 138th and 142nd streets, the Harlem River Drive, and Fifth Avenue, the project housed 624 families in slabs of eleven, sixteen, and nineteen stories (figure 9.10). In contrast to the free-

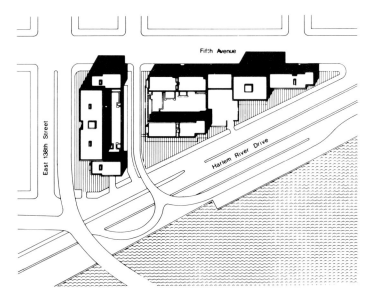

standing towers of the past, the Riverbend slabs were interconnected and surrounded a large plaza one level above grade. Riverbend had a higher density than
many earlier precedents, and it reversed the ideal of lowest possible site coverage.
A wide range of apartment types and sizes included duplexes which were linked
by two-story circulation galleries, each with porchlike "yards" (figure 9.11). Thus
the internal organization of the slab block took on an organizational complexity
previously unexplored.

Although the use of external galleries in New York housing has dated from
the Workingmen's Home of 1855 (see figure 1.4), Riverbend signaled the beginning of a wide application, encouraged not only by the aura of experimentation,
but also by expedience in fulfilling fire code requirements. Other more immediate
precedents for the "streets in the air" at Riverbend were European; the project
architect at Davis Brody had previous experience in England. Obvious antecedents were the projects and theories of Peter and Alison Smithson in England,
Candilis, Josic, and Woods in France, and Jakob Bakema in the Netherlands, all
members of Team Ten, which had gained some recognition in the United States
by the mid-1960s.[51]

Figure 9.11. Riverbend typical duplex apartment
section along a gallery "street," indicating the
raised "yard" at the entry.

NEW DIRECTIONS   295

Figure 9.12. Richard Meier and Associates. Twin Parks Northeast in the Bronx, completed in 1973 and seen at the time as a major breakthrough in high-rise massing, because of its fragmentation around small-scale public space in an effort to respect the surrounding low-rise context.

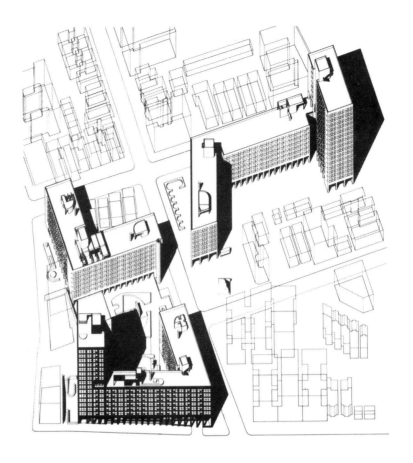

Several years after the completion of Riverbend considerable critical interest focused on the new Twin Parks projects in the Bronx. Most prominently published was Twin Parks Northeast, completed by Richard Meier and Associates in 1973.[52] Located on two irregular blocks at East 183rd Street between Crotona Avenue and the Bronx Botanical Gardens, the high-rise project was seen as a breakthrough in the way that it was integrated with the surrounding small-scale neighborhood. The massing was heavily fragmented, using two roughly U-shaped slabs of varying heights, from seven to sixteen stories (figure 9.12). The 523 apartments were tightly interwoven with parking, commercial, and community space. Two public plazas organized the open space, with an unusually high coverage of 53 percent, reflecting the growing tendency in that direction. The formal composition of the site organization reflected the growing influence of Colin Rowe, under whom the project architect from Meier's office had studied.[53] And as at Riverbend, some of the new European ideas were undoubtedly incorporated.[54] In Meier's words:

> The design approach, then, was to express an attitude toward integration into the pre-existing urban context. The main concerns were to relate the new buildings to the structures around them and to express the implicit social differentiation

between public and private spaces . . . in order to provide as much usable space as possible for the needs of both the residents and the community at large . . . .

Twin Parks Northeast Housing is not an architecture of isolated structures. Here there is reference to ideas of traditional building, preoccupation with urban continuity, and concepts of adaptive urban capability . . . . This idea involves the objective of a building to evolve from, to adapt to, and to reinforce existing urban conditions.[55]

In his evaluation of the project, Kenneth Frampton saw this kind of "contextualism" as an attempt to address issues of territoriality and defensibility for public space as posed by Oscar Newman's widely read book. Frampton said the project provided public space of "outstanding sensibility . . . both in relation to its existing urban context and in providing a viable public space for play; a space that seems to have been more than adequately supported by spontaneous use, even if, on occasions, this use had degenerated into violence."[56] The design paid far less attention to the apartments, which unlike many other recent new projects, were simple flats, contributing nothing to the new thinking. Unfortunately, the apartment space standards only adhered to FHA minimums rather than the higher UDC standards, which were not adopted until slightly later.[57]

Within the Twin Parks development several other projects contributed significantly to the exploration of the new site-planning sensibilities. For example, the relatively small Twin Parks Northwest by Prentice, Chan, and Olhausen posited a variation on the perimeter block, contributing to the revival of interest in that particular form of urbanism which had enjoyed wide application in the early period of the twentieth century.[58] Located along an escarpment parallel to Webster Avenue, both topography and the curve of East 184th Street were used to transform the simple perimeter massing (figure 9.13). Further down Webster Avenue at Twin Parks West a series of five sites designed by Giovanni Pasanella and Associates attempted to address the problem of site context through the use of the high-rise slab as monumental marker and gateway, within a pattern generated through the straightforward functional consideration of access and topography.[59] The triangular building at the intersection of Valentine and Webster avenues worked best in achieving this monumentality because of the dominance of the massing which was enhanced by the freestanding character of the site. As the project moved north, slab blocks paralleled the Webster Avenue escarpment. They contained duplex units organized in sections reminiscent of the Le Corbusier Unité (figure 9.14). Slightly later, in 1975, Pasanella also completed Twin Parks East, which again used the theme of urban marker.[60] Located at an important intersection involving Southern Boulevard, Prospect Avenue, and East 187th Street, both pylon and gate buildings were employed to mark entry, juxtaposed against the massive green landscape of the Bronx Zoological Garden (figure 9.15).

The planning for Battery Park City began with the creation of the Battery Park City Authority in 1968 as a nonprofit public corporation which followed the UDC precedent. Constructed on a large area of Hudson River landfill between Chambers Street and Battery Park, the proposal envisioned the creation of a new "city," with 19,000 new apartments and offices and commercial space involving

Figure 9.13. Prentice, Chan, and Olhausen. Twin Parks Northwest, completed in the Bronx in 1973; a partial perimeter block integrated with the sloping terrain.

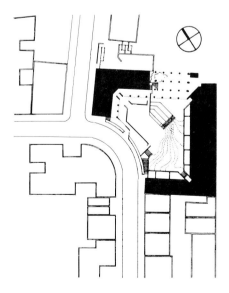

Figure 9.14. Giovanni Pasanella Twin Parks West duplex apartment sections, reminiscent of the Le Corbusier Unité organization.

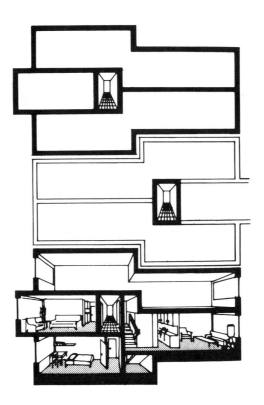

Figure 9.15. Giovanni Pasanella. Twin Parks East, completed in the Bronx in 1975; "pylon" and "gate" buildings opposite the Bronx Zoological Garden.

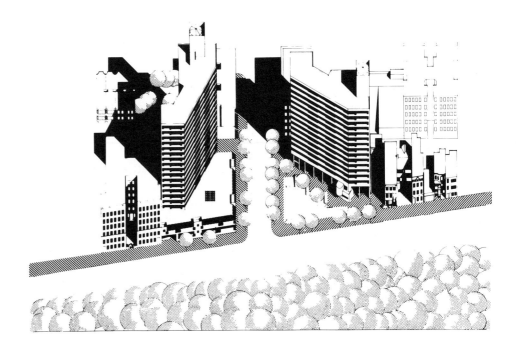

35,000 new jobs. The master plan was designed by Harrison and Abramovitz, Philip Johnson and John Burgee, and Conklin and Rossant.[61] The riverfront was organized as a promenade and park. A central "spine" of circulation and shopping was used to organize the buildings, which formed loosely defined plazas. Because of economic difficulties, Battery Park City was stalled for more then a decade, and the original master plan was discarded after completion of only one small portion. Slightly later, the Roosevelt Island development was initiated by the UDC and came to partial fruition much earlier. It followed the same model of the "city within the city," although it lacked the commercial and office development of Battery Park City. And because of its island setting, it fell more into the realm of urban enclave, in the tradition of Stuyvesant Town or Co-op City.

The Roosevelt Island master plan was designed for the UDC in 1969 by Philip Johnson and John Burgee. Like Battery Park City, it proposed a central "spine," noteworthy for its attempt to render a kind of high rise as picturesque. A winding "Main Street" tended to reduce vistas and make the perception of the whole less overwhelming.[62] All of the individual developments terraced down from this spine to the water's edge, with attention given to problems of maintaining views, especially of the Manhattan skyline (figure 9.16). Improved apartment space standards were a major concern at Roosevelt Island, which more than any other UDC project catered to a middle-income tenantry.

Of particular interest were the apartments designed by Sert, Jackson, and Associates for the Westview and Eastwood complexes completed in 1976.[63] These projects developed aspects of Sert's influential previous work elsewhere, like Peabody Terrace at Harvard, completed ten years earlier.[69] All involved further explorations of the Le Corbusier split-section apartments. Sert employed a gallery for access on every third level, gaining a very flexible organization of flats and duplexes while minimizing horizontal circulation (figure 9.17). Adjacent to Westview, the upper-middle-income Rivercross complex by Johansen and Bhavnani was particularly significant for its extremely generous space standards.[65]

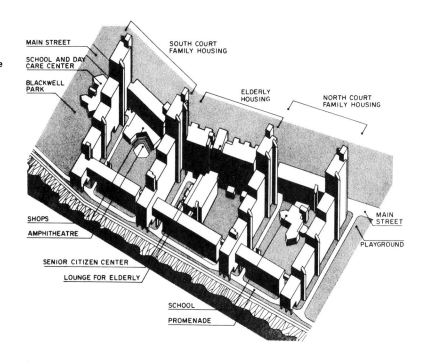

Figure 9.17. Sert, Jackson, and Associates. Eastwood on Roosevelt Island, completed in 1976, with open perimeters terracing toward the water and considerable exploration of the Le Corbusier Unité section.

Within the fabric of Manhattan, the imperative for contextualism had also emerged as an emblem of progressive design by the 1970s. But the freestanding tower tended to survive in various forms for reasons of economy if nothing else. Site planning for towers frequently became the domain of "plazas,"; in the highest-coverage situations these were combined with medium-rise housing and commercial building which tended to reinforce the street walls. Manhattan Plaza, completed in 1977 by David Todd and Associates, is an example of a relatively dispersed and open approach.[66] The site occupies an entire block between West 42nd and 43rd streets and Ninth and Tenth avenues. A forty-five-story tower at

Figure 9.18. David Todd and Associates. Manhattan Plaza on West 42nd Street, completed in 1977 as the archetype of the large raised plaza with parking and commercial space underneath, flanked by two forty-five-story towers at each end.

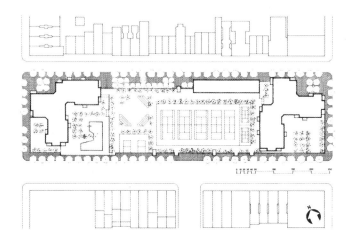

each end frames a large elevated plaza between them, which also serves as the roof of a parking garage (figure 9.18). One-story shops partially surround the block under the plaza level.

A more radical approach to site organization was used at East Midtown Plaza, completed in 1974 by Davis, Brody, and Associates.[67] The project integrates towers and a large plaza with a complex pattern of existing buildings. Two blocks adjoining East 24th Street between First and Second avenues are united by a plaza which spans the street, with the irregular parcels on each side unified by eleven-story buildings that maintain the street walls. Three towers are joined to the lower buildings to complete the composition, along with a number of existing buildings (figure 9.19). In a more monumental context, Confucius Plaza at the Bowery and Division and Canal streets attempted to address the scale of the adjacent Manhattan Bridge with its arch gateway.[68] Completed in 1976 by Horowitz and Chun, the curved slab steps up toward the bridge. The requisite plaza at the base is integrated with a parking garage, school, and shops.

Perhaps the most successful of this generation of high-rise housing in Manhattan was the 1199 Plaza, completed in 1975 in East Harlem between East 107th and 111th streets and FDR Drive.[69] The design by the Hodne/Stageburg Partnership was the result of extensive input from the project sponsors, Local 1199 of the Drug and Hospital Workers Union. It dated from the firm's winning entry to the 1963 Ruberoid competition for the same site, and the design development

Figure 9.19. Davis Brody and Associates. East Midtown Plaza, completed in 1974 with a large plaza spanning two blocks to unify the complex configuration of existing and new buildings.

Figure 9.20. Hodne/Stageburg Partnership. 1199 Plaza, a union cooperative completed in 1974 along the East River in Harlem after many years of study and revision of the original 1963 winning competition entry; four partial perimeters step down to the river, incorporating several building types within each whole.

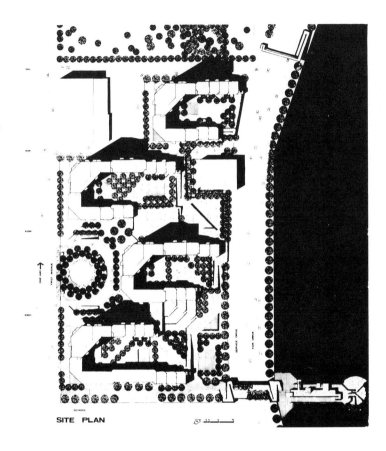

SITE PLAN

involved several subsequent schemes. Ultimately it evolved to its final configuration of four U-shaped buildings which step down toward the East River, dropping from thirty-two stories to six (figure 9.20). The massing is an interesting hybrid, combining characteristics of several housing types: the turn-of-the-century tower, the perimeter block, and the slab block. The forms also responded well to basic issues such as view, maximum sunlight, and security. Included among the 1,590 apartments were a variety of types; most prominently, the duplex units with gallery access. Compared with many other innovative projects of the same period, 1199 Plaza has been exceptionally successful.

The Roosevelt Island housing competition, sponsored in 1975 by the Urban Development Corporation, followed the precedent of the Ruberoid competition twelve years before, attempting to explore further design innovation for the problem of the high-rise neighborhood. The program called for an addition of one thousand apartments to the existing UDC development, and emphasized the architectural issues of "community, child supervision, security, maintenance, livability, and responsiveness to context."[70] Beyond the visual and verbal rhetoric, however, the winning schemes made little progress with these issues (figure 9.21). In comparison with some of the concrete achievements of the previous decade, the sub-

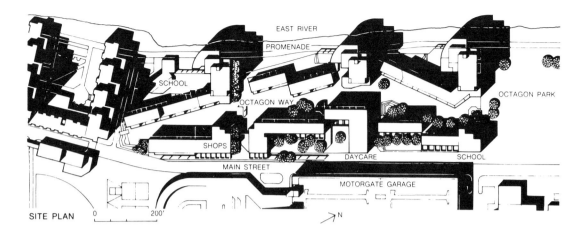

SITE PLAN 0 200' N

missions in general were disappointing; little further innovation emerged. Perhaps the only exceptions were the entries, which were exclusively visionary or polemical, and they signaled the growing dominance of that particular architectural mode within the decade (figure 9.22). The financial demise of the UDC, which occurred just after the competition also was a signal of the conclusion of a unique period of housing innovation.[71]

Figure 9.21. Robert A. M. Stern and John S. Hagmann. Placing entry to the Roosevelt Island housing competition sponsored by the New York State Urban Development Corporation in 1975.

Figure 9.22. O. M. Ungers. Entry to the Roosevelt Island housing competition using a miniature "Central Park" as a community focus. The design flexibility advocated a process which would include tenant groups and other architects.

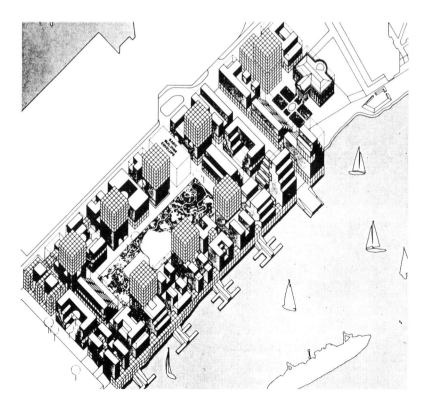

Figure 9.23 Richard Kaplan. Crown Gardens in
Brooklyn completed in 1971 as an informal
perimeter block; a high-rise slab faces two low-
rise courtyards partially composed of existing
rowhouses.

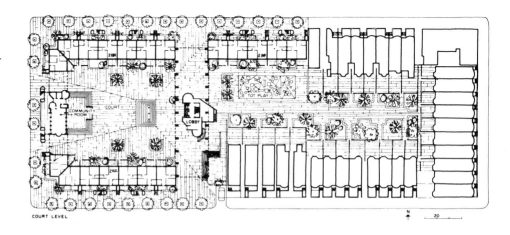

The increasing interest in lower housing led to reconsideration of the perimeter block after several decades of neglect. The traditional New York City application was reinterpreted in a number of ways. At Crown Gardens in Brooklyn, completed in 1971 by Richard Kaplan on a block bounded by Nostrand and New York avenues, and President and Carroll streets,[72] a high-rise slab at mid-block faced low-rise courtyards on each side. The project was composed partially of existing buildings (figure 9.23). Another approach more directly derivative of the perimeter block tradition in New York was Lambert Houses completed in the Bronx in 1973 along Bronx Park South between the Boston Post Road and East Tremont Avenue.[73] Designed by Davis, Brody, and Associates for the Phipps Houses, the site plan echoes the sensibilities of the Phipps Garden Apartments (see figure 5.42), which was one of the early pioneering efforts of that organization, designed by Clarence Stein in 1929 (figure 9.24). The Lambert Houses is a loosely organized series of repetitive perimeter clusters which also can be seen as simplified versions of Stein's Hillside Homes of 1935 (see figure 7.7). In general, the low massing combined with a relatively high coverage is reminiscent of the 1920s garden apartment tradition in the outer boroughs. Like that earlier generation of housing, Lambert Houses is only six stories, but the 736 apartments are served by elevators. Thus, at the moment of crisis with the tower, when the tower was pushed to its formal limits in an effort to reduce scale and to increase responsiveness to context, there also was the beginning of a historicist tendency which rejected the tower completely. These architects looked back to successful housing types of the earlier low-rise era in social housing.

Another low-rise project completed in the Bronx was the infill housing built by the South Bronx Community Housing Company in 1974 on several sites in the Mott Haven area, between East 137th and East 139th streets, Brooke and Willis avenues. Designed by Ciardullo-Ehrmann, it used simple row-type houses that had evolved from an important earlier infill experiment by the same architects in Red Hook in Brooklyn.[74] At Mott Haven, they were applied to three locations. The most interesting was the Plaza Borinquen, a small mid-block perimeter that surrounds a central garden[75] (figure 9.25). Eighty families were housed

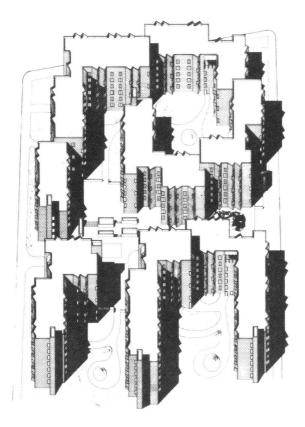

Figure 9.24. Davis, Brody, and Associates. Lambert Houses in the Bronx, a philanthropic project of Phipps Houses completed in 1973 using some of the same site organizational principles as the Phipps Garden Apartments, completed by the same philanthropic organization some fifty years earlier.

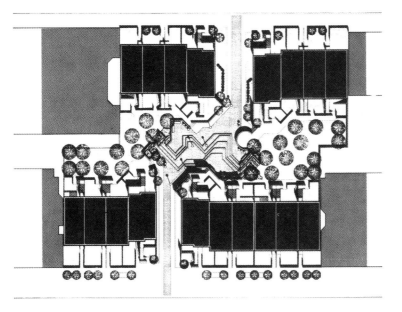

Figure 9.25. Ciardullo-Ehrmann. Plaza Boriquen at Mott Haven in the south Bronx; a low-rise mid-block perimeter completed in 1974, one of the simplest and best executed of the early low-rise, walk-up revival projects.

Figure 9.26. Urban Development Corporation and the Institute for Architecture and Urban Studies, with David Todd and Associates. Marcus Garvey Park Village in Brownsville, Brooklyn, completed in 1975 with walk-up apartments along mews cut across the mid-blocks in an attempt to maintain a small-scale fabric while increasing surveillance of the public space.

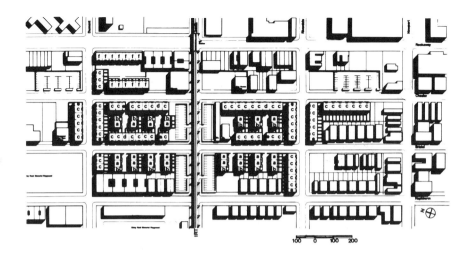

in total. Building height was limited to three stories, and an emphasis was placed on defining the territory of each family through provision of small private outdoor areas and through elmination of shared public stairs. The entire project, from the overall site planning to the studied simplicity of the architectural detail, represented a level of quality which was amply reflected in the success of the project from the tenants' point of view.

In Brooklyn, an equally important project within the new generation of low-rise housing in New York City was the Marcus Garvey Park Village completed in 1975.[76] It was a UDC project designed by a team from that agency and from the Institute for Architecture and Urban Studies, in collaboration with David Todd and Associates. The site consisted of several blocks in Brownsville, between Dumont, Riverdale, and Rockaway Avenues and Bristol Street. A tight-knit, low-rise, medium density configuration was used, integrating several existing buildings (figure 9.26). The site organization was particularly interesting, with several east-west pedestrian "mews" cut through the middle of the blocks in a manner reminiscent of Edward Potter's proposals for the New York City gridiron made almost a century earlier (see figures 1.16 to 1.18). The project paid careful consideration to the boundaries between public and private space. Maximum identity for each "house" was emphasized through provision of private "stoops" and entrances. The care given to the social organization was weakened, however, by the architectural expression. Overscaled "strip" windows were used in a revivalist attempt at a vernacular on the theme of the "International Style."

The move toward new lower housing also reached Manhattan, in spite of its propensity for high building. A perimeter had not been built in Manhattan since Knickerbocker Village in 1933 (see figure 7.2). But by the early 1960s, agitation on the Lower East Side led to a number of proposals for medium-rise perimeter fragments intended to repair partially destroyed blocks. The first and most sophisticated proposal for a complete perimeter was made in 1973 for the Cooper Square Committee, a local neighborhood association.[77] The project by Roger A.

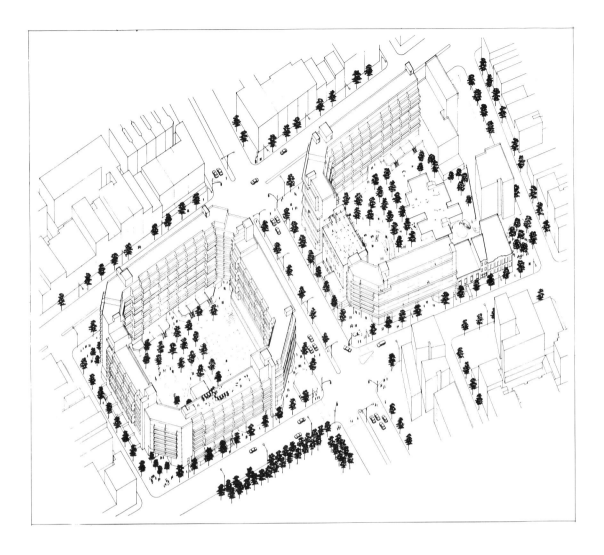

Figure 9.27. Roger A. Cumming with Waltraude Schleicher-Woods. Unbuilt 1973 proposal for Cooper Square on the Lower East Side; the first elaborate perimeter block proposed for Manhattan since the 1930s.

Cumming with Waltraude Schleicher-Woods, was proposed for a block bounded by the Bowery, East Houston, Stanton, and Chrystie streets. It reflected the designers' earlier association with Shadrach Woods and of many of the sensibilities the European projects of Candilis, Josic, and Woods, but it also was responsive to the tradition of the New York perimeter block. Its height varied from eight to fourteen stories, and the corners of the perimeter mass were chamfered in an attempt to improve the problematic corner apartments (figure 9.27). Parking was located under the central courtyard, with shops around the street edge. Roofs were developed for public use, and a children's day-care center was located in a small building at the center of the courtyard. Cooper Square was not built, and no others of the recent perimeter revival projects have been built in Manhattan. Frag-

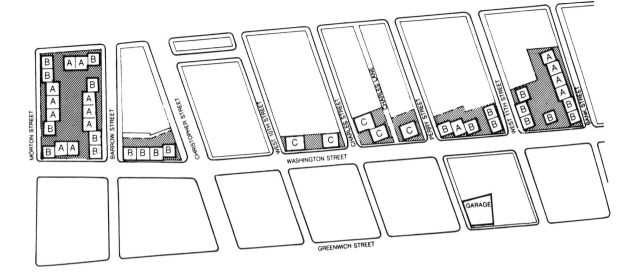

Figure 9.28. Perkins and Will. West Village Houses, the first and most controversial of the low-rise, walk-up projects, proposed in 1961 and not completed until fourteen years later. It attempted to preserve the existing fabric through small-scale infill and argued for a diversity of scale and use within the neighborhood.

mented versions of the perimeter type have been constructed in the Lower East Side, however, including a mediocre building on the Cooper Square site. Of these, the most notable was the project at Spring, Mulberry, and Mott streets, completed in 1982 by Pasanella and Klein.[78]

The most controversial and important precedent for the new low-rise initiatives was the West Village Houses, completed in Manhattan in 1975. Like Plaza Borinquen, it was an infill project, located among existing buildings on fourteen blocks in Greenwich Village bounded by Hudson, Christopher, Washington, Morton, and West streets (figure 9.28). It was designed by Perkins and Will with J. Raymond Matz as project architect. The project had a long and stormy history dating from 1961, and it paved the way for the succession of low-rise projects that has followed. The debate over West Village Houses is a microcosm of the issues which framed the national pathology involving the culture of urban housing. The project's history underscored the state of unrest in design ideology that followed the most prolific period for the production of social housing in the United States. The strength of the resistance to the project provides ample evidence of the force of its ideals and their almost heretical meaning in relation to the mainstream urbanism of that day.

The narrative begins in February 1961 when the New York City Housing and Redevelopment Board (HRB) announced an urban renewal plan for the West Village Houses site. The fabric of the existing neighborhood was a mixture of commercial and industrial buildings, and housing for approximately six hundred families. The HRB had designated it as a "blighted" area containing "slums," and called for massive clearance. New Mitchell-Lama housing would be constructed for middle-income families. Three fourteen-story towers and one twenty-one story tower were planned together with other low-rise buildings. All were designed by Barry Benepe, an architect collaborating with David Rose Associates, a developer.[79] The plan called for private development of the new middle-income housing at a cost of $13.5 million and industrial development at $15 million. A public subsidy of $6.75 million was also proposed.[80]

Led by Jane Jacobs, residents of the West Village immediately mobilized against the HRB proposal. Within two days of the project announcement they had managed to delay approval of funds for a preliminary planning study by the Board of Estimate,[81] and they began what would become the longest and hardest-fought battle for community self-control over development ever waged in New York City. It was a fight which perhaps could only have been sustained in Greenwich Village, the nation's most famous bohemia, with a long history of leftist politics.[82] Resistance coalesced into the Committee to Save the West Village, which argued that their neighborhood was not blighted; that there were few buildings that could be called slums; and that these could be rehabilitated by their owners. They also pointed out that they had not been consulted about plans which could drastically affect their lives. "Urban renewal," they charged, was only a euphemism for neighborhood destruction. City officials countered that Robert Moses' recent removal from office meant that public funds could be applied to rebuilding as well as clearance, and that the "bulldozer" approach of the 1950s would no longer be operative. The committee remained skeptical and announced its intention to stop the project completely.[83]

The long dispute touched most of the issues affecting housing design which had evolved during the previous three decades of government intervention in New York City. From the beginning, the design intentions of the New York City housing bureaucracy were suspect. When the Housing and Redevelopment Board hired the architect Victor Gruen to plan the project, Gruen attempted to pacify the committee members by assuring them that a design approach involving "wholesale demolition" would not be used. But Gruen advocated building housing and a park on platforms above the riverfront trucking area, which was hardly a small-scale enterprise.[84] Later it was discovered that another architect had been retained by the developer to plan the West Village project at least five months before any public announcements had been made or community involvement had been solicited.[85] And the Housing and Redevelopment Board was accused of setting up a counterorganization to promote the project, called the West Village Site Tenants Committee.

Community sentiment appeared to be overwhelmingly against the project. Several large organizations joined the protest, including the Greenwich Village Association and the local Planning Board, which had jurisdiction over the area.[86] By October 1961 the Housing and Redevelopment Board had officially dropped its plan for the area,[87] but the City Planning Commission continued to push for a study of the area while formulating an elaborate rebuttal to the public criticism, published by the Citizen's Housing Council.[88] Finally, on January 31, 1962, after almost a year had passed, the City Planning Commission, under continuing pressure from Mayor Wagner, voted to abandon its plans.[89] At this moment, the Committee to Save the West Village promised to develop its own housing proposal for the same fourteen-block area and hired the architectural firm of Perkins and Will to begin a study with J. Raymond Matz as project architect.

In May 1963 the Committee to Save the West Village plan was announced and published in a report.[90] It succinctly demonstrated the logic of a design alternative to the orthodox modernist urbanism of private developer and public bureaucracy alike. The plan called for a new kind of low-rise housing which would create 475 dwellings without demolishing existing housing. This strategy was envisioned as a prototype for the construction of new housing within an existing community without moving residents. The plan was economical in comparison with the earlier $35 million proposal, and provided 175 more dwellings. This high number was achieved because the existing dwellings were preserved. While the original proposal called for the destruction of 156 businesses, the new plan left all of them intact. Using a high ground coverage, the site planning was efficient, and apartment designs provided a maximum amount of livable space. Low-rise construction was proposed to respect the existing context. Low-rise also was considered to be less expensive to build because of its construction simplicity and capability of commanding increased rents over high-rise housing.

The proposal devised by the Committee to Save the West Village was intended to integrate the new housing into the existing community while maintaining the continuity of normal neighborhood activity. Flexibility of site design was achieved through the use of a formal language which was able to incorporate irregular and leftover pieces of land into the larger scheme. The apartment sizes were large enough for families, using a basic two-bedroom apartment adaptable to limited numbers of one- and three-bedrooms. The five-story buildings were planned without elevators. The communal and private spaces were carefully delineated to encourage public street life and maximum visual contact between dwellings and street, assuring a more secure environment. The varied apartment orientations and facades were intended to prevent visual monotony and to provide a choice for tenants. The same intentions applied to varied outdoor spaces. No large parking lots were used because they would disrupt the continuity of site usage. A broad range in family size and income was encouraged through application of Mitchell-Lama rent subsidies.

It took nine years for the Committee to Save the West Village to secure the necessary approvals from the city's building bureaucracy in order to begin their project. Preliminary approvals came toward the end of the 1960s, only after the progressive administration of Mayor John Lindsay had become firmly established. In 1969 the city began to pass the necessary zoning amendments which would allow the new West Village housing to be nestled among light industrial and commercial uses, a heresy according to the existing orthodox planning principles. Variances also had to be granted for the narrow spaces between buildings and other site-planning idiosyncrasies that were in conflict with Mitchell-Lama design requirements. By 1972 final approval was voted by the New York City Board of Estimate, granting a $24 million mortgage for construction of the 420 cooperative apartments as middle-income housing under the Mitchell-Lama program. The Greenwich Village Community Housing Corporation, an offspring of the Committee to Save the West Village, became the owner-sponsor. However, even as late as 1972, Albert A. Walsh, the administrator of the New York City Housing and Development Administration (the successor of the Housing Redevelopment Board), was so opposed to the project that he refused to sign the mortgage agreement. Instead, a subordinate signed under pressure from Mayor Lindsay.[91]

Predictably, the most vociferous opposition to West Village Houses came from the people and institutions that had promoted the orthodox tenets and practices of housing design in the postwar years. Obviously, opposition came from the City Planning Commission and its head, James Felt; but it also came from Roger Starr, the executive director of the Citizens Housing and Planning Council, a powerful private housing lobby which had existed since the 1930s. Starr had eagerly attacked Jane Jacobs' book in the *Village Voice* early on.[92] Both Felt and Starr argued for the clinical isolation of housing from other uses. They believed, for example, that in the West Village plan, children might be killed by the truck traffic, and that the surrounding loft buildings were out of character with adjacent new housing.[93] Resentful of the critique which the project implied, the old-guard housing bureaucracy was less than cooperative in processing its paperwork. Business interests were also outspoken opponents of the new thinking; as late as 1968, William Zeckendorf, the developer giant of New York City in the 1950s, was said to be assembling adjacent land in the West Village for his own luxury high-rise development.[94] Even later, in 1974, Hank Sopher, president of J. I. Sopher and Company, a large real estate firm, wrote in the *New York Times* that:

> The West Village Houses are a disastrous waste of taxpayers' money.
>
> I know we are in an economic recession, but that doesn't mean we have to bring back Depression-era walkups. They will have major security problems. They are bleak. They are totally out of tune with market preferences.
>
> As the City's largest leasing agent for luxury apartments, I believe I understand the public's taste. New Yorkers want to live in high-rise buildings with top security every inch of the way. They want a luxurious lobby, they want 24-hours doormen, luxurious halls, carpeted and well lit. What they don't want is a classless throwback to the past. West Village Houses is a disaster and Jane Jacobs should be pleased that she is living a thousand miles away, and doesn't have to face the criticism brought on her ill-conceived ideas.[95]

The era of the Vietnam War had motivated Jane Jacobs' family to leave the West Village for Toronto in 1969. By 1974 thirty of the forty-two buildings were completed, but the project was in deep trouble, and the theories of Jane Jacobs were targeted for blame. But the real problems for West Village Houses involved the larger economy. By fall 1975 only 5 of its 420 apartments had been sold.[96] The purchase prices of the apartments were simply too high for middle-income buyers, and inflation had caused the projected maintenance in 1963 to increase almost four times.[97] In addition, the economic recession of 1974–75 discouraged potential buyers, and cooperative mortgages were difficult to obtain from the banks. In November 1975 the city foreclosed on the $25 million Mitchell-Lama mortgage granted to the West Village Houses because of default on payments by the owner-sponsor. Ironically, Roger Starr of the Housing and Development Administration was named as receiver. Under city ownership, the project was quickly completed and rented for an average of $85 a room.[98] By the close of 1976, thirteen years after the plans were prepared, the first tenants had moved in.

In 1975 Jane Jacobs correctly argued that the project's fiscal problems were the result of the long delay in city approval: "What makes me very angry is that this could have gone ahead and been ready for occupancy in 1964 and 1965, when it could have been economical . . . this [project] isn't the only thing having trouble finding people who can afford it—this is a common denominator for all the new building that is being done."[99] And in fact, Mitchell-Lama housing all over New York City was in economic trouble. Even Manhattan Plaza, the $95 million Mitchell-Lama cooperative project located on West 42nd Street and completed shortly after West Village Houses, had similar economic difficulties.[100] Eventually, the city also foreclosed its mortgage, turning it into rental housing primarily for people in the performing arts.[101] Other projects were even less fortunate. Tiano Towers in Harlem, for example, was never completed, in spite of its extraordinary budget. It was the most expensive subsidized project ever built in New York City.[102]

In spite of the obvious economic pressures which contributed to the demise of the West Village Houses, critics persisted in blaming the design itself. Paul Goldberger of the *New York Times* even went so far as to hint that the lack of decoration on the facades could have been partially responsible for the demise of the project, pointing to the "success" of the "supergraphics" painted on the walls of the Church Street South housing in New Haven by its architect, Charles Moore.[103] It was true that economic cutbacks had considerably changed the appearance of the facades since the original proposal. The mansard roofs, floor-to-ceiling sliding windows, and exposed concrete frames were eliminated. But Jane Jacobs maintained that an architectural showpiece had never been intended, and that even before being occupied, the project had a positive effect on the neighborhood, stimulating the renovation of nearby vacant loft buildings into apartments.[104] As for the project by Charles Moore in New Haven, the "supergraphics" did not stem its rapid and considerable vandalization in the following year.

In the deepest sense, the criticism directed at the architectural design of West Village Houses was an emotional response to the challenges it posed to the middle-class ideals of New Yorkers. For a half century, walking up stairs had been an activity of the poor, and, since World War II, only for those who did not live in public housing towers. West Village Houses were said to appeal only to "unconventional tastes," a criticism which pushed the question to the brink of a moral issue. Indeed, neighborhood critics feared that West Village Houses would be taken over by a wealthy homosexual population, owing to its proximity to Christopher Street. Ironically, the existence of the West Village Houses did strengthen the West Village gay community, to the great annoyance of some West Villagers, many of whom had initially supported the project.[105] Perhaps it was true that in this particular phase of the evolution of new middle-class housing for New York City, walking up stairs and "unconventional tastes" were an essential equation. Yet this, too, would change.

10
Epilogue

W ITH the economic crisis of the Great Depression came the initiation of direct federal involvement with the production of social housing. This involvement increased steadily, with a major escalation in the decade of the 1960s. After the beginning of the Nixon Administration in 1969, however, the pattern was reversed. And, after the passage of the landmark Housing and Community Development Act of 1974, the mechanisms for the abandonment of federal social housing production were in place. For almost four decades, the United States Housing Act of 1937 had been the bulwark of the public housing era. In 1974 a new Section 8 was added to the 1937 legislation which turned government intervention away from direct development subsidies and toward the principle of rent subsidy. In effect this eclipsed the original purpose and legacy by turning production toward the private sector. The government would only enter into a contract with the developer to subsidize the difference between the fair market rent of an apartment and a fixed percentage of the tenant's income. Later on, new construction under Section 8 was effectively terminated in favor of housing rehabilitation. Finally in 1982 the Reagan administration terminated Section 8 altogether. Section 8 was replaced in 1984 with Housing Development Action Grants to assist localities with specific new projects. Their termination has also come to pass.[1]

The recent housing statistics for New York City reflect the changes in government policy. By 1982 the yearly net additions of housing units suffered a decline to about 10 percent of the peak figures of the 1960s.[2] At the same time, there was a surge in production of luxury apartments in Manhattan. And while new housing production declined, rehabilitation increased substantially for public programs as well as for private development. Rehabilitation also has been critical to the creation of new middle- and upper-middle-income enclaves in much of Manhattan and in other select locations, especially in Brooklyn. Critical to this process has been "rehabilitation" in the broadest sense, with the economic and physical transformation of entire neighborhoods. This process appears to represent a definitive stage in the development of the late capitalist city in the United

States.[3] It is connected to a dynamic between urban wealth and poverty in which the reconstitution of an urban upper middle class is beginning to figure prominently. For the first time in more than three decades, United States cities have begun to experience gains in population closely tied to this transition.[4] These signs are still very tentative, however.

The West Village struggle was perhaps most significant for the precedent it set in terms of this new dynamic, popularly called "gentrification."[5] It was a middle-class struggle, but it involved cultural values radically different from the mainstream middle-class suburban ideals of the period. As a political struggle it also was a radical development, with a threatened urban enclave staking its claim to a territory. In a limited but significant way, an increasing proportion of the middle class has shifted toward the same values, primarily focused on the "young urban professional." This shift was generated by diverse factors, including the increasing obsolescence of nineteenth-century urban industrial production and the changing modes of real property speculation and its relationship to the state. Also involved are changes in the economic function of cultural activity, especially in relation to urban development. And this is intertwined with shifts in the public conception of an artistic avant-garde, away from the "adversary culture" of the earlier part of this century. In New York, where the "culture industry" claims an increasing proportion of the city's economy, its relationship to the logistics of housing production has been critical.

The implication of the culture industry in real property development in New York can be traced to the same period as the West Village controversy. It involved the struggle for legalization of the use of industrial loft buildings for residential occupancy by artists. The artists' community in lower Manhattan unwittingly helped pave the way, with its need for large and cheap loft space for living and working. From its beginnings in Soho, gentrification through loft conversion became perfected and institutionalized, spreading to other neighborhoods such as Tribeca and the Lower West Side and even Brooklyn. Painters and sculptors in New York had occupied commercial space since the 1930s, especially as their spatial needs increased as an imperative to modernist work. Reinforcing this tendency were the well-known artists who had entered into the lore of modern art in New York and who helped thrust the city into the center of International postwar culture.[6]

By the 1960s the scale of loft conversion by artists had increased, concentrated on the cast-iron loft area south of Houston Street known as Soho. This development was partially due to the intense gentrification activity in the adjacent West Village which was placing increased pressure for redevelopment on surrounding neighborhoods, including Soho, the East Village, and the Lower East Side. The working-class and artist population of the West Village was being displaced to adjacent areas.[7] For the artists, Soho was especially ideal. An abundance of large-scale working space was cheap because of the high level of commercial vacancy in comparison with the East Village or the Lower East Side. To some extent, this condition in the loft district was caused by the obsolescence of the nineteenth-century industry that originally had created Soho.[8] It was also caused by the perceived obsolescence of the area urbanistically. The Moses-era city bureaucracy promoted this view with the Lower Manhattan Plan.[9] This proposal was prepared in coalition with banking interests who accordingly disinvested in the area for manufacturing uses.[10] The business community's sensibility was perhaps best reflected by a City Club of New York Plan authored by Ira D. Robbins in 1962 that called for all of Soho to be razed.[11]

By 1960 the Artists-Tenants Association had been formed to lobby for artists' rights as loft tenants.[12] The vast majority of their lofts were illegal because of building zone regulations and fire codes. In 1961 the city agreed to permit loft living for fewer than three families per building, thereby avoiding the requirements of the Multiple Dwelling Law. This limitation proved impracticable, however. By 1963 an estimated three thousand families were living in lofts which were almost all illegal.[13] In 1964 the Multiple Dwelling Law was revised to recognize artist occupancy,[14] but it was not until 1982 that the problems of legalization and stabilization were officially addressed in comprehensive legislation.[15] Ironically, this was a process which led to displacement of the artists by wealthier tenants, and it was orchestrated to include adjacent neighborhoods such as Tribeca.

In addition to artists, the early Soho coalitions included participants in the West Village struggle and other activists united by opposition to the years of Moses-dominated urbanism in New York City. Included were veterans of Joseph Papp's fight for free theater in Central Park, and opponents of Moses' plan to extend Fifth Avenue through Washington Square Park.[16] The Moses policies had remained a threat long after the beginning of his decline in 1960. An example was his aborted attempt to construct the Lower Manhattan Expressway across Broome Street, which alone could have destroyed Soho and adversely affected the West Village.[17] As late as 1968, demolition for the expressway still seemed imminent. The newly organized Artists Against the Expressway (AAE) led the opposition, arguing for the economic and cultural importance of the artists' community, which would be displaced. They completed the first loft-dwellers census in Soho, recording approximately 270 units.[18] In 1969 the expressway plan was finally killed.

In the early 1960s the city government's harassment of artists in lofts led to a number of important protests, including a threatened strike of New York art galleries in the fall of 1961.[19] This led to the first concessions by the city in December.[20] Such activity continued over several years. A demonstration at the Metropolitan Museum of Art during the winter of 1963 was particularly effective in bringing the issue closer to the patrons. Middle-class culture began to catch up.[21] The fledgling historic preservation movement, with considerable support from the architectural establishment, was spending as much time on saving Soho as on saving Pennsylvania Station or the Jefferson Market Courthouse.[22] Significantly, around the same time, legitimization of the art culture was further underlined by the precedent of philanthropic housing for artists, an enterprise unknown in New York since the days of the Tenth Street Studio (see figure 1.6). In April 1963 the J. M. Kaplan Fund began subsidizing artist housing, renting lofts for artists in the West Village at West 12th and Greenwich streets.[23] Later similar projects included cooperatives in Soho. Finally, in 1970, the Westbeth artist housing in the West Village was completed, in collaboration with the New York State Council on the Arts, using federal subsidies.[24]

The harbingers of the artists' impasse in relation to gentrification came as early as the beginning of the 1960s. What artists admired about loft living soon was admired by a new urban generation as well. Notice reached the popular media quite early. For example, in 1961 *Esquire* magazine published an article on the "loft generation," pointing out the advantages of low rents, large spaces, and the potential for individual initiative within urban housing. And in 1963, after the publicity surrounding the early Artists-Tenants Association fights against city evictions from lofts, *The Nation* pointed out that in other cities artists had proved to be a boon to real estate rather than a blight: "Where ever there has been a 'culture' of painters, writers, actors, musicians, rents have doubled, building has boomed, and small enterprises have sprung up like mushrooms."[25] Cited were Greenwich Village, Telegraph Hill, Taos, Provincetown, Chelsea, and Montparnasse. A decade later Soho and Tribeca were well on their way to achieving the same status; and two decades later the East Village joined the phenomenon. During a brief period around 1980, loft conversion was said to exceed new luxury apartment construction in Manhattan.[26]

Westbeth was a large loft building in the West Village at Bank and Washington streets. Its completion in 1969 was a turning point. For the first time an entire large commercial building was legally converted to artists' residences. It coincided with the growing interest on the part of national and local politicians in the relationship between art and real estate. This relationship became ever more complex as various forms of government patronage burgeoned to include the National Endowment for the Arts and the New York State Council on the Arts.[27] Westbeth also represented an architectural turning point. The renovation established space standards which were far lower than those of the cavernous lofts of the previous era (figure 10.1). Designed by Richard Meier, the project was his first large commission and received abundant publicity, definitively raising the prospects for loft living to the realm of high style.[28] By the mid-1970s, as wealthy residents began to move to Soho from uptown, lofts quickly became the newest entry in the lexicon of upper middle-class housing in Manhattan. Many young architects began their careers with well-publicized renovations (figure 10.2).[29] With incredible intensity, the phenomenon of loft conversion raged in Manhattan. By 1983, officials estimated there were up to 10,000 illegal lofts within the designated loft districts. Other figures reached 25,000.[30] These lofts were defined as illegal in that they had not received the minimum fire and safety approvals necessary for residential occupancy. The actual number was much larger in relation to the entire city, with other areas of Manhattan, Brooklyn, and Queens experiencing industrial loft conversion as well. Yet, as had been the case in many other episodes in the evolution of New York housing, the issue of legality was sidestepped to achieve the goal of development.

In spite of its public prominence, the loft phenomenon was only a small part of the recent changes in housing demography which reinforced a pattern of gentrification heavily oriented toward Manhattan. This transformation was evi-

Figure 10.1. Richard Meier and Associates. Westbeth Artists Colony in renovated industrial building in the West Village, completed in 1969; the lofts were smaller and more expensive than could still be obtained by artists elsewhere in lower Manhattan.

Westbeth: Artists' Housing
Richard Meier   Architect
1 Bedroom   0   5   10

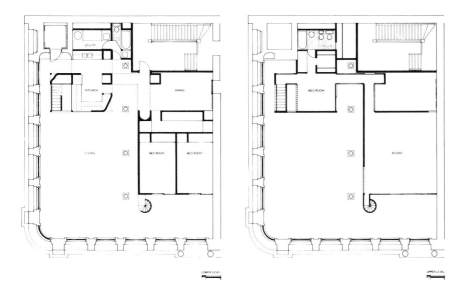

Figure 10.2. Jon Michael Schwarting. Loft on Broome Street in SoHo, completed in 1974 and one of the first architect's loft renovations to receive coverage in a major professional journal.

denced, for example, in an increase in home ownership in Manhattan between 1980 and 1983, while ownership in the other boroughs decreased.[31] In the same period, the average income of home owners in Manhattan also increased at a rate five times greater than for the other boroughs.[32] Most of this activity involved cooperative ownership of apartment buildings in Manhattan, where well over half of the recent total conversion from rental buildings has been concentrated.[33] By 1986, the average selling price of Manhattan cooperative apartments had increased 500 percent since 1978.[34] The demand was sustained by the decline in the rate of conversion after 1982,[35] presumably because of the reduced availability of suitable buildings for further conversion, among other factors. This activity has been concentrated south of 96th Street, putting enormous pressure on the existing neighborhoods to meet the demand. In 1986 21,500 luxury apartments were under construction in Manhattan, most on the Upper East and West sides.[36] Much recent new apartment construction is reminiscent of the West End Avenue and Park Avenue booms of the 1920s. Like the 1920s, however, it appears to have ended abruptly. According to one estimate, apartment starts have fallen from a high of 20,000 in 1985 to only 1,400 in 1987.[37]

A highly visible manifestation of the recent boom in Manhattan was the proliferation of new, privately developed high-rise luxury building. This activity was concentrated in select areas adjacent to the traditional luxury neighborhoods. Included was Third Avenue on the Upper East Side, where twelve major new buildings were completed between 1984 and 1986;[38] more recently, Broadway on the Upper West Side, seemed destined to follow the Third Avenue precedent.[39] The design and marketing of these buildings evoked a certain nostalgia for the luxury and ambiance of the 1920s boom. In some cases the nostalgia was quite literal, as in the form of the Montana on Broadway at West 87th Street, completed in 1984 by the Gruzen Partnership.[40] The dual-tower massing refered to the West

Figure 10.3. The Gruzen Partnership. The Montana, completed on upper Broadway in 1984, using a dual-tower massing reminiscent of Upper West Side landmarks like the Century, whose form had been generated by the 1929 Multiple Dwelling Law.

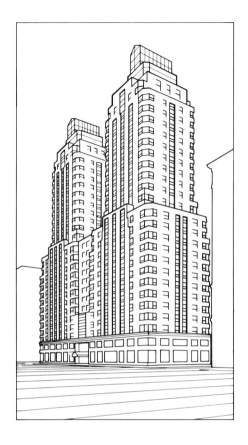

Side landmarks of fifty years ago—the Century (see figure 6.36), the Majestic, the San Remo, and the Eldorado along Central Park West (figure 10.3). But unlike the Montana, their forms were generated by the pragmatic mandate of the Multiple Dwelling Law (see figure 6.34), rather than by fashion.

The recent generation of luxury buildings has employed apartment design standards that are modest in relation to the high purchase price. In 1985, at the bottom of the luxury range, $200,000 could buy a studio apartment in the Saratoga, completed in 1984 by Lichtenstein, Schuman, Claman, and Efron on Third Avenue at East 75th Street; a one bedroom was $250,000, and two bedrooms began at $300,000.[41] These figures would require an income of between $75,000 and $150,000, with some considerable financial resources to begin with. Apartments in the tower completed by Cesar Pelli and Associates in 1984 over the Museum of Modern Art on West 53rd Street ranged in price from $370,000 to $1.3 million.[42] And in the Trump Tower on Fifth Avenue at 56th Street, completed in 1983 by Der Scutt with Swanke, Hayden, and Connell, a modest one-bedroom apartment could cost $775,000 (figure 10.4).[43] In 1985 a Trump Tower penthouse sold for $15 million.[44] Frequently for the purchaser, however, more important than domestic amenities is the opportunity for real property investment. In recent years,

the escalating price of Manhattan apartments has been quite lucrative for the home owner entrepreneur, as well as for the large-scale developer. Most concrete to the definition of "luxury" for the new housing has been geography. The long-time enclaves of the upper middle class such as the Upper East Side continued to preside, joined by the newly gentrifying areas. Underlying this definition of luxury were fears associated with security of investment, which were in turn related to personal security in a city in which the proportion of poor has increased drastically in recent decades.

In spite of the continuing erosion of the spatial dimension of luxury in housing, the superficial expression of affluence reached new levels. Apartment sales campaigns relied heavily on architectural scenography, including the names of "world class" designers. Each stylistic offering was designed to outmode the last in a manner similar to the apparel industry and intended to reflect the new values of the young urban professional. A bizarre high point was the proposal for Trump Castle, designed in 1984 by Johnson Burgee Architects for Donald Trump (figure 10.5). Located at East 59th Street and Madison Avenue, six circular high-rise "turrets" were planned to rise from a water-filled moat, a reference to medieval fortress. It also refers to the security of the drawbridge in a city with growing uncertainties about the dynamic between privilege and deprivation.[45] While

Figure 10.4. (*Right*) Lichtenstein, Schuman, Claman, and Efron. The Saratoga apartment plan with one bedroom. (*Middle*) Cesar Pelli and Associates Museum Tower apartment plan with one bedroom. (*Left*) Swanke, Hayden, and Connell, with Der Scutt. Trump Tower apartment plan with one bedroom.

Figure 10.5. Johnson Burgee Architects. Trump Castle, proposed in 1984 for Madison Avenue at 59th Street; a reflection of the new affluence in Manhattan with "turrets," "moat," and "drawbridge."

the Trump Castle remained unbuilt, the concept seems to have been transformed into a "Corinthian Column" at the Corinthian, a fifty-seven story condominium between First and Second avenues and East 37th and 38th streets, designed by Michael Schiment with Der Scutt.[46] In another approach, 100 United Nations Plaza, completed in 1985 on East 48th Street by Lichtenstein, Schuman, Claman, and Efron, advertised twenty-three penthouses. This apparition was sustained by the form of the upper ten floors designed by Der Scutt to recall the form of a gable.[47] The prolific advertising for the latter project was the product of an agency originated with the architect Robert A. M. Stern in a move consistent with the new spirit of the age.[48] In another vein, an indication of the new affluence has been the completion in 1983 of eleven new private town houses on East 67th Street at Second Avenue. Designed by Attia and Perkins for the Solow Development Corporation, they are the first such houses to be completed in Manhattan since the turn of the century. More interesting was a series of preliminary proposals for the project which included innovative designs by Richard Meier and James Stirling. In their own ways, both challenged the tradition of the New York brownstone, adding to the culture of the type. They were discarded, however, in favor of the more conservative scheme which comes close to replication of the appearance of the nineteenth-century brownstone.[49]

Recent years have seen a resurgence of planning for large-scale housing developments, after the lean years that followed the 1975 New York City fiscal "crisis." Most prominent has been the resumption of building at Battery Park City, which was begun in 1966. The project was stalled during the seventies, but in 1980 after resolution of the financial demise of the Battery Park City Authority, building activity began again, using a reformulated program and a new master plan developed by Alexander Cooper and Associates.[50] The new plan departed substantially from the original, establishing a gridiron of streets, producing a fabric resembling the mode of nineteenth-century infill, in contrast to the rather amoebic building clusters and parkland of the original project (figure 10.6). The new plan countered the reformist conventions of the past fifty years, which had argued against the gridiron for large-scale intervention, substituting variants on the "tower in the park" instead. In spite of the revised approach, the final result at Battery Park City does not have the cohesion of the nineteenth-century streetscape, at least partially because of the extreme juxtaposition of use and scale, with the resulting fragmentation of much of the public space. The physical continuity with the Manhattan gridiron is lost due to the traffic barrier created by West Street. Among the architects commissioned to infill the gridiron were veterans of the previous UDC housing era; for example, James Stewart Polshek and Partners, Bond Ryder James, Conklin Rossant, and Davis Brody and Associates. The sensibility of their previous work was modified considerably to meet the constraints of the Battery Park City plan. Other architects have included Charles Moore, Ulrich Franzen, the Gruzen Partnership, and Mitchell, Giurgola. The individual buildings have been of notable quality in relation to much of the privately developed housing of the same period for the same income level. In part, this is a result of the positive influence of the master plan and the luxury-level

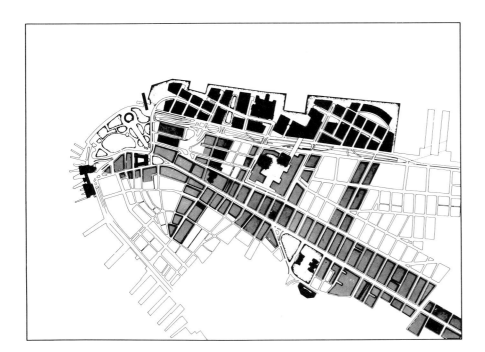

Figure 10.6. Alexander Cooper and Associates. Battery Park City master plan, completed in 1979; using an extension of the traditional Manhattan gridiron fabric, it definitively countered "tower in the park" planning.

subsidies.[51] Still, the apartments have been notably small, hardly sufficient for the young professional families which were targeted for the development.

Westway was another large-scale project which was part of the legacy of the pre-1975 era. It involved a proposal for a depressed superhighway along the West Side of Manhattan from 42nd Street to Battery Park City. By 1984 much of the demolition had been completed for the multibillion-dollar project, principally the dismantling of the old elevated West Side Highway and the piers along its path. But the project was effectively stopped in court by the opposition, which advocated a smaller-scale project, freeing most of the federal subsidy for more socially immediate causes such as mass transit.[52] Since its inception in 1973,[53] a somewhat hidden Westway agenda had been to "induce" a large-scale transformation of the Lower West Side of Manhattan, including a massive amount of new housing in keeping with the larger agenda for Manhattan development as an upper-middle-class enclave.[54] The empty blocks in the Westway site alternatives prepared in 1984 by Clarke and Rapuano with Venturi, Rauch, and Scott-Brown-Salmon Associates gave mute testimony to the scale of that strategy.[55] Local opposition was joined with congressional opposition from New Jersey, which protested the massive use of federal subsidy for a project so intertwined with the interests of private developers in New York.[56] The success of the campaign against the Westway project may one-day rank with the earlier fight to save the West Village as a turning point in recent New York City history; in this case, focusing development pressure away from an affluent urban center toward mass transit to stimulate rebuilding of the problematic periphery.

Massive pressure for West Side development continues, however, with the Lincoln West project, another large-scale housing proposal planned for the Penn Central rail yards along the Hudson River between 57th and 72nd streets. It is the largest single open site left in Manhattan, and the scale of proposals for its development have been unprecedented. The first, dating from 1982, projected 4,300 apartments with more than one million square feet of office space.[57] In 1985, with the acquisition of the site by Donald Trump, the scale of the proposed development was escalated to 7,900 apartments, with office space and television studios involving an investment of more than $1 billion. The design by Murphy-Jahn proposed an architectural megalith of 150 stories flanked by six 76-story buildings.[58] In its gigantism, the project, like its developer, has come to symbolize the recent period of fashionable self-interest and the cultivation of conspicuous affluence in New York, which have overshadowed the larger public good.[59] The public good has retained a constituency, however and like Westway, the Lincoln West proposals have not been without their opposition. Much the opposition has come from the adjacent Upper West Side neighborhood which has already experienced considerable recent new building, fueling fears of the disruptive scale and character of Lincoln West.[60] In the face of criticism, the project was given to Alexander Cooper and Partners in mid-1986, and the future of the development remains in question.[61] The site represents the last segment of the massive redevelopment of the Upper West Side that began over three decades ago, following a strategy of Robert Moses which included the Lincoln Center and West Park Village projects (see figure 9.1). At the same time, it represents the northern bulwark of an even more massive Lower and Middle West Side redevelopment, comprising Battery Park City and the waterfront development intended to follow in the shadow of Westway. All of this development reinforces the recent tendency to reconstitute mid- and lower Manhattan as a world apart from the problems of the rest of the city.

While the juxtaposition of extreme wealth and poverty have always been a conspicuous aspect of the culture of housing in New York City, the last decades have produced a physical commentary on this condition quite foreign to previous history. For the first time, fundamental changes in the economy of the city have produced a reduction in the housing stock, a worsening of the domestic living standards for the poor, and a widening gap between rich and poor in which old patterns of upward social mobility appear to have stagnated. By the 1970s, Manhattan had evolved toward a postindustrial economy, with an attendant class displacement involving substantial growth in the middle- and upper-income population, as evidenced by the recent boom in luxury housing. At the same time, for the entire city, the proportion of population officially counted as poor increased, from 14.9 percent in 1969 to 23.4 percent in 1983, far above the national increase of 2.9 percent for the same period. By 1987, the official percentage in poverty inched even higher. For blacks and Puerto Ricans it had reached 32 and 48 percent respectively.[62] The increase in poverty was accompanied by a substantial decline in the population of New York City between 1970 and 1980, from 7,894,862 to 7,071,030 or 10.4 percent overall. Yet the Manhattan decline was only 7.3 percent, compared with 14.3 percent in Brooklyn and 20.6 percent in the Bronx (Queens and Staten Island have remained stable). The differences between boroughs is further confirmed in the housing unit statistics for the same period, from a net increase in Manhattan of 5.6 percent to a decline of 2.4 percent in Brooklyn and 11.3 percent in the Bronx.[63] Such statistics are witnessed by the physical "ring" of destruction which surrounds the core of Manhattan.

The "New York ring" sweeps from the South Bronx and Harlem east to central Brooklyn and then south to the Lower East Side (figure 10.7).[64] In the remnants of once-stable residential areas, the urban rubble supports only scavengers in scenes reminiscent of Dresden or Berlin after the Allied bombing in World War II. Vast areas of the ring have experienced population decline of more than 40 percent, and in some areas more than 80 percent between the mid-1960s and the present.[65] Perhaps the most engaging public symbol of this process has been the fires which have finalized the devastation, occurring on a scale unknown in New York City since the Great Fires of the first half of the nineteenth century (see figure 1.1). Arson accounted for much of this destruction, with the documented incidence reaching approximately fifteen thousand annually in the mid-1970s.[66] Along with the fiscal crisis of 1975, the fires of the South Bronx became shocking symbols of decline in the public mind—an "epidemic of flame" as *New York Times Magazine* called it in one of the early public exposes.[67] The significance and meaning of "decline" in this context is debatable. A more cynical expression would be the "planned shrinkage" as outlined by Roger Starr.[68]

For New York City, the most remarkable statistics to emerge from the last decade were not simply the severe population losses, but the simultaneous extreme reduction in housing units. Instead of a housing surplus which would logically follow population decline, the housing shortage increased, presumably together with an increase in housing profits. In effect, through the massive devastation within the ring, the forces of the marketplace were thwarted, and if "shrinkage" was indeed "planned," it was to economic advantage. The fires of the Bronx, like the simultaneous gentrification in Manhattan, were stimulated by banking policy that dictated where investment money could be channeled. They were also stimulated by public policy, such as the J-51 tax abatement program, which became a notorious source of arson-related profits, facilitated through problematic insurance company policies.[69] Today there is less population, less housing, and higher housing costs than two decades ago, which is a remarkable reversal of the evolution of housing production in New York City. It is also a remarkable, if tainted, monument to the monied interests of the city, who have managed to weather the storm of "shrinkage" while maintaining record profits.[70]

In spite of the devastation within the ring, certain areas of the outer boroughs have been affected by the forces of gentrification. There has been renewal within parts of the ring, underlining the irony of the shortage of middle-income housing which coexists with the phenomenon of destruction of good housing stock. Mayor Edward Koch's notorious admonition that those who could not afford to live in Manhattan should leave applied to the middle class as well as to the poor,[71] and

Figure 10.7. The New York "ring" of devastation that surrounds Manhattan, indicating areas which have experienced a population loss of more than 40 percent since the 1960s.

THE NEW YORK "RING"

AREA OF POPULATION LOSS
EXCEEDING 40% 1960-1980

the outer boroughs, especially Brooklyn, have experienced an influx of a young, relatively affluent population fleeing the high rents of Manhattan. Areas of impressive nineteenth-century houses such as Park Slope or Brooklyn Heights have long been redeveloped. Adjacent areas such as Carroll Gardens, Fort Green, and Red Hook are quickly following. In Red Hook or even in Williamsburg, for example, the artist vanguard has been a telltale sign of the development which is supposed to come. It is this "first wave" that tends to surmount the social complexities that make many neighborhoods of the ring inaccessible to the white middle class, paving the way for the larger influx to follow.

In Manhattan the last frontier for gentrification is Harlem. In 1981, when the city was planning its first auction of brownstones in Harlem,[72] racial taboos made it inaccessible, at least to the white middle class. But this constraint seemed to be changing. Already, by 1980, the proportion of Manhattan blacks who lived in Harlem had declined to 25 percent from 32 percent in 1970.[73] A 1984 *New York* magazine article on the gentrification potential of Harlem was the harbinger of popular notice of the possibility of a previously unimaginable racial and economic transformation.[74] Harlem in many ways functions as the symbolic national black capital, and the political consequences of its loss would be profound to the black community. In addition, more than any other community in New York, the question of Harlem raises issues about the fate of New York's growing poor population. Given the eclipse of social housing programs, one scenario would displace the city's poor minorities to pockets of obsolesced suburban and inner-suburban housing, while segments of the middle and upper middle class continue to reinhabit the most desirable urban neighborhoods. As much as anything else, it will be city policy which decides such transformations.

By the end of the 1970s, the city government had become the largest single landlord in New York, with 40,000 apartments in receivership. Large concentrations of such city-controlled housing are within the ring.[75] In Harlem, for example, the city owns 40 percent of the buildings and vacant land.[76] Since 1981, it has actively pursued initiation of private development of select holdings.[77] In the Lower East Side, where city ownership is also high, the city also has moved definitively in the direction of developing its holdings. In 1981 the city attempted to sponsor artist-initiated development of loft buildings.[78] In 1984 it proposed selling 207 abandoned buildings and 219 vacant lots. The income would be used to renovate more than 1,200 city-owned apartments.[79]

The issue of redevelopment in the outer boroughs was the focus of a lengthy zoning study completed by the City Planning Commission in 1985.[80] It led to changes in the zoning law enacted in 1987.[81] The new regulations are intended to stimulate the construction of five thousand new private housing units per year by increasing the profitability of medium-density development. The new law focuses on the realm of six to twelve stories, which remains the domain of most of the housing in the city, apart from Manhattan. In particular it attempts to redress the problems engendered by the 1961 Zoning Resolution, which favored high-rise housing at densities that have tended to be economically impractical outside of Manhattan, except for housing built with subsidies. As a result, new private construction had stagnated in the boroughs. For example, until recently the last large,

Figure 10.8. Permissible massing configurations for comparable conditions in an R-7 zone under the 1961 Zoning Resolution (*left*) and the Quality Housing Amendment of 1987 (*right*). The coverage is increased from 25 to 60 percent of the lot.

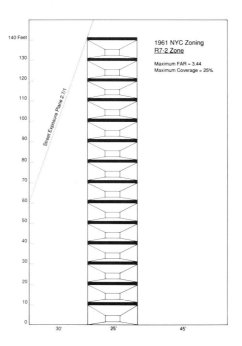

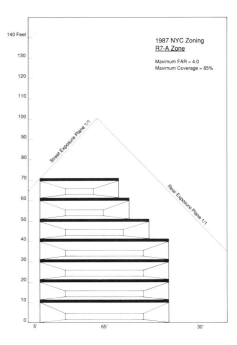

privately constructed apartment house to be built in Brooklyn was completed in Bensonhurst in 1969.[82] Through increased coverage and new bulk and height constraints, the zoning changes point toward a new generation of housing reminiscent of the 1920s garden apartment (figure 10.8). And they complete a circle as an important final step in the evolution away from domination of the "tower in the park." Combined with other stimulants such as the sale of city-held land and buildings and the new city rental subsidy programs,[83] the new zoning will be critical to the rebuilding of the ring. It reflects a private marketplace vision, however, which is focused toward the middle class for its success. In a city with one-quarter impoverished population, and where the cost of living forces families earning $20,000 into the poverty category,[84] the relevance of this particular vision may be limited.

In recent years the diminished scale of initiative for publicly assisted housing has been significant. Apart from the federal cut-backs, even major state programs like Mitchell-Lama have disappeared, after having constructed 139,000 apartments in New York City.[85] Construction of new social housing has declined from a high of 33,790 new units in 1965 to about one-tenth of that figure. Subsidized rehabilitation programs have grown, however, from only 60 units in 1965 to a 1981 high of 14,540.[86] These rehabilitation figures reflect to some extent the flurry of community development initiatives undertaken in the aftermath of the 1960s, embodied in such pioneering enterprises as the Bedford-Stuyvesant Restoration Corporation founded in 1967,[87] or the Manhattan Valley Development Corporation founded in 1968.[88] But given the intensity of the real estate market in New York City, the original mandates of many such initiatives has weakened to some degree, and their original accountability to a low-income constituency has been altered by funding cutbacks. From the point of view of design, rehabilitation at a reasonable cost is at best a compromise for much of the New York City housing stock. At Manhattan Valley or in East Harlem, as in other poor but "next to emerge" neighborhoods,[89] an undesired effect of rehabilitation is displacement of the poor families, as gentrification is further stimulated. With controls to reinforce the positive effects on neighborhood cohesion, however, the incremental nature of rehabilitation remains a compelling strategy for providing social housing. This revolutionary change in sensibility begun in the era of Jane Jacobs has come to influence social housing as well as the upper-middle-income housing for the new urban professional.

The most problematic building types for rehabilitation in New York City are the remaining Old Law and some New Law plans, which tend to defy rational and economic redesign, beginning with fundamental problems of light and air. Even some of the most important rehabilitation initiatives like those in Manhattan Valley have achieved mixed results in this regard.[90] For example, in a project at 927 Columbus Avenue by Levenson-Thaler Associates, a clever Old Law plan reorganization still could not overcome the problems of rooms which face into air shafts (figure 10.9). Old Law tenements are the most problematic. Light conditions are so restrictive that they can function well only as lofts, with entire floors opened up to the light at both ends. This strategy has been used in the East Village and the Lower East Side[91] (figure 10.10). At Manhattan Valley, the rehabilitated tenements contrast with the new Manhattan Valley Townhouses, a 77-unit condominium designed by Rosenblum-Harb Architects and completed in 1987 by the Manhattan Valley Development Corporation.[92] Located between West 104th and 105th streets along Manhattan Avenue, the U-shaped building repaired the destroyed block-end (figure 10.11). The facades attempted to maintain the rhythm of the surrounding rowhouses, pointing toward a housing type which can work with rehabilitation to restore partially destroyed areas. The new apartments

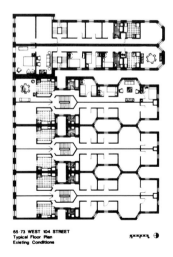
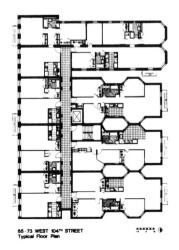

65-73 WEST 104 STREET
Typical Floor Plan
Existing Conditions

65-73 WEST 104TH STREET
Typical Floor Plan

Figure 10.9. Levenson-Thaler Associates. Rehabilitated tenements in Manhattan Valley; adjacent Old Law buildings have been joined to improve light and air and general plan efficiency.

Figure 10.10. Prelaw tenement on East 6th Street, converted to an artist's loft.

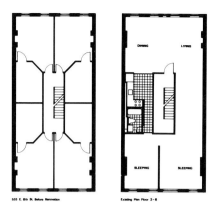

533 E. 6th St. Before Renovation

Existing Plan Floor 3–6

are almost luxury level in contrast to the surrounding buildings, however. The original purchase price of $65,000 more than tripled in several years. Together with the new "towers on the park," a large project designed by Bond, Ryder, James at West 110th Street and Central Park West, the destiny of the community has been sealed toward higher and higher income.[93]

Construction of much of the new social housing in the past decade has been beholden to Jacobs' vision. It would be difficult to find a single poor neighborhood in New York City with a preference for new high-rise towers, even if they were still within the realm of economic possibility. New low-rise social housing has become relatively commonplace, however. It is frequently lodged here and there

Figure 10.11. Rosenblum-Harb, Architects. Manhattan Valley townhouses completed on the Upper West Side in 1987. The low-rise massing was used to repair a destroyed block end.

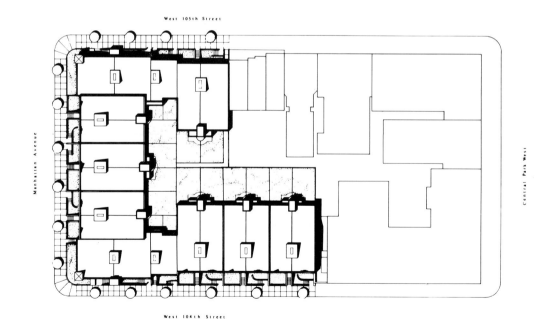

as infill within areas partially destroyed by urban renewal, abandonment, or arson. This infill strategy represents a drastic reversal in thinking in less than a decade. It prompted the eleventh and final housing competition in New York City history; for East Harlem infill housing sponsored by the New York State Council on the Arts.[94] The site was bounded by West 115th and 117th streets between Lenox Avenue and Adam Clayton Powell, Jr. Boulevard. It is an area where much of the nineteenth century fabric has been destroyed, with a diverse and fragmentary pattern of abandoned tenements, apartment buildings, and commercial and community uses. With the choice of site and with the program which placed particular emphasis on the cultural needs of a low-income constituency, the competition attempted to move closer than previously toward direct exploration of design responses to social imperatives. But in spite of this emphasis, the outlook of the program and the submissions could not help but be overshadowed by the diminished resources for building for poverty-level families.

At this time, the realities of the infill proposition can be found in any number of projects throughout the boroughs; for example at the Twin Parks renewal area in the South Bronx, where by the mid-1970s the UDC had completed some of its most publicized projects. They were large-scale, high-rise building ensembles which did attempt to respond to contextual issues. But the continuing redevelopment of the area has involved discarding the high-rise altogether. For example, the Crotona-Mapes Renewal Project, which is in the shadow of Richard Meier's Twin Parks Northeast development (see figure 9.12), consists of two hundred small-scale infill houses completed by Beyer, Blinder, and Belle in 1985.[94] Located between East 181st and 182d streets east of the Bronx Park, the new development consists of row houses which have been constructed with government subsidy for

Figure 10.12. Beyer, Blinder, Belle. Crotona-Mapes Renewal Project in the shadow of Twin Parks Northeast in the Bronx; new government-subsidized row houses constructed in 1985 for purchase by moderate-income families.

purchase by lower-middle-income families (figure 10.12). The new row houses can be considered as an extreme reaction to the failure of the experimentation at Twin Parks Northeast. They are also a pragmatic expression of the reduction in resources for social housing in recent years.

While at the time of its completion Twin Parks Northeast was considered a significant advance in housing in relation to the issue of context, within a few years the evidence had pointed toward failure. Ground-floor areas were vandalized, in spite of attempts to regain control, including chain-link barriers erected in the public spaces. In effect, most of the community areas were in a state of semi-abandonment. The burned-out apartments and high vacancy rate stood in mute testimony to the pressing need for rehabilitation, which has been in the planning stages since 1982, only ten years after its completion. The $1.7 million rehabilitation plan identified the project's problems as "36 percent design/construction deficiencies, 34 percent vandalism, and 20 percent deferred maintenance."[95] Other Twin Parks projects were said to suffer from even higher design and construction deficiencies, including Twin Parks Southeast and Twin Parks Northwest. And elsewhere, in the Coney Island projects, for example, the same situation exists.[96] But the failure of Twin Parks Northeast has been of particular significance given the faith placed in its contextualism to cancel the pathologies of large-scale institutionalized housing placed within a poor, racially tense neighborhood. Indeed, by 1976, only three years after occupation, its deterioration was already considerable.[97] The profound pathology of the context in comparison with the superficial contextualism of the project's design premise has affirmed its characterization by Romaldo Giurgola as "a perennial eclecticism that never touches anything fundamental."[98]

The policy of small-scale housing design and site-planning fragmentation is now widespread throughout the socially problematic areas of the outer boroughs. A major impetus for this activity was a federal subsidy program approved in 1980 under Section 235 to provide grants of up to $15,000 for a single-family house. In the same year, the city incorporated this subsidy into a program which called for 2,200 new houses to be constructed in ten neighborhoods using city and federal subsidies.[99] Additional projects soon followed, including those initiated by a new generation of philanthropic organizations, such as church coalitions like the East Brooklyn Coalition of Churches, or civic organizations like the New York City Partnership headed by David Rockefeller. This tendency toward fragmentation of housing production is the most extreme form of contextualism, holding forth the hope of minimizing the disruption of urban renewal while maximizing its potentially restorative effects. The strategy envisions a form of gentrification. A smaller government commitment is required than for large-scale high-rise construction because the level of technology involved is quite primitive. The building increments are quite small, allowing projects to easily be terminated without jeopardizing what has already been completed. Through private ownership, the issue of longer-range maintenance and other costs can be avoided entirely.

The Nehiamiah Houses in the Brownsville area of Brooklyn has been the largest new low-cost home-ownership initiative in New York City. In this initiative, begun in 1982 by the East Brooklyn Coalition of Churches, five thousand

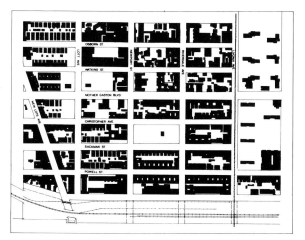

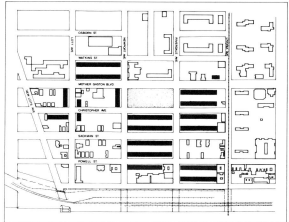

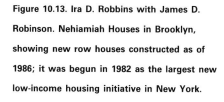

Figure 10.13. Ira D. Robbins with James D. Robinson. Nehiamiah Houses in Brooklyn, showing new row houses constructed as of 1986; it was begun in 1982 as the largest new low-income housing initiative in New York.

new row houses were projected to be built under the direction of developer Ira D. Robbins.[100] The project lies within the ring, in a devastated area adjacent to the Van Dyck Houses Public Housing project (see figure 8.23). The area of initial construction was bounded by New Lots and Livonia avenues, Mother Gaston Boulevard, and Junius Street (figure 10.13). Except for sporadic buildings, most of the area was reduced to rubble during the past decade. The Robbins plan, made in collaboration with architect James L. Robinson, places row houses along each street with approximately twenty-eight houses per row (figure 10.14). To achieve the five-thousand-house goal, the development would have to be extended to include approximately one hundred blocks.

The two-story Nehiamiah houses are only eighteen feet wide by fifty-five feet deep. Alternate interior arrangements can produce two or three bedrooms. Elevations are identical, except for the occasional reversal of the plan, which changes the entry placement (figure 10.15). The brick facades, with a relentless

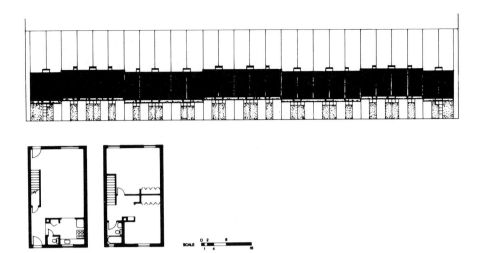

pattern of small windows, are reminiscent of nineteenth-century mill housing. The only significant difference is the setback from the street, which serves as parking for the family automobile. At the level of the individual house, the spatial standards are reasonable. At the collective level, however, the design conception is primitive and, in its own way, as reductive as the "tower in the park." The configuration is a horizontal barracks rather than vertical, with a density of only 14.6 dwellings per acre: *Zielenbau* planning (see figure 6.22) without the variety even of a corner house. With a loan from the churches and various forms of government subsidies, the initial houses cost just under $40,000, making them the least expensive new housing built in New York City at the time. The subsidy accrues from the land, which is donated by the city. There also is a direct subsidy from the city, a city tax abatement for twenty years, and a New York State mortgage subsidy.

The relationship between Nehiamiah Houses and the nineteenth century goes beyond appearance. The houses hearken back to Gilded Age private philanthropy for the "deserving poor." With a down payment of $5,000 and a twenty-year mortgage, a family income of $16,000 to $20,000 is needed to carry the costs, a figure far above the core poverty level. In 1983 households in public housing had a median income of $7,314, and 20 percent of the city's households had an average income of only $4,300.[101] Within this context, what emerges at Nehiamiah and other such home ownership programs is a profile of the twentieth-century "deserving poor," upwardly mobile families whose advanced status is rewarded with superior housing at reduced cost. For those left behind there is little housing available to pass down, a condition created by the devastation of the ring and exacerbated by displacement of the poor from redevelopment elsewhere.

The recent privatization of public philanthropy alludes to a nineteenth-century marketplace which today is only an apparition. But in the political marketplace, the purpose of Nehiamiah is well defined beyond the exigencies of philan-

Figure 10.15. Ira D. Robbins with James D. Robinson. Nehiamiah Houses, typical street front with yard and driveway.

thropy. Quite simply, the devastation of east Brooklyn was costing its churches their constituency, and the churches represent a major political force; the need for five thousand families was a matter of political survival.[102] Perhaps it was partially this urgency which has led to political difficulties at Nehiamiah over plans for the replacement of some sound existing buildings with the new row houses, resulting in vehement protest by their occupants.[103] Or could it be that Nehiamiah is simply a low-rise version of the same aggressive institutionalization as the urban renewal of decades past, with substitution of low-cost horizontal barracks for the "tower in the park"? Robbins has envisioned building as many as 200,000 new Nehiamiah-type houses in New York City.[104] He also has argued that cost efficiency dictates razing everything in the way. But the displaced families in East Brooklyn reasoned differently:

Now they're talking about building a one-family house out of inferior materials and putting my family in there, putting two families in a one-family house. The Nehiamiah plan started off by saying, we want to build on empty lots. Now they went from building on empty lots to now taking—acquiring this man's furniture store, acquiring our grocery store. Where will we have the shops? Where will we go? Where will my father go? He has finished paying for his house, now they want him to pay for another mortgage. Now we have reverends coming in, dressed up in cloth and giving us prayer while they're taking our homes and telling us we have to go.[105]

Another project which typifies the changes wrought by the recent United States political transformations is the Charlotte Gardens housing, begun in 1982 as a component of the South Bronx Development Organization (SBDO), a program within the East Tremont area of the ring. In a sense, the SBDO represented what was left of the Urban Development Corporation's former mandate. But it was a far smaller organization, localized in its concerns, although it was directed by Edward Logue, the former president of the UDC in its most active period. The Charlotte Street area was appropriate for its first SBDO building effort. A notorious symbol of the destruction of the South Bronx, the Charlotte street area lost 80 percent of its population between 1970 and 1980.[106] It received national attention after a visit by President Carter in October 1977, and by presidential candidate Reagan in August 1980. Weighing heavily on Charlotte Gardens project was the need for a symbolic gesture in keeping with the new national politics. The symbol chosen was the single-family house.[107] At Charlotte Gardens the houses stand in surreal contrast to the burned-out shells of apartment buildings nearby (figure 10.16). A resident recently described the equally surreal cultural contrast: "You see, I drive and then I take like let's say all Third Avenue, and then you see all these buildings are burned, and you see the people on the streets, and sometimes just seeing some neighborhoods, you feel depressing. And then coming back. And then when I come to my house, it's so different. It's just like living in Long Island."[108]

Thus, at the very end of the era of postwar suburbanization, the suburban single-family house has finally been attained by a few urban low-income families, albeit in minuscule numbers, and in the South Bronx rather than in Hempstead. The houses were completed exactly one hundred years after the first proposal for philanthropic cottage housing in the Bronx.[109] Charlotte Gardens is another variant on the philanthropy of the Gilded Age. It is not housing for the poor in the same sense that public housing programs were, with their legally enforced policy of open admissions for any family that needed housing, regardless of economic circumstance or social problems. Like Nehiamiah, Charlotte Gardens represents an opportunity only for the "deserving poor," which is to say the lower middle class, with the economic and social wherewithal for assimilation into the myths and privileges of cottage ownership.

The average selling price of the new houses was $52,000, with a 10 percent initial payment and a loan from the New York State Mortgage Agency. Actual construction cost was $81,000. In spite of the subsidies, it remains to be seen

Figure 10.16. South Bronx Development Corporation. Charlotte Gardens Housing, begun in 1983 and terminated in 1987; typical single-family house with burned-out apartment building behind.

Figure 10.17. Charlotte Gardens site plan, compared with the original neighborhood fabric, circa 1965.

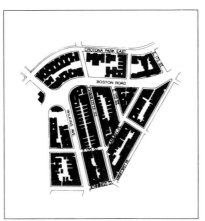

whether these houses will accrue the same long-term economic advantages as conventional private market houses in the suburbs, and whether their new owners will receive the same share in the "American dream." In terms of building equity alone, it is also questionable whether or not the prefabricated house-trailer-type construction will outlast the thirty-year mortgage. Charlotte Gardens is a literal suburban subdivision, along the lines of the early Levittown (see figure 8.26), although its curvilinear streets are due only to the happy circumstance of the preexisting irregularities in the Bronx gridiron in that particular location (figure 10.17). The density of 6.2 dwellings per acre is the lowest of any social housing ever constructed in New York City. By comparison, the nearby Governeur Morris Houses, a classic public housing tower project completed in 1965, maintains a density of 106 dwellings per acre. But more to the point is comparison with the building fabric which formerly existed on the site. With a density of well over 500 units per acre, it was a vibrant neighborhood, consisting primarily of New Law tenements built after 1901. The housing was far from substandard.

Elsewhere in New York City a small but highly visible new generation of owner-occupied, single-family, "social housing" has proliferated, although the extreme of the detached cottage has been limited to Charlotte Gardens. Several subsidy programs have been used. Typical are the 74 row houses in the Fulton Park area of Bedford-Stuyvesant, one of the first developments in the city's "small house ownership program." They were sold for $62,750 with approximately 10 percent down payment and a thirty-year mortgage.[110] In the realm of limited profit initiative were the 17 houses at Windsor Terrace adjoining Park Slope in Brooklyn, the first of 5,000 houses projected to be built by the New York City Housing Partnership. Other typical New York City Housing Partnership single-family projects have included 96 row houses in East Harlem and 255 prefabricated modular houses in Brownsville.[111] These are clearly middle income; the Windsor Terrace houses sold for $112,500. But still, they are cheaper than comparable private market-rate development. By comparison, for example, prefabricated modular two-family row houses built without subsidy at Carey Gardens in Bedford-Stuyvesant in Brooklyn sold at an average price of $164,500 per house in 1987.[112]

In spite of differences in development practice and selling price, all of these initiatives share the same questions about quality, related to the cost efficiency of the single-family house for social housing, in a time of subsidy austerity. The danger is drastic construction cost reduction, and reductive planning as at Nehiamiah. For example, at the Coney Island Town Houses Project in Brooklyn, the complaints from the new owners about the construction quality were widely publicized.[113] Sponsored by the city's small-house ownership program and completed in 1985, the 397 houses were designed by Scully, Thoresen, and Linard along west 31st and 37th streets.[114] In an attempt to reconstruct some of the remaining low-rise community on Coney Island, planning consisted of single-family row houses organized in a less reductive configuration than at Nehiamiah Houses. (figure 10.18). The project's problems were constructional, caused by economic constraints imposed by the Department of Housing and Urban Development, which set a selling price at $62,500 for a four-bedroom house, eliminating the possibility for quality construction. This approach to government philanthropy is simply reducing both construction cost and long-term maintenance costs by turning over the consequences of the cheapened construction to the home owners. Still, among the city's eligible lower middle class, with incomes between $20,000 and $35,000, the demand for the new houses is high. So strong is the desire for this vicarious piece of the "American dream" that at Charlotte Gardens the buyers were found long before the delivery of the houses.

The subsidized single-family houses fall primarily within the $65,000 to $75,000 range, which is within the means of lower-middle-income families. But in spite of the publicity, the actual numbers of all such small-home projects has been minuscule in relation to the overall housing need for low- and moderate-income groups in New York City. And in spite of this reality, these precedents are still characterized as a significant answer to the city's housing needs. According to the *New York Times* editorialist Roger Starr, "the small house is the Big Hope,"[115] which is perhaps the most sanguine assessment the liberal establishment can provide. With this, a curious circle has been closed by the formerly indefatigable opponents of Jane Jacobs more than two decades ago. Her theories have been given a strange new and pragmatic meaning in an age of new political realities.

Perhaps the most absurd symptom of this "new realism" was the Decal Program of the New York City Department of Housing Preservation and Development.[116] Beginning in 1980, a three-year program was initiated in which the windows of three hundred abandoned and burned-out buildings were covered with decals, pictures of windows and shutters with plants and cats and the like in them (figure 10.19). Within the void of the ring, these were intended to give an illusion of habitation—of a vicarious community created by scenographic effect rather than intercourse. They were thereby also intended to humor whatever residents remained. And they were said to be a help in attracting new investment in the ring by outsiders who would receive a better impression of things. In general, the

Figure 10.18. Scully, Thoresen, and Linard.
Coney Island Townhouses completed in 1985 to
replace similar houses destroyed less than two
decades earlier, with facades that are
reminiscent of turn-of-the-century working-class
housing in large sections of the outer boroughs.

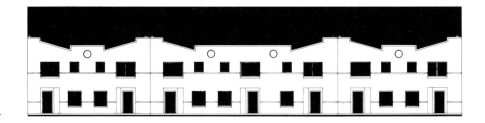

humor went unnoticed, although it was suggested that the city's poor might also receive decals of Mercedes Benz automobiles to park in front of their houses, or decals of beef steak in their refrigerators.[117]

Although government social housing programs continue in ad hoc fashion, one can point to the Decal Program as a symbolic "last gasp," an indication of a vast emptiness. The decals are a fitting final commentary on the state of the housing question, and of the culture at large.[118] The city of desperation is effectively covered over. An image of well-being was created for the same commuters along the Major Deegan Expressway who since the 1950s have watched the South Bronx pass successively from tenements to the vertical barracks of public housing, to a city of the dead, tranquil and orderly in its solemn dislocation. The decals were a powerful statement: death masks for a way of life replaced by the hyper-real domesticity of graphic cats, plants and blinds concealing a bitter reality. Much of the "Ring" exhibits the same characteristics. The South Bronx, for example, passed through successive stages within the same century: from farmland, to tenements, to inferno and dislocation, and finally to farmland again; a scenographic patrimony probably without precedent in urban history.

The reaction of the architectural profession to the course of urbanistic events in the last decade has mirrored that of the culture at large. The architectural mainstream turned away from the social and political concerns of the 1960s as quickly as it had embraced them. The programs that produced the new social architecture disappeared, along with an entire realm of concerns. At the same time, the architectural media promoted what might be described as the narcissistic phase in the history of the profession in the United States.[119] The mainstream has been oblivious to the worsening social conditions of the city, characterized by a poverty exceeding anything known in the 1960s. The 1980s was a decade of exaggerated juxtapositions: the ostentatious affluence of the new building in Manhattan, with the growing homeless population encountered at every turn.[120] While the number of soup kitchens increased from thirty in 1982 to five hundred in 1987,[121] the teapot emerged as a design object worthy of high discourse.[122] In the face of a profoundly worsening social condition, a mannered infatuation with "style" dominated the sensibility of the architectural thought, from Neo-Classicism to Neo-Constructivism and all the shades between.[123]

In the 1980s wealth and even greed became fashionable emblems of a status which is perversely enhanced by the deteriorating inner city. But while the allurement of wealth grew, signs have pointed toward an unraveling of the status quo. The market crash of October 19, 1987 underlined the discrepency between the self-interest of the economic system and rampant social problems. For housing the largest single indicator of change was the end of the luxury housing boom in Manhattan. Housing starts declined from 20,000 in 1985 to 1,400 in 1987, indicating a saturation point for luxury within the marketplace. But the economic infrastructure has also been saturated with poverty, as the gap between rich and poor continues to widen. The cost of housing has increased disporportionately for the poor.[124] In the next decade, the production of affordable, well-designed urban housing must become a national priority. If progressive architects are not ready to provide answers, discourse itself will become pointless.[125] Some prototypes do exist to work from, as the last twenty years have been filled with rich though scattered experimentation. Amid signs of renewed interest in social housing one emerging question involves the sources of patronage. A new amalgam of government and private production has yet to materialize on any scale.

The most encouraging potential of our period remains abstract. We under-

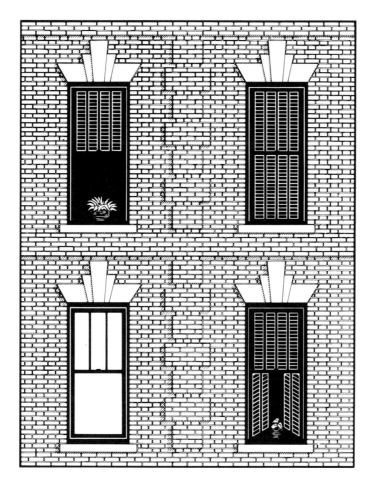

Figure 10.19. New York City Department of Housing Preservation and Development. Decal program for abandoned housing, 1980–83; typical "decals" covering window openings on East 116th Street, Manhattan.

stand the complex interplay of society, economics, and design better now than in 1850. The technical mechanisms to solve the housing question exist. What is missing is the political initiative to use them. We are immobilized by a fear of complexity. Escape into the private gratification of opulence and style is a predictable consequence for some, but it is an illusion which conspicuously overlooks our most crucial public issues. What is clear is that whatever social catastrophies await us will be the result of educated and cynical mistakes rather than uninformed and naive ones.

Notes

PREFACE

1. "Can We Have a Model City?" *The World,* (October 20, 1871), p. 4.

2. "Table-talk," *Appleton's Journal* IV (December 2, 1871), 4:638.

3. O. B. Bunce, "The City of the Future," pp. 156–158.

4. For a recent commentary on this relationship see: Warren I. Sussman, *Culture As History* (New York: Pantheon Books, 1973), ch. 12.

5. For example see: "Danger of An Epidemic," *New York Tribune,* (April 17, 1881), p. 1.

6. Howard D. Kramer, "Germ Theory and Early Health Program in the U.S.," p. 239.

7. William H. McNeill, *Plagues and Peoples,* p. 261.

8. Richard H. Shrylock, "Origins and Significance," n20.

9. E. Idell Zeisloft, *The New Metropolis,* p. 520.

10. Zeisloft, *The New Metropolis,* p. 272.

11. Useful but rather uncritical histories of the architectural profession in the United States are found in: Henry Saylor, "The AIA's First Hundred Years," part II; and Turpin C. Bannister, *The Architect at Mid-Century.*

12. Thomas Jefferson, *Notes on the State of Virginia,* p. 153.

13. For an interesting account of the architect-engineer rivalry from an engineering point of view see: William H. Wisely, *The America Civil Engineer,* pp. 300–306.

14. The writings of Alfred J. Bloor probably provide the best contemporary description of the sensibility surrounding the growth of the AIA, in particular a paper entitled" The Architectural and Other Art Societies of Europe." Also see: Alfred J. Bloor, "History of the American Institute of Architects," pp. 40–42.

15. For a comprehensive survey of this activity see: Dolores Hayden, *The Grand Domestic Revolution.*

1. EARLY PRECEDENTS

1. A. J. F. van Laer, ed., *Documents Relating to New Netherland,* pp. 160–168.

2. Detailed summaries of the evolution of legislation may be found in James Ford, *Slums and Housing;* and Joseph D. McGoldrick, Seymour Graubard, and Raymond Horowitz, *Building Regulation in New York City.* Also see Thelma E. Smith (ed.), *Guide to the Municipal Government of the City of New York.*

3. Berthold Fernow, ed., *The Records of New Amsterdam from 1653 to 1674.*

4. New York City, *Minutes of the Common Council: 1675–1776,* 1:137.

5. New York Colony, *Colonial Laws of New York,* (April 1, 1775), vol. 1, ch. 63, pp. 107–110.

6. David Grimm, "Account of the 1776 Fire for the New York State Historical Society."

7. New York State Legislature, *Laws* (1791), ch. 46, pp. 34–35.

8. New Amsterdam, *The Record of New Amsterdam* (February 19, 1657), p. 31.

9. New York Colony, *Colonial Laws of New York,* vol. 1, ch. 47, pp. 348–351.

10. James Hardie, *An Account of the Ma-*

lignant Fever Lately Prevalent in the City of New York; and Valentine Seaman, "Account of Yellow Fever in New York in 1795."

11. New York State Legislature, *Laws* (1800), ch. 16, pp. 24–26.

12. Robert Grier Monroe, "The Gas, Electric Light, and Street Railway Services in New York City," p. 112.

13. Charles H. Haswell, *Reminiscences of an Octogenarian of the City of New York,* p. 392.

14. Grant Thorburn, *Fifty Years of Reminiscences.*

15. Ira Rosenwaike, *Population History of New York City,* p. 18, table 3.

16. Edward Miller, *Report on the Malignant Disease Which Prevailed in the City of New York,* pp. 91–96.

17. New York City, *Minutes of the Common Council: 1784–1831* (April 30, 1804), 3:550–552.

18. Miller, *Report on the Malignant Disease,* p. 98.

19. New York City, *Minutes of the Common Council: 1675–1776* (April 18, 1678), 1:14.

20. New York State Legislature, *Laws* (1800), ch. 87, pp. 541–543.

21. New York City, *Minutes of the Common Council: 1784–1831* (June 15, 1829), 18:123.

22. William Ambrose Prendergast, *Record of Real Estate,* p. 49.

23. John H. Griscom, *Annual Report of the Interments in the City and County of New York, for the Year 1842,* p. 166.

24. Charles E. Rosenberg, *The Cholera Years. The United States in 1832, 1849, and 1866,* (Chicago: University of Chicago Press, 1962), pp. 187–225.

25. Haswell, *Reminiscences of an Octogenarian,* pp. 305–308.

26. New York State Legislature, *Laws* (1849), ch. 84, pp. 118–124.

27. Rosenwaike, *Population History of New York City,* p. 63, table 19.

28. *Ibid.,* pp. 39, 42.

29. The New York achievements which thrust this distinction upon it are described in Edward K. Spann, *The New Metropolis;* ch. 15. For related aspects of the transformation of its popular culture, see Paul Alan Marx, *This Is the City; An Examination of Changing Attitudes Toward New York as Reflected in Its Guidebook Literature, 1807–1860* (Ann Arbor, Mich.: University Microfilms International, 1983), parts 3 and 4.

30. Philip Hone, *The Diary of Philip Hone,*

1828–1851, Allan Nevins, ed. (New York: Dodd, Mead, 1927), p. 785.

31. John H. Griscom, *The Sanitary Condition of the Laboring Population of New York; Annual Report of 1842;* and *The Uses and Abuses of Air.*

32. Edwin Chadwick, *Report on the Sanitary Condition of the Labouring Population of Great Britain,* p. 203.

33. Griscom, *Annual Report of 1842,* p. 176.

34. *Ibid.*

35. Griscom, *The Sanitary Condition of the Labouring Population of New York* p. 6.

36. Griscom, *Annual Report of 1842,* pp. 175–176.

37. Gervet Forbes, "Remarks," p. 16.

38. *Plumber and Sanitary Engineer* (December 15, 1879), 3:26; Tenement House Building Company, *The Tenement Houses of New York;* and Haswell, *Reminiscences of an Octogenarian,* p. 332.

39. *Evening Post,* August 20, 1850.

40. Citizen's Association of New York, *Report Upon the Sanitary Condition of the City,* pp. 49–55; and "Gotham Court," *Frank Leslie's Sunday Magazine* (June 1879), 5:655.

41. "Gotham Court," p. 655.

42. Jacob A. Riis, *The Battle with the Slum,* p. 118.

43. For a detailed history of the AICP, see Lilian Brandt, *Growth and Development of AICP and COS.*

44. "Dwellings for the Poor," *Morning Courier* and *New York Enquirer,* January 30, 1847, p. 2.

45. Working Men's Home Association, *A Statement Relative to the Working Men's Home Association;* New York Association for Improving the Condition of the Poor, *Thirteenth Annual Report,* pp. 45–58; Robert H. Bremmer, "The Big Flat: History of a New York Tenement House." For a comparison of Gotham Court and the Workingmen's Home, see Anthony Jackson, *A Place Called Home,* ch. 1.

46. Ford, *Slums and Housing,* 2:878.

47. New York Association for Improving the Condition of the Poor, *Fifteenth Annual Report,* pp. 52–53.

48. Robert W. DeForest and Lawrence Veiller, eds., *The Tenement House Problem,* 1:86–87.

49. "The 'Big Flat' Tenement House," *New York Daily Tribune,* November 8, 1879, p. 3.

50. Jane Davies, "Llewellyn Park in West Orange, New Jersey."

51. Morton White and Lucia White, *The Intellectual Versus the City,* p. 31.

52. For a good survey of New York's suburban extensions by mid-century, see Edward K. Spann, *The New Metropolis,* ch. 8.

53. The origins of the ideological basis for the early suburban enclave is described in David Schuyler, *The New Urban Landscape,* ch. 8; Kenneth T. Jackson, *Crabgrass Frontier,* ch. 4.

54. Neil Harris, *The Artist in American Society,* ch. 10.

55. The contemporary guidebooks frequently noted the particulars of upper-middle-class New Yorkers' parvenu outlooks. See Paul Alan Marx, *This is the City.*

56. Alan Burnham, "The New York Architecture of Richard Morris Hunt," p. 11; Mary Sayre Haverstock, "The Tenth Street Studio"; Sarah Bradford Landau, "Richard Morris Hunt: Architectural Innovator and Father of a 'Distinctive' American School," pp. 49–50; Neil Harris, *The Artist in American Society,* pp. 268–270.

57. Citizen's Association of New York, *Report,* p. lxix.

58. New York State Legislature, *Laws of the State of New York* (1807); "Commissioners' Remarks," in William Bridges, *Map of Manhattan*; Isaac Newton Phelps-Stokes, *The Iconography of Manhattan Island,* vol. 3, plates 79, 80b, 86; vol. 5, pp. 1531, 1532, 1537. Also see John H. Reps, *The Making of Urban America: A History of City Planning in the United States.*

59. DeForest and Veiller, *The Tenement House Problem,* 1:293–300.

60. Citizen's Association of New York, p. 135.

61. "Homes of Poor People," *New York Daily Tribune,* January 8, 1882, p. 10; "Rear Tenements," *New York Herald,* January 23, 1881, p. 6.

62. DeForest and Veiller, *The Tenement House Problem,* 1:306–309.

63. This genre of "improved" tenements was discussed extensively in Citizen's Association of New York, *Report.*

64. George W. Morton, "Remarks," p. 211.

65. James Philip Noffsinger, *The Influence of the Ecole des Beaux-Arts on the Architects of the United States,* ch. 1.

66. Frederick Law Olmsted and J. J. R. Cross, "The 'Block' Building System of New York."

67. *Ibid.*

68. Stephen Smith, M.D. "Methods of Improving the Homes of the Laboring and Tenement House Classes of New York," pp. 150–152.

69. For a summary of Potter's contribution to housing, see Sarah Bradford Landau, *Edward T. and William A. Potter,* pp. 390–409. A compendium of Potter's research, "Concentrated Residence Studies," dated April 1903 is found in special collections at the Schaffer Memorial Library, Union College.

70. Edward T. Potter, "Urban Housing in New York I," "Urban Housing II," "Urban Housing II," and "Urban Housing V."

71. George W. Dresser, "Plan for a Colony of Tenements."

72. Brief mention of Potter's proposals were made in the *New York Times,* March 16, 1879; and Charles L. Brace, "Model Tenement Houses," p. 47. A description of the Derby proposal may be found in Nelson L. Derby, "A Model Tenement House."

2. LEGISLATING THE TENEMENT

1. Ford, *Slums and Housing,* pp. 117, 129; New York City, *Annual Report for the Year Ending December 31, 1854,* pp. 204, 234–235.

2. New York Association for Improving the Condition of the Poor, *Fifteenth Annual Report,* pp. 17–18.

3. New York State Assembly, *Report of the Special Committee on Tenement Houses; Report of the Select Committee on Tenement Houses.* Also see New York Association for Improving the Condition of the Poor.

4. Edward K. Spann, The New Metropolis, pp. 235–241, 389–395; James McCague, *The Second Rebellion: The Story of the New York City Draft Riots of 1865.*

5. Citizen's Association of New York, p. lxix.

6. New York State Assembly, *Report of the Committee on Public Health, Medical Colleges, and Societies Relative to the Condition of Tenement Houses in the Cities of New York and Brooklyn.*

7. New York State Legislature, *Laws* (1866), ch. 873, pp. 2009–2047.

8. New York State Legislature, *Laws* (1867), ch. 980, sec. 17, pp. 2265–2273.

9. McGoldrick, Graubard, and Horowitz, *Building Regulation in New York City,* pp. 49–66.

10. John P. Comer, *New York City Building Control,* ch. 2.

11. "The Qualifying of Architects," *American Architect and Building News* (April 20, 1878), 3:134–135.

12. Turpin C. Bannister, ed., *The Architect at Mid-Century,* vol. 1, ch. 9.

13. New York City, Health Department, *The Registration of Plumbers and the Laws and Regulations of All Buildings Hereafter Erected,* ch. 450.

14. Lawrence Veiller and Hugh Bonner, *Special Report on Housing Conditions and Tenement Laws,* pp. 5–6.

15. *Ibid.,* p. 17.

16. New York State Legislature, *Laws* (1879), ch. 504, pp. 554–556.

17. The competition program is found in: "Improved Homes for Workingmen," *Plumber and Sanitary Engineer* (December 1878), 2:1, 32. For an overview of housing competitions in New York, see Richard Plunz, "Strange Fruit: The Legacy of the Design Competition in New York Housing."

18. Plans of the first twelve winning schemes were published in "Model House Competition: Prize Plans," *Plumber and Sanitary Engineer* (March 1879), 2:103–106; (April, 1879), 2:131–132; (May, 1879), 2:158–159; (June 1, 1879), 2:180; (June 15, 1879), 2:212; and (July 1, 1879), 2:230.

19. "Prize Tenements," *New York Times,* March 16, 1879, p. 6. For additional contemporary criticism see: "The Tenement House Competition. Criticism of the Prize Plans," *New York Daily Tribune,* March 7, 1879, p. 1; Alfred J. Bloor, "Suggestions for a Better Method of Building Tenant-Houses in New York," p. 75.

20. Henry C. Meyer, *The Story of the Sanitary Engineer,* pp. 14–15.

21. "The Tenement-House Act," *New York Times,* May 25, 1879.

22. Alfred J. Bloor, "Suggestions for a Better Method of Building Tenant-Houses in New York," p. 75.

23. *Ibid.*

24. Nelson L. Derby, "A Model Tenement House."

25. "The Tenement House Competition: Criticism of the Prize Plans," *New York Tribune,* March 7, 1879, p. 1.

26. Edward T. Potter, "Plans for Apartment Houses" and "A Study of Some New York Tenement House Problems."

27. *Actes du congrès international des habitations à bon marché tenu à Bruxelles,* pp. 473–475. The paper given by Potter was published as *Étude de Quelques Problèmes de l'Habitation Concentree.*

28. Edward T. Potter, "System for Laying Out Town Lots."

29. Alfred J. Bloor, "The Late Edward T. Potter."

30. DeForest and Veiller, *The Tenement House Problem,* 1:94, 2:78.

31. Rosenwaike, *Population History of New York City,* p. 7, table 29; p. 110, table 49.

32. A summary of these changes may be found in McGoldrick, Graubard, and Horowitz, *Building Regulation in New York City,* pp. 51–56. For a history of the charter movement, see Barry J. Kaplan, "Metropolitics, Administrative Reform, and Political Theory.

33. New York State Legislature, *Laws* (1882), ch. 410, title 5, pp. 125–145.

34. New York State Legislature, *Report of the Special Committee Appointed to Investigate the Public Offices and Departments of the City of New York,* 4:4411.

35. New York State Senate, *Report of the Tenement House Committee of 1884,* Legislative Document no. 36 (February 17, 1885), pp. 42, 44.

36. *Ibid.,* p. 6.

37. New York State Legislature *Laws* (1887), ch. 566, pp. 738–772; and ch. 84, pp. 94–101.

38. New York State Legislature, *Laws* (1884), Ch. 272.

39. Theodore Roosevelt, *An Autobiography,* p. 82. Also see Jacob Riis, *How the Other Half Lives,* ch. 12.

40. "Matter of Jacobs," in New York State Court of Appeals, *New York Reports* (1885), Vol. 98, pp. 114–115.

41. Roosevelt, *An Autobiography,* p. 83. Also see Henry Steele Commager, *Documents of American History,* 2:116–118. Commager considered this decision important enough to include in his early editions, but dropped it from later ones.

42. Jacob Riis, "How the Other Half Lives" and *How the Other Half Lives.*

43. A good summary of Smith's contribution is found in Gordon Atkins, "Health, Housing, and Poverty in New York City," pp. 22–27.

44. For a general history of the AICP and COS, see Lilian Brandt, *Growth and Development of AICP and COS.*

45. Charles F. Wingate, "The Moral Side of the Tenement House Problem," pp. 162, 164.

46. Carrol D. Wright, *The Slums of Balti-*

more, *Chicago, New York, and Philadelphia*, pp. 19, 42, 45, 85–86.

47. Wingate, "The Moral Side of the Tenement House Problem," p. 161.

48. Allen Forman, "Some Adopted Americans," p. 50.

49. New York State Assembly, *Report of the Tenement House Committee of 1894*, Legislative Document no. 37, January 17, 1895, p. 11, 256.

50. New York State Legislature, *Laws* (1895), ch. 567, pp. 1099–1114.

51. Elgin R. L. Gould, *The Housing of the Working People*.

52. "Tenement House Reform. What the Government Should Do. The Last of Felix Adler's Lectures," *New York Daily Tribune*, March 10, 1884, p. 8.

53. Charles E. Emery, "The Lessons of the Columbian Year," p. 203.

54. For a good summary of this sensibility, see Michael T. Klare, "The Architecture of Imperial America."

55. Charles Mulford Robinson, *Modern Civic Art, or The City Made Beautiful*, pp. 257–258.

56. Louis H. Sullivan, *The Autobiography of an Idea*, p. 314.

57. A number of press clippings on the competition may be found in J. H. Freedlander, *Scrapbooks*, vol. 1. The competition results were published in "A Great International Competition: The University of California: Described with the Assistance of Mr. John Belcher, One of the Assessors," *Architectural Review* (January–June 1900), 7:109–118.

58. "American Architecture and Its Future," *Criterion* (October 22, 1898), in J. H. Freedlander, *Scrapbooks*, vol. 1.

59. "Why English Architects Did Not Succeed," *San Francisco Examiner*, October 8, 1898, in Freedlander, *Scrapbooks*, vol. 1.

60. Ernest Flagg, "The New York Tenement-House Evil and its Cure." Flagg describes the French influence in "The Planning of Apartment Houses and Tenements," pp. 85–90. For a survey of Flagg's work in tenement reform, see Mardges Bacon, *Ernest Flagg. Beaux-Arts Architect and Urban Reformer*, ch. 8.

61. The competition program is found in: Improved Housing Council, *Conditions of Competition for Plans of Model Apartment Houses* (New York 1896). For a discussion of the placing entries, see "New York's Great Movement for Housing Reform," *Review of Re-*views (December 1896), 14:692–701; "Model Apartment Houses," *Architecture and Building* (January 2, 1897), 26:7–10. Also see Robert DeForest and Lawrence Veiller, *The Tenement House Problem* 1:107–109; James Ford, *Slums and Housing*, plate 7; Anthony Jackson, *A Place Called Home. A History of Low-Cost Housing in Manhattan*, pp. 106–108.

62. The competition program is found in: Charity Organization Society of the City of New York, Tenement House Committee, *Competition for Plans of Model Tenements*. For discussion of the placing entries, see Lawrence Veiller, "The Charity Organization Society's Tenement House Competition;" "The Model Tenement House Competition," *Architecture* (March 15, 1900), 1:104–105; "Model Tenement Floors," *Real Estate Record and Builders' Guide* (March 17, 1900), 65:452–455; Robert DeForest and Lawrence Veiller, *The Tenement House Problem* 1:109–113; James Ford, *Slums and Housing*, plates 8,9.

63. Ford, *Slums and Housing*, plate 7E; "Model Tenements," *Municipal Affairs* (March 1899), 3:136.

64. Ford, *Slums and Housing*, vol. 2, pl.7F. For a survey of Phelps-Stokes' work in tenement reform see: Roy Lubov, "I. N. Phelps-Stokes: Tenement House Architect, Economist, Planner," pp. 75–87.

65. "Tenement House Show," *New York Times*, February 10, 1900, p. 7; DeForest and Veiller, *The Tenement House Problem*, 1:112–113.

66. Estimates from DeForest and Veiller, *The Tenement House Problem*, 1:8.

67. Some of these plans are published in Ford, *Slums and Housing*, plates 9B, 10A, 10B, 10D, 10E.

68. New York State Legislature, *Laws* (1901), ch. 334, pp. 889–923.

3. RICH AND POOR

1. Citizen's Association of New York, pp. lxiii–lxiv.

2. Griscom, *The Uses and Abuses of Air*, pp. 193–194.

3. New York Association for Improving the Condition of the Poor, *Sixteenth Annual Report*, p. 46.

4. "Congress in the Slums," *New York Herald*, July 27, 1888, p. 3; Jacob A. Riis, "The Clearing of Mulberry Bend."

5. New York City, *Minutes of the Common Council: 1784–1831* (April 20, 1829), 18:11–12.

6. Charles Dickens, *American Notes*, p. 213.

7. New York State Senate, *Report of the Tenement House Commitee*, pp. 232–235.

8. Jacob Riis, *How the Other Half Lives*, pp. 56–57.

9. *Ibid.*, p. 64.

10. Allen Forman, "Some Adopted Americans," p. 46.

11. New York State Senate, *Report of the Tenement House Committee*, pp. 102–104.

12. "The Charter Election—A Crying Evil," *New York Times*, November 21, 1864, p. 4.

13. "The Squatter Population of New York City," *New York Times*, November 25, 1864, p. 4.

14. One such case is described in "Squatter Life in New York," *Harper's New Monthly* (September 1880), 61:563.

15. These figures are included in Citizen's Association of New York, *Report*, pp. 291–292, 300–303, 334, 346.

16. "The Central Park," *Harper's Weekly* (November 28, 1857), 1:756–757.

17. Reps, *The Making of Urban America*, pp. 331–339.

18. For histories of the northward movement in Manhattan, see Charles Lockwood, *Manhattan Moves Uptown*; M. Christine Boyer, *Manhattan Manners*.

19. New York City, Central Park Commission, *First Annual Report*, p. 214.

20. The New York Association for Improving the Condition of the Poor, *Fifteenth Annual Report*, p. 18.

21. "The Charter Election—A Crying Evil," *New York Times*, November 21, 1864, p. 4. This removal process continued for over two decades. See "Squattors Shanties Torn Down," *New York Times*, April 17, 1881, p. 4.

22. Citizen's Association of New York, *Report*, p. 300.

23. *American Architect and Building News* (November 20, 1880), 13:242.

24. See street map in New York City, Department of Public Works, *Third Annual Report*.

25. H. C. Bunner, "Shantytown."

26. A. Blair Thaw, "A Record of Progress."

27. C. T. Hill, "The Growth of the Upper West Side of New York," p. 730.

28. "Squatter Life in New York," p. 568.

29. *Ibid.*, p. 563.

30. New York City, City Inspector, *Annual Report: 1856*, p. 199.

31. Hill, "The Growth of the Upper West Side of New York," p. 568. Also see "The Growing West Side," *New York Times*, April 17, 1881, p. 14.

32. Frank Richards, "The Rock Drill and Its Share in the Development of New York City."

33. Jay E. Cantor, "A Monument of Trade."

34. Anthony Trollope, *North America*, p. 214.

35. Edward K. Spann, *The New Metropolis*, p. 205.

36. A good record of the urban row house type is found in: William Tuthill, *The City Residence. Its Design and Construction*, (New York: W. T. Comstock, 1890). Charles Lockwood, *Bricks and Brownstone*.

37. Charles Astor Bristed, *The Upper Ten Thousand*, pp. 92–93.

38. "Alternative Designs for a City House, New York, N.Y.," *American Architect and Building News* (November 1, 1879), 6:140; plate follows p. 144.

39. Many contemporary observers remarked on this fact. For example, see Richard M. Hurd, *Principles of City Land Values*.

40. Descriptions of the turmoil of the 1870s may be found in Robert V. Bruce, *1877: Year of Violence*; Dennis Tilden Lynch, *The Wild Seventies*.

41. Definitions of housing terms from this period are given by the superintendent of buildings in "The Building Transactions of the Past Year," *American Architect and Building News* (February 7, 1880), 7:47.

42. For the characteristics of the new parisian bourgeosie see: David H. Pinkney, *Napoleon III and the Rebuilding of Paris*. For a general discussion of European precedents in relation to New York see: Elizabeth C. Cromley, "The Development of the New York Apartment, 1860–1905," Chapter 3.

43. Recently a passage from Edith Wharton's *Age of Innocence* has been popular in substantiating this moral issue. See Stephen Birmingham, *Life at the Dakota*, p. 17; Robert A. M. Stern, "With Rhetoric: The New York Apartment House," p. 80; Gwendolyn Wright, *Building the Dream*, p. 146.

44. Sarah Gilman Young, *European Modes of Living*, pp. 26–27.

45. *Ibid.*, p. 1.

46. James Richardson, "The New Homes of New York," *Scribner's Monthly* (May 1874), 8:67.

For a good introduction to the early New York apartment house and Hunt's seminal role, see Sarah Bradford Landau, "Richard Morris Hunt: Architectural Innovator and Father of a 'Distinctive' American School," pp. 61–66.

47. "The Apartment Houses of New York City," *Real Estate Record and Builder's Guide* (March 26, 1910), 85:644; and Raymond Roberts, "Building Management: Trend of Apartment House Buildings."

48. Calvert Vaux, "Parisian Buildings for City Residents," p. 809.

49. "Apartment House on East 21st Street, New York," *American Architect and Building News* (May 4, 1878), 3:157; plate follows p. 156.

50. A good sense discussion of the problems of middle-class flats can be found in Richardson, "The New Homes of New York."

51. *Appleton's Dictionary of New York and Vicinity* (New York: D. Appleton, 1879), pp. 11–12.

52. Charles Wingate, "The Moral Side of the Tenement House Problem," p. 160.

53. Richardson, "The New Homes of New York," pp. 63, 65.

54. John H. Jallings, *Elevators: A Practical Treatise*, p. 69. This study is still the best on the subject of early elevator development.

55. W. Sloan Kennedy, "The Vertical Railway," pp. 890–891.

56. "The 'Flats' of the Future," *The World*, October 8, 1871, p. 3.

57. "Parisian Flats," *Appleton's Journal* (November 18, 1871), 4:561–562, "The 'Flats' of the Future."

58. O. B. Bunce, "The City of the Future."

59. *Ibid.*, p. 6. This proposal or a similar one is described in detail in Arthur Gilman, "Family Hotels: The New Departure in Domestic Apartments" (letter), *New York Times*, November 19, 1871, p. 5.

60. Jean A. Follett, "The Hotel Pelham: A New Building Type for America," *American Art Journal* (Autumn 1983), 15:58–73.

61. Descriptions are in Arthur John Gale, "The Godwin Bursary," pp. 59–60; and "The Vancorlear, New York," *American Architect and Building News* (January 24, 1880), 7:28.

62. Hubert, Pirsson, and Co., *Where and How To Build*, pp. 74–75.

63. For a history of cooperative ownership in New York City, see Christopher Gray, "The 'Revolution' of 1881 is Now in its 2d Century," *New York Times*, October 28, 1984, sec. XII, p.

57. Also of interest is Dolores Hayden, *The Grand Domestic Revolution*, ch. 5.

64. Descriptions of the Dakota are in Historic American Building Survey, *New York City Architecture*; and Arthur John Gale, "The Godwin Bursary."

65. *Report on Elevated Dwellings in New York City*, p. 3. For a survey of p. 3.

66. *The Dalhousie Brochure.*

67. Andrew Alpern, *Apartments for the Affluent*, pp. 114–115; Joseph Giovannini, "The Osborne: Now 100 Years Old and Still a Nice Place To Live," *New York Times*, November 21, 1985, p. C-1.

68. These buildings were described as part of the Gale itinerary. See Arthur John Gale, "The Godwin Bursary," p. 58.

69. "A High House," *The Builder* (June 23, 1883), 44:867.

70. Gale's entire report was published in Arthur John Gale, "American Architecture from a Constructional Point of View."

71. "Architectural Style and Criticism in the States," *The Builder* (September 15, 1883), 45:344–345.

72. A complete description can be found in Gale, "The Godwin Bursary," pp. 61–63, figs. 70–77; and American Bank Note Co., *The Central Park Apartments Facing the Park*.

73. The popular press in New York tended to downplay the negative aspects of apartment life. For an indication of the kind of criticism that appeared, see Gwendolyn Wright, *Building the Dream*, pp. 141–151; David P. Handlin, *The American Home: Architecture and Society, 1815–1915* (Boston: Little, Brown, 1979), pp. 230–231.

74. Junius Henri Browne, "The Problem of Living in New York," pp. 919–920.

75. Everett Blanke, "The Cliffdwellers of New York," pp. 356–357.

76. John Vredenburgh Van Pelt, *A Monograph of the William K. Vanderbilt House*; and Cantor, "A Monument of Trade," p. 168.

77. George Edward Harding, "Electric Elevators," p. 31; Herbert T. Wade, "The Problem of Vertical Transportation," *American Review of Reviews* (December 1909), 40:705–712.

78. For surveys of the evolution of the NYC transit system, see James Blaine Walker, *Fifty Years of Rapid Transit*; Stan Fischler, *Uptown, Downtown*.

79. Reginald Pelham Bolton, "The Apartment Hotel in New York"; and New York City,

Landmarks Preservation Commission, "Ansonia Hotel: Designation Report."

80. Charles H. Israels, "New York Apartment Houses."

81. "The Apthorp," *Architecture* (July 15, 1909), 16:115; and "The Apthorp," *Architects' and Builders' Magazine* (September 1908), 40:531–543.

82. "The Belnord To Have Interesting Features," *Real Estate Record and Builders' Guide* (November 7, 1908), 82:873–875.

83. Ernest Flagg, "The Planning of Apartment Houses and Tenements," p. 86.

84. These statistics are from Reginald Pelham Bolton, "The Apartment Hotel in New York," pp. 27–32.

85. "270 Park Avenue," *Architecture* (May 1918), 37:143, plates 78–80.

86. "Apartment House, 277 Park Avenue. McKim, Mead, and White Architects," *Architecture and Building* (January 1925), 57:4.

87. "1185 Park Avenue," *Architecture and Building* (January 1930), 62:23, 24, 31.

88. For the development of the duplex apartment, see the three-part series "The Development of Duplex Apartments" by Elisha Harris Janes, in *The Brickbuilder*: "I. The Early Years" (June 1912), 21:159–161; "II. Studio Type" (July 1912), 21:183–186; "III. Residential Type" (August 1912), 21:203–206.

89. For recent surveys of the studio apartment type, see David P. Handlin, *The American Home,* pp. 377–385; Robert A. M. Stern, Gregory Gilmartin, and John Massengale, *New York 1900,* pp. 295–299.

90. "Studio Apartment at 70 Central Park West, New York City, Rich and Mathesius, Architects," *Architectural Review* (February 1920), 27:33.

91. New York State Legislature, *Laws* (1867), vol. 2, ch. 908, sec. 17, pp. 2265–2273.

92. Mention of this continuing problem is found in Hubert, Pirsson, and Hoddick, "New York Flats and French Flats," p. 61; McGoldrick, Graubard, and Horowitz, *Building Regulation in New York City,* pp. 6–7.

93. Arthur Gross, "The New Multiple Dwelling Law of New York," p. 273.

94. Edward T. Potter, "Tenement Houses," p. 62.

95. C. W. Buckham, "The Present and Future Development of the Apartment House."

96. By 1916, New York building law permitted self-service push-button elevators. See "The Building Code of the City of New York,"

in New York Society of Architects, *Yearbook* (1916), Art 27, Sec. 567. For further discussion of this change see chapter 5.

97. See early reports of the New York City Tenement House Department for typical plans.

98. "Modern Apartment Conveniences," *Real Estate Record and Builders' Guide* (September 12, 1908), 82:531.

99. Charles Griffith Moses, "A Mile and a Half Progress."

4. BEYOND THE TENEMENT

1. For an overview of English activity, see John Nelson Tarn, *Five Percent Philanthropy.* For an overview of U.S. activity see Eugenie C. Birch and Deborah S. Gardner, "The Seven-Percent Solution. A Review of Philanthropic Housing."

2. A description of these prototypes may be found in Henry Roberts, *The Dwellings of the Labouring Classes,* pp. 120–121. For a study of Roberts' contributions see James Stevens Curl, *The Life and Work of Henry Roberts.*

3. Citizens Association of New York, pp. lxxxvi–lxxxvii.

4. New York State Assembly, *Report of the Committee on Public Health,* pp. 12–14.

5. All projects are described in Alfred Treadway White, *Improved Dwellings for the Laboring Classes,* pp. 28–29.

6. "Prize Tenements," *New York Times,* March 16, 1879, p. 6.

7. "New York's Great Movement for Housing Reform," *Review of Reviews* (December 1896), 14:699.

8. Alfred Treadway White, *Sun-Lighted Tenements,* p. 3.

9. White, *Improved Dwellings for the Laboring Classes,* pp. 8–9.

10. *Ibid.,* p. 9.

11. *Ibid.,* p. 10.

12. *Ibid.,* p. 11.

13. For a general description of the phenomenon in Philadelphia at that time, see Addison B. Burk, "The City of Homes and Its Building Societies"; Stephen Smith, M.D., "Methods of Improving the Homes of the Laboring and Tenement House Classes of New York."

14. Seymour Dexter, "Cooperative Building and Loan Associations in the State of New York," p. 141; F. B. Sanborn, "Cooperative Building Associations, p. 115.

15. Figures cited in M. J. Daunton, *House and Home in the Victorian City*, p. 58.

16. White, *Improved Dwellings for the Laboring Classes*, p. 21.

17. E. Moberly Bell, *Octavia Hill*.

18. The Gotham Court rehabilitation was begun in 1879 by a "Mrs. Miles" and then continued with Dow. See *Some Results of an Effort to Reform the Homes of the Laboring Classes in New York City*, pp. 5–19; John Cotton Smith, *Improvement of the Tenement House System of New York* pp. 7–8; "The Good Work of the Misses Dow," *New York Tribune*, November 14, 1887, p. 2; "Housing of the Poor," *New York Evening Post*, January 2, 1885, p. 1.

19. See the description in New York State Assembly, *Report of the Tenement House Committee of 1894*, pp. 131–137.

20. See the descriptions in George W. Da Cunha, "Improved Tenements"; and "Model Tenement House," *American Architect and Building News* (April 17, 1880), 7:166.

21. Robert W. DeForest and Lawrence Veiller, *The Tenement House Problem*, 1:99.

22. As recorded in "Building Transactions of the Past Year," *American Architect and Building News* (February 7, 1880), 7:48. Also see James Gallatin, "Tenement House Reform in the city of New York."

23. New York Sanitary Reform Society, *First Annual Report*, p. 22; and Elgin R. L. Gould, *The Housing of the Working People*, pp. 196–200. Also see "Pleasant Homes at Little Cost: An Interesting Colony on the East Side," *New York Daily Tribune*, April 3, 1882, p. 5.

24. New York State Assembly, *Report of the Tenement House Committee*, pp. 137–142; "New Apartment Houses," *American Architect and Building News* (May 31, 1879), 5:175; "Improved Tenements," *New York Herald*, September 18, 1881, p. 9.

25. New York State Assembly, *ibid.*, pp. 126–131; Tenement House Building Company, *Report*; Tenement House Building Company, *The Tenement Houses of New York City*; New York State Assembly, Tenement House Committee, *Report*, pp. 126–131; and Gould, *The Housing of the Working People*, pp. 196–200.

26. These activities are described in some detail in "Model Tenements," *Harper's Weekly* (January 14, 1888), 32:31.

27. "The Astral Apartments, Greenpart, N.Y.," *American Architect and Building News* (November 13, 1886), 20:230–231.

28. *Ibid; The Astral Apartments.*

29. Elgin R. L. Gould, "The Housing Problem," pp. 123–127; and "Model Apartment Houses," *Architecture and Building* (January 2, 1897), 26:7–10.

30. City and Suburban Homes Company, *Model City and Suburban Homes*; New York City Housing Authority, Technical Division, *Survey*, pp. 67–71; Gould, "The Housing Problem," pp. 123–127; and "Model Apartment Houses," pp. 7–10.

31. Lawrence Veiller, "The Effect of the New Tenement House Law," pp. 108–109; New York City Housing Authority, Technical Division, *Survey*, pp. 60–66. A chronology of the City and Suburban Homes projects is found in: City and Suburban Homes Company, *Thirty-Sixth Annual Report* (New York: May 1932), p. 4.

32. "Housing of the Poor," *New York Times*, March 5, 1896, p. 2. For a reaction to Adler's talk, see: "Houses for the Poor," *New York Times*, March 6, 1896, p. 10.

33. For a general description of all City and Suburban Homes Company activities, see United States Federal Housing Administration, *Four Decades of Housing with Limited Dividend Corporation*; Gould, "The Housing Problem," pp. 122–131; and "New York's Great Movement for Housing Reform," pp. 693–701.

34. Adler actually advocated that the New York City government purchase large tracts of suburban land for social housing. See "Housing of the Poor," *New York Times*, March 5, 1896, p. 2; "For Improved Housing," *New York Times*, March 4, 1896, p. 2.

35. United States Federal Housing Administration, *Four Decades of Housing*, p. 9.

36. "Apartment Houses," *American Architect and Building News* (January 5, 1907), 91:3–11.

37. H. W. Desmond, "The Works of Ernest Flagg," pp. 38–39.

38. Ford, *Slums and Housing*, 2:902.

39. Ford, *Slums and Housing*, vol. 2, plate 12c. For an overview of the company's activities see Anthony T. Sutcliffe, "Why The Model Fireproof Tenement Company."

40. Henry L. Shively, "Hygienic and Economic Features of the East River Homes Foundation"; "Building for Health," *The Craftsman* (February 1910), 17:552–561; and Jonathan A. Rawson, Jr., "Modern Tenement Houses."

41. Charity Organization Society of the City of New York, *New York Charities Directory*, p. 335.

42. Will Walter Jackson, "A Peculiar Situation in Tenement Work"; and William Miller, *The Tenement House Committee and the Open Stair Tenements.*

43. Only cursory references to this organization are available. They are Miller, *The Tenement House Committee and Open Stair Tenements*; "Tenements That Are Safe in Fire," *Harper's Weekly* (April 29, 1911), 55:13; and Charity Organization Society, *New York Charities Directory,* p. 335.

44. "Modern Open Stair Tenements," *Real Estate Record and Builders' Guide* (April 29, 1916), 97:668; and Henry Atterbury Smith, "Economic Open Stair Communal Dwellings."

45. Arthur M. East, "Modern Tenements Needed in Chelsea." New York City Housing Authority, Technical Division, *Survey,* pp. 107–111.

46. New York City, Tenement House Department, *Eighth Report,* pp. 55–58.

47. "New Tenements for Negroes in City's Most Populous Block," *New York World,* January 21, 1901; and "New Model Tenements Uptown for East and West Side Families," in Howells and Stokes, *Scrapbook of Clippings*; City and Suburban Homes Company, *Model City and Suburban Homes.*

48. "New Model Tenements Just Completed," *Real Estate Record and Builders' Guide* (August 7, 1915), 96:246; and William Emerson, "The Open Stair Tenement," pp. 100–102, 105–106.

49. "Rogers Model Dwellings," *American Architect* (October 29, 1913), vol. 104, plates follow p. 172; and "The Rogers Tenements," *The Brickbuilder* (May 1915), 24:129, plates, 64, 65.

50. John Taylor Boyd, "Garden Apartments in Cities," pp. 66–68; "Modern Open Stair Tenements," p. 668; New York City Housing Authority, Technical Division, *Survey,* pp. 112–116.

51. Alfred Treadway White, *The Riverside Buildings of the Improved Dwellings.*

52. White, *Sun-Lighted Tenements,* p. 7.

53. "A Tenement Turns Outside In," *Architectural Forum* (November 1939), 71:406.

54. White, *The Riverside Buildings,* p. 8.

55. Hubert, Pirsson, and Hoddick, "New York Flats and French Flats."

56. J. F. Harder, "The City's Plan," pp. 41–44.

57. I. N. Phelps Stokes, "A Plan for Tenements in Connection with a Municipal Park," in DeForest and Veiller, *The Tenement House Problem,* 2:59–64.

58. Katherine Bement Davis, *Report on the Exhibit of the Workingman's Model Home.*

59. For contemporary material on model suburban factories, see Budgett Meakin, *Model Factories and Villages*; and Graham Romeyn Taylor, *Satellite Cities.* An excellent discussion of nineteenth-century New England factory towns may be found in John Coolidge, "Low Cost Housing: The New England Tradition," *New England Quarterly* (March 1941), 14:6–24.

60. For a history of the Tuxedo Park development, see Samuel H. Graybill, Jr., *Bruce Price,* 2:4. Tuxedo Park and Short Hills are contrasted in: "Some Suburbs of New York," *Lippincott's Magazine* (July 1884), 8:21–23.

61. Aaron Singer, *Labor-Management Relations at Steinway and Sons,* p. 88. In general, Singer gives a good overview of the phenomenon of nineteenth-century suburbanization of industry.

62. Charles L. Brace, "Model Tenement Houses."

63. "Houses for Workingmen," *New York Times,* September 8, 1891, p. 8.

64. For a general history of Garden City, see M. H. Smith, *History of Garden City.* Also see Kenneth Jackson, *Crabgrass Frontier,* pp. 81–84.

65. "The Hempstead Plains," *Harper's Weekly* (August 7, 1869), 13:503.

66. For a general source on the physical development of Steinway, see Singer, *Labor-Management Relations at Steinway and Sons,* ch. 4. Also see Theodore E. Steinway, *People and Pianos.*

67. J. S. Kelsy, *History of Long Island City,* p. 49.

68. For the evolution of strike activity during both periods, see Singer, *Labor-Management Relations at Steinway and Sons,* ch. 3 and ch. 5.

69. City and Suburban Homes Company, *Model City and Suburban Homes*; Elgin R. L. Gould, "Homewood—A Model Suburban Settlement"; Gould, "The Housing Problem," pp. 127–135; and DeForest and Veiller, *The Tenement House Problem,* 1:345–346.

70. United States Federal Housing Administration, *Four Decades of Housing,* p. 54.

71. Samuel Howe, "Forest Hills Gardens"; "Forest Hills Gardens, Long Island," *The Brickbuilder* (December 1912), 21:317–320; Charles C. May, "Forest Hills Gardens from the Town Planning Viewpoint."

72. *Forest Hills Gardens,* p. 8.

73. *Ibid.,* p. 13.

74. For a report of this research, see Grosvenor Atterbury, *The Economic Production of Workingmen's Homes.*

75. Walter I. Willis, *Queens Borough, New York City,* This representation was also made in Russell Sage Foundation, *A Forward Movement in Suburban Development,* p. 169.

76. Ebenezer Howard, *Garden Cities Tomorrow.*

77. Rego Park development is recorded in a clipping file in the local history collection at the Queens Borough Public Library.

78. For a summary of Queens development, see Works Progress Administration, Federal Writers' Project, *The WPA Guide To New York City,* pp. 555–561.

5. THE GARDEN APARTMENT

1. James Blaine Walker, *Fifty Years of Rapid Transit;* Stan Fischler, *Uptown, Downtown.*

2. New York State, State Board of Housing, *Annual Report, 1929,* table XXVII; New York City Department of City Planning, *New Housing in New York City, 1981–82,* p. 26.

3. Walker, *Fifty Years of Rapid Transit;* and James Ford, *Slums and Housing,* 1:214.

4. Ira Rosenwaike, *Population History of New York City,* p. 141, table 69.

5. Lawrence Veiller, *A Model Housing Law;* and "Widespread Movement for Good Housing," *Real Estate Record and Builders' Guide* (March 21, 1914), 93:501.

6. New York State Legislature, Joint Legislature Committee on Housing and the Reconstruction Commission of the State of New York, *Report of the Housing Committee,* pp. 6–8.

7. New York City, Board of Estimate and Apportionment, *Building Zone Plan;* for an interesting contemporary interpretation, see Robert Whitten, "The *Building Zone Plan* of New York City"; and "New Uses for the Zoning System," *Architectural Review* (April 1918), 6:66–67.

8. "Slight Effect of Changes in the Tenement House Law," *Real Estate Record and Builders' Guide* (June 21, 1919), 103:826.

9. Freeman Cromwell, "The Push Button Elevator as a Renting Aid," p. 9; and Bernard Lauren and James Whyte, *The Automatic Elevator in Residential Buildings,* part II, pp. 2–3.

10. The 1916 building code was amended to include mention of "full automatic push button elevators," but sources seem to indicate that it was not until several years later that this technology came into use. See *Code of Ordinances of the City of New York as Amended 9/15,* ch. 5, art. 29, p. 567; Cromwell, "The Push Button Elevator"; Henry Wright, "The Apartment House"; Alexander Marks, "Future Possibilities of Push-Button Control of Electric Elevators."

11. Mark Ash and William Ash, *The Building Code of the City of New York;* Henry Wright, "The Modern Apartment House," p. 237.

12. "Emery Roth Dies: Noted Architect," *New York Times,* August 21, 1948, p. 16; "Andrew Thomas, a City Architect," *New York Times,* July 27, 1965, p. 33; "G. W. Springsteen, Architect, 76, Dies," *New York Times,* October 6, 1954, p. 25; "Horace Ginsbern, 69, Dies; Founded Architects Firm," *New York Times,* September 22, 1969, p. 33.

13. For a brief summary of these programs, see Miles L. Colean, *Housing for Defense,* ch. 1.

14. United States Housing Corporation, *Report,* 2:397, table III.

15. *Ibid.,* 2:347–349.

16. Colean, *Housing for Defense,* pp. 14–15, 23–24.

17. For a history of the crisis in New York City, see Joseph A. Spencer, "The New York Tenant Organizations and the Post–World War I Housing Crisis."

18. The Real Estate Board of New York, *Apartment Building Construction—Manhattan, 1902–1953,* exhibit C. Also see "Supt. Miller Analyses Manhattan Building for Decade," *Real Estate Record and Builders' Guide* (September 4, 1920), 106: 313–314.

19. New York State, State Board of Housing, *Report Relative to the Housing Emergency in New York and Buffalo,* table V. By comparison, the rate in early 1987 was just under 2 percent, which is considered precipitously low; 5 percent is considered by law to represent an emergency situation. See William B. Eimicke, "New York State Housing Division Manages the Unmanageable."

20. New York State, State Board of Housing, *Report Relative to the Housing Emergency,* table V.

21. Charity Organization Society of the City of New York, Tenement House Committee, *The Present Status of Tenement House Regulation,*

p. 12. Also see Spencer, "The New York Tenant Organizations," pp. 53–54.

22. "Court To Hear Only 250 Landlord-Tenant Cases a Day Hereafter," *Bronx Home News,* November 2, 1919, p. 16.

23. "Offer To Aid Fight on Building Trust," *New York Times,* September 8, 1920, p. 16.

24. Julian F. Jaffe, *Crusade Against Radicalism,* ch. 7.

25. Zosa Szajkowski, *Jews, Wars, and Communism,* p. 123.

26. "Rent Strikes Largely Due to Bolshevik Propaganda," *Real Estate Record and Builders' Guide* (December 20, 1919), 104:625–626.

27. New York State Legislature, *Laws* (1915), ch. 454.

28. John Irwin Bright, "Housing and Community Planning."

29. "Strong Opposition Develops to Municipal Housing Legislation," *Real Estate Record and Builders' Guide* (January 31, 1920), 105:134.

30. "Architects Say Extra Story on Tenements Is Feasible," *Real Estate Record and Builders' Guide* (September 4, 1920), 106:312.

31. The Competition Program is found in: New York State Legislature. Joint Legislative Committee on Housing and the Reconstruction Commission, *Housing Conditions. Program of Architectural Competition for the Remodeling of a New York City Tenement Block.* For a discussion of the placing of entries, see "Architectural Competition for the Remodeling of a New York City Tenement Block," *Journal of the American Institute of Architects* (May 1920), 8:198–199; "Notes on an Architectural Competition For Remodeling of a Tenement Block," *American Architect* (September 8, 1920), 118:305–314; Andrew Thomas, Robert D. Kohn, "Is It Advisable to Remodel Slum Tenements?" pp. 417–426. For a general history of rehabilitation in New York City, see Alfred Medioli, "Housing Form and Rehabilitation in New York City."

32. John Taylor Boyd, Jr., "Garden Apartments in Cities," part I, pp. 69–73.

33. See the final committee report: New York State Legislature, Joint Legislative Committee on Housing and the Reconstruction Commission, *Report of the Housing Committee.* Notes and other documents from the committee are found with the Clarence S. Stein Papers, Department of Manuscripts and University Archives. Cornell University Libraries, Box 7 and 11.

34. For an overview of New York's suburban extensions by 1850, see Edward K. Spann, *The New Metropolis,* ch. 8.

35. For an overview of the Bronx situation, see Richard Plunz, "Reading Bronx Housing," pp. 67–70.

36. A chronological summary of NYC subway development is given in Stan Fischler, *Uptown, Downtown,* appendix.

37. A description of transit development in Queens can be found in Walter I. Willis, *Queens Borough, New York City,* pp. 5, 112.

38. *Ibid.,* pp. 66–85.

39. Historical sketches of Jackson Heights are found in the Queensboro Corporation, "A History of Jackson Heights," pp. 3, 18–19; Richard Plunz anad Marta Gutman, "The New York 'Ring,'" pp. 36–40.

40. For an early description of mass transit investment patterns, see Ray Stannard Baker, "The Subway 'Deal.'" Also see Henry A. Gordon, *Subway Nickels.*

41. For a list of real estate developers, see Willis, *Queens Borough, New York City,* p. 124.

42. The Queensboro Corporation, *Investment Features of Cooperative Apartment Ownership at Jackson Heights,* pp. 5–6.

43. "Jackson Heights: Will It Be Decay or Renaissance?" *Long Island Press,* April 7, 1975.

44. New York City Department of City Planning, *New Dwelling Units Completed 1921–1972 in New York City* (New York, December 1973).

45. New York City, Department of Parks, *Annual Report* (1914), p. 3.

46. C. Morris Horowitz and Lawrence J. Kaplan, *The Estimated Jewish Population of the New York Area, 1900 to 1975,* table 9.

47. Louis Wirth, "Urbanism as a Way of Life," pp. 1–24.

48. Among interesting recent work on this subject is Marshall Sklare, "Jews, Ethnics, and the American City," pp. 70–77; Deborah Dash Moore, *At Home In America.*

49. For further elaboration of this point, see Plunz, "Reading Bronx Housing," p. 63.

50. Horowitz and Kaplan, *The Estimated Jewish Population, op cit.*

51. New York State, *Report of the Tenement House Committee of 1894,* pp. 11, 256.

52. "Fine Construction for the Bronx," *Real Estate Record and Builders' Guide* (August 28, 1909), 84:384.

53. "New Long Island City Apartments Designed to Meet Popular Demand," *Real Estate*

Record and Builders' Guide (March 24, 1917), 99:392.

54. "Unique Departures in Bronx Apartment House Design," *Real Estate Record and Builders' Guide* (June 14, 1919), 103:791; "Bronx Apartment for 250 Families Will Cost $2,000,000," *Real Estate Record and Builders' Guide* (October 23, 1920), 106:583.

55. Considerable material related to the competition is found in the I. N. Phelps-Stokes Papers, New York Historical Society, box 12 and letter press book no. 17. The original program is no longer extant, but was republished in James Ford, *Slums and Housing,* pp. 915–918. For discussion of placing entries see: "Awards Announced in Tenement Plan Competition," *Real Estate Record and Builders' Guide* (February 11, 1922), 109:182; Frederick L. Ackerman, "The Phelps-Stokes Fund Tenement House Competition;" pp. 76–82; "Tenement House Planning," *The Architectural Forum* (April 1922), 36:157–159.

56. Frederick L. Ackerman, "The Phelps-Stokes Fund Tenement House Competition, pp. 76–82.

57. New York State Legislature, Joint Legislative Committee on Housing and Reconstruction Commission, *Report of the Housing Committee,* pp. 47–52.

58. For a summary of the early LCC work, see Susan Beattie, *A Revolution in London Housing.*

59. See Jean Taricat and Martine Villars, *Le logement à bon marché chronique Paris;* Jean-François Chiffard and Yves Roujon, "Les HBM et la ceinture de Paris."

60. For the evolution of Berlin tenement housing see: Horant Fassbinder, *Berliner Arbeiterviertel 1800–1918* Johann Friedrich Geist, *Das Berliner Meitshaus;* Goerd Peschken, "The Berlin 'Miethaus' and Renovation," pp. 49–54.

61. The English garden city movement is well known and documented. For the Belgian case, see Marcel Smets, *L'avènement de la cité-jardin en Belgique.*

62. John Taylor Boyd, Jr., "Garden Apartments in Cities," part I, p. 122.

63. Erich Haenel and Heinrich Tscharmann, *Das Mietwohnhaus der Neuzeit.* Also see Albert Gessner, *Das deutsche Miethaus.*

64. For example, see W. H. Frohne, "The Apartment House."

65. Helen Fuller Orton, "Jackson Heights. Its History and Growth."

66. Queensboro Corporation, *Garden Apartments, Jackson Heights;* John Taylor Boyd, Jr., "Garden Apartments in Cities," part II, pp. 130–132, 134; and "A New Idea in Apartment Houses," *Queensboro* (May 1917), 4:74.

67. "New Garden Apartments in Queens County, New York City," *Architectural Forum* (June 1919), 30:187–191; and Boyd, "Garden Apartments in Cities," part II, pp. 123, 125–129.

68. Queensboro Corporation, *Chateau Apartments, Jackson Heights Garden Apartments;* Andrew J. Thomas, "The Button-Control Elevator in a New Type of Moderate-Price Apartment Buildings"; and "New Jackson Heights Apartments Will Cost $5,000,000," *Real Estate Record and Builders' Guide* (March 11, 1922), 19:300.

69. "The Garden Homes at Jackson Heights, Long Island," *Architecture and Buildings* (May 1924), 56:55–57; and the Queensboro Corporation, *Investment Features of Cooperative Apartment Ownership at Jackson Heights.*

70. Frank Chouteau Brown, "Tendencies in Apartment House Design," p. 442–443, 445.

71. "Multi-Family House Development," *Real Estate Record and Builders' Guide* (February 9, 1918), 101:180.

72. Brown, "Tendencies in Apartment House Design," pp. 438–442.

73. *Ibid.,* pp. 438, 444.

74. Boyd, "Garden Apartments in Cities," part II, pp. 132–134.

75. Queensboro Corporation, *Cambridge Court, Jackson Heights;* "The Garden Homes at Jackson Heights, Long Island," pp. 55–57; and "Apartment House Group: Two Types, 4 and 5 Room Apartments, Borough of Queens, New York," *Architecture* (June 1921), vol. 43, plate LXXXII.

76. Thomas, "The Button-Control Elevator in a New Type of Moderate-Price Apartment Buildings," pp. 486–490.

77. "Jackson Heights Visit," *New York Times,* July 30, 1922, Sec. viii, p. 1.

78. The Queensboro Corporation, "Special Supplement to Record Visit of Delegates to the International Town, City, and Regional Planning Conference to Jackson Heights."

79. *Noonan Plaza;* Donald Sullivan, *Bronx Art Deco Architecture,* ch. 4.

80. R. W. Sexton, *American Apartment Houses,* pp. 162–163.

81. $4,000,000 Co-operative Project for Washington Heights," *Real Estate Record and Builders' Guide* (April 12, 1924), 113:9; *Hudson*

View Gardens Graphic, Dolores Hayden, *The Grand Domestic Revolution,* pp. 260–261.

82. "Real Estate Market in 1925 Most Active Yet Recorded," *Real Estate Record and Builders' Guide* (January 2, 1926), 117:7; "Tudor City: A Residential Center," *Architecture and Building* (July 1929), 61:202, 219–222, 227; H. Douglas Ives, "The Moderate Priced Apartment Hotel."

83. "Apartments Replacing Manhattan Landmarks," *New York Times,* March 10, 1929, sec. XIII, p. 1; "London Terrace Apartments, New York City," *Architecture and Building* (July 1930), 63:194, plates 205–208; "Recent Apartment Houses in New York," *Architectural Forum* (September 1930), 53:284.

84. Charles Lockwood, *Bricks and Brownstone,* pp. 88–89.

85. "Pomander Walk, New York," *Architecture and Building* (January 1922), 54:2–5; "New York Will Have a 'Pomander Walk' Colony," *New York Times,* April 24, 1921, sec. IX, p. 1; Solomon Asser and Hilary Roe, *Development of the Upper West Side to 1925,* pp. 36–46.

86. "High-Grade Apartment Homes For The Moderate Wage Earner," *New York Evening Post,* June 7, 1919, Sec. ii, p. 10; Boyd, "Garden Apartments in Cities Part I," pp. 64–65, 67; City and Suburban Homes Company, *Twenty-Fifth Annual Report*; and Federal Housing Administration, *Four Decades of Housing with a Limited Dividend Corporation* (Washington, D.C., 1939), p. 42.

87. Boyd, "Garden Apartments in Cities," part I, p. 67; and City and Suburban Homes Company, *Annual Report, 1917.*

88. An overview of this strategy is found in Anthony Jackson, *A Place Called Home,* ch. 2.

89. New York State Legislature, *Laws* (1920), ch. 949, p. 2487; and (1923), ch. 337, pp. 557–558.

90. *Ibid.* (1922), ch. 658, p. 1802.

91. For a general overview of life insurance company activities, see James Marquis, *The Metropolitan Life,* ch. 15; and Robert E. Schultz, *Life Insurance Housing Projects,* ch. 4.

92. John Taylor Boyd, Jr., "A Departure in Housing Finance"; "The Metropolitan Houses in New York City," *Architecture and Building* (May 1924), 56:42–44; "Metropolitan Life's $9-a-Room Housing Project Completed," *Real Estate Record and Builders' Guide* (July 5, 1924), 114:7–8; "How $9-a-Room Homes Were Made Possible" *Real Estate Record and Builders' Guide* (July 12, 1924), 114:5; Walter Stubler, *Comfortable Homes in New York City at $9.00 a Room a Month*; Metropolitan Life Insurance Company, *Just The Place For Your Children. Homes for 2125 Families. The Metropolitan Life's New City*; and New York City Housing Authority Technical Division, *Survey,* pp. 97–101.

93. New York State Legislature, *Laws* (1923), ch. 337, pp. 577–578.

94. *Ibid.* (1926), ch. 823, pp. 1507–1571; and Dorothy Schaffter, *State Housing Agencies,* pp. 251–256.

95. Miscellaneous material on labor movement housing is found in the Robert F. Wagner Labor Archives, New York University; and at the Labor-Management Documentation Center, Martin B. Catherwood Library, Cornell Library.

96. New York City Housing Authority, Technical Division, *Survey,* pp. 137–144; Calvin Trillin, "U.S. Journal: The Bronx: The Coops," p. 49.

97. B. A. Weinrebe, "Jewish Suburban Housing Movement," pp. 5–6. See also United Workers Cooperative Colony, *The Coops;* Trillin, "U.S. Journal," pp. 49–54; Delores Hayden, *The Grand Domestic Revolution,* pp. 255–257.

98. New York City Housing Authority, *Survey,* pp. 145–148.

99. Blanche Lichtenberg, interview. Lichtenberg and her husband were among the initial founding group.

100. New York City Housing Authority, Technical Division, *Survey,* pp. 77–81; New York State, State Board of Housing, *Annual Report, 1929,* pp. 27–29.

101. "More Cooperative Housing in New York," *Cooperation* (December 1928), 14:230–231; Weinrebe, "Jewish Suburban Housing Movement," p. 6.

102. Weinrebe, "Jewish Suburban Housing Movement," p. 7.

103. New York City Housing Authority, Technical Division, *Survey,* pp. 34–44; Sexton, *American Apartment Houses,* pp. 106–107; "Eleven Housing Development," *Architectural Forum* (March 1932), 56:234; New York State, State Board of Housing, *Annual Report, 1929,* and *Annual Report, 1931.* The completion of the later stages is also described in Amalgamated Housing Corporation, *Festival Journal: 20th Anniversary Amalgamated Cooperative Community, 1927–1947* (New York: A and L Consumer Society, 1947); and Amalgamated Hous-

ing Corporation, *30 Years of Amalgamated Cooperative Housing. 1927–1957* (New York: A and L Consumer Society, 1957).

104. Will Herberg, "The Jewish Labor Movement in the United States."

105. Calvin Trillin, "U.S. Journal," p. 49.

106. New York City Housing Authority, Technical Staff, *Survey,* pp. 28–33; George Springsteen, "The Practical Solution"; New York State, State Board of Housing, *Annual Report, 1930,* and *Annual Report, 1931.*

107. "Rockefeller Jr. Saves Needle Union Homes," *New York Herald Tribune,* September 19, 1925, p. 1; "Cooperative Homes for Garment Workers," *New York Times,* April 26, 1925, sec. II, p. 2; "Rockefeller Opens Cooperative Flats," *New York Times,* February 10, 1927, p. 48.

108. New York City Housing Authority, Technical Division, *Survey,* pp. 132–137; Thomas Garden Apartments, Inc., *Thomas Garden Apartments Prospectus;* Thomas Garden Apartments, New York City," *Architecture and Building* (March 1928), 59:111–112, 123–125; "Garden Apartment Building, East 158th Street, New York City," *Architectural Record* (March 1928), 63:273–275.

109. United Workers Cooperative Colony, *The Co-ops;* Herman Jessor, interview with Laurie Lieberman, in relation to coursework for "A4366 Historical Evolution of Housing in New York City," taught by me at Columbia University.

110. Blanche Lichtenberg, interview.

111. "More Cooperative Housing in New York," *Cooperation* (December 1928), 14:230.

112. "Clothing Workers Model Apartments Finished," *Real Estate Record and Builders' Guide* (December 31, 1927), 120:8.

113. "Amalgamated Cooperative Apartments," *Cooperation* (February 1928), 14:22, 23.

114. B. A. Weinrebe, "Jewish Suburban Housing Movement," p. 6.

115. "Cooperative Stores Run by Cooperative Housing Societies," *Cooperation* (June 1928), 14:102–104.

116. Herman Liebman, "Twenty Years of Community Activities"; United Workers Cooperative Colony, *The Coops.*

117. Michael Shallin, "The Story of Our Cooperative Services."

118. The Archive of the Shalom Aleichem Houses at the YIVO Institute for Jewish Research gives a good indication of the scope of this activity.

119. Lichtenberg, interview.

120. Fred L. Lavanburg Foundation, *First Annual Report, Levanburg Homes;* James Ford, *Slums and Housing* 2:902–903.

121. New York City Housing Authority, Technical Division, *Survey,* pp. 23–27; "Eleven Housing Developments," p. 244; New York State, State Board of Housing, *Annual Report, 1931.*

122. "The Paul Laurence Dunbar Apartments, New York City," *Architecture* (January 1929), 59:5–12; Roscoe Conkling Bruce, "The Dunbar Apartment House"; "New York Chapter of Architects Awards Medals for Best Apartment Houses," *Real Estate Record and Builders' Guide* (March 3, 1928), 121:6; *The Paul Laurence Dunbar Apartments and Dunbar National Bank;* New York City Housing Authority, Technical Division, *Survey,* pp. 72–76.

123. Gilbert Osofsky, *Harlem: The Making of a Ghetto,* pp. 155–158.

124. New York City Housing Authority, Technical Division, *Survey,* pp. 45–49; New York State, State Board of Housing, *Annual Report, 1931,* pp. 37–40.

125. Phipps Houses, Inc., *Phipps Garden Apartments;* Isadore Rosenfield, "Phipps Garden Apartments," pp. 112–124, 183–187; Clarence S. Stein, *Toward New Towns for America,* ch. 4.

126. Abraham E. Kazan, "Building and Financing Our Cooperative Homes."

127. "Farband Has Rent Relief Fund," *Cooperation* (May 1933), 19:94.

128. Calvin Trillin, "U.S. Journal," p. 50.

129. An extensive file of strike clippings is contained in the YIVO Institute archives.

130. Trillin, "U.S. Journal," p. 51.

131. By 1966 the news media were beginning to take notice of the decline of the Concourse, and in 1967 connected the decline to outer borough projects such as Co-op City. At the time, these reports were denied by the American Jewish Congress and public interest groups who sought to stabilize the situation. See "City Fights White Exodus from Grand Concourse," *New York Post,* March 9, 1967, p. 2; and David Stoloff, *The Grand Concourse.*

132. Lichtenberg, interview.

6. AESTHETICS AND REALITIES

1. "Modern Apartment at Kew Gardens," *Real Estate Record and Builders' Guide* (August 18, 1917), 100:215.

2. Herman Jessor, interview with Laurie Lieberman.

3. Joachim Schlandt, "Economic and Social Aspects of Council Housing in Vienna"; Manfredo Tafuri, *Vienne la rouge.*

4. *Who Was Who in America,* 5 vols. (Chicago: Marqui's Who's Who, 1973), 5:755.

5. New York State, State Board of Housing, *Annual Report, 1931,* p. 21; Talbot Hamlin, "The Prize-Winning Buildings of 1931," p. 26.

6. John Taylor Boyd, Jr., "A Departure in Housing Finance," p. 136. For other references to the Metropolitan Homes, see chapter 5.

7. See the first corporation brochure: City Housing Corporation, *Your Share in Better Housing.*

8. New York City Housing Authority, Technical Division, *Survey,* pp. 127–131; City Housing Corporation, *Sunnyside and the Housing Problem;* and Clarence S. Stein, *Toward New Towns for America.*

9. City Housing Corporation, *Fourth Annual Report,* p. 2.

10. Lewis Mumford, *The Culture of Cities,* p. 484.

11. Paul Byers, *Small Town in the Big City;* and *New York Times,* February 26, 1933, secs. X–XI, p. 1; February 28, 1933, p. 36; March 19, 1933, secs. XI–XII, p. 3; April 6, 1933, p. 3; April 17, 1933, p. 2; April 18, 1933, p. 14; April 21, 1933, p. 16. Extensive documents on the strike are also found in the Edith Elmer Wood Collection, Avery Architecture and Fine Arts Library, Columbia University, box 55.

12. For an indication of the range of concerns, see Henry Wright, "Outline of a Housing Research Prepared with the Cooperation of the Research Institute of Economic Housing."

13. Isadore Rosenfield, "Phipps Garden Apartments," pp. 112–114.

14. Henry Wright, "The Modern Apartment House," pp. 220–221. A representative record of Wright's research is found in the Henry Wright Papers, Department of Manuscripts and University Archives, Cornell University Libraries.

15. *Ibid.,* pp. 234–235.

16. Henry Atterbury Smith, "Economic Open Stair Communal Dwellings for Industrial Towns."

17. Henry Atterbury Smith, "Garden Apartments for Industrial Workers."

18. Ford, *Slums and Housing,* 2:891, plate 16A; and Open Stair Dwellings Company, *Open Stairs Applied to Industrial Towns and Villages.*

19. "First Elevator Apartment House in Queens," *Real Estate Record and Builders' Guide* (April 28, 1917), 100:583.

20. Frank Chouteau Brown, "Some Recent Apartment Buildings," pp. 262, 264; and "Eleven Housing Developments," *Architectural Forum* (March 1932), 56:236.

21. "Roosevelt Avenue Neighborhood: One of the Fastest Growing Sections of Queens," *Queensboro* (November 1925), 11:642.

22. John T. Moutoux, "The TVA Builds a Town," p. 331.

23. A useful comparative analysis of U.S. and European modernist housing in this respect is developed in Richard Pommer, "The Architecture of Urban Housing in the United States During the Early 1930's."

24. Congrès International d'Architecture Moderne, *Rationelle Bebauungsweisen.* Also see Jose Luis Sert, *Can Our Cities Survive?* Oscar Newman, *CIAM '59 in Otterloo,* pp. 11–16; Auke van der Woud, *Het Nievwe Bouwen.*

25. Museum of Modern Art, *Modern Architecture International Exhibition,* pp. 198–199.

26. Henry Russell Hitchcock, Jr., and Philip Johnson, *The International Style,* p. 38.

27. Museum of Modern Art, *Modern Architecture International Exhibition,* p. 20.

28. *Ibid.,* p. 22.

29. *Ibid.,* p. 20.

30. Hitchcock and Johnson, *The International Style,* ch. 8.

31. Museum of Modern Art, *Modern Architecture International Exhibition,* p. 179.

32. Hitchcock and Johnson, *The International Style,* p. 90.

33. For a contemporary account of this early movement, see "The Housing Movement," *Housing Betterment* (February 1912), 1:1.

34. For a survey of pre–World War I internationalism in the planning and design professions, see Anthony Sutcliffe, *Towards the Planned City,* ch. 6.

35. For an overview of these developments in the United States, see M. Christine Boyer, *Dreaming the Rational City,* chs. 3, 4.

36. Hitchcock and Johnson, *The International Style,* p. 90.

37. Tony Garnier, *Une cité industrielle.* Also see Dora Wiebenson, *Tony Garnier and the Cité Industrielle.*

38. Henry Wright, *Rehousing Urban Amer-*

ica, pp. 130–132; and Matilde Buffa Rivolta and Augusto Rossari, *Alexander Klein.*

39. Jean Labadie, "Les cathédrales de la cité moderne," and "À la recherche d'homme scientifique," pp. 547–556.

40. Le Corbusier, "Trois rappels à MM. les Architects," and *Urbanisme,* ch. 11.

41. "Maquette d'habitations à bon marché," *L'Architecture Vivante* (Fall and Winter 1927), plate 36.

42. The genesis of these schemes is shown in work included with the Gropius issue of "L'oeuvre architecturale de Walter Gropius," *L'Architecture Vivante* (Fall and Winter 1931), pp. 6–9, 14–15, 18–20, and plates 3–6, 10–17.

43. This study was first published in English in 1935; Walter Gropius, *The New Architecture and the Bauhaus,* pp. 72–73.

44. The most complete description can be found in Siegfried Giedion, *Walter Gropius,* p. 80, figs. 248–253.

45. "Portfolio of Apartment Houses," *The Architectural Record* (March 1932), 71:194–195; *Modern Architecture International Exhibition,* pp. 154–155; and "A Model Housing Development for Chrystie-Forsyth Streets," *Real Estate Record and Builders' Guide* (February 12, 1932), 79:6. Also see discussion of the project in: Robert A. M. Stern, *George Howe: Toward A Modern American Architecture,* pp. 101–104; Richard Pommer, "The Architecture of Urban Housing in the United States During the Early 1930s," pp. 250–252; Christian Hubert and Lindsay Stamm Shapiro, *William Lescaze,* pp. 76–77; Robert A. M. Stern, Gregory Gilmartin, Thomas Mellins, *New York 1930. Architecture and Urbanism Between the Two World Wars,* pp. 438–439; Lorraine Welling Lanmon, *William Lescaze, Architect,* pp. 83–85.

46. Plans and section from "Portfolio of Apartment Houses," pp. 194–195.

47. "St. Marks Tower," *Architectural Record* (January 1930), 67:1–4.

48. The towers were inserted in Broadacre City quite early in its development. See Frank Lloyd Wright, "Broadacre City."

49. "Lexington Terrace," *L'Architecture Vivante* (Spring and Summer 1930), pp. 70–71; Pfeiffer, Bruce Books, Yukio Futagawa, eds., *Frank Lloyd Wright, 1867–1859,* 1:80–81; 224–229.

50. A representation of this moment is found in "N.Y.C. of the Future," *Creative Art* (August, 1931), 9:128–171.

51. Hugh Ferris, *The Metropolis of Tomorrow.*

52. Herbert R. Houghton in "Experienced Observers Analyze Market Prospects," p. 7.

53. A typical early example is described in "First Small Suite Apartments Planned for West 86th Street," *Real Estate Record and Builders' Guide* (July 19, 1924), 114:10.

54. See the following exchange: "The Mayor's Discrimination Unjust," *Real Estate Record and Builders' Guide* (November 20, 1920), 106:701–702; and "Best Use of Terra Cotta," *Real Estate Record and Builders' Guide* (December 11, 1920), 106:798.

55. Joseph McGoldrick, Seymour Graubard, and Raymond Horowitz, *Building Regulation in New York City,* pp. 5–9; "Apartment Hotels Outside Tenement House Law," *Real Estate Record and Builders' Guide* (December 24, 1927), 120:7–8; and "Authorities Act To Bar Cooking in Hotel Apartments," *Real Estate Record and Builders' Guide* (October 16, 1926), 118:10.

56. "Upper Fifth Avenue Opens to Tall Apartments," *New York Times,* April 2, 1924, p. 1; "Plans To Transform 'Millionaire Row' Getting Under Way," *Real Estate Record and Builders' Guide* (April 26, 1924), 113:7.

57. "Brooklyn's First 12-Story Apartment Houses for Prospect Park Plaza Section," *Real Estate Record and Builders' Guide* (February 27, 1926), 117:9.

58. "Tallest Apartment House Project Planned for Park Avenue," *Real Estate Record and Builders' Guide* (August 30, 1924), 114:8.

59. "58-Story Apartment Hotel Planned for Tudor City," *Real Estate Record and Builders' Guide* (March 24, 1928), 121:10.

60. "World's Tallest Hotel Is Nearing Completion," *Real Estate Record and Builders' Guide* (May 1, 1926), 117:11; "The Ritz Apartment Hotel, New York City," *Architecture and Building* (December 1926), 58:128–129, plates 232–236; Steven Ruttenbaum, *Mansions in the Clouds.*

61. New York State Assembly, *Report to the Legislature of the Temporary Commission To Examine and Revise the Tenement House Law,* pp. 1–152, plates I–XIII.

62. "Commissioner Martin Analyzes Construction of Tenements Since 1902," *Real Estate Record and Builders' Guide* (May 28, 1927), 119:9; and Martin C. Walter, "Reports 83,459 Vacancies in Tenement Houses," *Real Estate*

Record and Builders' Guide (February 4, 1928), 121:10.

63. The magazine *Housing Betterment* closely monitored the "bootleg hotel" issue. For example, see "To Cook or Not To Cook: Where Law Evasion Ends" (May 1927), 16:69–82; "Too Many Cooks Spoil the Graft" (June 1929), 18:85–88; "Law Evasion Made Easy: The New York Apartment Hotel Issue" (December 1927), 16:310–315. Also see "Apartment Hotels Outside Tenement House Law," *Real Estate Record and Builders' Guide* (December 24, 1927), 120:7–8.

64. New York State Legislature, *Laws* (1929), ch. 713, pp. 1663–1756.

65. Arthur Gross, "The Multiple Dwelling Law of New York."

66. "San Remo Towers, New York City, Emery Roth, Architect," *Architectural Record* (March 1931), 69:212; "San Remo Apartment House, 145 Central Park West, New York City, Emery Roth, Architect," *Architecture and Building* (October 1930), 62:283, 289.

67. Ruttenbaum, *Mansions in the Clouds,* pp. 141–144.

68. Diana Agrest, ed., *A Romance with the City,* pp. 76–79; Ruttenbaum, *Mansions in the Clouds,* pp. 144–145.

69. "Portfolio of Apartment Houses," *Architectural Record* (March 1932), 71:190–191; Agrest, *A Romance with the City,* pp. 80–84.

70. "Air Conditioning Methods," *Real Estate Record and Builders' Guide* (April 19, 1930), 125:8.

71. Andrew Alpern, *Apartments for the Affluent,* pp. 114–115; Ruttenbaum, *Mansions in the Clouds,* pp. 127–133.

72. W. A. Swanberg, *Citizen Hearst,* p. 487, cited in Ruttenbaum, *Mansions in the Clouds,* p. 144.

73. Ruttenbaum, *Mansions in the Clouds,* p. 144.

74. Jacques Delamarre was a native American in spite of his French name. He completed an extraordinary body of Deco-Moderne work for Chanin. See Dan Klein, "The Chanin Building, New York."

75. "Room Count as Standard for Apartment Rentals Obsolete, Chanin Declares," *Real Estate Record and Builders' Guide* (October 17, 1931), 128:7–8.

76. "Apartment House of the Future Forecase by Electric Show," *Real Estate Record and Builders' Guide* (October 24, 1925), 116:10.

77. "Apartment House, 25 East 83rd Street, New York City," *Architectural Forum* (December 1938), 69:429–432; "Air Conditioned Apartments Placed on New York Market," *Real Estate Record and Builders' Guide* (May 1938), 141:25–29.

78. "Social Changes Create Small Apartment Demand," *New York Times,* March 10, 1929, sec. XIII, p. 1.

79. Otto V. St. Whitelock, "Planning Manhattan Homes for the Average Wage-Earner," p. 7.

80. Clarence Stein, *Toward New Towns for America,* frontispiece.

81. The significance of the domestic garage is discussed by J. B. Jackson, "The Domestication of the Garage," *The Necessity For Ruins,* pp. 103–111.

82. The Queensboro Corporation, *English Garden Homes in Jackson Heights*; Richard Plunz and Marta Gutman, "The New York 'Ring,'" pp. 40, 42.

83. "Building Boom in Borough of the Bronx Is Breaking All Records," *New York Times,* March 30, 1924, sec. IX, p. 2; Richard Plunz, "Reading Bronx Housing," pp. 57–58.

84. Plunz, "Reading Bronx Housing," p. 58.

85. Plunz and Gutman, "The New York 'Ring,'" pp. 39, 40, 41.

86. *Ibid.,* pp. 39, 41.

87. "'Forest Close,' Forest Hills, Long Island, N.Y., Robert Tappan, Architect," *Architectural Record* (March 1928), 63:232–235; Edith E. Elton, *Forest Close in Relation to Suburban Planning in England and America.*

88. "Fordham Road as a Business Center," *New York Times,* March 30, 1924, sec. IX, p. 2.

89. "Old Bronx Areas Must Be Rebuilt," *New York Times,* February 22, 1925, sec. X, p. 2.

90. City Housing Corporation, *Radburn Garden Homes*; City Housing Corporation, *Fourth Annual Report,* pp. 6–9), *Fifth Annual Report,* pp. 1–8, and *Sixth Annual Report,* pp. 1–11; Louis Brownlow, "Building for the Motor Age," ch. 15; and Stein, *Toward New Towns for America,* ch. 2.

91. Regional Plan of New York and Its Environs, "The Regional Highway System," pp. 210–305.

7. GOVERNMENT INTERVENTION

1. John H. Gries and James Ford, eds., *The President's Conference on Home Building and*

Home Ownership; Ford, *Slums and Housing*, 1:209–211.

2. Brief summaries of U.S. government housing programs may be found in Housing and Home Finance Agency, *Chronology of Major Federal Actions Affecting Housing and Community Development* (Washington, D.C.: GPO, 1963); and *Housing Activities of the Federal Government* (Washington, D.C.: GPO, 1952).

3. New York State, State Board of Housing, *Annual Report, 1934*, p. 17; a complete list of PWA projects nationwide is given in Ford, *Slums and Housing*, 2:718–719.

4. A brief summary of PWA activity is found in Robert Fisher, *Twenty Years of Public Housing*, pp. 82–91.

5. New York State Legislature, *Laws* (1934), ch. 4, pp. 13–25.

6. Schaffer, *State Housing Agencies*, pp. 268–278.

7. James Ford, *Slums and Housing*, 2:640.

8. Rosalie Genevro, "Site Selection and the New York City Housing Authority," pp. 334–352.

9. For the Andrew Thomas Proposal, see "A Proposal for Rebuilding the Lower East Side," *Real Estate Record and Builders' Guide* (May 6, 1933), 131:3–5; "New Plan for Garden Homes in Manhattan Slum Area," *New York Times*, May 7, 1933, Sec. X and XI, p. 1; For the John J. Klaber proposal, see John Klaber, "An Economic Housing Plan for the Chrystie-Forsyth Area," pp. 6–8; For the Howe and Lescaze proposal, see "Portfolio of Apartment Houses," *Architectural Record* (March 1932), pp. 194–195; "A Model Housing Development for Chrystie-Forsyth Streets," *Real Estate Record and Builders' Guide* (February 12, 1932), 79:6. For the Sloan and Robertson proposal, see "N.Y. Architects Apply for Federal Loan on Housing Project," *Architectural Record* (July 1933), 74:13–14; "$12,789,708 Housing on East Side Voted Over Cheaper Plan," *New York Times*, July 6, 1933, p. 1, 15. For the Holden, McLaughlin and Associates proposal, see Arthur C. Holden, "Facing Realities in Slum Clearance," p. 79. For the Jardine, Murdock, and Wright proposal, see Jardine, Murdock, and Wright, *Christie-Forsyth Street Housing*. For the Maurice Deutsch proposal, see "Submits Novel Plan For East Side Housing," *New York Times*, June 18, 1933, Sec. 11 and 12, p. 2.

10. Arthur C. Holden, "A Review of Proposals for the Chrystie–Forsyth Area," pp. 7–9; "Chrystie-Forsyth Development Plans Stim-ulated by Move to Mortgage City's Fee," *Real Estate Record and Builders' Guide* (April 9, 1932), 129:5–6; "LaGuardia Scraps Chrystie St. Plans," *New York Times*, February 1, 1934.

11. Robert A. Caro, *The Power Broker*, pp. 375–378.

12. New York City Housing Authority, *First Houses*. General descriptions of all NYCHA projects covered in this chapter may be found in: New York City Housing Authority, *Tenth Annual Report;* American Institute of Architects, New York Chapter, *The Significance of the Work of the New York Housing Authority.*

13. Langdon Post, *The Challenge of Housing*, ch. 6; Peter Marcuse, "The Beginning of Public Housing in New York," pp. 356–365.

14. "Model Housing in Woodside Started with Aid of Federal Funds," *New York Times*, January 28, 1934, secs. X–XI, p. 1. New York State, State Board of Housing, *Annual Report, 1934*, and *Annual Report, 1935.*

15. New York State, State Board of Housing, *Annual Report, 1934*, and *Annual Report, 1935;* "Knickerbocker Village," *The Architectural Forum* (December 1934), 61:458–464. Albert Mayer, "A Critique of Knickerbocker Village," pp. 5–10.

16. The competition program is found in an untitled pamphlet in the Phelps–Stokes Collection, Schomberg Center for Research in Black Culture, New York Public Library, box 9, A-50-A-75. The collection contains other material on the competition. For discussion of the placing entries, see "Garden Space Stressed in Low Cost Housing Design," *Real Estate Record and Builders' Guide* (June 3, 1933), 131:5; "Slum Block Which Won Phelps-Stokes Prize," *New York Herald Tribune*, June 13, 1933, Sec. X, p. 2; James Ford, *Slums and Housing*, fig. 127, plate 22.

17. Henry Saylor, "The Hillside Housing Development"; "Hillside Homes," *American Architect* (February 1936), 148:17–33.

18. Flagg's problematic involvement with the company is recounted in: Mardges Bacon, *Ernest Flagg. Beaux Arts Architect and Urban Reformer*, ch. 8. New York City Housing Authority, Technical Division, *Survey*, pp. 55–59; "Portfolio of Apartment Houses," *Architectural Record* (March 1932), 71:167–169.

20. *Flagg Court*, rental brochure; "Apartment Houses at Bay Ridge, Brooklyn," *Architectural Forum* (May 1937), 66: 414–415; New York City Housing Authority, Technical Divi-

sion, *Survey* pp. 55–59; Mardges Bacon, *Ernest Flagg*, pp. 261–265.

21. U.S. Federal Emergency Administration of Public Works, Housing Division, *Harlem River Houses*; and Talbot Hamlin, "New York Housing: Harlem River Houses and Williamsburg Houses." Also see James Sanders and Roy Strickland, "Harlem River Houses"; Peter Marcuse, "The Beginnings of Public Housing in New York," pp. 369–375.

22. U.S. Treasury Department, "Treasury Artists Working on PWA Housing Projects," *Bulletin No. 9: Treasury Department Art Projects* (March-May 1936), p. 14; and Olin Dows, "The New Deal's Treasury Art Program," pp. 28–29.

23. United States Federal Administration of Public Works, Housing Division. *Williamsburg Houses*; Talbot Hamlin, "Harlem River Houses and Williamsburg Houses," pp. 281–292; and *American Architect* (December 1935), 47:53; Peter Marcuse, "The Beginnings of Public Housing in New York," pp. 365–369.

24. Statistical data for all New York City Housing Authority projects may be found in New York City Housing Authority, *Project Data.*

25. Hamlin, "Harlem River and Williamsburg Houses," p. 286.

26. Lewis Mumford, *Roots of Contemporary American Architecture*, p. 420.

27. United States Federal Emergency Administration of Public Works, *Urban Housing*, p. 2.

28. Frederick Ackerman, "Note on New Site and Unit Plans."

29. For a general view of the Rockefellers' complicity in remolding cultural life in New York, see Russell Lynes, *Good Old Modern*; Edgar B. Young, *Lincoln Center.*

30. Frederick Ackerman and William Ballard, *Survey of Twenty-three Low Rental Housing Projects.*

31. New York City Housing Authority, "Proposed Low-Rental Housing Projects."

32. Preliminary schemes are recorded in: New York City Housing Authority, *Model Exhibit Showing Use of Urban Areas for Multi-Family Habitations,* plates 38 and 39. Also see Richard Pommer, "The Architecture of Urban Housing in the United States During the Early 1930s," p. 253.

33. Objections were recorded in Wilfred S. Lewis, "Architects Contracts."

34. The circumstances of this change in approaches is discussed further in Richard Pommer, "The Architecture of Urban Housing in the United States During the Early 1930's."

35. Museum of Modern Art, *Art in Our Time,* p. 329.

36. Frederick L. Ackerman, "Williamsburg, a Comment—Preliminary Submission of Elevations."

37. The competition program is found in: New York City Housing Authority, *Program of Competition for Qualification of Architects.* For discussion of the placing entries, see New York City Housing Authority, *Competition: Scrapbook of Placing Entries.* Other material related to the competition is found in the Fiorello H. La Guardia Archives, La Guardia Community College.

38. "Slum Clearance Housing Proposal: District Number 5, Manhattan," *Architectural Record* (March 1935), 77:220–223.

39. Bauer's lengthy discussion of the *Zielenbau* first brought that particular concept into the popular planning lexicon in the United States. See Catherine Bauer, *Modern Housing,* pp. 178–182.

40. Frederick Ackerman and William Ballard, *A Note on Site and Unit Planning.*

41. A record exists of the models and plans in: New York City Housing Authority, *Model Exhibit Showing Use of Urban Areas for Multi-Family Habitations.*

42. Ackerman and Ballard, *Survey of Twenty-three Low Rental Housing Projects,* pp. iii–iv.

43. See United States Federal Emergency Administration of Public Works, *Urban Housing,* pp. 25, viii.

44. "Higher Housing for Lower Rents," *Architectural Forum* (December 1934), 61:421–434.

45. Clarence Stein, "The Price of Slum Clearance," p. 157.

46. For the Housing Authority Technical Division proposal, see L. E. Cooper, "$6 Rentals Held Feasible on the East Side." *New York* For the Andrew Thomas Proposal, see "Architect Says His Plan for East Side Would Stamp Out World's Best Known Slums," *New York Herald Tribune,* May 7, 1933, Sec. 5, p. 2; "A Proposal For Rebuilding the Lower East Side," *Real Estate Record and Builders' Guide* (May 6, 1933), 131:3–5. For the Howe and Lescaze proposal, see Christian Hubert and Lindsay Stamm Shapiro, *William Lescaze;* Richard Pommer, "The Architecture of Urban Housing in the United States During the Early 1930s," p. 252. For the Holden, McLaughlen, and As-

sociates proposal, see Arthur C. Holden, "Facing Realities in Slum Clearance." pp. 75–82. For the John Taylor Boyd, Jr. proposal, see Peter A. Stone, "Rutgers Town Considered From a Social Viewpoint;" Rutgers Town Corporation, *Rutgers Town: Low Cost Housing Plan for the Lower East Side.*

47. Fred F. French, "394,000 Persons Eager to Live Downtown, French Survey Shows," pp. 1–3.

48. Rutgers Town Corporation, *Rutgers Town. Low Cost Housing Plan for the Lower East Side.* An earlier and smaller version of the same project was proposed in 1932: Robert W. Aldrich Roger, *Low Cost Housing Plan for the Lower East Side.*

49. "Ickes Bars Loan to Two Projects Here for Lack of Funds," *New York Times,* June 13, 1934, p. 4.

50. "Higher Housing for Lower Rents," p. 421.

51. Rutgers Town Corporation, *Rutgerstown and Queenstown: Low Cost Housing Projects for the Average Man.* Town Corporation, 1933).

52. Calls City Housing a Racket," *New York Sun,* March 27, 1939, p. 6.

53. A history of the Corlears Hook Planning is outlined in: Ann L. Buttenweiser, "Shelter For What And For Whom? pp. 391–413.

54. U.S. Federal Emergency Administration of Public Works, Housing Division, *Unit Plans.*

55. "Housing Number," *Architectural Record* (March 1935), 77:148–189.

56. "A Typical Project Illustrating Use of Block Models for Grouping of Unit Types," *Architectural Record* (March 1935), 77:154.

57. Henry Wright, "Are We Ready for American Housing Advance?" p. 311.

58. See entries under "Triborough Bridge" and "Triborough Bridge and Tunnel Authority" in Robert Caro, *The Power Broker.*

59. An excellent overview of this campaign is developed in John P. Dean, *Home Ownership: Is It Sound?* Also see Kenneth Jackson, *Crabgrass Frontier,* chs. 10, 11.

60. New York City Housing Authority, *Must We Have Slums?* p. 1.

61. Dean, *Home Ownership,* ch. 4.

62. "PWA Clears a Synthetic Slum," *Architectural Forum* (June 1937), 66:542; "The Second New York Own Your Own Home Exposition," *Building Age* (June 1920), 42:50–52.

63. Dean, *Home Ownership,* ch. 2; and "Publicizing the Model House," *Architectural Forum* (December 1937), 67:521–531, 552, 554, 556, 558. For an overview of the emergence of modern consumer advertising see: Roland Marchand, *Advertising the American Dream.*

64. John Chusman Fistere, "Tradition-Innovation"; and Henrietta Murdock, "The House of Tomorrow."

65. "Rus in Urbe," *Architectural Forum* (September 1934), 61:5.

66. Dean, *Home Ownership,* pp. 42–43.

67. "Prefabricated National Houses," *Architectural Forum* (February 1936), 64:137–138; "A House for Today," *New York Herald Tribune,* July 26, 1936), p. 14; "National Houses, Inc., Begins Production," *Architectural Record* (July 1936), 80:71; "The House of the Modern Age," *Architectural Forum* (September 1936), 65:254.

68. Small house issue, *Architectural Forum* (October 1935, November 1936, April 1937), vol. 63.

69. "Green Acres, a Residential Community," *Architectural Record* (October 1936), 80:285–286.

70. Dean, *Home Ownership,* p. 51.

71. One such campaign is described *Ibid.,* p. 124.

72. "G.E. Does It," *Fortune* (March 1942), 25:160.

73. G.E. competition issue: "A House for Modern Living," *Architectural Forum* (April 1935), 62:64–69.

74. "Publicizing the Model House," *Architectural Forum* (December 1937), 67:525–526.

75. "Small House Competition Sponsored by *Ladies Home Journal,*" *Architectural Forum* (October 1938), 69:275–294.

76. "American Gas Association Competition," *Architectural Forum* (July 1938), 69:2–74; and "American Gas Association Competition for Completed Houses," *Architectural Forum* (October 1939), 71:313–338.

77. Frank Dorman, "Managers Are Mayors of Small Cities," p. 18.

78. United States Congress, October 11, 1974, p. 35278.

79. For a survey description of these and many other exhibits which followed the same theme, see *"Building the World of Tomorrow": Official Guidebook of the World's Fair, 1939* (New York: Exposition Publications, 1939). Also see "Town of Tomorrow," *Architectural Forum* (April 1938), 68:287–308; The Queens Mu-

seum, *Dawn of a New Day, The New York World's Fair, 1939/40.*

80. A summary description of the beginning of the USHA program may be found in Fisher, *Twenty Years of Public Housing,* pp. 6–8, 92–125.

81. *Ibid.,* p. 8.

82. Schaffter, *State Housing Agencies,* pp. 251–256.

83. United States Housing Authority, *Summary of General Requirements and Minimum Standards for USHA-Aided Projects,* secs. 7, 8, 9.

84. These figures were calculated from New York City Housing Authority, *Project Data.*

85. Robert Moses, *Housing and Recreation.*

86. This episode was described in extensive detail in Caro, *The Power Broker,* pp. 610–612.

87. Carol Anonovici, W. F. R. Ballard, Henry S. Churchill, Carl Feiss, William Lescaze, Albert Mayer, Lewis Mumford, Ralph Walker, "Moses Turns Housing Expert." pp. 2–3. An adversarial relationship soon developed with progressive professionals, see Robert Moses, "Long-Haired Planners. Common Sense vs. Revolutionary Theories," pp. 16–17; Joseph Hudnut, "A Long-Haired Reply to Moses," p. 16.

88. United States Housing Authority, *Bulletin No. 11 on Planning and Policy Procedure.*

89. U.S. Federal Public Housing Authority, *Public Housing Design.*

90. U.S. Federal Housing Administration, *Architectural Planning and Procedure for Rental Housing;* see also U.S. Federal Housing Administration, *Rental Housing as Investment.*

91. United States Congress, *Housing Act,* sec. 15–5.

92. New York City Housing Authority, *Project Data.*

93. United States Housing Authority, *Summary of General Requirements and Minimum Standards for USHA-Aided Projects,* sec. 0.

94. An interesting official exposition of this argument may be found in Albert C. Shire, "Housing Standards and the USHA Program."

95. "A Lesson in Cost Reduction," *Architectural Forum* (November 1938), 69:405–408; New York City Housing Authority, *Fifth Annual Report,* pp. 6–14.

96. Preliminary schemes are recorded in: New York City Housing Authority, *New York City Housing Authority, 1934–1936;* New York City Housing Authority, *Model Exhibit Showing Use of Urban Areas for Multi-Family Hab-*

itations, plates 45 and 46. Also see: Richard Pommer, "The Architecture of Urban Housing in the United States During the Early 1930's," p. 356.

97. Richard Pommer, "The Architecture of Urban Housing in the United States During the Early 1930s," p. 256; New York City Housing Authority, *Fifth Annual Report,* pp. 6–14. Cost reductions for Queensbridge and other prewar projects are analyzed in New York City Housing Authority, *Large-Scale Low Rent Housing.*

98. The preliminary scheme is recorded in: Frederick Ackerman and William Ballard, *A Note On Site And Unit Planning,* p. 40; New York City Housing Authority, *Model Exhibit Showing Use of Urban Areas for Multi-Family Habitations,* plate 44. Also see Richard Pommer, "The Architecture of Urban Housing in the United States During the Early 1930s," p. 356.

99. New York City Housing Authority, *Vladeck Houses.*

100. New York City Housing Authority, *Clason Point Gardens,* pp. 2–3.

101. Le Corbusier, *Quand les cathédrales étaient blanches.*

102. "East River Houses: A High Density Project," *Pencil Points* (September 1940), 21:555–566; New York City Housing Authority, *East River Houses.*

103. Harold R. Sleeper, *A Realistic Approach to Private Investment in Urban Redevelopment.*

104. See map in New York City, Mayor's Committee on Slum Clearance, *Harlem Slum Clearance Plan.*

8. PATHOLOGY OF PUBLIC HOUSING

1. A summary of wartime programs may be found in U.S. Housing and Home Finance Agency, *Chronology of Major Federal Actions Affecting Housing and Community Development;* and Citizens Housing Council of New York, *Wartime Housing in the New York Metropolitan Area.*

2. Apartments Rented to Servicemen's Families," *New York City Housing Authority News* (November 1943), no. 17.

3. New York City Housing Authority, *Wallabout Houses,* p. 3.

4. "Architects' Emergency Committee," *Journal of the American Institute of Architects* (November 1931), 3:14; and "Unemployment

Relief in New York," *Journal of the American Institute of Architects* (February 1932), 4:29.

5. Louis La Beaume, "The Federal Building Program."

6. Theodore Rohdenburg, *A History of the School of Architecture, Columbia University*, pp. 35–40; Rosemarie Haap Bletter, "Modernism Rears Its Head."

7. "Architects' Craft and Code of Practice," *New York Times*, August 7, 1953, p. 5. Some documents pertaining to the architect membership of the FAECT are found with the Housing Study Guild Records, Department of Manuscripts and University Archives, Cornell University Libraries, folders 2–17 and 2–18.

8. "FAECT Four Years Old," *Technical America* (September 1939), 4:10.

9. "New York Architects in First 'Sit-Down Strike,'" *Architectural Record* (August 1936), 80:81; and "Jules Korchien Among Ten Fired for Organization," *Bulletin of the Federation of Architects, Engineers, Chemists, and Technicians* (July 1936), 3:2.

10. FAECT and AGA Win Big Increase in New York," *Architectural Record* (September 1936), 80:171.

11. Simon Breines, "'Designers of Shelter in America.'"

12. A brief description of post-Bauhaus activity in the U.S. may be found in Hans Wingler, *Bauhaus in America*.

13. Herbert Bayer, *Bauhaus, 1919–1928*.

14. Serge Chermayeff, "Telesis: The Birth of a Group."

15. Miscellaneous material on the architects' committees of the National Council of Soviet-American Friendship and the Committee of the Arts, Sciences and Professions may be found in the Chermayeff Papers Archive, Avery Architectural and Fine Arts Library, Columbia University.

16. Oscar Newman, *CIAM '59 in Otterloo*, pp. 11–16; Auke van der Woud, *Het Nieuwe Bouwen*.

17. Miscellaneous material on the American chapters of the Congrès Internationaux d'Architecture Moderne (CIAM) and on the American Society of Planners and Architects may be found with the Chermayeff ASPA papers, Widner Library, Harvard University.

18. "G.E. Does It," *Fortune* (March 1942), 25:165.

19. *Ladies Home Journal* (January, July, September, October, November 1944), vol. 61; (January, February, March, April, May, June,

July, August, September, November 1945), vol. 62; and (January, March, April, May, June, September, November 1946), vol. 63.

20. For an overview of the cultural context of Frank Lloyd Wright's urbanism, see Giorgio Ciucci, "The City in Agrarian Ideology and Frank Lloyd Wright," in Giorgio Ciucci, Francesco Dal Co, Mario Manieri–Elia, Manfredo Tafuri, *The American City From the Civil War to the New Deal*, pp. 293–376.

21. Museum of Modern Art, *Tomorrow's Small House*, p. 12.

22. *Ladies Home Journal* (February, March, July, September, November 1949), vol. 66; and (March, April, May, October 1950), vol. 67.

23. Serge Chermayeff and Christopher Alexander, *Community and Privacy*.

24. Robert E. Schultz, *Life Insurance Housing Projects*, pp. 30–39.

25. An overview of Metropolitan Life's plans was published in "New Housing Units for 12,000 Families," *New York Times*, October 21, 1945, p. 44.

26. "Metropolitan's Parkchester," *Architectural Forum* (December 1939), 71:412–426.

27. "Stuyvesant Town: Rebuilding a Blighted City Area," *Engineering News-Record* (February 5, 1948), 140:73–96; Arthur R. Simon, *Stuyvesant Town, U.S.A.*; and "Stuyvesant Town: Borough of Manhattan, New York City," *Architect and Engineer* (August 1948), 174:27–29.

28. "News," *Architectural Forum* (February, 1945), 82:7–8; "New Metropolitan Housing Project," *Architectural Record* (February, 1945), 97:116; "Gardens to Bloom on 'Gas House' Site," *New York Times*, January 4, 1945, p. 21.

29. An account of the hearings may be found in *CHC Housing News* (June–July 1943), pp. 1–5.

30. "Housing Project To Rise in Harlem," *New York Times*, September 18, 1944, p. 21; and "Metropolitan Life Plans Large Scale Housing Project for Harlem," *CHC Housing News* (September 1944), p. 4. Also see: Carlyle Douglas, "Ex-Residents Fondly Recall 'Island in Harlem'."

31. James Baldwin, "Fifth Avenue, Uptown," p. 73. Baldwin's view of the project was sharply refuted by the chairman of the Riverton Tenants Association. See Richard P. Jones, "Up the Riverton," p. 16.

32. Two excellent critiques of Stuyvesant Town were published in *Task* (1946), no. 4; Simon Breines, "Stuyvesant Town"; and Henry

Reed, "The Investment Policy of Metropolitan Life"; arguments favorable to Stuyvesant Town were developed by Tracy B. Augur, "An Analysis of the Plan of Stuyvesant Town."

33. "Stuyvesant Town Approved by Board," *New York Times,* June 4, 1943, p. 23; editorial reaction, June 5, 1943, p. 14. For a more general discussion of this problem, see: Kathryn Close, "New Homes With Insurance Dollars," pp. 450–454.

34. A lengthy discussion of these policies may be found in: Simon, *Stuyvesant Town.* Also see Algernon D. Black, "Negro Families in Stuyvesant Town," pp. 502–503; Joseph B. Robinson, "The Story of Stuyvesant Town," *Nation* (June 2, 1951), 172:516–518.

35. Lewis Mumford, "Stuyvesant Town Revisited," p. 71.

36. Schultz, *Life Insurance Housing Projects,* tables 8 and 9.

37. "Park Apartments," *Architectural Forum* (May 1943), 78:138–45.

38. "Stuyvesant Six: A Development Study," *Pencil Points* (June 1944), 25:66–70.

39. Henry Aaron, *Shelter and Subsidies,* p. 54.

40. *Ibid.,* table 10–1.

41. For a discussion of the true cost of the automobile, see Ezra J. Mishan, *The Costs of Economic Growth.* Also see James A. Bush, "Would America Have Been Automobilized in a Free Market?"

42. A summary of issues surrounding passage of the WET bill are found in *Congressional Digest* (November 1946), vol. 280. For an indication of the strength of opposition see: Lee F. Johnson, "How They Licked the TEW Bill," pp. 445–449.

43. Resolution dated January 19, 1946, in Chermayeff ASPA papers, Widner Library, Harvard University.

44. "An Emergency Housing Program," *Journal of the American Institute of Architects* (January 1948), 9:4–6.

45. Carl Koch, "What Is the Attitude of the Young Practitioner Toward the Profession?" pp. 264–269.

46. New York City Housing Authority, *Thirteenth Annual Report,* p. 2.

47. "Public Housing, Anticipating New Law, Looks at New York's High Density Planning Innovations," *Architectural Forum* (June 1949), 90:87–89.

48. New York City, Committee on Slum Clearance Plans, *North Harlem Slum Clear-ance Plan* and *Williamsburg Slum Clearance Plan* (New York, 1951).

49. Le Corbusier, "A Plan for St. Die"; and "Le Corbusier's Living Unit," *Architectural Forum* (January 1950), 92:88–89.

50. Jose Luis Sert, *Can Our Cities Survive?*

51. J. Tyrwhitt, J. L. Sert, and E. N. Rogers, *CIAM 8: The Heart of the City.*

52. Caro, "Mayor's Slum Clearance Committee," in *The Power Broker.*

53. "Post-War Housing Includes No Stores," *New York Times,* October 7, 1944, p. 15.

54. Richard Roth, "Baruch Houses: $30,000,000 Worth of Slum Clearance." New York City Housing Authority, *Baruch Houses and Playground.*

55. Oscar Newman, *Defensible Space: Crime Prevention Through Urban Design,* pp. 39–49.

56. A summary of early NYCHA tenant selection procedures is found in New York City Housing Authority, *Toward the End To Be Achieved,* pp. 12–13.

57. For an overview of tenant union activity in limited dividend and public housing see: Joel Schwartz, "Tenant Unions in New York Low-Rent Housing, 1933–1949," pp. 414–443.

58. Catherine Bauer, "Facts for Housing Program."

59. Catherine Bauer, "The Dreary Deadlock of Public Housing," pp. 140–143.

60. Caro, "Mayor's Slum Clearance Committee," in *The Power Broker.*

61. J. Anthony Panuch, *Building a Better New York,* p. 35.

62. Frank Kristof, *Changes in New York City's Housing Status,* p. 8.

63. "City Population Trails Suburbs," *New York Times,* February 23, 1961, p. 29.

64. "66% in City Area Moved in 1950's," *New York Times,* July 28, 1962, p. 21.

65. "4,000 Homes Per Year," *Architectural Forum* (April, 1949), 90:84–93; "The Most Popular Builder's House," *Architectural Forum* (April, 1950), 92:134–135. Also see: Kenneth Jackson, *Crabgrass Frontier,* pp. 234–245; Mark Robbins, "Growing Pains," pp. 72–79.

66. Eric Larrabee, "The Six Thousand Houses That Levitt Built," p. 84.

67. Figures cited in Charles Redford, "The Impact of Levittown on Local Government," p. 131. Also see: "The Most Popular Builder's House," *Architectural Forum* (April 1950), 92:134.

68. Larrabee, "The Six Thousand Houses," p. 82.

69. Urban dispersal issue, *Bulletin of the Atomic Scientists* (September 1951), vol. 7.

70. U.S. Federal Civil Defense Administration, *Operation Doorstep.*

71. For a general overview of the effects of the beginning of the atomic age on United States' culture see: Paul Boyer, *By The Bombs Early Light.*

72. John Lear, "Hiroshima, U.S.A."

9. NEW DIRECTIONS

1. Lewis Mumford, "High Buildings: An American View."

2. Lewis Mumford, "The Marseilles 'Folley.'"

3. New York City, Mayor's Committee on Slum Clearance, *Title 1 Slum Clearance Progress* (1956).

4. Robert Moses, *Public Works: A Dangerous Trade,* p. 426.

5. New York State Legislature, *Laws* (1955), ch. 407, art. 1, Braun Arthur, *The Limited Profit Housing Companies Law.*

6. For further statistics on Mitchell-Lama, see Joseph S. DeSalvo, *An Economic Analysis of New York City's Mitchell-Lama Housing Program*; and Barbara W. Woodfill, *New York City's Mitchell-Lama Program.*

7. United States Congress, *Laws,* Public Law 87–70, sec. 101, pp. 149–154.

8. Daniel S. Berman, *Urban Renewal, FHA, Mitchell-Lama,* p. 157.

9. "Four Housing Projects for City Approved," *New York Times,* May 23, 1952, p. 14.

10. "34 Million Co-op Housing Planned Near Penn Station," *New York Times,* August 19, 1957, p. 1.

11. See entries under "Manhattan Project," in Robert Caro, *The Power Broker.*

12. "Fresh Meadows," *Architectural Forum* (December 1949), 106:85–87; James Dahir, "Fresh Meadows," pp. 80–82. Also see: "New York Life Acquires Large Housing site," *New York Times,* March 23, 1946, p. 24.

13. Lewis Mumford, "From Utopia Parkway Turn East," pp. 102–106.

14. "Fordham Hill Apartments," *Architectural Record* (September 1950), 108:132–36.

15. Caro, *The Power Broker,* ch. 41.

16. New York City Planning Commission, *Zoning Maps and Resolution*; Thomas W. Ennis, "New Zoning Laws in Effect Friday," p. 1.

17. The zoning mechanism is explained in some detail in: New York City Planning Commission, *Rezoning New York City: A Guide to the Proposed Comprehensive Amendment of the Zoning Resolution of the City of New York.*

18. David B. Carlson, "Sam Lefrak: He Builds Them Cheaper by the Dozen," pp. 102–105.

19. "Big Development Due in Elmhurst," *New York Times,* May 11, 1960, p. 63; "Part of Warbasse Site Named Trump Village," *New York Times,* June 14, 1960, p. 60.

20. Carter B. Horsley, "Housing for 24,000 Begun in Brooklyn," p. 46; and Steven V. Roberts, "Project for 6,000 Families Approved for Canarsie Site," p. 1.

21. Thomas W. Ennis, "15,500-Apartment Co-op to Rise in Bronx," p. 1. Samuel E. Bleecker, *The Politics of Architecture,* pp. 64–73.

22. Caro, *The Power Broker,* p. 1151.

23. For interesting perspectives on this transition in the south Bronx, see Women's City Club of New York, *"With Love and Affection"*; and Bronx Museum of the Arts, *Devastation/Resurrection: The South Bronx.*

24. Robert Moses, *The Power Broker,* chs. 37 and 38. For a more personal assessment of the Moses urbanistic legacy in relation to expressway building, see Marshall Berman, *All That Is Solid Melts Into Air,* pp. 290–312.

25. Abel Silver, "City Fights White Exodus from Grand Concourse," *New York Post,* March 9, 1967, p. 2. This view was strongly countered in American Jewish Congress, *The Grand Concourse, Promise and Challenge* (New York, November 1967). Also see Bernard Weintraub, "Once-Grand Concourse," p. 35; Steven V. Roberts, "Grand Concourse: Hub of Bronx Is Undergoing Ethnic Changes," p. 35.

26. Denise Scott Brown and Robert Venturi, "Co-op City: Learning To Like It," *Progressive Architecture* (February 1970), 51:64–73. Criticism of the project has persisted from the first announcements. See William E. Farrell, "Architects Score Co-op City Design," p. 29. Sensationalist media coverage in 1977 recorded much of the project's deterioration.

27. "Quality in Quantity: Manhattan House, a Block of Swank New York Apartments," *Architectural Forum* (July 1952), 97:140–151.

28. "Variety and Open Space for New York," *Architectural Record* (July 1958), 124:175; and Edward L. Friedman, "Cast-in-Place Technique Restudied," pp. 158–169.

29. "Big City Two–and–a–half," *Architectural Record* (June 1959), 60:204–205.

30. New York City. Mayor's Committee on Slum Clearance, *Washington Square South, Slum Clearance Plan Under Title I of the Housing Act of 1949.*

31. United States Congress, House of Representatives, *Washington Square Southeast Slum Clearance Project Hearing.* Also see Robert Caro, *The Power Broker,* chs. 41, 45.

32. "Bright Landmarks on Changing Urban Scene," *Architectural Forum* (December 1966), 125:21–29.

33. Women's City Club of New York, *Tenant Relocation at West Park*; Elinor G. Black, *Manhattantown Two Years Later.*

34. For a detailed record of much of this research, see the Chermayeff Archive, Avery Library, Columbia University.

35. Jane Jacobs, *The Death and Life of Great American Cities,* p. 373.

36. The competition program and discussion of placing entries are found in: The Ruberoid Corporation, *Fifth Ruberoid Architectural Design Competition*; "Renewal Gains From Ruberoid Contest," *Architectural Forum* (September 1964), 119:7; "Minneapolitans Win Ruberoid Competition," *Progressive Architecture* (September 1963), 34:65–66; "Ruberoid Competition Gives New York Ideas for Urban Renewal," *Architectural Record* (October 1963), 139:14–15.

37. An abbreviated competition program and discussion of placing entries are found in: New York City Housing and Development Administration, *Record of Submissions and Awards. Competition for Middle-Income Housing at Brighton Beach, Brooklyn.* Also see "Development On A Brooklyn Beach," *Progressive Architecture* (May 1968) 34:62, 64; Robert A. M. Stern, *New Directions in American Architecture,* pp. 8–10; Stanislaus von Moos, *Venturi, Rauch, and Scott-Brown. Buildings and Projects,* pp. 288–289.

38. Robert Venturi, *Complexity And Contradiction in Architecture.*

39. New York City Housing and Development Administration, *Record of Submissions and Awards. Competition for Middle-Income Housing at Brighton Beach, Brooklyn.*

40. Caro, *The Power Broker,* ch. 45; New York City Planning Commission, *Tenant Relocation Report* (New York: January 20, 1954).

41. J. Anthony Panuch, *Building a Better New York.*

42. For more information on HDA, see New York State, Temporary State Commission, *HDA: A Superagency Evaluated.*

43. Lawrence Halpern and Associates, *New York, New York.*

44. Several of the early HDA projects are published in "Urban Housing: A Comprehensive Approach to Quality," *Architectural Record* (January 1969), 145:97–118.

45. New York State Legislature, *Laws* (1968), ch. 173–174.

46. For a detailed account of the Urban Development Corporation see Eleanor L. Brilliant, *The Urban Development Corporation.* Also see Charles Hoyt, "Crisis In Housing. What Did the New Super-Agency Mean for the Architect?"

47. Roger Katan, *Pueblos for El Barrio*; and Ellen Perry Berkeley, "*Vox Populi*: Many Voices from a Single Community," pp. 59–63.

48. Oscar Newman, *Defensible Space.*

49. New York State, Division of Housing and Community Renewal, *Statistical Summary of Programs*; New York City, Department of City Planning, *Housing Database,* table A-1.

50. "Upbeat in Harlem," *Architectural Forum* (January–February 1969), 130:65; and "A Riverside Co-op in New York City," *House and Home* (October 1971), 40:106–107.

51. By this time, several documents had received some exposure, including Alison Smithson, ed., "Team 10 Primer," *Architectural Design* (December 1962). It was republished by 1965. Also known in the United States was Oscar Newman, *CIAM '59 in Otterloo.*

52. Kenneth Frampton, "Twin Parks as Typology," pp. 56–61; Richard Meier, *Richard Meier, Architect,* pp. 129–137. For a general history of the total Twin Parks development, see Myles Weintraub and Reverend Mario Zicarelli, "Tale of Twin Parks,"pp. 54–67.

53. Rowe, who joined the Cornell faculty in 1962, influenced a critical number of young architects involved with urban design in New York. See Kenneth Frampton, Alessandra Latour, "Notes On American Architectural Education," pp. 27–31.

54. This observation was developed in an essay by Beyhan Karahanl in relation to coursework in "A4410 Origins of Design Attitudes in Modern Urbanism," taught by me at Columbia University, spring 1975.

55. Richard Meier, *Richard Meier, Architect,* pp. 129, 132, 133.

56. Kenneth Frampton, "Twin Parks As

Typology," p. 58. Even as the project was being constructed, it was entangled in youth gang warfare in the area. For example, on August 21, 1972, a youth was shot at East 181st Street and Crotona Avenue. See Emanuel Perlmutter, "Homicides in City Climbed to a Record of 13 for 24-Hour Period Ending at 12:01 Yesterday," p. 21.

57. The problem of unit standards at Twin Parks is discussed in Suzanne Stephens, "Learning from Twin Parks."

58. "Twin Parks Northwest," *Architecture and Urbanism* no. 43 (July 1974), pp. 65–70; Frampton, *Op. Cit.* p. 60.

59. Alessandra Latour, ed., *Pasanella and Klein,* pp. 27–72.

60. "Twin Parks East: Bronx Vest Pocket Housing with Two Schools and a Center for the Aged Tucked Under Its Towers," *Architectural Record* (August 1976), 159:110–113; Latour, *Pasanella and Klein,* pp. 73–98.

61. "Battery Park City," *Architectural Record* (June 1969), 145:145–148.

62. New York State Urban Development Corporation, *The Island Nobody Knows;* "Projekt Welfare Island, New York," *Baumeister* (February 1972), 79:166–170; Roger Rogin, "New York on a New York Island."

63. "Eastwood: A Low- to Moderate-Income Housing Development on Roosevelt Island . . . " *Architectural Record* (August 1976), 159:102–107.

64. Peabody Terrace was remarkably well regarded a decade after its completion. See Jonathan Hale, "Ten Years Past at Peabody Terrace."

65. Stanley Abercrombie, "Roosevelt Island Housing," *Architecture and Urbanism* (February 1978), pp. 91–103.

66. Paul Goldberger, "Manhattan Plaza: Quality Housing To Upgrade 42nd Street," *New York Times,* August 19, 1974, p. 27; Glenn Fowler, "Builders Hope to Lure Richer Tenants to Project," *New York Times,* August 19, 1974, p. 27; Suzanne Stephens, "The Last Gasp: New York City," p. 61.

67. Stanley Abercrombie. "New York Housing Breaks the Mold," 1:70–73.

68. Stephens, "The Last Gasp," p. 63.

69. "High-Rise in Harlem," *Progressive Architecture* (March 1976), 57:64–69; and "New York, N.Y.," *Architectural Forum* (May 1971), 134:42–45.

70. The competition program and discussion of entries are found in: New York State

Urban Development Corporation, *Roosevelt Island Housing Competition* (New York, 1974). Also see Suzanne Stephens, "This Side of Habitat," pp. 58–63; Gerald Allen, "Roosevelt Island Competition—Was It Really A Flop?" pp. 111–120.

71. Edward Logue, "The Future for New Housing in New York City." In 1985 the *New York Times* ran a series of five articles on the fiscal crisis: Martin Gottlieb, "A Decade After the Cutbacks, New York Is a Different City," p. 1; Martin Gottleib, "New York's Rescue: The Offstage Drama," p. 1; Maureen Dowd, "Hard Times in Brooklyn: How Two Neighborhoods Have Coped," p. 1; Michael Oreskes, "Fiscal Crisis Still Haunts the Police," p. 1; Sam Roberts, "75 Bankruptcy Scare Alters City Plans Into 21st Century," p. 1. For different interpretations of the "crisis," see Peter Marcuse, "The Targeted Crisis: On the Ideology of the Urban Fiscal Crisis and Its Uses," pp. 330–355; William K. Tabb, *The Long Default. New York City and the Urban Fiscal Crisis;* Eric Lichten, *Class, Power, and Austerity. The New York City Fiscal Crisis.*

72. Crown Gardens: Design to Reverse the Spread of Blight," *Architectural Record* (January 1969), 145:105–106.

73. "Lambert Houses: Urban Renewal with a Conscience," *Architectural Record* (January 1974), 145:133–140.

74. "Red Hook Housing, Phase One," *Architectural Record* (December 1972), 152:90.

75. "Mott-Haven Infill in the South Bronx . . . ," *Architectural Record* (August 1976), 159:114–116. For a description of the overall Mott Haven infill proposal, see New York City, Planning Commission, *Plan for New York City, 1969,* 2:54–57.

76. Museum of Modern Art, *Another Chance for Housing.*

77. Circumstances surrounding this project were recorded in an interview with Waltrude Schleicher Woods, May 1979. Also see Kenneth Frampton, "The Generic Street as a Continuous Built Forum."

78. Latour, *Pasanella and Klein,* pp. 99–112.

79. Suzanne Stephens, "Low-Rise Lemon," p. 56.

80. "Two Blighted Downtown Areas Are Chosen for Urban Renewal," *New York Times,* February 21, 1961, p. 37; "Huge Renewal Project Planned for W. Village," *Village Voice,* February 23, 1961, p. 1.

81. "Village Housing Study Finds Plea Put

Off, but Board Votes on Other Requests," *New York Times,* February 24, 1961, p. 31.

82. The special September 1961 issue of *Dissent* entitled "New York, N.Y." gives a good picture of Village sensibilities. See in particular Stephen Zoll, "The West Village: Let There Be Blight," pp. 289–296; Marc D. Schliefer, "The Village," pp. 360–365; Ned Polsky, "The Village Beat Scene: Summer 1960," pp. 339–359.

83. "Angry 'Villagers' To Fight Project," *New York Times,* February 27, 1961, p. 29.

84. "Architect Tells of Village Plan," *New York Times,* March 5, 1961, p. 52; "City Reassures 'Village' Groups," *New York Times,* March 8, 1961, p. 28; "City's West Village Project Hit By More Local Groups," *Village Voice,* March 23, 1961, p. 3.

85. Edith Evans Asbury, "Deceit Charges in 'Village' Plan," p. 68; Mary Perot Nichols, "West Village Renewal Fight Arouses Ire On Both Sides," *Village Voice,* October 26, 1961, p. 1.

86. "'Village' Group Protest Survey," *New York Times,* March 13, 1961, p. 31; "Project Foe Hits 'Village' Group," *New York Times,* March 14, 1961, p. 26; and "'Village' Board Assails Project," *New York Times,* March 18, 1961, p. 12.

87. "Board Ends Plan for West Village," *New York Times,* October 25, 1961, p. 39.

88. Citizens Housing and Planning Council of New York, *Renewal and Rebuttal: The City Planning Commission Tells the Public Its Decision on the Suitability of the So-Called West Village Area for Urban Renewal Study and Planning.*

89. Charles G. Bennett, "City Gives Up Plan for West Village," p. 33.

90. Perkins and Will, *The West Village Plan for Housing.*

91. Alan S. Oser, "Upturn for West Village Houses," p. 18.

92. Roger Starr, "Adventure in Mooritania," p. 5. The *Village Voice* had previously published a more sympathetic review. See Ira D. Robbins in "Books." The Death and Life of Great American Cities." p. 5. For an interesting rebuttal, see Elias S. Wilentz, "Good Planning or Bad?"

93. Roger Starr's arguments were set forth in his book *The Living End: The City and Its Critics,* pp. 162–167. A more heated reaction came from Ira S. Robbins who, according to the *Village Voice,* publicly called the opponents of the West Village urban renewal plan "igno-rant, neurotic, dishonest, slanderous, disorderly, and disgusting"; including "an infinestimal number of unstable people and those who are euphemistically called 'left-wingers,' who are just out and out communists." See Mary Perot Nichols, "City Official Blasts West Village Groups," p. 1.

94. Stephens, "Low-Rise Lemon," p. 56.

95. Letter to the Editor, *New York Times,* August 25, 1974, sec. VIII, p. 8.

96. "Co-op Scores Foreclosure Plan," *New York Times,* September 22, 1975, p. 37.

97. "City Is Foreclosing on 'Village' Project; Will Rent Complex," *New York Times,* November 22, 1975, p. 31.

98. Glenn Fowler, "Unsuccessful Cooperative Will Now Offer Rentals," p. 29.

99. Joseph P. Fried, "A Village Housing Project Becomes a Fiscal Nightmare,". Also see Peter Freiberg, "Jane Jacobs Defends 'White Elephant'." p. 29.

100. Joseph P. Fried, "Mitchell-Lama Housing Beset by Problems, but City Sees Progress in Solving Them," p. 79; Alan S. Oser, "Housing Subsidies a Paradox," p. 47; Stephens, "The Last Gasp," p. 61.

101. Joseph P. Fried, "Manhattan Plaza Wins Approval To Get Tenants," p. 73.

102. Stephens, "The Last Gasp," pp. 62–63; Robert Tomasson, "Four Luxury Towers To House the Poor Opening in Harlem," p. 35; and Michael Goodwin, "Project Admits Tenants To End a Three Year Delay," sec. II, p. 3.

103. Paul Goldberger, "Low-Rise, Low-Key Housing Gives Banality a Test in West Village," p. 33.

104. Peter Freiberg, "Jane Jacobs' Old Fight Lingers On," p. 5.

105. Part of this debate appears in Judith C. Lack, "Dispute Still Rages as West Village Meets Its Sales Test," sec. VIII, p. 1; and Chilton Williamson, Jr., "West Village Town Meeting," p. 944.

10. EPILOGUE

1. A summary of recent programs is found in Penelope Lemov, "Life After Section 8."

2. The peak year was 1963, with a net increase of 51,377 dwellings. See New York City, Department of City Planning, *New Housing in New York City, 1981–1982,* appendix.

3. Ernest Mendel, *Late Capitalism,* p. 387.

For a more local assessment see Emanuel Tobier, "Gentrification: The Manhattan Story."

4. Iver Peterson, "People Moving Back to Cities, U.S. Study Says," sec. I, p. 1. For the complete report, see U.S. Bureau of the Census, *Geographical Mobility: March 1983 to March 1984.*

5. "Gentrification" is a term which was apparently first used in relation to working class areas of London where, by the early 1960's, displacement by middle-class newcomers was widespread. See Ruth Glass, *London: Aspects of Change,* pp. xviii–xix.

6. Serge Guilbaut, *How New York Stole the Idea of Modern Art.*

7. By the early 1960s, some considerable public attention was given to this situation, not only, for example, in the *Village Voice,* but in *The New York Times* as well: Bernard Weintraub, "Renovations on Lower East Side Creating New Living Quarters," sec. VIII, p. 1; Weintraub, "Lower East Side Vexed by Housing," sec. VIII, p. 1. Also see Sharon Zukin, *Loft Living,* p. 113.

8. For a summary of the dynamic between New York City manufacturing jobs and loft space in Manhattan, see Suzanne O'Keefe, "Loft Conversion in Manhattan"; Emanual Tobier, "Setting the Record Straight on Loft Conversions."

9. *Lower Manhattan: Major Improvements, Land Use, Transportation, Traffic* (New York: Downtown–Lower Manhattan Association, 1963); *The Lower Manhattan Plan* (New York: New York City Planning Commission, 1966).

10. Zukin, *Loft Living,* pp. 37–43.

11. Ira D. Robbins, *The Wastelands of New York City.* Also see Charles R. Simpson, *SoHo: The Artist in the City,* p. 132.

12. Simpson, *SoHo,* pp. 123–126; Zukin, *Loft Living,* pp. 49–50.

13. New York State Legislature, *Report of the Joint Legislative Committee on Housing and Urban Development.*

14. New York State Legislature, *Laws* (1964), ch. 939.

15. New York State Legislature, *Laws* (1982), ch. 349. For a summary of loft-related legislation, see Zukin, *Loft Living,* table 7; O'Keefe, "Loft Conversion in Manhattan," pp. 29–35; Weisbrod, "Loft Conversions: Will Enforcement Bring Acceptance?"

16. Simpson makes this connection between the Soho struggle and other community initiatives: *SoHo,* p. 147.

17. As early as 1961, the Artists-Tenants Association was active in relation to the threat of massive clearance in Soho. See "Artists Face New Problem: Demolition of Loft Area," *Village Voice,* December 21, 1961, p. 3. A detailed history of the Lower Manhattan Expressway opposition is given in Simpson, *SoHo.* Also see Stanley Penkin, *The Lower Manhattan Expressway.*

18. Simpson, *SoHo,* p. 144.

19. Michael Duplaix, "The Loft Generation."

20. "Vote Indicates Art Strike Looms for City in Fall," *Village Voice,* July 27, 1961, p. 1; "Artists To Strike for Lofts in September," *Village Voice,* August 3, 1961, p. 16; "City May Move To Legalize Artists' Lofts, Stop Strike," *Village Voice,* August 24, 1961, p. 3.

21. In December 1961 the city issued its first Buildings Department rules for artist tenants in loft buildings, beginning the long process of legal recognition loft dwellings in New York. For an outline of the rules, see "City Cooperates, but Artists Face New Problems: Demolition of Loft Area," *Village Voice,* December 21, 1961, p. 3.

22. Stephanie Gervis, "Loftless Leonardos Picket as Mona Merely Smiles."

23. J. R. Goddard, "Village Area Artists Win/Lose This Week."

24. The origins of this collaboration are described in Ada Louise Huxtable, "Bending the Rules."

25. "Golden Touch," *The Nation* (January 5, 1963), 204:4; cited in "Artists Are Realtors' Best Friends, Edit Says," *Village Voice,* January 17, 1963, p. 25.

26. Carter B. Horsley, "Loft Conversions Exceeding New Apartment Construction."

27. Zukin, *Loft Living,* p. 114. Zukin outlines the activities of the J. D. Kaplan Fund in relation to the growing patrician interest in the economic impact of the arts.

28. "Westbeth's Rehabilitation Project: A Clue to Improving Our Cities," *Architectural Record* (March 1970), 137:103–109; "Westbeth Artists in Residence," *Architectural Forum* (October 1970), 133:45–49.

29. For example, in 1974 high-style loft design was first covered in the professional press. See Sharon Lee Ryder, "A Very Lofty Realm." Also see Paul Goldberger, "A Recycled Loft Restores the Luxury to City's Luxury Housing."

30. Official City Planning Department estimates were quoted in George W. Goodman,

"Illegal Loft Tenants Get Second Chance." For a higher unofficial estimate see Emanual Tobier, "Setting the Record Straight on Loft Conversions," p. 39. Also see James R. Hudson, *The Unanticipated City. Loft Conversions in Lower Manhattan* (Cambridge: MIT University Press, 1976).

31. Stegman, *The Dynamics of Rental Housing in New York City,* table 5–8.

32. *Ibid.,* table 5–4.

33. *Ibid.,* table 8–2.

34. According to figures released in 1985 by the Corcoran Group and Douglas, Elliman, and Ives, as published in the *New York Times,* April 28, 1985, sec. VIII, p. 1.

35. Kirk Johnson, "Pace of Co-op Conversion Slackening."

36. Michael de Courcy Hinds, "Frenzy of Building Activity Brings 18,000 Units to Market."

37. Anthony DePalma, "Construction of Apartments in Manhattan Falls Sharply," p. 1.

38. Michael de Courcy Hinds, "Marketing Third Avenue as a Chic Address."

39. Michael de Courcy Hinds, "Along Upper Broadway a Revival."

40. Alan S. Oser, "A Luxury Apartment House Will Rise on Broadway."

41. Figures cited in an advertisement in the *New York Times,* December 2, 1984, sec. VIII, p. 8.

42. Figures cited in an advertisement in the *New York Times,* April 15, 1984, sec. VIII, p. 4.

43. Figures cited by the Trump Organization in January 1985.

44. Figure quoted in Tony Schwartz, "The Show Must Go Up."

45. Susan Doubilet, "I'd Rather Be Interesting," p. 66.

46. "New Departure," *New York Times,* June 8, 1986, sec. VIII, p. 1; also see advertisement, sec. VIII, p. 14.

47. This design apparition was the central feature of a long series of advertisements. For example, see *New York Times Magazine,* September 28, 1986, p. 81; October 12, 1986, p. 63; October 26, 1986, p. 82; November 16, 1986, p. 117.

48. RAMS Marketing has handled other housing, including the St. Andrews Golf Community at Hastings-on-the-Hudson, designed by Robert A. M. Stern.

49. Paul Goldberger, "Architecture: Townhouse Rows," p. 15; "Eleven on 67," *New York Times,* April 4, 1982, sec. 8, p. 1; David Chipperfield, "Style or Pragmatism: Ciriani's Housing and Stirling's Apartments Contrasted"; "Richard Meier's New York Apartments Scheme," *International Architect* (1981), 1(5):6.

50. Alexander Cooper and Associates, *Battery Park City.*

51. The popular press has been positive: Carter Wiseman, "The Next Great Place," pp. 34–41; Paul Goldberger, "Battery Park City Is a Triumph of Urban Design," p. 23; Michael de Courcy Hinds, "Shaping a Landfill Into a Neighborhood."

52. Joe Conason, "The Westway Alternative."

53. Michael J. Lazar, *Land Use and the West Side Highway,* p. 8.

54. This lack of public attention to "induced development" was addressed in a critique of the Draft Environmental Impact Statement for Westway. See Beyer, Blinder, and Belle and Justin Gray Associates, *Combo: Critique, West Side Highway Project*; see also *Draft Environmental Impact Statement and Section 4(f) Statement for West Side Highway.*

55. Clark and Rapuano, Inc.; Venturi, Rauch and Scott Brown; Salmon Associates, "Westway. The Park." Brochure published by the Westway Management Group, September 1983; "Big Park for the Big Apple: Westway State Park, New York City," *Architectural Record* (January 1985), 173:124–131; "Westway Park," *The Princeton Journal* (1985), 2:196–199.

56. "New Attack on Westway," *New York Times,* May 19, 1985, sec. IV, p. 6; Arnold H. Lubasch, "Corps Aide Sees No Alternative to the Westway"; Representative James J. Howard, Letter to the Editor.

57. Joyce Purnick, "Estimate Board Gives Approval to Lincoln West"; also see figures in Martin Gottlieb, "Trump Set To Buy Lincoln West Site," Ethel Sheffer, "The Lessons of Lincoln West."

58. "Trump Planning 66th Street Tower, Tallest in World," *New York Times,* November 19, 1985, p. A–1; Paul Goldberger, "Height of 8 Towers Could Overwhelm Wide Open Space."

59. Unusually frank critical commentary on the phenomenon has centered around the personage of Donald Trump. See in particular: Paul Goldberger, "Trump: Symbol of a Gaudy, Impatient Time," John Kenneth Galbraith, "Big Shots."

60. Gottlieb, "Trump Set To Buy Lincoln

West Site"; Wolfgang Saxon, "West Siders Voice Opposition on Plan."

61. Paul Goldberger, "Developers Learned Some Lessons and Cut Back," Thomas C. Lueck, "Trump City Site May Be Sold."

62. Figures cited in "How Many Will Share New York's Prosperity?" *New York Times,* January 20, 1985, sec. 4, p. 6; Sam Roberts, "Gathering Cloud: The Poor Climb Toward 2 Million," B–1.

63. Michael A. Stegman, *The Dynamics of Rental Housing in New York City,* table 3–3.

64. Richard Plunz and Marta Gutman, "The New York 'Ring,'" pp. 18–33.

65. According to U.S. Census figures, the population total for the south Bronx (below the Cross Bronx Expressway) dropped from 499,346 in 1970 to 266,089 in 1980, a reduction of almost one-half. Some census tracts within the same area were reduced by up to 90 percent. Within the same approximate area, 67.6 percent of the remaining occupied buildings were adjacent to abandoned buildings, and 41.2 percent had maintenance deficiencies, which is the highest rate in New York City. In the same area, 54.7 percent of the population are below the official poverty level, which is also the highest rate in the city. See the 1980 United States Census and Stegman, *The Dynamics of Rental Housing in New York City,* tables 7–2 and 7–5.

66. See graph entitled "Structural Arson in New York City, 1967–1984," in *NYC Anti-Arson UPDATE* (Winter/Spring 1985), 2(3):7.

67. Fred C. Shapiro, "Raking the Ashes of the Epidemic of Flame."

68. Roger Starr, "Making New York Smaller"; Starr, "Letters," p. 16.

69. New York City Arson Strike Force, *A Study of Government Subsidized Housing Programs and Arson*; Michael Jacobson and Philip Kasinitz, "Burning the Bronx for Profit."

70. For an overview of this strategy in relation to the whole of the New York City "Fiscal Crisis," see: William K. Tabb, *The Long Default: New York and the Urban Fiscal Crisis,* chs. 5, 6.

71. In 1984 Mayor Koch was widely quoted as saying, "We're not catering to the poor anymore . . . there are four other boroughs they can live in. They don't have to live in Manhattan." See Arthur Brown, Dan Collins, and Michael Goodwin, *I Koch* (New York: Dodd, Mead, 1985), p. 290.

72. "Koch Says Lotteries To Sell City Hous-ing Are Not Ruled Out," *New York Times,* July 28, 1981, sec. II, p. 6; "Forms Available for Brownstones," *New York Times,* October 6, 1981, p. 3.

73. Michael Goodwin, "Census Finds Fewer Blacks in Harlem."

74. Craig Unger, "Can Harlem Be Born Again?" Also see: Neil Smith and Richard Schaffer, "Harlem Gentrification, A Catch 22?"

75. In 1983 the *New York Times* published a four-part series by Matthew L. Wald on city ownership. See "Saving Aging Housing: A Costly City Takeover," "New York City as an Apartment Owner: Three Case Histories," "Problems Persist When City Owns Houses," "No Simple Way for City To End Housing Burden."

76. New York City Harlem Task Force, *Redevelopment Strategy for Central Harlem* (New York: Office of the Mayor, August 25, 1982), p. 1.

77. For example, see Lee A. Daniels, "A Surge in Housing in Harlem Prompts Hopes for a Renewal," *New York Times,* September 12, 1981, p. 1; Lee A. Daniels, "Condominiums Planned for Harlem Brownstones," *New York Times,* January 26, 1983, sec. 2, p. 1.

78. Chuck DeLancy, "Lofts for Whose Living?"

79. Anthony DePalma, "Can City's Plan Rebuild the Lower East Side?"

80. Sandy Hornick, Arnold Kotlen, Tony Levy, David Vendor, "Quality Housing and Related Zoning Text Amendments;" Jesus Rangel, "Koch Promises New Zoning for Apartments;" Alan S. Oser, "Restructuring Zoning to Spur Apartment Construction;" Arnold S. Kotlen and David Vendor, "More and Better: Zoning for Quality Housing;" Anthony DePalma, "Developing New Housing Standards."

81. New York City Planning Commission. "Quality Housing Amendment Adopted by the Board of Estimate, August 14, 1987"; Bruce Lambert, "New York City Agrees to Allow Building of Bulkier Apartments," *New York Times,* August 15, 1987, sec. 1, p. 1.

82. Interview with David Vandor, Zoning Study Group, New York City Planning Commission, by me with David Smiley, November 27, 1984.

83. Alan S. Oser, "City's Rental-Subsidy Program To Get First Test Soon."

84. *Ibid.*

85. Figures quoted in Warren Moscow, "Mitchell-Lama: The Program That Was." p. 44.

Also see Robert T. Newsom, "Limited-Profit Housing—What Went Wrong?

86. New York City, Planning, *Housing Database,* tables A-1, A-2.

87. An account of the Bedford-Stuyvesant initiative was written by the corporation: "Restoration of Confidence: The Achievements of the Bedford-Stuyvesant Restoration Corporation. 1967–1981." Also see Carlyle C. Douglas, "In Brooklyn's Bedford-Stuyvesant, Glimmers of Resurgence Are Visible."

88. *Manhattan Valley Department Corporation.* Also see Richard D. Lyons, "If You're Thinking of Living in Manhattan Valley."

89. Kirk Johnson, "Rediscovering Cathedral Parkway;" Kirk Johnson, "Suddenly the Barrio Is Drawing Buyers;" Joseph Berger, "Hispanic Life Dims in Manhattan Valley;" Anthony DePalma, "Is The Upper East Side Moving North?"

90. For a general history of rehabilitation in New York City, see Alfred Medioli, "Housing Form and Rehabilitation in New York City." Also see Michael Winkleman, "Raising the Old Law Tenement Question."

91. Iver Peterson, "Tenements of 1880's Adapt to 1980s."

92. Alan S. Oser, "Project Evokes City's Brownstone Era."

93. Richard D. Lyons, "If You're Thinking of Living in Manhattan Valley."

94. The competition program is found in: New York State Council on the Arts, *Inner City Infill: A Housing Program for Harlem.* Representative entries are found in: New York State Council on the Arts, *Reweaving the Urban Fabric.* This catalogue provides an extensive survey of recent "infill" housing projects in New York City and elsewhere.

95. Perkins and Will, *MLC Rehabilitation Survey,* pp. 59–60.

96. Twin Parks Southeast, Northwest, and Southwest also induced heavy vandalism. Elsewhere, Ocean Village in Queens and Sea Rise on Coney Island was also notable for its rapid deterioration as a result of vandalism. *Ibid.,* pp. 50, 52, 55, 69, 85.

97. An analysis of the vandalism was developed in an essay by Beyhan Karahan in relation to course work for "A4410 Origins of Design Attitudes in Modern Urbanism," taught by me at Columbia University, Spring 1975.

98. Romaldo Giurgola, "The Discreet Charm of the Bourgeoisie," p. 57.

99. Michael Goodwin, "A Home Ownership Aid Program is Planned for City"; Lee A. Daniels, "City Is Sponsoring 2,200 Small Houses."

100. Alan S. Oser, "In Brownsville, Churches Joining to Build Homes;" George W. Goodman, "Housing in Brownsville Progresses;" Jim Sleeper, "East Brooklyn's Nehiamiah Opens Its Door and Answers Its Critics;" Anthony DePalma, "The Nehiamiah Plan: A Success;" Paul A. Crotty, "Nehiamiah Plan"; Jack Newfield, "Annual Thanksgiving Honor Roll," Sam Roberts, "Despite Success, Housing Effort Still Struggling," *New York Times,* September 24, 1987, p. B1.

101. Stegman, *The Dynamics of Rental Housing in New York City,* p. 5; table 5–11. An interesting profile of some of the early home owners is given in Utrice C. Leid, "A Neighborhood Grows in B'Klyn Ghost Town."

102. Wayne Barrett, "Why the Mayor Blessed Brownsville;" Sam Roberts, "In East Brooklyn, Churches Preach Gospel of Change." Also see: Sharon Zukin and Gilda Zweyman, "Housing for the Working Poor: A Historical View of Jews and Blacks in Brownsville."

103. Jeffrey Schmalz, "East New York Housing Stirs Emotions"; "Nehiamiah Slowed," *City Limits* (April 1986), 11:8.

104. I.D. Robbins, "Blueprints for a New York City Housing Program." Alan Finder, "A Queens Beachfront is Ground for a Fight Over Housing Goals." *New York Times,* December 25, 1988, sec. 4, p. 6.

105. "Building Alternatives: Housing for the Homeless," *Metroline # 208,* January 14, 1987, p. 13, transcript of WNET Channel 13 broadcast.

106. According to the U.S. Census, Tracts #153 and #155, in which Charlotte Gardens is located, suffered a combined drop in population from 20,747 to 4,066 between 1970 and 1980.

107. Kathleen Teltsch, "94 Factory-Built Houses Planned for South Bronx"; Philip Shenon, "Taste of Suburbia Arrives in the South Bronx"; Alan S. Oser, "Owner-Occupied Houses: New Test in South Bronx"; Winston Williams, "Rebuilding From the Grass Roots Up"; Letters to the Editor; *New York Times,* February 8, 1987, sec. VIII, p. 12; Sam Roberts, "Charlotte Street: Tortured Rebirth of a Wasteland." Also informative is the "Charlotte Gardens Information Kit" distributed by the South Bronx Development Organization, August 10, 1983.

108. "The Bronx Is Up," *Metroline Show 307.* p. 5. Transcript of WNET Thirteen telecast, February 10, 1988.

109. "Houses for Workingmen," *New York Times,* September 8, 1891, p. 8.

110. Alan S. Oser, "Brooklyn Renewal: Two Story Homes."

111. Lee A. Daniels, "Housing Partnership Begins In the Middle"; Lee A. Daniels, "Lots Are Drawn for New Middle-Income Homes"; Kirk Johnson, "One-Family Houses for East Harlem"; Michael de Courcy Hinds, "Delays Beset 255-Unit Modular Project in Brownsville."

112. Alan S. Oser, "New 2-Family Houses Without Subsidies."

113. David W. Dunlap, "Koch Proposes Shift in Coney Island Housing"; "Coney Island Residents Fault New Homes," *New York Times,* July 6, 1984, sec. II, p. 3; Matthew L. Wald, "New Coney Island Homes Called Flawed."

114. New York State Council on the Arts, *Reweaving the Urban Fabric.*

115. Roger Starr, "The Small House Is the Big Hope." See also "Ranch Houses? Where?" (editorial), *New York Times,* March 27, 1983, p. 30.

116. Robert D. McFadden, "City Puts Cheery Face on Crumbling Facades"; Robert D. McFadden, "Derelict Tenements In the Bronx To Get Fake Lived-In Look."

117. William E. Geist, "Residents Give a Bronx Cheer to Decal Plan."

118. Roger Starr, "The Editorial Notebook: Seals of Approval." A *Times* editorial in the following year was critical of the program: "Fake Blinds Can't Hide Blight," *New York Times,* November 14, 1983, p. 18. For the mayor's reply, see Edward I. Koch, "Of Decals and Priorities for the South Bronx."

119. The beginnings of this tendency are traced in: Alexander Tzonis and Liane Lefaivre, "The Narcissist Phase in Architecture."

120. As of 1986, there were estimated to be 100,000 families without homes (most currently living with others). There were 4,560 families in the emergency housing system (hotels or shelters). See Manhattan Borough President's Task Force on Housing for Homeless Families, *A Shelter Is Not a Home,* pp. 16–17. Also see: Peter Marcuse, "Why Are They Homeless?"

121. Figures were cited in, "A Million Meals," *Metroline Show 304,* p. 1. Transcript of WNET Thirteen telecast, December 23, 1987. According to Liz Krueger of the New York City Coalition Against Hunger, the numbers ranged from thirty in 1980, to five hundred fifty in 1988, but these include soup kitchens (approximately two hundred) and food pantries where foodstuffs are distributed (approximately three hundred fifty).

122. Officina Alessi, *Tea and Coffee Piazza;* Joseph Giovannini, "Tea Services with the Touch of an Architect;" "Architecture Argent," *Progressive Architecture* (January 1984), 65:23.

123. For further discussion of the current uses of "style," in New York, see: Richard Plunz and Kenneth Kaplan, "On 'Style'."

124. For a recent survey of housing and income conditions see Michael A. Stegman, *Housing and Vacancy Report: New York City 1987* (New York: Department of Housing Preservation and Development, 1988). Anthony DePalma, "Construction of Apartments in Manhattan Falls Sharply."

125. The point has been made more generally in William Julius Wilson, *The Truly Disadvantaged. The Inner City, the Underclass, and Public Policy,* pp. 18–19.

Bibliography

Aaron, Henry. *Shelter and Subsidies.* Washington, D.C.: Brookings Institution, 1972.

Abercrombie, Stanley. "New York Housing Breaks the Mold," *Architecture Plus* (November 1973), 1:62–75.

Achinstein, Asher. *The Standard of Living of Four Hundred Families in a Model Housing Project.* Albany, N.Y.: New York State Board of Housing, 1931.

Ackerman, Frederick L. "Note on New Site & Unit Plans." Memorandum to Commissioner Alfred Rheinstein, dated September 26, 1939. New York City Housing Authority Archive, Laguardia Community College, box 15E7, folder 3.

—— "The Phelps-Stokes Fund Tenement House Competition." *Journal of the American Institute of Architects* (March 1922), 10:76–82.

—— "Williamsburg, A Comment—Preliminary Submission of Evaluations." Memorandum to Langdon W. Post, dated August 21, 1935. New York City Housing Authority Archives, LaGuardia Community College, box 15B2, folder 3.

Ackerman, Frederick and William Ballard. *A Note on Site and Unit Planning.* New York: New York City Housing Authority, 1937.

—— *Survey of Twenty-three Low Rental Housing Projects.* New York: New York City Housing Authority, 1934.

Actes du congrès international des habitations à bon marché tenu à Bruxelles (Julliet 1897). Brussels, 1897.

Agrest, Diana, ed. *A Romance with the City: Irwin S. Chanin.* New York: Cooper Union Press, 1982.

Alessi, Officina. *Tea and Coffee Piazza.* New York: Shakespeare and Company, 1983.

Allen, Gerald. "Roosevelt Island Competition—Was It Really a Flop?" *Architectural Record* (October 1975), 158:111–120.

Alpern, Andrew. *Apartments for the Affluent: A Historical Survey of Buildings in New York.* New York: McGraw-Hill, 1975.

American Banknote Company. *The Central Park Apartments Facing the Park.* New York, 1882. New York Public Library.

American Institute of Architects, New York Chapter. *The Significance of the Work of the New York City Housing Authority.* New York, 1949.

Anderson, W. F. "Forest Hills Gardens—Building Construction." *The Brickbuilder* (December 1912), 21:319–320.

Aronovici, Carol, W. F. R. Ballard, Henry S. Churchill, Carl Feiss, William Lescaze, Albert Mayer, Lewis Mumford, and Ralph Walker. "Moses Turns Housing Expert." Letter to the Editor. *Shelter* (December 1938), 3:2–3.

Asbury, Edith Evans. "Deceit Charged in 'Village' Plan." *New York Times,* October 20, 1961, p. 68.

Ash, Mark and William Ash. *The Building Code of the City of New York.* New York: Baker, Voorhis, 1899.

Asser, Solomon and Hillary Roe. *Development of the Upper West Side to 1925: Thomas Healey and Pomander Walk.* New York Neighborhood Studies, Working Paper No. 5. New York: Columbia University, Division of Urban Planning, 1981.

Astral Apartments, The. Brooklyn, N.Y., circa 1885. New York Public Library.

Atkins, Gordon. "Health, Housing, and Poverty in New York City: 1865–1898." Ph.D. dissertation, Columbia University, 1947.

Atterbury, Grosvenor. *The Economic Production of Workingmen's Homes*. New York: Russell Sage Foundation, 1930.

—— "Forest Hills Gardens, Long Island." *The Brickbuilder* (December 1912), 21:317–318.

—— *Model Towns in America*. New York: National Housing Association Publication No. 17, January 1913.

Augur, Tracy B. "An Analysis of the Plan of Stuyvesant Town." *Journal of the American Institute of Planners* (Autumn 1944), 10:8–13.

Bacon, Mardges. *Ernest Flagg. Beaux-Arts Architect and Urban Reformer*. Cambridge, Mass.: The MIT Press, 1986.

Baker, Ray Stannard. "The Subway 'Deal': How New York City Built Its New Underground Railroad." *McClure's* (March 1905), 24:451–469.

Baldwin, James. "Fifth Avenue, Uptown." *Esquire* (July 1960), 54:70–76.

Bannister, Turpin C., ed. *The Architect at Mid-Century: Evolution and Achievement*. 2 vols. New York: Van Nostrand Reinhold, 1954.

Barrett, Wayne. "Why the Mayor Blessed Brownsville." *Village Voice*, September 10, 1982, p. 5.

—— "The Dreary Deadlock of Public Housing." *Architectural Forum* (May 1957), 106:140–143, 219, 221.

Bauer, Catherine. "Facts for a Housing Program." USHA 29139H. Washington, D.C., 1938 Mimeo. Avery Library, Columbia University.

—— *Modern Housing*. New York: Houghton Mifflin, 1934.

Bayer, Herbert. *Bauhaus, 1919–1928*. New York: Museum of Modern Art, 1938.

Beattie, Susan. *A Revolution in London Housing: LCC Architects and Their Work, 1893–1914*. London: Architectural Press, 1980.

Bedford Stuyvesant Restoration Corporation. "Restoration of Confidence: The Achievements of the Bedford-Stuyvesant Restoration Corporation, 1967–1981." April 1981 (typewritten).

Bell, E. Moberly. *Octavia Hill*. London: Constable, 1943.

Bennett, Charles G. "City Gives Up Plan for West Village." *New York Times*, February 1, 1962, p. 33.

Berger, Joseph. "Hispanic Life Dims in Manhattan Valley." *New York Times*, September 11, 1987. p. B1.

Berkeley, Ellen Perry. "Vox Populi: Many Voices from a Single Community." *Architectural Forum* (May 1968), 128:58–63.

Berman, Daniel S. *Urban Renewal, FHA, Mitchell-Lama: A Workshop Course*. New York: Beneson, 1967.

Berman, Marshall. *All That Is Solid Melts Into Air*. New York: Simon and Schuster, 1982.

Beyer, Blinder, and Belle and Justin Gray Associates. *Combo: Critique, West Side Highway Project*. New York: Community Boards 2, 7, and 9, January 1975.

Birch, Eugenie C., and Deborah Gardner. "The Seven Percent Solution. A Review of Philanthropic Housing, 1870–1910." *Journal of Urban History* (August 1981), 7:403–438.

Birmingham, Stephen. *Life at the Dakota: New York's Most Unusual Address*. New York: Random House, 1979.

Black, Algernon D. "Negro Families in Stuyvesant Town." *Survey* (November 1950), 86:502–503.

Black, Elinor G. *Manhattantown Two Years Later*. New York: Women's City Club of New York, April 1956.

Blanke, Everett. "The Cliffdwellers of New York." *Cosmopolitan* (July 1893), 15:354–362.

Bleecker, Samuel E. *The Politics of Architecture. A Perspective on Nelson A. Rockefeller*. New York: Rutledge Press, 1981.

Bletter, Rosemary Haag. "Modernism Rears Its Head—The Twenties and Thirties." in Richard Oliver, ed. *The Making of An Architect. 1881–1981*. New York: Rizzoli, 1981.

Bloom, Arthur, Dan Collins, and Michael Goodwin. *I Koch*. New York: Dodd, Mead, 1985.

Bloor, Alfred J. "The Architectural and Other Art Societies of Europe . . . with Suggestions as to Some of the Conditions Necessary for the Maximum Success of a National Art Society." Paper read before the New York chapter, AIA, February 16, 1869. Published copy in Avery Library, Columbia University.

—— "History of the American Institute of Architects." *Inland Architect and News Record* (October 1890), 16:40–42.

—— "The Late Edward T. Potter." *American Architect and Building News* (January 21, 1905), 87:1–22.

—— "Suggestions for a Better Method of Building Tenant-Houses in New York." *American Architect and Building News* (February 12, 1881), 9:75–76.

Bolton, Reginald Pelham. "The Apartment Hotel in New York." *Cassier's* (November 1903), 25:27–32.

Boyd, John Taylor, Jr. "A Departure in Housing Finance." *Architectural Record* (August 1922), 52:133–142.

—— "Garden Apartments in Cities." *Architectural Record*, part I (July 1920), 48:53–74; part II (August 1920), 48:121–135.

Boyer, M. Christine. *Dreaming of the Rational City: The Myth of American City Planning.* Cambridge, Mass.: MIT Press, 1983.

—— *Manhattan Manners: Architecture and Style, 1850–1900.* New York: Rizzoli, 1985.

Boyer, Paul. *By the Bomb's Early Light.* New York: Pantheon Books, 1985.

Brace, Charles L. "Model Tenement Houses." *Plumber and Sanitary Engineer* (February 1878), 1:47–48.

Brandt, Lilian. *Growth and Development of the AICP and COS: Report of the Committee on the Institute of Welfare Research.* New York: Community Service Society of New York, 1942.

Breines, Simon. "Designers of Shelter in America: A New Society Makes Its Bow." *Bulletin of the Federation of Architects, Engineers, Chemists, and Technicians* (November 1936), 3:4–5.

—— "Stuyvesant Town." *Task* (1946), no. 4, pp. 35–38.

Brenmer, Robert H. "The Big Flat: History of a New York Tenement House." *American Historical Review* (October 1958), 64(1):54–62.

Bridges, William. *Map of the City of New York & Island of Manhattan.* New York, November 16, 1811.

Bright, John Irwin. "Housing and Community Planning." *Journal of the American Institute of Architects* (July 1920), 8:276–277.

Brilliant, Eleanor L. *The Urban Development Corporation.* Lexington, Mass.: Lexington Books, 1975.

Bristed, Charles Astor. *The Upper Ten Thousand: Sketches of American Society.* New York: Stringer and Townsend, 1852.

Bronx Museum of the Arts. *Devastation/Resurrection: The South Bronx.* New York: Bronx Museum of the Arts, 1979.

Brown, Frank Chouteau. "Some Recent Apartment Buildings." *Architectural Record* (March 1928), 63:193–278.

—— "Tendencies in Apartment House Design, Part XI: The Unit Apartment Building and Its Grouping." *Architectural Record* (May 1922), 51:434–446.

Browne, Junius Henry. "The Problem of Living in New York." *Harper's New Monthly* (November 1882), 65:918–924.

Brownlow, Louis. "Building for the Motor Age." *Conference on Housing Proceedings.* New York: National Housing Association, 1929.

Bruan, Arthur. *The Limited Profit Housing Companies Laws.* November 15, 1955. Mimeo. Avery Library, Columbia University.

Bruce, Robert W. *1877, Year of Violence.* Chicago: Quadrangle Books, 1970.

Bruce, Roscoe Conkling. "The Dunbar Apartment House." *Southern Workman* (October 1931), 60:417–428.

Buckham, C. W. "The Present and Future Development of the Apartment House." *American Architect and Building News* (November 29, 1911), 100:224–227.

Bunce, O. B. "The City of the Future." *Appleton's Journal* (February 10, 1872), pp. 156–158.

Bunner, H. C. "Shantytown." *Scribner's* (October 1880), 20:855–869.

Burk, Addison B. "The City of Homes and Its Building Societies." *Journal of Social Science* (February 1882), 15:121–134.

Burnham, Alan. "The New York Architecture of Richard Morris Hunt." *Journal of the Society of Architectural Historians* (May 1952), 11:9–14.

Bush, James A. "Would America Have Been Automobilized in a Free Market?" Letter to the Editor, *New York Times*, February 10, 1985, Sec. IV, p. 20.

Buttenwieser, Anne L. "Shelter For What And For Whom? On The Route Toward Vladeck Houses, 1930 to 1940." *Journal of Urban History* (August 1986), 12:391–413.

Byers, Pam. *Small Town in the Big City: A History of Sunnyside and Woodside.* New York: Sunnyside Community Center, 1976.

Cantor, Jay E. "A Monument of Trade: A. T. Stewart and the Rise of the Millionaire's Mansion in New York." *Winterthur Portfolio*

10. Charlottesville: University Press of Virginia, 1975.

Carlson, David B. "Sam Lefrak: He Builds Them Cheaper by the Dozen." *Architectural Forum* (April 1963), vol. 119.

Caro, Robert A. *The Power Broker.* New York: Knopf, 1974.

Chadwick, Edwin. *Report on the Sanitary Condition of the Labouring Population of Great Britain: A Supplementary Report on the Results of a Special Inquiry Into the Practice of Interments in Towns.* London: W. Clowes, 1843.

Chandler, Charles F. *Ten Scrap Books of Tenement House Plans.* 10 vols. Filed with the New York City Department of Health, c. 1873–1883. Avery Library, Columbia University.

Charity Organization Society of the City of New York. *New York Charities Directory.* New York, 1912.

Charity Organization Society of the City of New York, Tenement House Committee. *Competition for Plans of Model Tenements.* New York, 1899. Butler Library, Columbia University.

Charity Organization Society of the City of New York, Tenement House Committee. *The Present Status of Tenement House Regulation.* (pamphlet) New York, 1921. New York City Municipal Archives.

Chermayeff–American Society of Planners and Architects Papers. Widner Library, Harvard University, Cambridge, Mass.

Chermayeff, Serge. "Telesis: The Birth of a Group." *Pencil Points* (July 1942), 23:45–48.

Chermayeff, Serge and Christopher Alexander. *Community and Privacy.* Garden City, N.Y.: Doubleday, 1963.

Chiffard, Jean-François and Yves Roujon. "Les HBM et la ceinture de Paris: Après les fortifs et la zone, la ceinture." *Architecture Movement Continuité* (1977), 43:9–25.

Chipperfield, David. "Style or Pragmatum: Ciriani's Housing and Stirling's Apartments Contrasted." *International Architecture* (No. 5, 1981), 1:26–34.

Citizen's Association of New York. Council of Hygiene and Public Health. *Report Upon the Sanitary Condition of the City.* New York: D. Appleton, 1865.

Citizens Housing Council of New York. *Wartime Housing in the New York Metropolitan Area.* New York, 1942.

Citizens Housing and Planning Council of New York. *Renewal and Rebuttal: the City Planning Commission Tells the Public Its Decisions on the Suitability of the So-Called West Village Area for Urban Renewal Study and Planning.* New York, 1961.

City and Suburban Homes Company, *Model City and Suburban Homes. The Meeting Ground of Business and Philanthropy.* New York, 1905. Edith Elmer Wood Collection, Avery Arts Library, Columbia University.

—— *Thirty-Sixth Annual Report.* New York, May 1932.

—— *Twenty-Fifth Annual Report.* New York, May 1921.

—— *Twenty-First Annual Report.* New York, May 1917.

City Housing Corporation. *Fourth Annual Report.* New York, 1928.

—— *Fifth Annual Report.* New York, 1929.

—— *Radburn Carden Homes.* New York, n.d. Edith Elmer Wood Collection, Avery Library, Columbia University.

—— *Sixth Annual Report.* New York, 1930.

—— *Sunnyside and the Housing Problem.* New York, n.d.

—— *Your Share in Better Housing.* New York, 1924.

Ciucci, Giorgio. Francesco Dal Co, Mario Manieri-Elia, Manfredo Tafuri. *The American City From the Civil War to the New Deal.* Cambridge, Mass.: The MIT Press, 1979.

Close, Katheryn. "New Homes With Insurance Dollars." *Survey Graphic* (November 1948), 37:450–454.

Code of Ordinances of the City of New York as Amended 9/15. New York: Chief, 1915.

Colean, Miles L. *Housing for Defense.* New York: Twentieth Century Fund, 1940.

Comer, John P. *New York City Building Control: 1800–1941.* New York: Columbia University Press, 1942.

Commager, Henry Steele. *Documents of American History.* 2 Vols. New York: F. S. Crofts & Co., 1935.

Conason, Joe. "The Westway Alternative." *Village Voice,* June 9, 1980, p. 1.

Congres International d'Architecture Moderne, *Rationelle Bebauungsweisen. Ergebnisse des 3. Internationalen Kongresses für Neues Bauen.* Stuggart-Julius Hoffman, 1931.

Cooper, Alexander and Associates. *Battery Park City: Draft Summary Report and 1979 Master Plan.* New York: Alexander Cooper Associates, October 1979.

Cooper, L. E. "$6 Rentals Held Feasible on the East Side." *New York Times*, April 29, 1934, sec. X and XI, p. 1.

Costello, Augustine E. *Our Firemen: A History of the New York Fire Departments*. New York: Costello, 1887.

Cromley, Elizabeth C. "The Development of the New York Apartment, 1860–1905." Doctor of Philosophy Dissertation, City College of the City University of New York, 1982.

Cromwell, Freeman. "The Push Button Elevator as a Renting Aid." *Real Estate Record and Builders' Guide* (January 17, 1931), 9, 117:39.

Crotty, Paul A. "Nehiamiah Plan." Letter to the Editor, *New York Times*, October 25, 1987, sec. VIII, p. 22.

Curl, James Stevens. *The Life and Work of Henry Roberts. 1803–1876*. Chichester, Sussex: Phillimore, 1983.

DaCunha, George W. "Improved Tenements." *American Architect and Building News.* (June 27, 1896), 52:123–124.

Dahir, James. "Fresh Meadows—New York Life's Big Rental Development in the Borough of Queens, N.Y." *The American City* (July 1948), 63:80–82.

The Dalhousie Brochure. New York, 1884. Avery Architectural and Fine Arts Library, Columbia University.

Daniels, Lee A. "City Is Sponsoring 2,200 Small Houses." *New York Times*, February 13, 1981, p. 1.

—— "Housing Partnership Begins in the Middle." *New York Times*, January 29, 1984, sec. IV, p. 7.

—— "Lots Are Drawn for New Middle-Income Homes." *New York Times*, December 9, 1983, sec. II, p. 3.

Daunton, M. J. *House and Home in the Victorian City*. London: Edward Arnold, 1983.

Davies, Jane. "Llewellyn Park in West Orange, New Jersey." *Antiques* (January 1975), 107:142–158.

Davis, Katherine Bement. *Report on the Exhibit of the Workingman's Model Home*. Albany: James B. Lyon, 1893.

Dean, John P. *Home Ownership: Is It Sound?* New York: Harper, 1945.

DeForest, Robert W. and Lawrence Veiller, eds. *The Tenement House Problem*. 2 vols. New York: Macmillan, 1903.

DeLancy, Chuck. "Lofts for Whose Living?" *City Limits* (October 1981), pp. 20–21.

DePalma, Anthony. "Can City's Plan Rebuild the Lower East Side?" *New York Times*, October 14, 1984, sec. IV, p. 6.

—— "Construction of Apartments in Manhattan Falls Sharply." *New York Times*, April 3, 1988, sec. X, p. 1.

—— "Developing New Housing Standards." *New York Times*, May 31, 1987, sec. VIII, p. 1.

—— "Is the Upper East Side Moving North?" *New York Times*, January 31, 1988, sec. VIII, p. 1.

—— "The Nehiamiah Plan: A Success But . . ." *New York Times,* September 27, 1987, sec. VIII, p. 1.

Derby, Nelson L. "A Model Tenement House." *American Architect and Building News* (January 20, 1877), 2:19–21.

DeSalvo, Joseph S. *An Economic Analysis of New York City's Mitchell-Lama Housing Program*. New York: New York City Rand Institute, June 1971.

Desmond, H. W. "The Works of Ernest Flagg." *Architectural Record* (April 1902), 11:1–104.

Dexter, Seymour. "Comparative Building and Loan Associations in the State of New York." *Journal of Social Science* (December 1888), 25:138–148.

Dorman, Frank. "Managers Are Mayors of Small Cities." *Shelter* (April 1938), 3:15–18.

Doubilet, Susan. "I'd Rather Be Interesting." *Progressive Architecture* (February 1984), 65:66.

Douglas, Carlyle. "Ex-Residents Fondly Recall 'Island in Harlem'." *New York Times*, March 15, 1985, p. B1.

—— "In Brooklyn's Bedford-Stuyvesant, Glimmers of Resurgence Are Visible." *New York Times*, April 19, 1985, p. B-1.

Dowd, Maureen. "Hard Times in Brooklyn: How Two Neighborhoods Have Coped." *New York Times*, July 4, 1985, sec. 11, p. 1.

Dickens, Charles. *American Notes*. 2 vols. London: Chapman and Hall, 1842.

Downtown–Lower Manhattan Association. *Lower Manhattan: Major Improvements, Land Use, Transportation, Traffic*. New York: Downtown–Lower Manhattan Association, 1963.

Dows, Olin. "The New Deal's Treasury Art Program: A Memoir." In Francis V. O'Connor, ed., *The New Deal Art Projects: An Anthology of Memoirs*, pp. 11–50. Washington, D.C.: Smithsonian Institution Press, 1972.

Draft Environmental Impact Statement and Section 4(f) Statement for West Side High-

way . . . U.S. Department of Transportation, April 25, 1974.

Dresser, George W. "Plan for a Colony of Tenements." *Plumber and Sanitary Engineer* (April 1879), 2:124.

The Paul Lawrence Dunbar Apartments and Dunbar National Bank. Promotional Brochure. New York, n.d. Edith Elmer Wood Collection, Avery Library, Columbia University.

Dunlap, David W. "Coney Island Residents Fault New Homes." *New York Times*, July 6, 1984, p. 3.

—— "Koch Proposes Shift in Coney Island Housing." *New York Times*, September 8, 1983, sec. II, p. 3.

Duplaix, Michael. "The Loft Generation." *Esquire* (June 1961), pp. 108–111.

East, Arthur M. "Modern Tenements Needed in Chelsea." *Real Estate Record and Builders' Guide* (February 7, 1914), 93:270–271.

Eimicke, William B. "New York State Housing Division Manages the Unmanageable" (Letter to the Editor). *New York Times*, March 23, 1987, p. 16.

Elsing, William T. "Life in New York Tenement Houses." *Scribner's* (June 1892), 11:697–721.

Elton, Edith E. *Forest Close in Relationship to Suburban Planning in England and America in the Early Twentieth Century*. M.A. thesis, Queens College, May 1986.

Emerson, William. "The Open Stair Tenement." *American Architect* (February 14, 1917), vol. 111.

Emery, Charles E. "The Lessons of the Columbian Year." *Cassier's* (January 1894), 5:203–210.

Ennis, Thomas W. "15,500-Apartment Co-op to Rise in Bronx." *New York Times*, February 10, 1965.

—— "New Zoning Law In Effect Friday." *New York Times*, December 10, 1961, sec. VIII, p. 1.

Farrell, William F. "Architects Score Co-op City Design." *New York Times*, February 20, 1965.

Fassbinder, Horant. *Berliner Arbeiterviertal 1800–1918*. West Berlin: Verlag fur das Stadium der Arbeiterbewegung GmbH, 1975.

Fernow, Berthold, ed. *The Records of New Amsterdam from 1653 to 1674*. 7 vols. New York: Knickerbocker Press, 1897. Reprint ed., Baltimore: Genealogical Publishing Co., 1976.

Ferris, Hugh. *The Metropolis of Tomorrow*. New York: I. Washburn, 1929.

Fischler, Stan. *Uptown, Downtown: A Trip Through Time on New York's Subways*. New York: Hawthorn Books, 1976.

Fisher, Robert. *Twenty Years of Public Housing*. New York: Harper, 1959.

Fistere, John Chusman. "Tradition-Innovation." *Ladies Home Journal* (June 1937), 54:28–31, 45.

Fitch, James Marston. *American Building: The Historical Forces That Shaped It*. Boston: Houghton Mifflin, 1946.

Flagg Court. Rental Brochure. New York: n.d. Ernest Flagg Archive, Avery Library, Columbia University.

Flagg, Ernest. "The New York Tenement-House Evil and Its Cure." *Scribner's* (July 1894), 16:108–117.

—— "The Planning of Apartment Houses and Tenements." *Architectural Review* (July 1903), 10:85–90.

Forbes, Gervet. "Remarks." *Annual Reports of Deaths in the City and County of New York for the Year 1834*. New York, 1835.

Ford, James. *Slums and Housing*. 2 vols. Cambridge, Mass.: Harvard University Press, 1936.

Forest Hills Gardens. Pamphlet No. 1. New York: Sage Foundation Homes, 1911.

Forman, Allen. "Some Adopted Americans." *The American* (November 1888), 9:46–53.

Fowler, Glenn. "Unsuccessful Cooperative Will Now Offer Rentals." *New York Times*, March 22, 1976.

Frampton, Kenneth. "The Generic Street as a Continuous Built Form." In Stanford Anderson, ed., *On Streets*, pp. 309–337. Cambridge, Mass.: MIT Press, 1978.

—— "Twin Parks as Typology." *Architectural Forum* (June 1973), 137:54–67.

Frampton, Kenneth, and Alessandra Latour. "Notes On American Architectural Education." *Lotus International* (1980), 27:5–39.

Freedlander, J. H. *Scrapbooks*. 4 vols. Avery Architectural and Fine Arts Library, Columbia University, New York, 1940.

Freidberg, Peter. "Jane Jacobs Defends 'White Elephant'." *New York Post*, October 15, 1975, p. 19.

—— "Jane Jacobs Old Fight Lingers On."

French, Fred F. "394,000 Persons Eager to Live Downtown, French Survey Shows." *New York Herald Tribune*, April 8, 1934, sec. X, p. 1.

Fred F. French Management Company. *Knickerbocker Village*. New York: 1933. Rental Brochure.

Fried, Joseph P. "Manhattan Plaza Wins Approval To Get Tenants." *New York Times*, March 15, 1977.

—— "Mitchell-Lama Housing Beset by Problems, but City Sees Progress in Solving Them." *New York Times*, December 8, 1974.

—— "A Village Housing Project Becomes a Fiscal Nightmare." *New York Times*, August 8, 1975.

Friedman, Edward L. "Cast-in-Place Technique Restudied." *Progressive Architecture* (October 1960), 41:158–175.

Frohne, W. H. "The Apartment House." *Architectural Record* (March 1910), 27:205–217.

Fryer, W. J. *Laws Relating to Buildings*. New York: Record and Guide, 1887.

Galbraith, John Kenneth. "Big Shots." *New York Review of Books* (May 12, 1988), 35:44–46.

Gale, Arthur John. "American Architecture from a Constructional Point of View." In *The Transactions, 1882–1883*, pp. 45–46. London: Royal Institute of British Architects, September 1883.

—— "The Godwin Bursary: Report of a Tour in the United States of America." In *The Transactions, 1882–1883*, pp. 57–64. London: Royal Institute of British Architects, September 1883.

Gallatin, James. "Tenement House Reform in the City of New York." *Public Health. Papers and Reports Presented at the Eighth Annual Meeting of the American Public Health Association*. Boston: Franklin Press, 1881, pp. 309–317.

Garnier, Tony. *Une cité industrielle: Etude pour la construction des villes*. Paris: Editions Vincent, 1918.

Geist, Johann Friedrich. *Das Berliner Meitshaus*. Munich: Prestel, 1980.

Geist, William E. "Residents Give a Bronx Cheer to Decal Plan." *New York Times*, November 12, 1983, p. 1.

Genevro, Rosalie. "Site Selection and the New York City Housing Authority." *Journal of Urban History* (August 1986), 12:334–352.

Gervis, Stephanie. "Loftless Leonardos Picket as Mona Merely Smiles." *Village Voice*, February 14, 1963, p. 1.

Gessner, Albert. *Das deutsche Miethaus*. Munich: F. Bruckmann, 1909.

Giedion, Siegfried. *Walter Gropius*. Paris: Editions G. Crès et Cie, 1931.

—— *Walter Gropius*. Stuttgart: G. Hatje, 1954.

Giovannini, Joseph. "Tea Services with the Touch of an Architect." *New York Times*, November 17, 1983, p. C12.

Giurgola, Romaldo. "The Discreet Charm of the Bourgeoisie." *Architectural Forum* (June 1973), 138:56–57.

Glass, Ruth. *London: Aspects of Change*. London: MacGibbon and Kee, 1964.

Goddard, J. R. "Village Area Artists Win/Lose This Week." *Village Voice*, April 13, 1963, p. 1.

Goldberger, Paul. "Architecture: Townhouse Rows." *New York Times*, June 16, 1980, sec. III, p. 15.

—— "Battery Park City Is a Triumph of Urban Design." *New York Times*, August 31, 1986, sec. II, p. 23.

—— "Developers Learned Some Lessons and Cut Back." *New York Times*, December 28, 1986, sec. II, p. 27.

—— "Eleven on 67." *New York Times*, April 4, 1982, sec. VIII, p. 1.

—— "Height of 8 Towers Could Overwhelm Wide Open Space." *New York Times*, November 19, 1985, sec. II, p. 4.

—— "Low-Rise, Low-Key Housing Gives Banality a Test in West Village." *New York Times*, September 28, 1974.

—— "A Recycled Loft Restores the Luxury to City's Luxury Housing." *New York Times*, July 7, 1977, p. C10.

—— "Trump: Symbol of a Gaudy, Impatient Time." *New York Times*, January 31, 1988, sec. II, p. 32.

Goodman, George W. "Housing in Brownsville Progresses." *New York Times*, November 6, 1983, sec. VIII, p. 6.

—— "Illegal Loft Tenants Get Second Chance." *New York Times*, June 12, 1983, sec. VIII, p. 6.

Goodwin, Michael. "Census Finds Fewer Blacks in Harlem." *New York Times*, May 30, 1981, p. 27.

—— "A Home Ownership Aid Program Is Planned for City." *New York Times*, February 22, 1980, sec. II, p. 3.

—— "Project Admits Tenants To End a Three-Year Delay." *New York Times*, August 16, 1979.

Gordon, Henry A. *Subway Nickels: A Survey of New York City's Transit Problem*. New

York, January 29, 1925. Pamphlet at New York Public Library.

Gottlieb, Martin. "A Decade After the Cutbacks, New York Is a Different City." *New York Times*, June 30, 1985, p. 1.

—— "New York's Rescue: The Offstage Drama." *New York Times*, July 2, 1985, p. 1.

—— "Trump Set To Buy Lincoln West Site." *New York Times*, December 1, 1984, p. 1.

Gould, Elgin R. L. *The Housing of the Working People: Eighth Special Report of the Commissioner of Labor*. Washington, D.C.: GPO, 1895.

—— "Homewood—A Model Suburban Settlement." Review of Reviews (July 1897), 16:43–51.

—— "The Housing Problem." *Municipal Affairs* (March 1899), 3:122–131.

Graybill, Samuel H. Jr. *Bruce Price, American Architect, 1845–1903*. 2 vols., Ann Arbor, Michigan: University Microfilms International, 1976.

Grimm, David. "Account of the 1776 Fire for the New York State Historical Society" (1870), Cited by I. N. Phelps Stokes, *The Iconography of Manhattan Island: 1498–1909*, 5:1021.

Gries, John M. and James Ford, eds. *The President's Conference on House Building and Home Ownership*. 11 vols. Washington, D.C.: GPO, 1932.

Griscom, John H. *Annual Report of the Interments in the City and County of New York for the Year 1842, with Remarks Thereon, and a Brief View of the Sanitary Condition of the City*. New York: James van Norden, 1843.

—— *The Sanitary Condition of the Laboring Population of New York with Suggestions for Its Improvement*. New York: Harper, 1845.

—— *The Uses and Abuses of Air: Showing Its Influence in Sustaining Life and Producing Disease, with Remarks on the Ventilation of Houses*, New York: Redfield, 1854.

Gropius, Walter. *The New Architecture and the Bauhaus*. London: Farber and Farber, 1935.

—— *Scope of Total Architecture*. New York: Harper and Row, 1955.

Gross, Arthur. "The New Multiple Dwelling Law of New York." *Architectural Forum* (September 1930), 53:273–276.

Guilbaut, Serge. *How New York Stole the Idea of Modern Art: Abstract Expressionism, Freedom, and the Cold War*. Chicago: University of Chicago Press, 1983.

Haenel, Erich, and Heinrich Tscharmann. *Das Mietwohnhaus der Neuzeit*. Leipzig: S. S. Weber, 1913.

Hale, Jonathan. "Ten Years Past at Peabody Terrace." *Progressive Architecture* (October 1974), 55:72–77.

Halpern, Lawrence and Associates. *New York, New York*. New York City Housing and Development Administration, 1968.

Hamlin, Talbot. "New York Housing: Harlem River Houses and Williamsburg Houses." *Pencil Points* (May 1938), 19:281–292.

—— "The Prize-Winning Buildings of 1931." *Architectural Record* (January 1932), 71:10–26.

Handlin, David P. *The American Home. Architecture and Society, 1815–1915*. Boston: Little, Brown, 1979.

Harder, Julius. "The City's Plan." *Municipal Affairs* (March 1898), 2:24–45.

Hardie, James. *An Account of the Malignant Fever Lately Prevalent in the City of New York*. New York: Hartin and McFarlane, 1799.

Harding, George Edward. "Electric Elevators." *American Architect and Building News* (October 27, 1894), 46:31–34.

Harlem Task Force. *Redevelopment Strategy for Central Harlem*. New York: Office of the Mayor, August 1982.

Harris, Neil. *The Artist in American Society: The Formative Years, 1790–1860*. New York: Braziller, 1966, ch. 10.

Haswell, Charles H. *Reminiscences of an Octogenarian of the City of New York: 1816–1860*. New York: Harper, 1896.

Haverstock, Mary Sayre. "The Tenth Street Studio." *Art in America* (September–October 1966), 54:18–57.

Hayden, Dolores. *The Grand Domestic Revolution: A History of Feminist Designs for American Homes, Neighborhoods, and Cities*. Cambridge, Mass.: MIT Press, 1981.

Hegemann, Werner. *City Planning; Housing*. 3 vols. New York: Architectural Book Publishing, 1938.

Herberg, Will. "The Jewish Labor Movement in the United States." *American Jewish Yearbook* (1952), 53:3–74.

Hill, C. T. "The Growth of the Upper West Side of New York." *Harper's Weekly* (July 25, 1896), 40:730–731, 734.

Hinds, Michael de Courcy. "Along Upper Broadway a Revival." *New York Times*, May 26, 1985, sec. VIII, p. 1.

—— "Delays Beset 255-Unit Modular Project in Brownsville." *New York Times*, June 29, 1986, sec. VIII, p. 7.

—— "Frenzy of Building Brings 18,000 Units to Market." *New York Times*, September 7, 1986, sec. XII, pp. 46–48.

—— "Marketing Third Avenue as a Chic Address." *New York Times*, March 24, 1985, sec. VIII, p. 1.

—— "Shaping a Landfill into a Neighborhood." *New York Times*, March 23, 1986, sec. VIII, p. 1.

Historic American Building Survey. *New York City Architecture: Selections*. Washington, D.C.: National Park Service, 1969.

Hitchcock, Henry Russell, Jr. and Philip Johnson. *The International Style: Architecture Since 1922*. New York: Norton, 1932.

Holden, Arthur C. "Facing Realities in Slum Clearance." *Architectural Record* (February 1932), 71:79.

—— "A Review of Proposals for the Chrystie-Forsyth Area." *Real Estate Record and Builders' Guide* (May 20, 1933), 131:7–9.

Hornick, Sandy, Arne Kotlen, Tony Levy, and David Vandor. "Quality Housing and Related Zoning Text Amendments." Memorandum. New York City Planning Commission, April 1985.

Horowitz, C. Morris and Lawrence J. Kaplan. *The Estimated Jewish Population of the New York Area, 1900–1975*. New York Federation of Jewish Philanthropies of New York, 1959.

Horsley, Carter B. "Housing for 24,000 Begun in Brooklyn." *New York Times*, July 16, 1972.

—— "Loft Conversions Exceeding New Apartment Construction." *New York Times*, October 12, 1980, sec. VIII, p. 1.

Houghton, Herbert R. "Experienced Observers Analyze Market Prospects." *Real Estate Record and Builders' Guide* (September 15, 1928), 122:7, 39.

Howard, Ebenezer. *Garden Cities of Tomorrow*. London: Swan Sonnenschein, 1902.

Howard, James J. Letter to the Editor. *New York Times*, May 28, 1985, p. A-18.

Howe, Samuel. "Forest Hills Gardens." *American Architect* (October 30, 1912), 102:153–160.

Howells and Stokes. *Scrapbook of Clippings*. Avery Architectural and Fine Arts Library Columbia University.

Hoyt, Charles. "Crisis in Housing. What Did the New Super-Agency Mean for the Architect?" *Architectural Record* (October 1975), 158:107–110.

Hubert, Christian, and Lindsay Stamm Shapiro. *William Lescaze*. Institute for Architecture and Urban Studies Catalogue 16. New York: Rizzoli, 1982.

Hubert, Pirsson, and Company. *Where and How To Build*. New York, 1892. New York Public Library.

Hubert, Pirsson, and Hoddick. "New York Flats and French Flats." *Architectural Record* (July–September 1892), 2:55–64.

Hudnut, Joseph. "A Long-Haired Reply to Moses." *New York Times Magazine* (July 23, 1944), p. 16.

—— "The Post-Modern House." *Architectural Record* (May 1945), 97:70–75.

Hurd, Richard M. *Principles of City Land Values*. New York: Record and Guide, 1903.

Huxtable, Ada Louise. "Bending the Rules." *New York Times*, May 10, 1970, sec. II, p. 23.

Improved Housing Council. *Conditions of Competition for Plans of Model Apartment Houses*. New York, 1896. New York Public Library.

Israels, Charles H. "New York Apartment Houses." *The Architectural Record* (July 1901), 2:490–93.

Ives, Douglas H. "The Moderate Priced Apartment Hotel." *Architectural Forum*. (September 1930), 53:309–312.

Jackson, Anthony. *A Place Called Home: A History of Low-Cost Housing in Manhattan*. Cambridge, Mass.: MIT Press, 1976.

Jackson, J. B. *The Necessity For Ruins*. Amherst, Mass.: University of Massachusetts Press, 1980.

Jackson, Kenneth T. *Crabgrass Frontier: The Suburbanization of the United States*. New York: Oxford University Press, 1985.

Jackson, Will Walter. "A Peculiar Situation in Tenement Work." *Real Estate Record and Builders' Guide* (February 28, 1914), 93:398.

Jacobs, Jane. *The Death and Life of Great American Cities*. New York: Random House, 1961.

Jacobson, Michael and Philip Kasinitz. "Burning the Bronx for Profit." *The Nation* (November 15, 1986), 242:512–515.

Jaffe, Julian F. *Crusade Against Radicalism: New York During the Red Scare, 1914–1924*. Port Washington, N.Y.: Kennikut Press, 1972.

Jallings, John H. *Elevators: A Practical Trea-*

tise on the Development and Design of Hand, Belt, Steam, Hydraulic, and Electric Elevators. Chicago: American Technical Society, 1915.

Jardine, Murdock, and Wright, Architects. *Chrystie–Forsyth Street Housing*. Untitled prospectus dated February 15, 1933. Edith Elmer Wood Collection, Avery Library, Columbia University.

Jefferson, Thomas. *Notes on the State of Virginia*. William Peden, ed. Chapel Hill: University of North Carolina Press, 1955.

Johnson, Kirk. "The 'Lumpy' Co-op Market Gets Tougher To Track as It Grows." *New York Times*, April 28, 1985, p. 1.

—— "One-Family Houses for East Harlem." *New York Times*, June 9, 1985, sec. VIII, p. 6.

—— "Pace of Co-op Conversion Slackening." *New York Times*, December 2, 1984, sec. VIII, p. 1.

—— "Rediscovering Cathedral Parkway." *New York Times*, May 5, 1985, sec. VIII, p. 6.

—— "Suddenly the Barrio Is Drawing Buyers." *New York Times*, June 2, 1985, sec. VIII, p. 1.

Johnson, Lee F. "How They Licked the TEW Bill." *Survey Graphic* (November 1948), 37:445–449.

Jones, Richard P. "Up the Riverton." Letter to the Editor, *Esquire* (September 1960), 46:16.

Kaplan, Barry J. "Metropolitics, Administrative Reform, and Political Theory: The Greater New York Charter of 1897." *Journal of Urban History* (February 1983), 9:164–194.

Katan, Roger. *Pueblos for El Bario*. New York: United Residents of Milbank–Frawley Circle–East Harlem Association, 1967. Avery Architectural and Fine Arts Library, Columbia University.

Kazan, Abraham E. "Building and Financing Our Cooperative Homes." *Festival Journal: 20th Anniversary Amalgamated Cooperative Community, 1927–1947*. New York: A and L Consumers Society, 1947.

Kelsey, J. S. *History of Long Island City*. Long Island City, N.Y.: Long Island Star, 1896.

Kennedy, W. Sloan. "The Vertical Railway." *Harper's New Monthly* (November 1882), 65:888–894.

Klaber, John J. "An Economic Housing Plan for the Chrystie-Forsyth Area." *Real Estate Record and Builders' Guide* (May 7, 1932), 129:6–8.

Klare, Michael T. "The Architecture of Imperial America." *Science and Society* (Summer-Fall 1969), 33:257–284.

Klein, Dan. "The Chanin Building, New York." *The Connoisseur* (July 1974), 181:162–169.

Koch, Carl. "What Is the Attitude of the Young Practitioner Toward the Profession?" *Journal of the American Institute of Architects* (June 1947), 7:265–269.

Koch, Edward I. "Of Deals and Priorities for the South Bronx" (Letter to the Editor). *New York Times*, November 19, 1983, p. 24.

Kotlen, Arnold S., and David Vandor. "More and Better. Zoning For Quality Housing." *New York Affairs* (No. 4, 1986), 9:99–108.

Kramer, Howard D. "The Germ Theory and the Early Public Health Program in the United States." *Bulletin of the History of Medicine*, (May–June, 1948), 21:233–247.

Kristoff, Frank. *Changes in New York City's Housing Status, 1950–1960*. New York: Housing and Redevelopment Board, 1961.

Labadie, Jean. "Les cathédrales de la cité moderne." *L'Illustration* CLX (August 12, 1922), 131–135.

—— "À la recherche d'homme scientifique." *Science et Vie* (December 1925), 28:546–556.

LaBeaume, Louis. "The Federal Building Program." *Octagon: A Journal of the American Institute of Architects* (April 1931), 3:13–15.

Lack, Judith C. "Dispute Still Rages as West Village Houses Meets Its Sales Test." *New York Times*, August 18, 1974.

Laer, A. J. F. van, ed. *Documents Relating to New Netherland: 1624–1626*. San Marino, Calif.: Henry E. Huntington Library, 1924.

Landau, Sarah Bradford. *Edward T. and William A. Potter: American Victorian Architects*. New York: Garland, 1979.

—— "Richard Morris Hunt: Architectural Innovator and Father of a 'Distinctive' American School." In Susan E. Stein, ed., *The Architecture of Richard Morris Hunt*. Chicago: University of Chicago Press, 1986.

Lanmon, Lorraine Welling. *William Lescaze, Architect*. Philadelphia: Art Alliance Press, 1987.

Larrabee, Eric. "The Six Thousand Houses That Levitt Built." *Harper's* (September 1948), 197:79–88.

Latour, Alessandra, ed. *Pasanella and Klein*. Rome: Edizion Kappa, 1983.

Lauren, Bernard and James Whyte. *The Au-*

tomatic Elevator in Residential Buildings. New York: Elevator Industries Association, 1952.

Fred L Lavanburg Foundation. *First-Annual Report.* New York, 1929. Edith Elmer Wood Archive, Avery Architectural and Fine Arts Library.

—— *Practices and Experiences of the Lavanberg Homes,* New York, 1934.

Lawson, Ronald and Mark Navon, eds. *The Tenant Movement in New York City, 1904–1984.* New Brunswick, N.J.: Rutgers University Press, 1986.

Lazar, Michael. *Land Use and the Westside Highway Recommendations: A Report of the Working Committee on the Westside Highway Project from Michael J. Lazar and John Zuccotti.* New York City Planning Commission, 1974.

Lear, John. "Hiroshima, USA." *Collier's* (August 5, 1950), 126:11–15.

Le Corbusier. *Le Corbusier.* Florence: Electra Editrice, 1951.

—— *Oeuvre Complete, 1938–1946.* Zurich: W. Boesiger, 1946.

—— "A Plan for St. Die." *Architectural Record* (October 1946), 100:79–80.

—— *Quand les cathédrales étaient blanches.* Paris: Plon, 1937.

—— "Trois rappels à MM. les Architects." *L'Esprit Noveau,* no. 4, pp. 457–470.

—— *Urbanisme.* Paris: Editions Vincent, Fréal, et cie, 1966.

Leid, Utrice C. "A Neighborhood Grows in Brooklyn Ghost Town." *City Sun,* October 24–30, 1984, p. 1.

Lemov, Penelope. "Life After Section 8." *Builder* (February 1985), pp. 110–117.

Lewis, Wilfred S. "Architects Contracts." Memorandum to Langdon W. Post, dated October 30, 1934. New York City Housing Authority Archives, LaGuardia Community College, box 15A4, folder 7.

Lichten, Eric. *Class, Power and Austerity. The New York City Fiscal Crisis.* South Hadley, Mass.: Bergin and Garvey Publishers, 1986.

Lichtenberg, Blanche. Interview with Richard Plunz, February 14, 1986.

Liebman, Herman. "Twenty Years of Community Activities." *Festival Journal: 20th Anniversary Amalgamated Cooperative Community, 1927–1947.* New York: A and L Consumers Society, 1947.

Lockwood, Charles. *Bricks and Brownstone: The New York Row House, 1783–1929, an Architectural and Social History.* New York: McGraw-Hill, 1972.

—— *Manhattan Moves Uptown: An Illustrated History.* Boston: Houghton Mifflin, 1976.

Logue, Edward. "The Future of Housing in New York City." in Richard Plunz, ed. *Housing Form and Public Policy in the United States.* New York: Praeger, 1980, ch. 2.

Lubasch, Arnold H. "Corps Aide Sees No Alternative to the Westway." *New York Times,* May 23, 1985, p. B-3.

Lubov, Roy. "I. N. Phelps-Stokes: Tenement House Architect, Economist, Planner." *Journal of the Society of Architectural Historians* (May 1964), 23:75–87.

Lubov, Roy. *The Progressives and the Slums: Tenement House Reform in New York City, 1890–1917.* Pittsburgh: University of Pittsburgh Press, 1963.

Lueck, Thomas C. "Trump City Site May Be Sold, Developer Says." *New York Times,* October 13, 1988, p. B1.

Lynch, Dennis Tilden. *The Wild Seventies.* 2 vols. Port Washington, N.Y.: Kennikat Press, 1971.

Lynes, Russell. *Good Old Modern. An Intimate Portrait of the Museum of Modern Art.* New York: Atheneum, 1973.

Lyons, Richard P. "If You're Thinking of Living in Manhattan Valley." *New York Times,* February 8, 1987, sec. VIII, p. 9.

Manhattan Borough President's Task Force on Housing for Homeless Families. *A Shelter is not a Home.* New York, March 1987.

Manhattan Valley Development Corporation. Brochure. New York: Manhattan Valley Development Corporation, 1983.

Marchand, Roland. *Advertising The American Dream. Making Way For Modernity, 1920–1940.* Berkeley: University of California Press, 1985.

Marcuse, Peter. "The Beginnings of Public Housing in New York." *Journal of Urban History* (August 1986), 12:353–390.

—— "The Targeted Crisis —on the Ideology of the Urban Fiscal Crisis and Its Uses." *International Journal of Urban and Regional Research* (September 1981), 5:330–355.

—— "Why Are They Homeless?" *The Nation* (April 4, 1987), 244:426–429.

Marks, Alexander. "Future Possibilities of Push-Button Control for Electric Elevators." *American Architect* (August 6, 1919), 116:187–194.

Marquis, James. *The Metropolitan Life*. New York: Viking Press, 1947.

Martin, Walter C. "Reports of 83,459 Vacancies in Tenement Houses." *Real Estate Record and Builders' Guide* (February 4, 1928), 121:10.

May, Charles C. "Forest Hills Gardens from the Town Planning Viewpoint." *Architecture* (August 1916), 34:161–172, plates CXIX–CXXVII.

Mayer, Albert. "A Critique of Knickerbocker Village." *Architecture* (January 1935), 71:5–10.

McCague, James. *The Second Rebellion: The Story of the New York City Draft Riots of 1865*. New York: Dial Press, 1968.

McFadden, Robert D. "City Puts Cheery Face on Crumbling Facades." *New York Times*, October 10, 1980, sec. II, p. 1.

—— "Derelict Tenements in the Bronx To Get Fake Lived-In Look." *New York Times*, November 7, 1983, p. 1.

McGoldrick, Joseph D., Seymour Graubard, and Raymond Horowitz. *Building Regulation in New York City: A Study in Administrative Law and Procedure*. New York: Commonwealth Fund, 1944.

McNeill, William H. *Plagues and Peoples*. Garden City, New York: Doubleday, 1976.

Meakin, Budgett. *Model Factories and Villages*. Philadelphia: Jacobs, 1905.

Medioli, Alfred. "Housing Form and Rehabilitation in New York City." In Richard Plunz, ed., *Housing Form and Public Policy in the United States*. New York: Praeger, 1980, ch. 14.

Meier, Richard. *Richard Meier, Architect*. New York: Oxford University Press, 1976.

Mendel, Ernest. *Late Capitalism*. Joris De Bres, tr. London: Verso, 1978.

The Metropolitan Life Insurance Company. *Just The Place For Your Children. Homes For 2125 Families. The Metropolitan Life's New City*. Promotional Brochure (New York, no date). Edith Elmer Wood Collection, Avery Library, Columbia University.

Meyer, Henry C. *The Story of the Sanitary Engineer, Later the Engineering Record Supplementary to Civil War Experiences*. New York, 1928.

Miller, Edward. *Report on the Malignant Disease Which Prevailed in the City of New York, in the Autumn of 1805*. New York, 1806. New York Public Library.

Miller, William P. *The Tenement House Committee and the Open Stair Tenements*. New York: American Institute of Architecture, 1912.

Mishan, Ezra J. *The Costs of Economic Growth*. New York: Frederick A. Praeger, 1967.

Monroe, Robert Grier. "The Gas, Electric Light, and Street Railway Services in New York City." *Annals of the American Academy of Political and Social Science* (January–June 1906), 27:111–119.

Moore, Deborah Dash. *At Home In America*. New York: Columbia University Press, 1981.

Morton, George W. "Remarks." *Annual Report of the City of New York, for the Year Ending December 31, 1857*. 1858.

Moscow, Warren. "Mitchell-Lama: The Program That Was." *New York Affairs* (No. 3, 1980), 6:42–45.

Moses, Charles Griffith. "A Mile and a Half of Progress." *Real Estate Record and Builders' Guide* (September 12, 1908), 82:505–506.

Moses, Robert. *Housing and Recreation*. New York: DeVinne-Brown, 1938.

—— "Long-Haired Planners. Common Sense vs. Revolutionary Theories." *New York Times Magazine* (June 25, 1944), pp. 16–17.

—— *Public Works: A Dangerous Trade*. New York: McGraw-Hill, 1970.

Moutoux, John T. "The TVA Builds a Town." *The New Republic* (January 31, 1934), pp. 330–331.

Mumford, Lewis. *The Brown Decades. A Study of the Arts in America, 1865–1895*. New York: Harcourt, Brace, 1931.

—— *The Culture of the Cities*. New York: Harcourt, Brace, 1944.

—— "From Utopia Parkway Turn East." *The New Yorker* (October 22, 1949), 25:102–106.

—— "High Buildings: An American View." *Architects' Journal* (October 1, 1924), 60:487.

—— "The Marseilles 'Folley.'" *The New Yorker* (October 5, 1957), 33:76–95.

—— *Roots of Contemporary American Architecture*. New York: Dover, 1972.

—— *Sticks and Stones: A Study of American Architecture and Civilization*. New York: Boni and Liveright, 1927.

—— "Stuyvesant Town Revisited." *The New Yorker* (November 27, 1948), 24:65–72.

Murdock, Henrietta. "The House of Tomorrow." *Ladies Home Journal* (September 1937), 54:24–26.

Museum of Modern Art. *Another Chance for*

Housing: Low Rise Alternatives: Browns-ville, Brooklyn; Fox Hills, Staten Island. New York: Museum of Modern Art, 1973.

—— *Art in Our Time.* New York: Museum of Modern Art, 1939.

—— *Modern Architecture International Exhibition.* New York: Museum of Modern Art, 1932.

—— *Tomorrow's Small House.* New York: Museum of Modern Art, 1945.

Nevins, Deborah, ed. *The Roosevelt Island Housing Competition.* New York: Wittenborn Art Books, 1975.

Newfield, Jack. "Annual Thanksgiving Honor Roll." *Village Voice*, December, 1986, p. 21.

Newman, Oscar. *Defensible Space: Crime Prevention Through Urban Design.* New York: Macmillan, 1972.

—— In Oscar Newman, ed., *CIAM '59 in Otterloo*, Stuttgart: Karl Kramer, 1961.

"New Model Tenements Uptown for East and West Side Families." In Howells and Stokes, *Scrapbook of Clippings.*

Newsom, Robert T. "Limited-Profit Housing—What Went Wrong?" *New York Affairs* (No. 4, 1975), 2:80–91.

New York Association for Improving the Condition of the Poor. *Thirteenth Annual Report.* New York, 1856.

—— *Fifteenth Annual Report.* New York, 1858.

—— *Sixteenth Annual Report.* New York, 1859.

New York City. *Annual Report of the City of New York for the Year Ending December 31, 1854.* 1855.

—— Board of Estimate and Apportionment. *Building Zone Plan.* 1916.

—— Central Park Commission. *First Annual Report.* New York: William C. Bryant, 1858.

—— City Inspector. *Annual Report, 1856.* 1857.

—— Committee on Slum Clearance Plans. *North Harlem Slum Clearance Plan.* 1951.

—— Department of City Planning. *Housing Database: Public and Publicly Aided Housing.* Vol. 1. August 1983.

—— Department of City Planning. *New Dwelling Units Completed 1921–1972 in New York City.* New York, December 1973.

—— Department of City Planning. *New Housing in New York City, 1981–82.* Pamphlet. December 1983.

—— Department of Parks. *New Parkways in New York City.* 1937.

—— Department of Public Works. *Third Annual Report.* 1893.

—— Health Department. *The Registration of Plumbers and the Laws and Regulations of All Buildings Hereafter Erected.* 1881.

—— Housing and Development Administration. *Record of Submissions and Awards. Competition for Middle-Income Housing at Brighton Beach, Brooklyn.* New York, 1968. Avery Library, Columbia University.

—— Landmarks Preservation Commission. "Ansonia Hotel: Designation Report." 1972.

—— Mayor's Committee on Slum Clearance. *Harlem Slum Clearance Plan Under Title I of the Housing Act of 1949.* 1951.

New York City. Mayor's Committee on Slum Clearance. *Washington Square South. Slum Clearance Plan Under Title I of the Housing Act of 1949.* New York, January 1951.

—— *Minutes of the Common Council of the City of New York: 1675–1776.* 5 vols. New York: Dodd, Mead, 1905.

—— *Minutes of the Common Council of the City of New York: 1784–1831.* 19 vols. New York: M. B. Brown's Printing and Binding, 1917.

—— Tenement House Commission. *First Report: January 1, 1902–July 1, 1903.* 1904.

—— Tenement House Department. *Eighth Report.* March 16, 1917. New York City Arson Strike Force. *A Study of Government Subsidized Housing Programs and Arson: Analysis of Programs Administered in New York City, 1978–1981.* September 1983.

New York City Housing Authority. *Baruch Houses and Playground.* New York: August 19, 1953. Promotional Brochure.

—— *Clason Point Gardens.* 1942.

—— *Competition: Scrapbook of Placing Entries.* New York, 1934. Avery Architectural and Fine Arts Library. Columbia University.

—— *East River Houses.* 1941.

—— *Fifth Annual Report*, New York, 1938.

—— *First Houses.* 1935.

—— *Housing: Cost Analysis.* 1945.

—— *Large-Scale Low Rent Housing: Construction Cost Analysis.* 2 vols. 1946.

—— *Model Exhibit Showing Use of Urban Areas for Multi-Family Habitations.* Works Progress Administration Project 65-97-201. New York, 1938. New York Public Library.

—— *Must We Have Slums?* 1937.

—— *New York City Housing Authority, 1934–1936: Examples of Types of Work.* 1936.

—— *Program of Competition for Qualification of Architects.* New York, June 18, 1934.

Fiorello H. LaGuardia Archives, LaGuardia Community College, box 15A4, folder 7.

—— *Project Data.* July 1, 1985.

—— "Proposed Low-Rental Housing Projects: Block 1670, Manhattan." Avery Architecture and Fine Arts Library. Columbia University (typed manuscript). December 4, 1935.

—— *Tenth Annual Report.* 1944.

—— *Thirteenth Annual Report.* 1947.

—— *Title I Slum Clearance Progress.* 1956.

—— *Toward the End To Be Achieved.* 1937.

—— *Vladeck Houses. A Lesson in Neighborhood History.* New York, 1940.

—— *Wallabout Houses.* 1942.

—— *Williamsburg Slum Clearance Plan.* 1951.

New York City Housing Authority. Technical Division. *Survey of Twenty-three Low-Rental Housing Projects in New York City.* Avery Architecture and Fine Arts Library, Columbia University (microfilm). September 1934.

New York City Planning Commission. *Community Planning Handbook.* New York: September, 1973.

—— *Plan for New York City, 1969.* 6 vols., 1969.

—— *Tenant Relocation Report.* January 20, 1954.

—— *The Lower Manhattan Plan.* 1966.

—— "Quality Housing Amendment Adopted by the Board of Estimate, August 14, 1987." New York, 1987.

New York City Planning Commission. *Rezoning New York City. A Guide to the Proposed Comprehensive Amendment of the Zoning Resolution of the City of New York.* New York, 1959.

New York City Planning Commission. *Zoning Maps and Resolution.* New York, 1961.

New York Colony. *Colonial Laws of New York from the Year 1664 to the Revolution.* 5 vols. Albany: J. B. Lyon, State Printer, 1894–96.

New York Sanitary Reform Society. *First Annual Report.* 1880.

New York Society of Architects, *Yearbook.* 1916.

—— *Yearbook.* 1918.

—— *Yearbook.* 1919.

New York State Court of Appeals. *New York Reports.* 1885.

New York State. Division of Housing. *Annual Report of the Commissioner of Housing to the Governor and the Legislature for the Year Ending March 31, 1950.* Legislative Document No. 14. 1950.

—— Division of Housing and Community Renewal. *Statistical Summary of Programs.* March 31, 1982.

—— Reconstruction Commission. Housing Committee. *Report.* 1920.

—— State Board of Housing. *Annual Report, 1929.* 1929.

—— State Board of Housing. *Annual Report, 1930.* 1930.

—— State Board of Housing. *Annual Report, 1931.* 1931.

—— State Board of Housing. *Annual Report, 1934.* 1934.

—— State Board of Housing. *Annual Report, 1935.* 1935.

—— State Board of Housing. *Report of the State Board of Housing Relative to the Housing Emergency in New York City and Buffalo and Extension of the Rent Laws.* Legislative Document No. 85. Albany: J. B. Lyon, 1928.

—— The Temporary State Commission To Make a Study of the Governmental Operation of the City of New York. *HDA: A Superagency Evaluated.* March 1973.

New York State Assembly. *Laws of the State of New York.* 1807, ch. 115.

—— *Report of the Committee on Public Health, Medical Colleges and Societies, Relative to the Condition of Tenement Houses in the Cities of New York and Brooklyn.* Legislative Document No. 156. March 8, 1867.

—— *Report to the Legislature of the Temporary Commission To Examine and Revise the Tenement House Commission.* Legislative Document No. 60. January 30, 1928.

New York State Assembly. *Report of the Select Committee Appointed to Examine into the Condition of the Tenement Houses in New York and Brooklyn.* Assembly Document no. 205, March 9, 1857.

New York State Assembly. *Report of the Special Committee on Tenement Houses in New York and Brooklyn.* Assembly Document no. 199, April 4, 1856.

—— *Report of the Tenement House Committee of 1894.* Legislative Document No. 37. January 17, 1895.

New York State Council on the Arts. *Inner City Infill: A Housing Competition for Harlem.* New York, 1985.

—— *Reweaving The Urban Fabric. Approaches to Infill Housing.* New York: Princeton Architectural Press, 1989.

New York State Legislature. Joint Legislative Committee on Housing and Reconstruction Commission of the State of New York. *Program of Architectural Competition for* the Remodeling of a New York City Block. Legislative Document No. 78. March 26, 1920.

—— Joint Legislative Committee on Housing and Reconstruction Commission of the State of New York. *Report of the Housing Committee*. Albany: J. B. Lyon, March 26, 1920.

—— *Report of the Board of General Managers of the State of New York at the World's Columbian Exposition*. 1894.

—— *Laws of the State of New York*. 1791, ch. 46.

—— *Laws of the State of New York*. 1800. ch. 16, 87.

—— *Laws of the State of New York*. 1849. ch. 84.

—— *Laws of the State of New York*. 1866. ch. 873.

—— *Laws of the State of New York*. 1867. ch. 908, Sec. 17.

—— *Laws of the State of New York*. 1879. ch. 504.

—— *Laws of the State of New York*. 1882. ch. 410, Title 5.

New York State Legislature. *Laws of the State of New York*. 1884. ch. 272.

—— *Laws of the State of New York*. 1887. ch. 84, 566.

—— *Laws of the State of New York*. 1895. ch. 567.

—— *Laws of the State of New York*, 1901. ch. 334.

New York State Legislature. *Laws of the State of New York*. 1915. ch. 454.

—— *Laws of the State of New York*. 1920. ch. 949.

—— *Laws of the State of New York*. 1922. ch. 658.

—— *Laws of the State of New York*. 1923. ch. 337.

—— *Laws of the State of New York*. 1926. ch. 823.

—— *Laws of the State of New York*. 1929. ch. 713.

—— *Laws of the State of New York*. 1934. ch. 4.

—— *Laws of the State of New York*. 1955, ch. 407, art. 1.

—— *Laws of the State of New York*. 1964. ch. 939.

—— *Laws of the State of New York*. 1968, chs. 173, 174.

—— *Laws of the State of New York*. 1982. ch. 349.

—— *Report of the Joint Legislative Committee on Housing and Urban Development*. Legislative Document No. 75. 1963.

—— *Report of the Special Committee Appointed to Investigate the Public Offices and Departments of the City of New York and of the Counties Therein Included*. 5 vols. 1900.

New York State Senate. *Report of the Tenement House Committee of 1884*. Legislative Document No. 36. February 17, 1885.

New York State Urban Development Corporation. The Island Nobody Knows. New York, 1969.

New York World's Fair. *"Building the World of Tomorrow." Official Guidebook of the World's Fair, 1939*. New York: Exposition Publications, 1939.

Nichols, Mary Perot. "City Official Blasts West Village Groups." *Village Voice*, November 23, 1969, p. 1.

Noffsinger, James Phillip. *The Influence of the Ecole des Beaux-Arts on the Architects of the United States*. Washington, D.C.: Catholic University of America Press, 1955.

Noonan Plaza. Pamphlet. New York: Nelden, 1931. Copy at the Office of Horace Ginsbern and Associates, New York.

Officina Alessi. *Tea and Coffee Piazza*. New York: Shakespeare and Company, 1983.

O'Keefe, Suzanne. "Loft Conversion in Manhattan." *Urban Resources* (Winter 1985), 2:30–31.

Olmsted, Frederick Law and J. J. R. Cross. "The 'Block' Building System of New York." *Plumber and Sanitary Engineer* (April 1879), 2:134.

Open Stair Dwellings Company. *Open Stairs Applied to Industrial Towns and Villages*. New York, June 1929.

Oreskes, Michael. "Fiscal Crisis Still Haunts the Police." *New York Times*, July 6, 1985, sec. II, p. 1.

Orton, Helen Fuller. "Jackson Heights. Its History and Growth." Typescript of paper read before the Newtown Historical Society. January 17, 1950. Queens Borough Public Library.

Oser, Alan S. "Brooklyn Renewal: Two-Story Homes." *New York Times*, April 13, 1984, sec. II, p. 1.

—— "City's Rental-Subsidy Program to Get First Test Soon." *New York Times*, November 18, 1984, sec. VIII, p. 7.

—— "Housing Subsidies a Paradox." *New York Times*, July 18, 1975.

—— "In Brownsville, Churches Joining To Build

Homes . . ." *New York Times*, May 1, 1983, sec. VIII, p. 7.

—— "Lessons from One-Family Housing in the South Bronx." *New York Times*, April 21, 1985, p. 7.

—— "A Luxury Apartment House Will Rise on Broadway." *New York Times*, January 14, 1983, p. B-7.

—— "New 2-Family Houses Without Subsidies." *New York Times*, November 15, 1987, p. 9.

—— "Owner-Occupied Houses: New Test in the South Bronx." *New York Times*, April 1, 1983, sec. VIII, p. 17.

—— "Project Evokes City's Brownstone Era." *New York Times*, January 13, 1984, p. B7.

—— "Restructuring Zoning To Spur Apartment Construction." *New York Times*, June 2, 1985, sec. VIII, p. 7.

—— "Upturn for West Village Houses." *New York Times*, August 20, 1976.

Osofsky, Gilbert. *Harlem: The Making of a Ghetto*. New York: Harper and Row, 1968.

Panuch, J. Anthony. *Building a Better New York*. New York: Office of the Mayor, 1960.

Penkin, Stanley. *The Lower Manhattan Expressway: The Life and Death of a Highway*. M.A. thesis, Avery Library, Columbia University, 1968.

Perkins and Will, Architects. *MLC Rehabilitation Survey*. New York: New York State Mortgage Loan Enforcement and Administration Corporation, July 1983.

—— *The West Village Plan for Housing*. New York: New York State Division of Housing and Community Renewal and the West Village Committee, 1963.

Perlmutter, Emanuel. "Homicides in City Climbed to a Record of 13 for 24-Hour period Ending at 12:01 Yesterday." *New York Times*. August 23, 1972, p. 21.

Perry, Clarence Arthur. *The Rebuilding of Blighted Areas*. New York: Regional Plan Association, 1933.

Peschken, Goerd. "The Berlin 'Meithaus' and Renovation." *Architectural Design* (1983), no. 11 and 12, 53:49–57.

Peterson, Iver. "People Moving Back to Cities, U.S. Study Says." *New York Times*, April 13, 1986.

—— "Tenements of 1880's Adapt to 1980's," *New York Times*, January 3, 1988, sec. VIII, p. 1.

Pfeiffer, Bruce Brooks, (Yukio Futagawa, ed.). *Frank Lloyd Wright, 1867–1959*. 12 vols. Tokyo: A.D.A. Edita, 1984–87.

Phipps Houses, Inc. *Phipps Garden Apartments*. Rental Brochure. New York, 1931. Edith Elmer Wood Collection, Avery Library, Columbia University.

Pinkney, David H. *Napoleon III and the Rebuilding of Paris*. Princeton, N.J.: Princeton University Press, 1958.

Plunz, Richard. "Reading Bronx Housing, 1890–1940." In Timothy Rub, ed., *Building a Borough: Architecture and Planning in the Bronx, 1890–1940*. New York: Bronx Museum of the Arts, 1986.

—— "Strange Fruit. The Legacy of the Design Competition in New York City Housing." in New York State Council on the Arts. *Reweaving The Urban Fabric*. New York: Princeton Architectural Press, 1989.

Plunz, Richard and Marta Gutman. "The New York 'Ring.'" *Eupalino 1* (1983), pp. 32–47.

Plunz, Richard and Kenneth Kaplan. "On 'Style'." *Precis* (Fall 1984), 5:32–43.

Plunz, Richard, ed. *Housing Form and Public Policy in the United States*. New York: Praeger, 1980.

Polsky, Ned. "The Village Beat Scene: Summer, 1960." *Dissent* (September 1961), 8:339–59.

Pommer, Richard. "The Architecture of Urban Housing in the United States During the Early 1930's." *Journal of the Society of Architectural Historians* (December 1978), 37:235–264.

Post, Langdon. *The Challenge of Housing*. New York: Farrar and Rinehart, 1938.

Potter, Edward T. *Etude de Quelques Problemes de L'Habitation Concentrée*. Paris: Librairie Guillaumin et cie, 1897. New York Public Library.

—— "Plans for Apartment Houses." *American Architect and Building News* (May 5, 1888), vol. 23, plate follows p. 210.

—— "A Study of Some New York Tenement House Problems." *Charities Review* (January 1892), 1:129–140.

—— "System for Laying Out Town Lots." *American Architect and Building News* (October 15, 1887), vol. 22, plate follows p. 188.

—— "Tenement Houses." *American Architect and Building News* (November 24, 1900), 70:59–62.

—— "Urban Housing in New York I: The Influence of the Size of the City Lots." *American Architect and Building News* (March 16, 1878), 3:90–92.

—— "Urban Housing II: What May Be Done

with Smaller Lots." *American Architect and Building News* (April 20, 1878), 3:137–138.

—— "Urban Housing III: Use of Frontage, Width of Streets—the Tenement Houses Possible on Smaller Lots." *American Architect and Building News* (May 18, 1878), 3:171–173.

—— "Urban Housing V." *American Architect and Building News* (September 27, 1879), 6:98–99.

Prendergast, William Ambrose. *Record of Real Estate* (1914). Cited by I. N. Phelps Stokes. *The Iconography of Manhattan Island: 1498–1909*, 5:1746.

Purnick, Joyce. "Estimate Board Gives Approval to Lincoln West." *New York Times*, September 17, 1982, p. 1.

Queensboro Corporation. *Cambridge Court, Jackson Heights*. Rental Brochure. New York, 1923. Edith Elmer Wood Collection, Avery Library, Columbia University.

—— *Chateau Apartments. Jackson Heights Garden Apartments*. Rental Brochure. New York, n.d. Edith Elmer Wood Collection, Avery Library, Columbia University.

—— *English Garden Homes in Jackson Heights*. New York, 1927. Edith Elmer Wood Collection, Avery Architectural and Fine Arts Library, Columbia University, box 58.

—— *Garden Apartments. Jackson Heights*. Rental Brochure. New York, n.d.. Edith Elmer Wood Collection, Avery Library, Columbia University.

—— "A History of Jackson Heights." *Jackson Heights, New York: General Information and Shopping Directory*. New York, 1955.

—— *Investment Features of Cooperative Apartment Ownership at Jackson Heights*. New York, 1925. Avery Architectural and Fine Arts Library, Columbia University.

—— "Special Supplement to Record Visit of Delegates to the International Town, City, and Regional Planning Conference to Jackson Heights." *Jackson Heights News*. April 24, 1925. Edith Elmer Wood Collection, Avery Library, Columbia University.

The Queens Museum, *Dawn of a New Day. The New York World's Fair. 1939/40*. New York: New York University Press, 1980.

Rangel, Jesus. "Koch Proposes New Zoning for Apartments." *New York Times*, May 15, 1985, p. B-5.

Rawson, Jonathan A., Jr. "Modern Tenement Houses." *Popular Science* (February 1912), 80:191–196.

Real Estate Board of New York. *Apartment Building Construction—Manhattan, 1902–53*. New York, 1953.

The Records of New Amsterdam. 7 vols. Avery Library, Columbia University, Chermayeff Papers Archive.

Redfield, Charles. "The Impact of Levittown on Local Government." *Journal of the American Institute of Planners* (Summer 1951), 17:130–141.

Reed, Henry. "The Investment Policy of Metropolitan Life." *Task* (1946), no. 4, pp. 38–40.

Regional Plan of New York and Its Environs. "The Regional Highway System." *Regional Plan of New York and Its Environs*. 2 vols. New York, 1929–1931.

—— *Regional Survey of New York and Its Environs*. 10 vols. New York, 1927–1931.

Rentschler, D. and W. Schirmer, eds. *Berlin und seine Bauten, Teil IV, Wohnungsbau: Band B, die Wohngebäude-Mehrfamilienhäuser*. Berlin: Wilhelm Ernst, 1974.

Report on Elevated Dwellings in New York City. New York: Evening Post Job Printing Office, 1883.

Reps, John H. *The Making of Urban America: A History of City Planning in the United States*. Princeton, N.J.: Princeton University Press, 1965.

Richards, Frank. "The Rock Drill and Its Share in the Development of New York City." *Cassier's* (June 1907), 32:160–177.

Riis, Jacob A. *The Battle with the Slum*. New York: Macmillan, 1902.

—— "The Clearing of Mulberry Bend." *Review of Reviews* (August 1895), 12:172–178.

—— "How the Other Half Lives." *Scribner's* (December 1889), 6:643–662.

—— *How the Other Half Lives*. New York: Scribner, 1890.

Rivolta, Matilde Buffa and Augusto Rossari. *Alexander Klein: Scrittie progetti dal 1906 al 1957*. Milano: Gabriele Mazzotta Editore, 1975.

Robbins, Ira. D. "Blueprint for a New York City Housing Program." Letter to the Editor, *New York Times*, November 20, 1985, p. A30.

—— "Books. The Death and Life of Great American Cities." *Village Voice*, November 16, 1961, p. 5.

—— *The Wastelands of New York City: A Preliminary Inquiry Into the Nature of Commercial Slum Areas, Their Potential for*

Housing and Business Development. New York: City Club of New York, 1962.

Robbins, Joseph B. "The Story of Stuyvesant Town." *Nation* (June 2, 1951), 172:516–518.

Robbins, Mark. "Growing Pains." *Metropolis* (October 1987), pp. 72–79.

Roberts, Henry. *The Dwellings of the Labouring Classes.* London: Society for the Improvement of the Labouring Classes, 1850.

Roberts, Raymond. "Building Management: Trend of Apartment House Buildings." *Real Estate Record and Builders' Guide* (July 17, 1915), 96:111–112.

Roberts, Sam. "Charlotte Street. Tortured Rebirth of a Wasteland." *New York Times,* March 9, 1987. p. B1.

—— "In East Brooklyn, Churches Preach Gospel of Change." *New York Times,* March 24, 1988, p. B1.

—— "Gathering Cloud: The Poor Climb Toward 2 Million." *New York Times,* June 11, 1987, p. B1.

—— " '75 Bankruptcy Scare Alters City Plans into 21st Century." *New York Times,* July 8, 1986, p. 1.

Roberts, Steven V. "Grand Concourse: Hub of Bronx Is Undergoing Ethnic Changes." *New York Times,* July 21, 1966, p. 35.

—— "Project for 6,000 Families Approved for Canarsie Site." *New York Times,* June 28, 1967.

Robinson, Charles Mulford. *Modern Civic Art, or The City Made Beautiful.* New York: Putnam, 1903.

Roger, Robert W. Aldrich. *Low Cost Housing Plan for the Lower East Side.* New York, 1932. Avery Architectural and Fine Arts Library, Columbia University (mimeographed).

Rogin, Roger. "New Town on a New York Island." *City* (May–June 1971), 5:42–47.

Rohdenburg, Theodore. *A History of the School of Architecture, Columbia University.* New York: Columbia University Press, 1954.

Roosevelt, Theodore. *An Autobiography.* New York: The MacMillan Company, 1914.

Rosenberg, Charles E. *The Cholera Years. The United States in 1832, 1849, and 1866.* Chicago: University of Chicago Press, 1962.

Rosenfield, Isadore. "Phipps Garden Apartments." *Architectural Forum* (February 1932), 56:110–124, 183–187.

Rosenwaike, Ira. *Population History of New York City.* Syracuse, N.Y.: Syracuse University Press, 1972.

Roth, Richard. "Baruch Houses: $30,000,000 Worth of Slum Clearance." *Empire State Architect* (July–August 1954), 14:9–11.

Ruberoid Company. *Fifth Ruberoid Architectural Design Competition: East River Urban Renewal Project.* New York, 1964.

Russell Sage Foundation. *A Forward Movement in Suburban Development.* Promotional Brochure, New York, 1916. Russell Sage Collection, City College Library.

Rutgers Town Corporation. *Rutgers Town: Low Cost Housing Plan for the Lower East Side.* New York, 1933.

—— *Rutgers Town and Queenstown. Low Cost Housing for the Average Man.* New York, 1933.

Ruttenbaum, Steven. *Mansions in the Clouds: The Skyscraper Palazzi of Emery Roth.* New York: Balsam Press, 1986, ch. 6.

Ryder, Sharon Lee. "A Very Lofty Realm." *Progressive Architecture* (October 1974), 55:92–97.

Sanborn, F. B. "Cooperative Building Associations." *Journal of Social Science* (December 1888), 25:112–124.

Sanders, James and Roy Strickland. "Harlem River Houses." *Harvard Architectural Review* (Spring 1981), 2:48–59.

Saxon, Wolfgang. "West Siders Voice Opposition on Plan." *New York Times,* November 19, 1985, sec. II, p. 4.

Saylor, Henry. "The AIA's First Hundred Years." *Journal of the American Institute of Architects* (May 1957), vol. 27, part II.

—— "The Hillside Housing Development." *Architecture* (May 1935), 71:245–252.

Schaffter, Dorothy. *State Housing Agencies.* New York: Columbia University Press, 1942.

Schlandt, Joachim. "Economic and Social Aspects of Council Housing in Vienna Between 1922 and 1934." *Lotus* (1975), 10:161–175.

Schliefer, Marc D. "The Village." *Dissent* (September 1961), 8:360–365.

Schmalz, Jeffrey. "East New York Housing Stirs Emotions." *New York Times,* November 21, 1986, p. B-1.

Schultz, Robert E. *Life Insurance Housing Projects.* Homewood, Ill.: S.S. Huebner Foundation for Insurance Education, 1956.

Schuyler, David. *The New Urban Landscape: The Redefinition of a City Form in Nineteenth-Century America.* Baltimore: Johns Hopkins University Press, 1986.

Schwartz, Joel. "Tenant Unions in New York

Low-Rent Housing, 1933–1949." *Journal of Urban History* (August 1986), 12:414–443.

Schwartz, Tony. "The Show Must Go Up." *New York* (December 24–31, 1984), pp. 48–49.

Scott Brown, Denise and Robert Venturi. "Co-op City: Learning To Like It." *Progressive Architecture* (February 1970), 51:64–73.

Seaman, Valentine. "Account of Yellow Fever in New York in 1795." In Noah Webster, ed., *A Collection of Papers on the Subject of Bilious Fevers Prevalent in the United States for a Few Years Past*, pp. 4–7. New York: Hopkins, Webb, 1776.

Sert, Jose Luis. *Can Our Cities Survive?* Cambridge, Mass.: Harvard University Press, 1942.

Sexton, R. W. *American Apartment Houses, Hotels, and Apartment Hotels of Today*. New York: Architectural Book Publishing, 1929.

Shallin, Michael. "The Story of Our Cooperative Services." *Festival Journal: 20th Anniversary Amalgamated Cooperative Community, 1927–1947*. New York: A and L Consumers Society, 1947.

Shapiro, Fred C. "Raking the Ashes of the Epidemic of Flame." *New York Times*, July 13, 1975, p. 12.

Sheffer, Ethel. "The Lessons of Lincoln West." *News York Affairs* (No. 3, 1984), 8:127–141.

Shenon, Philip. "Taste of Suburbia Arrives in the South Bronx." *New York Times*, March 19, 1983, p. 1.

Shire, Albert C. "Housing Standards and the USHA Program." USHA 29140H. Washington, D.C., 1938. Avery Architectural and Fine Arts Library, Columbia University (mimeographed).

Shively, Henry L. "Hygienic and Economic Features of the East River Homes Foundation." *New York Architect* (November–December 1911), 5:197–203 and plates.

Shrylock, Richard H. "The Origins and Significance of the Public Health Movement in the United States." *Annals of Medical History*. I n.s. (1929), pp. 645–665.

Simon, Arthur R. *Stuyvesant Town, USA*. New York: New York University Press, 1970.

Simpson, Charles R. *SoHo: The Artist in the City*. Chicago: University of Chicago Press, 1981.

Singer, Aaron. *Labor Management Relations at Steinway and Sons, 1853–1896*. Ann Arbor, Mich.: University Microfilms International, 1977.

Sklare, Marshall. "Jews, Ethnics, and the American City." *Commentary* (April 1972), vol. 53.

Sleeper, Harold R. *A Realistic Approach to Private Investment in Urban Redevelopment Applied to East Harlem as a Blighted Area*. New York: Architectural Forum, 1945.

Sleeper, Jim. "East Brooklyn's Nehiamiah Opens Its Doors and Answers Its Critics." *City Limits* (June–July 1984), pp. 14–15.

Smets, Marcel. *L'avènment de la cité-jardin en Belgique*. Liège: Pierre Mardaga Editeur, 1977.

Smith, Henry Atterbury. "Economic Open Stair Communal Dwellings." *Real Estate Record and Builders' Guide* (February 10, 1917), 99:184.

—— "Economic Open Stair Communal Dwellings for Industrial Towns." *Architecture* (May 1917), 35:81–84.

—— "Garden Apartments for Industrial Workers." *American Architect and Building News* (May 22, 1918), 113:686–689.

Smith, John Cotton. *Improvement of the Tenement House System of New York*. New York: American Church Press, 1879. New York Public Library.

Smith, Matthew Hale. *History of Garden City*. Manhasset, N.Y.: Channel Press, 1963.

—— *Sunshine and Shadow in New York*. Hartford, Conn.: J. B. Burr, 1868.

Smith, Neil, and Richard Schaffer. "Harlem Gentrification. A Catch 22?" *New York Affairs* (Winter 1987), 10:59–78.

Smith, Stephen, M.D. "Methods of Improving the Homes of the Laboring and Tenement House Classes of New York." *The Sanitarian* (July 1875), 3:145–162.

Smith, Thelma E., ed. *Guide to the Municipal Government of the City of New York*. New York: Meilen Press, 1973.

Smithson, Alison (ed.). "Team 10 Primer." *Architectural Design* (December 1962), 32:559–602.

Some Results of an Effort To Reform the Homes of the Laboring Classes in New York City. New York: Henry Bessey, 1881. New York Public Library.

Spann, Edward K. *The New Metropolis: New York City, 1840–1857*. New York: Columbia University Press, 1981.

Spencer, Joseph A. "New York Tenant Organizations and the Post–World War I Housing Crisis." In Ronald Lawson and Mark Navon, eds., *The Tenant Movement in New*

York City, 1904–1984, ch. 2. New Brunswick, N.J.: Rutgers University Press, 1986.

Springsteen, George. "The Practical Solution." *Architectural Forum* (February 1931), 54:242–246.

Starr, Roger. "Adventure in Mooritania." *Village Voice*, January 11, 1962, p. 5.

—— "The Editorial Notebook—Seals of Approval." *New York Times*, June 7, 1982, p. 18.

—— "Letters." *New York* (December 12, 1976), p. 16.

—— *The Living End: The City and Its Critics*. New York: Coward, McCann, 1966.

—— "Making New York Smaller." *New York Times Magazine*, November 14, 1976, p. 32.

—— "The Small House Is the Big Hope." *New York Times*, December 30, 1983, p. 22.

Stegman, Michael A. *The Dynamics of Rental Housing in New York City*. New York: Department of Housing Preservation and Development, February 1982.

Stein, Clarence. "The Price of Slum Clearance." *Architectural Forum* (February 1934), 60:154–157.

Stein, Clarence S. *Toward New Towns for America*. Liverpool-University Press of Liverpool and Chicago, 1951.

Steinway, Theodore E. *People and Pianos*. New York: Steinway and Sons, 1961.

Stephens, Suzanne. "The Last Gasp: New York City." *Progressive Architecture* (March 1976), 157:61.

—— "Learning from Twin Parks." *Architectural Forum* (June 1973), 138:62–67.

—— "Low-Rise Lemon." *Progressive Architecture* (March 1976), 57:54–57.

—— "This Side of Habitat." *Progressive Architecture* (July 1975), 54:58–63.

Stern, Robert A. M. *George Howe, Toward A Modern American Architecture*. New Haven: Yale University Press, 1975.

—— *New Directions in American Architecture*. New York: George Braziller, 1969.

—— "With Rhetoric: The New York Apartment House." *VIA* (1980), pp. 78–111.

Stern, Robert A. M., Gregory Gilmartin, and John Massengale. *New York 1900: Metropolitan Architecture and Urbanism, 1890–1915*. New York: Rizzoli, 1983.

Stern, Robert A. M., Gregory Gilmartin, Thomas Mellins, *New York 1930, Architecture and Urbanism Between the Two World Wars*. New York: Rizzoli, 1987.

Stokes, Isaac Newton Phelps. *The Iconography of Manhattan Island: 1498–1909*. 6 vols. New York: Robert H. Dodd, 1926.

—— "A Plan for Tenements in Connection with a Municipal Park." In DeForest and Veiller, *The Tenement House Problem*, 2:59–64.

Stoloff, David. *The Grand Concourse—Promise and Challenge*. New York: American Jewish Congress, 1967.

Stone, Peter A. "Rutgers Town Considered From a Social Viewpoint." *Real Estate Record and Builders' Guide* (July 29, 1933), 132:5–8.

Stubler, Walter. *Comfortable Homes in New York City at $9.00 a Room a Month*. New York: Metropolitan Life Insurance, 1925.

Sturgis, Russell. "The City House." *Scribner's* (June 1890), 7:694–713.

Sullivan, Donald. *Bronx Art Deco Architecture: An Exposition*. New York: Hunter College Graduate Program in Urban Planning, 1976.

Sullivan, Louis H. *The Autobiography of an Idea*. New York: Peter Smith, 1949.

Sutcliffe, Anthony. *Towards the Planned City: Germany, Britain, the United States, and France, 1780–1914*. New York: St. Martin's Press, 1981.

Sutcliffe, Arthur T. "Why The Model Fireproof Tenement Company?" Typescript. 1958. Ernest Flagg Archive, Avery Library, Columbia University.

Swanberg, W. A. *Citizen Hearst: A Biography of William Randolph Hearst*. New York: Scribner, 1961.

Szajkowski, Zosa. *Jews, World Wars, and Communism*. 2 vols. New York: KTAV, 1972.

Tabb, William K. *The Long Default. New York City and the Urban Fiscal Crisis*. New York: Monthly Review Press, 1982.

Tafuri, Manfredo. *Vienne la rouge*. Liège: Pierre Mardaga Editeur, 1981.

Taricat, Jean and Martine Villars. *Le logement à bon marché cronique par J. 1850–1930*. Boulogne: Edition Apogée, 1982.

Tarn, John Nelson. *Five Percent Philanthropy: An Account of Housing in Urban Areas Between 1840 and 1914*. Cambridge: Cambridge University Press, 1973.

Taylor, Graham Romeyn. *Satellite Cities: A Study of Industrial Suburbs*. New York: D. Appleton, 1915.

Teltsch, Kathleen. "94 Factory-Built Houses Planned for South Bronx." *New York Times*, June 27, 1982, p. 39.

Tenement House Building Company. *Report*. New York, October 1890.

—— *The Tenement Houses of New York City.* New York: Albert B. King Press, 1891.

Thaw, A. Blair. "A Record of Progress." *Lend a Hand* (May 1893), 10:309–317.

Thomas, Andrew J. "The Button-Control Elevator in a New Type of Moderate–Price Apartment Buildings at Jackson Heights, New York City." *Architectural Record* (June 1922), 51:486–490.

Thomas, Andrew, and Robert D. Kohn. "Is It Advisable To Remodel Slum Tenements?" *Architectural Record* (November 1920), 48:417–426.

Thomas Garden Apartments, Inc. *Thomas Garden Apartments. Prospectus.* Promotional Brochure. New York, 1927. Edith Elmer Wood Collection, Avery Library, Columbia University.

Thorburn, Grant. *Fifty Years of Reminiscences* (1845). Cited by I. N. Phelps Stokes, *The Iconography of Manhattan Island: 1498–1909,* 5:1664.

Tobier, Emanuel. "Gentrification: The Manhattan Story." *New York Affairs* (No. 4, 1979), 5:13–25.

—— "Setting the Record Straight on Loft Conversions." *New York Affairs* (No. 4, 1981), 6:33–44.

Tomasson, Robert. "Four Luxury Towers To House the Poor Opening in Harlem." *New York Times,* October 28, 1975.

Trillin, Calvin. "U.S. Journal: The Bronx: The Coops." *The New Yorker* (August 1, 1977), 53:49–54.

Trollope, Anthony. *North America.* Donald Smalley and Bradford Allen Booth, eds. New York: Knopf, 1951.

Tuthill, William. *The City Residence. Its Design and Construction.* New York: W. T. Comstock, 1890.

Tyrwhitt, Jaqueline, Jose Luis Sert, and Ernesto Rogers. *CIAM 8: The Heart of the City.* London: Lund Humphries, 1952.

Tzonis, Alexander, and Liane Lefaivre. "The Narcissist Phase in Architecture." *Harvard Architectural Review* (Spring 1986), 1:53–61.

Unger, Craig. "Can Harlem Be Born Again?" *New York* (November 19, 1984), pp. 28–36.

United States Bureau of the Census. *Geographical Mobility: March 1983 to March 1984.* Current Population Reports. Series P-20, no. 407. Washington, D.C.: GPO, September 1986.

United States Congress. *Congressional Digest* (November 1946), vol. 27.

—— *Congressional Record* (October 11, 1974), vol. 120.

—— *Housing Act.* 1937.

—— House of Representatives, Subcommittee No. 2. of the Select Committee on Small Business, Eighty-Fourth Congress. *Washington Square Southeast Slum Clearance Project Hearing.* Washington, D.C.: U.S. Government Printing Office, 1955.

—— *Laws.* 1961.

United States Federal Civil Defense Administration. *Operation Doorstep.* Washington, D.C.: GPO, 1953.

United States Federal Administration of Public Works. Housing Division. *Harlem River Houses.* Washington, D.C.: GPO, 1937.

—— *Unit Plans,* Washington, D.C.: GPO, 1935.

—— *Urban Housing: The Story of the PWA Housing Division, 1933–36.* Washington, D.C.: GPO, 1936.

—— *Williamsburg Houses. A Case History of Housing.* Washington, D.C.: U.S. Government Printing Office, 1937. Edith Elmer Wood Collection, Avery Library, Columbia University.

United States Federal Housing Administration. *Architectural Planning and Procedure for Rental Housing.* Washington, D.C.: GPO, 1938.

—— *Four Decades of Housing with a Limited Division Corporation.* Washington, D.C.: GPO, 1939.

—— *Rental Housing as Investment.* Washington, D.C.: GPO, 1938.

United States Federal Public Housing Authority. *Public Housing Design.* Washington, D.C.: GPO, 1946.

United States Housing and Home Finance Agency. *Chronology of Major Federal Actions Affecting Housing and Community Development.* Washington, D.C.: GPO, 1963.

—— *Housing Activities of the Federal Government.* Washington, D.C.: GPO, 1952.

United States Housing Authority. *Bulletin No. 11 on Planning and Policy Procedure: Planning the Site.* Washington, D.C.: GPO, 1939.

—— *Summary of General Requirements and Minimum Standards for USHA-Aided Projects.* USHA 699.69192H. 1939 (mimeographed).

United States Housing Corporation. *Report,* 2 vols. Washington, D.C.: GPO, 1919.

United Workers Cooperative Colony. *The Coops: The United Workers Cooperative Colony 50th*

Anniversary, 1927–1977. New York: Semi-Centennial Coop Reunion, 1977.

Van Pelt, John Vredenburgh. *A Monograph of the William K. Vanderbilt House*. New York: John Vredenburgh Van Pelt, 1925.

Vaux, Calvert. "Parisian Buildings for City Residents." *Harper's Weekly* (December 19, 1857), 2:809–810.

Veiller, Lawrence. "The Charity Organization Society's Tenement House Competition." *American Architect and Building News* (March 10, 1900), 67:77–79.

—— "The Effect of the New Tenement House Law." *Real Estate Record and Builders' Guide* (January 18, 1902), 62:105–109.

—— *A Model Housing Law*. New York: Survey Associates, 1914.

Veiller, Lawrence and Hugh Bonner. *Special Report on Housing Conditions and Tenement Laws in Leading American Cities*. New York: Evening Post Job Printing House, 1900.

Venturi, Robert. *Complexity and Contradiction in Architecture*. New York: Museum of Modern Art, 1966.

Von Moos, Stanislaus. *Venturi, Rauch, and Scott-Brown. Buildings and Projects*. New York: Rizzoli, 1987.

Wald, Matthew L. "New Coney Island Homes Called Flawed." *New York Times*, July 16, 1984, sec. II, p. 2.

—— "New York City as an Apartment Owner: Three Case Histories." *New York Times*, November 29, 1983, p. B-1.

—— "No Simple Ways for City To End Housing Burden." *New York Times*, December 3, 1983, p. 25.

—— "Problems Persist When City Owns Houses." *New York Times*, December 1, 1983, p. B-1.

—— "Saving Aging Housing: A Costly City Takeover." *New York Times*, November 27, 1983, p. 1.

Walker, James Blaine. *Fifty Years of Rapid Transit: 1864–1917*. New York: Law Printing, 1918.

Weinrebe, B. A. "The Jewish Suburban Housing Movement. Part II: Cooperative Apartment Houses" (typescript). Anna Richter, tr. Works Progress Administration, Federal Writers Project, "Jews of New York," box 3628, New York City Municipal Archives.

Weintraub, Bernard. "Lower East Side Vexed by Housing." *New York Times*, July 7, 1963.

—— "Once-Grand Concourse." *New York Times*, February 2, 1965, p. 35.

—— "Renovations on the Lower East Side Creating Living Quarters." *New York Times*, May 5, 1963.

Weintraub, Myles and Mario Zicarelli. "Tale of Twin Parks." *Architectural Forum* (June 1973), 137:54–67.

Weisbrod, Carl B. "Loft Conversions: Will Enforcement Bring Acceptance?" *New York Affairs* (No. 4, 1981), 6:45–56.

White, Alfred Treadway. *Better Homes for Workingmen*. New York: Putnam, 1885.

—— *Improved Dwellings for the Laboring Classes*. New York: Putnam, 1877; rev. ed., 1879.

—— *The Riverside Buildings of the Improved Dwellings Company*. Brooklyn, N.Y., 1890.

—— *Sun-Lighted Tenements: Thirty-Five Years' Experience as an Owner*. Publication 12. New York: National Housing Association Publications, March 1912.

White, Morton and Lucia White. *The Intellectual Versus the City*. Cambridge, Mass.: MIT Press, 1962.

Whitelock, Otto V. St. "Planning Manhattan Homes for the Average Wage-Earner." *Real Estate Record and Builders' Guide* (December 13, 1930), 126:7–9, 42.

Whitten, Robert. "The *Building Zone Plan* of New York City." Avery Library, Columbia University, c. 1917 (typewritten).

Wiebenson, Dora. *Tony Garnier and the Cité Industrielle*. New York: Braziller, 1969.

Wilentz, Elias S. "Good Planning or Bad?" Letter to the Editor *Village Voice*, November 23, 1961, p. 4.

Williams, Winston. "Rebuilding from the Grass Roots Up." Letter to the Editor, *New York Times*, December 21, 1986, sec. IV, p. 6.

Williamson, Chilton, Jr. "West Village Town Meeting." *National Review* (August 29, 1975), 27:944.

Willis, Walter I. *Queens Borough, New York City: 1910–1920*. New York: Queens Chamber of Commerce, 1920.

Wilson, William Julius. *The Truly Disadvantaged. The Inner City, the Underclass, and Public Policy*. Chicago: University of Chicago Press, 1987.

Wingate, Charles F. "The Moral Side of the Tenement House Problem." *Catholic World* (May 1885), 41:160–164.

Wingler, Hans. *Bauhaus in America*. Berlin: Bauhaus-Archiv, 1972.

Winkleman, Michael. "Raising the Old Law Tenement Question." *New York Affairs* (No. 4, 1981), 6:20–28.

Wirth, Louis. "Urbanism as a Way of Life." *American Journal of Sociology* 44 (July 1938), 1–34.

Wisely, William H. *The American Civil Engineer, 1852–1974.* New York: American Society of Civil Engineers, 1974.

Wiseman, Carter. "The Next Great Place." *New York* (June 16, 1986), pp. 34–41.

Women's City Club of New York. *"With Love and Affection": A Study of Building Abandonment.* New York, 1977.

Women's Club of New York. *Tenant Relocation at West Park: A Report Based on Field Services.* New York, March 1954.

Woodfill, Barbara M. *New York City's Mitchell-Lama Program: Middle Income Housing.* New York: New York City Rand Institute, June 1971.

Working Men's Home Association. *A Statement Relative to the Working Men's Home Association.* New York, December 31, 1857. New York Public Library.

Works Progress Administration, Federal Writers' Project. *The WPA Guide to New York City.* New York: Pantheon Books, 1982.

Woud, Auke van der. *Het Nievwe Bouwen. International. CIAM Heyying Town Planning.* Delft: Delft University Press, 1983.

Wright, Carrol D. *The Slums of Baltimore, Chicago, New York, and Philadelphia: Seventh Special Report of the Commissioner of Labor.* Washington, D.C.: GPO, 1894.

Wright, Frank Lloyd. "Broadacre City: A New Community Plan." *Architectural Record* (April 1935), 77:244–245.

Wright, Gwendolyn. *Building the Dream: A Social History of Housing in America.* New York: Pantheon Books, 1981.

Wright, Henry. "The Apartment House." *Architectural Record* (March 1931), 69:187–224.

—— "Are We Ready for American Housing Advance?" *Architecture* (June 1933), 67:309–316.

—— "The Modern Apartment House." *Architectural Record* (March 1929), 65:213–245.

—— "Outline of a Housing Research Prepared with the Cooperation of the Research Institute of Economic Housing." Avery Architecture and Fine Arts Library, Columbia University, New York, 1930.

—— *Rehousing Urban America.* New York: Columbia University Press, 1935.

Young, Edgar B. *Lincoln Center. The Building of an Institution.* New York, New York University Press, 1980.

Young, Sarah Gilman. *European Modes of Living; or The Question of Apartment Houses.* New York: Putnam, 1881.

Zeisloft, E. Idell. *The New Metropolis.* New York: D. Appleton, 1899.

Zoll, Stephen. "The West Village: Let There Be Blight." *Dissent* (September 1961), 8:289–96.

Zukin, Sharon. *Loft Living: Culture and Capital in Urban Change.* Baltimore; Johns Hopkins University Press, 1982.

Zukin, Sharon, and Gilda Zweyman. "Housing For the Working Poor: A Historical View of Jews and Blacks in Brownsville." *New York Affairs* (No. 2, 1985), 9:3–18.

Illustration Credits

Frontispiece: Reprinted from *the New York Mirror* (November 15, 1834), 12:1.

1.1. Reprinted from *Harper's New Monthly Magazine* (January 1881), 42:193.

1.2. Reprinted from *Frank Leslie's Sunday Magazine* (June, 1879), 5:643. Scale: 1″=30′.

1.3. Reprinted from *Frank Leslie's Sunday Magazine* (June 1879), 5:648.

1.4. Reprinted from New York Association for Improving the Condition of the Poor, *Thirteenth Annual Report,* p. 50. Scale: 1″=50′.

1.5. Used with permission from the New York Public Library. Scale: 1″=1500′.

1.6. Reprinted from *Frank Leslie's Illustrated Newspaper* (January 23, 1869), p. 297.

1.7. Reprinted from J. Stubben, *Der Stadtebau* (Handbuches der Architektur, Entwerfen, Anlage, und Einrichtung der Gebaude, vol. 9, fig. 574.

1.8. Drawn by the author. Scale: 1″=200′.

1.9. Reprinted from New York State Assembly, Tenement House Committee, *Report of 1895,* plate faces p. 13. Scale: 1″=30′.

1.10. Photograph by Jessie Tarbox Beals. Used with permission from the Museum of the City of New York.

1.11. Reprinted from Citizen's Association of New York, *Report of the Council of Hygiene and Public Health,* p. 136. Scale: 1″=50′.

1.12. Reprinted from Jacob Riis, *How the Other Half Lives,* p. 163.

1.13. Reprinted from Citizen's Association of New York, *Report of the Council of Hygiene and Public Health,* p. 275. Scale: 1″=20′.

1.14. Reprinted from Citizen's Association of New York, *Report of the Council of Hygiene and Public Health,* pp. 122, 204. Scale: 1″=30′.

1.15. Redrawn from Charles F. Chandler, *Ten Scrap Books of Tenement House Plans,* vol. 5, plate 954. Scale: 1″=30′.

1.16. Reprinted from *American Architect and Building News* (March 16, 1878), 3:92; and *American Architect and Building News* (May 18, 1878), 3:175.

1.17. Reprinted from *American Architect and Building News* (April 20, 1878), 3:137, and *American Architect and Building News* (May 18, 1878), 3:172.

1.18. Reprinted from *American Architect and Building News* (September 6, 1879), 6:99, Scale: 1″=50′; 1″=30′.

1.19. Reprinted from *Plumber and Sanitary Engineer* (April 1879), 2:124. Scale 1″=80′.

2.1. Reprinted from *Plumber and Sanitary Engineer* (March 1879), 2:103. Scale: 1″=30′.

2.2. Reprinted from *Plumber and Sanitary Engineer* (April 1879), 2:132; *Plumber and Sanitary Engineer* (May 1879), 2:159; and *Plumber and Sanitary Engineer* (June 1879), 2:180. Scale: 1″=30′.

2.3. Reprinted from New York State Assembly, Tenement House Committee, *Report of 1895,* plate faces p. 13. Scale: 1″=30′.

2.4. Reprinted from *American Architect and Building News* (February 12, 1881), 9:75. Scale: 1″=30′.

2.5. Reprinted from *American Architect and Building News* (January 20, 1877), 2:20. Scale: 1″=50′.

2.6. Reprinted from *Charities Review* (January 1892), 1:137. Scale: 1″=50′.

2.7. Courtesy of the Avery Architectural and Fine Arts Library, Columbia University.

2.8. Reprinted from *American Architect and*

Building News (October 15, 1887), vol. 22, plate follows p. 188. Scale: 1″=50′.

2.9. Reprinted from W. J. Fryer, Laws Relating to Buildings, pp. 140–142. Scale: 1″=50′.

2.10. Photograph by Jacob Riis. Used with permission from the Museum of the City of New York.

2.11. Reprinted from New York State, Assembly, Tenement House Committee, Report of 1895, fig. 9.

2.12. Reprinted from The Builder (March 6, 1858), 16:159. Scale: 1″=50′.

2.13. Reprinted from Scribner's Magazine (July 1894), 16:108, 112–114. Scale: 1″=50′.

2.14. Reworked from James Ford, Slums and Housing, vol. 2, plate 7C. Scale: 1″=50′.

2.15. Reprinted from Architecture and Building (January 2, 1897), 26:9. Scale: 1″=200′.

2.16. Reprinted from William P. Miller, The Tenement House Committee and the Open Stair Tenements. Scale: 1″=50′.

2.17. Reprinted from Robert W. DeForest and Lawrence Veiller, The Tenement House Problem 1:116. Scale: 1″=50′.

2.18. Reprinted from Municipal Affairs (March 1899), 3:136. Scale: 1″=50′.

2.19. Reworked from I. N. Phelps Stokes, Random Recollections of a Happy Life, plate opposite p. 122. Scale: 1″=30′.

2.20. Reprinted from Robert W. DeForest and Lawrence Veiller, eds., The Tenement House Problem, vol. 1, plate opposite p. 112.

2.21. Reprinted from Robert W. DeForest and Lawrence Veiller, eds., The Tenement House Problem, vol. 1, plate opposite p. 10.

2.22. Reprinted from James Ford, Slums and Housing, plate 10E. Scale: 1″=30′.

2.23. Reprinted from James Ford, Slums and Housing, plate 10D. Scale: 1″=30′.

2.24. Drawn by the author. Scale: 1″=100′.

2.25. Reprinted from Architectural Record (July 1920), 48:55. Scale: 1″=200′.

2.26. Reprinted from American Architect and Building News (January 5, 1907), 91:8. Scale: 1″=30′.

2.27. Reprinted from City Housing Corporation, Sunnyside and the Housing Problem, p. 16. Scale: 1″=50′.

3.1. Reprinted from Citizen's Association of New York, Report of the Council of Hygiene and Public Health, pp. 198, 200. Scale: 1″=20′.

3.2. Reprinted from Review of Reviews (August 1895), 12:177. Scale: 1″=200′.

3.3. Photograph by Jacob Riis. Used with

permission from the Museum of the City of New York.

3.4. Reprinted from Harper's Weekly (November 28, 1857), 1:757.

3.5. Reprinted from Harper's Weekly (November 28, 1857), 1:757. Scale: 1–2000′.

3.6. Reprinted from Harper's New Monthly Magazine (September 1880), 61:566.

3.7. Reprinted from Harper's Weekly (July 25, 1896), 40:730.

3.8. Reprinted from Matthew Hale Smith, Sunshine and Shadow in New York, frontispiece.

3.9. Reprinted from Scribner's Magazine (June 1890), 7:695. Scale: 1″=20′.

3.10. Reprinted from Harper's New Monthly Magazine (September 1883), 67:564; and Augustine E. Costello, Our Firemen: A History of the New York Fire Departments, p. 80.

3.11. Reprinted from American Architect and Building News (November 1, 1879), 6:140. Scale: 1″=30′.

3.12. Reprinted from Richard Hurd, Principles of City Land Values, p. 53. Scale: 1″=80′.

3.13. Reprinted from Architectural Record (July 1901–April 1902), 11:479. Scale 1″=30′.

3.14. Reprinted from Harper's Weekly (December 19, 1857), 1:809. Scale: 1″=30′.

3.15. Reprinted from American Architect and Building News (March 4, 1878), vol. 3, plate opposite p. 156. Scale: 1″=30′.

3.16. Reprinted from Scribner's Monthly (May 1874), 8:65, 66. Scale: 1″=30′.

3.17. Reprinted from Scribner's Monthly (May 1874), 8:67. Scale: 1″=30′.

3.18. Photograph used with permission from the New York Historical Society.

3.19. Reprinted from Appleton's Journal (November 18, 1871), 6:561.

3.20. Reprinted from Scribner's Monthly (May 1874), 8:64, 68. Scale: 1″=50′.

3.21. Reprinted from Royal Institute of British Architects, The Transactions, 1882–1883, fig. 68. Scale: 1″=80′.

3.22. Reprinted from Andrew Alpern, Apartments for the Affluent, p. 18. Scale: 1″=80′.

3.23. Reprinted from Frank Leslie's Illustrated Magazine, (September 9, 1889), 69:81.

3.24. Reprinted from Royal Institute of British Architects, The Transactions, 1882–1883, fig. 65. Scale: 1″=50′.

3.25. Reprinted from Augustine E. Costello, Our Firemen: A History of the New York Fire Department, p. 1038.

3.26. Photograph used with permission from the New York Historical Society.

3.27. Reprinted from American Bank Note Company, *The Central Park Apartments Facing the Park*. Scale: 1"=100'.

3.28. Reprinted from *Cosmopolitan* (July 1893), 15:357.

3.29. Reprinted from *the American Architect* (January 5, 1907), 91:7. Scale: 1"=80'.

3.30. Reprinted from *Architect's and Builder's Magazine* (September, 1908), 9:532. Scale: 1"=80'.

3.31. Reprinted from *Real Estate Record and Builder's Guide* (November 7, 1908), 82:874. Scale: 1"=80'.

3.32. Reprinted from *Architectural Review* (August 1903), 10:128.

3.33. Reprinted from *Real Estate Record and Builder's Guide* (December 19, 1908), 82:1215.

3.34. Reprinted from *Architecture,* (May 1918), vol. 37, plate LXXIX. Scale: 1"=200'.

3.35. Reprinted from *American Architect* (November 29, 1911), 100:225. Scale: 1"=50'.

3.36. Reprinted from New York City, Tenement House Commission, *First Report,* plates 122; 123. Scale: 1"=30'.

3.37. Reprinted from *Real Estate Record and Builder's Guide* (September 12, 1908), 82:531. Scale: 1"=30'.

3.38. Reprinted from *Real Estate Record and Builders' Guide* (September 12, 1908), 82:505. Scale: 1"=2000'.

4.1. Reprinted from Henry Roberts, *The Dwellings of the Labouring Classes,* p. 121. Scale: 1"=30'.

4.2. Reprinted from Citizen's Association of New York, *Report of the Council on Hygiene,* plate opposite p. LXXXVI. Scale: 1"=30'.

4.3. Reprinted from New York State, Assembly, *Report of The Committee on Public Health, Medical Colleges and Societies, Relative to the Condition of Tenement Houses in the Cities of New York and Brooklyn,* plate opposite p. 12. Scale: 1"=30'.

4.4. Reprinted from Alfred Treadway White, *Improved Dwellings for the Laboring Classes* (1877). Scale: 1"=50'.

4.5. Courtesy of the Slide Library of the Graduate School of Architecture and Planning, Columbia University, New York. Scale: 1"=100'.

4.6. Reprinted from Alfred Treadway White, *Improved Dwellings for the Laboring Classes,* plate follows p. 45. Scale: 1"=50'.

4.7. Reprinted from Alfred Treadway White, *Better Homes for Workingmen,* plate follows p. 13. Scale: 1"=80'.

4.8. Reprinted from *American Architect and Building News* (April 17, 1880), 7:166; and *American Architect and Building News* (July 27, 1896), 52:123, Scale: 1"=50'.

4.9. Reprinted from New York Sanitary Reform Society, First Annual Report, plate opposite p. 24. Scale: 1"=50'.

4.10. Reprinted from New York Sanitary Reform Society, *First Annual Report,* frontispiece.

4.11. Reprinted from William P. Miller, *The Tenement House Committee and the Open Stair Tenements;* and from *Scribner's Magazine* (June 1892), 11:707. Scale: 1"=30'.

4.12. Reprinted from Tenement House Building Company, *Report,* p. 6. Scale: 1"=50'.

4.13. Reprinted from E. R. L. Gould, *The Housing of Working People,* p. 788. Scale: 1"=50'.

4.14. Reprinted from *Architecture and Building* (January 2, 1897), 26:7, 8. Scale: 1"=100'; 1"=50'.

4.15. Reprinted from *Municipal Affairs* (March 1899), 3:126. Scale: 1"=80'.

4.16. Reprinted from *Real Estate Record and Builders' Guide* (January 18, 1902), 69:108. Scale: 1"=80'.

4.17. Reprinted from *American Architect and Building News* (January 5, 1907), 91:9. Scale: 1"=30'.

4.18. Upper and Lower Right: Reprinted from James Ford, *Slums and Housing,* plates 13B, 13A. Upper Left: *Real Estate Record and Builders' Guide* (January 18, 1902) 69:108. Scale: 1"=200'.

4.19. Reprinted from *New York Architect* (November–December 1911), vol. 5, plate faces p. 201. Scale: 1"=80'.

4.20. Reprinted from *New York Architect* (November–December 1911), vol. 5, plate opposite p. 197.

4.21. Reprinted from *New York Architect* (November–December 1911), 5:198, 199.

4.22. Reprinted from *Real Estate Record and Builders' Guide* (February 28, 1914), 93:398.

4.23. Reprinted from *American Architect* (October 29, 1913), 104:174. Scale: 1"=50'.

4.24. Reprinted from *Architectural Record* (July 1920), 48:67, 68. Scale: 1"=100'.

4.25. Reprinted from *American Architect and Building News* (April 18, 1896), 52:25, Scale: 1"=100'; 1"=30'.

4.26. Photograph by Jacob Riis. Used with permission from the Museum of the City of New York.

4.27. Reprinted from *Architectural Record* (July–September 1892), 2:62. Scale: 1″=100′.

4.28. Reprinted from *Municipal Affairs* (March 1898), 2:42. Scale: 1″=500′.

4.29. Reprinted from Robert DeForest and Lawrence Veiller, eds., *The Tenement House Problem* 2:57. Scale: 1″=100′.

4.30. Reprinted from New York Legislature, *Report of the Board of General Manager of the State of New York at the World's Columbian Exposition* (Albany: James B. Lyon, 1894), pp. 400, 409. Scale: 1″=30′.

4.31. Reprinted from *Harper's Weekly* (August 7, 1869), 13:503.

4.32. Reprinted from *Abstract of the Title of Steinway and Sons to Property at Long Island City,* frontispiece. Scale: 1″=1000′.

4.33. Reprinted from *Municipal Affairs* (March 1899), 3:133. Scale: 1″=30′.

4.34. Reprinted from *Architectural Forum* (May 1935), 62:438.

4.35. Reprinted from *The Brickbuilder* (December 1912), 21:318; and G. W. Bromley and Co., *Atlas of the City of New York, Borough of Queens,* plate 18. Scale: 1″=1000′.

4.36. Reprinted from Grosvenor Atterbury, *Model Towns in America,* pp. 13, 15. Scale: 1″=200′.

4.37. Reprinted from *Real Estate Record and Builders' Guide* (June 24, 1922), 109:778.

4.38. Reprinted from the *Journal of the American Institute of Architects* (November 1920), 8:384.

5.1. Reprinted from *Real Estate Record and Builders' Guide* (April 22, 1916), 97:615.

5.2. Reprinted from United States Housing Corporation, *Report* 2:347. Scale: 1″=500′.

5.3. Reprinted from *American Architect* (September 8, 1920), 108:306, 309. Scale: 1″=100′.

5.4. Reprinted from *Architectural Record* (July 1920), 48:71. Scale: 1″=200′.

5.5. Reprinted from Umberto Toschi, *La Citta* (Torino: Topografia Sociale Torinese, 1966), p. 346.

5.6. Reprinted from *Real Estate Record and Builders' Guide* (April 21, 1917), 99:553.

5.7. Reprinted from *Real Estate Record and Builders' Guide* (August 28, 1909), 84:384. Scale: 1″=30′.

5.8. Reprinted from *Real Estate Record and Builders' Guide* (March 24, 1917), 99:392. Scale: 1″=30′.

5.9. Reprinted from *Real Estate Record and Builders' Guide* (October 23, 1920), 106:584. Scale: 1″=150′.

5.10. Reprinted from *Architectural Forum* (April 1922), 36:158. Scale: 1″=50′.

5.11. Reprinted from *Journal of the American Institute of Architects* (March 1922), 10:82. Scale: 1″=80′.

5.12. Reprinted from *Architectural Record* (July 1920), 48:63. Scale: 1″=200′.

5.13. Reprinted from Erich Haenel and Heinrich Tscharmann, *Das Mietwohnhaus der Neuzeit,* p. 83. Scale: 1″=200′.

5.14. Reprinted from Queensboro Corporation, *Investment Features of Cooperative Apartment Ownership at Jackson Heights* Pamphlet (New York, 1925), p. 32. Scale: 1″=200′.

5.15. Reprinted from *Queensboro* (May 1917), 4:17.

5.16. Reprinted from *American Architect* (May 22, 1918), 113:686.

5.17. Reprinted from *Architectural Forum* (June 1919), 30:189. Scale: 1″=30′.

5.18. Reprinted from *Architectural Record* (August 1920), 48:123.

5.19. Reprinted from *Architectural Record* (June 1922), 51:489; and *Architecture and Building* (June 1924), 56:56. Scale: 1″=30′.

5.20. Reprinted from Queensboro Corporation, *Chateau Apartments, Jackson Heights Garden Apartments.* Scale: 1″=80′. Courtesy Avery Architectural and Fine Arts Library. Columbia University.

5.21. Reprinted from *Architectural Record* (May 1922), 51:442. Scale: 1″=50′.

5.22. Reprinted from *Real Estate Record and Builders' Guide* (February 9, 1918), 101:180. Scale: 1″=80.

5.23. Reprinted from *Architectural Record* (May 1922), 51:438.

5.24. Reprinted from *Architectural Record* (August 1920), 48:132. Scale: 1″=30′.

5.25. Reprinted from *Architecture and Building* (May 1924), 56:55–57. Scale: 1″=30′.

5.26. Reprinted from *Architecture and Building* (May 1924), 56:55–57. Scale: 1″=200′.

5.27. Courtesy of Horace Ginsbern and Associates. Scale: 1″=100′.

5.28. Reworked from *Architectural Forum* (September 1930), 53:284. Scale: 1″=200′.

5.29. Reworked from *Architecture and Building* (January, 1922), 54:5. Scale: 1″=80′.

5.30. Reprinted from *Architectural Record* (July 1920), 48:64. Scale: 1″=80′.

5.31. Reprinted from Walter Stubler, *Comfortable Homes in New York City at $9.00 a Room a Month,* pp. 6–7.

5.32. Drawn by Nancy Josephson. Scale: 1″=100′.

5.33. Reprinted from *Architectural Forum* (March 1932), 56:234. Scale: 1″=80′.

5.34. Courtesy of the Museum of the City of New York.

5.35. Reprinted from New York State, Board of Housing, *Report, 1929,* p. 16. Scale: 1″=200′.

5.36. Reprinted from *Architectural Record* (March 1928), 63:273. Scale: 1″=80′.

5.37. Reprinted from *Architectural Record* (March 1928), 63:273.

5.38. Courtesy of the YIVO Institute for Jewish Research.

5.39. Reprinted from Fred L. Lavanburg Foundation, *Practices and Experiences at the Lavanburg Homes,* p. 5. Scale: 1″=80′.

5.40. Reprinted from *Architectural Forum* (March 1932), 56:244. Scale: 1″=200′.

5.41. Reprinted from *Architectural Record* (March 1928),63:272. Scale: 1″=200′.

5.42. Reprinted from *Architectural Forum* (February 1932), 56:114, 115, 120. Scale: 1″=200′; 1″=400′.

6.1. Reprinted from *Architectural Record* (March 1931), 69:196.

6.2. Reprinted from James Ford, *Slums and Housing,* vol. 2, plate 16B, Scale: 1″=200′.

6.3. Reprinted from Walter Stubler, *Comfortable Homes in New York City at $9.00 a Room a Month,* p. 8. Scale: 1″=50′.

6.4. Reprinted from *Architectural Record* (August 1922), 52:135.

6.5. Reprinted from *Architecture and Building* (May 1924), vol. 56, plate 100.

6.6. Reprinted from City Housing Corporation, *Sunnyside and the Housing Problem,* p. 31.

6.7. Reprinted from *Architectural Forum* (February 1932), 56:112. Scale: 1″=1000′.

6.8. Reprinted from New York State, Board of Housing, *Report, 1930,* p. 70.

6.9. Reprinted from City Housing Corporation, *Sunnyside and the Housing Problem,* p. 22.

6.10. Reprinted from City Housing Corporation, *Sunnyside and the Housing Problem,* p. 17. Scale: 1″=30′.

6.11. Reprinted from *Architectural Record* (March 1929), 65:220, 221.

6.12. Reprinted from *Architectural Record* (March 1929), 65:213. Scale: 1″=80′.

6.13. Reprinted from *Architecture* (May 1917), 35:81–84.

6.14. Reprinted from *the American Architect* (May 22, 1918), 113:687–688. Scale: 1″=1000′.

6.15. Reprinted from James Ford, *Slums and Housing,* vol. 2, plate 16A. Scale: 1″=50′.

6.16. Reprinted from *Real Estate Record and Builders' Guide* (April 28, 1917), 99:583. Scale: 1″=50′.

6.17. Reprinted from James Ford, *Slums and Housing,* vol. 2, plate 18A. Scale: 1″=200′.

6.18. Reprinted from *Queensboro* (November 1925), 11:642.

6.19. Reprinted from *Architectural Record* (March 1928), 63:262. Scale: 1″=50′.

6.20. Reprinted from *Architectural Forum* (March 1932), 56:236.

6.21. Reprinted from *Architectural Forum* (March 1932), 56:236.

6.22. Reprinted from Museum of Modern Art, *Modern Architecture International Exhibition,* p. 198.

6.23. Reprinted from *L'Illustration* (August 12, 1922), 160:133.

6.24. Reworked from *L'Esprit Nouveau,* No. 4, pp. 465, 466.

6.25. Reprinted from Le Corbusier, *Le Corbusier,* p. III.

6.26. Reprinted from *L'Architecture Vivante* (Fall and Winter 1927), p. 36.

6.27. Reprinted from Siegfried Giedion, *Walter Gropius,* plate 14.

6.28. Reprinted from Walter Gropius, *Scope of Total Architecture,* fig. 40.

6.29. Reprinted from Siegfried Giedion, *Walter Gropius,* p. 202, Scale: 1″=50′.

6.30. Upper: Redrawn from *Architectural Record* (March 1932), 71:194; Lower-Reprinted from *New York Times,* June 18, 1933, Sec XI and XII, p. 2. Scale 1″=100′.

6.31. Reprinted from *Architectural Record* (March 1932), 71:195.

6.32. Reprinted from *Architectural Record* (March 1932), 71:196. Scale: 1″=400′.

6.33. Reprinted from *Architectural Record* (January 1930), 67:1.

6.34. Reprinted from Regional Plan Association, Inc., *Regional Survey of New York and its Environs* 6:329. Scale: 1″=150′.

6.35. Photograph by the author.

6.36. Reprinted from *Architectural Record* (March 1932), 71:190.

6.37. Reprinted from *Real Estate Record and Builders' Guide* (October 17, 1931), 128:7. Scale: 1″=30″.

6.38. Drawn by Tracy Dillon.

6.39. Reprinted from *Real Estate Record and Builders' Guide* (December 13, 1930), 126:7. Scale: 1″=30′.

6.40. Drawn by Harry Kendall and George Schieferdecker from plans at the New York City Department of Building. Scale: 1″=100′.

6.41. Drawn by Stephen Day from plans at the New York City Department of Buildings. Scale: 1″=30′.

6.42. Drawn by Stefano Paci and Stephen Day from plans at the New York City Department of Buildings. Scale: 1″=30′.

6.43. Drawn by Amy Dreifus and Michele Noe from plans at the New York City Department of Buildings. Scale 1″=100′.

6.44. Reprinted from *Architectural Record* (March 1928), 63:232. Scale: 1″=200′.

6.45. Reworked from City Housing Corporation, *Sixth Annual Report,* plate opposite p. 1. Scale: 1″=1200′.

7.1. Reprinted from New York City Housing Authority, *Tenth Annual Report,* p. 25; with drawing by the author. Scale: 1″=150′.

7.2. Reprinted from Fred F. French Management Company, *Knickerbocker Village;* and Clarence Arthur Perry, *The Rebuilding of Blighted Areas,* p. 46. Scales: 1″=200′; 1″=400′.

7.3. Reprinted from New York City Housing Authority, *Housing: Cost Analysis,* p. 27. Scale: 1″=30′.

7.4. Drawn by Tracy Dillon from a plan in James Ford, *Slums and Housing,* plate 22A. Scale: 1″=100′.

7.5. Reprinted from *Architecture* (May 1935), 71:249. Scale: 1″=50′.

7.6. Reprinted from *Architecture* (May 1935), 71:247, 249, 250. Scales: 1″=150′; 1″=750′.

7.7. Reprinted from New York State, Board of Housing, *Annual Report, 1934,* p. 26. Scale: 1″=500′.

7.8. Reprinted from *Flagg Court.* Scale: 1″=200′.

7.9. Reprinted from *Pencil Points* (May 1938), 19:282. Scale: 1″=400′.

7.10. Reprinted from United States, Federal Emergency Administration of Public Works, Housing Division. *Harlem River Houses.*

7.11. Upper: Drawing by the author. Scale: 1″=400′. Middle and Lower: Reprinted from Werner Hegemann, *City Planning; Housing* 3:141 with permission from the Architectural Book Publishing Company.

7.12. Courtesy of Fiorello H. LaGuardia Archives. Fiorello H. LaGuardia Community College, New York.

7.13. Reprinted from Werner Hegemann, *City Planning; Housing* 3:140. Courtesy of Architectural Book Publishing Company, Inc.

7.14. Reprinted from New York City Housing Authority, *Proposed Low Rental Housing Project, Block 1670-Manhattan.* Scale: 1″=200′.

7.15. Redrawn from New York Housing Authority, *Competition: Scrapbook of Placing Entries.* Scale: 1″=500′.

7.16. Reprinted from *Architectural Record* (March 1935), 77:223.

7.17. Reworked from Frederick Ackerman and William Ballard, *A Note on Site and Unit Planning,* pp. 42, 46.

7.18. Reprinted from Rutgers Town Corporation, *Rutgers Town: A Low Cost Housing Plan for the Lower East Side,* Scale: 1″=1500′.

7.19. Reprinted from *Architectural Record* (March 1935), 77:155.

7.20. Reworked from *Architectural Record* (March 1935), 77:155. Scale: 1″=150′.

7.21. Reprinted from New York City, Department of Parks, *New Parkways in New York City,* p. 16.

7.22. Reprinted from *Architectural Forum* (September 1934), 61:5.

7.23. Reprinted from *Architectural Record* (October 1936), 80:286. Scale: 1″=200′.

7.24. Reprinted from *Architectural Record* (April 1935), 77:287.

7.25. Reprinted from *Architectural Record* (April 1935), 62:356.

7.26. Reprinted from United States Federal Public Housing Authority, *Public Housing Design,* p. 32.

7.27. Reprinted from United States Federal Housing Administration, *Architectural Planning and Procedure for Rental Housing,* pp. 17–18.

7.28. Reprinted from United States, Federal Housing Administration, *Architectural and Rental Procedure for Rental Housing,* p. 8.

7.29. Redrawn from New York City Housing Authority, *New York City Housing Authority, 1934–1936. Examples of Types of Work,* Scale: 1″=500′.

7.30. Reprinted from New York City Housing Authority, *Tenth Annual Report,* p. 37. Scale: 1"=500'.

7.31. Reprinted from *Architectural Forum* (November 1938), 69:406, 407. Scales: 1"=50''; 1"=80'.

7.32. Reprinted from Frederick Ackerman and William Ballard, *A Note on Site and Unit Planning,* p. 40. Scale: 1"=500'.

7.33. Reprinted from New York City Housing Authority, *Tenth Annual Report,* p. 41. Scale: 1"=500'.

7.34. Reprinted from Jose Luis Sert, *Can Our Cities Survive?,* p. 39.

7.35. Reprinted from New York City Housing Authority, *Tenth Annual Report,* p. 45. Scale: 1"=500'.

7.36. Reprinted from New York City Housing Authority, *Tenth Annual Report,* p. 61. Scale: 1"=500'.

7.37. Reprinted from Le Corbusier, *When the Cathedrals Were White,* p. 188.

7.38. Reprinted from *The New Republic* (April 6, 1938), 94:276.

7.39. Reprinted from New York City Housing Authority, *East River Houses,* p. 2.

7.40. Reworked from *Pencil Points* (September 1940), 21:556. Scale: 1"=500'.

7.41. Reprinted from *CHPC Housing News* (July 1950), 8:1, Scale: 1"=1200'.

8.1. Redrawn by Yvonne Yao from Museum of Modern Art, *Tomorrow's Small House,* p. 12. Scale: 1"=30'.

8.2. Reprinted from *Architectural Forum* (December 1939), 71:416. Scale: 1"=1000'.

8.3. Reprinted from *Architectural Forum* (December 1939), 71:419. Scale: 1"=200'.

8.4. Reworked from a map courtesy of the Stuyvesant Town Administration Office. Scale: 1"=500'.

8.5. Courtesy of the Stuyvesant Town Administration Office; and New York City Housing Administration, *East River Houses,* p. 14. Scale: 1"=30'.

8.6. Reprinted from *CHC Housing News* (September 1944), 3:4. Scale: 1"=200'.

8.7. Reprinted from *CHC Housing News* (June–July 1943), p. 5.

8.8. Reworked from *Architectural Forum* (May 1942), 77:140. Scale: 1"=50'.

8.9. Reprinted from *Pencil Points* (June 1944), 25:87. Scale: 1"=1000'.

8.10. Reprinted from New York City Housing Authority, *Tenth Annual Report,* p. 75. Scale: 1"=300'.

8.11. Reprinted from New York City Housing Authority, *Tenth Annual Report,* p. 78. Scale: 1"=300'.

8.12. Courtesy New York City Housing Authority. Scale: 1"=50'.

8.13. Reworked from *Architectural Forum* (June 1949), 90:87.

8.14. Reprinted from New York City Committee on Slum Clearance Plans, *North Harlem Slum Clearance Plan Under Title I of the Housing Act of 1949,* pp. 12–13.

8.15. Reworked from New York City, Committee on Slum Clearance Plans, *North Harlem Slum Clearance Plan Under title I of the Housing Act of 1949,* p. 15. Scale: 1"=50'.

8.16. Courtesy New York City Housing Authority. Scale: 1"=200'.

8.17. Reprinted from Le Corbusier, *Oeuvre Complete, 1938–46,* p. 172.

8.18. Courtesy New York City Housing Authority. Scale: 1"=500'.

8.19. Courtesy Fiorello H. LaGuardia Archives. Fiorello H. LaGuardia Community College, New York.

8.20. Courtesy New York City Housing Authority. Scale: 1"=500'.

8.21. Reprinted from *Empire State Architect* (July–August 1954), 14:9.

8.22. Drawn by Christine Hunter from Sanborn Map Company, Inc., *Manhattan Land Book, 1978–79.* Scale: 1"=1500'.

8.23. Drawn by Christine Hunter from plans courtesy of the New York City Housing Authority.

8.24. Reprinted from *Architectural Record* (July 1958), 124:184.

8.25. Used with permission from the New York Public Library. Scale: 1"=6000'.

8.26. Reworked from *Architectural Forum* (April 1950), 92:134. Scale: 1"=20'.

8.27. Reprinted from *Bulletin of Atomic Scientists* (September 1951), 7:268.

8.28. Reprinted from United States, Federal Civil Defense Administration, *Operation Doorstep,* cover.

8.29. Reprinted from *Collier's* (August 5, 1950), 126:12.

9.1. Drawn by Stephen Day from New York City Committee on Slum Clearance Plans, *Manhattantown Slum Clearance Plan Under Title I of the Housing Act of 1949,* p. 10–11; and from Sanborn Map Company, Inc., *Manhattan Land Book 1985–86.* Scale: 1"=500; 1"=1000'.

9.2. Reprinted from *American City* (July,

1948), 63:81. Scale: 1″=1000′. Courtesy of Haines, Lunberg, Waehler.

9.3. Reprinted from *Architectural Record* (September 1950), 108:133. Scale: 1″=300′.

9.4. Reworked from plans courtesy of the Lefrack Organization, Inc. Scale: 1″=300′.

9.5. Reprinted from *Progressive Architecture* (February 1970), 51:68. Scale: 1″=1200′.

9.6. Courtesy of Skidmore, Owings, and Merrill. Scale: 1″=200′.

9.7. Courtesy of I. M. Pei and Partners. Scale: 1″=200′.

9.8. Courtesy of Edvin Stromsten.

9.9. Redrawn by Stephen Day from Lawrence Halpern and Associates, *New York, New York,* pp. 16–19. Scale: 1″=500′; 1″=1000′.

9.10. Courtesy of Davis, Brody, and Associates. Scale: 1″=300″.

9.11. Courtesy of Davis, Brody, and Associates. Scale: 1″=20′.

9.12. Courtesy of Richard Meier and Associates. Scale: 1″=80.

9.13. Reworked from *Architecture and Urbanism* (July 1974), no. 30, p. 67. Scale: 1″=200′.

9.14. Courtesy of Pasanella and Klein. Scale: 1″=20′.

9.15. Courtesy of Pasanella and Klein.

9.16. Drawn by Tracy Dillon. Scale: 1″=1000′.

9.17. Reprinted from *Architectural Record* (August 1976), 160:107. Scale: 1″=400′.

9.18. Courtesy of David Todd, Architect. Scale: 1″=200′.

9.19. Courtesy of Davis, Brody, and Associates. Scale: 1″=200′.

9.20. Courtesy of Thomas Hodne Architects, Inc. Scale: 1″=300′.

9.21. Reprinted from *Progressive Architecture* (July 1975), 54:61. Scale: 1″=300′. Courtesy of Robert A. M. Stern.

9.22. Reprinted from Deborah Nevins, ed., *The Roosevelt Island Housing Competition.* Courtesy of Oswald Matias Ungers.

9.23. Reprinted from *Architectural Record* (January 1969), 145:105. Scale: 1″=150′.

9.24. Courtesy of Davis, Brody, and Associates.

9.25. Courtesy of John Ciardullo. Scale: 1″=80′.

9.26. Reprinted from Museum of Modern Art, *Another Chance for Housing,* p. 20. Scale: 1″=500′.

9.27. Courtesy of Roger A. Cumming. Scale: 1″=200′.

9.28. Reworked from *Progressive Architecture* (March 1976), 57:54 Scale: 1″=300′.

10.1. Courtesy of Richard Meier and Associates. Scale: 1″=20′.

10.2. Courtesy of Michael Schwarting. Scale: 1″=30′.

10.3. Drawn by Nancy Josephson from information courtesy of the Gruzen Partnership.

10.4. *Left:* Courtesy of the Trump Organization; *middle:* reprinted from *New York Times* (April 15, 1984), sec. VIII, p. 4; *right:* reprinted from *New York Times* (December 2, 1984), sec. VIII, p. 8. Scale: 1″=30′.

10.5. Drawn by Jose Alfano from Information courtesy of Johnson Burgee Architects. Scale: 1″=80′.

10.6. Courtesy of Alexander Cooper Architect. Scale: 1″=2000′.

10.7. Drawn by Wiebke Novack.

10.8. Drawn by Yvonne Yao. Scale: 1″=50′.

10.9. Courtesy of Conrad Levenson Architect and Allan Thaler Architect. Scale: 1″=50′.

10.10. Drawn by Stephen Day from information compiled by Jeffery Schofield. Scale: 1″=30′.

10.11. Courtesy of Rosenblum-Harb Architects. Scale: 1″=80′.

10.12. Drawn by David Smiley from maps in the City Planning Commission, *Community Planning Handbook,* and information courtesy of Beyer, Blinder, Belle, Architects. Scale: 1″=500′.

10.13. Drawn by David Smiley and Stephen Day from City Planning Commission, *Community Planning Handbook,* and from site inspection. Scale: 1″=1000′.

10.14. Drawn by David Smiley and Stephen Day from information courtesy of James D. Robinson, Architect. Scale: 1″=200′; 1″=30′.

10.15. Photograph by the Author.

10.16. Photograph by the Author.

10.17. Drawn by Marta Gutman from information courtesy of the South Bronx Redevelopment Corporation. Scale: 1″=1000′.

10.18. Redrawn by Yvonne Yao from information courtesy of Scully, Thoreson, Linard, Architects. Scale: 1″=30′.

10.19. Drawn by Ludmilla Pavlova.

Index

Aaron, Henry, 260
Absentee landlords, 5
Academy Housing Corporation, 159
Ackerman, Frederick, xv, 125, 127, 135, 17, 198-99, 209-11, 219, 222, 238, 294
Adler, Felix, 33, 39, 101
Aesthetics: civic, 40; vs. functionalism, xiv, 164-206; totalitarian, 289
Air-conditioning, central, 198
Air rights, 16, 293
Air shafts, 43
Albany Houses, 262, 268-69
Alexander Cooper and Associates, 320, 322
Alfred Hopkins and Associates, 264
Alhambra, The, 148
Allaire, James, 6
Allen, Arthur I., 203-4
Alleys, 11, 18
Amalgamated Clothing Workers of America, 151, 153, 161, 165-67
Amalgamated Housing Corporation, 151
American Architect and Building News, 55
American Institute of Architects (AIA), xiv, 27, 126, 248-50
American Institute of Architects Journal, 126
American Notes (Dickens), 51
American Society of Civil Engineers and Architects, xiv
American Society of Planners and Architects (ASPA), 251-52, 261
Amon, Will R., 215
Andrews, Adolphus, 248
Annexation, mass transit and, 138
Ansonia, The, 78, 79
Antwerp Competition, *see* University of California at Berkeley

Apartments: for affluent class, 62, 287-89, 322, 337; conversion to co-ops, 317-18; cooperatives, 71; definition of, 123; duplex units, 83; elevators for, 66, 78, 123-24, 176; FHA and, 235; financing of, 156-57; hotels, 69, 194; loft conversion, 316; palazzo-type plan, 71; PWA design guidelines, 225-27; receivership, 325; size, 198, 310; small-scale, 306-12; split-section, 299; suburban, 128; two-level, 76, 83; vertical space, 84; *see also* High-rise apartments; Public housing; Tenements
Appleton's Dictionary, 64
Appleton's Journal, ix, 69
Appliances, 198, 229
Apthorp, The, 80
Architects: building bureaucracy, 23; Emergency Employment Committee, 248; European influence, 40-41, 138, 165, 181-82, 192, 250; market crash and, 248; narcissism and, 339; New Deal programs, 248; post-war conservatism, 251; professional institutionalization, xiv; progressivism, 126, 261, 340; PWA fees, 227; registration laws, 22-23, 126; social class of, 124
Architectural draftsmen, 249
Architectural Forum, 230, 231, 251, 259, 262
Architectural Guild of America (AGA), 249
Architectural League of New York, xiv, 251, 259
Architectural Planning and Procedure for Rental Housing (FHA), 235
Architectural Record, 226, 227
Architecture, profession of: education, xiv, 16-17, 39, 124, 250; vs. engineering, 182; identity for, 39; labor unions and, 249; political

ideals and, 126, 172-73, 251, 261; social vs. style concerns, xv, 337; standards for practice, 23; tenement design and, 16

Armour Institute, *see* Illinois Institute of Technology

Aronovici, Carol, 183, 249

Arson, 323

Artists: civic art, 40; collective housing of, 10-11; loft conversions, 314-16; New Deal, 216-20; real estate and, 315-16; studios for, 83, 157

Artists Against the Expressway (AAE), 315

Artists-Tenants Association, 315

Art Students' League, xiv

Association for Improving the Condition of the Poor (AICP), 6-8, 21, 36, 100-1

Asterisk-type plan, 270

Astor, Vincent, 210

Astor House, 66

Astoria, Queens, 114

Astoria Ferry, 115

Astral Apartments, 98

Atomic bomb, 277-79

Atterbury, Grosvenor, xv, 41, 103, 106, 118, 219

Attia and Perkins, 320

Attics, 276

Automobile, effect of, 141, 175, 200-6, 233, 260, 287, 288

Avant-garde, European, 184

Bachelor apartments, 66

Back-building, 15, 24

Bakema, Jakob, 295

Baldwin, James, 256-57

Ballard, William F., 222, 238, 239, 264

Barr, Alfred H., 251

Barracks style, 221

Barthe, Richard, 216

Baruch Houses, 268, 270, 271

Battery Park, 297, 320-21

Battery Park City, 274, 294, 297, 320

Battery Park City Authority, 291, 320

Bauer, Catherine, 221, 274

Bauhaus, 250

Beals, Jesse Tarbox, 14

Beaux-Arts style: decline, 165, 190, 249; *Ecole de Beaux Arts,* 17, 39-41, 44; facades, 168, 192; historicism, 181-82

Bedford-Stuyvesant, Brooklyn, 336

Bedford-Stuyvesant Restoration Corporation, 326

Beecher, Catherine, xv

Bel Geddes, Norman, 233

Belnord, The, 79, 80, 110, 210

Bendix Corporation, 277

Benepe, Barry, 309

Bensonhurst, Brooklyn, 326

Beresford, The, 196-97

Berlin, 138, 323

Better Homes and Gardens, 276

Beyer, Blinder, and Belle, 329

Bien, Sylvan, 239

Big Flat, *see* Workingmen's Home

Blacks: apartments for, 7-8, 214-19; cooperative ownership, 160; displacement of, 325, 327; Harlem and, 256-57; philanthropic project for, 106; poverty of, 322-23

Bloor, Alfred J., 27, 29-30

Bly, James F., 216

Bohemianism, 84, 309, 316

Bond, Ryder, James, 328

Bonner, Hugh, 23

Bootleg hotels, 194-95

Borough development: automobile and, 200-6; gentrification and, 323, 325; land costs, 122; Manhattan unification with, 129; mass transit and, 9-10; site-planning, 336; technology and, 123

Boston, 69, 248

Bottle Alley, 52

Boulevard Gardens, 208, 210-11

Boyd, John Taylor, Jr., 224-25

Breakfast nook, 167

Breines, Simon, 258

Breuer, Marcel, 186-187, 250, 251, 252, 259, 267, 281

Bright, John Irwin, 219

Brighton Beach Housing Competition, 290, 292

Bristed, Charles Astor, 59

Broadacre City, 192

Bronx, 128-29, 208, 286, 323; Jews in, 151-59; labor cooperatives, 151-52, 158; South, 304-5, 323, 334-36; urbanization of, 130-32

Bronx River Parkway, 205

Brook Farm, 9

Brookings Institution, 260

Brooklyn, 306, 323; row houses in, 65; philanthropic tenements in, 98; urbanization of, 130-32

Brooklyn Bridge, 129

Brooklyn College, 250

Brooklyn Heights, 9, 325

Brooklyn-Manhattan Transit Corp. (BMT), 121, 130

Brounn and Muschenheim, 221

Brown, Archibald Manning, 214, 262

Brown, Denise Scott, 287

Brown, Jack, 285
Brownstones, 59-62, 77, 320
Brownsville, Brooklyn, 294, 306, 330-34, 337
Brownsville Houses, 262-63, 272, 294
Buckham, Charles W., 85
Buckley, Richard W., 215
Buell, William P., 50
Builder, The, 74
Building construction: accelerated techniques, 155; bureaucracy and, 22-23, 49; fire prevention, 1, 3, 4, 23-24, 73, 124; government-initiated, 38-39; legislation and, 1, 31, 208; materials, 180, 237; NYC Code, 123; technology and, 50, 57, 66, 69, 71-74, 78, 123
Buildings Bureau, 49
Building Zone Plan (1916), 85, 123, 195, 284-85
Bullard and Wendehack, 229
Bulletin of the Atomic Scientists, 277
Bunshaft, Gordon, 251, 252, 264, 265, 268, 287
Bureau of Buildings, 49, 73
Bureau of Inspection, 49
Bureau of Records, 49
Burnham, Daniel, 39, 40, 41
Burton and Bohm, 240, 242
Buses, 233

Cafeterias, cooperative, 152, 157
Cambridge Court, 144, 146
Camp Nigedaiget (Workers Cooperative Colony), 152
Can Our Cities Survive? (Sert), 267, 289
Candilis, Josic, and Woods, 295, 307
Capitalism: co-ops and, 161; lower class housing and, 4-5
Carey Gardens, 337
Carrère, John, 17
Carrère and Hastings, 194
Carroll Gardens, Brooklyn, 325
Carter, Jimmy, 334
Cathedral Ayrocourt Apartments, 176
Cellars, 3, 5, 22, 50-51
Celtic Park Apartments, 213
Central Park, 11; high-rises, 74; plan, 55; squatting, 54
Central Park Apartments, 76, 78, 83
Central courtyard, 29
Century, The, 196, 198, 230, 318
Cesar Pelli and Associates, 318
Chadwick, Sir Edwin, 4
Chandler, Charles F., 27, 105
Chanin, Irwin S., 196, 198, 230

Charity Organization Society, 36, 43-44
Charity Organization Society Competition (1900), 103-4, 106
Charlotte Gardens, 334-336, 337
Charlottenburg, Berlin, 138
Chateau, The, 141, 146, 164
Chelsea, The, 71, 78
Chermayeff, Serge, 250, 251, 252, 259, 289
Chicago, ix, 39, 112, 192
Cholera, xii, 3, 21, 50
Chrystie-Forsyth Project, 132, 208-9
Churchill, Henry S., 238
Ciardullo-Ehrmann, 304
Cigar-Maker's Union, 34
CIO (Congress of Industrial Organizations), 249
Citizens' Association of New York, Council of Hygiene and Public Health, 21
Citizens Housing and Planning Council, 258, 311
City and Suburban Homes Company, 99-101, 116, 149-50, 168, 213
City Beautiful movement, 40
City Club of New York, 315-16
City Housing Corporation, 168, 205
City in a park planning, 184-90, 243
Civil defense, housing policy and, 277-79
Civil engineering, architecture and, xiv
Civil War, 21
Clark, Edwin Severin, 71
Clarke, Gilmore D., 254, 255
Clarke and Rapuano, 321
Clark Buildings, 99
Clason Point Gardens, 240, 248
Clauss and Daub, 191
Clavin, Irwin, 254, 255
Clerks' and Mechanics' House Company Limited, 113
Cleveland, 248
Clinton and Russell, 78
Co-op City, 258, 286
Co-ops, *see* Cooperatives
Collective housing, 10-11
Colliers, 277
Collins, Ellen, 93
Columbia Broadcasting System, 230
Columbia College, 18
Columbian Exposition (1893), 39, 112
Columbia University, 124, 249, 250, 294
Columbus Park, 52; *see also* Mulberry Bend
Commercial development, major traffic arteries of, 204
Commercial space, in public housing, 268
Committee to Save the West Village, 309, 310

Communal living, 157; of artists, 10-11; meals, 66, 152, 157; uses and, 92, 94

Community and Privacy (Chermayeff and Alexander), 252, 289

Community self-control, development of, 309

Commuting, 9, 116, 141, 200-6, 233, 287, 288; *see also* Mass transit

Company towns, 114

Complexity and Contradiction in Architecture (Venturi), 290

Condemnation, 281; *see also* Slum clearance

Condominiums, 320

Coney Island, 294, 330

Coney Island Town Houses Project, 337

Confucius Plaza, 301

Congrès Internationaux d'Architecture Moderne, 180, 250-51, 267, 295

Conklin and Rossant, 299, 320

Construction, *see* Building construction

Consumer culture, 233, 251

Contextualism, 300, 329-30

Cooper, Edward, 94

Cooper, Alexander, *see* Alexander Cooper and Associates

Cooper Square, 307

Cooper Square Committee, 306

Cooper Union, 124

Cooperatives, 71, 74, 84, 113, 131, 317; for artists, 10-11, 83-84, 315-16; depression and, 160-62; financing of, 156-57; working-class, 151-59

Coops, *see* Workers Cooperative Colony

Corbett, Harvey Wiley, 192

Corinthian, The, 320

Corlears Hook, 224

Corona, Queens, 130

Cosmopolitan, 77

Costs, 200; federal limits, 236-40; of lots, 59; of lower-income housing, 334; of luxury apartments, 318; politics of, 208-9, 261; profitability and, 135-38; societal change and, 223

Council of Hygiene and Public Health, 21, 54, 88

Courtyards, 41, 47, 76; central, 28, 71; garden apartments, 122; introverted form, 210

Crime, 272, 294, 330

Cross Bronx Expressway, 287

Cross-type plan, 262-63

Crotona-Mapes Renewal Project, 329

Crotona Park, Bronx, 287

Croton Aqueduct, 2, 50, 61

Crown Gardens, 304

Culture industry, 314

Cumming, Roger, 307

Da Cunha, George, 24, 94-95

Dakota, The, 71-73, 77, 78

Dalhousie, The, 74, 76

David Rose Associates, 309

David Todd and Associates, 300-1, 306

Davis, Andrew Jackson, 9, 148

Davis, Brody and Associates, 294, 301, 304, 320

Day, Joseph P., 205

Day care programs, 157

Death and Life of Great American Cities, The (Jacobs), 289

Decal Program, 336, 338-339

Decentralization, xi-xii, 277

Deco-Moderne style, 182, 196

Defensible Space (Newman), 272, 294

DeForest, Robert, 45

Delamarre, Jacques, 196, 198

Delano and Aldrich, 125

Del Gaudio, Matthew, 216

Density: back building and, 15; co-ops and, 158; disease and, 2-3; Jewish culture and, 132; land value assessments and, 194-95; population and, 2; vertical, xi-xii, 11; zoning and, 285

Derby, Nelson, 20, 28

Der Scutt, 318, 320

Design: aesthetic approach, 40, 164-206, 289; apartment standards, 123; competitions, 24, 41-45, 103, 106, 127, 135, 210, 221, 231-33, 290-91, 302; conservatism, 252; cultural nihilism, 290-91; 1806 mandate for, 2; functionalism vs. style, 40; government guidelines, 225-27, 235-36; high-rise standards, 69, 195-96, 302; housing research, 173; institutionalization of, xiii, xv; international study (1895), 37; jurisdiction over, xiv-xv; legislation, 33, 133-35; low-cost, 223, 261-65; low-rise revival, 304-12; populism and, ix, 274; prefabs, 230, 294; profits and, 135-38; review of, 5; social housing, 219

Designers of Shelter in America (DSA), 250

Deutsch, Maurice, 190, 209

Development, x, xv; community self-control, 309; culture industry and, 314-16; private sector, 130, 281-82, 313; strip, 205; subways and, 129-31; U.D.C., 302-3

DeYoung and Moscowitz, 248

Dickens, Charles, 51

Discrimination, 131

Disease, urban, xii-xiii, 1, 2, 3, 50

Division of Defense Housing Coordination, 247

Domestic staffing, 68

Dominick, William F., 236
Douglaston, Queens, 130
Dow, Olivia, xv, 93
Dowling, Robert W., 254
Draft Riots, 21
Drainage, 31
Dresden, 323
Dresser, George, 20
Dressler, Benjamin, Jr., 203
Drug and Hospital Workers Union, 301-2
Duboy, Paul, 79
Duenkel, Louis E., 89
Dumbell tenements, *see* Old Law Tenement
Dunbar Apartments, *see* Paul Lawrence Dunbar Apartments
Duplexes, 11, 83, 201, 295
Dutch Colonial period, viii, ix
Dutchtown, 56, 71
Dutch West India Company, 1
Dyckman Houses, 264

East Brooklyn Coalition of Churches, 330-34
East Harlem, 245, 270, 274, 290, 329-37
East Midtown Plaza, 301
East River Homes (Vanderbilt), xii, 103-5, 175
East River Houses, 245, 248, 256
East Tremont, Bronx, 132, 334
East Village, 314, 327
Eastwood, 299
Ecole des Beaux-Arts, 17, 39; *see also* Beaux Arts style
Educational programs, for tenants, 93
Edwin Markham Houses, 248
Eken, Andrew J., 254, 255
Eldorado, The, 195, 196, 318
Electricity, 78
Elevators, 66, 123-24, 176
1185 Park Avenue, 83
1199 Plaza, 301-2
Elliott Houses, 262
Embury, Aymar, II, 240, 242
Emergency Fleet Corporation, 125, 207
Emergency Home Relief Bureau, 162
Emerson Apartments, 106
Emerson, William, 106
Emery, Charles, 39
Emery Roth and Sons, 268, 270, 271
Enforcement, 23, 27, 33, 126
Englehardt, Theodore H., 210-11
English Tudor style, 165, 202
Epidemics, xii, 2, 3, 50
Equitable Life Assurance Company, 253, 284
Erb, William E., 133
Erie Canal, xi

Esquire, 316
Evictions, 162, 292, 315-16

Facades, 98, 160, 165
Factory housing, 112, 322
Fairlawn New Jersey, 205
Farband Houses, 152, 156
Farband Housing Corporation, 151
Farragut Houses, 268-69
Farrar and Watmaugh, 148
Federal government, 125; abandonment of social housing, 313; AIA and, 126-27; Civil Defense Agency, 277; Department of Housing and Urban Development, 337; Federal Home Loan Bank, 260, 261; Federal Home Loan Bank Board, 207, 260; Federal Housing Administration (FHA), 207, 228, 230, 231, 235-236, 247, 252, 260-61, 277, 293, 297; Federal Public Housing Administration, 261; Federal Public Housing Authority, 234; Federal Relief Administration, 210; Federal Works Agency, 234; Housing and Community Development act (1974), 313; Housing and Home Finance Agency, 234; Housing Development Action Grants, 313; intervention by, 1, 37, 39, 207-46, 304, 313; National Housing Agency, 234, 247, 261; National Housing Association, 183; Public Housing Administration, 234; Public Works Administration, 234; Section 8 housing, 313; Section 221d3 housing, 282; Section 235 housing, 330; subsidies to private sector, 150, 260; Title I projects, 281, 284, 289, 291-92; U.S. Department of Housing and Urban Development, 337; U.S. Department of Labor, 37, 228; World War I and, 125-26; World War II and, 247, 277-79; *see also* Public housing
Federation of Architects, Engineers, Chemists and Technicians (FAECT), 249
Fellheimer, Wagner, and Vollmer, 262, 268-69
Felt, James, 311
Ferries, 129
Ferriss, Hugh, 129, 192, 284
Fifth Avenue Hotel, 66
Fine Arts Society, xiv
Fire Department, 22
Fire prevention, 1, 3, 4, 23-24, 73, 124
First Houses, 209, 268
Five Points, 51, 58
Flagg Court, 214
Flagg, Ernest, xv, 31, 33, 41, 47, 79, 99, 101, 213-14
Flagg-type plan, 41-48, 99-106, 150

Floor Area Ratio (FAR), 285
Ford, James, xv, 208
Flushing, Queens, 113
Fordham Hill Apartments, 284
Forest Close, 204
Forest Hills Gardens, 117-20
Forest Hills West, 121
Forman, Allen, 36, 52
Forster, Frank J., 215
Fort Green, Brooklyn, 325
Fort Green Houses, 248
Fouiboux, J. Andre, 229
Frampton, Kenneth, 297
François I style, 78
Franzen, Ulrich, 320
Frappier, Arthur J., 192
Frederick F. French Company, 148, 176
French, Fred F., 210, 224
French Flats, 62, 65
French Renaissance style, 164
Fresh Meadows, 282-84, 287
Frost, Frederick G., 238
Fuller, Charles F., 214
Functionalism, 29, 40; aesthetics and, 184;
    European, 180-81, 221; growth of middle
    class and, 167-68; public works, 248

Gallery access, 7, 295, 299
Garages, 80, 175, 201-2
Garden apartments, 122-63, 275, 304; auto-
    mobiles and, 141, 175; elevators for, 124,
    141, 176, 178; experimentation, 164, 168,
    169; philanthropic, 149-63; reappearance of,
    325; scenographic devices, 164; types, 139-
    40, 147, 148, 178
Garden City, Long Island, 113-14, 120, 121
Garden City Company, 114
Gardstein, Samuel, 217
Garnier, Tony, 184
Gay community, 312
General Electric, 231, 232, 251, 277
General Motors, 233
Gentrification, 314-16, 325, 327
Genug, George, 209
George Washington Bridge, 206
Germ theory, xii
German Cabinetmakers Association, 113
Ghettoes, see Slum clearance; Tenements
Gilbert, Cass, 184
Gilded Age, 332, 334
Gilman, Arthur, 69
Ginsbern, Horace, 124, 147, 164, 214-19
Giovanni Passanella and Associates, 297-98
Giurgola, Romaldo, 330

Glass block, 198
Goldberger, Paul, 312
Golden, Robert E., 148
Goldhill Court, 133
Goodelman, Aaron, 157
Gore, George, 254, 255
Gotham Court, 6, 18
Gould, Elgin R. L., 101
Gould, Jay, 78
Governeur Morris Houses, 336
Graham Court, 78
Gramercy Park, 110
Grand Concourse, 132, 287
Graves and Duboy, 78
Great Depression, 219, 248, 252, 290, 313
Greater New York Charter (1897), 31
Greater New York Tenants League, 126
Green Acres, 230
Greenwich Village, 290, 308, 315-17
Greenwich Village Community Housing Cor-
    poration, 310-11
Greystone, The, 139, 147-48
Gridiron block 11, 16; limitiations of, 60, 180;
    modification of, 18-20, 29; reorganization,
    111, 118, 149, 255, 306; revival, 320; saw-
    tooth geometry, 174-79; single family house
    and, 60
Griffin, Percy, 44, 100, 116
Griscom, John H., 4, 36
Gropius, Walter, 186-89, 250, 251, 252, 265,
    267, 281
Gruen, Victor, 309
Gruzen Partnership, 317-18, 320
Gun Hill Houses, 264
Gurney, G. Harmon, 217

Haight House, 66
Haesler, Otto, 180-81
Halpern, Lawrence, 292
Hamburg, 165
Hamlin, Talbot, 216-20
Harde and Short, 100
Hardenbergh, Henry, 71-73
Harder, Julius F., 111
Harlem, 65, 325
Harlem River Houses, 208, 214-19, 227, 236,
    268
Harper's New Monthly, 76-77
Harrison, Wallace K., 229, 251
Harrison and Abramovitz, 299
Hartley Dwellings, 106
Harvard University, 124, 250, 289, 299
Haskell, Llewellyn, 9
Haussmann, Baron, 62

Hayes Avenue Apartments, 143
Healey, Thomas, 149
Heart of the City, The (CIAM), 267
Height restrictions, 85, 123, 194, 235
Henkel, Paul R., 133
High rise apartments, 16, 92, 141-42, 194,
    243; building setbacks, 29; crime and, 272,
    330; dual-tower massing, 317-18; elevators
    for, 66, 78; evolution of, 68; height restric-
    tions, 84, 123, 194, 235; in-line form, 264;
    low-rise debate, 224, 261, 312, 328-29; lux-
    ury, xi, 66-87, 192, 194, 287-89, 317-20;
    middle class, 253-72, 281; New Law plans,
    85; outer boroughs and, 282-90; palazzo
    type, 79-80; pathology of, 270-75, 330; pe-
    rimeter designs, 111; plazas, 300-1; privacy
    and, 76, 272; public housing projects, 240,
    243, 261-74; site context, 297, 330; skyscra-
    pers, 184-86; slab block, 186, 191, 281, 282,
    295; technology and, 79-80; *see also* Towers
    in the park
Highway programs, 233, 287, 288
Hilbersheimer, Ludwig, 186, 250
Hillside Homes, 208, 212-13, 304
Hindu style, 214
Hiroshima, 277
Hiss and Weeks, 79
Historic preservation movement, 315
Hitchcock, Henry Russell, Jr., 181, 182-83,
    251
Hoddesdon, England, 267
Hodne Associates, 290
Hodne/Stageburg Partnership, 301-2
Hohauser, William I., 236, 247
Holden, Arthur, 216
Holden, McLaughlen and Associates, 209, 224
Holland Tunnel, 205
Home Buildings, 89
Homeless population, 337
Home ownership: American dream of, 227-33,
    251, 276, 336, 337; by blacks, 160; econom-
    ics of, 260; fixation, 62; low-cost, 330-34;
    Manhattan increases in, 317; working-
    class, 92, 93, 116
Homewood, 116-17, 149, 164
Hone, Philip, 4
Hood, Raymond, 135-36, 192
Hoover administration, 207
Horizontal garden city, 284
Horowitz and Chun, 301
Hotel Pelham, 69
Housing and Community Development Act
    (1974), 313
Housing design, *see* Design
Housing Development Action Grants, 313

Housing and Development Administration
    (HOA), 292, 293, 311-12
Housing and Home Finance Agency, 234
Housing and Recreation (Moses), 234
Housing and Redevelopment Board (HRB),
    274, 292, 308-9
Housing of the Working People, The, (US
    Dept of Labor), 37
Housing projects, *see* Public housing
Housing research, xv, 16-17, 28, 173, 219,
    261
Housing shortages, 261, 274, 323
Housing starts, 340
Housing Study Guild, 224
How the Other Half Lives (Riis), 51
Howard, Ebenezer, 120, 142
Howe, George, 190, 209, 251
Howe and Lescaze, 190-91, 192, 209, 224
Howells and Stokes, 106
Hubert, Philip, 71, 74
Hubert, Pirsson, and Company, 76, 110
Hubert Home Clubs, 71
Hudnut, Joseph, 249, 250
Hudson View Gardens, 148
Hunt, Richard Morris, xiv, 10, 17, 29, 62, 68,
    78
Hutaff, Richard, 210
Hygiene, 104

Illinois Institute of Technology, 250
Immigrants: architects, 124; cooperatives of,
    151-59; first large-scale, xiii, 4; mobility of,
    123, 132; social disruption by, 36-37
I. M. Pei and Partners, 288
Improved Dwellings Association, 94-95
Improved Dwellings Company (London), 88,
    98
Improved Housing Council of the Association
    for the Improving the Condition of the
    Poor, 41, 43, 99, 100-1
Independence Houses, 292
Independent Subway System (IND), 129
Indian style, 164
Industrial architecture, 221
Infill housing, 293, 304, 308, 329-30
Ingle, John W., Jr., 217, 221
Institute for Architecture and Urban Studies,
    306
Insurance companies, 150-51, 167, 253, 257,
    282-84, 287
Interborough Rapid Transit Corp. (IRT), 78,
    129
International Congress on Low Cost Housing
    (1897), 29

International Ladies Garment Workers Union, 155-56
International Regional Planning Conference (1925), 147
International style, 181, 182, 190, 191, 306
Investments: banking policy and, 323; real property, 318-19
Irving Park, 10
Iser, Gustav W., 209
Italian Renaissance style, 80, 196
Italians, 52

Jackson Heights, Queens, 130-31, 138, 146, 201
Jacob Riis Houses, 257
Jacobs, Jane, 309, 311, 312, 327, 328, 338
James, Bond Ryder, 320
James Stewart Polshek and Partners, 320
Japanese style, 164
Jardine, Murdock and Wright, 209
Jefferson Market Courthouse, 315
Jenkins, Helen Hartley, 106
Jessor, Herman J., 152, 165, 282, 286
Jewish National Workers Alliance of America (Natsionaler Yiddisher Arbeter Farband), 151, 152-53
Jews, cooperative projects of, 151-59, 162, 163, 173
J. M. Kaplan Fund, 315
Johansen, John M., 251
Johansen and Bhavnani, 299
Johnson, James Boorman, 10
Johnson, Philip, 181-83, 251, 299
Johnson Burgee Architects, 319; see also Philip Johnson and John Burgee

Kahn, Louis, 251, 252
Kaplan, Richard, 304
Karl Marx Hof, 165
Katan, Roger, 293
Kaufman, Edgar, Jr. 251
Kellum, John, 58, 113
Kennedy, Robert G., 24
Kessler S. J. and Sons, 288-89
Kew Gardens, Queens, 121
King and Campbell, 149
Kips Bay Plaza, 288
Klaber, John J., 209
Klein, Joseph, 202
Knickerbocker Village, 207, 210-11
Koch, Carl, 261
Koch, Edward, 323
Korn, Louis, 85
Kreymbourg, Charles, 133, 147

Labor: company towns, 113-16; government workers, 125; housing built by, 151, 155; piano strikes, 116; Zionism, 153; see also Working class
Labor Homes Building Corporation, 155
Ladies Home Journal, 229, 251, 252
LaGuardia, Fiorello, 224, 234
Lamb and Rich, 98
Lambert, Jacques, 185
Lambert Houses, 304
Land: assessments, 194-95; costs, 92, 122, 148; speculation in, xv, 20, 126, 314; uses of, 1; see also Development
Landlords, 5, 126
Lanham Act (1941), 247
Laurel, 139
Lavanburg Foundation, 159
Lavanburg Homes, 159
Lear, John, 277
Le Corbusier, 184-86, 240, 257, 267, 268, 280, 288, 290, 299
Lefrak, Samuel J., 285
Lefrak City, 285
Legislation, 22; AIA and, 261; civil rights and, 34; 1882 consolidation of, 31; enforcement of, 23, 27; scientific basis for, 36, 37
Lengh, Charles, 200
Leonard Schultze and Associates, 284
Lescaze, William, 190-91, 209, 216, 262
Lescaze, Holden, McLaughlan and Associates, 224-25
Levenson-Thaler Associates, 327
Levitt, William, 276-77
Levitt and Sons, 275-77
Levittown, 275-77
Lichtenstein, Schuman, Claman, and Efron, 318, 320
Light, 5-7; building setbacks, 123; inferior design standards, 13, 15, 61, 195-96; laws, 31, 33; slots, 29; solar control, 214; solar orientation, 18, 29
Limited Dividend Housing Companies Law (1926), 151, 155, 156, 159
Limited Profit Housing Companies Law (1955), 281; see also Mitchell-Lama program
Lincoln Center, 322
Lincoln West project, 322
Linden Court, 141, 146, 204
Lindsay, John, 292, 310
Litchfield, Electus D., 236
Llewellyn Park, New Jersey, 9-10, 112
Lodging houses, 2
Loft buildings, 331, 312, 314-16, 327
Logue, Edward, 334

London, 88, 138
London County Council, 138
London Terrace, 148
Long Island, 113-14, 121, 230, 275-77
Long Island City, Queens, 114, 151, 167, 170, 191, 214
Long Island Railroad, 115, 118-21
Long Island State Park Commission, 206
Lot costs, 59
Lot size, 18, 135; *see also* Gridiron block
Lower East Side, 96, 239, 268, 276, 279, 306, 314, 323, 235, 327
Lower Manhattan Expressway, 315
Lower Manhattan Plan, 315
Lower classes, xiii; cultural needs of, 329; displacement and, 325, 327; high-rise vs. low rise housing, 224; government subsidies for, 208, 260-61; recent increases in, 322-23; Section 8 housing, 313; social control of, 4; substandard new housing, 6; suburbs and, 10; squatters, 5, 52-58; Title I projects, 281-82, 284, 289, 291-92; *see also* Public housing; Working-class
Low-rise projects, 304-12, 328
Luxury housing, 58, 67-87, 192, 194, 287-89, 290, 317-20, 322, 337

McCarthy, W. T., 236
MacDougal, Edward A., 130
McFadden, Howard, 209
MacKay, John W., Jr., 78
McKim, Charles Follen, xiv, 17
McKim, Meade, and White, 83
Majestic, The, 195, 196, 230, 318
Major Deegan Expressway, 339
Manhattan: early infrastructure, 2-4; gridiron plan, 11-12, 17-20; housing types, ix, xiii; land costs in, 92, 122, 148; ownership and, 317; population 2, 4, 11-13, 30, 323; ring of devastation in, 323-24
Manhattan House, 287
Manhattanization, 285
Manhattan Plaza, 300, 312
Manhattantown, *see* West Park Village
Manhattan Valley, 327
Manhattan Valley Development Corporation, 326, 327
Manhattan Valley Townhouses, 327-28
Maniewich, Abraham, 157
Mansions, 58, 78
Marcus Garvey Park Village, 306
Margon and Holder, 195
Mariner's Harbor, 125
Marseilles Unité (Le Corbusier), 267, 280, 288

Marshall Plan, 267
Martorano, Felix, 290
Mass national media, ix, 35
Mass transit, 65, 101; annexation and, 138; commuting on, 9; vs. highways, 322; land development and, 129-30; suburbs and, 28; West Side expansion and, 78; working-class housing and, 92, 101, 113-21
Massachusetts Institute of Technology, 17
Mathesius, Frederick, 248
Matz, J. Raymond, 308, 310
Mayan Deco style, 147, 164, 196
Mayor's Committee on Slum Clearance, 266, 268, 281, 282, 289, 291
Meier, Richard, 296, 316, 320, 329
Mesa Verde, The, 176-79
Metropolis of Tomorrow, The (Ferriss), 192
Metropolitan Association, 88
Metropolitan Board of Health, *see* New York City Board of Health
Metropolitan Life Housing, Long Island City, 167-69
Metropolitan Life Insurance Company, 151, 167, 253, 257
Metropolitan Museum of Art, 315
Mews, 18, 89-92, 148-49, 204, 306
Meyer, Jr., Henry C., 254
Middle class: anti-urban ideals of, 132; apartments for, 62, 64, 122-63; borough redevelopment and, 325; communal outdoor space, 92, 94; gentrification by, 314, 323; government incentives for, 253, 281; limited housing for, 200; mass isolation of, 253; suburbs and, 10, 65, 274
Mies van der Rohe, Ludwig, 250
Miller, Julius, 200
Mitchell, Giurgola, 320
Mitchell-Lama program, 281-282, 286, 294, 308, 310-11, 310-12, 326
Mobility, and ethnicity, 123, 132
Model Fireproof Tenement Company, 101, 214
Model homes, 228-30, 251
Model Housing Law, A (Veiller), 123
Modern Housing (Bauer), 221
Modernism: European, 180-81, 219; functional, 198; U.S., 190-92
Moholy-Nagy, Laszlo, 250
Monroe Model Tenement, 96-97
Montana, The, 317
Moore, Charles, 312, 320
Moorish style, 1264
Morgen Freiheit, 156
Mortality rates, xii, 51
Mortgage guarantees, 116, 207, 235, 247

Morton, George W., 16-17
Moscowitz, Jacob, 236, 248
Moses, Robert, 29, 206, 209, 227, 234-35, 245, 249, 255, 257, 281, 282, 286, 289, 291-92, 309, 314, 315, 322
Mott Haven, Bronx, 304
Mulberry Bend, 51-52
Multiple Dwelling Law (1929), 85, 195, 196, 200, 210, 315, 318
Multiple dwellings, *see* Apartments
Mumford, Lewis, xv, 172, 182, 219, 257, 280, 282-84
Municipal Art Society, xiv
Municipal Housing Authorities Law (1934), 208
Municipal Housing Authority Act (1934), 208
Murphy-Jahn, 322
Museum of Modern Art, 181, 191, 220, 250, 251, 318
Mussel Shoals, 180

Nation, The 316
National Better Homes in America, 230
National Board of Health, 36
National defense, and housing, 247, 277-79
National Endowment for the Arts (NEA), 316
National Housing Act (1941), Title VI, 247
National Housing Act (1961), 282
National Housing Agency, 234, 247, 261
National Housing Association, 183
National Industrial Recovery Act (1933), 207, 249
Nehiamiah Houses, 330-32
Neo-classicism, 340
Neo-constructivism, 340
Neutra, Richard, 232, 251
New Bauhaus, 250
New Deal, 13, 125, 206, 208, 228, 233, 248, 260
New Deal Treasury Art Projects Program, 216
New Law, *see* Tenement House Acts (1901)
New Law Tenements, 47-49, 85-86, 133-35, 194, 327
Newman, Oscar, 272, 294, 297
New towns, 120, 294
New York Association for Improving the Condition of the Poor (AICP), *see* Association for Improving the Condition of the Poor
New York City Board of Estimate, 309, 316
New York City Board of Examiners, 23
New York City Board of Health, 2, 3, 22, 96
New York City Common Council, 1, 2, 3, 21
New York City Department of Buildings, 31
New York City Department of Housing Pres-
ervation and Development, 338-39
New York City Department of Parks, 249
New York City Department of Survey and Inspection of Buildings, 22, 23
New York City Housing and Redevelopment Board, (HRB), 290, 308, 309
New York City Housing Authority, 208, 209-10, 219, 234, 262, 270, 273; Technical Division, 209, 224
New York City Housing Partnership, 330, 338
New York City Planning Commission, 183, 309, 311, 325
New York Daily Tribune, 15
New York Fireproof Tenement Association, 101
New York Life Insurance Company, 253, 282-84, 287
New York Magazine, 325
New York Post, 163
New York Regional Plan (1929), 206
New York Ring, 323-24
New York Sanitary Reform Society, 27
New York State Board of Housing, 207
New York State Commissioner's Plan of 1811, xii, 11
New York State Council on the Arts (NYSCA), 316, 329
New York State Housing Board, 151
New York State Housing Law (1926), 208
New York State Insurance Code, 150
New York State Mortgage Agency, 334
New York State Reconstruction Commission, 127, 141
New York State Tenement House Commission (1900), 23, 194
New York State Tenement House committee (1884), 21, 33, 36
New York State Urban Development Corporation (UDC), 292-93, 294, 297, 302-3, 334
New York Times, 53-54, 90, 311, 312, 323, 338
New York World's Fair (1939), 233
Noonan Plaza, 147, 164
Note on Site and Unit Planning, A (Ackerman and Ballard), 222

Ohm, Philip, 99-100
Old Law Tenement, 24, 27, 28, 30, 35, 43, 45, 47, 57, 123, 126, 127, 194, 261, 276, 327
Olmsted, Frederick Law, 17, 54
Olmsted, Frederick Law, Jr., 118-19
One Hundred United Nations Plaza, 320
Open Stair Dwellings Company, 106, 176-79
Open Stair Tenement Company, 105-8

Open space: building mass and, 164; concentrated, 174; *see also* Courtyards; Garden apartments

Osborn, The, 74, 76

Palazzo-type plan, 79-80, 83, 137, 143, 149

Panuch, J. Anthony, 292

Panuch Report (1960), 274, 292

Papp, Joseph, 315

Parapets, fire and, 1

Paris, 39, 41, 44, 62, 69, 138

Paris Exhibition (1925), 182

Parkchester, 253-54, 258, 282-84

Parker, Louis N., 149

Parking, 80, 201-2, 289, 307

Parkside Houses, 264

Park Slope, Brooklyn, 325, 337

Pasanella, Giovanni, *see* Giovanni Passanella and Associates

Pasanella and Klein, 308

Paul Lawrence Dunbar Apartments, 159, 174

Peabody, Elizabeth, 9

Peabody, George, 98

Peabody Trust, 88, 98

Peace movements, 183

Pei, I. M., 251, 252; *see also* I. M. Pei and Partners

Pelham, George F., 85-86, 148

Pelham Parkway, 132, 148

Pennell, Richard, 3

Penn Station South, 282, 292

Pennsylvania Station, 118, 282, 292, 315

Penthouses, 320

Perimeter blocks, 108-10, 133, 135, 141-43, 148; garden apartments, 147; medium-rise, 306-8; reconsideration, 297, 304, 307; U-form, 137

Perkins and Will, 308, 310

Perret, Auguste, 184-85

Peter Cooper Village, 253, 255

Phelps Stokes Fund, 106, 135-37, 210, 222-23

Philadelphia, 93, 248

Philanthropic housing, 4-6, 88-121, 159; for artists, 10-11, 315; city vs. suburb, 93-94; federally owned, 207-24; functionalism and, 178, 180; garden apartments and, 149; middle income, 281; motor age and, 205-6; new forms of, 150, 332; working-class cottage and, 116

Philip Johnson and John Burgee, Architects, 299

Phipps, Henry, 103

Phipps Garden Apartments, 160, 173, 212-13, 304

Phipps Houses, 304-5

Phipps Tenements, 103

Photojournalism, 35

Pike, Benjamin, Jr., 114

Planning: architectural review, 22-23; community-initiated, 293; international exchange, 183; mixed use and, 310; motor age and, 205-6; superprojects, 286; towns, 112-16, 183; zoning study (1985), 325

Planning the Site, (USHA), 235

Playgrounds, 128

Plaza Borinquen, 304-5

Plazas, 300-1

Plumber and Sanitary Engineer, 24, 27

Plumbing, 31, 61

Pneumatic rock drill, 57

Pollution, water supply, 2, 50, 55

Polshek, James Stewart, *see* James Stewart Polshek and Partners

Pomander Walk, 149

Poor, *see* Lower classes; Public housing; Tenements

Poor, Alfred Easton, 236, 243-45

Population growth, 4, 11-13, 30, 123, 274, 323

Porte cochère, 41

Porter, Charles C., 232

Post, George, 20

Potter, Edward T., xv, 18, 29, 124, 149, 178, 306

Poverty, 322-23

Pratt, Charles, 98

Pratt Institute, 124

Prefabricated houses, 230, 294

Prelaw Tenement, 51, 127, 328

Prentice, Chan, and Olhausen, 297

President's Conference on Home Building and Home Ownership (1931), 207

Price, Bruce, 60, 64

Price, Thompson, 6

Princeton University, 124

Private property, threats to, 34

Profitability, 135-38, 281

Property tax exemptions, 281

Public health, xii-xiii, 1-3, 50, 88

Public housing, xiii, xv; costs vs. design, 223; cultural nihilism and, 290-91; early years of, 207-46; isolation of, 268; low-cost and, 261; low-rise projects, 308, 312, 328; median income, 332; middle income, 281, 282; New York State, 234, 248; open admissions, 334; owner-occupied single family, 337; reductions in, 325-30; Section 8, 313; subsides, 257, 330-34, 337; tenant selection, 273; tower projects, 270-73, 336; *see also* Federal government; Philanthropic housing

Public Housing Administration, 234
Public Housing Design (USHA), 235
Public philanthropy, privatization of, 332; *see also* Philanthropic housing
Public works, and functionalism, 180
Public Works Administration (PWA), 207-216, 224-27, 233-34, 236

Quand les cathedrales etaient blanches (Le Corbusier), 243
Queen Anne style, 149
Queens, 323; company towns, 114; philanthropic housing in, 117-20; super projects, 282-84, 285; transportation and, 121; urbanization of, 130-31
Queensboro Bridge, 116, 121, 130, 230
Queensboro Corporation, 130, 138-39, 144, 146, 201
Queensbridge Houses, 219, 238-39, 268
Queenstown, 224

Racism, 256-57, 287, *see also* Blacks
Radburn, 205, 230
Rafford Hall, 86
Railroad flats, 13, 18
Railroads, xi, 113
Reagan, Ronald, 334
Real Estate Board of New York, 127
Real Estate Record and Builder's Guide, 198
Reconstruction Finance Corporation (RFC), 207
Red Hook, Brooklyn, 325
Red Hook Houses, 219, 236-38, 268
Redevelopment: displacement of poor, 272, 289, 292, 332; gentrification, 314-16, 325, 327; outer boroughs, 323-25; social disruption of, 289; Title I projects, 281, 284, 291-92; West Side, 294
Red Scare, 126
Reform, in housing, 4, 34-37, 95; architects, 29; federal tenement study, 37; movements, 24; populism and, ix, 34-37; rehabilitation and, 127; towers in the park and, 268
Refrigeration, central, 78
Rego Construction Company, 121
Rego Park, Queens, 121
Rehabilitation, 93, 289, 290, 313; city-owned apartments, 325; vs. new construction, 209-10; subsidized, 325; tenements, 127; *see also* Redevelopment
Relocation, 272, 289, 292
Renovation, *see* Rehabilitation
Rensselaer Polytechnic Institute, xiv, 92

Rent: restrictions, 167; strikes, 126, 173; subsidies, 218, 281, 286, 294, 310-12, 313, 325
Report of the Council of Hygiene, 88
Research, *see* Housing research
Ribbon forms, *see Zielenbau* planning
Richard Meier and Associates, 296-97; *see also* Richard Meier
Richardson, H. F., 255
Richardson, Henry Hobson, 17
Richmond Terrace, Staten Island, 248
Riis, Jacob, 35, 51
Riley, Champlain L., 105
Riots, 21
Ritch, John W., 7
Ritz Tower, 194
Riverbend Houses, 294-95
Rivercross, 299
Riverside Buildings, 108-10
Riverton, 253, 256
Robbins, Ira D., 315, 331-34
Roberts, Henry, 88
Robin, Edwin J., 236
Robinson, Allan, 150
Robinson, Charles Mulford, 40
Robinson, James L., 331
Rockefeller, David, 330
Rockefeller, John D., Jr., 155, 160
Rockefeller, Nelson, 268, 286
Rockefeller Center, 192
Rockefeller family, 219
Rogers Model Dwellings, 106
Rogers and Hanneman, 201
Roofs, 178, 307
Rookeries, *see* Prelaw Tenement
Rookery, 15
Roosevelt, Franklin D., 247
Roosevelt, Theodore, 34
Roosevelt Island, 294, 299, 302-3
Roosevelt Island Competition, 302-3
Rosenblum-Harb Architects, 327-28
Rosenfield, Isadore, 272
Rosenfield, Zachary, 272
Roth, Emery, 124, 133, 194, 195, 196, 200, 268, 270, 271
Rothenberg Housing, Kassel, 180-81
Rowe, Colin, 296
Row houses, 58-62, 149, 304; automobile and, 202-4; sudsidies for, 65, 329
Ruberoid Corporation, 290, 301-2
Russell Sage Foundation, 117-20
Rutgers Town, 224-25, 270
Rutgers Town Corporation, 224

Saarinen, Eero, 251, 252

Saarinen, Eliel, 147
St. Die, 267
St. Gaudens, Augustus, xiv
St. Louis, 270
St. Marks Place, 192
Sage, Russell, 78
Sajo, Stefan S., 165
San Remo, 195, 318
Sanitary Inspection Districts, 21
Sanitation, 21; cellars, 50; laws, 1, 33; legislation, 4, 31; squatters and, 54-56
Saratoga, The, 318
Sass and Smallheiser, 101
Savings and Loan associations, 93
Sawtooth geometry, 174-79
Scenography, architectural, 164-65, 214
Schafer, Charles, Jr., 202
Schickel, William, 96
Schiment, Michael, 320
Schleicher-Woods, Waltrude, 307
Schlusing, C. W., 243-45
School sinks, 16
Schwarting, Jon Michael, 317
Schwartz and Gross, 83
Scofidio, Ricardo, 290
Scott Brown, Denise, 287
Scribner's, 65
Scully, Thoresen, and Linard, 337
Second Empire style, 58, 71
Section 8 housing, 313
Section 221d3 housing, 282
Section 235 housing, 330
Sedgwick Houses, 264, 268
Sert, Jackson, and Associates, 299
Sert, Jose Luis, 250, 251, 252, 267, 289
Setback laws, 85
Sewage, see Sanitation
Shalom Aleichem Cooperative, 151, 156
Shalom Aleichem Houses, 152, 156, 157-58, 162, 163, 173
Shantyhill, 56
Shantytowns, 53-57
Shelter (T-Square Club), 248
Short, R. Thomas, 43
Short Hills, 112
Shortages, see Housing shortages
Shreve, Lamb, and Harmon, 239
Shreve, Richmond H., 216, 239, 253
Sibley and Fetherston, 127, 135
Single family housing, 58-62; automobile and, 202-6; conversion of, 123; mass-produced, 275; outer boroughs, 200; post-war boom in, 251-52; row, 11, 58-62, 65, 149, 202-4, 304, 329; small house competitions, 233; suburban houses, 228-33, 334-35; subsidized, 330-34, 337-39
Site planning: contextualism and, 292-300; flexibility of, 310; outer boroughs, 330
Skidmore, Owings, and Merrill, 264-66, 282, 287-88
Skyscrapers, see High-rise towers
Slab block, 186-91, 264, 270, 281, 282, 287, 295
Sloan and Robertson, 209
Slum clearance, 2, 6, 52, 123, 148, 245, 261; Mayor's Committee on, 281, 289, 291-92; outer boroughs, 282-84; Title I, 281-82, 284, 289, 291-92; United States Housing Act, 272; see also Redevelopment; Tenements
Slums and Housing (Ford), 208
Small-home projects, subsidized, 337-39
Smith, Alfred E., 127
Smith, Henry Atterbury, xv, 43, 103-5, 174-80
Smith, Perry Coke, 245
Smith, Stephen, 18, 36
Smithson, Alison, 295
Smithson, Peter, 295
Social architecture, xv, 88, 167; see also Functionalism
Social class: dwelling type, xiii; home ownership and, 62; housing inequity and, 50; luxury high-rises and, 77
Social control, of poor, 4
Social housing, 294, 304, 313, 325; see also Philanthropic housing; Public housing
Society for Ethical Culture, 39
Society of American Artists, xiv
Society for Improving the Condition of the Laboring Classes (London), 88
Soho, 314
Solow Development Corporation, 320
Sommerfeld and Sass, 159
Sopher, Hank, 311
South Bronx, 294, 323, 329, 334-36, 339
South Bronx Community Housing Company, 304-5
South Bronx Development Organization (SBDO), 334
South Jamaica Houses, 240
Soviet Russia, 277
Spanish Flats, see Central Park Apartments
Speculation, xv, 20, 126, 314
Springsteen, George, 124
Springsteen and Goldhammer, 148, 152, 153, 159, 165
Squatter's shacks, 5, 52-58

Stairs, 105
Starr, Roger, 311, 312, 323, 338
Starrett City, 286
Staten Island, 125, 323
Steam heat, 78
Stein, Clarence, xv, 125, 127, 159, 170, 173, 182, 200, 205, 212-13, 224, 304
Steinway, Queens, 114-16
Steinway, William, 114
Steinway, Strikes, 116
Stern, Robert A. M., 320
Stevens House, xi, 68-69, 78
Stewart, Alexander T., 58, 113-14
Stewart House, 58, 78
Stirling, James, 320
Stockmar, Severin, 210
Stokes, Isaac Newton Phelps, xv, 41, 44, 111
Stokes, William, 79
Stonorov, Oscar, 251
Straus, Nathan, 240, 242
Strikes, 116, 162
Strip development, automobile-oriented, 205
Stromsten, Edvin, 290
Stübben, Joseph, 147
Stubbins, Hugh, 251
Studio building type, 83
Stuyvesant, The 62-63, 68
Stuyvesant Town, 253, 255, 256-59, 281, 282, 284
Style, 164, 196, 337, see also Design
Subdivisions, 206, 230, 275-77; see also Suburbs
Subsidized housing, 150, 304, 313, 325; see also Philanthropic housing; Public Housing
Suburbs: commuting, 28, 116; government intervention, 150, 207, 228, 230, 235, 247, 260, 274; ideal, 9; middle class and, 65, 230, 260-61, 275-77; post-war boom, 251; working class cottages, 28, 112-13
Subways, 122, 129
Suffolk County, Long Island, 274
Sullivan, Louis, 17, 40, 219
Sunnysidee Gardens, 168, 170-73, 174
Swanke, Hayden, and Connell, 318

Taft Houses, 293
Tappan, Robert, 201, 204
Task, 250
Taxes, 332; abatement program, J-52, 323, 332; exemptions, 150-151, 260, 281; waivers, 257
Team Ten, 295
Technical America (FAECT), 249
Technology; see Building construction

Telesis, 250
Tenants movements, 126, 162
Tenant unions, 273
Tenement(s): vs. apartments, 64; case studies, 21-22, 37; condemnation of, 281; density report, 37; design competitions, 24-28, 41-45, 135-36; dumbell, 24, 27, 28, 30, 43, 45, 47, 57; evolution of, 13-15; health and, xii, 1-3, 50; legally defined, 22; legislation, xv, 21-49; non-residential uses, 33; philanthropic, 96-97; rehabilitation, 127, 327; social order, 21; studies for, 37, 41; see also Slum clearance
Tenement Economies Society, 105
Tenement House Acts: (1867), 22, 23, 84; (1879), 24, 37, 135; (1901), 85, 135, 194, 196; (1919), 123
Tenement House Building Company, 96
Tenement House Department, 31, 49, 106
Tenement House Problem, The (DeForest and Veiller), 45
Tenth Street Studio, 10-11, 315
Terra-cotta, 194
Thomas, Andrew, xv, 124, 125, 127-28, 133, 135-37, 141, 143, 146, 149, 151, 159, 164, 167, 209
Thomas Garden Apartments, 155, 164
Tiano Towers, 312
Title I projects, 281, 284, 289, 291-92
Todd, David, see David Todd and Associates
Towers; see High-rise apartments
Tower in the park planning, 184-90, 192, 261-74; crime and, 272, 294; demise of, 270, 280, 291, 292; design concerns, 267-68; government subsidies for, 253-72; ideology, 256-58; legislation and, 195; luxury projects, 289; new, 328; vandalism, 294; urbanism social housing, 190, 275, 280
Towers, The, 141-43
Towns, planned, 112-16, 183
Trains, diesel vs. electric, 233
Trapani, Paul, 217
Trash disposal, 1
Tribeca, 314, 315
Trillin, Calvin, 162
Trolley service, 115
Trollope, Anthony, 59
Trump, Donald, 319-20, 322
Trump, Fred C., 286
Trump Castle, 319
Trump Tower, 318
Trump Village, 285
Tudor City, 148
Turner, Burnett C., 238

Tuscan style, 150, 164
Tuskeegee, The, 106
Tuxedo Park, 10
Twin Parks, Bronx, 294, 296, 329
Twin Parks East, 297
Twin Parks Northeast, 296-97, 329-30
Twin Parks Northwest, 297, 330
Twin Parks Southeast, 330
Twin Parks West, 297
277 Park Avenue, 83
Typographical Union, 153

U buildings, 137, 141-48, 151, 152
Ungers, O. M., 303
Unions, coop housing of, 151-59
Unite d'Habitation, 267, 297
United Residents of Milbank-Frawley Circle-
  East Harlem Association, 293
United States agencies, *see* Federal govern-
  ment
United States Shipping Board, 125
United States Housing Acts: Housing, inter-
  national exchange, 183; Housing Act
  (1937), 235, 236, 240, 313; Housing Act
  (1949), 261, 272; Housing Act (1961), Sec-
  tion 221d3, 282
United States Housing Authority (USHA),
  234-35, 237, 243, 247, 274
United States Housing Corporation, 125, 207
United Workers Cooperative Association, 152,
  156; *see also* Workers Cooperative Colony
University Plaza, 289
University of California at Berkeley, 40
Unwin, Raymond, 147
Upper East Side, 319
Upper West Side, 57, 322
Upper class, 9-10, 58, 78, 287-89, 290, 322,
  337
Upper middle class: art scene, 10-11; lofts
  and, 316; public subsidies and, 282; row
  houses of, 58-60; slab block housing and,
  287-89; suburbs and, 230
Urban centers, dismantling of, xi
Urban development, debate, x
Urban Development Corporation, *see* New
  York State Urban Development Corpora-
  tion
Urban marker, 297
Urban renewal, 273, 309-10, 333; *see also* Re-
  development; Rehabilitation
Urbanism: conservative, 308:12; critique of,
  289; decentralization, 277; Europeans and,

184; ideal visions, 192; tower in the park,
  261-74; urban studies, 183
Utopianism, 184, 192

Vacancy rates, war and, 126
Van Alen, William, 230
Vancorlear, The, 71
Vandalism, 330
Vanderbilt, Ann Harriman, 103
Vanderbilt, Cornelius, 95
Vanderbilt mansion, 78, 95
Van Dyck Houses, 272, 294, 331
Van Wart, John S., 210-11
Vaux, Calvert, 63
Vaux and Radford, 95
Veiller, Lawerence, 23, 44, 45, 105, 123, 194
Ventilation, 5-7, 13-15, 31; air shafts, 16; in-
  ferior design standards, 195-96; plumbing
  and, 61, 88
Venturi, Rauch, and Scott-Brown-Salmon As-
  sociates, 321
Venturi, Robert, 287
Vertical space, 84
Veterans' Emergency Housing Act (1946),
  261
Veterans' Home Loan Guaranty Program,
  260
Victory Gardens, 139
Viele, Egbert, 54
Vienna, 165, 273
Vietnam War, 311
Village Voice, 311
Villard, Henry, 78
Ville Radieuse, 184, 290
Vladeck Houses, 225, 239
Vollmer, Carl A., 247
Voorhees, Gemlin, and Walker, 224
Voorhees, Walker, Foley and Smith, 243-45,
  282-84

Wachsmann, Konrad, 251
Wagner, Robert, 274, 292
Wagner-Ellender Taft (WET) Bill (1945), 261
Wagner-Steagall Bill, 233
Walker, Harry, 217
Walker and Poor, 264
Wallabout Houses, 247-48, 262
Wallhigh, 56
Walsh, Albert A., 311
Wank, Roland, 165, 180
War, and housing programs, 125, 277-79
Ware, James E., 24, 41, 74, 99, 101, 102

Ware, William Robert, 17
Warnecke, Heinz, 216
Warren and Wetmore, 80
Warren Place Mews, 89-92
Washington Square, 59, 315
Washington Square Village, 288-89
Water closets, 16, 22, 33, 88; *see also* School
  sinks
Waterlow, Sydney, 88, 92, 95, 98
Waterlow-type plan, 88-89, 98
Water supply, pollution of, 2
Wefferling, Walter, 247
Weiner, Paul Lester, 289
Wells, George H., 139-40, 144, 146
Wells-Koetter, 290
Westbeth artist housing, 315-16
West Park Village, 282, 289, 292, 322
West Point, xiv
Westview, 299
West Village, *see* Greenwich Village
West Village Houses, 308-12
West Village Site Tenants Committee, 309
Westway, 294, 321, 322
White, Alfred Treadway, 89, 92, 94, 108, 110,
  111, 121
Whitman-Ingersoll, *see* Fort Green Houses
William Field and Son, 89, 96, 108
Williamsburg Houses, 208, 214-20, 227, 253,
  268
Wilson, John, L., 215
Windsor Terrace, 337
Wingate, Charles F., 36
Wirth, Louis, 132
Women's Club of New York, 289
Wood, Silas, 6
Woods, Shadrach, 307

Woodside, Queens, 208
Woolworth building, 184
Workers Cooperative Colony, 151, 152, 156,
  165, 167, 173, 286
Working class: company towns and, 114; co-
  operative housing, 151-59; model suburban
  cottage, 112; transportation and, 121; *see
  also* Lower classes
Workingmen's Home, 7, 18, 106, 295
Workmen's Circle, 152, 153
Works Progress Administration, 222
World, The, ix-xi
Wright, Frank Lloyd, 182, 192, 251
Wright, Henry, xv, 125, 170, 172, 173-74,
  183, 212-13, 227, 249
Wyoming, The, 74

Yale University, 124, 250
Yard areas, 203
Yellow fever, 2, 3
Yiddish culture, 151-59
Yiddish Cooperative Heimgesellschaft
  (Shalom Aleichem Cooperative), 151, 156
York and Sawyer, 240, 242
York Avenue Estate, 99-100
Young, Sarah Gilman, 62
Y-shaped units, 239

Zeckendorf, William, 311
Zeisloft, E. Idell, xiii
Zielenbau planning, 180, 221-22, 223, 240,
  244, 332
Zionism, 153
Zoning, 28; CPC study (1985), 325; 1987
  changes in, 326; 1961, 285